I0091985

Eastern Africa Series

The Oromo and the Christian Kingdom of Ethiopia 1300–1700

MOHAMMED HASSEN

Department of History
Georgia State University

JC JAMES CURREY

James Currey
is an imprint of Boydell & Brewer Ltd
PO Box 9, Woodbridge, Suffolk IP12 3DF (GB)
www.jamescurrey.com

and of

Boydell & Brewer Inc.
668 Mt Hope Avenue, Rochester, NY 14620-2731 (US)
www.boydellandbrewer.com

British Library Cataloguing in Publication Data

A catalogue record for this book is available from the British Library

ISBN 978-1-84701-117-6 (James Currey cloth)
ISBN 978-1-84701-161-9 (James Currey paperback)

Typeset in 10 on 12pt Cordale with Gill Bold display
by Avocet Typeset, Somerton, Somerset TA11 6RT

Dedication

To Paul Baxter, Asmarom Legesse and Bonnie Holcomb for their commitment to Oromo studies at the time when it was actively discouraged in Ethiopia, and their contribution to its development, and to my wife, Aziza, and our sons, Birmaji and Robale.

Contents

Preface and Acknowledgements

The Oromo and the Christian Kingdom 1300–1700 has had an unusually long gestation period. It was originally conceived as part of the Oromo democracy project, initiated by five scholars: Abas Haji Gnamo, Asmarom Legesse, Belletech Deressa, Lemmu Bassia and myself. The project expanded beyond the scope of a single edited volume. Asmarom Legesse's contribution developed into a magnificent book that, with remarkable erudition and eloquence, discusses the Oromo democratic heritage, 'a rich source of ideas that can inspire and inform constitutional makers in Africa'.[1] Belletech Deressa's exploratory essay developed into an important book on the role women played in Oromo and Ethiopian history. Belletech identifies Oromo women leaders 'who made significant contributions to the survival of the Oromo nation' as well as the survival of the imperial state.[2] My original exploratory essay on the Oromo in Ethiopian historiography developed into a book manuscript that will be published separately. *The Oromo and the Christian Kingdom, 1300–1700* is the fourth volume of the Oromo democracy project series. Its completion was hampered for years by other commitments coupled with a combination of factors beyond my control. Another volume in the Oromo democracy project series is in its final stage of completion.[3]

The single largest national group in Ethiopia, the Oromo constitute about 40 per cent of the population. Oromia, the Oromo regional state in central and southern Ethiopia, is the largest, most densely populated and richest part of Ethiopia. Oromia forms the backbone of the Ethiopian economy. More than 50 per cent of Ethiopia's export items and the Ethiopian government's annual revenue comes from Oromia. As a

[1] Asmarom Legesse, *Oromo Democracy: An Indigenous African Political System* (Trenton, NJ: The Red Sea Press, expanded edition 2006 [2000]), xiii.
[2] Belletech Deressa, *Oromtitti: The Forgotten Women in Ethiopian History* (Raleigh, NC: Ivy House, 2003), ix.
[3] The fifth edited volume in the Oromo democracy project series deals with the conquest of the Oromo by King Menelik of Shawa and later the emperor of Ethiopia (1889–1916), pending publication. Though the completion of the Oromo democracy project was delayed for a long time, the end result – the publication of five separate books – undoubtedly will add to the expansion of knowledge in the field of Oromo studies.

result, the survival of Ethiopia as a united and prosperous country will depend on integrating the history of the Oromo into Ethiopian historiography and treating the Oromo today as equal citizens of the country.

Considered as people without history, the Oromo were supposed not to have been in Ethiopia before the first half of the sixteenth century. However, this book will demonstrate the existence of a long-ignored relationship between the Christian Amhara society and the Oromo communities in and south of the region of Shawa at least since the fourteenth century. The presence of some Oromo groups within the medieval Christian kingdom is confirmed by a number of sources, including the Chronicle of Emperor Amda-Siyon (1314–44), which refers to a people in their own country, called Galla.[4] Galla was the old pejorative name for the Oromo. In the first three chapters, I will assemble evidence that reveal glimpses of the presence of Oromo groups within the medieval Christian kingdom. These sedentary Oromo groups that lived under the Christian administration were not part of the sixteenth-century pastoral Oromo population movement.

During the sixteenth century the Christian society confronted lightly armed, fast-moving and strategically sophisticated Oromo warriors. Because of the size of their population and the superiority of their weapons the Christian leaders at first did not take seriously the war against the Oromo. They were confident of conquering the Oromo as they had conquered their Muslim enemies. The Christian chroniclers, who articulated the views of the Christian leaders towards the Oromo, understood the new enemy faced by their society only through their Christian world view. Thus to the Christian chroniclers the Oromo appeared to be 'uncivilized' because they were not Christians, their society was not hierarchically organized like the Christian and Muslim societies, and they lacked the institution of monarchy. In short, the Oromo replaced the Muslims as the perceived enemy of the Christians.

The Oromo and the Christian Kingdom 1300–1700 has three major goals. The first is to establish the historical narrative by distilling evidence from royal chronicles, hagiographies, Amhara Christian written and oral traditions, local Muslim chronicles, Oromo oral traditions, anthropology, archaeology, linguistics, ethnonyms, toponyms and cultural texts. With these sources the book will explore the Oromo presence inside the borders of the medieval Christian kingdom from at least the beginning of the fourteenth century. While Christian and Muslim sources from that period mention such Oromo communities, these sources have been overlooked in Ethiopian historiography. They were de-emphasized partly because of the firmly entrenched theory claiming that the Oromo entered the medieval Christian kingdom around the middle of the sixteenth century following the disastrous jihad of Imam Ahmad (1529–43). There were two important reasons why historians did not suspect, much less discuss, the pre-sixteenth-

---

[4] Getatchew Haile, *The Works of Abba Bahriy and Other Documents Concerning the Oromo* (in Amharic, Avon, MN: self-published, 2002), 26.

century Oromo presence within the medieval Christian kingdom of Ethiopia. The first was the credence given to Abba Bahrey's 'Zenahu le Galla', a short manuscript written in 1593 that dates the arrival of pastoral Oromo on the border of the Christian state to the 1520s. The second was the scholarly assumption that placed the original homeland of the Oromo beyond the boundaries of modern Ethiopia, thus depicting them as 'alien invaders' entering the country as immigrants only during the first half of the sixteenth century. The representation of the Oromo as 'alien invaders' originates from confusing the territorial extent of the medieval Christian kingdom with modern-day Ethiopia. The former constituted only about one-third of the latter. In all their traditions the Oromo remember Ethiopia as their original homeland. Historical evidence confirms the validity of this widely agreed Oromo origins narrative. Beyond any doubt the Oromo did not originate from outside the boundaries of modern Ethiopia.

The second goal is to discuss the dynamics of Oromo migration within and beyond Ethiopia during the sixteenth century. Pastoral Oromo migrated from the southern to the northern regions of Ethiopia, including Gojjam, Begameder, Tigray and Wallo, all in the heartlands of the Christian kingdom. Though population movements were massive and well documented in African history, the sixteenth-century pastoral Oromo population movement had its distinct patterns both in the Horn and in Africa generally. The book will demonstrate that the basic dynamics of Ethiopian history were population movements, interactions and transformations. Sixteenth-century Oromo population movement revolutionized the contacts between the Christians and the Oromo. To a large measure, these new types of interactions were shaped by periods of long warfare interposed by times of peace between the two communities, merging their destinies and histories.

My third goal is to show that there is a general tendency in Ethiopian historiography to contextualize the study of sixteenth- and seventeenth-century pastoral Oromo population movement and settlement mainly in terms of the adverse impact on the Christian society. No study has delineated how the Oromo themselves were affected by the people they encountered, by the religions they embraced, and by the political institutions in which they actively participated. My more-inclusive narrative traces the intertwined history of the Amhara and Oromo communities in Christian society. The involvement of the Christianized Oromo in the military, political and cultural institutions of the Christian state impelled dynamic interactions between the two societies at various levels. A significant segment of the Oromo elite became defenders of the Christian state itself. During the eighteenth century, Oromo influence on the Christian kingdom was demonstrated by Christianized Oromo leaders' role in determining the royal sucession and royal policies.[5] Moreover, while the Christianized Oromo estab-

[5] For instance, Mordechai Abir, *Ethiopia: The Era of the Princes – The Challenge of Islam and the Re-Unification of the Christian Empire 1769–1855* (New York: Praeger, 1968), chapters 2, 5 and 6.

lished two regional dynasties in Gojjam, Islamized Oromo in the region of Wallo formed a number of states, two of which strongly challenged the Christian state itself.[6] In short, this book is a history of the Christian kingdom from 1300 to1700, as much as it is a history of the Oromo people in Ethiopia.

Writing a history of the interactions between the Christians and the Oromo across four centuries requires using various sources, including, but not limited to royal chronicles, hagiographies, Amhara and Oromo oral traditions, myths and legends, together with local Muslim and European missionary and travellers accounts. I have also drawn on some sections of my PhD dissertation.[7] Of the many royal chronicles, I relied heavily on the chronicles of Emperors Amda-Siyon (1314–44), Sarsa Dengel (1563–97)[8] and Susenyos (1607–32).[9] I used the Arabic, English and French versions of *Futuh Al-Habasha, the Conquest of Abyssinia,*[10] the classic book that deals with the epic drama of the jihad conducted by Imam Ahmad (1529–43). I have also used the recently translated two volumes of *Pedro Páez's History of Ethiopia, 1662.*[11] More importantly, I have made extensive use of Abba Bahrey's 1593 manuscript, *Zenahu le Galla,* relying on both versions of Huntingford's 1954 translation as well as Getatchew Haile's 2002 Amharic and English translations.[12] Abba Bahrey was a fascinating scholar of his age, and his manuscript is a major contribution to our understanding of Oromo social organization and migration and the class structure of the Christian society during the second half of the sixteenth century. As a researcher who seeks to understand the geographically intertwined existence between the Christian society and the Oromo, including the impact of the pastoral

[6] For instance, Hussein Ahmed, *Islam in Nineteenth-Century Wallo, Ethiopia: Revival, Reform and Reaction* (Boston, MA: Brill, 2001), chapters 4 and 6.

[7] Mohammed Hassen, 'The Oromo of Ethiopia, 1500–1850: With Special Emphasis on the Gibe Region' (PhD diss., University of London, School of Oriental and African Studies, 1983), chapter 1, 36–68, chapter 3, 135–75, and chapter 4.

[8] G.W.B. Huntingford, trans. and ed., 'The History of King Sarsa Dengel (Malak Sagad) 1563–1597' (unpublished manuscript, School of Oriental and African Studies, University of London, 1976).

[9] F.M.E. Pereira, *Chronica de Susenyos Rei de Ethiopia* (Lisbon: Impresa National, 1892–1900).

[10] Chihab Eddin B. Abdel Qadir, surname Arab Faqih, *Futuh Al-Habasha (Histoire de la conquête de l'Abyssinie XVI siècle),* trans. and ed. M.R. Basset (Paris: 1897); Sihab ad-Din Ahmad bin Abd al-Qader bin Salem bin Utman, also known as Arab Faqih, trans. Paul Lester Stenhouse, annotated Richard Pankhurst, *Futuh Al-Habasha: The Conquest of Abyssinia by* (Hollywood, CA: Tsehai, 2003); Arab Faqih, Arabic text of *Futuh Al-Habasha* (Cairo: 1974).

[11] Isabel Boavida, Hervé Pennec and Manuel João Ramos, eds, trans. Christopher J. Tribe, *Pedro Páez's History of Ethiopia, 1662.* 2 vols (Farnham: Ashgate/ Hakluyt Society, 2011).

[12] Abba Bahrey, *Zenahu le Galla* 'History of the Galla', in *Some Records of Ethiopia, 1593–1646,* trans. and ed. C.F. Beckingham and G.W.B. Huntingford (London: Hakluyt Society, 1954), 111–29. I also relied heavily on Getatchew Haile, *The Works of Abba Bahriy and Other Documents Concerning the Oromo.*

Oromo population movements on the Christian kingdom as well as on the Oromo themselves up to 1700, I stand on the shoulders of Merid Wolde Aregay's meticulous scholarship aligning cultural transformations with shifting frontiers.[13]

This study is intended as a modest contribution towards the need for a paradigm shift in Ethiopian historiography, as suggested by Ayele Bekerie: 'Contrary to the popular belief that describes the Oromo as sixteenth-century immigrants and settlers in the Ethiopian highlands, the Oromo appeared to be as ancient and indigenous, just like the Amhara, the Tigreans, Agaws and the Bejas.'[14] As an integral part of the Cushitic-language-speaking family of peoples, the Oromo have been one of the original inhabitants of Ethiopia. Such a paradigm shift in Ethiopian historiography, it is hoped, will create an intellectual climate in which the young men and women of Ethiopia will be able to learn each other's authentic history, not grotesque distortions; truth, not falsehood; cultural achievements, not demeaning stereotypes; various religious traditions, not only Christianity; Cushitic-language speakers' achievements, not only those of the Semitic peoples. Such historical knowledge will enable the Oromo and other peoples of Ethiopia to be conscious of their dignity and unity in diversity, and promote respect for each other's cultural heritage and strengthen mutual understanding.[15]

Finally, if this study provokes more informed discussion about the pre-sixteenth-century Oromo presence within the medieval Christian kingdom and kindles enthusiasm for producing objective and dispassionate scholarship on the subject, its purpose of enriching and expanding the horizon of Ethiopian historiography will have been fulfilled.

It is not easy to acknowledge the full range of my indebtedness. I am grateful to my colleagues in the Department of History at Georgia State University for supporting this project, especially Professor David Sehat, for his technical assistance with the computer. I am also grateful to the chair people of the Department for supporting my scholarly endeavour. I am indebted to Dr Jill Anderson for her help with all library-related issues and much more. I am profoundly indebted to Dr Yael Fletcher for editing the manuscript with care and for her guidance.

I would like express my profound gratitude to the remarkable editing team at James Currey. I owe a huge debt of gratitude to Jaqueline Mitchell, Commissioning Editor, for her insightful comments and suggestions and for continuously encouraging me to complete the manuscript. I

[13] Merid Wolde Aregay, 'Southern Ethiopia and the Christian Kingdom, 1508–1708, With Special Reference to the Galla Migrations and Their Consequences', (PhD diss., University of London, 1971).
[14] Ayele Bekerie, 'Ethiopica: Some Historical Reflections on the Origin of the Word Ethiopia', *International Journal of Ethiopian Studies* 1, 2 (2004), 116.
[15] Mohammed Hassen, 'The Significance of Abba Bahrey in Oromo Studies: A Commentary on *The Works of Abba Bahriy and Other Documents Concerning the Oromo*', *The Journal of Oromo Studies* 14, 2 (July 2007), 153.

owe a debt of gratitude to Lynn Taylor for her gentle guidance in facilitating publication. I offer my profound gratitude to Nicholas Jewitt for his excellent copy-editing of the manuscript, graciously and patiently providing me with meticulous comments and insightful suggestions, all of which improved the quality of the manuscript in more ways than one. I am profoundly grateful to Bonnie Holcomb who sacrificed her own project to proofread the typeset manuscript at a short notice. I am honoured and touched by her generosity.

I have been very fortunate to have friends and colleagues who contributed to the completion of this book. I am greatly indebted, more than I can express in words, to the following scholars. Professor Daniel Ayana read the manuscript at short notice and responded with many suggestions. I am very grateful for his timely comments and friendship. Rev. Dr Harwood Schaffer generously read the entire draft of the book and provided me with helpful comments and suggestions. I am deeply thankful for his guidance with Hebrew and Christian ideas that are reflected in Oromo traditions. I am indebted to Professor Ezekiel Gebissa for his insightful suggestions and critical comments on draft chapters of the manuscript. I am indebted to Haile Larebo for his translation of the relevant sections of Susenyos's Chronicle from Geez into English.

I owe a debt of gratitude to the late Dr Paul Baxter, my mentor since 1977. His friendship and that of Pat Baxter have been the source of joy and inspiration for me for over three decades. I am deeply indebted to my departmental colleague, Professor Charles Steffen, for providing me with very helpful suggestions on the first four chapters of the manuscript. I am also deeply indebted to Professor Asmarom Legesse for his insightful comments on the exploratory essay that eventually developed into an unpublished book manuscript on the Oromo in Ethiopian historiography. I am indebted to the late Professor Merid Wolde Aregay for his excellent PhD dissertation, a path-breaking work in the field of medieval history of the Christian kingdom of Ethiopia.[16] I am also indebted to Professor Getatchew Haile, especially for his book on the works of Abba Bahrey.[17] I am grateful to my graduate student, Zachary Bates, for his generous help with index. Of the fourteen maps used in the manuscript, seven were adapted from other sources by kind permission. All efforts have been made to track copyright holders of source material and the author and publisher would be grateful of any additional information that can be provided.

I owe a profound debt of gratitude to my wife Aziza, who is my anchor and whose support and enthusiasm for my entire scholarly endeavour is the source of joy and inspiration for me. It was her love and the force of her personality that kept my focus on completing this book. Our sons, Birmaji and Robale, tirelessly encouraged me to finish this work and move onto my other long-overdue projects.

[16] Aregay, 'Southern Ethiopia and the Christian Kingdom'.
[17] Haile, *The Works of Abba Bahriy and Other Documents Concerning the Oromo*.

Oromo Glossary

Abba	father, owner of, or title of respect
Abba Bokku	father or keeper of the *bokku*, a leader of the *gada* in power
Abba Dula	father of war (i.e. commander of an Oromo army)
Abba Gada	father of the *gada* in power (i.e. a leader)
Abba Muudaa	the spiritual head of traditional Oromo religion (i.e. a holy person to whom pilgrimage is due)
Abbay	river
Angafa	first-born son
Awraja	sub-province
Ayyaanaa	a guardian angel or 'spirit double'
Bokku	wooden sceptre kept by the Abba Gada in power
Butta	a very joyous Oromo festival, celebrated by each member of a *gada* group in power by slaughtering a bull
Butta war	a war which followed a *butta* festival
Chaffee assembly	meadow assembly (the Oromo parliament)
Chibbra	traditional Oromo method of conducting warfare
Chiffra	an Amharic term for Oromo Chibbra
Dajazmach	commander of the vanguard
Dhalatta	'those who are born', i.e. those who are adopted into an Oromo clan
Gabbaro	conquered men who were required to serve
Galma	the sacred house of Abba Muudaa
Gosa	clan or descent group
Guddifacha	adoption or an adopted son
Ilma gosa	a son of a clan (i.e. one who is adopted into a clan)
Ilma Oromo	son of the Oromo, (i.e. the Oromo people)
Jila	pilgrim(s) to the Abba Muudaa
Moggaasaa	naming an individual or groups through adoption into an Oromo clan
Nagaa (*nagyaa*)	peace, moral code
Oda	the 'sacred' sycamore (tree)
Ogessa	the skilled ones

Qaalluu	a priest of traditional Oromo religion, who performed sacrifice
Tullu	hill
Wadaja	individual or group prayer
Waaqa	traditional Oromo god
Uumaa	creation
Yahabata	cavalry of *gabbaro* or conquered people

Standardization of the
Spelling of Ethiopian Names

There are no standard spellings in English of Ethiopian names, nor of words in the Amharic and Oromo languages. As a result, there are variant spellings of the same name that a reader may find confusing. The following list shows the spellings which have been used in the study.

Variant spellings	Version used
Aba, Abbaa	Abba
Abba Bahriy	Abba Bahrey
Abba Muda, Abbaa Muuda	Abba Muudaa
Abay, Abai	Abbay
Abassa, Abessinia	Abyssinia
Amda Seyon, Amda Siyon	Amda-Siyon
Amaras	Amharas
Awsa	Awssa
Ayana, Ayaana	Ayyaanaa
Azzaj	Azaj
Azzaj Tinno	Azaj Tino
Bagemder, Begemder, Bagemdir (province)	Begameder
Barentuma, Barettuma, Barettum	Barentu
Boran, Booranna	Borana
Caffe, chafe	*Chaffee*
Dejazmach, Dedjazmatch, Djazmach	*Dajazmach*
Dembya, Dembia (province)	Dambiya
Dewaro, Doaro (province)	Dawaro
Enarya, Narea, Inarya (province)	Ennarya
Fetegar (province)	Fatagar
Gabaro	Gabbaro
Gala, Gaallaa	Galla
Gallaan	Galan
Geda	Gada
Gojam, Gozzam (province)	Gojjam
Harer, Herer	Harar

Hererge	Hararghe
Itu	Ittu
Jawe, Dawe, Jawwi	Jaawwii
Jele, Jelle	Jille
Koran, Kuran	Qur'an
Kushitic	Cushitic
Laalo, Laalloo	Lalo
Libina Dengel, Lebena Dengel	Libena Dengel
Macca, Matacha	Macha
Mada Walabu	Madda Waallaabuu
Qallu, Kallu	Qaalluu
Quereban	Qurban
Shew, Shoa, Showa (province)	Shawa
Tigre, Tigrai (province)	Tigray
Tigrean	Tigrayan
Tuloma, Tolama	Tulama
Waalagga, Wollaga, Wellaga (province)	Wallaga
Waka, Waqa	Waaqa
Walabu	Waallaabu
Warra Dhaayyee, Warr Dae, Wardai, Wardey	Warra Daya
Warra Himanu	Warra Himano
Wara Qallu	Warra Qaalluu
Wello, Wollo (province)	Wallo
Yaayyaa	Yaya

List of Maps

Chronology

1586–88 Susenyos lived in captivity among the Oromo and he becomes the first Amhara prince to be adopted by the Oromo

1593   Abba Bahrey writes his famous manuscript *Zenahu le Galla*

1603   Beginning of Emperor Za-Dengel's spirited campaign against the Oromo

1604   The death of Emperor Za-Dengel

1607   Susenyos makes himself an emperor with Oromo support and the intensifies the policy of settling friendly Oromo groups among the Christians

1622   Emperor Susenyos' official conversion to Catholicism and his attempt at imposing this on Ethiopian Orthodox Christians

1632   Emperor Fasilada's restoration of the Ethiopian Orthodox Church

1682   The beginning of Emperor Iyasu's spirited campaign against the Oromo

1706   The death of Emperor Iyasu I

1855   The beginning of Emperor Tewodros' punishing campaign in Wallo

Introduction

The history, way of life, political and religious institutions, and even the name of the Oromo is in large part ignored in Ethiopian historiography. The source of such widespread neglect is partly due to lack of accurate information from the Oromo perspective. Since the Oromo, as a preliterate people, did not write about their encounter with the Christian society, existing records reflect the views of Christian monks and court chroniclers. These perspectives presented the Oromo as enemies of the Amhara and the Christian state. The magnified enmity between the Amhara and the Oromo was compounded by religious and cultural differences, thus perpetuating the negative image of the Oromo in Ethiopian historiography. It is precisely for this reason that the scholar Richard Reid wrote:

> There can be few peoples in African history who have been as misunderstood, and indeed as misrepresented, as the Oromo – or pejoratively 'Galla' in the older literature. They have been, arguably, even more demonized by Ethiopian chroniclers of various hues and over a longer timeframe than the Somali, historically the other great rival 'bloc' confronting the Amhara in northeast Africa.[1]

European travellers and missionary accounts since the sixteenth century took on the anti-Oromo perceptions of Ethiopian Christian chroniclers. As a result, the Oromo were 'made scapegoats for much that was held to be "wrong" with highland state and society in the nineteenth century'.[2] In other words, no systematic account of the Oromo was written by a first-hand unprejudiced observer before the 1840s. Even the monk Abba Bahrey, whose manuscript of 1593 is examined in Chapter 6, was not free from prejudice in his presentation of Oromo history. Earlier accounts were most probably compiled from hearsay by individuals with little or no experience of southern Ethiopia;[3] by Portuguese missionaries[4] who knew little or nothing about the region;

---

[1] Richard J. Reid, *Frontiers of Violence in Northeast Africa: Genealogies of Conflict since c. 1800* (New York: Oxford University Press, 2011), 30.
[2] Ibid., 31.
[3] See for instance, Conti-Rossini, 'Lauto Biografia de Pawlos Monaco Abissina del Secola XVI', Rendiconti della Reule Accademia dei Lincei 27 (1918), 285–6.
[4] See for instance, R.S. Whiteway, trans. and ed., *The Portuguese Expedition*

by royal chroniclers who exaggerated Christian victories against the Oromo; or by Christian monks who connected the sixteenth-century pastoral Oromo population movement with the contemporaneous religious wars that nearly destroyed the medieval Christian kingdom of Ethiopia. In other words, earlier accounts about the Oromo were compiled by individuals who did not know the Oromo language, who were not familiar with Oromo history, and who had no experience of the Oromo way of life, political processes, or religious institutions. As with the eighteenth-[5] and nineteenth-century[6] European travellers, these accounts were not only fragmentary but also biased and, as a consequence, the human qualities of the Oromo and their egalitarian culture were ignored.

Since the Oromo were not literate, what was written about them was mainly recorded by the Amhara and Tigrayan monks and court chroniclers. The Oromo had contact with the Amhara from at least the fourteenth century, and these interactions varied between peaceful co-existence and warfare. The warfare between the Amhara and the Oromo to no small extent influenced what the Christian monks and court chroniclers wrote about the Galla, the name by which they described the Oromo. From the fourteenth to the twentieth centuries, the local Christian and Muslim literature from the Horn of Africa and the Swahili city-states along the coast of East Africa, as well as the accounts of European missionaries, travellers, diplomats and merchants, make considerable reference to the 'Galla', the name by which the Oromo were officially called up to 1974.

Since the sixteenth century, a fundamental theme in the literature of the Christian kingdom of Ethiopia was the confrontation between the Amhara and the Oromo. According to Bairu Tafla, the result was that the Oromo were assumed to be enemies of the Amhara for all of their history.[7] As Bairu has indicated, the enmity between the two communities, magnified by religious and cultural differences, created an 'intense prejudice deeply rooted in the [Amhara]-Tigray society, a prejudice which, to the disadvantage of science and art, undermined the objective

(contd) *to Abyssinia in 1541–1543, as Narrated by Castanhoso with Some Contemporary Letters, The Short Account of Bermudez, and Certain Extracts from Correa* (London: Hakluyt Society/Kraus 1902/1967), 228–9; also, Manuel de Almeida, 'The History of High Ethiopia or Abassia Book IV', in *Some Records of Ethiopia 1593–1646*, trans. and ed. C.F. Beckingham and G.W.B. Huntingford (London: Hakluyt Society, 1954), 134–7.

[5] James Bruce, *Travels to Discover the Source of the Nile in the Years 1768, 1769, 1770, 1771, 1772, and 1773* (London: J. Ruthwen for G.G.J. and J. Robinson, 1790), vol. 2, 403. See also C.R. Markham, *A History of the Abyssinian Expedition* (London: Macmillan, 1869), 39–40.

[6] W.C. Harris, *The Highlands of Ethiopia* (London: Longman, Brown, Green and Longmans, 1844), vol. 3: 72–73. See also S. Gobat, *Journal of Three Years' Residence in Abyssinia*, 2nd edn (New York: Negro Universities Press, 1969), 52.

[7] Bairu Tafla, *Asma Giyorgis and His Work: History of the Galla and The Kingdom of Šawā*, (Stuttgart: Franz Steiner, 1987), 48.

[recording of Oromo history]'.[8] Consequently, the term 'Galla' acquired crude stereotype to the extent that Kesete Berhan Tesema, in his 1970 Amharic dictionary, defines Galla as 'uncivilized, cruel, pagan, and the enemy of the Amhara'.[9] Gadaa Melbaa has noted that 'the Abyssinians attach a derogatory connotation to the Galla, namely "pagan, savage, uncivilized, uncultured, enemy, slave or inherently inferior"'.[10] These negative concepts have become permanent attributes of Galla. In short, in the Christian literature, the Amhara and the Galla are depicted in sets of interlocking images built up out of centuries of conflict. Where the Amhara are civilized, the Galla are 'barbarians'. Where the Amhara are indigenous to Ethiopia, the Galla are 'newcomers' to the same country. Thus the Oromo past was erased by the crude representations associated with Galla, which were so often repeated and embellished that the notion of the 'savage Oromo' took on a life of its own.[11]

In his 1960 classic work, *The Name 'Negro': Its Origin and Evil Use*, Richard Moore convincingly argued that 'it is the right and duty of free and self-respecting people to name themselves fittingly as a necessary condition for placing their relationship with all other people on the plane of human dignity and mutual self-respect'.[12] Up until 1974, the Oromo were denied the basic democratic right to name themselves and to define their own identity. 'The important thing about a name is the impression which it makes in the minds of others and the reactions which it invokes through . . . association [with vicious] ideas'.[13] According to Ayele Bekerie: 'Naming plays a critical dual role either in defining or distorting one's identity, in articulating or blunting the essence of being human, and in evoking respect or disrespect from the human community.'[14]

The Oromo did not and do not call themselves 'Galla' and resist being so called. Out of over two thousand and eight hundred named Oromo clans or *gosas* (clans or descent groups), not a single one 'uses [Galla] as a self-identification'.[15] The Oromo generally used their *gosa* or clan names when referring to each other. The origin of the term Oromo is inextricably connected with the eponym Horo, who is supposed to have been 'born' at Madda Waallaabuu, the Oromo sacred land, where funda-

[8] Ibid., 49.

[9] Quoted in Toleeraa Tasmaa and Hundassa Waaqwayoo, *Seenaa Saba Oromoofi Sirna Gadaa Kitaaba Duraa* (Finfinnee: Pberna Printing, 1995), 17.

[10] Gadaa Melbaa, *Oromia: An Introduction to the History of the Oromo People* (Minneapolis, MN: Kirk House, 1999), 14.

[11] Teshale Tibebu, *The Making of Modern Ethiopia, 1896–1974* (Lawrenceville, NJ: The Red Sea Press, 1995), 17–18.

[12] Richard B. Moore, ed. W. Burghardt Turner and Joyce Moore Turner, *The Name 'Negro': Its Origin and Evil Use* (Baltimore, MD: Black Classic Press, 1992 [1960]), 97.

[13] Ibid., 48.

[14] Ayele Bekerie, 'Ethiopica: Some Historical Reflections on the Origin of the Word Ethiopia', *International Journal of Ethiopian Studies* 1, 2 (2004), 110.

[15] Gene Gragg, *Oromo Dictionary* (East Lansing, MI: Michigan State University Press, 1982), xiii.

mental Oromo institutions appear to have developed (see Chapter 3). Like most national or ethnic names, it appears that the Oromo first used the term to distinguish themselves from their non-Oromo neighbours. 'Name is surely the simplest, most literal, most obvious of all symbols of identity.'[16] As the core of their identity, Oromo has always been a collective name, 'the identifying mark' of their separate national identity. With the rise of modern political consciousness during and after the 1960s, the name Oromo has become the source of pride and hope: pride in past cultural achievements and hope for a democratic and prosperous future. Today the name Oromo 'evokes an atmosphere and drama that has power and meaning for those whom it includes'.[17] The 'magic power that has always been attributed to names'[18] is not limited only to the Oromo.

> Names keep turning up in one way or another in all the ongoing rediscoveries of group identities. The name of a country, of an individual, of a group, carries in it all the cargo of the past. A name will seldom itself be the heart of the matter of group identity, but it can often take us to where the heart can be found, leading us deep into the history, the relationships, and the emotions that lie at the center of any such affair.[19]

For the people it includes, the name Oromo represents the exact opposite of the name Galla. While Galla conveys all the negative connotations about the people and their institutions, Oromo encapsulates their positive attributes. As a collective name, Oromo is a sure sign and emblem 'of their separate identity ... by which they distinguish themselves and summarize their "essence" to themselves – as if in a name lay the magic of their existence and guarantee of their survival'.[20] According to Thomas Zitelmann, the name Oromo 'stresses the qualities of being human, free-born, a people'.[21] Zitelmann goes on to argue that 'Oromo is the ancient self-definition'.[22] It is this ancient self-definition that I employ in this book.

At the heart of Ethiopian historiography is what has been dubbed 'the sixteenth century sudden arrival of the Oromo'.[23] The underlying assumption is that the Oromo are 'newcomers to Ethiopia',

[16] Harold Isaacs, *Idols of the Tribe: Group Identity and Political Change* (New York: Harper & Row, 1975), 71.
[17] I have drawn on Anthony Smith, *The Ethnic Origins of Nations* (New York: Basil Blackwell, 1987), 23.
[18] Isaacs, *Idols of the Tribe*, 72.
[19] Ibid., 73.
[20] Smith, *Ethnic Origins of Nations*, 23.
[21] Thomas Zitelmann, 'Re-Examining the Galla/Oromo Relationship: The Stranger as a Structural Topic', in *Being and Becoming Oromo: Historical and Anthropological Enquiries*, ed. P.T.W. Baxter, Jan Hultin and Alessandro Truilzi (Uppsala: Nordiska Afrikainstitutet, 1996), 106.
[22] Ibid., 106. See also Gene Gragg, 'Oromo of Wellegga', in *The Non-Semitic Languages of Ethiopia*, ed. M. Lionel Bender (East Lansing, MI: African Studies Center, Michigan State University Press, 1976), 166.
[23] Donald Levine, *Greater Ethiopia: The Evolution of a Multiethnic Society*, 2nd edn (Chicago IL: University of Chicago Press, 2000), 78.

a historical fallacy, itself a product of anti-Oromo prejudice, nourished by long warfare between the Oromo and the Amhara. This means that, although the Oromo have been an integral part of the Cushitic-language-speaking family of peoples who have lived in the Ethiopian region for thousands of years, they were not and are still not considered as one of the original inhabitants of the country in Ethiopian historiography. While focusing on the large pastoral Oromo population movement of the sixteenth century, Ethiopianist scholars have ignored the important dynamics of the history of the country: population movements, interactions and transformations. According to Richard Olaniyan, the 'stuff of history includes migrations, wars, triumphs and tragedies, the extinction and the emergence of ... kingdoms, and much else'.[24] In other words, population movement belongs in history, whether it was in Ethiopia, elsewhere in Africa or the rest of the world. As Paul Kennedy has noted, 'human history has always been shaped by the growth of and migration of population'.[25] Though unrecorded by historians, such is the case in the Ethiopian region. In fact, the fourteenth- and sixteenth-century Christian-Muslim conflicts in Ethiopia were partly a response to population movements.[26] Population movement, especially from the northern region to southern parts of Ethiopia still continues.

Oromo population movement followed patterns that were well established in the Horn of Africa. For instance, the Afar and the Somali migrated from southern Ethiopia to their present locations. A number of Semitic-speaking groups such as the Adare (Harari), the Gurage and the Amhara migrated early in their history. As the Amhara people slowly moved from their original homeland of Beta Amhara (in what is today the Wallo region) to what is today the Shawa region and beyond, a number of Oromo groups appear to have moved from the region of Bale to the region of Shawa. Though limited, we find references to Oromo groups already living in the medieval Christian kingdom during the fourteenth century, possibly earlier (see Chapter 2). Who is to say when their forefathers arrived there? 'Whole populations seldom suddenly arrive in regions. Migration is more often an ongoing process over decades and even centuries'.[27] What is certain is that while the Amhara communities moved from the north to the south, Oromo *gosas* moved from the south to the north. Both groups were not moving at the same time. Nevertheless, it appears that they met most likely in what is today the Shawa region.

[24] Richard Olaniyan, ed., *African History and Culture* (Lagos: Longman, 1990 [1982]), 2.
[25] Paul Kennedy, *Preparing for the Twenty-First Century* (New York: Random House, 1993), cover page.
[26] See for instance, Merid Wolde Aregay, 'Population Movement as a Possible Factor in the Christian-Muslim Conflict of Medieval Ethiopia', in *Symposium Leo Frobenius* (Munich: Derlag Dokumentation, 1974), 261–81.
[27] Richard Greenfield and Mohammed Hassen, 'Interpretation of Oromo Nationality', *Horn of Africa* 3, 3 (1980), 6.

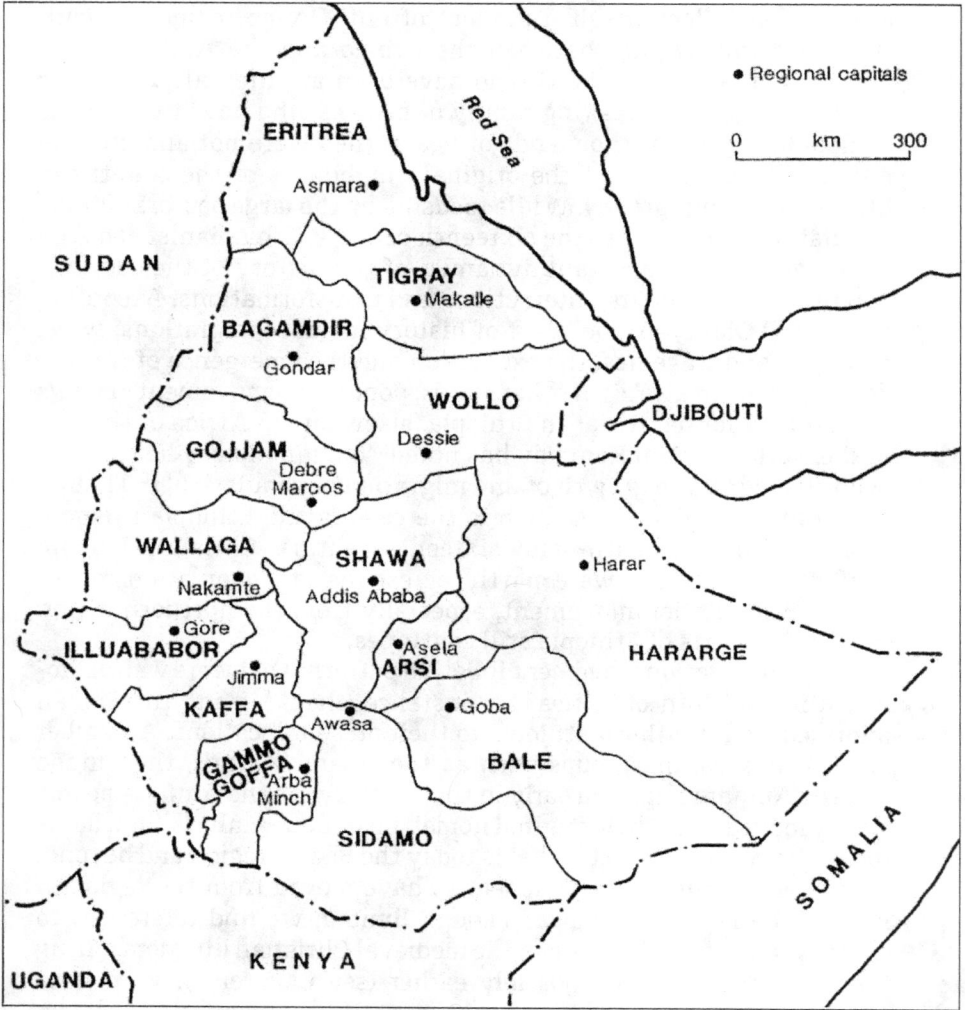

Map 1   Modern administrative regions of Ethiopia to 1974 (adapted from Hassen, *The Oromo of Ethiopia: a history 1570–1860*, Cambridge: Cambridge University Press, 1990).

The Oromo, who constitute at least 40 per cent of the population of Ethiopia, are the single largest Cushitic-language-speaking national group in Africa: 'Cushitic is the third largest Afro-Asiatic language in the world after Arabic and Hausa.'[28] How did the Oromo achieve this distinction? I believe the answer to this question lies in the *gada* system, the dynamic institution that enabled the pastoral Oromo not only to expand over a wider territory within and beyond Ethiopia but also to absorb and assimilate a very large non-Oromo population. There is no doubt that the Oromo nation was shaped by the *gada* system. In fact, it is very difficult, if not impossible, to account for the rise of the Oromo into prominence in the Horn of Africa, their increase in population, and their impressive movement within and beyond Ethiopia without reference to the *gada* system.

In the first three chapters, I assemble evidence that demonstrates the presence of Oromo groups within the medieval Christian kingdom. Those sedentary Oromo-language-speaking groups that lived under the Christian administration since the fourteenth century were not part of the sixteenth-century pastoral Oromo population movement. This pre-sixteenth-century Oromo presence within the medieval Christian kingdom is generally ignored or overlooked in Ethiopian historiography.

In Chapter 1, I explore the pre-sixteenth-century Oromo interactions with Christian and Muslim peoples in and south of the region of Shawa and the influences those interactions had on the Oromo creation myth, the story of the Sacred Book of the Oromo, the Borana and Barentu moiety system and the Qalluu institution. The influences may be direct or indirect, but their impact is visible. The Oromo creation myth shares with the Hebrew, Christian and Muslim myths of origin a single Creator, the elements of darkness and water, and the creation of the earth, sky and sun. In the Oromo cosmology it is Waaqa (God) who 'created heaven and earth and all that is found on and in them'.[29] Like the God of the 'Peoples of the Book' (Hebrews, Christians and Muslims), the Oromo God is universal. Although not one of the Peoples of the Book, through early interactions with their Christian and Muslim neighbours the Oromo may have realized that their neighbours' holy books provided significant guidance and wisdom. To overcome their lack of such a book, with its 'magic' of reading and writing, the Oromo invented a story of a lost sacred text. That and other legends appear to be highly influenced by Christian and Muslim concepts. For example, the explanation for the early division of the Oromo into the two moieties of Borana and Barentu (Barentuma) is 'caught up in a mytho-poetical past that is shared with the Peoples of the Book'.[30]

---

[28] Gragg, *Oromo Dictionary*, xvi.
[29] Gemetchu Megerssa, 'Knowledge, Identity and the Colonizing Structure: The Case of the Oromo in East and Northeast Africa' (PhD diss., University of London, 1994), 90, 146.
[30] Zitelmann, 'Re-Examining the Galla/Oromo Relationship', 106.

The Qalluu institution was the core of traditional Oromo religion,[31] 'believed to have existed since mythical times'.[32] The Qalluu was the person who performed ritual sacrifices, interpreted the laws of Waaqa, and served as a link between Waaqa and the Oromo. As the spiritual leader of traditional Oromo religion, the Qalluu himself became the Abba Muudaa, which literally means the 'father' of the *muudaa* rituals. *Muudaa* refers to both the ceremony held every eight years to honour the holy person – the Qalluu – and the pilgrimage to his shrine, which is a sacred site. Those who went on pilgrimage to honour the Qalluu were known as *jila*. Just as Christian and Muslim pilgrims visited the birth-places of their religions, for centuries Oromo pilgrims – *jila* – visited the land of Abba Muudaa located in what are today the regions of Bale and Sidamo in southern Ethiopia. For the Oromo the land of Abba Muudaa is said to be a place of righteousness, wisdom, harmony, peace and *gada* democracy. There is clear evidence that the highland Oromo calendar was influenced by Christian and Muslim concepts. However, this aspect cannot be discussed here. It should suffice to say that the measurement of time was important for the *gada* system: rituals, ceremonies, political, military and religious activities were regulated by an elaborate calendar, considered one of 'the highest cultural achievements of the Oromo society'.[33]

In Chapter 2, I present evidence that establishes the presence of Oromo-speaking groups in some parts of Shawa, Arsi, northern and southern Bale, and western Hararghe before the sixteenth century. The region of Shawa was the heartland of the fourteenth-century medieval Christian kingdom. It appears that the term Galla probably came into use during the Zagwe period, traditionally dated from 1137 to 1270. However, the recent archaeological work of David Phillipson suggests that the Zagwe Dynasty existed from 1000 to 1270.[34] These latter dates are followed in this study. By the time Yikunno Amlak established the Shawn Amhara dynasty (1270–85), there is a clear reference to a Galla group as 'trouble makers'.[35] This information is written in the hagiography of Bishop Zena-Markos, whose death was accompanied by a conflict between his disciples and the Oromo. The presence of some Oromo groups within the medieval Christian kingdom is also confirmed by the Chronicle of Emperor Amda-Siyon (1314–44), which refers to a people called Galla and their country, '*Hagara Galla*' (the country of the Galla).[36]

---

[31] In this section, I have heavily drawn on Mohammed Hassen, 'Pilgrimage to the Abba Muudaa', *Journal of Oromo Studies* 12, 1–2 (July 2005). 142–57.
[32] Karl Knutsson, *Authority and Change: A Study of the Kallu Institution among the Macha Galla of Ethiopia* (Gothenburg: Etnografiska Museet, 1967), 65.
[33] Asmarom Legesse, *Gada: Three Approaches to the Study of African Society* (New York: The Free Press, 1973), 282.
[34] David W. Phillipson, *Foundations of an African Civilisation: Aksum & The Northern Horn 1000 BC – AD 1300* (Woodbridge: James Currey, 2012), 228.
[35] Haile, *The Works of Abba Bahriy*, 27.
[36] Ibid., 26.

Map 2 Fra Mauro's map of 1460, showing the location of the Galla River (from Crawford, *Ethiopian Itineraries circa 1400–1524 including those collected by Alessandro Zorzi at Venice in the years 1519–1524*, Cambridge: Hakluyt Society / Cambridge University Press, 1858, reproduced by kind permission of Hakluyt Society).

The designation Galla appears for the first time in European sources on a map made for Prince Henry the Navigator of Portugal by Fra Maura (see Map 2), created in 1460.[37] The Galla River of Mauro's map is also at the very centre of an important Amhara tradition that deals with Galla Forest. The use of Galla in these sources indicates long historic contacts between the Amhara and at least some Oromo groups. Christian hagiographies also refer to Oromo clans or putative descent groups, such as the Galan, Yaya, Liban and Lalo, living in and around the region of Shawa during the thirteenth and fourteenth centuries.[38] Arab Faqih, a historian of the sixteenth-century jihad, refers to a number of sedentary Oromo groups who lived under the Christian administration, including the Warra Qaalluu.[39] This further confirms the pre-sixteenth-century Oromo presence in the kingdom.

The sixteenth-century pastoral Oromo population originated in the southern regions of Ethiopia. However, as an integral part of the Cushitic-language-speaking family of peoples, who is to say that the Oromo did not live centuries earlier in the northern parts of what is today Ethiopia? Christopher Ehret states that the movement of 'proto-Cushitic language speakers' was 'initially along the roughly north/south axis through the middle of the Ethiopian highlands'.[40] Most likely the Oromo developed their separate identity in the southern region of Ethiopia. What is not in doubt is the fact that the Oromo lived within central and southern regions of present-day Ethiopia. What some Ethiopianist scholars do not realize is that while the Oromo migrated within Ethiopia before, during and after the sixteenth century, they did not come into Ethiopia from outside the country. Indeed, Oromo internal migration within Ethiopia is a fact beyond dispute; their immigration into Ethiopia is a myth perpetuated by confusing historical Abyssinia and modern Ethiopia. Historical Abyssinia was no more than one-third of modern Ethiopia, the boundaries of which were determined in the last two decades of the nineteenth century. The claim that the Oromo

[37] O.G.S. Crawford, ed., *Ethiopian Itineraries circa 1400–1524 including those collected by Alessandro Zorzi at Venice in the years 1519–1524* (Cambridge: Hakluyt Society / Cambridge University Press, 1958), 16.

[38] Among others, see Tadesse Tamrat, *Church and State in Ethiopia, 1270–1527* (Oxford: Clarendon Press, 1972), 184. See also Negaso Gidada, *History of the Sayyoo Oromoo of Southwestern Wallaga, Ethiopia from about 1730 to 1886* (Addis Ababa: Mega Printing Enterprise, 2001), chapter 2; Alemayehu Haile et al., eds., *History of the Oromo to the Sixteenth Century*, 2nd ed. (Finfinnee: Oromia Culture and Tourism Bureau, 2006), 42–76; Mekuria Bulcha, *Contours of the Emergent and Ancient Oromo Nation: Dilemmas in the Ethiopian Politics of State and Nation-Building* (Cape Town: Centre for Advanced Studies of African Society, 2011), chapter 4.

[39] Arab Faqih (Chihab Eddin B. Abdel Qadir), *Futuh Al-Habasha (Histoire de la conquête de l'Abyssinie XVI siècle)*, trans. and ed. M.R. Basset (Paris, 1897), 135–7, 269, 298. See also Arab Faqih, Futuh *Al-Habasha*, Arabic text, (Cairo: 1974), 254–5.

[40] Christopher Ehret, 'Cushitic Prehistory', in *The Non-Semitic Languages of Ethiopia*, ed. M. Lionel Bender (African Studies Center, East Lansing, MI: Michigan State University Press, 1976), 88.

migrated into Ethiopia is based on an inaccurate historical premise that seeks to establish their homeland outside the contemporary borders of the modern state, thus making them 'newcomers to the country'[41] rather than indigenous inhabitants.

In Chapter 3, I explore various theories about the origins of the Oromo, followed by discussion of the homelands of pastoral Oromo on the eve of the sixteenth century. Some writers claimed that the Oromo originated from beyond Africa,[42] while others speculated that they came from central Africa.[43] Still others assumed that they originated in northern Somalia[44] or northern Kenya.[45] The pastoral Oromo themselves, the protagonists of the massive sixteenth-century migrations, have never claimed any homeland other than the regions of Bale, Sidamo and Gamu Gofa. Yet very few writers have paid attention to what the pastoral Oromo oral tradition had to say about their homelands. Careful interpretation of such narratives provides insight into the political economy of their different homelands on the eve of their epoch-making migrations. I try to establish the area in which the Oromo first appear to have become conscious of their distinct identity, separate from their neighbours, with their own political, cultural and religious institutions, and to designate their six homelands. Among the major factors that led to the large pastoral Oromo population movement were increases in the human and animal populations and the militarization of the *gada* system, which was most likely a response to the pressure from the southward-expanding Christian kingdom.

In Chapters 4 and 5, I discuss the factors that facilitated the rapid spread of pastoral Oromo from southern to northern and western regions of Ethiopia. These included the destructive jihads of 1529–43 and of 1559, civil war that created instability within the Christian kingdom, and effective guerrilla tactics with which Oromo warriors unnerved the unarmed Christian peasantry. In fact, 1559 was a landmark in the history of the Christian kingdom, the Muslim state of Harar, and pastoral Oromo population movements. The power of both Chris-

---

[41] Mohammed Hassen, *The Oromo of Ethiopia: A History 1570–1860* (Cambridge: Cambridge University Press, 1990), xii–xiii.

[42] Asma Giyorgis, followed by others, claimed that the Oromo originated in Asia and came to Ethiopia via Madagscar. See Tafla, *The Works of Asma Giyorgis*, 137, note 166. Martial de Salviac connected the Oromo with ancient Gauls in France. See Martial de Salviac, *An Ancient People, a Great African Nation: The Oromo*, ed. and trans. Ayalew Kanno (Self-published, 2005), 367–9.

[43] Charles Beke believed that the Oromo came from Central Africa. See his 'On the Origin of the Galla', *Report to the 1847 meeting of the British Association for the Advancement of Science* (London, 1848), 6–7. See also Antoine d'Abbadie, 'On the Oromo: Great African Nation Often Designated under the Name "Galla",' trans. Ayalew Kanno, *Journal of Oromo Studies* 14, 1 (March 2007), 119.

[44] I.M. Lewis, 'The Galla in Northern Somaliland', *Rassegna di Studi Etiopici* 15 (1959), 21–38.

[45] Richard Pankhurst, *The Ethiopian Borderlands: Essays in Regional History from Ancient Times to the End of the 18th Century* (Lawrenceville, NJ: Red Sea Press, 1997), 279.

tians and Muslims dramatically decreased after the jihad of 1559, while the power of the pastoral Oromo substantially increased. The sudden and radical transformation in the balance of power quickly brought to an end two centuries of struggle between Muslims and Christians, replacing it by the struggle of both against the Oromo for the next three centuries.

Chapter 6 is devoted to Abba Bahrey, the famous sixteenth-century historian and poet, and his campaign against the Oromo. Among other works, Abba Bahrey authored *Zenahu le Galla*, which is can be translated as 'News of the Galla', 'Ethnography of the Galla' or 'History of the Galla'. It was *Zenahu le Galla* that in so many ways shaped the presentation of Oromo history in Ethiopian historiography. Bahrey's manuscript is an invaluable eye-witness account about the warfare between the Oromo and his Christian society. As the first detailed description of Oromo social organization, their clan or sectional names and their population movements, it is a major contribution to our understanding of the pastoral Oromo population movements of the second half of the sixteenth century and their impact on both the Christian and Muslim communities. His manuscript also contains detailed explanations of how the class structure of the Christian society severely weakened its defences against Oromo attacks. As an eye-witness account, Abba Bahrey's manuscript has been celebrated as an original text. Nevertheless, such status does not mean that the manuscript is free from inaccuracies and prejudices. Surprisingly there is not a single critical analysis of Bahrey's manuscript. Rather, modern Ethiopianist scholars display a willingness, even an eagerness, to endorse Bahrey's anti-Oromo prejudice. Abba Bahrey wrote *Zenahu le Galla* not to emphasize the human qualities of the Oromo, but to exaggerate their brutality. However, the brutality that Bahrey attributes exclusively to Oromo warriors was also shared by Christian soldiers (see Chapters 5, 7 and 8). Abba Bahrey could understand the Oromo society of his time only from the viewpoint of his culture. Therefore his work must be interpreted with caution; he was a man of his time, a product of his Christian society, and its anti-Oromo prejudice was shaped by the experience of long warfare between the Amhara Christians and the Oromo, of which Bahrey himself was a victim. He had a concrete purpose in writing about Oromo military strength as well as their alien customs. styling them as less human than members of his own Christian society. If we ignore the anti-Oromo prejudice of Bahrey's Christian society that coloured his views about the Oromo, we run the risk of accepting everything he wrote as an objective work of a neutral scholar, thus canonizing all his negative views of the Oromo. His writings must be analysed within the background of knowledge production in an environment of conflict, i.e. the warfare between the Christians and the Oromo during the second half of the sixteenth century. Finally, Abba Bahrey's *Zenahu le Galla* appears to have inspired at least three Amhara emperors to conduct aggressive campaigns against the Oromo. Of those three emperors, I examine in Chapter 6 the impact that Bahrey's manuscript had on Emperor Za-Dengel (1603–04).

Chapter 7 deals with the Oromo and the Christian kingdom *c.* 1600–18 during the first part of the reign of Emperor Susenyos (1607–32). As a young man, he lived in captivity for two years among the Oromo. He was adopted and became the 'son' of a Borana[46] Oromo clan, thus becoming the first Amhara prince to have been adopted by the Oromo. For the Oromo, once adopted, Susenyos was one of them. According to his chronicle, 'the [Oromo] who captured him liked and treated him as [his own] child'.[47] He was the first Amhara prince who had command of the Oromo language, learned their manners and acquired their fighting skill. He was also the first Amhara prince to marry an Oromo woman, a daughter of an influential *gada* official.[48] In the process, Susenyos initiated a tradition of an Amhara prince marrying a woman from an influential Oromo clan, the process by which enterprising Oromo leaders came to dominate the Christian kingdom itself by the middle of the eighteenth century. Above all, Susenyos was the first Amhara prince who discovered the secret of Oromo strength – their effective fighting method. He made it an integral part of his own war strategy. It was with Oromo warriors and Oromo tactics that he made himself the Christian emperor. In gratitude for their support, Susenyos settled several friendly Oromo groups in regions under his control. However, the presence of a sizable contingent of Oromo in his army intensified Christian suspicion. In order to allay their fears and dilute opposition, Susenyos had to demonstrate his concern for defending the country by a relentless attack on non-Christian Oromo. Few Amhara kings of the century had been more driven by the desire to gain back lost territory or, at the very least, to make the Oromo into loyal subjects, than Susenyos.[49] Although he was not able to turn the tide militarily against the Oromo, Susenyos was very successful in settling numerous Oromo groups in Gojjam and Begameder, where they were converted to Christianity and adopted Amharic language and culture, thus becoming an integral part of the dominant Amhara society. In other words, Susenyos was able to cause irreparable damage to Oromo unity by permanently alienating a significant part of the Oromo from their nation and integrating them into Amhara Christian society.

Chapter 8 examines Oromo Christianization and the beginning of the breakdown of Oromo social organization, their deeper involvement in the seventeenth-century religious conflicts within the Christian kingdom, the conflation of Oromo interests with those of the people they wanted to conquer, and their assimilation into Amhara society. Like Susenyos,

---

[46] The adoption ceremony was undertaken by the Abba Gada on behalf of his *gosa* or clan or confederacy. Once adopted, Susenyos became the 'son' of the Borana group that adopted him. By their adoption criteria, Susenyos was the first Oromo 'son' to be the emperor of the Christian kingdom. On adoption see pp. 156–8.

[47] Esteves Pereira, ed., *Chronica de Susenyos, Rei d'Ethiopia* (Lisbon: Impresa Nacional, 1892–1900), 4.

[48] Harold Marcus, *A History of Ethiopia* (Los Angeles, CA: University of California Press, 1994), 39.

[49] Philip Caraman, *The Lost Empire: The Story of the Jesuits in Ethiopia, 1555–1634* (Notre Dame, IN: University of Notre Dame Press, 1985), 59.

Emperor Iyasu (1681–1706) conducted aggressive wars against the Oromo. His objective was to reverse the tide of Oromo victory and force them into submission. The strategy and tactics of Iyasu's campaigns reveal the influence on him of Bahrey's *Zenahu le Galla*. What is more, Iyasu was the most powerful Christian emperor since the time of Susenyos; he was able to marshal and make effective use of a significant number of firearms.[50] He was therefore militarily in a much better position than the Oromo, 'many of whom he sought to assimilate or bring under his control'.[51] It was during Iyasu's reign that the Christianized Oromo elite first attempted to influence the royal succession, albeit unsuccessfully.[52] To integrate Christianized Oromo into his administration, Iyasu elevated the famous Christianized Oromo Tullu to the rank of *dajazmach* (commander of the vanguard) and appointed him as the governor of the region of Damot in Gojjam. Emperor Iyasu gave in marriage his own daughter to Tullu, reflecting the undeniable rise of the power of Christianized Oromo elite.[53] He thus began the practice of integrating powerful individuals of Oromo origin into the royal family. Iyasu also promoted the Dajazmach Tige, an enterprising warrior, 'to the prestigious rank of Behtwadad, or "Beloved" of the king, apparently the first Oromo to enjoy the highly esteemed status'.[54] Despite his aggressive campaigns against the Oromo east of the Abby River (Blue Nile), Iyasu was not able to achieve the desired victories. Instead, by 1700, a Christianized Oromo elite had emerged as a major force in the political landscape of the Christian kingdom itself. In the Epilogue I discuss how in the following century Christianized Oromo gained substantial behind-the-throne influence on royal successions and imperial decisions.

The Oromo and the Christian Kingdom, 1300–1700 is as much history of the Christian kingdom itself as it is history of the Oromo and their interaction with Christians, which ultimately shaped and transformed the destiny of both communities.

[50] Pankhurst, *The Ethiopian Borderlands*, 315.
[51] Ibid., 309.
[52] Merid Wolde Aregay, 'Southern Ethiopia and the Christian Kingdom, 1508–1708, with special reference to the Galla migrations and their Consequences' (PhD diss., University of London, 1971), 578–9.
[53] Tafla, *Asma Giyorgis and His Work*, 415.
[54] Pankhurst, *The Ethiopian Borderlands*, 317.

I

Early Interactions among the Oromo, Christian and Muslim Peoples: Traditions and Institutions

There is a long history of interactions among the Oromo, Christian, and Muslim communities in and south of the region of Shawa. These interactions influenced how the Oromo constructed their uniquely enriched African cosmology. History of interactions among the three communities goes back to the thirteenth and fourteenth centuries. However, the topic of early Christian and Muslim influences on some Oromo institutions has hardly been imagined, much less covered, in the Ethiopian scholarly discourse. Established historical wisdom asserts that neither Christian nor Muslim ideas influenced Oromo institutions and, if there ever were any such influence, it must have happened after 1522. Why after 1522? In his 1593 manuscript, *Zenahu le Galla*, Abba Bahrey suggested 1522 as the time when the Oromo attacked the province of Bali for first time during the reign of King Libna Dengel (1508–40). Bali was one of the most-important Muslim states that was conquered by Emperor Amda-Siyon and incorporated into the southward-expanding Christian kingdom between 1330–32 (see Map 3). The state of Bali was located in the northern most part of the current regions of Arsi/ Bale. Though 1522 is a misleading date, it has become accepted as marking the arrival of the Oromo as 'newcomers' on the border of the Christian Kingdom of Abyssinia. It also marks the popularization of the name of Galla in Ethiopian historiography. The untenability of 1522 as the date of the 'Oromo arrival' will be examined in Chapters 2 and 3.

The main argument of this chapter is that the Oromo had long maintained interactions with Christian and Muslim peoples in the region of what is today Shawa and southern Ethiopia and, consequently, were exposed to the Christian and Muslim ideas that influenced aspects of Oromo traditions and institutions. This argument is based partly on previously untapped sources and partly on fresh interpretation of existing data coupled with an examination of some Oromo oral traditions that have been ignored in Ethiopian historiography. Some scholars continue to assert that 1522 marks the beginning of documented Oromo history[1] and that re-examining earlier data is 'inventing

---

[1] Ulrich Braukämper, 'Oromo Country of Origin: A Reconsideration of Hypotheses', *Ethiopian Studies: Proceedings of the Sixth International Conference, 14–17 April 1980*, ed. Gideon Goldenberg (Boston: A.A. Balkema, 1986), 35.

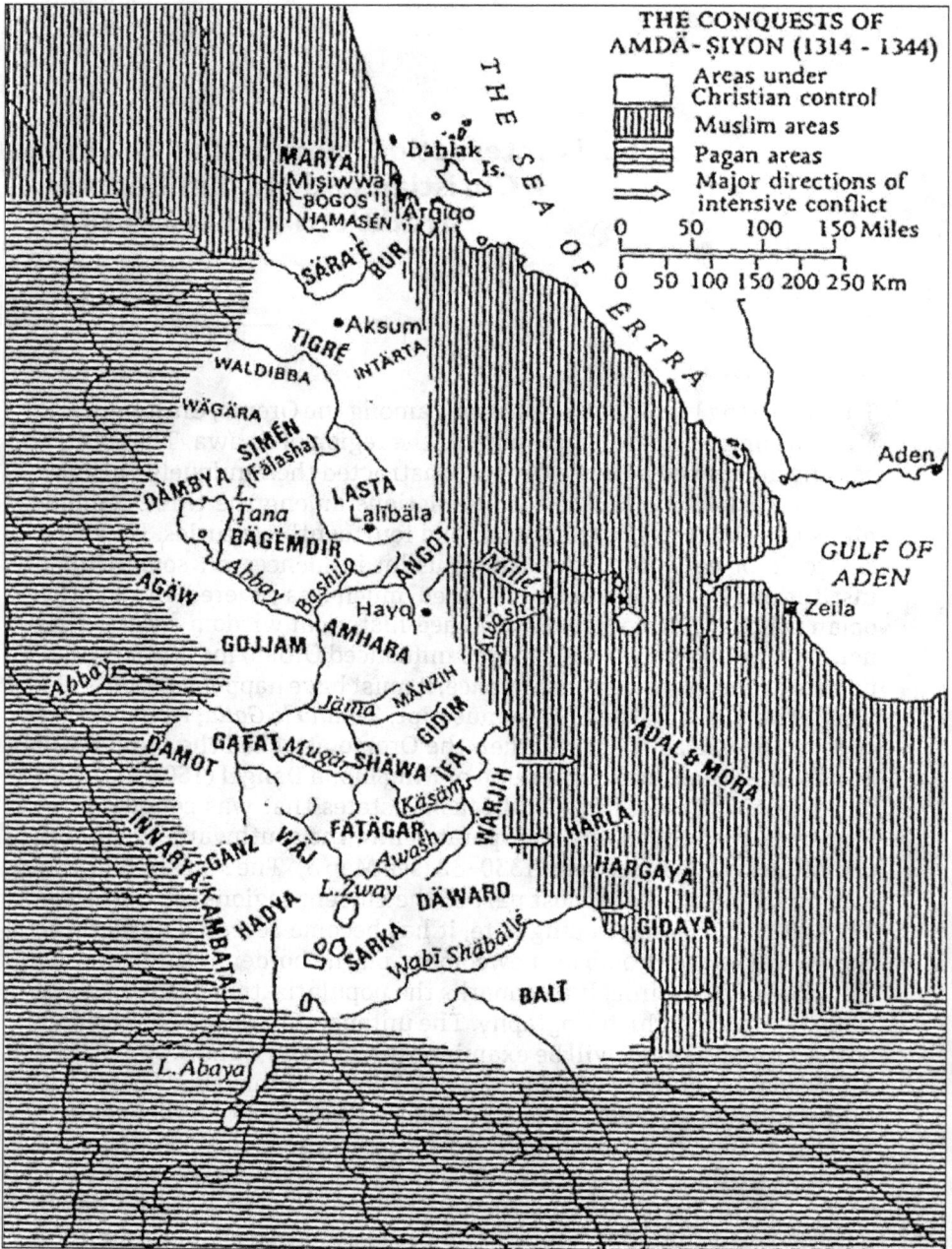

Map 3 Territorial expansion of the Christian kingdom 1314–1344 (adapted from Tamrat, *Church and State in Ethiopia, 1270–1527*, Los Angeles: Tsehai Publishers, reprinted 2009, adapted by kind permission of Tsehai Publishers).

history'.[2] I, however, agree with Jan Vansina that 'The discipline of history evolves as much through reconsideration of older evidence as through the adduction of new evidence, and oral data should be part of this process.'[3] Furthermore, Vansina emphasizes the importance of oral tradition in the reconstruction of the past.

> Oral traditions have a part to play in the reconstruction of the past. The importance of this part varies according to place and time. It is a part similar to that played by written sources because both are messages from the past to the present, and messages are key elements in historical reconstruction. When writing fails tradition comes on stage. This is wrong. Wherever oral traditions are extant they remain an indispensable source for reconstruction. They correct other perspectives just as much as other perspectives correct them.[4]

This chapter and the next one will examine the existing data from a new perspective and establish that the Oromo were exposed to both Christian and Muslim ideas that, in turn, may have influenced their traditions and some key institutions. Let me make one point very clear. By discussing the Christian and Muslim influence on some aspects of Oromo institutions, I am not suggesting that the Oromo borrowed their idea of one God from their Christian and Muslim neighbours. Far from it: the Oromo belief in one God was rooted in the Cushitic-speaking peoples' belief in Waaqa (this being an ancient Cushitic name for God). Christopher Ehret argues that the Cushitic-language-speaking peoples' concept of Waaqa 'is the earliest instance of religious syncretism yet known in world history'.[5] This, according to Ehret, had occurred 'sometime in the eighth or seventh millennium BCE' when the early Cushitic-speaking peoples, living in what are today eastern parts of northern Sudan and northern parts of Ethiopia, adopted the eastern Saharo-Sahelian peoples' concept of divinity. 'They chose their own word for the new concept of spirit, expanding the meaning of the old Cushitic root word *waaq'a* for "sky" to apply to both "sky" and "Divinity."'[6] Though Oromo belief in one God predates those of their Christian and Muslim neighbours, their basic institutions appear to have been influenced by ideas radiating from these at least since the twelfth century. Even Mekuria Bulcha, who appears to reject the thesis of Christian and Islamic influences on Oromo institutions, admits that 'the traditional Oromo religion contains many concepts which are similar in meaning to Semitic religious concepts'.[7] As indicated below, striking similarities among the

---

[2] See for instance, Harold Marcus, 'Does the Past Have any Authority in Ethiopia?' *The Ethiopian Review* (April 1992), 18–21.

[3] Jan Vansina, *Oral Tradition as History* (Madison, WI: University of Wisconsin Press, 1985), 200.

[4] Ibid., 199.

[5] Christopher Ehret, *The Civilizations of Africa: A History To 1800* (Charlottesville, VA: University Press of Virginia, 2002), 91.

[6] Ibid., 79.

[7] Mekuria Bulcha, *Contours of the Emergent and Ancient Oromo Nation: Dilemmas in the Ethiopian Politics of State and Nation-Building* (Cape Town, South Africa: The Centre for Advanced Studies of African Society, 2011), 238.

Christian, Muslim and Oromo religious ideas reflect the long interaction among the three communities.

Christian traditions show the existence of contact between the Oromo and the Amhara during the thirteenth century, and possibly earlier. Muslim narratives, as reported by Arthur Starkie, show that some Oromo groups may have had contact with the people of the City of Harar 'since the thirteenth century'.[8] What is more, a Muslim source from Harar mentions an Oromo presence in the Ramis River Valley during the fourteenth century. This was the earliest reference in a Muslim source to the name Oromo, which indicates that the name was an ancient self-designation. Somali narratives also mention an Oromo presence within the Muslim states of southern Ethiopia during the fourteenth century. The hagiographical traditions that mention early interaction between some Oromo groups and the Christian society are believed to have been written during the thirteenth century.[9] Professor Getatchew Haile's book also mentions the contact between Christians and some Oromo groups during the thirteenth century.[10]

The narratives that deal with increasing contacts between the Amhara and some Oromo groups during the fourteenth century were written down during the sixteenth century and possibly earlier.[11] The Muslim stories from the city of Harar were written during the eighteenth century,[12] while the Somali tradition that dealt with the subject was collected over the centuries but published only in 1974.[13] Oromo oral narratives that reflect Christian and Muslim influence upon their institutions were recorded during the nineteenth and twentieth centuries.[14] The recorded Amhara and Muslim traditions that deal with early Oromo history will be examined in this and the following chapters.

This chapter focuses primarily on the Oromo traditions. We have to allow a measure of validity to these traditions for three obvious reasons. These narratives provide an Oromo perspective that deserves scholarly investigation. Jan Vansina writes: 'such sources are irreplaceable, not

[8] Enid Starkie, *Arthur Rimbaud in Abyssinia* (Oxford: Clarendon Press, 1937), 8.
[9] See for instance, E.A.W. Budge, trans. and ed., *The Book of the Mysteries of Heaven and Earth, and other works of Bakhayla Mîkâ'êl,-Zôsîmâs* (London: Oxford University Press 1935), xix.
[10] Getachew Haile, *The Works of Abba Bahriy and Other Documents Concerning the Oromo*, in Amharic (Avon, MN: self-published, 2002), 27.
[11] Mohammed Hassen, 'The Pre-Sixteenth Century Oromo Presence Within the Medieval Christian Kingdom of Ethiopia', in *A River of Blessings: Essays in Honor of Paul Baxter*, ed. David Brokensha (Syracuse, NY: Syracuse University, 1994), 47.
[12] E. Wagner, trans. and ed., *Legende und Geschichte: der Fatah Madinat Harar von Yahya Nasrallah* (Wiesbaden: Steiner, 1978), 120–1.
[13] Sheikh Ahmad Abdullahi Rirash, *Kashf as Sudul Can Tarikhas-Sumal: Wahamalikahumas-Sabca* (Uncovering the Somali History and their Seven Kingdoms) (Mogadishu: 1974), 36–37.
[14] A. Cecchi, *Da Zeila alle Frontiere del Caffa* (Rome: Ermanno Loescher, 1886–1887), vol. 2, 30, translation in K.E. Knutsson, *Authority and Change: A Study of the Kallu Institution Among the Macha Galla of Ethiopia* (Gothenburg: Etnografiska Museet, 1967), 148.

only because information would otherwise be lost, but because they are sources "from the inside"'.[15] Inside sources not only provide insight into the Oromo world-view but also facilitate the construction of a broader and more accurate picture of early Oromo history. What is more, Oromo oral traditions provide us with a source of information that has not been previously tapped. Vansina underlines the importance of oral tradition in recording the past of non-literate societies.

> It follows that oral traditions are not just a source about the past, but a histo-riology (one dare not write historiography!) of the past, an account of how people have interpreted it. As such oral tradition is not only a raw source. It is a hypothesis, similar to the historian's own interpretation of the past. Therefore oral traditions should be treated as hypotheses, and as the first hypothesis the modern scholar must test before he or she considers others. To consider them first means not to accept them literally, uncritically. It means to give them the attention they deserve, to take pains to prove or disprove them systematically for each case on its own merits.[16]

Additionally, like other traditions, Oromo oral traditions have messages that are sometimes direct, at other times indirect, sometimes clear and at other times ambiguous. They are presented in the form of legends and myths, which, on closer inspection, show Christian and Muslim influence on Oromo traditions and on some of their basic institutions. This chapter explores four examples, starting with the simple and yet interesting Oromo creation myth and the 'Sacred Book of the Oromo', which will be followed by a detailed discussion of the Oromo moiety system and the Qaalluu institution.

THE OROMO CREATION MYTH

The Oromo creation myth shares many elements with the cosmology of other African peoples. However, unlike some Africans, such as the Dogon of Mali who produced a highly complex creation myth, the Oromo creation story is not elaborate. Father Lambert Bartels' book shows that the Oromo do not have 'impressive creation myths as there are to be found with the Jews and other peoples'.[17] Additional information about the Oromo creation myth will be discussed in Chapter 3. In this section I will attempt to show shared elements with Biblical tradition, monotheism, God, creation, while pointing out significant differences revealing originality of Oromo concepts.

The Oromo creation myth appears to have been influenced either by Christian or Muslim ideas or a combination of both. The influence may be direct or indirect. But the impact is visible. To show that influence, let me start by quoting from the Hebrew/ Christian creation myth.

[15] Vansina, *Oral Tradition as History*, 197.
[16] Ibid., 196.
[17] Lambert Bartels, *Oromo Religion: Myths and Rites of the Western Oromo of Ethiopia: An Attempt to Understand* (Berlin: Dietrich Reimer, 1983), 360.

> In the beginning God created the heavens and the earth. Now the earth was formless and empty, darkness was over the surface of the deep, and the Spirit of God was hovering over the waters. And God said, 'Let there be light', and there was light. God saw that the light was good, and he separated the light from the darkness. God called the light 'day', and the darkness he called 'night'. And there was evening, and there was morning – the first day. And God said, 'Let there be an expanse between the waters to separate water from water.' So God made the expanse and separated the water under the expanse from the water above it. And it was so. God called the expanse 'sky'. And there was evening, and there was morning – the second day.[18]

The Muslim creation myth is not as elaborate as the Hebrew/Christian one. The Qur'an states that it is 'Allah who created the heavens and the earth in six days', and 'made the darkness and the light'. The Qur'an adds that it is Allah 'who created the heavens and the earth in true (proportions): the day He saith, "Be," behold it is: His word is the truth'.[19] For the Oromo creation is *uumaa*. The term refers 'to the entire physical world and the living things and divine beings contained within it ... The term *uumaa* is derived from the verb *uumu* meaning literally "to create". The nominal form of *uumaa* therefore refers to everything that is created, in short, to *Waaqa's* (God's) creation.'[20] Though limited in its scope, the Oromo creation myth does have an order of creation that it shares with the above Hebrew/Christian myth, including the Creator, indirectly the Spirit of the Creator, the elements of darkness and water, and creation of the earth and the sky and the sun. In the Oromo cosmology it is Waaqa, who 'created heaven and earth and all that is found on and in them'.[21] The Oromo creation myth according to Dabasssa Guyyo's account as presented by Gemechtu Megerssa states:

> In the beginning there was nothing but water. The Creator divided the water into that of the *gubba* or 'above' and into that of *goola* or 'below.' This Waaqa created in the dim light, resembling that of *boru* [first light]. Then Waaqa created the sky (*qollo*) out of the upper water, separating from the sky. In the sky, Waaqa placed *bakkalcha*, the morning star. Waaqa then brought forth dry land out of the water of below. This was followed by the rising sun. Before this time, the sun did not exist ... Once the sun was set in motion, its movement created day and night. Then using *bakkalcha*, the morning star, Waaqa created all the numerous stars of heaven, the animals and plants of the dry land and all the creatures that float in the air and those that swim in water.[22]

In the creation myths of the Hebrews, Christians and Muslims, the Creator 'is an infinitely perfect spiritual being that creates a physical

---

[18] International Bible Society, *The Holy Bible: New International Version* (Hodder & Stoughton, 1986), Genesis 1: 1–8.
[19] Abdallah Yusuf Ali, new edn and rev. trans. *The Meaning of the Holy Qur'an* (Beltsville, MD: Amana Publications, 1996), 294, 313, 359.
[20] Gemetchu Megerssa, 'The Oromo World View', *Journal of Oromo Studies* 12, 1–2 (July 2005), 70.
[21] Gemetchu Megerssa, 'Knowledge, Identity and the Colonizing Structure: The Case of the Oromo in East and Northeast Africa' (PhD diss., University of London, School of Oriental and African Studies, 1994), 90, 146.
[22] Ibid., 91.

universe out of nothing'. [23] In contrast to the Peoples of the Book, the Oromo Waaqa 'creates the universe out of itself'.[24] While the Christian God's nature is not mysterious, in the sense that He is revealed as a divine personage in the sacred scripts, that of Waaqa is mysterious, 'unknowable or incomprehensible'.[25] This is because, for the Oromo, '*Waaqa* exists at the same time through His creation and independently of it. He is both the Creator and his Creation'.[26] The Peoples of the Book are the Hebrews, the Christians and the Muslims. The Oromo were not one of the Peoples of the Book. We will shortly examine how the Oromo tackled their lack of their own Book. For now it is important to stress that water is central to the Oromo creation myth. What is more, every Oromo clan claims that early in their history their forefathers crossed a river. This tradition of crossing a river is similar to Moses crossing the Red Sea. As Sumner explains:

> Water, as a material reality existing in nature, is one of the least used images in Ethiopian written literature, but in [Oromo] oral literature, water (rainy season, flood, spring, lake, river, brook) is a characteristic feature of the green and fertile regions of Ethiopia where most of the Oromo live.[27]

The water that is connected with the Oromo creation myth is that of *Waallaabuu*, 'the original water out of which *Waaqa* created the universe becomes the origin of life and therefore of the Oromo'.[28] *Waallaabuu* was the water of the above, out of which Waaqa created humanity. For the Oromo, the locality of Madda *Waallaabuu* (whose importance will be discussed in Chapter 3) was similar to the Christian and Muslim Garden of Eden from which Adam and Eve were expelled when Eve gave the forbidden fruit of the Tree of Knowledge of Good and Evil to Adam to eat. The Borana Oromo, too, were forced to move out of their 'heaven on earth' – *Madda Waallaabuu* – in this case by a dangerous 'beast' known as Liqimssa (the swallower) that devoured people one by one.[29]

For the Oromo, Waaqa is the God of all creation.[30] Like the God of the Peoples of the Book, the Oromo God is universal. Like the Christians and the Muslims, the Oromo believed in one God, the Creator of the universe,

---

[23] Charles Verharen, 'Comparing Oromo and Ancient Egyptian Philosophy', *Journal of Oromo Studies* 15, 2 (July 2008), 10.
[24] Ibid., 11.
[25] Gemetchu Megerssa, quoted in ibid., 10. I am indebted to Nicholas Jewitt for his help in reformulating this statement.
[26] Megerssa, 'The Oromo World View', 73–74.
[27] Claude Sumner, *Oromo Wisdom Literature,* vol. 1: *Proverbs: Collection and Analysis* (Addis Ababa: Gudina Tumsa Foundation, 1995), 352.
[28] Megerssa, 'Knowledge, Identity and the Colonizing Structure', 146.
[29] E. Cerulli, *Etiopia occidentale : dallo Scioa alla frontiera dela Sudan, note del viaggai, 1927–1928,* (Rome: Sindicato Italiano Arti Grafiche, 1930–1933), vol. II, 169–72. See also E. Cerulli, *Somalia: Scritti Vari editi ed inditi* (Rome: 1964 [1959]), vol. 2, 127.
[30] Rev. Ronald Ward, 'Pilgrimage in Oromia – Madda Wallaabuu', *Qunamtii Oromia* 3, 1 (September 1992), 15.

whom they called Waaqa Tokkicha (the only God or the one God). Care-fully studying Oromo prayers Charles Tutschek concluded that the Oromo 'adore a supreme being [Waaqa] ... who is almighty, omniscient, all good, all wise, in short possessing all the qualities which we Chris-tians attribute to our God'.[31] F.B. Azaïs, an archaeologist missionary who travelled extensively among the Oromo in Hararghe, Shawa, Arsi, Sidamo, and Bale, states that the Oromo 'were able to maintain the belief in one God – the Great God that [they] worship, without symbol, without figurative representation'.[32] Martial de Salviac believed that Oromo monotheism was 'a glory incomparable in the world of the infidel'.[33] He adds that the blessed name of Waaqa 'has been continually on the lips of this people' and through 'their prayers, their worship, their chants',[34] they affirm their fundamental belief in the existence of only one God.

> O God, O Lord! O my Master
> O our father who dominates in the skies;
> You know all creatures and all men;
> You are master above all masters;
> Besides your kingdom, there is no other kingdom.[35]

The above beautiful prayer aptly reflects the influence of Christian ideas on the Oromo. This is because early in their history, the Oromo did not have the idiom of kingdom in their political vocabulary. The concepts of lord, master and father also reflect similar influence. The Ittu Oromo in western Haraghe chant the following prayer, reflecting the influence of Christian ideas.

> O God, O Lord!
> Master, without any master;
> Rich, never poor,
> Boundless wealth, you do not need more;
> king, whose throne is uncontested;
> 'Today mount, tomorrow dismount'

The most striking influence of Christian ideas on some Oromo groups' religious ideas is expressed in the sacred chants of Arsi, who repeat the following phrases in their private prayers. 'Our Father who reigns in the skies ... send us Your word.'[36] Father Wilhelm Schmidt's analysis of Oromo monotheism, as presented by Thomas Zitelmann, suggests the possibility of early Oromo contacts with Christianity.[37] The following

---

[31] Charles Tutschek, ed. L. Tutschek, *A Grammar of the Galla Language* (Munich: published privately, 1845), 24.

[32] F.B. Azaïs, 'Etude sur la religion du peuple Galla', *Revue d'ethnographie et des traditions populaires* 7, 26 (1926), 113.

[33] Martial de Salviac, trans. Ayalew Kanno, *An Ancient People: Great African Nation: The Oromo* (Self-published, 2005 [1901]), 29.

[34] Ibid., 143, 145.

[35] Ibid., 151.

[36] Ibid., 152.

[37] Thomas Zitelmann 'Oromo Religion, Ayyaana and the Possibility of A Sufi Legacy', *Journal of Oromo Studies* 12, nos 1–2 (July 2005), 88.

discussion intermittently establishes the validity of Father Schmidt's observation. What is more, the Oromo belief in one supreme being is shared in common with Christian and Muslim monotheism. For instance, Azaïs noted that for the Oromo Waaqa 'is the Sovereign king, Master of all the thrones on earth. He is the Creator of the universe, which is at his service.'[38] This is strikingly similar to the monotheism of the People of the Book. However, Oromo monotheism also differs from that of the People of the Book, a topic that will be discussed shortly.

The Oromo refer to their God as Waaqa Tokkicha (the only God) 'that one before which nothing existed'.[39] The Oromo also refer to their Creator as Waaqa Guraacha, 'Waaqa', Cushitic for God, and 'Guraacha', an Oromo term for black. Waaqa Guraacha

> [is] usually translated as the 'Black God.' This qualification stands however for much more than colour. Guraacha refers rather to the idea of absolute origin: Waaqa as the ultimate source of all things. It is that which is in its original state. That which has not been interfered with. It also carries the sense of mystery, of that which still in the shadow or not yet revealed.[40]

We have seen above the possibility of early Oromo contact with Christianity. The following short popular prayer among Christian Oromo in the region of Shawa shows unmistakable influence of Islamic ideas on Waaqa Guraacha.

> God the creator; of all creature
> Kind and clement black God
> Evaluator God
> Magnanimous ... One God with hundred names[41]

One God with hundred names is strikingly similar to the hundred names of Allah in Islam. In the Qur'an it is stated that 'Al-bari, the Creator, is one of the hundred names of Allah'.[42] Interestingly for the Oromo, the most popular and most-favoured colour is black, the colour of the Creator himself. Thus for the Oromo black is more than colour – it 'represents the notion of purity, truth, originality and divine mystery'.[43] It also symbolized good fortune. Today among the Borana in southern Ethiopia and northern Kenya, black is the colour of good fortune, good luck, and success, while white is the colour of bad luck and misfortune. The Borana say '*waan addii nagarsisse*' – 'I faced a white thing', which actually means 'I faced incredible misery or hardship'.[44] Among

[38] Azaïs, 'Etude sur la religion du peuple Galla', 113.
[39] Megerssa, 'Knowledge, Identity and the Colonizing Structure', 90.
[40] Ibid.
[41] Quoted in Alemayehu Haile et al., eds, *History of the Oromo to the Sixteenth Century*, 2nd edn. (Finfinnee: Oromia Culture and Tourism Bureau, 2006), 27.
[42] Quoted in Zitelmann, 'Oromo Religion, Ayyaana and the Possibility of A Sufi Legacy', 89.
[43] Megerssa, 'Knowledge, Identity and the Colonizing Structure', 15–16, 289.
[44] I am deeply indebted to Borru Dhaddacha, a highly educated and a very knowledge Borana himself for providing me with this information. I interviewed him on September 26, 2005, during his short visit to Georgia.

the Borana, Guraacha still has a connotation of divine. Guraacha, also means something in its original state, 'the mystery that cannot be revealed, that which is unknowable or incomprehensible'. Thus, 'Waaqa Guraacha' resonates: firstly, it stands for a God who is 'one and the same for all, the creator of everything, source of life, Omni-present, infinite, incomprehensible and He can do and undo anything'.[45] Such a description is very similar to the God of the Bible and the Qur'an. In addition, Waaqa Guraacha is blue sky or heaven, the habitation of Waaqa.

Like the God of Christian and Muslim tradition, Waaqa 'is the source of all life',[46] and, as the giver and sustainer of life, is the fountainhead of knowledge: Waaqa is 'all-knowing'.[47] In Islam, Allah is 'all-knowing and all-seeing'.[48] The Oromo believe Waaqa to be 'Almighty Master, inexhaustible benefactor of men who, lacking nothing, need not refuse us anything'.[49] In Islam it is said that Allah is 'dependent on nothing, but everything is dependent on Him'.[50] As Creator of the universe, including the earth and all things living on it, Waaqa has existed from the beginning. Such description of the nature of Waaqa is similar, if not identical with the God of the Peoples of the Book. For instance, in Islam it is said that Allah is 'Infinite and Eternal. He has no beginning nor end'.[51] What is more, Waaqa, the Creator of the universe, has the power to extend it. 'It is said that God supports everything without Himself being supported. In the second form is added the idea of extending the earth. In the Psalms, it is said that Yahweh stretches "the heavens out like a tent".'[52] According to Professor Sumner,

> Starting with water and rocks going through the vegetables and animal world to man, [Waaqa] has appointed to every being its own place in a cosmic order of which He is also the guardian. Sin is a breaking of this cosmic order. [Waaqa]'s creative and ordering activity manifests itself in all things. It manifests itself in the specific characteristics of man in general, of every species of plant and every species of animal. It is manifested also in the individual characteristics of every man, of each plant and each animal taken singly.[53]

In the Qur'an, it is said 'to Allah doth belong the dominion of the heavens and the earth, and all that is therein, and it is He who hath power over all things.'[54] For the Oromo, Waaqa 'exists at the same time through His creation and independently of it. He is both the Creator and

[45] Megerssa, 'Knowledge, Identity and the Colonizing Structure', 15.
[46] Claude Sumner, *Proverbs, Songs, Folktales: An Anthology of Oromo Literature* (Addis Ababa: Gudina Tumsa Foundation, 1996), 106.
[47] Sumner, *Oromo Wisdom Literature*, vol. 1, 313.
[48] Ali, *The Meaning of the Holy Qur'an*, 317.
[49] Sumner, *Proverbs, Songs, Folktales*, 106.
[50] Ali, *The Meaning of the Holy Qur'an*, 318, 287.
[51] Ibid., 126.
[52] Sumner, *Proverbs, Songs, Folktales*, 25.
[53] Sumner, *Oromo Wisdom Literature*, vol. 1, 33.
[54] *Qur'an*, Surah Al Mai'da, verse 120, quoted in Ali, *The Meaning of the Holy Qur'an*, 287.

his Creation.'[55] In the Hebrew/Christian myth, God created everything, including human beings within six days and rested on the seventh day. For the Oromo Waaqa created everything, including human beings within 27 days. This means while creation in the Hebrew/Christian myth was completed within six days, for the Oromo creation was completed in a month since every Oromo month has 27 days. Where the Oromo Waaqa differs from the Gods of the Peoples of the Book, is in the belief that Waaqa is one and many at the same time. In Islam the unity of Allah is absolute. However, the Oromo concept of Waaqa being one and many at the same time is reminiscent of Christian theology where God is said to be 'three in one' – the doctrine of the Trinity.[56]

'These multiple aspects of the Supreme Deity are designated by the word *ayyaana*. *Ayyaana* emanates out of [Waaqa], penetrates out of the womb of this mysterious absolute, as the morning light penetrates darkness, marking the beginning of time.'[57] In the Oromo cosmology, *ayyaana*, 'appeared with the first rising sun' when Waaqa 'created the universe out of itself'.[58] Ayyaana is a comprehensive Oromo word, which is impossible to express in a single English word or phrase. According to Tamene Bitima, the author of *A Dictionary of Oromo Technical Terms*, *ayyaana* has varied definitions: fortune, luck; celebration, ceremony, festival; a day free of work; divinity, spirit; grace; angel.[59] Even these definitions do not fully cover the whole range of the meanings of *ayyaana*. This is because, to the speakers of Oromo language *ayyaana*, has various shades of meanings depending on the context in which it is used. At one level *ayyaana* means spirit, in the sense that everything on earth, including trees, rivers, seas, mountains, rocks, animals, and human beings, have their particular *ayyaanas*. Even every day of a month has its own particular *ayyaana*. Just like the 'character of a day is influenced by the [*ayyaana*] it possesses',[60] the fate of an individual is determined from birth to death by the *ayyaana* he/she possesses.

In many ways the concept of *ayyaana* is similar to the Ibo (Igbo) people's concept of '*chi*', which according to Chinua Achebe is 'so powerful in Igbo religion and thought', and without understanding it, 'one could not make sense of the Igbo world-view'. Achebe adds, that 'every person has ... *chi* ... a person's fortunes in life are controlled more or less completely by his *chi*'.[61] Like *chi* for Igbo, *ayyaana* is central to Oromo thought and

55 Megerssa, 'The Oromo World View', 73–74.
56 I am indebted to Nicholas Jewitt for bringing to my attention the similarity of the Christian doctrine of the Trinity and the Oromo belief of Waaqa being one and many at the same time.
57 Megerssa, 'Knowledge, Identity and the Colonizing Structure,' 90–91.
58 Ibid.
59 Tamene Bitima, *A Dictionary of Oromo Technical Terms* (Cologne: Rüdiger Köppe, 2000), 41.
60 Hassan Wario, 'Journey to the Shrine of Nura Symbols of Gada Ornaments, Space and the Puff Adder in Somatic and Ritual Transformation' (MA thesis, Norwich: University of East Anglia, 1998), 13.
61 Chinua Achebe, 'Chi in Igbo Cosmology' (1975), in *Chinua Achebe Things Fall*

without understanding it 'one cannot make sense' of Oromo world view. Achebe argues that *chi* has 'central place in Igbo thought of the notion of duality. Wherever, Something stands, Something Else will stand beside it.'[62] This is true of *ayyaana* also. In Oromo cosmology everyone is born with her/ his *ayyaana*, a guardian angel or 'spirit-double' just as in Igbo cosmology. As the fate of an individual is tied to his *chi* in Igbo thought, the fate of an individual is tied to her/ his *ayyaana* from birth to death in Oromo religion. Among the Borana Oromo in southern Ethiopia and northern Kenya 'the concept [of *ayyaana*] unites all forces-human, natural, or supernatural and encapsulates the essential force of life and fertility'. [63] There are good *ayyaanas* as there are bad ones. According to Oromo cosmology, Waaqa gives either good or bad *ayyaana* to every individual, which means that the fate of every individual has already been determined from before birth to death by the Creator himself. This has a clear parallel with the religions of the Peoples of the Book. *Ayyaana* also has other meanings 'many of which are religious and/or philosophical in nature'. According to Gemetchu Megeressa:

> At the highest level of abstraction, *ayyaana* is that by which and/or through which *Waaqa* creates everything in the universe. In this sense, *ayyaana* causes the coming into being of everything ... *Ayyaana*, for the Oromo, is just as much the creative act of thinking in which a thought becomes that [which] it mentally represents. In other words, it constitutes the recognition that there exists dialectical relationship between thought and the object of thought ... In this sense, *ayyaana* represents knowledge. This knowledge is not only externalized, it is not only knowledge about the object, but is also internalized, in that it also generates reflective thought about the object.[64]

One can observe a parallel in Hebrew scripture in the concept of the ongoing creation and being of Yahweh: 'The LORD possessed me in the beginning of his way, before his works of old. I was set up from everlasting, from the beginning, or ever the earth was.'[65] There is also some relationship between the concept of *ayyaana*, for example 'by which and/ or through which Waaqa creates everything in the Universe' and the concept in Christian literature (in the Gospel of John) of wisdom or 'the Word' – '*Logos*' (Greek) – of God through which He created the universe.[66]

> In the beginning was the Word, and the Word was with God, and the Word was God. He was in the beginning with God, all things were made through, and without him was not anything made that was made. In him was life, and the life was the light of men. The light shines in the darkness, and the darkness has not overcome it.[67]

(contd) *Apart: Authoritative Text, Contexts and Criticism*, ed. Francis Abiola Irele (New York: Norton, 2009), 159–60.

[62] Ibid., 160.

[63] Wario, 'Journey to the Shrine of Nura Symbols', 14.

[64] Megerssa, 'The Oromo World View', 71–72.

[65] *The Holy Bible*: King James Version, Proverbs 8: 22–23.

[66] I am indebted to Rev. Dr Harwood Schaffer for bringing this aspect to my attention. Personal correspondence.

[67] *The Holy Bible Revised Standard Version Containing the Old and New Testaments* (Toronto: Thomas Nelson & Sons, 1952), John 1: 1–5.

Interestingly the Oromo concept of *ayyaana* also appears to have been influenced by Islamic ideas. According to Thomas Zitelman, *ayyaana* 'carries also a specific legacy that links it to a class of terms that are Arabic-Islamic loans with the Oromo language. The Arabic-Islamic equivalent of *ayyaana* has several meanings. In a secular sense, Arabic *aiyan* can mean anything that is clear, visible or public. In a religious sense, it can mean a 'personal revelation' (of God).'[68] Zitelman convincingly establishes that *ayyaana* 'is strongly linked to the metaphysical philosophy of Muhyddin Ibn Arabi' (1165–1242). For Ibn Arabi, 'the whole universe [is] expressed [through] creative possibilities, which are eternally fixed in God's knowledge. These 'creative possibilities' were called the *aiyan thabita* (*thabita*, fixed permanent).'[69] Besides the similarity between the terms *aiyan* and *ayyaana*, both concepts express 'dialectical relationship between thought and the object of thought'. Father Bartels, the author of an invaluable book on Oromo religion, observes that *ayyaana* is 'Waaqa's creative power manifesting itself through his creatures'.[70] Thus for Bartels, *ayyaana* is Waaqa's 'creative capacity', which 'is very close to Ibn's Arabi's' 'creative possibilities'. This is not an isolated example of an influence of Islamic ideas on an Oromo institution. The very concept of Waaqa Tokkicha (the only God) is similar, if not identical, with the Islamic idea which says that there is only one God (Allah). Haberland gathered massive data on different aspects of Oromo society, including their early monotheism. He believes that Oromo monotheism developed under Islamic influence. Haberland favours 'the idea of an early Islamic influence on the Oromo religious and social belief. Legal terms like *sera/hera* (given law), *aadaa* (traditional law), *lubbu/nafsi* (soul) and *awulia* (saint) were seen as Islamic loans.'[71]

There are many similarities between the Oromo and Biblical proverbs.[72] Father Angelo Mizzi, who lived among the Oromo for decades and gathered extensive data on Oromo social organization, tradition, proverbs, and religious life, was surprised by the extent of the similarities between Oromo and Biblical proverbs. Mizzi gathered Oromo proverbs over a six years period and 'underlines, hundred times, the similarities between Oromo and Biblical proverbs.'[73] In the table below are a set of six examples to make the point.

[68] Zitelmann, 'Oromo Religion, Ayyaana and the Possibility of A Sufi Legacy,' 83.
[69] Ibid.
[70] Bartels, *Oromo Religion*, 371.
[71] Zitelmann, 'Oromo Religion, Ayyaana and the Possibility of A Sufi Legacy', 88.
[72] Angelo Mizzi, *I Proverbi Galla* prima serie (Malta: The Empire Press, 1935), 1–53.
[73] Sumner, *Oromo Wisdom Literature*, vol. 1: 54.

Oromo proverb[74]	English translation[75]	Biblical parallel[76]
Baharri bishaan ifirra in-barbaadu.	The sea does not ask for water.	'Into the sea all the rivers go, and yet the sea is never filled.' Ecclesiastes 1: 7
Aarri Arrii namaan baasa.	Anger makes white hair grow.	'[A]nger shorten[s] your days, and worry brings premature old age.' Ecclesiasticus 30: 2
Aara nama tokkootti, hundi bada.	The wrath of a single man produces a general illness.	'The hot-headed man provokes disputes.' Proverbs 15: 18
Ballaan bordoo [ulee] duraa fuudhan, garuu in-dhaqu.	The stick was taken away from the blind man: he could not go anywhere.	'You must not put an obstacle in the blind man's way.' Leviticus 19: 14
Obboleeyyan walitti maxxanan, namuu in-dandayu.	The brothers are united: no one can vanquish them.	'Brother helped by brother is a fortress.' Proverbs 18: 19
Ibiddi nama itti aanu guba.	Fire burns one who comes near it.	'Can a man hug fire to his breast, without setting his clothes alight?' Proverbs 6: 27

Angelo Mizzi explained the striking similarities between the Oromo proverbs and Biblical parallels, through an ingenious but untenable theory, which makes the Oromo 'ancient Syrians'.[77] Fortunately Mizzi abandoned his theory about Oromo origin and explained the similarities in terms of borrowing and importation – that the similarities could be explained in terms of Biblical ideals borrowed by the Oromo rather 'than the natural product of their own natural genius'.[78] But he did not explain how the ideals of Oromo proverbs were borrowed and imported and, therefore, were not the creation of the Oromo people. Indeed, they were their own creation as thousands of Oromo proverbs that have no analogue in Christian and Muslim traditions abundantly demonstrate. However, since the Oromo lived as neighbours with both Christian and Muslim societies, ideas radiating from those societies may have influenced some Oromo proverbs. The few examples given above show such influence.

---

[74] Mizzi, *I proverbi Galla*, 14, 7, 13, 15, 44, 29, respectively.

[75] Sumner, *Oromo Wisdom Literature*, vol. 1, 72, 75, 99, 119, 90, 20, respectively.

[76] All biblical quotations in Table 1 are from the *Jerusalem Bible* (Darton, Longman & Todd, 1966), except the second (Ecclesiasticus), which is from the *New Jerusalem Bible* (Darton, Longman & Todd, 1985).

[77] Angelo Mizzi, *L'apostolato Maltese Nei secoli Passati, con speciale riguardo all' ozione missionaria svolta nelbacino Mediterraneo*, vol. 2, *Menologio Missionario* (Malta: The Empire Press, 1938), 265, trans. Claude Sumner, *Oromo Wisdom Literature*, vol. 1: *Proverbs: Collection and Analysis* (Addis Ababa: Gudina Tumsa Foundation, 1995), 55.

[78] Ibid.

TWO VIEWS ON TRADITIONAL OROMO RELIGION
AND PHILOSOPHY

Recently two scholars added new dimensions to our understanding of traditional Oromo religion and philosophy. While Mekuria Bulcha observes strong similarities between traditional Oromo religion and Judaism, Charles Verharen establishes links between Oromo cosmology and that of ancient Egyptian philosophy, both of which are discussed briefly in this section. Mekuria Bulcha provides five examples that, in his view, demonstrate 'striking analogies between' traditional Oromo religion and Judaism. According to Bulcha they include (1) the ritual sacrifices, the practice of male circumcision, the observance of the Sabbath among the Oromo in Wallaga in the 1920s; (2) that 'the Oromo law of levirate has similarity with that of the biblical law of levirate' (Deuteronomy 25: 5); (3) the similarities between the Oromo ethical code of *safuu* and the Ten Commandments; (4) 'the myth about the sacrificial lamb'; (5) 'religious significance of mountains'. After discussing these examples in some detail Bulcha asks an important question. 'How can we explain these similarities?'[79]

In my opinion the similarities can be attributed to the following four factors. First, the ritual sacrifices and the practice of male circumcision were and still are common practices among both the Cushitic- and Semitic-speaking peoples. Second, observance of the Sabbath among the Oromo in Wallaga is a striking example of the influence of the Ethiopian Orthodox Church, after the conquest of the Oromo and establishment of modern Ethiopian empire during the 1880s. Since the Ethiopian Orthodox Church combines in its teaching both the Old and the New Testaments, observance of the Sabbath among local Orthodox Christians has a long history.[80] Third, some of the above-mentioned similarities may reflect the shared cultural roots of both Cushitic- and Semitic-speaking peoples going back probably to their Afro-Asiatic proto-family.[81] Fourth, and even more important, for centuries the Oromo lived among or as neighbours of both Christians and Muslims. As we have seen above, and will see further, Oromo institutions were influenced by ideas radiating from both Christian and Muslim societies. In short, the similarities between the traditional Oromo religion and Judaism may reflect not only the long contact the Oromo had with the Peoples of the Book, but also their very long presence in north-east Africa, where the presence of Judaic ideas, rituals and practices have been long observed. As an important branch of the Cushitic-speaking peoples who have lived for centuries in north-east Africa, the Oromo may have been exposed indirectly or directly to Judaic ideas and practices. Of course the influences on the Oromo were not part of a one-way process. There are numerous examples that show that the Oromo in

[79] Bulcha, *Contours of the Emergent and Ancient Oromo Nation*, 241–5.
[80] Taddesse Tamrat, *Church and State in Ethiopia 1270–1527* (London: Oxford University Press, 1972), 207–9.
[81] Ehret, *The Civilizations of Africa*, 35–42.

turn influenced the customs, practices and traditions of their Christian and Muslim neighbours in many ways, as discussed in later chapters.

Charles Verharen 'posits the possibility of linkages'[82] between Oromo cosmology and that of the ancient Egyptian philosophy. In his own words:

> The strongest analogues to Oromo cosmology ... are to be discovered in ancient Egypt. Both philosophies insist on the mysterious nature of the origins of the universe. Both claim that the first principle of creation is a primordial water, although the Egyptians further specify its nature as chaotic ... The Oromo call this creative water *walaabu*, which must be distinguished from *Madda Walaabu*, water in a specific geographic location. The ancient Egyptians call it *Nun*. Both philosophies hold that primordial water is organized by creative principles, called *ayyaana* by the Oromo and *khepera* by the Egyptians. *Khepera* is translated as *becoming*. The principles of *khepera* are immanent within *Nun*, and their self-organizing process creates the powerful force manifested as the sun or *Ra* ... [T]he creative principles of *ayyaana* are also linked to the sun. Both traditions postulate an evolution from an inert substance, water, to an active principle, the sun. The *ayyaana* in the Oromo tradition constitute the ordering process whereby the sun emerges from the primordial water. The *ayyaana* through the sun start 'the process of time and creation, through which all things come to life'.[83]

Verharen observes 'the ontological similarities' between the Oromo and ancient Egyptian ethics 'may not be accidental'. The key to understanding the core of Oromo ethics is the concept of *nagaa*, 'which is defined literally as "peace" but carries extended meanings such as "harmony", "order", "balance", "justice"'.[84] Verharen finds parallel between the Oromo concept of *nagaa* and ancient Egyptian concept of *maat*.

> The Oromo use of the concept of *nagaa* or peace to test their adherence to *saffu* or the moral code calls to mind the ancient Egyptian concept of *maat*, the peace, harmony, order, balance that must characterize our responsibility to the continuance of life ... Like the ancient Egyptians, the Oromo share the idea that all humans are subject to a universal principle of harmony and order, *nagaa* – from the elected leaders of the *gada* to the lowliest herd boy.[85]

Verharen concludes his comparison of the Oromo and ancient Egyptian philosophy with this observation. 'Both Oromo and ancient Egyptian philosophy agree that life is good in itself and not for the sake of something else. Chaos erupts into life through natural or human causes, but it is manageable. Ethics in both philosophies demands the restoration of order and harmony, *nagaa* and *maat*.'[86] Charles Verharen's fascinating article establishes some linkages between Oromo and ancient Egyptian philosophies. Possible explanation for such linkages may include, but are not limited to the following three points. First, available evidence indicates that ancient Egyptians had contact with the

[82] Bulcha, *Contours of the Emergent and Ancient Oromo Nation*, 250.
[83] Verharen, 'Comparing Oromo and Ancient Egyptian Philosophy', 12–13.
[84] Ibid., 15, 19.
[85] Ibid., 19–20.
[86] Verharen, 'Comparing Oromo and Ancient Egyptian Philosophy', 25.

famous land of Punt, which was located in the Horn of Africa.[87] Second, 'scattered proper names found in ancient Egyptian [which are] identified as Cushitic'[88] may provide additional evidence for contact between ancient Egyptians and Cushitic-language speakers in the Horn of Africa. Third and most important, historical evidence demonstrates that ancient Egyptians had long-established commercial relations[89] with the Cushitic-language-speaking peoples in the Horn of Africa. As a two-way process, the commercial relations ancient Egyptians had with the peoples of the Horn of Africa may have influenced both sides. The similarities between Oromo and ancient Egyptian philosophy may reflect such an influence. However, how such obvious similarities between the Oromo and ancient Egyptian philosophy came about is a matter for further research.

THE 'SACRED BOOK OF THE OROMO'

Another example of Christian and Muslim influence on Oromo tradition is reflected in the invention of the tradition of the 'Sacred Book of the Oromo'. There is not a single scholar who considered the possibility that the Oromo were particularly aware of their lack of written words, when compared to their Christian and Muslim neighbours. In the Qur'an, the Christians, the Jews and the Muslims are repeatedly referred to as the People of the Book. It is said that the Book was sent down by God to guide the people. Since the thirteenth century, if not earlier, some Oromo groups have lived among or as neighbours with both Christians and Muslims who hold their holy books – the Bible and the Qur'an – with reverence. Like other non-literate societies, it is not far-fetched to argue that the Oromo scriptures were contained in their oral tradition. However, probably through their contacts and interactions with their Christian and Muslim neighbours, the Oromo may have realized that their holy books provided them with guidance, wisdom, knowledge and the 'magic' of writing. Since the educated elements of both the Christian and the Muslim societies were able to read their holy books, the skill of reading opened up for them a new intellectual world that was closed for the Oromo. Because of their inability to read, the Oromo may have felt that they were victims of ignorance. To overcome their lack of a holy book, with its magic of reading and writing, the Oromo invented a story about their Sacred Book, which is presented in two similar traditions both among the Orma group in Kenya and the Oromo in Ethiopia. The

[87] G. Mokhtar, ed., *UNESCO General History of Africa, Vol. 2, Ancient Civilizations of Africa* (Berkeley: The University of California Press, 1981), 144–8, 341.
[88] Carleton T. Hodge, 'Lisramic (Afroasiatic): An Overview', in *The Non-Semitic Languages of Ethiopia*, M. Lionel Bender, ed. (East Lansing, MI: Michigan State University, 1976), 45.
[89] Among others, see Richard Pankhurst, *The Ethiopian Borderlands: Essays in Regional History from Ancient Times to The End of the 18th Century* (Lawrenceville, NJ: Red Sea Press, 1997), 1–15.

Orma were a powerful branch of the Oromo people, who started their slow movement from southern Ethiopia into what is now Kenya probably during the second half of the fourteenth century or the fifteenth. The tradition of the Oromo Sacred Book was so widespread among the Oromo-speaking people in the Horn of Africa that it is reasonable to assume that it developed before the large-scale population movement of the Oromo began during the second half of the fifteenth and the beginning of the sixteenth centuries. What is certain is that this tradition developed in some of the Muslim states in southern Ethiopia, most likely in the state of Bali, or Dawaro or Fatagar or Waj where the Oromo lived as neighbours with both the Christian and Muslim societies (see Chapter 2).

The Orma tradition in Kenya was collected in 1890, while the Oromo traditions in Ethiopia were collected between the 1840s and 1930s. What the two traditions have in common is that originally the Oromo had their own Sacred Book which they lost because of their carelessness. In both traditions, it is claimed that their Sacred Book was devoured by an ox (Kenya) and a cow (Ethiopia) and that this lost book could be found by carefully examining the entrails of an ox or a cow. Where the two traditions differ is that the Orma believe that if the lost book is found, they will become once again a powerful people, whereas the traditions in Ethiopia state that the lost book itself cannot be found, because Waaqa became angry with the Oromo and refused to provide them with another Book. However, Oromo experts know how to make use of the traces of the lost Book. The following Orma tradition from Kenya as presented by Hilarie Kelly reflects a strong influence from Muslim ideas.

> A man and a woman were the first people created and God gave them a book in which all his orders were written and told them that as long as these were obeyed they would be the first great people on earth. For a long time they carefully preserved the book and carried out the orders, and became a great and powerful race, until at length getting tired of living according to rules they became careless of the book and left it lying about. One day an ox passing saw it and swallowed it and from that day their power gradually declined. Hence the custom whenever an ox dies or killed of carefully examining its stomach for any traces of the lost book. If they could once more obtain it they would again become the first race on earth.[90]

There is a parallel between this tradition and that of the Christians and the Muslims

in the story of Adam and Eve. Both the Bible and the Qur'an command the believers to live according to the teachings of their holy books. In the Qur'an, Allah says 'We have sent unto you a light' (i.e. the Qur'an)[91] which provides guidance.

[90] Hilarie Ann Kelly, 'From Gada to Islam: The Moral Authority of Gender Relations among the Pastoral Oromo of Kenya' (PhD diss., University of California, Los Angeles, 1992), 302, quoting from unpublished typescript by J.S.S. Rowland, 'An Outline of Tana River History' (1955), 1.

[91] Ali, *The Meaning of the Holy Qur'an*, 240.

An alternate version among the Oromo in Ethiopia relates that from the beginning God sent down three books, one each for the Christians, the Muslims and the Oromo. The Christians and the Muslims kept their books safely, while the Oromo, through negligence, allowed their book to be eaten by a cow. The story goes on to say that when Christians and Muslims wanted to know hidden things they find them in their books by reading. The Oromo could not do this because their book had been eaten. However, the Oromo wise men were able to find traces of the lost book in the stomach of the cow. When a cow is slaughtered, the wise men could read from the inside of the stomach about the hidden secrets. Those 'who read the Oromo book are called *ogessa*.[92] The tradition makes it clear that the Oromo loss of their book resulted in their inability to read, which was the cause for their ignorance.

> Waaqa, in the beginning, had given a book [to the Oromo]. A cow devoured it. Waaqa was irritated and did not want to give [the Oromo] another book. We have thus been reduced to looking for the book there where it was lost, inside the peritoneum of the cows that we consult to know the future. Also the Oromo makes mistakes only through ignorance. When an Oromo just dies, his soul ascends toward Waaqa who asks: – who are you? – It is an Oromo replies the Awulia. An Oromo, responds Waaqa, but he is ignorant. Does not know how to read better than a cow ... he does not know how to distinguish between good and bad. How do you punish him? Find him a corner in paradise.[93]

In many parts of the world the reading of entrails was practised by many people, including the ancient Israelites. What is probably unique about the Oromo practice was how it was explained in terms of their lack of a sacred book. From start to finish, the above quotation reflects strong Islamic influence on Oromo tradition. Let me substantiate this statement. First, Oromo concern about their ignorance most likely reflects their 'internalization of the rhetoric of superiority of the societies within which they lived'.[94] Second, the notion that the Oromo making 'mistakes only through ignorance', is meant to encourage repentance and seeking forgiveness. The Qur'an says, 'If any of you did evil in ignorance, and thereafter, repented and amended (his conduct)' Allah will forgive him.[95] Third, the concept of an Oromo soul ascending toward Waaqa, could be as a result of either Christian or Islamic influence. However, the notion of a soul accounting for its deeds while on earth is undoubtedly Islamic. Fourth, the Qur'an repeatedly mentions that, after a dead person is buried, he or she is subjected to a series of questions, not by Allah Himself but by His angels. Only those who conduct their lives while on earth according to the command of Allah as elaborated in the Qur'an will be able to answer any question. In the above story an Oromo soul was unable to answer who he was. An *Awulia*, (a Muslim holy man, favoured with the blessing of Allah) answered for him: 'he is an Oromo'.

[92] G. Massaja, *Lettere e scritti minori, 1836–66, A cura di Antonino Rosso I* (Rome: Istituto Storico dei Cappuccini, 1978), 96–97.
[93] de Salviac, *An Ancient People: Great African Nation*, 158.
[94] Personal correspondence with Rev. Dr Harwood Schaffer.
[95] Ali, *The Meaning of the Holy Qur'an*, 307–8.

Fifth, it was an *awulia* that pleaded with Waaqa the case of an Oromo soul, on the ground of his ignorance. He is ignorant because he lacks a sacred book and therefore 'does not know how to distinguish between good and bad'. Finally, the *awulia* asks Waaqa not to punish the ignorant Oromo but instead to find for him 'a corner in paradise', which is a clear expression of Islamic influence on the shaping of the story of the Oromo Sacred Book.

In short, the tradition about the Oromo Sacred Book is so widely diffused that it must have developed before the Orma branch of the Oromo began their slow migration from southern Ethiopia into Kenya: 'It is probably, because of their exposure to Islamic ideas before their migration from southern Ethiopia to Kenya ... that the Orma, Borana, Gabbra and Sakuye all have traditions that say they have been Muslim in the distant past.'[96]

BORANA AND BARENTU

Before discussing the Qaalluu institution, following Professor Vansina, I will treat oral traditions as hypotheses and analyse the meanings of the names of the two Oromo moiety systems – Borana and Barentu – to test the order of their seniority. Oromo tradition and scholarly works establish that the two moieties systems and the Qaalluu institutions (the sphere of religious activities) were inextricably interwoven. It is not possible to separate one from the other. According to Asmarom Legesse, 'the Qallu institution is the organization at the head of the two great moieties or societal halves of the Oromo nation. The moieties cut across the age and generation classes.'[97] The connection between the two moieties and the Qaalluu institution will be examined later. Here we focus on the traditions of the moieties, the meaning of their names and their political economy.

Early in their history, the Oromo were divided into two moieties, named Borana and Barentu (Barentuma). In the Christian literature and among the Oromo in southern Ethiopia and Kenya, Barentu is known as Barettuma. Eastern Oromo do not use the term Barettuma and instead use Barentu and Barentuma interchangeably. The 'ma' that is added to Barentu simply means of Barentu or belonging to Barentu. It is a collective name of the Oromo of Wallo, Arsi, Bale and Hararghe. I prefer to use Barentu rather than Barettuma.

In the course of the following discussion, I will attempt to show how the Christian and Muslim ideas were reflected, whether directly or indirectly, in the legend of the separation of the Borana from Barentu moiety. While it remains difficult to explain the origins of the terms Borana and Barentu, it appears that Barentu was an old Cushitic name (see below), while Borana was an Oromo term of later origin.

[96] Kelly, 'From Gada to Islam', 302.
[97] Asmarom Legesse, *Oromo Democracy: An Indigenous African Political System* (Lawrenceville, NJ: The Red Sea Press, 2000), 32.

Asmarom Legesse notes: 'Moieties may be exogamous or territorial or non-territorial entities ... structurally linked to each other and sharing activities that cause them to be interdependent.'[98] In the Oromo case, the moieties were originally non-territorial. It appears to me that the exogamous character of the two moieties did not make them entirely interdependent for three practical reasons. First, because 'wives were often taken from among non-Oromo, often from politically subordinated groups'.[99] Second, if two Oromo *gosas* (descent groups or clans} quarrelled, their dispute was settled according to the law of Borana or Barentu. This was in regard to blood price, which varied according to the degree of relationships.[100] Finally, it appears that there was 'a degree of autonomy enjoyed by each moiety'.[101]

GOSA OR DESCENT GROUP

At this juncture it is relevant to discuss briefly the pervasive importance of *gosa* in traditional Oromo society. The term *gosa* is difficult to define precisely. In a number of sources, *gosa* is defined as a lineage, or a clan, or sub-clan, or a tribe, species or people or a nation.[102] There is no exact Oromo term for clan. The closer term is *gosa*, which is not just a clan, but 'a large category of descent groups which includes all peoples descended from'[103] a mythical or common ancestor. *Gosa* is also 'one of the mechanisms for defining individual and collective identity'[104] within Oromo society. Throughout this study I prefer using *gosa*, descent group and clan interchangeably.

Together with the *gada* system and Qaalluu institution, *gosa* appears to have shaped the course of Oromo history. Members of *gosa* have rights and obligations for helping each other in different situations. As Paul Baxter observed among the Borana, members of a *gosa* 'should render each other every sort of assistance, contributions to fines, hospitality, help with herding, gifts in misfortune and distributions from fortunes of bounty.'[105] It was precisely for these reasons that young boys were taught about family tree within a *gosa*. According to Haberland, a boy of five years knows the names of his forefathers to the depth of 12 to 15 generations.[106] The basic rules of *gosa* include descent through paternal line, strict exogamous marriage, territorially defined area that bears a

[98] Ibid., 134.

[99] Kelly, 'From Gada to Islam', 36.

[100] Tasawo Merga, 'Senna Umatta Oromo: Jalqaba jarra Kudha Jahafti hamma dhumiti jarra Kudda Sagalafanti' (unpublished manuscript, 1976), 12.

[101] Wario, 'Journey to the Shrine of Nura Symbols', 11.

[102] Paul Baxter, 'Social Organization of the Galla of Northern Kenya' (PhD diss., Oxford University, 1954), 77.

[103] Abbas H. Gnamo, *Conquest and Resistance in the Ethiopian Empire, 1880–1974. The Case of the Arsi Oromo* (Boston: Brill, 2014), 34.

[104] Ibid., 56–60, 68–9.

[105] Baxter, 'Social Organization of the Galla of Northern Kenya', 102.

[106] E. Haberland, *Galla Süd-Aethiopiens* (Stuttgart: W. Kohlhammer, 1963), 115.

name of a particular *gosa*, political autonomy and its dynamic nature through the process of segmentation, fission and fusion giving birth to hundreds of *gosa*s each with its own name. What this means is that Barentu or Borana descent groups generally tended to dominate some areas and lived near to one another.[107] This does not mean that *gosa*s were not mixed. Indeed they were mixed extensively. The reason for this is obvious.

> A *gosa* name can be a structural and territorial term. However, the groups are not territorial in themselves. A territory is inhabited not only by a *gosa* groups whose name it bears but many others. Almost everywhere, different descent groups live interspersed with other groups. As a structural feature, a *gosa* name can be used to denote a sub-branch or a federation of several sub-branches of the Oromo nation.[108]

Although exogamous, members of the two moieties did not necessarily have always to balance each other and move together. According to Asmarom Legesse we 'do not know why the name of one or the other moiety predominated in different regions.'[109] I suspect that it was probably because of the widespread Oromo practice of marrying non-Oromo as well as the issue of blood price together with their tradition of adopting non-Oromo that led to this development. This tendency was already observable even before the sixteenth-century pastoral Oromo population movement (see Map 4 on page 87). During and after the pastoral Oromo expanded over an extensive territory, the Oromo moiety system underwent profound changes, some of which will be discussed in the chapters on population movements. In what follows I attempt to show some influence from the Christian ideas as they are related to the traditions of Borana and Barentu, while examining the theory that Barentu was an old Cushitic name with Borana being an Oromo term of later origin.

INFLUENCE OF SEMITIC LEGEND ON THE 'FATHER' OF BORANA AND BARENTU

In the national myth, Oromo was the common 'father' of both Borana and Barentu. But in the separate Borana genealogy, first recorded by Bahrey, Borana had a 'father' called Sapera.[110] What is the meaning and origin of Sapera? According to Getachew Haile, 'Sappira [Sapera] in Geez ... means "band of people" from the Greek Speira, or "military unit"'.[111] In light of its Greek meaning, it is tempting to suggest that Sapera refers to the Oromo *chibbra* (Amharic *chiffra*) method of fighting (see Chapters 7 and 8).

---

[107] Merga, 'Senna Umatta Oromo', 12.
[108] Bulcha, *Contours of the Emergent and Ancient Oromo Nation*, 135–6.
[109] Legesse, *Oromo Democracy*, 149.
[110] Bahrey, 'History of the Galla', in *Some Records of Ethiopia*, 112.
[111] Haile, *The Works of Abba Bahriy*, 196.

Interestingly, Sapera, the 'father' of Borana, was considered to be 'the son of the serpent'. The serpent plays a crucial role in the mythologies of many peoples, including the ancient Egyptians, whose many 'gods and goddesses took the forms of snakes to impress their foes with terror'.[112] Even the rod of Moses, the liberator of his people from the Egyptian oppression, 'was a type of serpent'.[113] It appears that snake legends are very common throughout Africa and Semitic regions of western Asia, as in the Garden of Eden, where Eve was tempted by a snake.[114] The snake is often a phallic symbol in Oromo. However, the story of the father of Sapera as serpent is quite similar to the Aksumite story of the serpent king that was worshipped. That was probably before the people of the Axumite empire were converted to Christianity during and after the fourth century of the common era. Even after their conversion to Christianity, serpent worship may have continued among the Axumite people. This is because 'some serpent worship has Biblical connections while some does not'.[115] Interestingly 'the use of the serpent by God as a source of mystical power' is clearly expressed in the story of Moses' staff in the Bible.[116] The story of Sapera as 'the son of the serpent' is one of the areas where Semitic Christian legend penetrated into Oromo culture, probably earlier than the thirteenth century.[117]

Another Christian story that is reflected in Oromo tradition is that of the widespread legend of Akkoo Manooyee. Akkoo (grandmother) Manooyee was a very powerful, decisive leader, who inspired fear and terror. She was reported to have been a wondrous beauty who ruled for forty years, and is characterized, as a 'cruel, bloodthirsty', and destructive warrior, whose bravery had no equal.[118] Perhaps this legend is related to the story of a certain equally beautiful woman leader known as Yodit, who is reported to have come to power sometime between 970 and 980 CE, ruling for forty years. Her Amharic nickname was Guidit, a terrible or a monster queen. Although the history of Guidit is clouded in mist of legends, one thing is for certain. 'All written sources as well as oral tradition ... speak of the existence of a cruel Queen', who devastated the city of Axum, the political and spiritual capital of the Axumite empire.[119] Guidit was a historical figure and a very powerful Agaw queen, who rebelled against the Axumite domination and 'lashed back with a campaign in which Aksum was sacked, her churches were

---

[112] Ali, *The Meaning of the Holy Qur'an*, 375, see note 1075.
[113] Ibid.
[114] *The Holy Bible*, Exodus 4: 2–5.
[115] Personal communication with Rev. Dr Harwood Schaffer.
[116] *The Holy Bible*, Exodus 7: 8–12.
[117] For instance, Paulitchke stated that the Oromo were already in the region of Ethiopia during the Axumite period. P.V. Paulitchke, 'Die Wanderungen der Oromo oder Gallas Ost-Afrikas', *Mittheilungen de Anthropologischen Gessellschaaft zu Wien* 19 (1889), 165–78.
[118] 'The Legend of Akkoo Manooyee', 1, 11–12, 38 (www.gubirmans.com?Manooyee.htm, accessed 20 March 2008).
[119] Sergew Hable Sellassie, *Ancient and Medieval Ethiopian History to 1270* (Addis Ababa: Printing Press, 1972), 225.

burned, and most of her royalty were killed'.[120] It appears that the Agaw queen dealt the final *coup de grâce* from which the Axumite empire never fully recovered. The Agaws were Cushitic-language speakers, who formed the Zagwe Dynasty (*c.*1000–1270).[121] An Amhara tradition, recorded in the nineteenth century, states that Guidit led military expeditions against the Oromo.[122] Hopefully future research may show that this Amhara tradition reflects the presence of some Oromo groups in the region during this period. Be that as it may, the parallel between the legend of Guidit and that of Akkoo Manooyee is striking. The period of forty years may seem insignificant, but the number forty was also very important in the Judeo-Christian and Muslim traditions. In the legends both Guidit and Akkoo Manooyee were cruel and destructive leaders, who demanded difficult tasks from the people they terrorized. For example, Akkoo Manooyee demanded from the Oromo the impossible task of building for her a 'floating structure in the sky without touching the ground'.[123] This is redolent of the Judeo-Christian and Muslim myth of the Tower of Babel.

This inferred connection is also supported by a legend of the Arroojjii Oromo. In this widespread legend, the Arroojjii were reported to have been the most powerful and most sophisticated Oromo clan who had advanced civilization.[124] Because of their high level of civilization, the Arroojjii were puffed up with pride and arrogance, which propelled them to rebel against Waaqa. To complete their rebellion, the legend says, the Arroojjii started building a bridge that would take them beyond the sky. For the Oromo the sky was the habitation of Waaqa. The Arroojjii design was an obvious challenge to the authority of Waaqa. Their pride and arrogance angered Waaqa so much that he destroyed their bridge[125] and scattered them among all major Oromo clans. In short, the stories of the serpent father of Sapera, of Akkoo Manooyyee and of the arrogance of Arroojjii appear to indicate that some Oromo groups had contact with Christian communities probably during the time of Guidit or shortly after. Such contact between them probably took place in the region of Shawa.

By the eleventh century, Oromo appear in the records of the Christian kingdom. Alaqa Tayya, a famous traditional historian, the 'father of Ethiopian history',[126] states forcefully that the Oromo were present during the reign of Mera Tekle Haimanot, the first emperor of the Zagwe Dynasty.[127] It is not surprising then that the name Galla, as a designa-

[120] Donald N. Levine, *Greater Ethiopia: The Evolution of a Multiethnic Society*, 2nd edn (Chicago, IL: University of Chicago Press, 2000), 70–71.

[121] Ibid., 71.

[122] H. Blanc, *A Narrative of Captivity in Abyssinia* (London: Smith, Elder and Co., 1868), 339–40.

[123] 'The Legend of Akkoo Manooyee', 2.

[124] Ibid., 6.

[125] Ibid., 7.

[126] Taddesse Tamrat, 'Introduction', *Alaqa Tayya's Ye Ityopya Hizeb Tarik*, rev. ed. (Addis Ababa: 1971/72), 9.

[127] Haile, *The Works of Abba Bahriy*, 216.

tion for the Oromo people, appeared for the first time (see Chapter 2) in the Orthodox Church hagiography during the Zagwe period (*c.* 1000–1270). Most of the Zagwe emperors are said to have ruled for forty years each. According to Getachew Haile, the Zagwe emperors' reign of forty years was probably related to the Oromo *gada* system.[128] A forty-year cycle is at the core of the *gada* system and, as mentioned, is also a very important number in the Judeo-Christian and Islamic traditions. It was said that Moses had forty nights of communion with God on Mount Sinai.[129] The Israelites wandered in the wilderness for forty years. Jesus is said to have fasted forty days in the wilderness before he took up his Ministry.[130] During the Biblical Flood Noah is said to have stayed in the ark for forty days. 'At the end of forty days Noah opened the window of the ark which he had made.'[131] It was at the age of forty that Prophet Muhammad started preaching the religion of Islam. In Ethiopian Christian legend, it is said that Saint Takla Hamanot stood on one leg and prayed for forty years.

The Borana Oromo, who now live in southern Ethiopia and northern Kenya, are divided into two moieties, Sabo and Gona. They have two ritual leaders, Qaalluu Karayu and Qaalluu Oditu. The former, who is the senior and ritually the more important of the two, is said to be 'a mythical leader believed to have been sent to earth by [Waaqaa]'.[132] The senior Qaalluu's heavenly origin is confirmed by another version of the legend.[133] It claims that he was of a non-Oromo origin. Thus he was 'stranger', who was found in the forest by the Wata, hunter-gathers, together with nine things, one of which was *buuti*, 'a poisonous puff adder snake'.[134] The Qaalluu Oditu is the most-important ritual leader for the Gona moiety. Both the Karayyu and Oditu Qaalluus keep puff adder snakes, which serve them as the highest symbols of their authority.[135] The myth of the Borana gives another striking example of Christian influence on an Oromo institution. It 'states clearly that [Qaalluu] is [Waaqa]'s son'.[136] Of course, there are other religions in which an individual is called the son of God. The Oromo could have independently developed the concept of the son of Waaqa, but it appears to me that the concept of the Son of Waaqa is a Christian influence on the Qaalluu institution.

As with other ritual leaders, snakes play a prominent role in the ritual activities of the Gujji Qaalluu. The Gujji are an important branch of the Oromo society, who live in the region of Sidamo. They belong to

[128] Ibid., 101.
[129] Ali, *The Meaning of the Holy Qur'an*, 383, see note 1100.
[130] *The Holy Bible*, Matthew 4: 2.
[131] *The Holy Bible*, Genesis 8: 6.
[132] Wario, 'Journey to the Shrine of Nura Symbols', 25.
[133] Knutsson, *Authority and Change*, 144–5: see also Haberland, *Galla Süd-Aethiopiens*, 158.
[134] Wario, 'Journey to the Shrine of Nura Symbols', 27.
[135] Ibid., 6, 29.
[136] Ibid., 147.

the Borana moiety. The senior Borana Qaalluu still keeps *buuti*, a puff adder, and cares for it for purpose of enchanting 'its power to harm'.[137] Each moiety respects a certain type of snake. This respect for snakes is probably a common cultural trait underlying both Cushitic and Semitic cultures. In the form it is presented, the myth of Sapera reflects that the Semitic legend had filtered into Oromo tradition much earlier than previously suspected.

'FOUNDING FATHERS'

Abba Bahrey's *Zenahu le Galla*, Amhara Christian literature, and Oromo tradition unanimously make Borana and Barentu eponymous heroes and founders of the two moieties respectively. One widely diffused Oromo legend relates that the two 'founding fathers' were brothers. Both were the sons of Ilma Oroma, the first son of the Oromo. However, there is a twist in this legend, which makes Borana the son of Ana, while his sister, Antu, was Barentu's 'mother', thus making the two cousins rather than siblings. The twist is meant to reflect the gendered distinction between the two siblings. In this legend, Antu is presented as older than her brother. However, since tradition did not allow a girl to be considered as *angafa* (the first-born son), with all the privileges to inherit most of the property and the authority of the father after the death of the latter, Ana became *angafa*. As a result, all his descendants are regarded as the first born among the Oromo.[138] On the surface, this seems to reflect the division of the Oromo into two exogamous moieties, of which one was called Borana – 'the masculine' – and the other Barentu – 'the feminine'.[139] Under the legendary cloak, this tradition actually makes the name Barentu older than Borana, and, as we shall soon see, there are other traditions that support this conclusion. What is difficult to explain are the terms Ana and Antu.

Ana, as a name of one of the oldest Oromo clans, is found in the genealogies of both Borana and Barentu moieties and are scattered throughout most of Oromo territory. As will be shown in a number of chapters, during the sixteenth and seventeenth centuries, one section of Ana, a major branch of the Barentu, spearheaded pastoral Oromo population movement into the northern parts of the Christian kingdom. Eventually, the Ana Oromo were absorbed and assimilated into Amhara culture in the region of Begameder, Gojjam and Wallo. The other section of Ana directed their movement to the east, where their descendants formed widespread Oromo *gosa*s in Hararghe. It is likely that Ana is a Cushitic term. According to Father Angelo Mizzi, Ana was the divinity of heat, 'the God of the sky', while Anat and

---

[137] Father F. Azaïs, trans. Ayalew Kanno, 'A Study of the Religion of the Oromo People', *Journal of Oromo Studies* 19, nos. 1–2 (July 2012), 177.

[138] Father Angelo Mizzi, *Cenni Etnografici Galla ossia Organizzazione Civile, usi e costumi Oromonici* (Malta: The Empire Press, 1935), 70–75.

[139] Haberland, *Galla Süd-Aethiopiens*, 775.

Anaities were north-west Semitic divinities representing the feminine principle in nature.[140] Harwood Schaffer, emphasizes that 'the connection of Anat is generally to Ugarit and the Canaanites not to Jerusalem and Christianity', reflecting Anat's indirect connection with Judeo-Christian tradition.[141] The Kunama people, who live in the northern part of Eritrea, have a supreme god whom they call Ana. In their religion, Ana is supposed to have created the sky and the earth, including humankind. Again, according to Schaffer, Ana was imported into Egypt during the Hyksos Period' (i.e. *c.* 1700–1567 BCE).[142] The Hyksos were Semitic-language speakers, who invaded Egypt from their base in Palestine. While the name of the Kunama's supreme God is Ana, the name of their sacred capital is Barentu. For the Kunama the latter is the centre of their tradition and religion.[143] The appearance of the terms Ana and Barentu among the Kunama may suggest something more than an accidental coincidence with the Oromo words. It is known that the Narya, previously known as Barya, who are the close neighbours of the Kunama, have a language with Cushitic characteristics.[144] This must have influenced the Kunama, which in turn suggests that the terms Ana and Barentu were of earlier Cushitic and possibly Semitic origin.

According to a third tradition, Borana was a composite term composed of *bori* – 'east, light' – and *ana* – masculine divinity. Thus Borana would mean 'the light of the east', whose descendants settled in the west. In other words, Borana was the name of the moiety whose descendants settled in the west. The following few words from a girls' song in Wallaga, western Ethiopia, may reflect the above tradition. 'Look at my eyes, eyes of a Borana, beaming forth pure morning light.'[145] The term Barentu is also a composite term. *Bari* – 'morning, light, east' – and *antu* – 'feminine divinity'; thus Barentu would mean 'the morning light of the east', whose descendants remained in the east. In other words, Barentu was the name of the moiety, whose descendants settled in the east. This means Borana and Barentu reflect the settlement patterns of the descendants of the two major moieties. Amazingly, for both the Borana and the Barentu, the East is a cardinal point of orientation connected with their origin. It was the 'sacred direction'[146] that had symbolic significance in their ceremonies. East is the direction to which the Borana turn during prayer as well as at moments of tense social drama. Asmarom Legesse reports a

[140] Father Angelo Mizzi, *Semplici Constatzioni Filogico-etnologiche Galla* (Malta: The Empire Press, 1935), 24–26.
[141] Personal communication with Rev. Dr Harwood Schaffer.
[142] Ibid.
[143] *Adveniat Regnum Tuum*, 30 (1975), 49–51; 31 (1976), 38–42.
[144] See for instance, G.W.B. Huntingford, *Historical Geography of Ethiopia from the 1st Century A.D. to 1704*, rev. edition, ed. R. Pankhurst and D. Appleyard (London: Oxford University Press, 1989), 227.
[145] Bartels, *Oromo Religion*, 133.
[146] I have drawn on Jan Vansina, *Oral Tradition as History*, 126.

very interesting event that unfolded while he was observing a tense Borana assembly meeting:

> The meeting was virtually out of control when the Abba Gada made a surprise announcement: he told the assembly to turn their faces toward the East. All the participants who were seated in a circular arrangement around the Abba Gada sat up and turned toward 'il boru' the place 'where the sun rises', the place of origin of the Borana. In that position the Abba Gada gave a blessing that lasted some 15 minutes: a type of slow call and response cycle of blessings that suspended all feelings of hostility. When the meeting resumed, tempers had greatly subsided.[147]

For both Borana and Barentu, East – the direction of the sunrise – is the place of their origin. There appears to be indirect connection between the Oromo orientation to the East, and the Muslim orientation toward Mecca, which is north-east of Ethiopia. In other words, through 'formal and informal processes' the Oromo, as neighbours of both Christian and Muslim people, appear to have made foreign ideas their own. For instance, Bari is the morning light of the east for the Barentu Oromo. 'Al-bari, the Creator, is one of the hundred names of Allah' in Islam.[148] According to Anga'a Dhugumaa, the Oromo say 'Waaqa is Tokkicha maqaa Dhibbaa' (the only God with hundred names)',[149] which is strikingly similar to the hundred names of Allah in Islam. Some of the names of Waaqa according to Azaïs, are:

> the master or the Almighty, before whom all powers disappear. Another name is, everlasting benefactor to man, inexhaustible benefactor, who has everything and never refuses to give away; another name is the one whose signs (knowledge) is boundless. One cannot enumerate all the titles that the [Oromo] people give to God in their prayers and sacred hymns.[150]

Bori is the morning light of the east for the Borana. 'Bore, the Creator [was] a term used by Jewish thinkers during the Babylonian exile.'[151] This appears to suggest that any discussion of Borana and Barentu will be 'caught up in a mytho-poetical past that is shared with the Peoples of the Book'.[152] However, what is certain is that Borana represented the 'masculine' attribute while Barentu represented the 'feminine' attribute. Both terms convey exactly the same meaning except that one is 'masculine' and the other 'feminine'. The light of the east conveys a strong religious concept, which becomes clearer from the following prayer.

[147] Legesse, *Oromo Democracy*, 119.
[148] Zitelmann, 'Oromo Religion, Ayyaana and the Possibility of a Sufi Legacy', 89.
[149] Anga'a Dhugumaa, *From the Revised Gadda to Macca-Tuulama Association* (New York: self-published, 1998), 18.
[150] Azaïs, 'Etude sur la religion du peuple Galla', 113.
[151] Personal correspondence with Rev. Dr Harwood Schaffer.
[152] Zitelmann, 'Oromo Religion, Ayyaana and the Possibility of A Sufi Legacy', 89.

Ya waaqa barii[153] *waaqa Barentumaa*
Waaqa barii waaqa lallabaa
Bokkun guraacha tahe.[154]

Oh God of the east, God of the sunrise,
God of Barentu
God of the East, God of the sunrise
God of proclamation
bokku [the wooden sceptre kept by a leader
of the *gada* class] has become divine.[155]

What becomes clear from the literature collected by Mizzi, who had lived among the Oromo for decades and gathered extensive oral tradition from both the Borana and Barentu groups, is that in the final analysis both the Borana and Barentu are associated with divinity. As *barantecca* was some sort of divinity for the Barentu Oromo, *borantecca* for the Borana was the divinity of the river to which tribute had to be given on crossing.[156] What is more, these were both serpents, regarded as sacred.[157] In short, what has been written so far demonstrates how difficult it is to untangle the discussion of the terms Borana[158] and Barentu from the ideas of the Peoples of the Book.

---

[153] *Bari* has a double meaning: 'the direction of sunrise' and 'eternal'.
[154] Mizzi, *Semplici constatazioni*, 76.
[155] i.e. the *bokku* has become divine through the presence of Waaqa in the Proclamation ceremony. I am indebted to Borru Dhuddacha for his help with the translation of this text.
[156] Knutsson, *Authority and Change*, 45; see also A. Cecchi, *Da Zeila alle frontiere del caffa* (Rome: Ermanno Loescher, 1886), vol. 2, 29.
[157] Azaïs, 'Etude sur la religion du peuple Galla', 73–4.
[158] Legesse, *Oromo Democaracy*, 140, states that Borana is the senior moiety while Barentu is the junior. 'Legend has it that one moiety was "born" before the other and that is the main reason why they are ranked. As such, seniority simply represents the 'order of birth' of the moieties. It is possible that one moiety did indeed precede the other in terms of historical social formation', 144. Asmarom adds: 'We know that the senior moiety in the 16th century was called "Borana" and there is no debate about that.' However, the story about Ana and Antu mentioned above makes the same point and the ranking was not in terms of order of birth, but gender-determined. What is more, the following tradition reverses Asmarom's conclusion and suggests that it was the Barentu and not the Borana that was the senior moiety. Asmarom also mentions a very interesting point in relation to Gona and Sabbo moieties among the Borana in southern Ethiopia. According to his information, 'one moiety appears to contain more assimilated aliens than the other ... the half that resorts to corporate assimilation of aliens is the one that is thought of as the big moiety ... Furthermore, it is the senior moiety that behaves in this way and is thought to be bigger', 141. If we apply this criterion to the Borana and Barentu moieties at the beginning of the sixteenth century, it was the Barentu moiety that resorted to corporate assimilation of aliens and was therefore bigger. Evidence in support of this conclusion will be presented in Chapters 3 and 4.

AN OROMO LEGEND THAT HAS PARALLELS WITH THE OLD TESTAMENT

This legend relates that Borana and Barentu were brothers, who lived together 'for a long time', until one day they quarrelled. In spite of Barentu's dutiful yet unaffectionate respect towards Borana, the latter looked down upon his 'younger brother'. Then one day a son of Borana killed a son of Barentu. Since it was not permitted for a younger brother to fight his elder brother, Barentu decided to leave the country, crossing the frontier near a river. However, since the river was running over its banks at the time, Barentu was not able to cross it without the help of a woman from the family of Galan (the first-born son of Borana). The following quotation expresses the currency of this tradition:

> *Lagni baasuu dide (ceesisuu dide)*
> *intala warra Galan uf-dura buusani*
> *raada warra Buroo itti aansani*
> *intalti warra Galan jirrman dhoofite*
> *bisaan gargar-citee isaan ba'an*
> *Ormi (Borana) yogga dhufan bisaan ceehuu dhoorke.*
> *Akkasittti Barentumti dagi-dufte.*[159]

> The river prevented them [Barentu] from crossing'[160]
> With the daughter of the family[161] of Galan[162] at their head'[163]
> Followed by the heifer[164] from the family of Buroo;[165]
> the daughter from the family of Galan hit the water with her staff,[166]
> The Water was divided or separated for the Barentu to cross,[167]
> The Borana were prevented from crossing by the water.
> That is how the Barentu came here in stealth.[168]

This tradition is similar to that of the story of the two sons of Adam, namely 'Abel and Cain. Cain was the elder and Abel the younger. Cain was puffed up with arrogance and jealousy which led him to commit the crime of murder.'[169] In the tradition cited above, reference is made to a river that 'cut' or prevented the Borana from catching up with the Barentu. In this story, one may detect a pointed Biblical echo of the Red

[159] Mizzi, *Cenni etnografici Galla ossia organizzazione civile*, 71.
[160] i.e. the Borana wanted to cross the river in order to catch up with the Barentu.
[161] *Warra* has the meaning of family, clan and tribe.
[162] Galan was an important Oromo clan, which was believed to have been the 'first born son' of the Borana moiety.
[163] 'The daughter of Galan' was to marry 'the son of Barentu' for the purpose of reconciling the two brothers.
[164] Bride wealth.
[165] A neutral brother who was not a party to the quarrel.
[166] Her staff was reference to her *siiqqee*, a symbol of women's power in Oromo tradition.
[167] After the Barentu crossed, the river joined together to prevent the Borana from crossing.
[168] I am indebted to Borr Dhuddacha for his help with the translation of this text.
[169] Ali, *The Meaning of the Holy Qur'an*, 255, see note 731.

Sea, which prevented Pharaoh's soldiers from catching up with Moses and the Israelites for the purpose of returning them to Egypt. The story of crossing a river is a universal feature of early Oromo history. This tradition also supports Asmarom's thesis that the two moieties were exogamous.[170] What is more, the tradition expresses the role of the first-born son, *angafa,* in Oromo society. It confirms that Galan was the first-born son of the Borana. The importance of mentioning Galan at this point is to show that members of this descent groups were already living in the region of Shawa before the thirteenth and fourteenth centuries, as will be shown in the next chapter. The institution of *angafa* (first born) seems to have given sustained stimulus to the continuous process of migration over several centuries. According to the Oromo tradition of primogeniture, the *angafa* inherited two-thirds of the father's property.[171] This seems to have caused considerable tension among younger brothers, who had to make their fortunes on their own, which often entailed migrating beyond the reach of the elder brother's authority.[172] The above tradition also reflects a long process that actually took place. On the surface the part that deals with the son of Borana killing the son of Barentu is very similar to the Biblical story of Cain (the senior brother) killing Abel (the junior brother) because of his favour with God and the separation of their descendants. Underneath the common Biblical theme we observe the factual core of difference in economic specialization between the Borana and Barentu areas. The Barentu moiety, from its base in the highlands of Bale, was engaged in mixed economy, while the Borana, from its base in the lowlands of Ganale River specialized in pastoralism.

There is juxtaposition here with the Biblical story where Cain, the elder brother, was an agriculturalist, while his younger brother, Abel, was a pastoralist. Because God regarded favourably Abel's offering over that of Cain, the latter got jealous and killed his younger brother.[173]

> In the Oromo case it is the pastoralist who kills the agriculturalist. In both stories we have the issue of economic specialization and the conflict between pastoralists who need open land and agriculturalists who need enclosed lands for grain and seed production. This juxtaposition does not necessarily contradict [the] thesis about the connection to Christian tradition and themes, but points to a deeper parallel with the agriculturalist/pastoralist struggle over the nature of the use of land.[174]

The problem of discussing differences in economic specialization between the Borana and Barentu areas becomes all the more difficult when one attempts to define how and when it happened. We can guess how it happened, but there is no way of knowing when it happened. The only safe way of putting it is that it was a slow process that took centu-

---

[170] Legesse, *Oromo Democracy*, 151.
[171] d'Abbadie, 'On the Oromo: Great African Nation', 135.
[172] d'Abbadie, Nouv. Acq. Fran. No. 21300, folio 778.
[173] *The Holy Bible*, Genesis 4: 2–16.
[174] Personal communication with Rev. Dr Harwood Schaffer.

ries to evolve. However, it gathered momentum during the first half of the fourteenth century when dramatic developments were taking place in the region (see next chapter). It seems that at the initial stage of economic specialization, the moiety that specialized in pastoralism acquired the appellation Borana, for reasons that will be suggested, while the moiety that was involved in mixed economy retained the old Cushitic name of Barentu. According to Schaffer:

> There is a similar parallel with Cain and Abel. In Hebrew Cain is a strong word beginning with a hard consonant. Abel, by way of contrast is the Hebrew word Hevel which means breath or vapor and signifies weakness. As the story begins the listener knows which one is going to live and which one is going to die, just by the nature of their names. The names foretell the story.[175]

Due to the 'masculine' attribute associated with Borana, members of this moiety acquired the status of the 'eldest son' in the national legend which accorded to its descendants seniority in the national myth'.[176] Eventually, the term Borana became a mark of distinction to express one's feelings of cultural and social superiority, or it was used to emphasize the fictitious or real 'purity' of one's genealogy. To this day, the Borana signifies to Oromo speakers a 'cultural and linguistic purity' which is more apparent than real. It also signifies close association between Borana and pastoralism. For the Oromo, the Borana are pastoralists par excellence, who maintain a traditional Oromo way of life.

According to Professor Roland Oliver:

> The Rift valley and its adjacent highlands seem, during the latter Iron Age, to have been occupied by a whole series of societies whose economic strategies embraced both mountain agriculture and valley, with a constant interaction between one and the other. In the Ethiopian sector of the Rift, it is clear that the ancestors of the Oromo people occupied both the valley floor and the Bali highlands to the east of it keeping their cattle in the valley and cultivating barley and other crops on the hills.[177]

This specialization in terms of cultivating crops in the highlands and keeping cattle in the lowlands appears to have developed slowly over a long period. Probably it was the *fora* expedition that led to this development. *Fora* was the practice of dividing the cattle into 'dry' and 'lactating' cows, keeping the latter near the village, while the former were taken to the lowlands where there was enough pasture in the wet season.

Asmarom Legesse thinks *fora* started assuming a progressively larger role in the life of the adolescent Borana with the decline of inter-tribal wars.[178] But one thing is for certain: *fora* was an old prac-

---

[175] Ibid.

[176] Martial de Salviac, *Un peuple antique au pays de Ménélik: les Galla, grande nation Africaine* (Paris: H. Oudin, 1905), 20–36. See also Cerulli, *Etiopia occidentale*, vols. II, 139–43.

[177] Roland Oliver, *The African Experience* (New York: Harper Collins, 1991), 108.

[178] Legesse, *Gada: Three Approaches*, 97.

tice among the Oromo. It was one aspect of the transhumant economy that accounts for the development of economic strategies based on crop cultivation in the highlands and cattle keeping in the lowlands. A Gujji Oromo legend reported by Haberland brings an important point to light.[179] The legend claims that the Borana originated in fora. According to this legend, Borana came from Gujji herdsmen 'who wandered off' (*wronite inboronte*). This legend is very important, because it introduces an interesting concept, *inboronte*, which means wandered off or went somewhere and did not come back. In fact, the term Borana conveys a very strong concept of a 'wanderer' who moves from place to place sticking to the simple but noble tradition of the pastoral life. Possibly the term Borana developed to express the concept of those 'who wandered off' and did not return, which could be the reason why the term Borana evolved later than the old Cushitic name, Barentu.[180] Currently, among the Borana, *fora* is 'the time when men take the family herds into the untamed river valleys. Borana land is rich in wildlife and no part of it is better endowed than the Dawa and Ganale basins',[181] as are the lowlands by Lake Abaya for the Gujji.[182] The same is true of the Ramis valley for the Anniya, the only pastoral group in Hararghe that still calls itself Barentu.

ISLAMIC INFLUENCES ON THE QAALLUU INSTITUTION

There is a fair amount of literature on the Qaalluu institution, which was the core of traditional Oromo religion.[183] It is 'believed to have existed since mythical times'.[184] Close examination of existing data shows 'that traditional Oromo religion had institutions, ritual practices, ritual experts, calendars, and ritual terminologies and texts that were common for the different branches of the Oromo nation in the past'.[185] The noun *qaalluu* is derived from the verb *qalu* – 'to slaughter' or 'to sacrifice'. Qaalluu was the person who performed ritual sacrifices, interpreted the laws of Waaqa and served as a link between Waaqa and the Oromo. As the spiritual leader of traditional Oromo religion, the Qaalluu legitimated the institution of Abba Muudaa and validated the pilgrimage to his shrine. In other words, the Qaalluu himself became the Abba Muudaa, which literally means the 'father' of the *muudaa* rituals. *Muudaa* refers to both the ceremony held every eight years to honour the holy person – the Qaalluu – and the pilgrimage to his shrine, which is a sacred site. Traditionally, there were two Qaalluu who were

---

179 Haberland, *Galla Süd-Aethiopiens*, 277.
180 This is my tentative conclusion.
181 Legesse, *Gada: Three Approaches*, 57.
182 Haberland, *Galla Süd-Aethiopiens*, 286.
183 In this section, I have heavily drawn on my short article, 'Pilgrimage to the Abba Muuda', *Journal of Oromo Studies* 12, nos. 1–2 (July 2005), 142–57.
184 Knutsson, *Authority and Change*, 65.
185 Bulcha, *Contours of the Emergent and Ancient Oromo Nation*, 254.

the ritual leaders of the two original moieties, 'whose shrines were historically associated with cradle lands of the Borana and Barettuma Oromo'.[186] According to Asmarom Legesse,

> The Qallu, the men with the highest ritual authority, are the men of bless-ings and men of peace par excellence. They are prohibited from bearing arms, shedding blood and making laws. They are excluded from the highest deci-sion-making body in the land. [187]

Yet, because of their ritual authority and prestige, they oversaw the election of *gada* leaders, those who provided political and military lead-ership. Above all else, the Qalluu were 'holy men' and men of peace and, hence, they were greatly honoured and showered with gifts by the pilgrims. The national myths about the finding of the first Qaalluu, though varied in form, are very similar in content. According to these myths, the first Qaalluu was of divine origin. Some say he 'fell from the sky itself'. Others say that he was found with the first black heifer, and still others say that he was the 'eldest son of Ilma Orma'[188] (or the Oromo). Because of the myth of origin of the first Qaalluu and his successors' role in ritual ceremonies, the Qaalluu were the centre of traditional Oromo religion. As the 'eldest son' of Ilma Orma (the Oromo), the national myth confers upon him the title of the father, the source of all traditions. In this role, a Qaalluu was 'the prophet of the nation' who guarded the law of Waaqa and its interpretation.[189] The law of Waaqa dealt with rituals while the laws made by the Oromo assembly dealt with maintaining social order. Waaqa was both God and the sky, the habitation of Waaqa, manifesting the dual nature of the two moieties within the nation. Waaqa had to do with fertility, peace, and the life-giving rains necessary for farming and pastoralism and the reason why prayers for peace, fertility and rain are at the centre of Borana religion.[190] The title of the 'prophet' of the nation confers upon the Abba Muudaa the title of father, the source of all tradi-tions. Azaj Tino, who first wrote about the Abba Muudaa, described him as 'the prophet of the nation', who guards the laws of Waaqa and its inter-pretation. Indeed, the pilgrimage to the Abba Muudaa was integral to the practice of the traditional Oromo religion.

As indicated above, for the Oromo, Waaqa is one and the same for all human beings, the Creator of everything, source of all life, omnipresent, infinite, incomprehensible, who can do and undo anything. He is pure, intolerant of injustice, crime, sin and falsehood.[191] According to Harwood

---

[186] Legesse, *Gada: Three Approaches*, 101.

[187] Ibid., 121.

[188] de Salviac, *An Ancient People: Great African Nation*, 177; Haberland, *Galla Süd-Aethiopiens*, 151–8; Knutsson, *Authority and Change*, 144–5.

[189] F.M. Esteves Pereira, ed., *Chronica de Susenyos, Rei de Ethiopia* (Lisbon: Impresa National, 1892–1900), 214.

[190] Baxter, 'The Social Organization of the Galla of Northern Kenya', 48. See also Legasse, *Gada: Three Approaches*, 216.

[191] Mengesha Rikitu, *Oromia Recollected* (London: Magic Press, 1998), 99; see also Gada Melba, *Oromia: A Brief Introduction* (Khartoum, 1980), 23.

Schaffer, 'the attributes of Waaqa have similarities to Yahweh, the God of the Abrahamic faith. These similarities are astounding'.[192] This means, in contrast with their neighbours' polytheistic religions, Oromo monotheism shares a lot in common with that of the Peoples of the Book.

Islamic influences stemmed from the contacts the Oromo people had with Muslims (most likely in the old Muslim states of Shawa, Ifat, Fatagar, Dawaro and, above all, Bali); in particular, there are indications of specific practices radiating from the shrine of Sheik Hussein of Bali in the Qalluu institution. The annals of these contacts are shrouded in uncertainty and a full reconstruction of their impact must await further research in the field. The following circumstantial evidence, however, does suggest Islamic influence on the Qalluu institution. Even though the national myths surrounding the origin of the first Qalluu cited above make him either of divine origin or the eldest son of Ilma Orma (the eldest son of Oromo), there is a popular tradition that makes the first Barentu Qalluu of non-Oromo origin. As we saw above, the Borana tradition also makes the first and the most senior Qalluu a 'stranger'[193] (i.e. a non-Oromo).

THE STORY OF ABBA MUUDAA

The story of Abba Muudaa suggests that the first Qalluu were probably exposed to some rudimentary form of Islamic ideas. However, before showing that aspect it is important to state that, 'the Qalluu and the Abba Muudaa are one and the same ritual leader'.[194] As indicated above, Muudaa refers to both the ceremony held every eight years to honour the holy person – the Qalluu – and the pilgrimage to his shrine, which is a sacred site. Those who went on pilgrimage to honour the Qalluu were known as *jila*. Asmarom Legesse notes:

> The great ritual significance of the Muda ritual derives from the fact that it was and is the point in their respective cycles when the two systems intersect. It represents the encounter between the two principle institutions of the Oromo. As such Muda is laden with meaning and stands on par, in its significance, with the *gada* power handover ceremony (Balli) and the octennial meetings of the national assembly (Gumi or Chaffe).[195]

The Qalluu institution and the pilgrimage to honour the Abba Muudaa were the heart, the soul, and the spirit of traditional Oromo religion, centred around *Waaqa*, the Creator of the universe and the sustainer of life on earth. In all their ceremonies, the Oromo prayed and still pray to *Waaqa,* whom they trust and to whom they turn in their moments of joy and distress. According to Claude Sumner: 'The Oromo know that what comes from [*Waaqa*], whether it is adversity or prosperity, is the best.

192 Personal communication with Rev. Dr Harwood Schaffer.
193 Wario, 'Journey to the Shrine of Nura Symbols', 27–28.
194 Legesse, *Oromo Democracy*, 94.
195 Ibid.

The important thing is that one should go forth before God: to do otherwise is reprehensible.'[196] The Oromo go forth before *Waaqa* in prayer and trust in Him. 'To trust *Waaqa* is an indication of the fundamental belief that *Waaqa*, who is the source and origin of all that exists, also cares for creation by protecting it and by bestowing it with fertility, abundance and peace.'[197]

Azaj Tino, one of the authors of the Chronicle of Emperor Susenyos (1607–32), provides us with the earliest written record we have about traditional Oromo religion. A contemporary of Abba Bahrey,[198] Azaj Tino states that the Abba Muudaa was spiritual head of and played an important part in the workings of the Oromo traditional religion. Azaj Tino was a learned man who gathered information from the Oromo themselves and showed respect for Oromo culture and customs about which he was most knowledgeable. He demonstrated the important role played by the Abba Muudaa and wrote in detail about the pilgrimage to honour him. He stated that the Oromo believe in their Abba Muudaa 'as the Jews believe in Moses and the Muslims in Muhammad. They all go to him from far and near to honour him and receive his blessings.'[199] The Oromo pilgrims went to either the Borana or Barentu sacred lands from as far as Wallaga in the west, Hararghe in the east, Wallo in the north and from what is today Kenya in the south. The extant literature reveals Oromo emotional attachments to the hills, mountains, rivers and valleys of the sacred lands of the Borana and Barentu – the feeling well preserved in Oromo oral tradition and religious songs.[200]

A number of important points emerge from Azaj Tino's remarkably perceptive information about traditional Oromo religion, that the Abba Muudaa was the spiritual head of the Oromo religion. 'He is the centre of religious life and the rallying point of the nation, though he has no civil or executive authority. In him are personified and centralized the laws and traditions...and [Waaqa] is said to speak through him.'[201] It was in that context that Azaj Tino presented the Abba Muudaa as the prophet of the Oromo nation who guarded and interpreted the laws of Waaqa.[202] When Azaj Tino was writing, the sacred lands of the Abba Muudaa, comparable to Mecca for Muslims and the Holy Land for Christians, were located in southern Ethiopia.[203] Just as Muslims and Chris-

---

[196] Sumner, *Proverbs, Songs, Folktales*, 106.

[197] Joseph Van de Loo, *Guji Oromo Culture in Southern Ethiopia: Religious Capabilities in Rituals and Songs* (Berlin: Dietrich Reimer, 1991), 284.

[198] Interestingly, Abba Bahrey, who wrote his *Zenahu le Galla* in 1593, did not mention the pilgrimage to honour the Abba Muudaa. This failure is one of the many indications that his knowledge of Oromo society of the time was limited.

[199] Pereira, *Chronica de Susenyos*, 214.

[200] de Salviac, *An Ancient People: Great African Nation*, 177–87.

[201] G.W.B. Huntingford, *The Galla of Ethiopia: The Kingdom of Kafa and Janjero* (London: International African Institute, 1955), 83.

[202] Pereira, *Chronica de Susenyos*, 214.

[203] Antoine d'Abbadie, 'On the Oromo: Great African Nation Often Designated under the Name of "Galla"', trans. Ayalew Kanno, *Journal of Oromo Studies* 14, 1 (March 2007), 133.

tians, as individuals trying to save their souls and earn salvation, went on pilgrimage to the birthplaces of their religions, so did the Oromo: but the Oromo pilgrims were representatives of Borana and Barentu, thus keeping alive the roots of the two ancient moieties.

THE *JILA*

Pilgrimages were made every eight years and those who went on pilgrimages were known as *jila*. The term *jila* has double meanings; a pilgrim who went to receive personally the blessings of the Abba Muudaa and a delegate who went on pilgrimage to receive the blessings of the spiritual leader of traditional Oromo religion on behalf of his descent group. On their way to the Abba Muudaa the *jila* chanted numerous songs including the following.

> We are going to the spiritual Father;
> We brave the frost of the night;
> Morning dews inundated me;
> The wet grass bathed me;
> All my clothes are soaked.
> O my perfume, O fragrant Pontiff![204]

Upon their arrival at the shrine of Abba Muudaa, the *jila* sang the following song which expresses their longing for good reception.

> Give us good reception, O fragrant father!
> The pilgrims from all parts emerge, they arrive;
> It is Waaqa that guided them.
> They brave depths and precipices;
> They overcame the marshes;
> They disregarded fatigues;
> Not a coward has turned back.
> Give us good reception, O fragrant father!
> Our heifers and our fecund ewes are scattered on the plain;
> We want the Unction, the Unction;
> The pilgrims reclaim the Unction.
> O my perfume, O fragrant pontiff![205]

The *jila* were received by the Abba Muudaa with marks of honour and questioned by him on Oromo laws and customs. According to Haberland's account, as presented by Knutsson, the pilgrims arrived at the Abba Muudaa's residence in the evening.

> They wait until all the calves that they have brought have arrived, whereupon they drive them into the kallu's [Qaalluu] kraal. Thereafter they proceed singing to the ritual house (galma) where the kallu awaits them with his wife, kalitti, at his side. The kallu has wrapped his head in a lion's mane on which he has fastened two [*kalacha*[206]]. He is treated with the utmost reverence and no

[204] de Salviac, *An Ancient People: Great African Nation*, 184.
[205] Ibid., 185.
[206] *Kalacha* is a greatly respected ritual object. According to Knutsson, 'it consists of a phallic ornament worn on the forehead by certain officials in

one dares to raise his eyes to him. All take places as though they were seeking to hide from him. The pilgrims are generously entertained with meat and honey wine and pass the night dancing and feasting.[207]

Early the next morning the pilgrims passed before the Abba Muudaa who, after communal prayers, gave them gifts of myrrh and showered blessings upon them, which they valued highly. One of the important blessings was anointment with butter, which led Huntingford to translate Abba Muudaa as 'father of anointing'.[208] Muslim kings from the Gibe region not only sent gifts to the Abba Muudaa, in recognition of his ritual authority, but also regarded the presence of *jila* in their countries as conferring blessings on them. This was reported by Antoine d'Abbadie, who in 1846 saw the *jila* from Limmu-Ennarya, Gumma, Jimma and Gera gathered in Limmu-Ennarya before their departure on the long journey to the land of Abba Muudaa.[209] The pilgrimage to honour the Abba Muudaa served as the focal point of Oromo unity. This is because for 'centuries, Oromo land was crisscrossed by routes, arising from the different regions and converging at the shrines' of Abba Muudaas in the southern highlands. Thus the pilgrimage not only maintained contact among Oromo, but it also gave them 'a sense of Oromo national community'.[210] Similarly, one of the major purposes of Muslim pilgrimage to Mecca is to maintain unity of the *umma* – the Muslim community. Finally, the Oromo maintained contact with each other and with the spiritual force of their traditional religion through the pilgrimage. So did the Christians and Muslims maintain contact with spiritual force of their religions through their pilgrimage to the birthplaces of their religions.

Azaj Tino most likely wrote about the pilgrimage to the land of Abba Muudaa during the 1610s. Almeida, a Portuguese missionary and contemporary of Azaj Tino, wrote that 'the [Oromo] are neither Christians nor Moors nor heathens for they have no idols to worship'.[211] Asma Giyorgis, a Catholic missionary writing shortly after 1900, stated that 'from among the Ten Commandments given to Moses by God, the [Oromo] lack only the first one, which says, "I am the Lord thy God ... thou shalt have no other gods before me." This is the only natural law they lack.'[212] Asma Giyorgis also clearly indicated that the pilgrimage to honour the Abba Muudaa had crucial importance to Oromo religion.[213]

(contd) the *gada* system and by the foremost ritual experts of the tribe'. Knutsson, *Authority and Change*, 89.

[207] Ibid., 151–2.

[208] Huntingford, *The Galla of Ethiopia*, 83.

[209] Antoine d'Abbadie, 'The papers of Antoine and Arnauld d'Abbadie', Bibliothèque nationale, Paris, 21, 300, folios 788–90.

[210] Bulcha, *Contours of the Emergent and Ancient Oromo Nation*, 256.

[211] de Almeida, 'The History of High Ethiopia or Abassia Book IV', in *Some Records of Ethiopia*, 136.

[212] Tafla, *Asma Giyorgis and his Work*, 125.

[213] Ibid., 133.

Several reports by nineteenth- and twentieth-century European travellers and missionaries contain accounts of the pilgrimages that are strikingly similar to those of Azaj Tino.[214] Perhaps Cecchi's account of the journey to the land of Abba Muudaa sums up most, though not all, of the important points:

> The journey to the Abba Muda is made partly to honour him and partly to receive his blessing and anointment, which qualify the pilgrims for ritual functions in their own home region. Only those who have committed no serious crimes may make the journey ... They must be married and circumcised. This means that they must have undergone the butta ceremony and thereby completed their forty-year participation in the *gada* system. During the journey they are said to be dressed as women and to receive food from women. They wear their hair cut short and bear no weapons. As an offering to Abba Muda they bring a bull, and as a sign of their peaceful intentions they drive a sheep. When they reach Abba Muda, the pilgrim's leader offers food to the snake that guards Abba Muda's grotto. After communal prayers Abba Muda anoints the *jila*s and gives them myrrh. He commands them not to cut their hair and to be righteous, not to recognize any leader who tries to get absolute power, and not to fight among themselves.[215]

The Abba Muudaa also commands the *jila* to teach the people to live according to the laws of Alanga (a whip carried by *gada* leaders symbolizing the rule of *gada* law and as an indication of their authority): that is, to judge justly, not to allow forced labour, not to fight each other but to drive the Sidama (Abyssinians) from their lands. From this perspective, the Abba Muudaa was a ritual leader who inspired Oromo resistance to Abyssinian occupation of their lands.

Because the pilgrims received the Abba Muudaa's blessings and anointment, they were regarded as 'saintly people', men without sin and, therefore, closer to Waaqa. Similarly, Muslims believe that those who went on pilgrimage to Mecca and Medina are forgiven for all their past sins. The Oromo pilgrims could pass 'between warring groups of people, no one maltreats them, for they are identifiable'. Even the animals the *jila* drove as gifts for the Abba Muudaa were protected just like the *jila* themselves. Likewise, Muslims who went on pilgrimage were provided with protection, which was also extended to the animals brought as offerings for sacrifice.[216] As Muslim pilgrims returning from Mecca were accorded the tile of Haj, Oromo pilgrims were accorded the title of *jila*. Upon the Oromo pilgrims' return home, Asma Giyorgis emphasized, the *jila* were received 'with pomp and ceremony'.[217] The pilgrims were given gifts by the Abba Muudaa, 'whose presence is regarded as mysterious benefit for the tribe'. Upon the Muslim pilgrims' return home, they are received with great celebration and entertained by their neighbours. The *jila* were considered to be 'saints' and as a link

---

[214] The literature on the Qaalluu institution and Abba Muudaa is not only rich but also covers the major part of Oromo land.

[215] Cecchi, *Da Zeila alla frontiere del Caffa*, vol. 2, 30, trans. Knutsson, *Authority and Change*, 148.

[216] Ali, *The Meaning of the Holy Qur'an*, 244, see note 688.

[217] Tafla, *Asma Giyorgis and his Work*, 133.

between the spiritual father and the nation.[218] As a *jila* was inviolable, no one touched his cattle in war or in raids between villagers. The people who kept their cattle went unarmed as a sign of their peacefulness. The story went that *jila* were 'brothers' to both Borana and Barentu. The 'rule of *jila*' – maintaining peace between the two brothers – was set against the rule of rivalry between different descent groups.

When the pilgrims arrived at the spiritual centre, the Abba Muudaa used to question them about the laws of Waaqa and the customs of the Oromo. Before their departure the *jila* individually requested the Abba Muudaa to bless them and the Oromo people. They articulated their requests with the following words, which reflect the unmistakable influence of Christian ideas.

> I have come to you to receive the Unction, now I want to return to my hearth; Bless me. O my pontiff. Fill me up with your benediction. Say your words over me. That your flocks multiply! That a long line of offspring comes out of you! ... Bless the sons of Orma, O my pontiff! O pontiff, you my benediction and my support ... O pontiff my Healer! ... O pontiff of Waaqa, O my benediction.[219]

Before blessing the *jila* the Abba Muudaa urged them to teach the people the laws of Waaqa and the customs of the Oromo. He impressed upon the *jila* that they should warn the Oromo against abandoning the way of life of their fathers, and urged them to preserve the pastoral way of life that guaranteed the continuity of the ancient traditions. The prayers and blessings that the Abba Muudaa showered on the pilgrims demonstrate the ideal type of prosperity that he envisaged.

> Prosper, O sons of Orma, O sons of the race, prosper! Go, see again the threshold of your house; return to the midst of your own; return to the bosom of your tribe; arrive in the territory of your Abba Bokku [Abba Gada]. May the milk of your herds flow abundant! May it overflow your vases very full! May every village drink from your superfluity! May all be filled with wealth. May the udders of your favourite cows be puffed up, whose milk only the father of the family drinks, whose milk only the mother of the family drinks, whose milk only those who have received the Unction drink! Prosper! This is the will of my heart, the will that I make for the pilgrims. Enjoy happy days and happy nights! May Waaqa be with you! May he accept your sacrifices and your wadaja [communal prayer]! Prosperity to all: such is the will of my soul.[220]

On their return journey the *jila* chanted the following song that shows their satisfaction with the blessings they received and the long arduous journey home.

> We have received the Unction;
> We hurry to return;
> The distance is frightful ...
> It will soon be six months that I slept outside ...

[218] Mizzi, *Cenni Etnografici Galla Organizzazione Civile*, 9. See also de Salviac, *An Ancient People: Great African Nation*, 155–6.
[219] Ibid., 186.
[220] Ibid., 186–7.

>The whole crowd has received the unction.
>Yes, yes, the unction! ...
>The vase of the pontiff
>has poured the benediction.[221]

In Islam, communal prayer is highly emphasized and encouraged. It is regarded as much more important than individual or private prayer. In Oromo tradition, *wadaja* or communal prayer, is the heart and soul of Oromo traditional religion. According to Martial de Salviac, *wadaja* is the only form of prayer universally recognized by the Oromo. 'The principal act of the Oromo religion is the Wadaja ... That is the pivot on which rest all the other rites, the centre around which they gravitate. That is the national prayer, the universal form of the profession of the Oromo faith, in use among all the tribes.'[222] In the above-quoted prayer for the pilgrims, the Abba Muudaa prayed for Oromo prosperity both in its general sense and in its spiritual sense. In the general sense his prayer means material prosperity produced by peace under the rule of an Abba Bokku, the foundation of Oromo democracy. The core of his prayer was *nagaya*, peace, which emphasized peace with Waaqa, with the community, with the land, the animals and the environment. In the spiritual sense, it means maintaining the old way of life and traditional Oromo religion based on Waaqa, opening the door to their happiness and greatness as people.

Getatchew Haile claims that the Abba Muudaa not only blessed the stock of the pilgrims by saying multiply, may God maximize the fruit of your labour, etc., but also wished them victory over their enemies and booty in war.[223] The last is an oversimplification, but the thought is not so different from that of those Christian and Muslim religious leaders who offered similar prayers for victory on behalf of their co-religionists and believed that God was on their side. Christian and Muslim religious leaders also admonished their co-religionists not to fight among themselves. Of course, the Abba Muudaa prayed for Oromo victory on battlefield. He was confident that if they were united and maintained their way of life they would be victorious. But the Abba Muudaa differed from these Christian and Muslims religious leaders, whose societies often did not have democratic institutions, in that he urged the Oromo not to recognize any leader who tried to gain absolute power. These admonitions expressed the common, central Oromo democratic value, which always sought to limit the power of leaders by a variety of social and political mechanisms. Most Muslim and Christian political systems had no similar in-built mechanisms for limiting the power of their leaders.

---

[221] Ibid., 185–6.
[222] Ibid., 162.
[223] Haile, *The Works of Abba Bahriy*, 146.

THE *GALMA*

The house of the Abba Muudaa, his *galma*, was the centre of his spiritual activities and a symbol of peace and moral force. Today among the Borana in southern Ethiopia and northern Kenya, the term *galma* has double meaning. First, it means '"the return" and this may refer to the symbolic return to the land of Qallu which is the original land of the Borana'. Second, *galma* is believed to be the 'symbolic "container of the power of Qallu"'.[224] According to Hassan Wario, *galma* was and still is a sacred shrine, a 'space created to signify return to sanctity, fertility, regeneration and continuity'.[225] In short, the *galma* was the centre of worship and learning where people went for prayer, asking the Abba Muudaa (the link between Waaqa and the Oromo) to bless them with peace, rain, fertility and prosperity. Those who sought knowledge about the Oromo spiritual universe visited the *galma*, which was a focal point of learning and religious activities, once or twice a week. They would dance, sing, and beat drums in a ritual called *dalaga* or *dalaqa* in order to achieve a state of ecstasy.[226] This is very similar, if not identical, with the Muslim prayer known as *manzuma*. The essence of the teaching at *galma* was peace and harmony or *nagaya* (*nagaa*). Oromo begin and end all their prayers with *nagaya*, peace, in its broadest sense, which includes the safety and well-being of the individual and of the community. For the community, peace is the maintenance of law and order, care for the poor, the weak and sick. For an individual, it is inner peace: peace of the body, mind, and soul, which is close to the Jewish concept of Shalom and the Muslim concept of Salam. Peace relates to an individual's imaginative sense of well-tempered, balanced inter-relations with other persons, the environment and with Waaqa. The Abba Muudaa connects Oromo with this universal peace through his prayers.

Jila were considered to be 'men of God' and imbued with a sort of 'sacred quality', as men without sin. The concept is similar to that attached to Muslim pilgrims to Sheikh Hussein of Bali, or even to Mecca. Oromo pilgrims were protected from violence and might even be helped on their journey by their former enemies. What is more, the *jila* were provided with the necessities of life while on journey even in enemy territories. We have noted above that the Qur'an commands Muslims to provide protection and necessities of life for pilgrims. *Jila* and their wives had to be sexually abstinent for two weeks before their departure and throughout the pilgrimage, which might take six months both ways. Indeed, they should both sleep on the floor rather than on a bed. This is similar to the simplicity that is required of a Muslim during pilgrimage. Once en route Oromo pilgrims should not look back, for to do so was regarded as breaking the pilgrimage. These

---

[224] Wario, 'Journey to the Shrine of Nura Symbols', 55.
[225] Ibid.
[226] Melbaa, *Oromia: A Brief Introduction*, 25–26.

concepts of ritual purity appear to have parallels with those maintained by Muslim pilgrims to Mecca. To show that they were men of Waaqa, pilgrims distinguished themselves by three signs. First, *jila* took along with them sheep, 'animals of peace', which were the ideal sacrifice to Waaqa.[227] For Muslim pilgrims, sheep were also the ideal animal for sacrifice while they were in Mecca. Second, Oromo pilgrims wore trophies not associated with war on their wrists and necks, 'which marked them for the occasion as *nama waaqa*, men of God'; and they did not carry spears or other arms which were the mark of manhood for the Oromo. Third, while on pilgrimage, the *jila* carried other insignia such as a forked staff, which had three prongs at the top, standing for, we are told, the peace, unity and knowledge of tradition. These restrictions and signs, such as the three- pronged staff, are similar to those maintained by pilgrims to the tomb of Sheikh Hussein today, but with one crucial difference: pilgrims to the tomb of Sheikh Hussein go as individuals whereas those who go to the Abba Muudaa went as representatives of their clans.

It is probably this 'cultural fit' or similarity that led two scholars, Cerulli and Trimingham, to consider that Sheikh Hussein, for Muslim Oromo, was a continuation of the old Abba Muudaa.[228] According to Asmrom Legesse, such a connection was maintained by the Arsi Oromo:

> When the Arsi lost their institutions under the double impact of a most ruthless branch of the Abyssinian imperial army led by Ras Darghe and their enthusiastic acceptance of Islam as their religion and their shield ... Many of the ethical ideas surrounding pilgrims have been transferred from Muda to Sheikh Hussein.[229]

There may be a cross-fertilization of the 'benevolence' of the Abba Muudaa and that attributed to Sheikh Hussein.[230] Probably, there is a common cultural tradition underlying the prayers chanted by *jila* and those pilgrims who today go to the tomb of Sheikh Hussein. There are also similarities between the ideas of generosity in traditional Oromo society and the powerful image of Sheikh Hussein, which inspires people to show charity and kindness to pilgrims. In essence, the two pilgrimages probably have a common origin. The Abba Muudaa's 'two hands, one holding a blessing and the other a curse',[231] the former so much sought after and latter so much dreaded, are also not very different from the tradition of Sheikh Hussein.[232] Moreover, the remote

227 Bartels, *Oromo Religion*, 357.
228 Cerulli, *Etiopia Occidentale*, vol. 2, 145; J.S. Trimingham, *Islam in Ethiopia* (London: Oxford University Press, 1952), 256.
229 Legesse, *Oromo Democracy*, 95.
230 B.W. Andrzejewski, 'Sheikh Hussein of Bali in Galla Oral Tradition', *IV Congresso Internationale di Studi Etiopici* (Rome: Accademia Nazionale dei Lincei, 1974), 33–34.
231 Knutsson, *Authority and Change*, 150.
232 Hadj Yusuf Abdul Rahman, ed., *Kitab Rabi al-Qulub fi Dhikr Manaqib Fada'il Sayyidina al-Shaikh Nur Husain* (Cairo: 1927), *passim*.

tomb of Sheikh Hussein in Bali does not seem to have suffered from Oromo attacks in the sixteenth century; perhaps the shrine may have served as a neutral ground for settling internal disputes among themselves and with their enemies.[233]

Finally, there is a tradition that the Barentu Abba Muudaa was of non-Oromo origin. Hassan Wario's research clearly demonstrates that the Borana Qaalluu was of non-Oromo origin, the only person who is allowed to break the law of strict Borana exogamy, marrying into his clan, 'Warra Qaalich'.[234] This means that the Abba Muudaa of both the Borana and the Barentu were originally of non-Oromo origins. Of the two original Abba Muudaas, it appears to me that it was the Barentu Abba Muudaa that was influenced by Islamic ideas. The difference between the Abba Muudaas of the two moieties probably arose from the Barentu's geographical proximity to the Muslim society in southern Ethiopia. This moiety, with its base area in the highlands of Arsi/ Bali, appears to have been exposed more to Islamic ideas radiating from the shrine of Sheikh Hussein of Bali than that of the Borana, who were probably beyond the reach of Islamic influence. The following Barentu song, which was popularly chanted by *jila* on their way to and from Abba Muudaa, says that he was originally a 'stranger', a non-Oromo.

> *Bareentu achi Debanuu gale: Barentitti Tabbo galte*
> *Tabbo Mormor duuba, Asta warra Tabbo gale muuda*
> *Warra Muuda dide, Barrentuma in-qabu: inni dhalata.*[235]
> From there the Barentu has come to Debanu, the people are from Tabbo. Tabbo is behind Mormor, Asta the family that comes to Tabbo Muuda, those who refuse Muuda. He is not Barentu: He is 'born into it'.[236]

'Born into it' is a metaphor for adoption. This Barentu tradition makes it clear that their original Abba Muudaa was a non-Oromo. The claim of this tradition is supported by the early 1970s research in the field. According to Braukämper, the influential Abba Muudaa who now resides in Dollo Bale 'is not of "true" Oromo origin, but is descended from the offspring of a mixed ... clan called Raitu (Rayya)".[237] It is plausible that individuals with rudimentary knowledge of Islam may have served as Oromo ritual leaders or shaped religious views of some Abba Muudaas.

Another popular Barentu song chanted by *jila* going to and from Abba Muudaa implies that the spiritual leader saved the nation by giving his 'blessing' and advice from a situation of terrible crisis caused by hunger.

---

[233] See for example, R. Caulk, 'Harar Town and Its Neighbours in the Nineteenth Century', *Journal of African History* 18, 3 (1977)' 372.

[234] Wario, 'Journey to the Shrine of Nura Symbols', 28.

[235] Mizzi, *Semplici constatzioni*, 74.

[236] Author's free translation.

[237] Ulrich Braukämper, 'Islamic Principalities in Southeast Ethiopia between the Thirteenth and Sixteenth Centuries', *Ethiopianist Notes* 1, 2 (1977), 27–8.

Eega Muuda godaane godaana soraa
Soraara[238]*nuttti roobe qollee*[239] *qallise (ifire)*
Wayaa a bututeesese (ifire)
Warri Muudaa in beekne jaalo waata moo tumtu jaalo.[240]

[With the advice of Abba Muudaa]
We moved away [in search of water and grass]
the move caused by shortage of rain
[lack of] isolated rains, ruined us [made us destitute]
our clothes were worn out into pieces on our body
We were so impoverished [and hungry]
The hunger that skinned and killed men and animals
It rained and plenty showered upon us
Those who do not know the beloved Muudaa, comrade
They are *waata* and *tumtu*,[241] comrade[242]

It is almost impossible to capture the literal and figurative meaning of the above short prayer that was chanted by *jila* during their pilgrimage. However, it seems certain that the Oromo were at some point forced to move away by forces beyond their control. They were so impoverished, so destitute that everything they had was wiped out. It was under such a circumstance that the Abba Muudaa blessed them and told them to move away from the situation of serious crisis. Hassan Wario's research also confirms that the Borana Abba Muudaa's miraculous descent was connected with situation of severe drought. In fact, it was the 'birth' of the Abba Muudaa that brought rain and saved the Borana from destruction.[243] The traditions of both Borana and Barentu stress that during the time of serious drought, the Abba Muudaa encouraged the Oromo to move to areas blessed with water, plenty of pasturage and other resources. The pressure that forced the Oromo to move away could either be connected with severe drought of the late 1320s or early 1330s or the expansion of the Christian kingdom to the south or it was connected with the conflict between the Christians and Muslim communities or the combination of all of them. When did the said crisis brought about by drought and resulting in terrible hunger take place? There is no historical evidence for existence of a major drought accompanied by famine at the beginning of sixteenth century. However, there is strong evidence for existence of a major drought and widespread famine during the first half of the fourteenth century. Therefore, it appears to me that the said drought took place probably during the reign of the warrior-emperor

---

[238] *Soraara* is 'isolated rains or showers in the dry season, after the rainy season is over'. See for instance, Ton Leus with Cynthia Salvadori, *Aadaa Boraanaa: A Dictionary of Borana Culture* (Addis Ababa: Shama Books, 2006), 601.

[239] According to *Aadaa Boraanaa: A Dictionary of Borana Culture*, 'qollee is someone who has lost everything, is wiped out', 529.

[240] d'Abbadie, Nouv. acq. tran. No. 238452, 'Lettres sur La Mission Catholique du pays des Galla, 1845–1895', letter of Taurin Cahagne Harar, 3 December 1883.

[241] *Waata* and *tumtu*, (those who worked forges and blacksmiths) were not allowed to go on pilgrimage to honour the Abba Muudaa.

[242] Author's free broad translation.

[243] Wario, 'Journey to the Shrine of Nura Symbols', 26–27.

Amda-Siyon (1314–44) when a major upheaval took place in the region followed by a devastating famine (see Chapter 2). If this assumption is accurate, it appears that the tradition of Abba Muudaa developed probably during the first half of the fourteenth century under the influence of Christian and Muslim ideas and as a response to dramatic developments in the region.

As noted earlier, the residence of the Abba Muudaa, the *galma*, was a spiritual centre, which people visited both to learn and to participate in prayers for peace, rain, fertility and plenty. It might almost be said that, just as Muslims have their mosques and Christians have their churches, the Oromo have *galma*. The Qaalluu of the Borana in southern Ethiopia personify peace and truth and, though they do not wield political power, they have been described as 'the life spirits of the Borana'.[244]

> Neither Boran society nor culture can be understood without consideration of the part played by the Qallu. All Boran acknowledge the sanctity of the Qallu; it is by the Qallu that all their essential customs were ordained, and by them endowed with a moral force and divine order. Further, it is their possession of the Qallu, which, above all else, distinguishes the Boran 'tribe' from the 'junior tribes' and makes them all superior to their neighbours.[245]

It would seem that during and after the sixteenth century, and for some time afterwards, every fully-fledged Oromo group that formed part of the confederacy had its own ritual leaders who accompanied them, just as Christian clergy and Muslim preachers joined the territorial expansions of their respective religious communities. The ritual leaders who accompanied the migrating clans or descent groups were not Qaalluu in the real sense of the term. They were called *irreessa*, the 'right hand of the Qaalluu', and were his emissaries who had the 'right to exercise their functions from the [Qaalluu] who resided at the cradle land of the moiety'.[246] This connection helps explain the continuous link maintained through the eight-year cycle of *jila* pilgrimages to the sacred southern cradle lands. Thus 'the Qallu institution became the ritual force that kept the roots of the ancient moiety system alive and the pilgrimages were branches linking the far-flung communities to those roots'.[247] Before pilgrimages to the Abba Muudaa were officially abolished around 1900 by Emperor Menelik, who saw the danger of promoting Oromo unity by this practice, pilgrims from Hararghe used to go to Mormor in Bali. Those from Shawa, Wallaga and the Gibe region either went to Wallal or Harro Waallabuu. The Arsi went to Dallo Baruk or Debanu.[248] The different groups sent their representatives (*jila*) to

---

[244] Baxter, 'Social Organization of the Galla in Northern Kenya', 157
[245] Ibid.
[246] de Salviac, *An Ancient People: Great African Nation*, 165. See also Tafla, *Asma Giyorgis and his Work*, 133, 179–83, 311.
[247] Legesse, *Oromo Democracy*, 32.
[248] Cerulli, *Etiopia Occidentale*, vol. II: 249–43, 169, 172; see also Paul Soleillet, *Voyages en Ethiopie Janvier 1882–Octobre 1884: Notes, Lettres et Documents Divers* (Rouen: Cagniard, 1886), 261; de Salviac, *An Ancient People: A Great African Nation*, 181.

their spiritual father in the country from where their pastoral ancestors embarked on the sixteenth-century pastoral Oromo population movement (see Chapter 4).

CONCLUSION

In the above discussion, I have tried to show pre-sixteenth century Christian and Muslim direct and indirect influences on Oromo traditions and institutions stemming from interactions among the Oromo, Christians, and Muslims. Though the history of interactions between the Oromo and Amhara society was remembered in the form of oral legends, myths and fables, these sources do demonstrate that some form of contact did exist. Oromo contact with Christian communities definitely goes back to the thirteenth century, and possibly earlier, as recounted in Christian hagiographies. Contemporary written records of early interactions between some Oromo groups and Christian Amhara provide indisputable evidence of this contact. The next chapter explores how the interactions among the Christians, Muslims and some Oromo groups expanded during the fourteenth and subsequent centuries.

The Oromo creation myth, the myth of the Sacred Book of the Oromo, the Borana and Barentu moiety system, and the Qaalluu institution all appear to have been influenced by both Christian and Muslim ideas. Just as Christian and Muslim pilgrims visited the birthplaces of their religions, for centuries Oromo pilgrims – *jila* – visited the land of Abba Muudaa located in what are today the region of Bale and Sidamo. For the Oromo the land of Abba Muudaa is said to be a place of righteousness, wisdom, harmony, peace and *gada* democracy. The land of Abba Muudaa, as will be shown in Chapter Three, was the place where all the important Oromo religious and political institutions developed; it was the rich source of their historic beginnings and of their view of the universe. In short, the land of the Abba Muudaa provides the cultural templates for Oromo religious beliefs, their political philosophy, based on *gada*, and their knowledge of themselves and their history. For the Oromo, the land of Abba Muudaa was sacred ground, like Mecca for the Muslims and the Holy Land for the Christians. Further, the Qaalluu institution developed among the Macha Oromo in central and western Ethiopia only after 1900, when Emperor Menelik (1889–1913) banned the pilgrimage.[249] Although the Oromo pilgrimage to the land of Abba Muudaa was the core of traditional Oromo religion, for Emperor Menelik the pilgrimages were not so much religious acts as opportunities to stir up pan-Oromo feelings and to form a plan for rebellion.[250] By banning the pilgrimages to the land of Abba Muudaa, Emperor Menelik 'knowingly aimed to destroy the crucial links that sustained Oromo cultural, political and religious unity'.[251]

[249] Knutsson, *Authority and Change*, 155.
[250] Huntingford, *The Galla of Ethiopia*, 83–84.
[251] Hassen, 'Pilgrimage to the Abba Muudaa', 154.

2

Oromo Peoples in the Medieval Christian Kingdom of Ethiopia before 1500[1]

With the sources at our disposal, it is not difficult to establish the pre-sixteenth century Oromo presence within the medieval Christian kingdom of Ethiopia, more appropriately identified as the Christian kingdom of Abyssinia. Though Christian sources mention some Oromo groups during the thirteenth and fourteenth centuries, these were ignored or overlooked, possibly because of the firmly entrenched theory claiming that the Oromo entered the Christian kingdom around the middle of the sixteenth century in the wake of the disastrous jihadic war of Imam Ahmad.[2] Even Merid Wolde Aregay, who in his earlier study established the Oromo presence in the southern parts of the Christian kingdom during the fifteenth century, claims that they were 'relatively speaking, newcomers to the central highlands'.[3] The central highlands include the present region of Shawa, the heartland of the medieval Christian kingdom, far from its frontiers.

The literature on the pre-sixteenth-century Oromo presence within the medieval Christian kingdom is limited. Besides my own short chapter of 1994, only three recent sources discuss the pre-sixteenth century Oromo presence in the region of Shawa.[4] There appear to have

[1] This is a revised and expanded version of my chapter, 'The Pre-Sixteenth Century Oromo Presence within the Medieval Christian Kingdom of Ethiopia', in *River of Blessings: Essays in Honor of Paul Baxter*, ed. David Brokensha (Syracuse, NY: Syracuse University Press, 1994), 43–65. I am indebted to David Brokensha for giving me permission to include it in this work.
[2] Tadesse Tamrat, *Church and State in Ethiopia, 1270–1527* (Oxford: Clarendon Press, 1972), 301.
[3] Merid Wolde Aregay, 'Population Movement as a Possible Factor in the Christian-Muslim Conflict of Medieval Ethiopia', in *Symposium Leo Frobenius: Perspectives des études Africaines*, Rapport final d'un symposium international organisé par les Commissions Allemande et Camerounaise pour l'UNESCO du 3 au 7 décembre 1973 à Yaoundé (Cameroun) (Cologne: German UNESCO Commission/ Berlag Dokumentation, 1974), 266–81.
[4] Negaso Gidada, *History of the Sayyoo Oromoo of Southwestern Wallaga, Ethiopia from about 1730 to 1886* (Addis Ababa: Mega Printing Enterprise, 2001), chapter 2. See also Alemayehu Haile et al., eds, *History of the Oromo to the Sixteenth Century*, 2nd edn (Finfinne: Oromia Culture and Tourism Bureau, 2006), 42–76; Mekuria Bulcha, *Contours of the Emergent and Ancient Oromo Nation: Dilemmas in the Ethiopian Politics of State and Nation-Building* (Cape

been two principal reasons why other scholars did not suspect, much less discuss, this issue. The first was the credence attached to Abba Bahrey's *Zenahu le Galla*, which dates their arrival on the border of the southern province of Bali in the early 1520s. The second was the scholarly assumption that placed the original homeland of the Oromo either in northern Somalia[5] or northern Kenya or southern Ethiopia but far from the frontiers of the medieval Christian kingdom, thus excluding the possibility of an Oromo presence in and around the region of Shawa before the sixteenth century.

As indicated earlier, the presence of some Oromo groups within the medieval Christian kingdom is confirmed by, among others, the Chronicle of Emperor Amda-Siyon (1313–44), which makes clear reference to a people called Galla and their country as '*Hagara Galla*' (the country of the Galla).[6] Despite such unmistakable reference to the Galla and their country, Jules Perruchon, who translated Amda-Siyon's Chronicle from Geez into French, and G.W.B. Huntingford, who translated it into English,[7] replaced Galla by Gala and the country of the Galla by the country of Gala. They did this most probably because they assumed Gala to be a different people from Galla, who were not thought to be within the Christian kingdom before the middle of the sixteenth century. The information contained in the Chronicle of Amda-Siyon is important to early Oromo history in four major ways. First, it confirms the presence of sedentary Oromo groups around the Awash River during the 1330s. Second, it implies that Amda-Siyon may have conducted war against some rebellious Oromo groups. Third, as the result of Christian and Muslim conflicts and drought and famine that appear to have engulfed the region during the reign of Amda-Siyon, a number of Oromo groups were probably displaced and forced to move further to the south beyond the control of the Christian kingdom. Finally, it appears that the establishment and expansion of the Amhara Kingdom of Shawa since 1270 may have precipitated the process of the displacement of some of the Oromo-speaking groups in the region and probably halted the northward flow of Oromo penetration from the south, especially during the reign of Amda-Siyon that, during its southward expansion, organized regular garrisons along the frontiers. Nevertheless, some Oromo groups who were already living in the region of Shawa before the formation of the Shawan Amhara Empire during the first half of the fourteenth century remained an integral part of that empire during and after the fourteenth century. In this chapter I attempt to substantiate the presence of some Oromo groups within the medieval Christian kingdom in and south of the region of Shawa in the fourteenth century.

(contd) Town, South Africa: The Centre for Advanced Studies of African Society, 2011), chapter 4.

[5] Bulcha, *Contours of the Emergent and Ancient Oromo Nation*, chapter 4.

[6] Jules M. Perruchon, 'Histoire des guerres d'Amda Seyon, roi d'Ethiopie', *Journal Asiatique* 8 (1889), 294, 305.

[7] G.W.B. Huntingford, trans., *The Glorious Victories of Amda Seyon, King of Ethiopia* (Oxford: Clarendon Press, 1965), 62.

This could have a far-reaching impact on the long-ignored relationship between the Christian Amhara society and the Oromo in and south of the region of Shawa. While the evidence is not new, this fresh interpretation of written Amhara oral tradition and religious literature allows us to establish the pre-sixteenth-century Oromo presence within the medieval Christian kingdom of Abyssinia. These sedentary Oromo groups lived under the Christian administration and they were not part of the sixteenth-century pastoral Oromo population movement. Later in the sixteenth century, Oromo immigrants found that a basic framework of Oromo culture in and south of the present region of Shawa had already been established. This presence was subsequently built upon and consolidated by the large population movement of pastoral Oromo during the sixteenth century.

THE TERM 'GALLA'

Since the language of the Oromo had yet to be put in written form, what was written about them was primarily written by Amhara and Tigrayan monks and court chroniclers. The Oromo had had contact with the Amhara since at least the thirteenth century, contact which alternated between peaceful co-existence and warfare. The warfare, to no small extent, influenced what the Christian monks and court chroniclers wrote about the Galla, the name they gave the Oromo. 'Galla' was an identity-related name imposed by others on the Oromo, it was not one the Oromo called themselves. Though reference to the term seems to have been limited, Galla has been used in Christian literature since the thirteenth century, if not earlier (see below). In one Geez hagiography, believed to have been written in the thirteenth century,[8] there is a reference to a people called Galle.[9] Who were the Galle? It is tempting to suggest that Galle was the early form in which the term Galla came into Ethiopian Orthodox Church literature. The term Galla probably came into use during the Zagwe period (*c.* 1000–1270). By the time Yikunno Amlak (1270–85) established the Shawn Amhara dynasty, there is a clear reference to a Galla group as 'trouble makers'[10] who caused trepidation for the disciples of Bishop Zena-Markos. This is written in the hagiography of the bishop himself, whose death was accompanied by a conflict between his disciples and that of the Oromo. The cause of the conflict is not mentioned in the hagiography of Bishop Zena-Markos, but Mekuria Bulcha believes it 'was between the followers of the traditional Oromo religion ... and Christian settlers who wished to impose

---

[8] E.A.W. Budge, trans. and ed., *The Book of Mysteries of Heaven and Earth* (London: 1935), xix.

[9] J. Halevy, 'Notes pour l' histoire d' Ethiopie le pays de Zague', *Revue Sémitique* 5 (1897), 275–84.

[10] Getatchew Haile, *The Works of Abba Bahriy and other Documents Concerning the Oromo* (Avon, MN: self-published, 2002), 27, citing his work, Haile (Catalogue of Ethiopian Manuscripts, Vol. IX, 270).

their religion on the indigenous population'.[11] This may or may not have been the case. What is not in doubt is that the information about the Oromo as troublemakers establishes their presence in the central part of the Christian kingdom,[12] during the reign of Yikunno Amlak, as indicated below.

What is important to consider here is the origin of the term Galla itself. It now appears that the name came from an Oromo descent group or *gosa* name of Galan (also spelled as Gallan). As the following discussion will show, the Galan were one of the most important and the largest Oromo descent group, whose members had lived in the region of Shawa during and probably before the thirteenth century. It appears that Christian settlers and Galan Oromo had 'a long history of contact and conflict' in the region of Shawa. According to Mekuria Bulcha, it was the Amhara people who first changed Galan to Galla because of phonemic discrepancies between the Amharic and Oromo languages. Bulcha argues:

> It is plausible to state that the Amharic term 'Galla' came from ... a group of people called Galaan ... It seems that the phonemic discrepancy occurred because the letter 'n' in Galaan [Galan] is silent and it could be inaudible to ears unused to the Oromo language ... Although Galla was a result of a phonemic distortion it was generalized to all those who spoke the Oromo language, who were non-Christians and were considered enemies of the Amhara.[13]

Bulcha's conclusion is supported by information from an earlier reliable source. Job Ludolphus, the seventeenth-century German scholar was told by his learned Amhara informant, Abba Gregory, that they call themselves Oromo, but 'we give them the name of Gallans'.[14] According to Edward Ullendorff, Abba Gregory was 'from Makana Sellasie in the Amhara province'. He was a learned priest and 'an informant of truth and reliability'.[15] His information about the Gallans confirms his truthfulness and reliability. Although the term Galla originated most likely during the Zagwe period, it was popularized after the establishment of the Shawan Amhara kingdom in 1270, whose expansion to the south brought more Amhara and Oromo groups into contact with one another.

---

[11] Bulcha, *Contours of the Emergent and Ancient Oromo Nation*, 213.

[12] Haile, *The Works of Abba Bahriy*, 27. Haile goes further and suggests a factor that may have made invisible some Oromo individuals' service within the Christian administration. This was because once an Oromo was converted to Christianity he was given a Christian name and classified as Amhara.

[13] Bulcha, *Contours of the Emergent and Ancient Oromo Nation*, 170.

[14] Job Ludolphus, trans. J.P. Gent, *A New History of Ethiopia: Being a Full and Accurate Description of the Kingdom of Abessinia, vulgarly, though erroneously called The Empire of Prester John* (London: Samuel Smith, 1682), 81. See also Thomas Zitelmann, 'Reexamining the Galla/Oromo Relationship: The Stranger as a Structural Topic', in P.T.W. Baxter, Jan Hultin, and Alessandro Triulzi, eds, *Being and Becoming Oromo: Historical and Anthropological Enquiries*, (Uppsala: Nordiska Afrika Institutet, 1996), 106.

[15] Edward Ullendorff, *The Ethiopians: An Introduction to the Country and People* (London: Oxford University Press, 1960), 10–11.

During the fourteenth and subsequent centuries, Galla was adopted by the local Muslim chroniclers and European missionaries, travellers, and diplomats.

THE APPEARANCE OF 'GALLA' IN EUROPEAN SOURCES

The designation Galla appears for the first time in European sources on a map made for Prince Henry the Navigator of Portugal by Fra Mauro. This map embodied the best and most up-to-date information about Africa that was available in Venice in the years preceding its completion on 26 August 1460.[16] Fra Mauro's map contains an indispensable piece of information that throws much light on early Oromo history (see Map 2, page 9). It not only locates the Oromo people just south of the Christian kingdom, but it also gives concrete historical validity to the numerous Amhara written and oral traditions.

> Mauro completed his map ... using information he obtained from Ethiopian monks who had come to attend the Council of Florence. The monks came to Italy in 1441 and, as they had been living in Jerusalem for some time, the information they gave to Mauro could be on developments which had occurred much earlier. Mauro's map shows a river to which he gave the two names of Xebe and Galla. The part Galla, which is the lower course of Mauro's river, is placed directly below the river Auasi and the province of Vaidi, namely south of Awash and Waj. Kammerer has identified the Galla river with the Omo, while Crawford thinks it is one of the tributaries of the Gibe. From its direction of flow and its position in relation to the Awash and Waj, the most likely identification is with the Ganale Doria, since the Wabi is named elsewhere on the map.[17]

All three identifications, especially the last, extend the river a very long distance to the south, which is unlikely to have been true. First and foremost, Fra Mauro's river is the last major river south of the Christian kingdom that flows into the Indian Ocean. Recently Mekuria Bulcha has identified Fra Mauro's Galla River with the Gibe River. Bulcha argues that Fra Mauro's location of the source of the Gibe River was 'quite right, but he laid its course in the wrong direction'.[18] On the contrary, Fra Mauro laid the course of the Galla River in the right direction. Bulcha's identification of the Gibe with the Galla River is based on the faulty assumption that the two rivers are one and the same. However, they are two separate rivers that flow in different directions. Fra Mauro's map locates the Galla River a short distance south of the Awash River and the historical province of Waj. The source of the Galla River and its course correspond almost exactly with the source and course of the

[16] O.G.S. Crawford, ed., *Ethiopian Itineraries circa 1400–1524 including those collected by Alessandro Zorzi at Venice in the years 1519–1524* (Cambridge: Hakluyt Society/ Cambridge University Press, 1958), 16.
[17] Merid Wolde Aregay,'Southern Ethiopia and the Christian Kingdom, 1508–1708, with Special Reference to the Galla Migrations and their Consequences' (PhD dissertation, University of London, 1971), 148–9.
[18] Bulcha, *Contours of the Emergent and Ancient Oromo Nation*, 207.

Wabi Shebelle River. Wabi is marked on Mauro's map as a small river in the eastern part of the Horn that empties into the Red Sea. Thus it is not the real Wabi Shebelle. To all intents and purposes, the Galla River could be identified only with the headwaters of the Wabi Shebelle. The reason for such identification will become clear in the following discussion, which focuses on that area. Second, though Kammerer identified the upper course of the Galla River with the Omo, which is missing from Mauro's map, he placed the lower course of that river on the actual course of the Wabi Shebelle River.[19] By so doing, Kammerer unintentionally identified the Galla River with the Wabi Shebelle. As we shall see in the next chapter, Bahrey states that the Oromo crossed the river of their country, called Galana, when they attacked historical Bali in the early 1520s. Schleicher identified Bahrey's Galana with Wabi Shebelle,[20] which formed the boundary between the medieval Christian kingdom and Oromo cattle-keepers who lived south of the river. The Oromo who lived within the Christian kingdom were sedentary farmers. In his study of Fra Mauro's map, P. Zurla concludes that 'the people described as fierce enemies of the Christians and located south of the Galla River were the Galla themselves'.[21] According to Zurla, Fra Mauro separated the Christian kingdom from the land of the Oromo by mountains, fortresses and the Galla River itself.[22] By placing the Oromo territory in a mountainous region, Mauro provided us with striking confirmation about one aspect of Oromo history: that they lived in the highlands of southern Ethiopia. The implication of his information will become clearer further on in this discussion. As we know from other sources, Mauro also confirmed that the Oromo lived in highlands of what is today southern Ethiopia. This is supported by Haberland's research, which establishes that the Oromo lived in the region of Bale, practising a mixed economy based on agriculture and cattle keeping.[23] Furthermore, Mauro's information provides evidence for long contact between some Oromo groups and the Christian kingdom.

GALLA IN AMHARA TRADITION

The Galla River of Mauro's map is also at the very centre of an important Amhara tradition. This river is supposed to be the natural boundary between the Christian kingdom and what Almeida called 'the orig-

---

[19] A Kammerer, *La mer rouge l'Abyssinie et l'Arabie depuis l'antiquité* (Cairo: Société Royale Géographie d'Egypte, 1929–35), 377.

[20] A.W. Schleicher, *Geschichte der Galla Berichte eines Abessinischen menschen über die invasion der Galla in Sechzehnten Jahrhundert* (Berlin, 1893), 17; quoted in Bariu Tafla, trans. and ed., *Asma Giyorgis and his Work: History of the Gāllā and The Kingdom of Sawa* (Stuttgart: Franz Steiner, 1987), 137, note 166.

[21] D.P. Zurla, *Il Mappomondo di Fra Mauro Camaldolese* (Venice, 1806), 136.

[22] Ibid.

[23] See for instance, E. Haberland, *Galla Süd-Aethiopiens* (Stuttgart: Kohlhammer, 1963), 772.

inal home and fatherland of the [Oromo]'.[24] The two Christian monks who participated in the Council of Florence in 1441 and supplied the vital information to Mauro may have known the name Galla either through the Orthodox Church literature of earlier times or through first-hand knowledge of it.[25] Whatever the source, the information Mauro received from them concerned developments that had occurred much earlier. The appearance of this name on the supposed boundary is important in two ways. First, it provides solid historical evidence that some Oromo people may have lived in this area before the supposed boundary became part of the Christian kingdom through the conquests of Christian emperors. Besides, a natural boundary presupposes some kind of contact, be it peaceful exchange or conflict or both, between the peoples of the two adjacent countries. Second and most important, the appearance of the name 'Galla' on Mauro's map provides definitive historical validity to the numerous Amhara written and oral traditions.

Scholarly work so far undertaken by both Ethiopians and Western scholars has neglected to take this into account. A critical re-reading of the early Christian literature can on occasion prove revealing, both in what is included and perhaps misinterpreted and in what is unconsciously ignored. A great task lies before future scholars in the vigorous re-examination of the rich Christian literature. My emphasis stems from the belief that, so far, these sources have not been carefully and widely consulted for the pre-sixteenth-century history of the Oromo. Beke, while trying to find the etymology of the term Galla, came across a tradition that says the name is taken from the river in Gurage province in the south-west of Shawa, on the banks of which a great battle is said to have been fought between the Oromo and the Abyssinians.[26] This river most likely refers to the Wabi Shebelle River as it is a major river in the region. The connection between the term Galla and a river is very important, partly because almost all Oromo, including those in Kenya, claim that their ancestors crossed a river Galana, and partly because one Amhara tradition categorically asserts that the Oromo acquired the name Galla from the name of the river of their country, Galana.[27] On 18 April 1840, the missionary J.L. Krapf reported a detailed version of the same tradition:

> A Debtera afterward came and spoke about the origin of the Gallas. He said that the mother of the Gallas had been a *woizoro* lady of the Abyssinian kings when they resided on the mountain Entoto, in the neighborhood of Gurague – that the lady was given in marriage to a slave from the south of Gurague, by whom she had seven sons, who were educated in their father's language and

[24] Manuel de Almeida, 'The History of High Ethiopia or Abyssinia Book IV', trans. and ed. C. F. Beckingham and G.W. B. Huntingford, *Some Records of Ethiopia, 1593–1646* (London: Hakluyt Society, 1954), 133–4.
[25] Crawford, *Ethiopian Itineraries*, 10; See also Girma Beshah and Merid Wolde Aregay, *The Question of the Union of the Churches in Luso-Ethiopian Relations, 1500–1632* (Lisbon: Junta de Investigações do Ultramar & Centro de Estudos Históricos Ultramarinos, 1964), 16.
[26] Charles Beke, 'On the Origin of the Gallas', *Report to the 1847 meeting of the British Association for the Advancement of Science* (London, 1848), 3.
[27] Tafla, *Asma Giyorgis and his Work*, 155.

custom, as well as in his business, which was that of a herdsman – that the sons became robbers, having fathered many people with them ... That when they thought they were strong enough, they began to fight with the Abyssinians, and frequently vanquished them, particularly on one occasion near the river Galla, in Gurague; and hence they have been called Gallas to the present day ... All this is written in a small treatise, of which I have procured a copy. This account of the origin of the Gallas I think is very probable.[28]

The above tradition deals with a historical legend which combines both fact and fiction or myth. The factual part deals with a long history of contact and conflict between the Amhara and Oromo communities in the region of Shawa, which will be discussed shortly. The fictional part deals with the Amhara myth of Oromo origin which, most probably was invented for the purpose of portraying the Oromo people 'as an inferior and immoral *alter ego* of the Amhara, which embodies the Ethiopian national model'.[29]

EVIDENCE FOR OROMO PRESENCE FROM THE CHRONICLE OF AMDA-SIYON (1313–1344)

The question that cannot be answered with certainty concerns the date of the supposed battle between the Christians and the Oromo. Was it during the reign of Amda-Siyon? Or was it later, or even earlier? Christian traditions are unanimous in asserting that it was during the reign of this warrior-king. Historical evidence shows that between 1329 and 1332 Amda-Siyon defeated seven Muslim states, one after the other (see Map 3, page 16). When the Muslim leader Sabradin challenged the authority of Amda-Siyon in 1329, the king called together his military commanders, including 'Ya'akel Gada commander of the cavalry of the right'.[30] This officer was probably one of the most-important commanders: his father's name Gada is an unmistakable Oromo name, a proper name as well as the name of the famous Oromo political institution. In one of the engagements with Muslim forces, Amda-Siyon's soldiers killed their enemies and brought to the king the spoils of war, some of which were *salaba* (genital organs of dead enemies). The custom of *salaba* was practised by the Afar, Amhara, Oromo, Somali, Tigrayan and other warriors in Ethiopia. While Asma Giyorgis claimed that the Oromo learned 'the evil practice' of *salaba* from the Amhara, Huntingford speculated that the custom was introduced by the Oromo during the sixteenth

---

[28] C.W. Isenberg and J.L. Krapf, *The Journals of C.W. Isenberg and J.L. Krapf detailing their proceedings in the kingdom of Shoa and journeys in other parts of Abyssinia in the years 1839, 1840, 1841, and 1842* (London: Frank Cass, 1968 [1843]), 25.

[29] Eloi Ficquet, 'Fabrication of Oromo Origins', trans. Ayalew Kanno ('La Fabrique des Origins Oromo', *Annales d'Ethiopie* 18 (2002), 55–71), *Journal of Oromo Studies* 14, 2 (July 2007), 109.

[30] Huntingford, *The Glorious Victories of Amda Seyon*, 60.

century.[31] Huntingford never suspected an Oromo presence in the region during the time of Amda-Siyon but, since the king's Chronicle mentions it, the custom must have existed during and probably even before Amda-Siyon established a powerful Christian empire. According to Getatchew Haile, it is recorded in King Amda-Siyon's Chronicle that

> during his reign he had been to the country of the Galla. On April 28 [1332] the king first passed through and reached the Galla country. On June 7, he left the Galla country, along with his army. These statements refer to the king's movement within the country. They do not imply that the king ever left Ethiopia.[32]

By Ethiopia, Haile means the medieval Christian kingdom. From the time he arrived until the time he left *Hagara Galla* (the country of the Galla), Amda-Siyon appears to have stayed in this district located near Dawaro. This district must have been heavily cultivated and densely populated to have supported Amda-Siyon's large army for five weeks. His victories were accompanied by appalling carnage and destruction that probably sent different groups fleeing from the centre of the storm, abandoning their property and territory to seek refuge in difficult areas where geographic features or distance held out hope of asylum.[33] The chronicler himself describes the first massacre in the land of the Hadiya people in these words. '[Amda-siyon committed] a great massacre of the people of this country [Hadiya], killing or massacring some ... and carrying away others into captivity with their king, big and small, men and women, old and young, whom he transported into his kingdom.'[34] The chronicler adds that mosques were demolished, towns burned, thousands were killed, and even cattle and food crops were destroyed, exposing the survivors to the ravages of hunger. 'Men's blood flowed like water, and bodies lay like grass on the earth.'[35]

According to Professor Taddesse Tamrat, the purpose for such destruction was to establish the absolute power of the king over the lives and property of the conquered people.

> He [Amda-Siyon] appropriated all the people and their land, and reserved every right to dispose of them according to his wishes. He executed all resistance fighters who fell into his hands, and reduced to slavery other captives of war. The conquering army then raided the country, burning and looting and taking away the cattle, horses, and other possessions of the local people. These acts of cruel repression were deliberately committed not only to replenish the

[31] Tafla, *Asma Giyorgis and his Work*, 323; Huntingford, *The Glorious Victories of Amda Seyon*, 61.

[32] Haile, *The Works of Abba Bahriy*, 26.

[33] I have drawn on J.D. Omer-Cooper, *The Zulu Aftermath: A Nineteenth Century Revolution in Bantu Africa* (London: Longman, 1966), 1–7. See also Takla Sadiq Makurya, *Ya Gragn Ahmed Warara* (Addis Ababa: Artistic Press, 1975/76), iv, 708.

[34] Quoted in Taddesse Tamrat, *Church and State in Ethiopia 1270–1527* (Oxford: Clarendon, 1972, 106.

[35] Huntingford, *The Glorious Victories of Amda Seyon*, 92, 104.

ever-failing provisions of the huge Christian army, but also to force the people to surrender, and to give them a terrible example of the destructive force of the Christian army in case of further revolts.[36]

Those who were taken into captivity were enslaved and given as gifts to important Christian families, 'including those of local saints ... [and] prominent monks'. Taddesse Tamrat adds: 'The terms used by Amda-Siyon's chroniclers in describing his successes clearly indicate that slave raiding was an important by-product of many of his campaigns.'[37]Amda-Siyon's warfare and slaving raids appear to have led to massive displacement of people, which seems to have altered the pattern of ethnic distribution during the first half of the fourteenth century.[38] While some groups fled Amda-Siyon's sword, others may have fled from the famine that afflicted the region. Probably it was the drought and the famine that triggered intense conflict between the Christians and Muslim communities at the time. Be that as it may, Christian traditions are unanimous about the severity of that famine.

> A terrible famine occurred in the time of *Ase* Amda-Sayon [sic]. At that time, there was a noble lady in great distress in the country called Fatagar. A certain *Azmach* Endreyas was governor of Katata and Dawaro. He had a slave called Lalo, who was his *ya-llam-ras*.[39] Because she was starving, the lady entered the service of Lalo so that he would provide her with milk. He took her for his wife, and she gave birth to seven children ... As these children grew up, they became thieves, outlaws and robbers ... *Azmach* Endreyas led an expedition against them and when they fought, Lalo was defeated and fled with his cattle to a forest called Galla.[40]

The above tradition or legend appears to be an allegorical representation of contact between the Amhara and the Oromo in the region of Shawa. Interestingly the various versions of this tradition mentions Katata and Fatagar, where according to the legend the seven children of Lalo were born, perhaps reflecting the long Oromo presence on Shawan plateau.

Mekuria Bulcha interprets this legend in terms of the 'famine, migration, conquest, displacement' of the Oromo. In his own words:

> The legend indicates that famine had caused Amhara migration to the Shawan Plateau, and the contact with the Oromo ... Conflict arises when the offspring [marriage between noble lady and Lalo] maintain their identity; they follow in the footsteps of their father and learn [Oromo] language. That is followed by an Abyssinian conquest represented by the figure of Azmach Endreyas. The result is Oromo displacement.[41]

Bulcha's interpretation of famine causing Amhara migration to the Shawan plateau is, however, historically inaccurate. This is because

[36] Tamrat, *Church and State in Ethiopia*, 99.
[37] Ibid., 87.
[38] Ibid., 150, see note 1.
[39] A person who was responsible for the cattle of the governor.
[40] Tafla, *Asma Giyorgis and his Work*, 85–91.
[41] Bulcha, *Contours of the Emergent and Ancient Oromo Nation*, 189.

the expansion of Amharic-speaking Christians from the region of Amhara to the Shawan plateau was a very long process which probably started during the eleventh century. It is said that there 'are traditions of a slow movement of isolated Christian families from Amhara to the region of Shawan plateau'.[42] However, Christian traditions do not show directly or indirectly that movement of isolated Christian families was triggered by famine. Most likely Bulcha's interpretation is telescoping the situation of the first half of the fourteenth century back to the eleventh century. Nevertheless, Bulcha's interpretation of the fourteenth-century conflict between the Amhara and Oromo communities and displacement of the latter is historically valid, as will be shown shortly.

The above-quoted legend or tradition is similar to the one already cited, and both seem to have come from the same source. In 1840, the missionary Krapf procured the earlier version, whereas the latter version, according to Asma Giyorgis, was brought to the Emperor Menelik (1889–1913) by a certain monk named Abba Balaynah.[43] It appears that the original manuscript was written during the reign of Emperor Zara Yaeqob (1434–68) and kept on the island of Lake Zeway, where other Christian manuscripts escaped Muslim destruction during the first half of the sixteenth century. At least some part of the story was written either before or during the jihadic wars, or perhaps shortly after, when Imam Ahmad's destruction was still vivid in memory and all possible explanations for his success were enumerated. The main thrust of the second version is that Imam Ahmad's victory over the Christians was the result of the wrath of God because Emperor Libna Dengel (1508–40) was lax in his religion and had adopted certain pagan Oromo traditions. How did Libna Dengel adopt Oromo traditions, if they were not already in the region, asked the famous historian Takla Sadiq Makurya?[44] He answered his own question by concluding that the Oromo were within the medieval Christian kingdom much longer than hitherto had been suspected.

The above-quoted tradition refers to a certain historical reality. Several interesting points are raised, first about the Galla Forest itself. From the topographical description of the tradition, which especially mentions Dawaro, it appears that the Galla Forest was in the direction of the Galla River of Mauro's map. Both names refer to the same region. As we have seen above, Amda-Siyon was in the country of the Galla for about five weeks in 1332. His Chronicle mentions Hagara Galla as a district near Dawaro and not far from the Awash River.[45] It appears that Hagara Galla, Galla River and the Galla Forest were all located in the same vicinity.

[42] Tamrat, *Church and State in Ethiopia*, 64–65.
[43] Tafla, *Asma Giyorgis and his Work*, 85.
[44] Takla Sadiq Makurya, *Ya Ityopiyya Tao Rik Ka Aste Aste Lebna Dengel Eska Aste Tewodros* (Addis Ababa: Berhanena Selam Printing Press, 1945, i.e. 1952/53), 75. Quoted in Gidada, *History of the Sayyoo Oromoo*, 57, note 145.
[45] Perruchon, 'Histoire des guerres d' Amda Seyon, roi d'Etiopie', 294, 305.

CONTACT BETWEEN THE LALO OROMO DESCENT GROUP AND THE AMHARA

In the above tradition the marriage between the slave Lalo and the Amhara woman seems to suggest a contact, before or during the first half of the fourteenth century, between some Oromo groups and the Amhara. Which Oromo group was this? In this tradition, Lalo is presented as the father of seven children. In Oromo oral tradition and genealogy, Lalo is also the eponym of the founder of the Lalo sub-moiety, a large and powerful group that was part of the Borana Confederacy. The Lalo group is still an important Oromo sub-moiety in Wallaga,[46] Jimma, and Illubabor. Could it be that this Amhara tradition refers to an historical contact between the Lalo group and the Amhara in the region of Katata or Fatagar or Dawaro? An account in 'Taarika Zagalla' (unpublished 'History of the Galla'), extensively quoted by Negaso Gidada, clearly states that Amda-Siyon attacked, displaced, and resettled the Lalo group 'in the regions of Katata, Fatagar and Dawaro'.[47] Most likely it was in Katata that a river mentioned by Conti-Rossini and known as Jimma River, which separates Shawa from northern provinces, was located.[48] Jimma is an Oromo personal name, the name of a clan as well as the name of a place. That is why Arab Faqih, in his *Conquest of Abyssinia*, mentioned Jimma as a personal name as well as the name of a descent group.[49] Third, according to another tradition reported by Conti-Rossini, the Wallo Oromo descended from the seven sons of a certain Lalo from Dawaro, the founder of the nation, at 'their place of origin in Dawaro.'[50] Knutsson recorded an oral tradition from the Macha Oromo that claims that Lalo was the ancestor of several groups that lived during the reign of Emperor Azara Yaeqob from 1434 to 1468.[51] Lalo is not only the name of a large putative descent group that is widespread, but it is also a place name. This is because Oromo descent groups usually give their names to the territory or land in which they live. There are a number of places known by the name of Lalo, including but not limited to, Lalo Qile, Lalo Qumba, and Lalo Jimma.[52] What all the

[46] Gidada, *History of the Sayyoo Oromoo*, 23, 53, note 51.

[47] Ibid., 68

[48] C. Conti-Rossini, *Storia d'Etiopia* (Milan: 1928), 34–35. It was only in the twentieth century that Jimma River was changed into Amharic Jamma/Zhama River. 'Jamma is still Oromo'. I am indebted to Daniel Ayana for providing me with this information. Personal correspondence dated September 25, 2013.

[49] P.L. Stenhouse, trans., R. Pankhurst, ann. *Futuh Al-Habasha: The Conquest of Abyssinia by Sihab ad-Din Ahmad bin Abd al-Qader bin Salem bin Utman, also known as Arab Faqih*, (Hollywood, CA: Tsehai, 2003), 56, 170. See also Arab Faqih, *Futuh Al-Habasha (Histoire de la conquête de l'Abyssinie XVI siècle)* trans. and ed. M.R. Basset (Paris, 1897), 135–7.

[50] C. Conti-Rossini, 'Domenico Brielli-Ricordi Storici de Wallo', in *Studi Etiopica Raccolta du C. Conti-Rossini* (Rome: Instituto per L'Oriente, 1945), 87.

[51] K.E. Knutsson, *Authority and Change: A Study of the Kallu Institution among the Macha Galla of Ethiopia* (Gothenburg: Ethnografiska Museet, 1967), 37.

[52] Bulcha, *Contours of the Emergent and Ancient Oromo Nation*, 192.

above-mentioned traditions have in common is that the Lalo putative descent groups had long contact with the Amhara in the core areas of the Shawan plateau, including Katata. Bairu Tafla thinks that Katata may have been 'the old name of Lalo Meder in Manz'.[53] Tafla adds,

> Manz ... constituted a distinct province within the Christian kingdom of Ethiopia as early as, and probably earlier than, the fourteenth century. It lay to the west of the Adal lowlands and to the north of Tagulat. It consisted mainly of Mamma Meder, Gera Meder and Lalo Meder, all of which were autonomous units within Manz.[54]

Though limited, there is evidence that shows some Oromo groups' presence in the region of Manz during the thirteenth and first half of the fourteenth centuries. First, Mekuria Bulcha claims that 'Mamma, Laalo and Geera, to which the Amharic word "meder" (land) is suffixed, are Oromo *gosa* and place names. That indicates that Oromo descent groups with the same names were the inhabitants of Manz when the Amhara communities arrived in the area in the twelfth and thirteenth centuries or even earlier.'[55] Second, Negaso Gidada also connects *Lalo Meder* ('lalo land') in Manz (Northern Shawa) with the Oromo putative descent group of Lalo.[56] Gidada further claims that 'the Oromo may have constituted the majority of the population'[57] in some districts of Shawa in the fifteenth century. Such a claim may have been an exaggeration. However, there is no doubt that the Oromo constituted a significant part of the population of the Christian kingdom, to such an extent that the Chronicle of Amda-Siyon designates a particular district as the country of the Galla. Third, one recent study supports some Oromo groups' presence in the region of Manz (see below). Additional evidence for the presence of some Oromo groups in northern Shawa during the reign of Yikunno Amlak (1270–1285) is presented below.

According to one Amhara tradition of later origin, Lalo was one of the three founders of Manz; the other two were Mama and Gera. 'Although their deeds were recorded in the form of legends, Mama, Lalo and Gera were historical personages. They appeared to have lived in the latter part of the seventeenth century', writes Donald Levine,[58] but he appears to have been unaware that the historical personages he presents have Oromo names. However, this Lalo of Manz tradition who lived in the latter part of the seventeenth century is quite distinct from the Lalo

---

[53] Tafla, *Asma Giyorgis and his Work*, 933.
[54] Ibid., 944. In northern Shawa even the term Oromo was also used as a *toponym*. Tafla has noted that there is a river and an area known as Oromo or 'Oramo or Woromo: an area and a river bordering Marhabete and Salale. The river rises from the slopes of Dabra Libanos and flows into the Abbay [River]', 955.
[55] Bulcha, *Contours of the Emergent and Ancient Oromo Nation*, 191.
[56] Gidada, *History of the Sayyoo Oromoo*, 42.
[57] Ibid.
[58] D.N. Levine, *Wax and Gold: Tradition and Innovation in Ethiopian Culture* 2nd edn (Chicago: University of Chicago Press, 1972), 31.

about whom Azaj Tino (Chief Steward Takla Sellase) wrote in the first quarter of the seventeenth century.

Azaj Tino, a contemporary of Abba Bahrey, presented early Oromo history in a manner that was radically different from that of the latter. Tino, a highly learned man, seems to have belonged to the core of the Abyssinian elite who did not seriously oppose the imposition of the Catholicism on the Abyssinian Orthodox Christians (see Chapter 8). He was among the dignitaries at the court of Emperor Susenyos (1607–32) who gladly embraced Catholicism.[59] The Oromo word *tino*, which means 'little' or 'short,' was his nickname, attributed to him on account of his small stature. Azaj Tino appears to have had intimate knowledge of Oromo society, language and culture. Sometimes his unconscious admiration for some aspect of the Oromo culture, which Bahrey abhorred, makes one suspect that he probably belonged to the second generation of converted Oromo. Most likely his father may have been among the first generation of Oromo who were settled by Sarsa Dengel (1563–97), either in Gojjam or Begameder (see Chapter 5). What is certain is that Azaj Tino was brought up in a Christian household and was provided with the best Christian education. His enthusiastic espousal of Catholicism, which other Orthodox clergy opposed violently, also suggests that he probably did not have deep roots within Orthodox Christianity. According to Getatchew Haile, no one was more knowledgeable about the Oromo than Azaj Tino.[60] What is not in doubt is that Azaj Tino was well-educated in Geez, the language of high culture in the kingdom. He was among the leading scholars in Abyssinia during the first half of the seventeenth century. He wrote the greater part of the Chronicle of Susenyos, which is the richest, the best and the longest chronicle in the entire history of the Christian kingdom. As the second generation of a probably converted Oromo to Orthodox Christianity, he was supposed to have been integrated into the Abyssinian society, adopting that society's prejudices against the Oromo.

Azaj Tino knew Oromo society, language and culture, and had a unique perspective on early Oromo history. It appears that Tino gathered much oral tradition from numerous Oromo who served in the army of Emperor Susenoys (1607–32). As a result, his presentation of early Oromo history was based on the Oromo view of their own history. Unlike Abba Bahrey, who claimed that the Oromo arrived on the border of historical Bali only during the early 1520s, Tino indirectly refutes this claim and establishes conclusively that the Oromo lived for centuries before the 1520s in Dawaro in what today is the northern part of the region of Arsi/Bale and western Hararghe (Charachar). Azaj Tino's central thesis, which establishes the presence of the Oromo in Dawaro long before the 1520s, is supported by irrefutable

---

[59] Boavida et al., *Pedro Páez's History of Ethiopia*, vol. 2: 259. See also A. Bartnicki and J. Mantel-Niećko, 'The Role and Significance of the Religious Conflicts and People's Movements in the Political Life of Ethiopia in the Seventeenth and Eighteenth Centuries', *Rassegna di studi Etiopici* 24 (1970), 29.

[60] Haile, *The Works of Abba Bahriy*, 145.

historical evidence.[61] In this respect, Tino's contribution to our understanding of early Oromo history is quite remarkable.

Gabra Sellassie, another traditional historian, confirms Azaj Tino's thesis about the pre-sixteenth-century Oromo presence within the Christian kingdom. During the fourteenth century, the Oromo who lived there were loyal subjects of the Christian Emperors.[62] Takla Sadiq Makurya also supports the same conclusions.[63] What this amounts to is that four leading Ethiopian traditional historians, Asma Giyorgis, Gabra Sellassie, Alaqa Tayya and Takla Sadiq Makurya, all follow in the footstep of Azaj Tino and unanimously confirm the Oromo presence within the Christian kingdom during the fourteenth century. Of these historians, it was Alaqa Tayya who made an interesting conclusion about the pre-fourteenth-century Oromo history. Although Tayya was described by Taddesse Tamrat as 'the father of Ethiopian history,' his version of Oromo history was not taken seriously.[64]

ALAQA TAYYA'S VIEW ABOUT EARLY OROMO PRESENCE WITHIN THE CHRISTIAN KINGDOM

Of the above-mentioned four historians, it is Takla Sadiq Makurya who essentially re-states that Tayya's version of Oromo history is accurate.[65] Like other historians, Alaka Tayya assumed that the Oromo came from beyond the boundaries of modern Ethiopia, which is historically inaccurate. However, his information is very interesting in one respect. He shows the presence of some Oromo groups within the Christian kingdom five hundred years before the beginning of the sixteenth century. According to Tayya, the truth 'about (the time of) the coming of the [Oromo] to Ethiopia is in the tenth year of the reign of Zagwe (during Merra Tekle Haymanot, whose regal name was Zagwe), in 930 year of Mercy.'[66] This may reflect the reality of some Oromo groups' presence in the region, which means that around the middle of the tenth century, some Oromo groups were already living within the Christian kingdom itself. Tayya states succinctly: 'The history of the [Oromo] that the Westerners have written is from their personal knowledge and research. But we [write], having seen the history

[61] Arab Faqih, *Futuh Al-Habasha*, 135–7, 254–5.

[62] Gabra Sellassie, *Tàrika Zàmen Zà-Dagmawi Menelik Negusà-Nàgast Zà-Ityopya* (Addis Ababa: Berhanena Selam Printing Press, 1965), 29–30.

[63] Takla Sadiq Makurya, *Ya Gragn Ahmed Warara* (The Invasion of Gran Ahmad) (Addis Ababa: Artistic Press, 1967 Ethiopian calendar), 801–804.

[64] Taddesse Tamrat, 'Introduction', in Alaqa Tayya, *Ye Ityopya Hizeb Tarik* (Addis Ababa: Berhanena Selam Printing Press, 1971/72), 9. It is surprising that Professor Taddesse Tamrat in a major study, *Church and State in Ethiopia*, covers the history of the Oromo up to 1527 with one footnote. See Tamrat, *Church and State in Ethiopia*, 150, note 1, 298, map.

[65] Makurya, *Ya Gragn Ahmed Warara*, 802–803.

[66] Haile, *The Works of Abba Bahriy*, 216.

which Azzaj Tinno [Tino] has written.'[67] Tayya appears to have used the ancient manuscript written by Azaj Tino, which was seemingly based on Oromo oral tradition and on earlier work. Unfortunately, Azaj Tino's manuscript that Tayya consulted has not been located. If it should ever be located, it may clarify many issues. For now it suffices to say that his claim cannot be easily dismissed as irrelevant because traditional Christian sources have not been carefully consulted for the presence of some Oromo groups in the Christian kingdom before the sixteenth century. As indicated in Chapter 1, there were Christian ideas, myths and traditions that in some measure influenced some aspects of Oromo traditions probably during the Zagwe period, if not earlier. Professor Getatchew Haile makes an interesting observation about the similarity of the Zagwe administration to that of the Oromo *gada* system.

> It is probably [*sic*] that the Zagwe possessed an administration similar to the Gada System. For instance, there are two separate lists indicating the reigns of various (Zagwe) kings. Seven of the eleven kings in the first list and eight of the nine kings in the second reigned for forty years each. It is highly likely that the forty-year reign signifies a period in office. It is very unlikely that the similarities are a matter of mere coincidence. In addition, attributing the similarities to a scribe's error cannot be a satisfactory explanation.[68]

The forty-year cycle was the core of the *gada* system.[69] The above-quoted observation of Getatchew Haile indicates not only possible contact between the Christian communities and some Oromo groups, but also the likelihood that the term Galla came into use during the Zagwe period. Here I merely add the items relating to the Zagwe period that have some relevance to Oromo history and show that at least two Oromo *gosa*/clan names were mentioned in the Christian sources of the period.

The first piece of relevant information is mentioned in the hagiography of Abba Libanos, who is said to have lived around A.D. 1015 'in the region of zegamel or Debre Asebbo' in northern Shawa. Abba Libanos abandoned Zegamel after the local 'ruler named Hora killed about twelve of his students.'[70] Hora is an Oromo proper name, which implies that some Oromo groups may have lived in the region during the first half of the eleventh century. The second piece of relevant information is contained in *The Book of the Mysteries of Heaven and Earth*, believed to have been composed by Bahaya-Mikae'el.[71] According to

---

[67] Ibid.

[68] Ibid, 101.

[69] Asmarom Legesse, *Gada: Three Approaches to the Study of African Society* (New York: Free Press, 1973), 124.

[70] Haile et al., *History of the Oromo to the Sixteenth Century*, 62. See also E.A.W. Budge, *The Life of Takla Hâymânôt in the version of Dabra Lîbanôs and the Miracles of Takla Hâymânôt in the version of Dabra Lîbanôs* (London, 1906), 187–9.

[71] Bahaya Mika'el, *Mashafa Mistirata – Samay Wamider*, partial trans., J. Perruchon, *Patrologia Orientalis* 1 (1904), 1–97. In 1935 it was edited and translated in full by E.A.W. Budge, *The Book of the Mysteries of Heaven and Earth* (London: 1935).

Budge, nothing is known about the author. 'In a general manner, his work suggests that it was the product of the fifteenth century, although parts of it may be older.' It is the older parts of this work that concern us here that may have come from the work of 'the famous monk of the same name, who flourished in the thirteenth century, who was believed to have received many remarkable revelations'.[72]

This book mentions the names of thirty people and countries: 'the children of Ham and their habitations'. Among the countries mentioned are Shawa, Angot, Enderta, Beguna and Bali. Among the names of people mentioned are the Zagwe (perhaps the then-ruling dynasty), the Habash (Amhara and Tigrayan), the Saho, the Danakale (the Muslim people of the lowlands who call themselves Afar) and Libi or Liba, which Perruchon, Basset and Budge have identified as Liban, a very powerful and widely scattered Oromo group whose *gosa* name is found over most of Oromo territory.[73] In the same book the term Galan is mentioned as the name of an individual. Galan is a typical Oromo personal name of an individual. As we shall see, Galan was also the name of an important Oromo *gosa* that lived in the region of Shawa.[74] In the same book there is a statement that strongly implies the migration of the people called Galle.[75] Probably Galle may have been the early form in which the term Galla came into the Christian literature.

With the establishment of Shawan Amhara Dynasty by Yikunno Amlak (1270–85) we find a few more references to Oromo groups in the Orthodox Church literature. Probably Yikunno Amlak 'was involved in the power struggle for succession between Yitbarak and Na'akuto-Laab'.[76] When Yitbarak emerged victorious, he imprisoned Yikunno Amlak. The latter managed to escape and 'organized an effective military revolt against King Yitbarak within the crucial area of Amhara and Shawan plateau'[77] eventually killing the Zagwe king and founding a new dynasty. According to Taddesse Tamrat, the mother of Yikunno Amlak is 'said to have been one of the slaves of a rich Amhara chief in Sagarat'.[78] However, Conti-Rossini claims that the mother of Yikunno Amlak was 'a slave of commander Challa'.[79] The latter is a typical Oromo name. It was also the name of an Oromo clan that settled in southern Wallo much earlier than hitherto suspected. Yikunno Amlak is said to have 'established the Church of St. Gabriel in the village of Galla Gurr [in Manz]. The name Gurr is a derivative of the Oromo word

---

[72] Budge, *The Book of the Mysteries of Heaven and Earth*, xix.
[73] Ibid., 27, 31–32. See also Halevy, 'Notes pour l'histoire d'Ethiopie,' 275–84; M.R. Basset, *Études sur l'histoire d'Éthiopie*, extrait du *Journal Asiatique* (Paris, 1882), 18, 233 (hereafter cited as Basset, *Journal Asiatique*).
[74] Mohammed Hassen, 'The Oromo of Ethiopia, 1500–1850: With Special Emphasis on the Gibe Region' (PhD dissertation, University of London, 1983), 47, 50.
[75] Halevy, 'Notes pour l'histoire d'Ethiopie', 275–84, 360–72.
[76] Tamrat, *Church and State in Ethiopia*, 66.
[77] Ibid., 67.
[78] Ibid., 66.
[79] Conti-Rossini, *Storia di Etiopia*, 317–18.

for a "pile of rock."' How could a village be called Galla, if that name was not already familiar even before the reign of Yikunno Amlak? There are several 'piles of rocks' in the region of Manz. Excavation by a team of archaeologists at some of piles of rocks 'uncovered cattle and human fossils, beads, bracelets and leg laces as well as varieties of broken potteries that were reminiscent of house furniture', which could be dated back to the tenth century or earlier. The use of beads and bracelets indicates the existence of *Atete*, the famous traditional ritual practised by Oromo women and adopted by several other ethnic groups including Amhara women. Unmistakable Oromo place names such as Girja and Wadera also hint at the possibility of some Oromo groups presence in the region of Manz probably during the Zawge period, if not earlier.[80]

Getatchew Haile's work mentions a 'Galla' group, regarded as 'trouble makers' and living within the Christian kingdom during the last quarter of the thirteenth century or the early fourteenth century.[81] Alaka Tayya's work also attests to the presence of some Oromo groups within the Christian kingdom during the reign of Widm Asferre (1299–1314).

> [D]uring the second year of his reign, when the Galla on one hand and the Muslims on the other continued to rise up and wreaked havoc on them, the king, the officials, and the clergy came together and counseled in unity to make peace with these Muslims of Yifat [Ifat] and Wello [Wallo] in order to combat only the Galla. They not only counseled, but indeed made peace with the Muslims.[82]

There was a precedent for such an alliance between the Christians and the Muslims directed against the 'pagan' kingdom of Damot. Common enmity against Damot and common economic interest created an alliance between the ambitious Yikunno Amlak and the Muslim leaders of Ifat. As a result, it was with Muslim support that Yikunno Amlak defeated and killed the last Zagwe king and established the new Amhara dynasty in 1270.[83] As we have already seen, Amda-Siyon, the son and successor of Widm Asferre and the grandson of Yikunno Amlak, is reported to have led a military expedition into *Hagara Galla* (the country of Galla) in 1332.[84] Getatchew Haile adds a profound observation that has tremendous significance for Oromo history during the reign of Amda-Siyon: 'Perhaps an apparently difficult circumstance they encountered might have forced the Oromo to leave Ethiopia and move further south.'[85] By Ethiopia, Getatchew Haile means the medieval Christian kingdom. The difficult circumstances that forced the Oromo to move further south during the reign

---

[80] Haile et al., *History of the Oromo to the Sixteenth Century*, 47, 48.

[81] Getatchew Haile, *A Catalogue of Ethiopian Manuscripts*, Volume IX (1987), 270. See also, Haile, *The Works of Abba Bahriy*, 27.

[82] Haile, *The Works of Abba Bahriy*, 233.

[83] Sergew Hable Sellassie, *Ancient and Medieval Ethiopian History to 1270* (Addis Ababa: Addis Ababa Printing Press, 1972), 254.

[84] Haile, *The Works of Abba Bahriy*, 26.

[85] Ibid.

of Amda-Siyon were warfare, slaving raids, and famine that followed in their train.

The famine during the reign of Amda-Siyon, probably coming as it did at the time when a colossal upheaval was taking place because of the struggle between the Christians and the Muslims, must have been severe, most likely forcing some people to abandon their land and move in search of food and safety. The Amhara tradition cited earlier unanimously asserts that the Christian governor of Katata and Dawaro drove away the rebellious and uncontrollable 'children' of Lalo. This tradition perhaps reflects the actual flight of some Oromo groups from the regions of Katata and Dawaro during the reign of Amda-Siyon. Perhaps two simultaneous events took place during his reign. First, there was the pressure from the warfare between the Muslims and the Christians, which was accompanied by the consolidation of an empire, where there was strong state control, to move further south, where there was no state control. Second, the drought, which was most likely accompanied by severe famine, may have forced some people to move further south with their cattle and children.

REFERENCE TO OROMO CLAN NAMES IN THE ORTHODOX CHURCH LITERATURE

Ethiopian Orthodox Church literature, which seems to have flourished during and after the reign of Amda-Siyon, provides us with bits and pieces of evidence that, when taken together, prove the presence of some Oromo groups in the region of Katata and Grarya. The narratives of Saint Takla Haymanot (c. 1215–1315) and Saint Filipo (1323–1406) furnish us with unmistakable Oromo place names in the region.[86] Haymanot is said to have been born in the village of Itisa[87] in northern Shawa. According to Taddesse Tamrat, Silalish is an ancient name for Itisa.[88] Interestingly Silalish appears to have been derived from Salale, a name of an important Oromo descent group. This means both Itisa and Salale are Oromo names. Could names of places be given Oromo names, if Oromo speakers were not in the area? Haymanot is said to have used 'Ella' water for baptism.[89] 'Ella' means 'water', as well as a 'well' in the Oromo language. The hagiographical tradition of Saint Qawistos, one of Haymanot's disciples, who founded a monastery at Nibge in the neighbourhood of the Muslim state of Ifat, is particularly relevant in this regard. The narratives of his life furnish us with two important Oromo

[86] See for example, G.W.B. Huntingford, *The Historical Geography of Ethiopia from the 1st Century A.D. to 1704*, rev. edn, ed. R. Pankhurst and D. Appleyard (London: Oxford University Press, 1989), 83. See also E.A.W. Budge, *Life and Miracles of Takla Hâymânôt* (London: 1906), 76–86; Taddesse Tamrat, *Church and State in Ethiopia*, 160–74.

[87] Haile et al., *History of the Oromo to the Sixteenth Century*, 62.

[88] Tamrat, *Church and State in Ethiopia*, 119, see note 3.

[89] Haile et al., *History of the Oromo to the Sixteenth Century*, 63

clan or descent group names. This saint is reported to have conducted extensive proselytization among the pagan people of Galan and Yaya, who worshipped the God Qorke.[90]

> [Saint Qawistos] found the inhabitants of the country worshipping the devils at the foot of a kobal [?] tree. They were sitting there eating, drinking and amusing themselves in the fashion of the Muslims. They fanned the fire with their hands and held hot flames in their mouths and chanted saying 'O people of Galan and Yay, see what your god Qorke (can) do!' ... And they brought for [Qorke a daily present of] two fat cows, five sheep, five goats, and twenty-one baskets of white [wheat?] bread. All these were eaten by the functionaries of the gods.[91]

A number of important points emerge from what is reported above. First, the religious practice of the Galan and Yaya is similar to traditional Oromo religion, briefly discussed in the previous chapter. As the Oromo traditionally prayed under the shade of the sacred *oda* (sycomore) tree, the Galan and Yaya worshipped Qorke, (possibly Waaqa) at the foot of a Kobal, probably corruption of *oda*, tree. Second, according to Taddesse Tamrat, the Galan and Yaya people lived near Mount Yay, east of Katata, the land which Amhara tradition connects with rebellious Oromo groups. Third, Yaya is still the name of important putative Oromo descent groups in Hararghe[92] as well as among the other major sub-moieties or Oromo confederacies such as the Arsi, the Tulama, the Macha, the Guji and the Karrayu.

Fourth, Galan is another important Oromo putative descent groups that appears from Hararghe in the east to Wallaga in the west and from Wallo in the north to Kenya in the south. In fact, Galan is traditionally considered as 'the first son' (*angafa*) of the Borana, the eponymous founder of the Western Oromo moiety. Because of the special privileges and role given to the *angafa* in Oromo society, the Galan had a unique position in the *gada* system, as well as in the Qaalluu (Oromo religious) institution. Galan appears as a *gosa* name in the genealogies of all major Oromo groups. According to Bulcha, the Galan 'are numerically the largest Oromo *gosa*-cluster. The cluster dominates the Shawan plateau: more than 40 per cent of the putative descent groups located here belong to Galaan or reckon their lineage back to it.'[93] An Italian traveller of the nineteenth century, A. Cecchi, reported a tradition that says that the Galan have prestige as the oldest Oromo *gosa* group.[94] Knuttson reported the same.[95]

Yaya is an important putative descent group within the Karrayu (also spelled Karrayyuu) Confederacy. Karrayu, according to Bahrey,

[90] Tamrat, *Church and State in Ethiopia*, 184.
[91] Ibid.
[92] Haile et al., *History of the Oromo to the Sixteenth Century*, 250–1, 257.
[93] Bulcha, *Contours of the Emergent and Ancient Oromo Nation*, 222.
[94] A. Cecchi, *Da Zeila alle Frontiere del Caffa: Viaggi di Antionio Cecci Spedizione Italiana nell'Africa Equatoriale, 1876–82* (Rome: Ermanno Loescher, 1886), vol. 1: 252.
[95] Knutsson, *Authority and Change*, 172.

is the 'first son' of Barentu and the father of six powerful sub-moieties. In other words, the Karrayu are part of the Eastern Oromo moiety, which itself is broken into six powerful confederations.[96] Like Galan, Karrayu appears almost all over Oromo territory either as a *gosa* or confederacy. In fact, Karrayu appears among the Borana in southern Ethiopia and northern Kenya, where Galan turns up as Gallantu. 'It is interesting to note', writes Negaso Gidada, 'that the Yaya or Yaye in Booranaa [Borana] section of the Oromo in the south are given as sub-groups of the Galantu and the Karryyu'.[97] Haberland recorded a song that points out that the Yaya among the Borana in the south came from Dawway,[98] or what is known today as southern Wallo, which indirectly confirms the movement of some Oromo groups from the north to the southern regions of Ethiopia. There are also pre-sixteenth-century Oromo place names in southern Wallo and northern Shawa. According to Bulcha, there are' fifteenth-century place names' such as:

> Masara, Teso, Gora, Ganamo, Gombo, Gandawallo (Ganda Wallo), Salagan, Badabayi (Baddaa Bayii), all of which were located in the regions of Wallo and Shawa and all of which are typical Oromo names also elsewhere in Oromo even today. What is important to note here is that, besides being toponyms, each word has also a meaning in the Oromo language providing thereby a linguistic evidence for Oromo presence in those places.[99]

What is fascinating about the Borana in southern Ethiopia and northern Kenya is that the Karrayu – the largest Borana sub-moiety – is, in turn, divided into thirty-six sub-*gosas*.[100] Karrayu is also the clan of the Qaalluu, the hereditary religious leader. Asmarom Legesse observes that the Karrayu were 'the most expansive and dynamic part of the nation'. As we will see in later chapters on pastoral Oromo population movements, the Karrayu spread to the northern regions of the Christian kingdom. The Karrayu also formed 'the vanguards of the southward migration of the Borana into Kenya' and spread 'as far south as the Tana River in Kenya, among the Orma'.[101] In the Borana *gada* system in southern Ethiopia, the Karrayu clan still performs what the Galan performed among the northern Oromo before the *chaffee* assemblies (parliaments), which, according to Alaka Tayya, 'were banned by a proclamation (issued) by Emperor Menelik II [1889–1913], in order to prevent an eventual disturbance emanating from the gatherings'.[102] According to Mekuria Bulcha,

[96] Bahrey, 'History of the Galla', in *Some Records of Ethiopia*, 114.

[97] Gidada, *History of the Sayyoo Oromoo*, 50–51.

[98] Haberland, *Galla Süd-Athiopiens*, 118, 173.

[99] Bulcha, *Contours of the Emergent and Ancient Oromo Nation*, 218.

[100] Sahlu Kidane, *Boran Folktales: A Contextual Study* (London: Haan Publishing, 2002), 5.

[101] Asmarom Legesse, *Oromo Democracy an Indigenous African Political System* (Trenton, NJ: The Red Sea Press, 2006), 163.

[102] Haile, *The Works of Abba Bahriy*, 222.

> The Galaan [Galan] and Yaayyaa (Yaya) are Oromo putative descent groups who live today not only on the Shawan Plateau, but also all over the Oromo country. They are among the most important building-blocks of a pan-Oromo kinship structure ... They were also part of the Oromo kinship structure described ... by Baharey [in 1593].[103]

The people of Galan and Yaya, according to Taddesse Tamrat, lived near Mount Yay, somewhere east of Katata, where Saint Takla Haymanot baptized the pagan people in the river Meesot.[104] The word 'lived' should be noted because the reference is to the sedentary people after whom these places, including the river (with their unmistakable Oromo origin) are named. According to Negaso Gidada, the Galan and Yaya were:

> living in Shawa not far from Dabra Berhan during the reign of Amda Seyon [sic] and during the expansion of Christianity in the region. From the sacrificial food they used then, it can be assumed that the Yaayyaa [Yaya] and the Galaan [Galan] cultivated wheat and raised cattle, goats and sheep.[105]

As indicated above, Taddesse Tamrat states that Galan and Yaya worshipped their God known as Qorke, which is probably a linguistic corruption of Waaqa. In the sense of worship in which it is presented in Taddesse Tamrat's seminal book, it is hard to think of anything other than Waaqa. Both words are two syllables of similar sounds with the second syllable introduced by a glottal stop.[106] There is no doubt that *qorke* is an Oromo word, which today may have different meanings. Qorke, according to Gidada was a festival that the Yaya and the Galan held during the dry season months of February and March.[107] He maintains that a similar ritual is still being performed by the Oromo during 'one of the months of the dry season'.[108] Among the Oromo in Hararghe, Qorke is the name of a deity who dwells in sacred places, such as sycamore trees or any 'big tree,' the source of a river or spring, or the centre of a deep forest. There are still a number of places in the Hararghe region by the name of Qorke where traditional ceremonies are performed.

Finally, the already-cited Amhara tradition connects Katata, Dawaro and Lalo, the name of one of the major Oromo putative descent groups. As we have seen above, Azaj Tino connects Lalo and Dawaro, which he regards as the birthplace of the Oromo nation. Haberland 'refers to the local historical tradition [which confirms] that the Oromo had settled'[109] in the region of Shawa before the sixteenth century. Further,

---

[103] Bulcha, *Contours of the Emergent and Ancient Oromo Nation*, 157–8.
[104] Tamrat, *Church and State in Ethiopia*, 184, see note 1.
[105] Gidada, *History of the Sayyoo Oromoo*, 38.
[106] I am indebted to Rev. Dr Schaffer Harwood for his suggestion about *qorke*.
[107] Gidada, *History of the Sayyoo Oromoo*, 38.
[108] Ibid.
[109] Quoted in Odd Eirik Arnesen, 'The Becoming of Place: A Tulama-Oromo Region of Northern Shoa', in P.T.W. Baxter, Jan Hultin and Alessandro Triulzi, ed., *Being and Becoming Oromo: Historical and Anthropological Enquiries* (Uppsala: Nordiska Afrikainstitutet, 1996), 216.

Arab Faqih, an historian of the sixteenth-century jihad, establishes conclusively the presence of a sedentary Oromo group in Dawaro.[110] I have already indicated that the Galla River, the Galla Forest and *Hagara Galla* were all located in the same vicinity. This district, which unanimous Amhara tradition connects with Galla, was not far from Dawaro, Fatagar, Katata and Waj, where some Oromo groups, including Galan and Yaya, may have lived. The unpublished 'Tarika Zagalla' ('History of the Galla') states that when Emperor Galawdewos and the Portuguese soldiers returned to Shawa in 1543 (after the death of Imam Ahmad in 1543), they stayed among the Galan along the Galana River (i.e. Galla River, which means the headwaters of Wabi Shebelle River).[111] Bermudez, the Portuguese bishop, who stayed with Galawdewos, confirms the presence of the Galan in the region.

> The Asmache de galan [the commander of the Galan], too, came soon, who was married to the princess, aunt of the king; he brought several baskets of bread, sheep ... calves, capons, and fifty jars of mead, all on the part of the King, his lord.[112]

The above-mentioned commander of the Galan must have been an important officer, and was connected with the royal family through marriage. This does not appear to be an isolated example of Christianized and Amharized individuals, possibly of Oromo origin, who achieved a high position of power during the reign of Galawedos (1540–49). Amhara tradition claims that a certain Tullu (a very common Oromo name) was the *agafri* (literally, Chief of the Palace Guard) and a brave warrior who fought for King Libna Dengel (1508–40) against Imam Ahmad.[113] During the six years (1520–26) when the Portuguese Embassy stayed at the court of King Libna Dengel, Alvares provides us with the names of two individuals who served as *Bahar Nagash* (the title of the governor of the province of the Sea). They were Dori and Bulla. Alvares tells us that when Bahar Nagash Dori died he was succeeded by his son, Bulla.[114] There is no doubt that Dori and Bulla are unmistakable Oromo names. What these few examples demonstrate is that during the sixteenth century some of the prominent individuals, who were from the background of sedentary Oromo communities were integrated into the heart and soul of Christian administration. Getatchew Haile suggests that there may have been more individuals of

[110] Arab Faqih, *Futuh Al-Habasha*, 135–7, 254–5.

[111] Quoted in Gidada, *History of the Sayyoo Oromoo*, 40.

[112] R.S. Whiteway, trans. and ed., *The Portuguese Expedition to Abyssinia in 1541–1543 as Narrated by Castanhoso with some Contemporary Letters, the Short Account of Bermudez and Certain Extracts from Correa* ([1902] London: Hakluyt Society, 1967), 205.

[113] Makurya, *Ye Gragn Ahmad Warara*, 803.

[114] Father Francisco Alvares, trans. Lord Stanley, *The Prester John of The Indies: A true Relation of the Lands of The Prester John, being the Narrative of the Portuguese Embassy to Ethiopia in 1520*, rev. edn, ed. C.F. Beckingham and G.W.B. Huntingford (Cambridge: Hakluyt Society / University Press, 1961 [1881]), vol. 1, 114.

Oromo background who served in position of power under the Christian administration. However, their identity was unknown because after their conversion, those individuals were given Christian names and they adopted an 'Amhara identity',[115] as was the custom of the time.

As already mentioned, the unpublished 'Tarik Zagalla' ('History of the Galla') makes extensive reference to the Oromo during the reign of Emperor Amda-Siyon. In fact this document, as quoted by Negaso Gidada, categorically states that as the result of Amda-Siyon's war, some Oromo groups were displaced.[116]

To summarize: first, there is no doubt that the Liban, the Galan, the Yaya, the Lalo and other groups, to be mentioned later, were Oromo-speaking communities who lived in the region of Shawa during the thirteenth century, if not earlier. Second, it appears that by the time of Amda-Siyon (1314–44), there were some Oromo groups who lived in the region of what is today Shawa. 'Tarika Zagalla' and several other sources, including the Chronicle of Amda-Siyon, confirm Oromo presence in the region during the reign of this warrior emperor.[117] Takla Sadiq Makurya implies that it was the Christian defence establishment that checked a large-scale pastoral Oromo population movement before the jihad of Imam Ahmad (1529–43) cleared the way for them.[118] From another angle, Taddesse Tamrat arrives at the same conclusion when he states 'Christian Ethiopia was never the same again after the wars of Ahmad Gragn'.[119] The Christian defence establishment, which was destroyed by the jihad of Imam Ahmad, was first built during the reign of Emperor Amda-Siyon. What is not in doubt is that the Galan, Yaya, Liban and Lalo were among the Oromo groups who were living in the region of Katata during the reign of Amda-Siyon. According to Alaka Tayya, Amda-Siyon had settled some Oromo groups between Lake Tana and Damot in north-western parts of the Christian kingdom, where they accepted Christianity and adopted the language of the people among whom they settled.[120] There is no reason to doubt this information because the transfer of people from one part of the Christian kingdom to another for military purposes was a tested policy of Amda-Siyon. Second, the Galla River of Fra Mauro's map, the Galla Forest of the Christian tradition, the Galla River of the Amhara tradition and the *Hagara Galla* of Amda-Siyon's

---

[115] Haile, *The Works of Abba Bahriy*, 27.

[116] 'Tarikra Zagalla' [History of the Galla], quoted in Gidada, *History of the Sayyoo Oromoo*, 40–45.

[117] Gidada, *History of the Sayyoo Oromoo*, 41.

[118] Makurya, *Ye Gragn Ahmad Warara*, 803.

[119] See Taddesse Tamrat, *Church and State in Ethiopia*, 301, where he states: 'Indeed, many of the difficulties which befell the Christian Kingdom in the Sixteenth and Seventeenth centuries can be attributed directly or indirectly to the disastrous effects of the Muslim wars. The Galla expansion could never be contained in the Sixteenth century largely because Ahmad Gragn's forces had effectively disrupted the system of frontier defence of the medieval Christian empire.'

[120] Tayya, *Ye Ityopya Hizeb Tarik*, 37.

Chronicle were all in the same region, near Waj, Dawaro, Fatagar and Katata, and the said Galla River could possibly be identified with the Wabi Shebelle River.

Third, it appears that during the first half of the fourteenth century, the pattern of ethnic distribution may have been altered. Finally, the creation of the powerful Amhara empire seems to have checked the large-scale population movements from the east to the west; and, more important, from south to the north. The military colonies in the southern provinces acted as a dam that stemmed the normal flow of population movement to the north.

THE PASTORAL OROMO PRESSURE ON THE CHRISTIAN KINGDOM

During the fifteenth century, the Christian defence system seems to have frustrated a number of large-scale pastoral Oromo population movements to the north. For example, according to a tradition reported by Haberland, the northern Gujj, the Allabadu Oromo pastoralists, had already reached around Lake Langano by the middle of the fifteenth century. However, they were driven back from the region by the soldiers of Emperor Zara Ya'eqob (1434–68).[121] During the reign of Baeda-Maryam (1468–78), the Christian governor of Bali, a certain Jan Zeg is reported to have led an expedition into unknown country, where he was killed along with all of his forces.[122] The crucial question is, where was this unknown country? It is difficult to believe that any of the Muslim principalities that bordered Bali on the east, north and west (Adal, Hadiya, Dawaro and Sharka) were unknown to the writers of the Christian chronicles (see Map 4). The most likely region unknown to the chroniclers would be the region south of Bali, which was not under Christian administration. This would mean that the Christian governor of Bali led an expedition against the pastoral Oromo who lived in the lowlands south of the old Bali during the reign of Baeda-Maryam. (This will be explored further in Chapter 4.) Oromo pressure upon the Christian kingdom continued up to the first three decades of the sixteenth century, when taking advantage of the jihadic war of Imam Ahmad (1529–43), it became irreversible.

It appears that Darrell Bates made a valid observation in 1979 when he stated: 'The [Oromo people] ... watched [the struggle between the Christians and Muslims] ... with interest. They had suffered in their time from both parties, and were waiting in the wings for opportunities to exact revenge and to recover lands which had been taken from them.'[123]

---

[121] Haberland, *Galla Süd-Aethiopiens*, 276.
[122] Basset, *Journal Asiatique*, 96, 139.
[123] Darrell Bates, *The Abyssinian Difficulty: The Emperor Theodorus and the Magdala Campaign* (Oxford: Oxford University Press, 1979), 7.

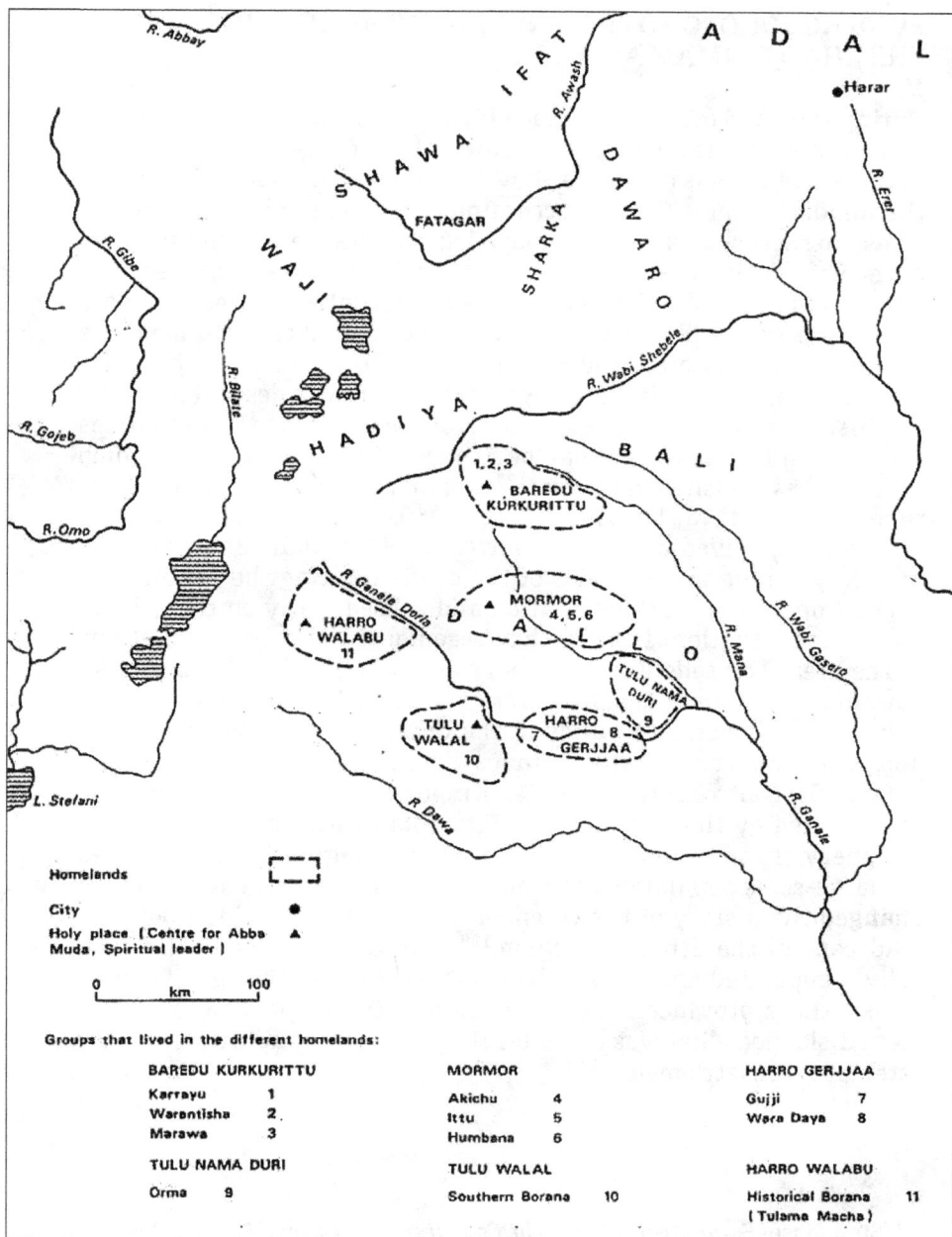

Map 4 Homelands of the Pastoral Oromo c. 1500 (adapted from Hassen, 'The Oromo of Ethiopia, 1500–1850, PhD diss., University of London, 1983).

EVIDENCE OF OROMO PRESENCE FROM THE HISTORIAN OF THE JIHAD OF IMAM AHMAD

During the jihad of Imam Ahmad (1529–43), Christians and Muslims fought bitterly. The sedentary agricultural Oromo, who already lived in and south of what is today the Shawa region, lost their identity during the jihadic struggle. Hence, according to the general view of historians, no section of the Oromo played an integral part in the struggle of the period. However, Arab Faqih makes it clear that some sections of the Oromo people who lived in the hotly contested areas suffered severely from the jihadic war. He mentions a number of Oromo clans by name, such as Jimma and Warra Qaalluu, to cite just two. Jimma is mentioned as personal name as well as the name of a descent group.[124] The historian of the jihad makes numerous references to Oromo groups from which the following may be deduced. There were some Oromo groups,[125] established in Dawaro[126] (northern Bale and western Hararghe) in Ifat and Waj, both in what is today the Shawa[127] region. These Oromo groups lived under the control of a Christian administration and they fought on both sides of the conflict during the jihadic war, depending at first on their location and subsequently on the exigencies of the situation. In this, they resembled the other populations of the area. The sedentary Oromo groups who lived under Christian administration were separate from the sixteenth century pastoral Oromo who lived in the valley of the Ganale River in southern Bale and in Sidamo. Those pastoral groups lived beyond the boundaries and outside the control of the Christian Kingdom of Abyssinia. They were not affected by the devastation of the jihad since they lived on the periphery of the conflict. It was these pastoral groups who launched the large-scale population movement of the sixteenth century, which changed the history of the Oromo and radically altered the political landscape of the Ethiopian region.[128] Before the Christian kingdom fully recuperated and re-established its strong military garrisons in the southern provinces, the large pastoral Oromo population movement dislodged what was left after the jihadic war and thwarted new attempts at resettlement.[129]

---

[124] Stenhouse, *Futuh Al-Habasha, The Conquest of Abyssinia*, 56, 170. See also Arab Faqih, *Futuh Al-Habasha*, 135–7.
[125] Ibid.,135–7, 269, 298.
[126] Ibid.
[127] Ibid., 269, 291, 298, 355, 382.
[128] This section is summarized from Mohammed Hassen, 'Some Aspects of Oromo History that have been Misunderstood', *The Oromo Commentary* (1993), 28–29.
[129] Hassen, *The Oromo of Ethiopia: A History 1570–1860*, (Cambridge: Cambridge University Press, 1990), 20.

THE PRE-SIXTEENTH-CENTURY YAJJU OROMO PRESENCE IN IFAT

When Imam Ahmad invaded Ifat in 1531, his forces came to a district called Qawat, which, according to Arab Faqih, was 'so excellent a land' that it was known as a smaller Gojjam[130]. He further states that this fertile land was inhabited by a sedentary people called El-Ejju, who spoke a language different from that of the Muslims and the Christians. After his victory, Imam Ahmad appointed Kalid al-Waradi in charge of the people of Qawat. The Muslim leaders converted the leaders of the people of Qawat, namely Haizu, Dalo and Daballa. 'These three became Muslims and their submission was genuine, for they gave witness at the memorable events that were to follow.'[131] When Imam Ahmad himself visited Qawat, he urged El-Ejju's cavalry and 'four-thousand infantry to become Muslims and all of them did so'. They in turn converted 'their wives and children and their conversion was sincere'.[132] The El-Ejju people then furnished the Muslim force with a large contingent of cavalry and infantry. As the warriors for the cause of Islam, the El-Ejju followed the jihadic war to Beta Amhara and then settled in Angot, a uniquely strategic position.

> [T]he highlands of Angot ... served as a great water divide for three river systems of the central plateau of Ethiopia. Here rise the upper waters of the Takaze, the Bashilo ... and numerous other rivers flowing eastwards into the basin of the Awash.[133]

From here the El-Ejju were to dominate the history of the Christian kingdom with its capital at Gondar, especially from the 1750s to the 1850s. Three views about the El-Ejju are presented here. According to Trimingham:

> It is possible that the foundational element of the Yajju were 'Afar-Saho peoples who have penetrated this region both before, as well as during, the great Muslim conquest after which they were conquered by [Oromo]. A process of mutual absorption took place, shown in hybrid tribal names like the Warra Shaikh; the [Oromo] social and family life was profoundly modified and also their religion after they accepted Islam, but the [Oromo] language and traditions predominated, whereby the Yajju continue to regard themselves as [Oromo]. The Warra Shaikh family which produced Rāses Gugsa and 'Ali, whose control over central Abyssinia strangled the empire, was the chief branch of Yajju. It has acquired the usual legend tracing its descent back to 'Umar Shaikh who came from across the sea.[134]

Trimingham related Yajju (the foundational element) with Afar-Saho primarily on two grounds. First, like Afar, the Yajju 'wear feathers in

---

[130] On the larger and most fertile province of Gojjam, located west of the Blue Nile, see Chapters 5, 7 and 8.
[131] Stenhouse, *Futuh Al-Habasha, The Conquest of Abyssinia*, 207.
[132] Ibid., 207–8.
[133] Tamrat, *Church and State in Ethiopia*, 35.
[134] J.S. Trimingham, *Islam in Ethiopia* (London: Oxford University Press, 1952), 35.

their hair after their first killing'.[135] As we know from other sources, the Oromo also wore feathers in their hair after killing.[136] Second, the Yajju 'seem to combine the agricultural and pastoral life, living by their flocks and by agriculture in which irrigation plays an important part'.[137] Once again, as we know, all sedentary Oromo combined agricultural and pastoral lives, living off of their flocks and agriculture.[138] In fact, on the basis of these two grounds, Trimingham unintentionally makes the Yajju more closely related to the Oromo than they are to the Afar-Saho. As far as the history of the Yajju is concerned, Trimingham seemingly did not consult what Arab Faqih had said about the history of the El-Ejju people. Had he done so, he would have realized that the El-Ejju left their country Qawat in Ifat around 1531. To all intents and purposes, the Yajju Trimingham writes of were the El-Ejju of *Futuh Al-Habasha* who moved to Angot around 1531.

Without actually identifying who the El-Ejju were, Merid Wolde Aregay has provided an ingenious but untenable explanation for their permanent settlement in Angot.

> The Muslim peoples under Ahmad comprised ... nomads, pastoralists and agri-culturalists. It appears that much of the sedentary population had moved into the nearby highland province leaving to the other two sections some space in which to spread themselves. The case of El-ijju is an indication of such a movement ... The El-ijju must have moved to Angot in large numbers and the reason why they did not return to their fertile country after the collapse of Ahmad's empire must be because Muslims from across the Awash had occupied Qawat.[139]

This explanation is untenable, first, because there is no historical evidence to show that, during the early phase of the jihad, the sedentary agriculturalists from across the Awash moved to Qawat or any other place to provide space for the nomads and pastoralists to spread themselves. Second, and more important, Arab Faqih makes it clear that the El-Ejju were taken to Angot as auxiliaries of the Muslim forces.[140] The real reason why the El-Ejju did not return to Qawat after the collapse of the jihad is suggested below; neither Trimingham nor Aregay acknowledged that the El-Ejju could have been an Oromo-speaking group that may have lived in Ifat long before the sixteenth century.

According to Gabra Sellassie and Alaqa Tayya, the Yajju trace their family ancestry to Shaikh Umar from Arabia, who came at the time of Imam Ahmad and settled in Yajju. He married many women and produced many children, and their village consequently became

---

[135] Ibid., 195.
[136] E. Cerulli, *The Folk Literature of the Galla of Southern Abyssinia*, Harvard African Studies Vol. 3 (Cambridge, MA: Harvard University Press, 1922), 102.
[137] Trimingham, *Islam in Ethiopia*, 195.
[138] A.H.S. Landor, *Across Widest Africa: An Account of the Country and the People of Eastern, Central and Western Africa, as Seen During a Twelve-Month's Journey from Djibuti to Cape Verde* (London: Hurst and Blackett, 1907), 120–1.
[139] Aregay, 'Southern Ethiopia and the Christian Kingdom', 138–9.
[140] Arab Faqih, *Futuh Al-Habasha* (Arabic text, Cairo, 1974), 269, 298, 355, 382.

known as *Warra Shihu* (the family of a thousand).[141] Some scholars have accepted this view uncritically. Merid Wolde Aregay goes even further and claims 'the [Oromo] failed to subdue or assimilate them completely, and therefore the Yajju are known to the [Oromo] as *Warra Shaikh*'.[142] Alaqa Tayya offers an ingenious explanation for the name *Warra Shaikh* (the family of Shaikh), the appellation by which Muslim Yajju were known to non-Muslim Oromo. However, he unintentionally mentions a name that belies his explanation. He says the first-born son of Shaikh Umar was named Wale, a most common and an unmistakable Oromo name. This suggests that Alaqa Tayya is bent on establishing an acceptable genealogy for the *Warra Shaikh* because these people became very important to the Christian kingdom during the Gondar period. If he makes the 'founding father' of the Yajju come from Arabia, he again mentions the name of a people who are supposed to be different from the Oromo. For example, a certain woman of *Warra Shaikh* was married to the chief of *Ilma Oromo* (literally, children of Oromo) and gave rise to the chain of leaders who dominated the politics of the Christian kingdom. The term *Ilma Oroma*, which is mentioned only once in Alaqa Tayya's book, literally means 'the children of Oromo' and is another collective name for the Oromo people. His claim about the origin of the Yajju is incorrect on four grounds. First, the claim that the ancestry of the Yajju is traceable to Arabia at the time of Imam Ahmad cannot be accurate. We have seen that the El-Ejju of Arab Faqih went to Angot from Ifat in 1531 when the jihadic war reached there. The El-Ejju settled in an equally fertile area of Angot. After the failure of the jihad in 1543, they remained in their new domicile and the new Christian emperor pardoned them, as he did all who had accepted Islam. Because their conversion had been only superficial, it was not seen as a threat to the Christian kingdom. Second, the name Yajju is a derivation of the name of the people Arab Faqih calls El-Ejju. Third, the claim of an Arab ancestry is an innocent expression of Islamic values and is a common phenomenon among the Muslims in north-east Africa and elsewhere. Islamized Oromo have consistently fabricated genealogies. For example, the Oromo of Wallo claim to have come from Harar following the jihadic war of Imam Ahmad.[143] In the Gibe region, where most Oromo kings accepted Islam only during the first two decades of the nineteenth century, they claim that their ancestors were Muslims for many centuries.[144] The claim that the ancestors of the *Warra Shaikh* came from Arabia in the sixteenth century is extremely unlikely.

Nevertheless, the name Umar, the supposed ancestor of the *Warra Shaikh* in connection with the jihad of Imam Ahmad, may refer to a true historical figure. Arab Faqih refers to a number of Muslim commanders by that name, including one brother of Wazir Adole.[145] It is not

141 Tayya, *Ye Ityopya Hizeb Tarik*, 198.
142 Aregay, 'Southern Ethiopia and the Christian Kingdom', 139.
143 Conti-Rossini, 'Domenico Buelli-Recordi Storici di Wallo', 87.
144 Hassen, *The Oromo of Ethiopia: A History 1570–1860*, 85.
145 Arab Faqih, Futuh Al-Habasha, *The Conquest of Abyssinia*, 197–8, 324, 396.

far-fetched to assume that the Umar who is supposed to have come from Arabia at the time of the jihad may have been one of the Muslim leaders under whose command the El-Ejju of Qawat went to Angot and settled. What may have happened is that after the arrival of the pastoral Oromo in Angot in the second half of the sixteenth century, the El-Ejju, who were probably only nominal Muslims, may have referred to themselves as *Warra Shaikh*, and hence they were called so by their non-Muslim Oromo neighbours to demonstrate the difference in religion between the two. We have numerous examples of this phenomenon in the Gibe region as well as in the region Hararghe. Fourth and finally, of the three already mentioned names of Haizu, Dalou and Daballa (the traditional leaders of the people of Qawat who accepted Islam and joined the Muslim forces), Dalou and Daballa are still very common Oromo proper names throughout Oromo territory. If these leaders with unmistakable Oromo names submitted to the Imam and fought on his behalf, a written Amhara tradition claims that a certain Tullu (another very common Oromo name) was the *agafri* (literally, Chief of the Palace Guard) and a brave warrior who fought for King Libna Dengel (1508–40) against Imam Ahmad. This indicates that during the jihad the Oromo fought on both sides.[146]

We also find unmistakable Oromo place names in *Futuh Al-Habasha* in or near Qawat, the land of the El-Ejju, which suggests that these people were Oromo speakers. The place name Genda Belo (the village of Belo), inhabited by Christians and even mentioned in the Chronicle of Baeda-Maryam, is one example.[147] It was in this village that the Imam astonished his commanders and followers by refusing to accept the twenty ounces of gold that the frightened inhabitants presented as a gift. In the words of Arab Faqih: 'In those days the Imam was poor, and the soldiers and [commanders] took some of the gold and said to the Imam "we will give this gold to your wife Delwanbara". The Imam resisted, saying "this is for the conducting of the *jihad*".'[148] In or near Qawat are also mentioned the place names Wan Jara and Ledjabh. The first is clearly an Oromo place name. The second has been identified by Basset as Laga Ambo ('the river of mineral water' in Oromo language), which as a source of water for cattle is one of the most common names throughout Oromo country. In addition, the El-Ejju of Arab Faqih may be Ejju, the name of an Oromo clan. The Yajju of the Christian literature was derived probably either from Ejju, an Oromo name of a clan or from Arab Faqih's El-Ejju. According to Asmarom Legesse the clearest evidence that the Yajju belonged to the Oromo nation comes from their tradition itself. 'They called themselves "Ilman Orma" as recorded in Antoine d'Abbadie's account of the great ancestors of the northern most Oromo.'[149] What is more, the French traveller Antoine d'Abbadie met

[146] Makurya, *Ya Gragn Ahmed Warara*, 803.
[147] J. Perruchon, *Les Chroniques de Zar'a Yâ'eqôb et de Ba'eda Mâryâm, Rois d'Éthiopie de 1434 à 1478* (Paris: Emile Bouillon, 1893), 182.
[148] Arab Faqih, Futuh Al-Habasha, *The Conquest of Abyssinia*, 38.
[149] Legesse, *Oromo Democracy*, 171.

Ras Ali, the last Yajju ruler of Gondar, in 1843, and recorded the latter's long genealogy, in which a certain Sibu is reported to have migrated from Walal and crossed the river Awash early in their history.[150] Sibu was a powerful Oromo confederacy that spread to Shawa, Wallaga and the Gibe region. From this, it appears that the Ejju putative descent group was probably the vanguard party of the Sibu sub-moiety that lived in the region of Ifat much earlier than the sixteenth century. Interestingly, a document that deals with the rise and fall of the Yajju Dynasty claims that the earliest Oromo clan to settle in the region of Wallo was the Bokoji putative descent group, whose settlement in the region of southern Wallo goes back to the fourteenth century.[151] If the claim of this document is established, the pre-sixteenth-century presence of some Oromo groups was not limited only to the region of Shawa during the fourteenth century. It may have also extended to the region of southern Wallo.

THE PRE-SIXTEENTH-CENTURY OROMO PRESENCE IN THE HISTORIC PROVINCE OF WAJ (SEE MAP 4, ABOVE)

I have suggested earlier that the appellation Galla was connected with an Oromo clan by the name of Galan. As Galan probably gave rise to the appellation, so did the province of Waj to the Waji Oromo putative descent group. While Cohen thinks that the Waji Oromo clan got its name from the old political denomination, [152] Bulcha argues that 'the territory got its name from Waaji[Waji] Oromo, and not the other way round'.[153] Yet Ulrich Braukämper claims that, with the exception of Waji Oromo *gosa*, the Oromo had no 'traceable connection with Wag [Waj]'.[154] Waji Oromo *gosa* members are scattered among all major Oromo confederacies, and lived in the regions of Shawa and Arsi. They are also found

> in numerous places in the region of Wallaga where they constitute large descent groups among the Leeqaa Naqamte of eastern, and the sayyoo of southwestern, Wallaga. In southern Oromia, they are found among the Borana and the Gujii Oromo, and in the north among the Raayyaa in Tigray.[155]

Among the Arsi Oromo there are Waji Shanan (the five Wajis) together constituting one of the major *gosa* family of Arsi Oromo. Waji Shanan in turn are divided into eighteen sub-clans all of them tracing back their genealogy to the 'founding father' – Waji.[156] Braukämper did

[150] A. d'Abbadie, unpublished papers, Papers of Antoine and Arnauld d'Abbadie, no. 21300, folio 796.
[151] Quoted in Haile et al., *History of the Oromo to the Sixteenth Century*, 43.
[152] M. Cohen, *Etudes d'Ethiopien méridional* (Paris: Paul Geuthner, 1931), 78–80.
[153] Bulcha, *Contours of the Emergent and Ancient Oromo Nation*, 175.
[154] Ulrich Braukämper, *Islamic History and Culture in Southern Ethiopia: Collected Essays* (New Brunswick, NJ: Transaction Publishers, 2002), 46–47.
[155] Bulcha, *Contours of the Emergent and Ancient Oromo Nation*, 174.
[156] Haile et al., *History of the Oromo to the Sixteenth Century*, 217–18.

not explain why a single clan is not adequate to establish a traceable Oromo connection with the province of Waj.[157] In any event, his claim that the Oromo arrived in Waj only 'after the middle of the sixteenth century' is historically untenable because his own data confirms an early Oromo presence in Waj. Besides the obvious linguistic association, Braukämper's reference to the 'genealogical traditions in Arsi [that] report a marriage connection between the Oromo ancestor [Waji] and the Ulbarag, Semetic-speaking Hadiyya'[158] confirms early Oromo presence in Waj. This conclusion in turn matches Borana Oromo tradition recorded by Haberland that describes Waj as the place where the original Oromo fell from heaven.[159] This tradition, which makes Waj the original home of the first Oromo, perhaps reflects the long presence of one or more *Oromo* groups in the province. All these traditions agree with Arba Faqih's reference to the land of Orm (the land of an Oromo group) in the province of Waj. He also mentions typical Oromo place names, such as Jitu and Arkatlu.[160] According to Arab Faqih's record, when Wazir Adole, the commander of Imam Ahmad's army, was either in or near Waj, in 1531,

> [h]e sent scouts of a hundred horsemen to Maya, under the command of Zahroubi Osman. From Maya, the Muslim army went to the land of Aran where they looted and destroyed. From there, they went to the land of Orm ... where the Muslim force was attacked by the infidels. After defeating the infidels, the Muslim army left the land of Orm.[161]

From this Arabic record, it is clear that there was a group known as Orm (Oromo) in Waj. Given the unanimity of oral traditions from different sources and the support of a written record, the Oromo presence in Waj before the sixteenth century is an established historical fact by any standard of historical interpretation.

The Maya were known to have lived in the province of Waj and the surrounding areas and were pastoralists and expert archers who used poisoned arrows to slaughter their enemies. As the land of Maya was in Waj, so was the land of Orm. These Orm were most likely the Waji Oromo. What is not clear from the monumental book of Arab Faqih is the connection, if any, between the Maya people and the Waji Oromo. In 2005 Merid Wolde Aregay made two suppositions about the possible origin of the Maya people. First, and less certainly,

> a Tegrean origin for the Maya ... In all likelihood the Maya were Afar pastoralists who lived in the lowlands to the east of Harar city and who, soon after their displacement from the area, might have sojourned for some years at a place to the west of the city. The name Maya has survived in both places.

---

[157] The following section is summarized from Hassen 'The Oromo in the Medieval Muslim States of Southern Ethiopia', *Journal of Oromo Studies* 15, 1 (March 2008), 211–12.

[158] Braukämper, *Islamic History and Culture in Southern Ethiopia*, 47.

[159] Haberland, *Galla Süd-Aethiopiens*, 137–8.

[160] Arab Faqih, Futuh Al-Habasha, *The Conquest of Abyssinia*, 298.

[161] Arab Faqih, *Futuh Al-Habasha* (Arabic text, Cairo, 1974), 254–5.

> Their resistance to [Imam Ahmad in the early 1530s] could indicate that they blamed some people who followed him, perhaps the Harla for their displacement.[162]

This is far-fetched on several grounds. First, there is no doubt whatsoever that the Maya were not a Tigrayan military unit that was settled in the region of Waj during the fifteenth century. The Maya were a Cushitic-speaking nomadic people, who were feared and dreaded by their neighbours for their use of deadly poisoned arrows. Second, there is no historical evidence which shows that the Afar nomads lived east of the city of Harar during the fifteenth and sixteenth centuries. In reality the region was in habited by sedentary Adare people, who were famous for their extensive farming. Third, there is no place name known as Maya east of the city of Harar. As we will see below, there are two names of fertile valleys known as Maya both located west and south-west of the city of Harar. Fourth, the Maya people resisted not only the Muslim force under Imam Ahmad, but all their enemies, including the Christians and the Oromo. Amazingly Aregay's work itself confirms that it was the poisoned arrow of the Maya people that killed Emperor Iskindir (1478–94).[163] (On the Maya resistance against the Oromo see Chapters 4 and 5). Fifth, and above all, there is no historical record which shows that the Maya people were displaced and forced to move from the region of Harar to the region of what is today Shawa. On the contrary, historical evidence shows that the Maya people lived in and around the region of Waj during the fifteenth and sixteenth centuries.

What is known about the Maya is that their history is shrouded in a number of uncertainties that make generalizations difficult. First and foremost, the name Maya itself is famous. 'Maya Devi – the goddess Maya, as she became known' was the mother of Buddha in India.[164] Maya was also the name of the people who created one of the most sophisticated civilizations in Central America between 300–900 CE. Second, Maya was an important genealogical name among the Oromo in Hararghe, in the Gibe region, and Wallaga. In Hararghe, the *Warra Maya* (the house of Maya) are regarded not only as 'the purest' of the Oromo but also as the sons of Babile, the founder of a sub-confederacy within the grand Qallo confederacy (see Map 5). Maya, in turn, is regarded as the founder of five *gosas*.[165] It does not appear that the Maya Oromo in Hararghe were the descendants of the Maya conquered and assimilated by the Borana Oromo pastoralists in Waj toward the

[162] Merid W. Aregay, 'Military Elites in Medieval Ethiopia', in Donald Crummey, ed., *Land, Literacy and the State in Sudanic Africa* (Trenton, NJ: The Red Sea Press, 2005), 177–8.

[163] Ibid., 177. See also J. Perruchon, trans. and ed., 'Histoire d'Eskender, d'Amda Seyon II et de Nâ'od, rois d'Ethiopie', in *Journal Asiatique*, 9, iii (1894), 343; Basset, *Journal Asiatique*, 12–13, 103.

[164] Deepak Chopra, *Buddha: A Story of Enlightenment* (New York: Harper Collins, 2007), 7.

[165] P. Paulitschke, 'Die Wanderungen der Oromo oder Gallas Ost-Afrikas', *Mittheilungen de Anthropologischen Gessellschaaft zu Wien* 19 (1889), 165–78.

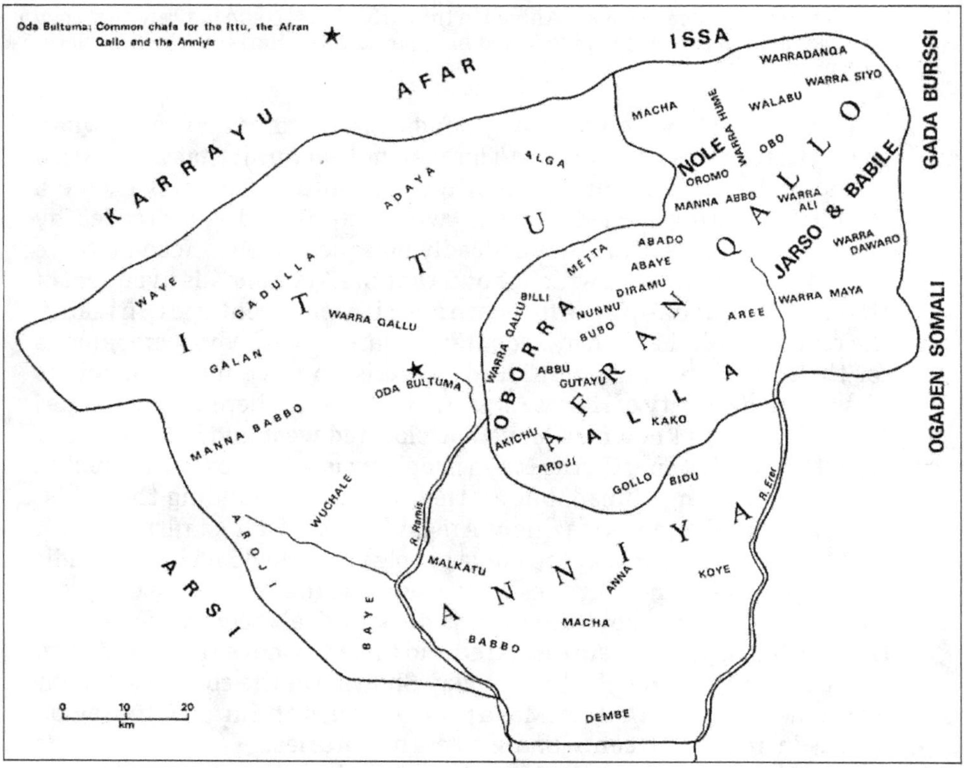

Map 5   The Eastern Oromo settlement area (adapted from Huntingford, *The Galla of Ethiopia: The Kingdoms of Kaffa and Janjero*, London: International African Institute, 1955, adapted by kind permission of the International African Institute).

end of the sixteenth century. The Hararghe Oromo, to which the Maya belonged, embarked on large-scale population movement from Dawaro and attacked the city of Harar in 1559, almost two or three decades before the Maya were conquered by the Borana Oromo during the 1570s and 1580s. This excludes the possibility that the Maya were assimilated by Hararghe Oromo in Waj. Maya is also the name of two fertile valleys not far from the city of Harar, Maya Guddo (the broad Maya) and Maya Qello (the narrow Maya), about seventeen to twenty-five kilometres (ten to fifteen miles) west and south-west of the city of Harar. The small rivers that run through the two valleys are also known by that name. Maya is also a name of a town and a lake, about twenty kilometres (twelve miles) west of the city of Harar on the way to Dire Dawa. In addition, Maya is an important proper name among the Oromo both in Hararghe and elsewhere.

Among the Oromo in Wallaga, Ulla Maya (the door of Maya), the last stop of the Oromo before they crossed the Birbir River to Qellem, had special significance in the *gada* system. The Sayyo Oromo depended on Ulla Maya for their *bokku*, the wooden sceptre kept by the leader of the assembly. It was also to Ulla Maya that the Sayyo Oromo went for the final decision of court cases that could not be solved at the *bokku* council.[166] Today, we also find Ammaya Oromo in the district of Gurage west of Nonno in the modern region of Shawa. These are certainly the descendants of Bahrey's Ameye, who were mentioned as an important *gosa* group within the huge Macha confederacy.[167]

PRE-SIXTEENTH-CENTURY OROMO PRESENCE IN DAWARO (SEE MAP 6)

The province of Dawaro was bordered by Adal in the north and east, by Bali in the south, by Hadiya and Sharka in the east, and by the country of Maya in the north-east.[168] This was the most easterly of the Christian provinces and the richest. Braukämper states that the inhabitants of Dawaro were probably Hadiya/Sidam.[169] Aregay claims that the population was heterogeneous Christian and Muslim, speaking Amharic as well as Argobba, who lived in the districts near Fatagar and Ifat, whereas the people living in the eastern parts were probably related to Adare. Neither scholar suspects that some Oromo groups may have lived in Dawaro long before the sixteenth century.[170]

---

[166] Gidada, *History of Sayyoo Oromo*, 29–30.

[167] Bahrey, 'History of the Galla', in *Some Records of Ethiopia*, 113.

[168] Ulrich Braukämper, 'Islamic Principalities in Southeast Ethiopia between the Thirteenth and Sixteenth Centuries', *Ethiopianist Notes* 1, 2 (1977), 18–19. See also E. Cerulli, *Studi Etiopici 1: La Lingua e la Storia di Harar* (Rome: Istituto per l'Oriente, 1936), 18.

[169] Braukämper, *Islamic History and Culture in Southern Ethiopia*, 75.

[170] Ibid., 20. See also Merid Wolde Aregay, 'Political Geography of Ethiopia at the Beginning of the Sixteenth Century', in *IV Congresso Internazionale di Studi*

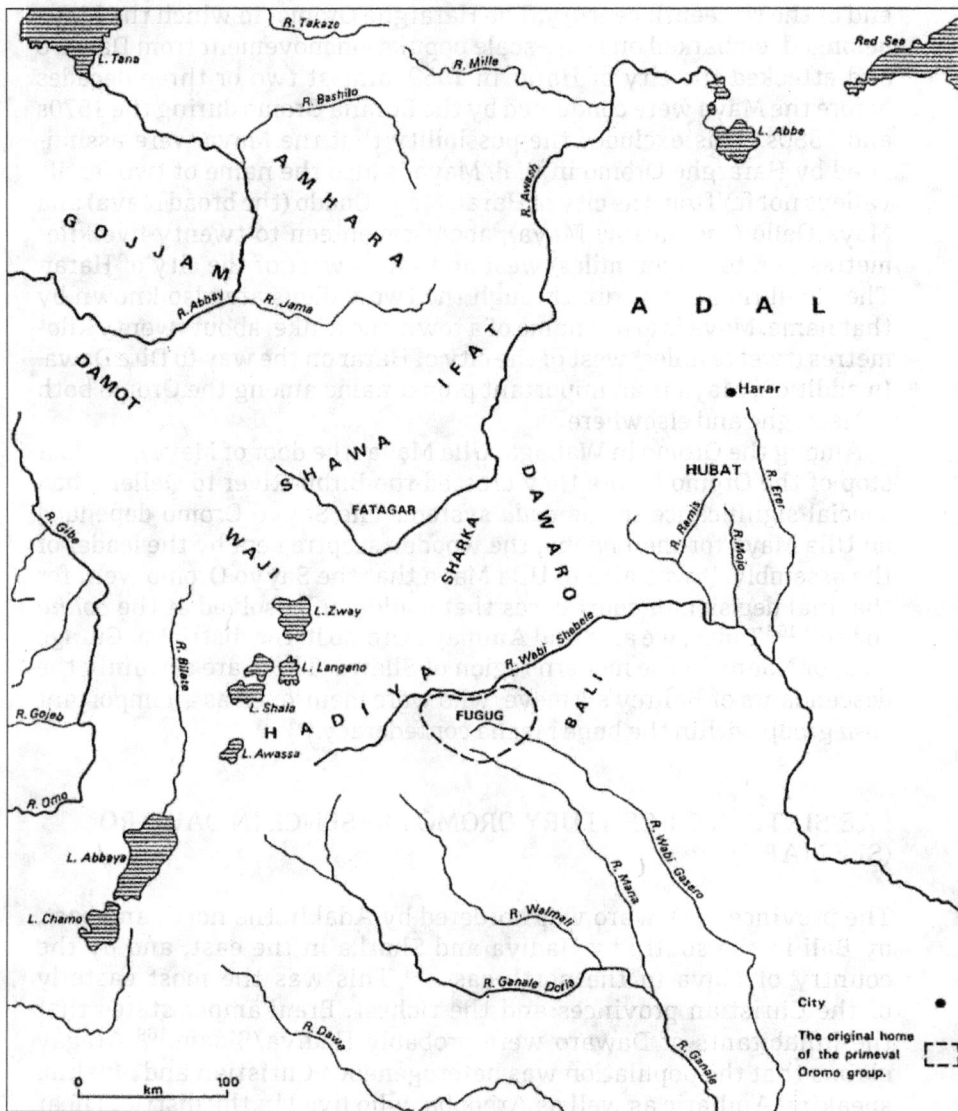

Map 6   The probable location of Fugug around 1330 (adapted from Hassen, 'The Oromo of Ethiopia, 1500–1850', PhD diss., University of London, 1983).

Braukämper[171] goes on to claim that the vast area between the Omo River and the Indian Ocean coast 'was occupied in the thirteenth century by groups of Ethiopic race who partly spoke Cushitic or Semitic languages'.[172] To what 'Ethiopic' race refers is not clear from Braukämper's work. What is clear is that he is intent on establishing as a fact his opinion that the Oromo did not exist in this vast area before the middle of the sixteenth century. His view was probably influenced by Eike Haberland's theory that the entire area stretching from the Gibe Valley to the highlands of Hararghe was occupied by a large group of Semitic-speaking people who were split up and fragmented after the middle of the sixteenth century during the pastoral Oromo population movement.[173] In reality no single Muslim state that extended from the highlands of Hararghe to the Gibe Valley did exist for the Oromo to split. Instead there were several Muslim states that were conquered by King Amda-Siyon, (during 1329–32) and incorporated into the expanding Christian empire. In fact Haberland's theory is not different in content from that of Cerulli, who claimed that the whole region between Bali and Gibe region was peopled with Sidama.[174]

Interestingly Braukämper replaced the theories of Haberland and Cerrlli by his own, positing that the Hadiya people inhabited the area from Hararghe to the Gibe region. The evidence he presents in support of this is the oral tradition he gathered in 1972 and 1973 in Hadiya land.

> The intensity with which the original connection is perceived is manifested in the fact that the ancestor of Hadiyya is considered the son of Abadir, the legendary founder of Harar, and an indigenous (Sidama) woman. This indicates that the Hadiyya ethnogenices [ethnogenesis; i.e. the birth or formation of Hadiya identity] probably took place in the Hararge region and that the forefathers were representatives of a relatively homogenous culture based on a symbiosis of autochthonous Africans with a thin substratum of Muslim Arabs. The study of historical and ethnological details proves this.[175]

There is no study that proves what Braukämper claims to be true. In fact, his conclusion is untenable historically. First, the Hadiya are part of the eastern-Cushitic-language-speaking people, who have lived in the region for thousands of years. It is historically inaccurate to establish an Arab ancestry for the Hadiya based on traditions that may have only symbolic value. For instance, just like the Hadiya, some Oromo groups in the Gibe region claimed that Sheikh Abadir (the thirteenth-century

(contd) *Etiopici* (Rome: Accademia Nazionale dei Lincei, 1974), 624–5; Cerulli, *Studi Etiopici* 1, 18. The Argobba were a Semitic-language-speaking Muslim population of Ifat, who fiercely resisted the expansion of the Christian kingdom.
[171] The following section is summarized from Hassen 'The Oromo in the Medieval Muslim States of Southern Ethiopia', 206–9.
[172] Braukämper, *Islamic History and Culture*, 15.
[173] Haberland, *Galla Süd-Aethiopiens*, 77–78.
[174] E. Cerulli, *Studi Etiopici 2: La Lingua e La Storia del Sidamo* (Rome: Istituto per l'Oriente 1938), 1–2, 31–33.
[175] Braukämper, *Islamic History and Culture*, 61

Arab missionary) was their ancestor. Such a claim only reflects the importance of Abadir as the standard- bearer of Islam and had nothing to do with Oromo ancestry. Even more confusingly, Braukämper also makes the Hadiya both Cushitic- and Semitic-language speakers.[176] How could they become both Cushitic- and Semitic-language speakers at the same time?

Braukämper did not seem to realize that oral traditions collected in 1972/73 are not helpful about the events of the fourteenth and fifteenth centuries. Oral traditions about remote events need to be supported by corroborating evidence. Without corroborating evidence, the scholar's conclusion is nothing more than a conjecture. In fact, Braukämper himself provides evidence for the presence of some Oromo groups in Dawaro when he writes 'the Tullu Moti (Oromo: "king's hill") near Asba Tafari [Chiro in western Hararghe] was so named because it is said to have served as a place of residence for Christian rulers ... This place Tullu Moti is especially connected with Zara Yai'eqob.'[177] If the Oromo were not in the region mentioned by Braukämper, what explains the fact that the Christian rulers' palace was named Tullu Moti or 'the hill of the king' in the Oromo language? Could non-Oromo speakers give an unmistakable Oromo place name, without the presence of the Oromo themselves? What Braukämper fails to realize is that there are a number of pieces of historical evidence, briefly mentioned below, confirming the presence of some Oromo groups in Dawaro during the fourteenth and fifteenth centuries.

Notwithstanding Braukämper's conclusive assertions, even Amhara oral traditions are unanimous that the ancestor of the Oromo was born in Dawaro. These traditions, which are considered no more than fables,[178] are supported by Arab Faqih, historian of the Jihad of Imam Ahmad (1527–43), who strongly suggests that the Amhara traditions reflect some form of historical reality. In 1529, Muslim forces chasing the Christian general Ras Nabyat in Dawaro arrived in the village of Mashib in the country of Warra Qaalluu, where they ravaged and burned the countryside, captured weapons and carried inhabitants into slavery.[179] Arab Faqih also mentions a river called Buro in the country of Warra Qaalluu, a name of unmistakable Oromo origin. The Warra Qaalluu was an important Oromo sub-moiety whose descendants are still found in Wallo, Hararghe and Wallaga regions as well as among the Borana in southern Ethiopia and northern Kenya. In this Arabic source, the Warra Qaalluu are referred to not as nomads but as seden-tary agriculturalists. Following the jihadic turmoil and the subsequent pastoral Oromo population movement, the Warra Qaalluu seem to have joined the migrating Oromo, abandoning farming in favour of pasto-ralism. Several other groups (both Oromo and non-Oromo) followed a similar path, mainly because of the unsettled situation that exposed

[176] Ibid., 66.
[177] Ibid., 36.
[178] Aregay, 'Southern Ethiopia and the Christian Kingdom', 153.
[179] Arab Faqih, *Futuh Al-Habasha*, 135–7.

the farming communities to a series of disasters. Arab Faqih also mentions an important Oromo place name, Andourah or Andhura (literally centre or umbilical cord), in Dawaro. This was where the famous Christian general Wasan Sagad had built a church, whose construction took eleven years and was described as magnificent and without comparison in the province.[180] The church was later looted and burned by the Muslims. Andourah seems to have been the headquarters of the Christian forces in the province. It was also the headquarters for Muslims, and the Imam stayed there on a number of occasions.[181] From Andourah, on one occasion, the Imam went to Qonburah (a common Oromo place name), above the market of Dawaro, where the inhabitants received him warmly. What is more, Arab Faqih also mentions Oromo personal names 'such as Dallu and Jalati'.[182] What is intriguing but difficult to explain is that, according to Harar tradition, an Oromo group lived in the fourteenth century on the banks of the Ramis River, a tributary of the Wabi Shebelle. Oromo Ramis[183] were located by the tradition of Abadir around the Wabi bend, where the provinces of Bali, Dawaro and Hararghe had a common boundary. It is impossible to draw any firm conclusion, because Arab Faqih is silent on the topography of this area. However, three points may be added here. First, Muslim tradition maintains that Awu Said, a disciple and a contemporary of Sheikh Abadir (the early thirteenth-century standard bearer of Islam in the city of Harar), is reported to have conducted missionary activities among some Oromo groups in western Hararghe, which was part of historical Dawaro.[184] Secondly, 'the hagiography of Sheikh Yusuf Aw Barkhadale' (who died after 1289), reports the miracles that caused the death of 'a pagan Galla [chief] called Qanana',[185] who resisted conversion to Islam. Although this may have an element of a legend, it is astonishing that the term Galla already entered written Somali sources before or around the beginning of the fourteenth century. Third, the oldest reference to an Oromo clan or sectional name was first made 'in the hagiography of Sheik Ishaq Ahmed of Alawi', who is said to have travelled among the Arsi Oromo. 'The mention of Arsi proves that the Oromo were mostly known by their sectional names as early as the twelfth century'.[186] Finally, the Oromo putative descent groups who use the political denomination of Dawaro are still found in Hararghe among the Nole Daga Warre Hume[187] (see Map 5). Besides, several Oromo groups in

[180] Stenhouse, *Futuh Al-Habasha, The Conquest of Abyssinia*, 144.

[181] Ibid.

[182] Quoted in Daniel Ayana, 'The "Galla" that Never Was: Its Origin and Reformulation in a Hinterland of Comparative Disadvantage', *Journal of Oromo Studies* 17, 1 (March 2010), 16.

[183] E. Wagner, trans. & ed., *Legende und Geschichte: Der Fath Madinat Harar von Yahya Nasrallah* (Wiesbaden: Steiner, 1978), 120–1.

[184] Haile, *History of the Oromo to the Sixteenth Century*, 81–82.

[185] Ayana, 'The "Galla" that Never Was', 15.

[186] Ibid., 16.

[187] E. Scarin, *Hararino Ricerche e Studi Geografici* (Florence: Centro di Studi Colonial, 1942), 86. See also M. Mokhtar, 'Notes sur le pays de Harrar', *Bulletin*

Hararghe repeatedly mention Dawaro as the place of their origin, probably reflecting the long Oromo presence in that historic province.[188]
Another Oromo descent group that uses the name Dawaro is also found
in Wallaga and other regions. What all the above demonstrates is the
long Oromo presence in the region of historical province of Dawaro.

PRE-SIXTEENTH-CENTURY OROMO PRESENCE IN FATAGAR (SEE MAP 6, ABOVE)

Fatagar was one of the Muslim states conquered by Emperor
Amda-Siyon between 1329 and 1332. It appears that some Oromo
groups including Galan, Yaya and Lalo may have lived in Fatagar.
According to widespread Oromo tradition, the famous Oromo political and religious centre, known as Oda Nabe, was located in Fatagar.
Negaso Gidada claims that Oda Nabe, located in Fatagar about thirty
kilometres east of the present city of Addis Ababa, emerged as an
Oromo political and religious centre in 1230 CE. Gidada's date is based
on oral traditions that are not supported by written evidence.[189]
Although the time for the beginning of Oda Nabe is suspect, Oromo
traditions are unanimous in asserting that Oda Nabe served as the
centre of Abba Muudaa pilgrimage during the second half of the
thirteenth century. Two factors are given for the movement of Abba
Muudaa pilgrimage from Oda Nabe in Fatagar to Oda Roba in Bale.
First, tradition claims that it was the assassination of the influential
Oditu Qaalluu, from Galan family[190] which led to the movement of the
centre of the Abba Muudaa pilgrimage from Oda Nabe to Oda Roba, in
Bale, in 1316.[191] The second and more plausible reason for this change
was the pressure exerted by the expansion of the Christian kingdom
during the reign of Emperor Amda-Siyon.[192] It is important to note
here that during the first half of the fourteenth century, Oda Roba was
located beyond the control of the Christian kingdom.

PRE-SIXTEENTH-CENTURY OROMO PRESENCE IN BALI (SEE MAP 6, ABOVE)

The important Muslim trading state of Bali, where the shrine of Shaikh
Hussein is the rallying point for all the Muslims in the southern region
of Ethiopia, was bordered by Dawaro and Sharka in the north, Hadiya
in the west, Adal and Dawaro in the east, and the huge grazing ground

---

(contd) *de la Société Khédiviale de Géographie* (Cairo, 1877), 357–97.

[188] Haile et al., *History of the Oromo to the Sixteenth Century*, 81.

[189] Gidada, *History of Sayyoo Oromo*, 28–30.

[190] Haile et al., *History of the Oromo to the Sixteenth Century*, 55.

[191] Ibid., 56. The cause for the assassination of Oditu Qaalluu is given as his
involvement in political conflict, which his religious role forbids.

[192] Bulcha, *Contours of the Emergent and Ancient Oromo Nation*, 162.

of the Oromo pastoralists in the south. In the past, it has been claimed that the historical Bali was the 'original home' of all Sidama peoples. This theory, which was first propagated by Cerulli and later perpetuated by many scholars, no longer seems valid. In the next chapter, I will show the Oromo presence within and in the immediate surroundings of the historical province of Bali in or before the sixteenth century. Here it should suffice to say that the majority of the eastern Oromo pastoralists lived in the lowlands of what is today referred to as the Bale region, the *awraja* (sub-province) of Fasil, in Dallo on the banks of the Ganale River, whereas the agriculturalists lived in the highlands of the historical Bali itself.[193] This is supported by the information in the book of Arab Faqih, where unmistakable place names, such as Qaqmah and Malu, among others, have been mentioned. It was in Qaqmah where the forces of Imam Ahmad captured the governor of the district Takla Haymanot, whose wife became the concubine of the Muslim leader. Imam Ahmad called her Hajrah and took her with him in the conquest of Abyssinia. 'She bore him a son.'[194] According to Arab Faqih, 'The land of Malu is the center of Bale,' which was 'plundered of its wealth, ravaged and burnt and then reduced it to ashes.'[195] Qaqmah and Malu are typical Oromo place names. On the whole his 'reference to the "people of Bali" ... was a generalized identification of the Oromo in the lower altitudes of Bali'.[196]

Interestingly, Arab Faqih makes a clear distinction between the two types of fighting tactics that were used in Bali against the Muslim forces. On the one hand, there were Christians, who 'were indefatigable in fighting. They harassed the Muslims, attacking them from right and left.'[197] On the other hand, there was a typical guerrilla-type fighting practised in the province of Bali. Garad Kamal, the brother-in-law of Imam Ahmad, explained the tactics of the people of Bali:

> The people of Bali never fight in battle lines, and only fight by subterfuge. If you and your soldiers march at the front of your force, they will attack the stragglers at the rear of the army, and if you move against them, they will run away, but not far away. If you march in the rearguard, they will attack the vanguard of the army, and if you move against them they will run away, but not far. That is their ruse and their way of acting .... The Imam Ahmad said, 'we will outwit them with a trick of our own'.[198]

This sophisticated form of guerrilla fighting, which from Arab Faqih's report seems to have been highly developed and used in Bali, was similar if not identical to the type of guerrilla warfare with which the pastoral Oromo terrified the entire region during their epoch-making population movement (see Chapters 4, 5, 7 and 8). It is very likely that the Oromo

---

[193] Tasawo Merga, 'Senna Umatta Oromo : Jalqaba jarra kudha Jahafti hamma dhumiti jarra kudha Sagalafanti' (Addis Ababa: 1976, unpublished manuscript), 8–9.
[194] Arab Faqih, *Futuh Al-Habasha, The Conquest of Abyssinia*, 112.
[195] Ibid., 131.
[196] Ayana, 'The "Galla" that Never Was', 16.
[197] Arab Faqih, *Futuh Al-Habasha, The Conquest of Abyssinia*, 135.
[198] Ibid., 116.

developed a guerrilla style of hit-and-run fighting method in response to the pressure of the southward-expanding Christian kingdom. The Oromo may not have invented the hit-and-run tactics of wearing down an enemy, but they do appear to have developed it into an effective fighting method that transformed them into formidable warriors.

Haberland reports an important tradition claiming that the Arsi Oromo, who were part of the eastern Oromo, had already broken away from the main body some 'sixty' years – or two generations – before 1522, leaving their area near Wabi Shebelle River and moving to the central highlands.[199]

Finally, the evidence variously presented has clearly established the pre-sixteenth-century Oromo presence within the medieval Christian kingdom of Ethiopia. The *Hagara Galla of Amda Siyon's Chronicle*, the Galla River and the Galla Forest of the local Christian literature, and the Galla River of Fra Mauro's map point to a long contact between the Amhara and some Oromo groups. The Galan, Yaya, Liban, Lalo and Waji Oromo, were putative descent groups that lived in and around the region of Shawa long before the sixteenth century. Arab Faqih refers to a number of sedentary Oromo groups, including the large Warra Qaalluu group, who lived under Christian administration. This further confirms the pre-sixteenth-century Oromo presence in the kingdom.

The sedentary agricultural Oromo communities who lived in and to the south of the present region of Shawa in the pre-sixteenth-century period were under the control of Christian administration. However, the pastoral Oromo groups who lived in some parts of what are today the regions of Bale, Sidamo and Gamu Gofa lived beyond the boundaries and outside the control of the Christian kingdom. It was these pastoral groups who launched the massive sixteenth century population move-ment that changed the history of the Oromo and radically altered the political landscape of the region. The chapters on pastoral Oromo popu-lation movements of the sixteenth and seventeenth centuries will extensively depict this process.

---

[199] Haberland, *Galla Süd-Aethiopiens*, 511.

3

The Homelands of the Pastoral Oromo before 1500

A book dealing with history of the Oromo and the Christian kingdom of Ethiopia c. 1300–1700 cannot avoid addressing the location of the Oromo cradleland. The search for this began in the 1620s[1] and continues in recent publications by scholars Mekuria Bulcha and Eloi Ficquet.[2] According to Bairu Tafla, the question remains, by and large, unresolved.[3] The Oromo, however, claim only Ethiopia as their land of origin. The aim of this chapter is to synthesize the available information on the controversial subject of the Oromo cradleland and clearly establish an area that may be designated as the birthplace of Oromo national institutions, sanctioned as sacred land in their traditional religion, as well as to indicate the locations of the homelands of the Borana and Barentu moieties. I argue that it was from six separate homelands within the boundaries of the modern Ethiopia that the pastoral Oromo groups launched their large population movements from the mid-fifteenth century to the mid-sixteenth century. My analysis is based on oral traditions, early chronicles and linguistic evidence.

There have been persistent attempts in Ethiopian historiography to present the Oromo as the sixteenth-century 'New Invaders' of Ethiopia, in spite of the fact that the Oromo are one of the original inhabitants of that country.[4] Some scholars assumed that the Oromo originated beyond Africa,[5] others that they came from central

[1] See for instance, Manoel de Almeida, trans. and ed. by C.F. Beckingham and G.W.B. Huntingford, *Some Records of Ethiopia 1593–1646*, (London: Hakluyt Society, 1954), 133–4.

[2] Mekuria Bulcha, *Contours of the Emergent and Ancient Oromo Nation: Dilemmas in the Ethiopian Politics of State and Nation-Building* (Cape Town: The Centre for Advanced Studies of African Society, 2011), chapter 4. See also Eloi Ficquet, (trans. Ayalew Kanno) 'Fabrication of Oromo Origins', *Journal of Oromo Studies* 14, 2 (July 2007), 105–30 (originally 'La Fabrique des origines Oromo', *Annales d'Ethiopie* 18 (2002), 55–71).

[3] Bairu Tafla, (trans. and ed.) *Asma Giyorgis and His Work: History of the Galla and the Kingdom of Sawa* (Stuttgart: Franz Steiner, 1987), 50.

[4] Darrel Bates, *The Abyssinian Difficulties: The Emperor Theodorus and the Magdala Campaign, 1867–68*, (Oxford: Oxford University Press, 1979), 7.

[5] Asma Giyorgis, followed by others, claimed that the Oromo originated in Asia and came to Ethiopia via Madagascar. See Tafla, *The Works of Asma*

Africa,[6] others still that the Oromo originated either in Somalia[7] or Northern Kenya,[8] all thus placing their cradleland outside the boundaries of modern Ethiopia. This hypothesis finds support in the works of the sixteenth- and seventeenth-century Portuguese writers and in Somali oral traditions, if the latter are taken at face value. The Portuguese writings depend heavily on the works of the Christian monk, Abba Bahrey.[9] For some scholars, Bahrey's manuscript *Zenahu le Galla* establishes 1522 as the beginning of documented Oromo history.[10] The pastoral Oromo themselves, however, have never claimed any homeland other than the regions of Bale, Sidamo and Gamu Gofa, yet very few authors have paid attention to what their oral tradition had to say about their homelands. Careful interpretation of these traditions provides insight into the political economy of their different homelands on the eve of their history-making massive population movement.

As indicated in the previous chapters, received wisdom about early Oromo history is limited to the time of their population movement, which began during the second half of the fifteenth century but gathered dramatic momentum in the aftermath of the devastating Christian and Muslim conflict between 1529 and 1543. Wanting to explain the reasons for the Muslims' spectacular victories, the Christian chroniclers claimed that the 'lax morals' of the Christian leadership in conjunction with certain 'pagan Oromo practices' resulted in the Christian defeat.[11] In other words:

> the 'coming of the Galla' is perceived ... as a punishment and a form of expiation for the country's sins, particularly those of its ruler Lebna Dengel whose

(contd) *Giyorgis*, 137 note 166. Martial de Salviac connected the Oromo with ancient Gauls in France. See his *An Ancient People: A Great African Nation – The Oromo,* Translation from the Original French Edition, Ayalew Kanno (Self-published, 2005), 367–9.

[6] Charles Beke believed that the Oromo came from Central Asia. See his article 'On the Origin of the Galla'. Reprint from *The British Association for the Advancement of Science* (London: 1847), 6–7. See also Antoine d' Abbadie, 'On the Oromo', 119.

[7] I.M. Lewis, 'The Galla in Northern Somaliland', *Rassegna di Studi Etiopici 15* (1959), 21–38.

[8] Richard Pankhurst, 1997. *The Ethiopian Borderlands*, 279. See also his *The Ethiopians* (Malden, MA: Blackwell Publishers Inc., 1998), 96. Pankhurst, who has studied Ethiopia for more than half a century claims that the existence of the Oromo 'seems to have been first recognized in Fra Mauro's Mappamondo of 1460', 96. Such a claim betrays the author's unfamiliarity with early Oromo history.

[9] On Abba Bahrey, see Mohammed Hassen, 'The Historian Abba Bahrey and the Importance of His "History of the Galla"', *Horn of Africa*, 13, 3 & 4/14, 1 & 2 (July–December 1990 / January–June 1991), 90–106.

[10] U. Braukämper, 'Oromo Country of Origin: A Reconsideration of Hypotheses', *Ethiopian Studies: Proceedings of the Sixth International Conference*, 14–17 April 1980, ed. Gideon Goldenberg (Boston: A.A. Balkema, 1986), 35.

[11] Gabra Sellassie, *Tarikà Zàman Zâ Dagmawi Menelik Negusà-Nàgast Zà-Ityopya* (Addis Ababa: Berhanena Selam Printing Press, 1965), 31.

unwarranted pride and pagan practices (allegedly modeled upon 'Galla' customs) opened the country to its fiercest enemies – Gran's [Imam Ahmad] conquests followed by the Oromo migration and to their threatening inroads into the heart of the Ethiopian state.[12]

In this way the story of the sudden arrival of the 'Galla' took root in the minds of the Christian monks and court chroniclers. Imagination transformed the Oromo into 'newcomers', the new enemy, envisioned as one half of 'a two-headed hydra: one "Galla" and another Muslim'.[13] This image contributed to the replacement of the struggle between the Christians and Muslims with the struggle of both against the Oromo. On the one hand, the 'newcomer' that emerges in the Christian tradition is a reflection of the sixteenth-century pastoral Oromo pressure on the Christian kingdom. On the other hand, it is partly a myth because some Oromo groups were indeed living in the Christian kingdom during the thirteenth and the fourteenth centuries. As a myth, it 'has a place and function in the society that has created it. Myths support cultural values and mediate points of stress.'[14] By the 1540s, pastoral Oromo population movements severely impacted Christian society in general and the ruling Amhara elite in particular. Consequently, since the sixteenth century, 'fears of Islam and of the Oromo have dominated the political consciousness of the Amhara ruling elite, and the thought of the two in combination has been a recurring nightmare'.[15]

In the previous chapter we have seen evidence that shows the presence of some Oromo groups in a number of provinces under Christian administration, including Bali, Dawaro, Waj, Fatagar and Ifat, at least since the fourteenth century. By the fifteenth century, if not much earlier, pastoral Oromo pressure was being felt within the Christian kingdom, particularly during the reign of King Baeda-Maryam (1468–78). Based on the evidence, M.R. Basset concludes that the Oromo were in the Christian kingdom during the fifteenth century.[16]

This chapter first looks at conceptions of the Oromo cradleland, from the sixteenth century to the present. It presents the perspectives of early chroniclers, traces the influence of Bahrey, and explores the views of scholars over the past fifty years. It focuses on how and where earlier

[12] Alessandro Triulzi, 'Oromo Traditions of Origin', *Etudes Ethiopiennes* Volume I, *Actes de la Xe Conférence Internationale des Études Éthiopiennes* (Paris, 24–28 August 1988), ed. Claude Lepage et al., (Paris: Publication de la Societe Francaise pour les Études Éthiopiennes, 1994), 596.

[13] Teshale Tibebu, *The Making of Modern Ethiopia, 1896–1974* (Lawrenceville, NJ: Red Sea Press, 1995), 17.

[14] I have drawn on Dorothy Hammond and Alta Jablow, *The Africa that Never Was: Four Centuries of British Writing about Africa* (Prospect Heights, IL: Waveland Press, 1992 (1970) reprint), 8.

[15] Paul Baxter, 'The Problem of the Oromo or the Problem for the Oromo', in I.M. Lewis, ed. *Nationalism and Self Determination in the Horn of Africa* (London: Ithaca Press, 1983), 132.

[16] M.R. Basset, *Études sur l'histoire d'Éthiopie I, Chronique Ethiopienne, extrait du Journal Asiatique*, 7, 18 (1882), 96, 139 (hereafter cited as Basset, *Journal Asiatique*).

historians have located the Oromo cradleland, presents a new argument for its location evidenced by oral sources, and looks at the pastoral Oromo population movement between 1300 and 1500.

THE QUESTION OF THE OROMO CRADLELAND

'Where did the Oromo come from?'[17] asks the eminent historian Bairu Tafla in a characteristically perceptive approach to the debate on the subject. He answers it by saying that the question about their homeland remains by and large open. Both the question and his answer, however, appear to have been based on the assumption that the Oromo arrived in the medieval Christian kingdom of Abyssinia only during the sixteenth century as sanctioned by Bahrey's *Zenahu le Galla*[18] and royal chronicles of the period. This section discusses the views of eight scholars on the question of Oromo cradleland, namely M.de. Almeida, C. Beke, E. Cerulli, I.M. Lewis, H.S. Lewis, E. Haberland, U. Braukämper and M. Bulcha.

The influence of early accounts
At the outset let me state clearly that the search for Oromo cradleland is hampered by reliance on biased sources and the misreading of Bahrey's manuscript. Abba Bahrey, who first wrote about Oromo social organization and the impact of their warfare on his Christian society, never claimed that they originated from outside Ethiopia. Bahrey stated that the Oromo, coming from the west, 'crossed the river of their country', and 'came to the frontier of Bali during the reign of Emperor Libna Dengel' (1508–40). [19] By 'their country', Bahrey means the region of Harroo Waallaabu. Bali indicates the historical province of Bali, the northern part of the present region of Arsi/Bale. W. Schleicher has identified 'the river of their country' with the Wabi Shebelle River.[20] Bahrey's information not only makes one section of the Oromo (i.e. the Borana) neighbours with the Christian kingdom, but also places their country squarely within the highlands of southern Ethiopia. The import of Bahrey's information was lost on subsequent scholars, who only concentrated on one aspect of his statement: the Oromo attack on the province of Bali. That attack probably took place around 1522. Bahrey, writing in 1593 – about seventy-one years after the first major Oromo attack on Bali, was emphasizing their military pressure on the Christian kingdom rather than identifying the location of their cradleland. The interpreters of Bahrey's information perpetuated the myth

---

[17] Tafla, *Asma Giyorgis and His Work*, 50.
[18] Of course Bahrey did not mention the exact date of the Oromo attack on Bali. It was on the basis of internal evidence that Huntingford suggested 1522 as the date of that event.
[19] Bahrey, 'History of the Galla' in *Some Records of Ethiopia, 1593–1646*, 111.
[20] Schleicher, *Geschichte der Galla*, 17, quoted in Tafla, *Asma Giyorgis and His Work*, 137, note 166.

about the 'sudden arrival of the Oromo' on the border of or within the medieval Christian kingdom.

The major weakness of Bahrey's manuscript is that while it dealt primarily with one section of Oromo society, it appeared to give accounts of the two major Oromo moieties named Borana and Baray-tuma (Barentu). Most scholars have accepted that his history discussed both groups adequately, even though he made it clear that he wrote mainly about the Borana. Even a superficial reading of the manuscript demonstrates that Bahrey was well acquainted with the Borana, who attacked his homeland of Gamo, which was located not far from the modern town of Shashemene in the region of what is today Shawa.[21] By contrast, Bahrey did not have first-hand knowledge about the Barentu groups, for whom he gathered information from others. He specifically states:

> Those who are accurately informed declare that when Boran [Borana] quit their country they do not all go, but those who wish to stay do so, and those who wish to leave do so ... Those of the Boran who stayed came out of their country by way of Kuera.[22]

This information seems to have led many scholars to assume that it was meant to apply to all Oromo pastoralists including the Barentu. Both Bahrey and other historical sources provide us with information to the contrary. A close examination of Bahrey's genealogical description of the two Oromo moieties reveals that his information on the Barentu is far from satisfactory, while that on the Borana is almost complete. For instance, Bahrey includes in his Borana genealogies more than sixty major *gosa* (putative descent groups) and sub-*gosa* names and around twenty-four for the Barentu, notwithstanding the fact that, at the time he was writing, the Barentu contained seven fully-fledged confederacies, while the Borana had only three. What is more, as I will briefly demonstrate in the next chapter, it was the larger Barentu groups who opened the drama of the large sixteenth-century pastoral Oromo population movement, repeatedly defeated the well-armed Christian and Muslim forces, and spread out over a wide territory. From what will be discussed in the next chapter and documented history, it is clear that the Barentu moiety of the Oromo was much larger than the Borana, but Bahrey's history[23] has it the other way around. In short, Bahrey's manuscript deals mainly with the Borana.

Based on Bahrey's incomplete information, the seventeenth-century Jesuit historian M. de Almeida places the land of *Ilma Orma* ('children of Oromo', i.e. the Oromo people) on the southern border of the medieval Christian kingdom of Abyssinia (see Map 7 below). 'They invaded', he tells us, 'the [province] of Bali, with which they had a common fron-

---

[21] Aregay, 'Southern Ethiopia and the Christian Kingdom, 309.
[22] Bahrey, 'History of the Galla', 112.
[23] Ibid., 113–14.

tier, or of which they were close neighbours.'[24] The significance of this statement seems to have been lost on scholars who accepted the year 1522 as the beginning of Oromo arrival in Bali. In the previous chapter we have seen four highly respected traditional historians, specifically Asma Giyorgis, Alaka Tayya, Gabra Sellassie and Takla Sadiq Makurya, conclude that some Oromo groups were living within the medieval Christian kingdom before, during and after the reign of Emperor Amda-Siyon (1314–44). It is interesting to note in passing that some Oromo groups were probably living within the medieval Christian kingdom for several centuries before Bahrey wrote his manuscript in 1593. Even if one accepts Asma Giyorgis' report that the Oromo arrived in the Christian kingdom at the beginning of the fifteenth century,[25] this was almost two centuries before the date of Bahrey's writing.

The nineteenth-century English traveller and scholar Charles Beke, basing his argument on the Amhara traditions of Oromo origin (which in essence placed the Oromo homeland somewhere south of the frontier of the Christian kingdom) and on traditions of the Oromo of Shawa, Wallo and Wallagga, which unanimously refer to either Bahr Gamo, Tullu Walal or Wallaabu (all located in the region Bahrey and Almeida indicated), arrives at the following conclusion:

> The name thus given by the [Oromo] to the country of their ancestors ... may seemingly be regarded as a proof that the primitive [Oromo] were the inhabitants, not of the plain country bordering on the Indian Ocean, where they were known to have settled upwards of two centuries, but rather of some high mountainous country.[26]

The thrust of this argument was that pastoral Oromo came from a high mountain-country south of the Christian kingdom. The essence of this conclusion is correct. However, it suffers from two shortcomings. First, Oromo oral traditions upon which Beke based his argument were mainly from the Borana section, and therefore do not give a complete picture. Second, and even more important, Beke believed that the Oromo entered the Christian kingdom through Wallagga from beyond the Baro River, in the west coming from central Africa.[27] This reflects the prevailing nineteenth-century conception that the Oromo came from outside Ethiopia.[28]

[24] M. de Almeida, 'The History of High Ethiopia or Abassia', in *Some Records of Ethiopia*, 134.

[25] Bairu Tafla, *Asma Giyorgis and His Work*, 137.

[26] C. Beke, 'On the Origin of the Gallas', *Report to the 1847 meeting of the British Association for the Advancement of Science*, (London, 1848), 7.

[27] Ibid., 6–7. See also Antoine d'Abbadie, Nouv. Acq. Franc. No. 21300, Folio, 729.

[28] In the nineteenth century a number of writers assumed that the Oromo came from outside Ethiopia. Among others, see C.E.X. Rochet d'Héricourt, *Voyage sur la Côte Orientale de la Mer Rouge: dans le pays d'Adel et le Royaume de Choa* (Paris: Arthus-Bertrand, 1841), 205–6. See also Paul Soleillet, *Voyages en Éthiopie: Janvier 1882–Octobre 1884: Notes, Lettres et Documents Divers* (Rouen: Cagniard, 1886), 253.

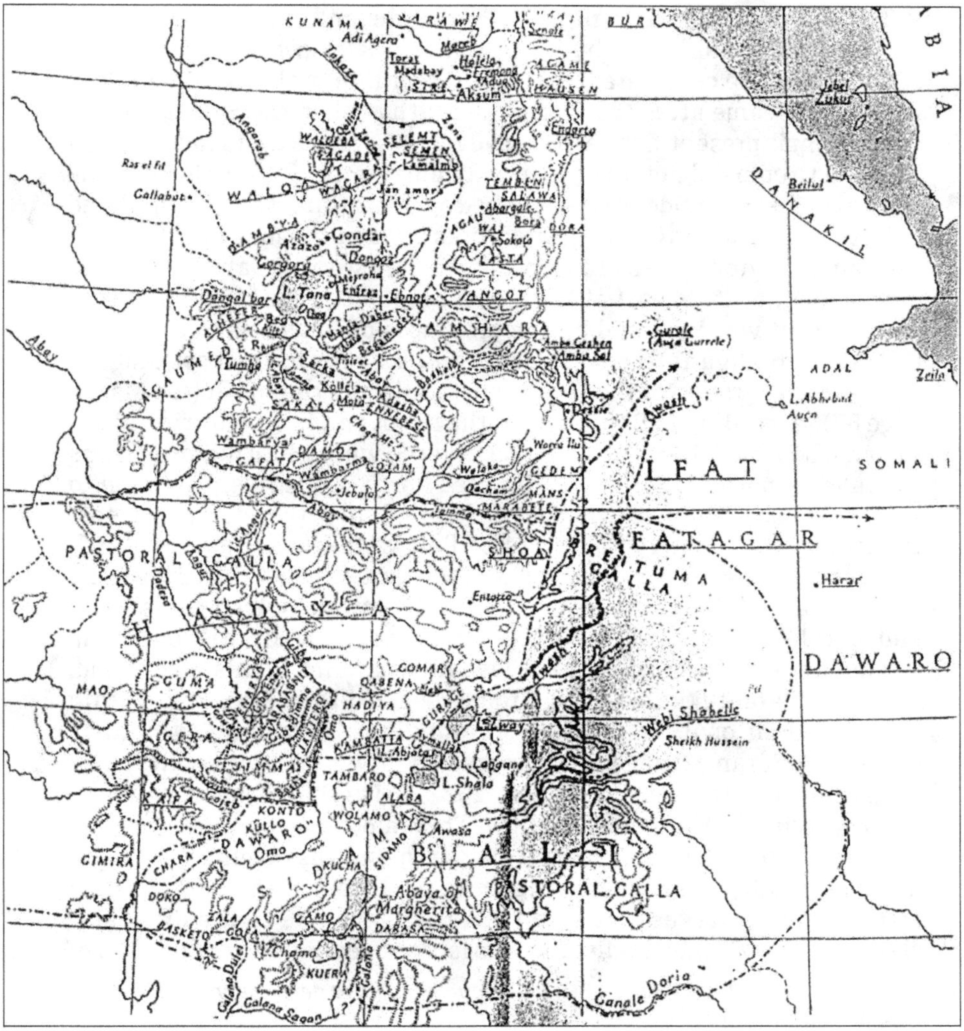

Map 7   Almeida's map of Abyssinia, showing the original homeland of the Oromo according to the seventeenth-century Portuguese missionary, Almeida (adapted from Beckingham and Huntingford, *Some Records of Ethiopia 1593–1646*, London: Hakluyt Society, 1954, by kind permission of Hakluyt Society).

The suggestion that Bali was the 'cradleland' of all the Sidama people, first promulgated by E. Cerulli and later accepted by others, can no longer be considered plausible. According to this argument, the Oromo who came after 1522 from the south pushed the Sidama people west to their present habitat.[29] However, two researchers have shown that the Oromo did not dislodge the Sidama people from Bali.[30] On the contrary, there is evidence that settled agricultural Oromo groups lived in Bali[31] itself, while Oromo pastoralists lived in the lowlands south of the same province.[32] As already indicated, historical Bali was located in the north-eastern part of the present regions of Arsi/Bale (see Map 1, page 6). It was bordered by the provinces of Dawaro and Sharka to the north, Hadiya to the west, Adal and Dawaro to the east and the large grazing ground of the Oromo pastoralists to the south (see Map 4, page 87). According to Braukämper, the major part of Bali territory was situated south of the Wabi Shabelle River[33], while Huntingford claims that a large portion of Bali was situated north of the river.[34] For Merid Wolde Aregay, 'the most densely inhabited and, therefore, the most effectively administered districts of Bali were in the more elevated northern and western region'.[35] These scholars suggest that the Oromo lived outside of historical Bali. E. Cerulli (followed by J.S. Trimingham and Merid Wolde Aregay) has extended the southern frontier of Bali up to the Ganale, which includes the lowlands of Dallo. If this is accepted, the entire Barentu (i.e. eastern) Oromo seem to have been either within historical Bali or its immediate surroundings. According to Bahrey, it was the Borana Oromo who crossed the river of their country and arrived on the frontiers of Bali in 1522.[36] The Barentu Oromo were already living in the same province. This important fact, the implication of which will become clearer further on in this documented argument, is totally overlooked or ignored or distorted in the Ethiopian historiography. It was this distortion that gave rise to the untenable claim that the Oromo cradleland was located beyond the boundaries of

[29] E. Cerulli, *Studi Etiopici*, Vol II, *La Lingua e la Storia del Sidamo*, (Rome: Istituto per l'Oriente 1938), 6.

[30] Tasawo Merga, 'Senna Umatta Oromo: Jalqaba jarra kudha Jahafti hamma dhumiti jarra kudha Sagalafanti' (Addis Ababa: 1976), unpublished manuscript ('History of the Oromo People: From the Beginning of the Sixteenth Century to the End of the Nineteenth Century', 6–8. (Hereafter cited as 'Senna Umatta Oromo'). See also S. Stanley, *History of the Sidama* (Addis Ababa: 1967), 19, quoted in U. Braukämper, 'Islamic Principalities in Southeast Ethiopia between the Thirteenth and Sixteenth Centuries', *Ethiopianist Notes* 1, 2 (1977), 25–26.

[31] Haberland, *Galla Süd-Aethiopians*, 772. See also his map on page 6.

[32] Merga, ibid., 8.

[33] Braukämper, 'Islamic Principalities in Southeast Ethiopia', 25.

[34] Huntingford, *The Glorious Victories of Amda Seyon, King of Ethiopia* (Oxford: Clarendon Press, 1965), 22.

[35] Merid Wolde Aregay, 'Political Geography of Ethiopia at the Beginning of Sixteenth Century' in *IV Congresso International di Studi Etiopici*, vol. 1 (Rome: Accademia Nazionale dei Lincei, 1974), 625–6.

[36] Bahrey, 'History of the Galla', 111.

modern Ethiopia. However, I will demonstrate in this chapter that the cradleland and the homelands of pastoral Oromo were located in what is today Ethiopia, in the regions of Bale, Sidamo and Gamu Gofa.

Misleading information about the Oromo cradleland began in the 1620s and 1630s with Almeida who, using Bahrey's account, extended this area from the frontier of historical Bali to the Indian Ocean. 'These lands lying between Bali and the sea, the coast of which sailors call "the desert" is the real home and fatherland of the [Oromo]'[37] (see Map 7 above). However, closer inspection of Almeida's map shows clearly that the area referred to was quite distinct from the coast and lay to the south-west of Bali, as Abba Bahrey had suggested. B. Tellez, writing in 1710 using Almeida's information, concluded that 'these lands that lie between Bali and the ocean are the proper country and habitation of the [Oromo]', thus placing the Oromo cradleland in Somalia.[38] By the early twentieth century, the hypothesis that stemmed from Bahrey's incomplete account and Almeida's innocent geographical ignorance was firmly established and fortified in a corpus of scholarly works. This was further reinforced by the addition of 'new' elements such as Somali pressure, Somali oral traditions, the remnants of Oromo-speaking communities in northern Somalia and the so-called 'Galla graves' in northern Somalia.[39] Trimingham claimed that it was the social upheaval amongst Somalis clans at the beginning of the sixteenth century that 'so utterly uprooted' the Oromo from Ogaden region in what is today eastern Ethiopia and southern Somalia 'that the very whereabouts of their former home can only be conjectured and they migrated en masse to find new ranges'.[40]

I.M. Lewis: northern Somalia

I.M. Lewis suggests that the Oromo lived in northern Somalia as far back as the eleventh century. He argues that around the twelfth century the Dir Darod (a powerful Somali confederacy) had already begun the long process that expelled the Ishaq (another powerful confederacy) from their original dwelling place in northern Somalia.[41] It was presumably the Ishaq who, in turn, pushed the Oromo towards central Somalia, from where they were again perhaps pushed by Somali pressure in the sixteenth century.

[37] M. de Almeida, 'The History of High Ethiopia or Abassia', in *Some Records of Ethiopia 1593–1646*, 133–4.
[38] B. Tellez, trans., John Stevens, *The Travels of the Jesuits in Ethiopia* (London: J. Knapton, Bell & Baker, 1710), 64.
[39] The residual Oromo-speaking communities in Northern Somalia were the remnants of those who migrated there in the sixteenth century. See, for instance, Mohammed Hassen, 'The Oromo of Ethiopia, 1500–1850: With Special Emphasis on the Gibe Region', 216–17.
[40] Trimingham, *Islam in Ethiopia* (London: Oxford University Press, 1952), 80.
[41] See, for instance, I.M. Lewis, 'The Galla in Northern Somaliland', 21–38; also I. M. Lewis, 'The Somali Conquest of the Horn of Africa', *Journal of African History* 1, 2 (July 1960), 213–30.

> To some extent this Somali expansion and [Oromo] withdrawal coincided with Imam Ahmad's invasion of Abyssinia ... Certainly prior to their retreat to the south and south-west .... the [Oromo] occupied central Somalia to the north of the Shebelle River, and part of north-eastern Ethiopia including the Haud now occupied by the Ogaden Somali.[42]

This interpretation of Somali pressure, which depends heavily on Somali oral traditions, actually deals with Somali groups other than the Oromo. Perhaps one reason why scholars such as I.M. Lewis and E. Cerulli tend to interpret the struggle between the major Somali tribal groups as the struggle between the Somali and the Oromo was the great importance they attached to Somali oral traditions, which unanimously claim that the Somali fought continuously against the *Galo* ('pagan') or camel-owners who inhabited the land before them. Since pastoral Oromo lived in the highlands of southern Ethiopia, they did not originally own camels. They became camel-owners only after they moved to semi-arid lowland areas probably during the fifteenth and subsequent centuries. Somali oral tradition, which revolves around the term *Galo*, seems to have been uncritically taken by scholars to refer to the Galla (the Oromo) people. Ali Abdurahman Hersi, a Somali historian, has proven that the references in the Somali oral tradition were to non-Muslim Somali and not the Oromo people, at least during the thirteenth century.[43]

H.S. Lewis: Lakes Shamo and Stephane

H.S. Lewis, a scholar who has made immense contributions to our knowledge of Oromo society, provides us with useful information about the original home of the pastoral Oromo. Like most scholars of the 1960s, H.S. Lewis did not suspect the pre-sixteenth-century Oromo presence within the medieval Christian kingdom. Basing his analysis mainly on linguistic data, H.S. Lewis rejects the theses advanced by Cerulli and I.M. Lewis and argues that the Horn was the original home of neither the Oromo nor the Somali people. Instead, he states that the region of southern Ethiopia and northern Kenya was the original home for both groups. From this general standpoint, H.S. Lewis proceeds to the specific question of defining the exact location of what he termed as the original Oromo homeland in southern Ethiopia. He analyses the Oromo traditions of origin, Bahrey's *Zenahu le Galla* and Almeida's map, all in conjunction with linguistic data,[44] and arrives at the following conclusion:

[42] I.M. Lewis, *A Pastoral Democracy: A Study of Pastoralism and Politics among the Northern Somali of the Horn of Africa* (Oxford: Oxford University Press, 1960), 23.

[43] Ali Abdurahman Hersi, 'The Arab Factor in Somali History: The Origins and the Development of Arab Enterprise and Cultural Influence in the Somali Peninsula', PhD diss., U.C.L.A., 1977, 20–24. See also Shaikh Ahmad Abdullahi Risash, *Kashf As-Sudul con Tarikh as Sumal wa Hama Likahum*, (Mogadishu: 1974), 36–57.

[44] The usefulness of linguistic evidence for reconstructing early history in Africa has already been shown by many scholars. Among others, see Roland Oliver, 'The Problem of Bantu Expansion', *Journal of African History* 7, 3 (1966), 361.

The [Oromo] originated in the area between and around Lakes Shamo and Stephanie, in the area of the Galana Sagan and Galana Dulei just south of Bahrgamo and Mt. Walabo in north-west Borana. It is here that the closest linguistic relatives of the [Oromo] – Konso, Gato, Gidole, Arbore, Gawata, Warazi, Tsamai, Geleb – are found. The [Oromo] language was once one with these, and [Oromo] speakers even today live in this area. This is striking confirmation of Bahrey, of Almeida's map and of the oral traditions of the [Oromo] themselves.[45]

H.S. Lewis assumes that all pastoral Oromo lived in a single homeland[46] up to the time of their sixteenth century population movement, but this small area was just one of several homelands for Borana Oromo pastoralists. Lewis' claim that northern Kenya was part of original Oromo homeland is not supported by historical evidence. Furthermore, Lewis is incorrect in saying that Bahrey's home, Gamo, 'was one of the earliest areas to be attacked by the [Oromo]'[47] because we know from Bahrey's *Zenahu le Galla* that his province of Gamo was attacked only in the 1570s,[48] almost half a century after the first reported attack on Bali in 1522, and long after the pastoral Oromo had attacked many provinces in many regions.

What is more, Lewis claims that the Oromo 'began their expansion about 1540 from south-central Ethiopia, probably south of Lake Abaya'.[49] This applies partly to the Borana Oromo movement, which had begun much earlier than 1540. However, Lewis does not seem to have realized that the population movement of the Barentu group began long before the sixteenth century.[50] Like several other scholars, H.S. Lewis assumed that the Oromo were nomads before and during their population movement, and that they all lived more or less in the same area. But we know for certain that the Oromo originally practised a mixed economy, which involved grain growing and cattle breeding.[51]

H. S. Lewis claims that the closest linguistic relatives to the Oromo, the Konso, Gidole and others, are found in the region which he describes as 'the original homeland of the [Oromo]'.[52] However, two studies that appeared after the 1963 Lewis article have clearly shown that the Konso and Gidole were dislodged from the Negelle area in Sidamo region across the Sagan River to their present habitat by the pressure of Borana Oromo. The Darassa also claim that they were expelled from their original home in Shakiro or Adola by the pressure of Guji Oromo, who now occupy the

[45] H.S. Lewis, 'The Origins of the Galla and Somali', *Journal of African History* 7, 1 (March 1966), 41.
[46] Toleera Tasmaa and Hundassa Waaqwayoo, *Sena Saba Oromoofi Sirna Gadaa*, (Addis Ababa: Artistic Press, 1995), 24.
[47] H.S. Lewis, 'The Origins of the Galla and Somali', 32.
[48] See, for instance, Hassen, 'The Oromo of Ethiopia, 1500–1850', 322.
[49] H.S. Lewis, ibid., 38.
[50] See for instance, Aregay, 'Southern Ethiopia and the Christian Kingdom', 153–7.
[51] Haberland, *Galla Süd-Aethiopiens*, 772.
[52] H.S. Lewis, 'The Origins of the Galla and Somali', 39.

region.[53] Finally, the area indicated by H.S. Lewis as the original home-land of the Oromo was the homeland of only the Borana Oromo. Despite minor shortcomings in his argument, Lewis has greatly contributed to establishing conclusively that the Oromo did not migrate to Ethiopia from outside the modern boundaries of that country.

Eike Haberland: Bali highlands

Haberland's ideas about the Oromo cradleland are particularly insightful because he based his analysis on massive data gathered from the Oromo themselves. His interpretation was a radical departure from the received wisdom about the Oromo cradleland. He writes:

> It appears quite certain to me that their [Oromo] true ancestral home was the cool highlands in the region of Bali. There they lived in a tribe with mixed cattle-rearing and grain-growing economy, until for reasons unknown to us there was a rapid rise in the population.[54]

In support of his conclusion, Haberland presents a number of salient points. First, Oromo themselves locate their origin in the highlands of the middle south. Second, to their traditions may be added other evidence, such as the myths surrounding the origin of their high priests (Qaalluu) and pilgrimage to the Abba Muudaa. Third, their main cereal crop, barley, is a highland crop. Fourth, their domestic animals, the cow and especially the long-tailed sheep, are likewise typical to a highland environment. Fifth, the Oromo calendar was conceived in the highland region, since the beginning of the year is placed at the end of the rainy season (the question of Oromo calendar will not be discussed in this study). Sixth, the central pillar of the Oromo house presupposes that originally they lived in permanent dwellings.[55]

Among the Oromo of Hararghe, barley still holds a special place in the ceremony or rituals. According to M. de Salviac, barley played a pivotal part in rituals and prayers; this was especially the case for the universal national prayer *wadaja*, practised by all:

> The *Wadaja* is a religious pact par excellence which gathers all the Oromo clans under the same worship and the same religion. All the Oromo ceremonies are connected to the *Wadaja* and have value only with it. The *Wadaja* ceremony has the objective of honoring God, to praise Him, to glorify Him, by rendering to Him an appropriate worship under the mysterious word of *Wadai*. The *Wadaja* is always used for attracting divine benedictions over the families, the village and the land, or for the removal of plagues. In one word, they go to the kind God and obtain his favors for all their needs; such was the practical end of their homage.[56]

[53] Paul Black, 'Linguistic Evidence on the Origins of the Konsoid Peoples', in Harold G. Marcus and John Hinnant, eds, *Proceedings of the First United States Conference on Ethiopian Studies 1973* (East Lansing, MI: Michigan State University, 1975), 299–300. See also Tasawo Merga, 'Senna Umatta Oromo', 9.
[54] Haberland, *Galla Süd-Aethiopens*, 772.
[55] Ibid., 773–4.
[56] Father F. Azaïs, 'A Study of the Religion of the Oromo People', translation from French by Ayalew Kanno, *Journal of Oromo Studies* 19, 1–2 (July 2012), 179.

The *wadaja* could be performed by a family, sub-*gosa* or *gosa*, and it could relate either to individual or group affairs. A family that needed such a prayer was expected to prepare food for the guest, which had to include some bread of barley or some roasted barley.[57] Even today, when Islam has replaced the traditional religion and *cha'at* (a leafy green plant chewed as a stimulant during a prayer or other social occasions) has replaced barley in *wadaja*, barley is still used when praying for rain, for fertility and health, and in the ceremony of sowing seed when harvesting and when people die. In all ceremonial usage, it is either roasted or boiled. Before its consumption, a short prayer is said and a small portion is spread in four directions for the 'persons of the other world'. Among the Hararghe Oromo today, sorghum is the staple, a multi-purpose crop in that the grain is food, the leaf is fodder, and the dried stalk is building material for thatching and also fuel.[58] However, sorghum, as a life-sustaining crop that dominates the economy, has not yet replaced barley's special role. Barley holds a central place in many rituals of the Arsi and Guji, both as grain and as porridge.[59] Barley, which is an indigenous and a highland crop, must have been a major crop that together with milk, butter and meat, provided staple food. It seems that barley was consumed largely in the highlands, where milk was in short supply. In the lowlands it must have been used as a supplementary food.

Historically cattle were certainly the most useful animals for the Oromo. The cow played an important role in ritual and in the economy. The Oromo drank its milk and ate its meat and butter. Its skin was used for sleeping mats and shelter, and its entrails for divination. As indicated in Chapter 1, the Oromo say they lost their Book due to carelessness. However, the Oromo wise men, *ogessa*,[60] were able to find the lost book: they found it in the stomach of the cow. By killing a cow wise men can read the inside of the stomach for the hidden secrets. Thus the cow not only provided sustenance for the Oromo, but also gave them the key for unlocking sacred secrets. The cow was more than an animal for the pastoral Oromo. It was the gift of Waaqa (God). The first black cow was found with the first Qaalluu[61] (the religious leader). As such, a cow was addressed, like a person, by a particular name.[62] In general,

[57] de Salviac, *An Ancient People: A Great African Nation – The Oromo*, 162.

[58] Seifu Metaferia, 'The Eastern Oromo (K'ottus) of Ethiopia and Their Time Reckoning "System"', *Africa Rivista Trimestrale di Studi e Documentazione dell'Istituto Italo-Africano*, 33, 4 (1978), 487.

[59] For the importance of barley among other Oromo, see Joseph Van Deloo, *Guji Oromo Culture in Southern Ethiopia* (Berlin: Dietrich Reimer Verlag, 1991), 30; see also P.T.W. Baxter, 'Butter for Barley and Barley for Cash: Petty Transactions and Small Transformations in an Arssi Market', in Sven Rubenson, ed., *Proceedings of the Seventh International Conference of Ethiopian Studies* (East Lansing, MI: Michigan State University, 1984), 459–72.

[60] Guglielmo Massaja, *Lettere e scritti minori III Anni 1863–1866*, A cura di Antonino Rosso (Roma: Istituto storico dei Cappuccini, 1978), 96–7.

[61] According to widely diffused tradition, the first Qaalluu was of divine origin.

[62] Asmarom Legesse, *Gada: Three Approaches to the Study of African Society* (New York: The Free Press, 1973), 281.

cattle were the main item of bride wealth, blood price as the measure of wealth, and the main medium of exchange. Among domestic animals, cows and sheep hold a special place for the Oromo of Hararghe. Like barley, the sheep was used in traditional ceremonies. It was used in *rako* (marriage), which was for life.[63] It was very important in traditional oath taking. What is more, as a sign of their peaceful intentions, Oromo pilgrims to the Abba Muudaa took sheep with them, and neither pilgrims nor sheep were molested even in enemy territory.[64]

In Hararghe, the central pillar of a house (*utuba*) holds a special place. People are not allowed to be near the central pillar when it is raining. It is supposed that in a storm lightning could strike the person near the pillar. When a person of high social standing in a community gets seriously sick, the elders pray for him or her, mentioning repeatedly the *utuba* (pillar) when they refer to God. At the height of the prayer the leader of the praying group stands under the central pillar stretching out his arms and crying. This prayer is supposed 'to reach God' soon. Even among the nomadic Borana Oromo in southern Ethiopia and northern Kenya, who depend on easily constructed mobile homes with which they moved around, the sacred quality of *utuba* is well established. According to Hassan Wario:

> The *utuba* is an analogous to the backbone of the house and therefore it has important symbolic meanings. Water used for washing the sacrificed coffee called bun is to be poured under the *utuba*…. When asking for blessings from waqa, women in labour touch the *utuba* and pray for it for safe delivery of the baby.[65]

Among the Oromo in Hararghe the central pillar is a sacred spot in a house, through which the soul 'passes' when a person dies. It remains to be established whether this practice is common among Oromo in other parts of Ethiopia. However, the sacred quality of the central pillar of a house would seem to be a sufficiently general characteristic to confirm Haberland's conclusion that the Oromo originally lived in permanent dwellings rather than easily constructed mobile homes used by nomads.

Ulrich Braukämper: the highland area between the Darassa country and the upper Dawa

Ulrich Braukämper, who added to our knowledge of Hadiya and Kambatta history, has tried to identify or locate the Oromo cradleland in an area different from the ones suggested by Haberland and H. S. Lewis.[66] Braukämper situates Oromo cradleland in the highland area between the Darassa country and the upper Dawa. However, the area

---

[63] This was marriage by binding unbreakable oath.
[64] A. Mizzi, *Cenni Etnografici Galla Ossia Organizzazione Civile, usi e costumi Oromonici* (Malta, 1935), 9. See also de Salviac. *An Ancient People: A Great African Nation – The Oromo*, 179.
[65] Wario, 'Journey to the Shrine of Nura', 15.
[66] Braukämper, *Geschichte der Hadiya Süd-Aethiopiens*, 130–3.

which Braukämper designates as 'the original home of the Oromo' was actually the home of the Darassa, another Cushitic-language-speaking people of southern Ethiopia. What is more, Braukämper's identification suffers from serious shortcomings. He not only relies on Bahrey's *Zenahu le Galla*, but also misreads several sections. For Braukämper , Bahrey's manuscript establishes 1522 as the beginning of documented Oromo history,[67] which, as we have shown, is historically incorrect. He claims that the name Galla originated from what he calls *Daudi Galla* ('the time of dispersal in Hadiya language'),[68] an event that took place during the second half of the sixteenth century. The term Galla, however, was already in use at least since the last quarter of the thirteenth century.

Braukämper exaggerates the significance of 1522, stating that, according to Bahrey's text, 'The two main fractions of the Oromo, the Borana and Barentu, invaded the Ethiopian province of Bali from the West.'[69] But we know that Bahrey specifically mentioned that only the Borana attacked Bali in 1522. Braukämper also assumes that 'the fission into the two main moieties of the Northern Oromo, Borana and Barentu, took place in Dallo'.[70] This division ostensibly took place between 1522, when the Oromo were said to have attacked Bali, and 1530, when they presumably made their law to attack the territory of the Christian kingdom at a place called Koss on the boundary between Dallo and Bali. Braukämper neither tells us how he came to know that the Borana and Barentu made a law in 1530 to attack a territory for the Christian kingdom nor why they made that law at Koss.

Furthermore, Braukämper did not explain how the two groups supposedly at odds overcame their division and made a pact to attack the territory of the Christian kingdom. According to Bahrey's manuscript, however, 'it was in the 1570s and 1580s'[71] that the Borana and Barentu separated, and not between 1522 and 1530. Braukämper asserts that the Borana and Barentu fought separately after their supposed 'fission' in Dallo between 1522 and 1530. However, the division of the Oromo into the Borana and Barentu moieties was a phenomenon that took much longer than the eight years suggested by Braukämper. Even after the separation into Borana and Barentu, the Oromo obeyed the same law, lived under the same *gada* system, moved together and jointly fought against common enemies. While the Barentu began the major

---

[67] Braukämper, 'Oromo Country of Origin', 198.

[68] Braukämper, *Geschichte der Hadiya Süd-Aethiopiens*, 130–3.

[69] Braukämper, 'Oromo Country of Origin', *Ethiopian Studies: Proceedings of the Sixth International Conference, 14–17 April 1980*, ed. Gideon Goldenberg (Boston: A.A. Balkema, 1986), 35.

Braukämper, 'Oromo Country of Origin', 29; Braukämper, *Geschichte der Hadiya Süd-Aethiopiens*, 136–39; Braukämper, 'Islamic Principalities in Southeast Ethiopia', 27–8.

[70] Braukämper, 'Oromo Country of Origin', 34.

[71] Bahrey, 'History of the Galla', 112.

sixteenth-century population movement, the Borana quickly joined them. According to Yilma Deressa, when the news of the Barentu's population movement and their military success reached Wallal, it stirred the Borana warriors to join the great adventure.[72] From this it follows that at least during the first phase of pastoral Oromo population movement, the leaders of the Borana and Barentu were in contact in order to coordinate their forces, determine what route to follow, when to advance or retreat, and how to settle disputes peacefully. Asmarom Legesse states that the Borana and the Barentu fought against their enemies 'with one joint army under the leadership of a single Abba Gada'.[73] Such joint action continued intermittently up to the seventeenth century, as will be shown in the last two chapters of this study. In short, it was the unity of the Borana and Barentu that made them a formidable force. Several contemporary sources, including Bahrey's manuscript, the Chronicles of Emperor Sarsa Dengel (1563–97), those of Emperor Susenyos, (1607–32) and other documents of the period confirm that the Borana and Barentu conducted joint military activities.

What is more, Braukämper claims that 'the ancestors of the Oromo did not expand [into Bali] ... before the beginning of the sixteenth century'.[74] In truth, as will be shown below, most if not all Barentu Oromo were living within historical Bali. Even if one accepts the historically inaccurate notion that the Oromo did not live in Bali before the sixteenth century, it is surprising that Braukämper did not even suspect that a pastoral society that lived on the frontier of a neighbouring territory, but was not subjected to any law, save its own, could have crossed into that territory, even though Bahrey's *Zenahu le Galla* did not record the event. This is a static view of a frontier dynamic. In any case, Braukämper's data contradicts his assertion and established that 'a mixed Oromo-Hadiyya population'[75] lived in Dallo, which was part of historic Bali.

Mekuria Bulcha: Shawan plateau

In a book published in 2011 Mekuria Bulcha presented a new thesis about the Oromo cradleland. For Bulcha, 'The Shawan Plateau [was the] Cradle of Oromo Civilization'. His main argument 'is that the Shawan Plateau was inhabited by the Oromo during the medieval period and probably even before that'.[76] The information presented in the previous two chapters in this study clearly establishes that a number of Oromo groups were inhabitants of the Shawan plateau at least since the twelfth and thirteenth centuries. Bulcha suggests that the Oromo had always lived in the region of Shawa. In the absence of historical

[72] Yilma Deressa, *Ya Ityopya Tarik Ba'asra Sedestanyaw Kefla Zaman* (Addis Ababa: Berhanena Selam Printing Press, 1967), 228.
[73] Legesse, *Oromo Democracy*, 188.
[74] U. Braukämper, *Islamic History and Culture in Southern Ethiopia: Collected Essays* (New Brunswick, NJ: Transaction, 2002), 135.
[75] Ibid., 81.
[76] Bulcha, *Contours of the Emergent and Ancient Oromo Nation*, 131.

evidence it is impossible to know if that was the case. What is known and knowable is that the expansion of the Christian kingdom during the reign of Emperor Amda-Siyon was accompanied by the displacement of some Oromo groups from the Shawan plateau. Bulcha states that 'the available data does not indicate any compelling need which made [the Oromo] move from south to north before or after the sixteenth century'. [77] On the contrary, the available data demonstrates the movement of the Oromo from the north to the south during the first half of the fourteenth century and, significantly, from the south to the north, most spectacularly during the sixteenth century. This study shows the continuous movements of the Oromo from the south to the north. Oromo population movement within and beyond Ethiopia followed patterns of population movements which were well established in the Horn of Africa, to be mentioned further in this presentation. Despite the evidence presented by previous scholars, Bulcha claims that the highlands of southern Ethiopia were neither the Oromo cradlelands nor the centre of their dispersal. For him, the Shawan plateau was both of these. He explains:

> Had the Arsi/Bale region been a point of dispersal, we would expect a denser cluster of the bigger and more expansive descent groups here than elsewhere. Among the descent groups that proliferate and flourish here, we do not find many that branch-out to other parts of the Oromo country as, for example, the Galaan, Karrayyuu, Jiddaa, Yaayyaa, and Liiban who, while flourishing and clustering on the Shawan Plateau, are widely spread outside of it ... The point I want to make here is that the denser the clustering of the descent groups, the nearer they are to the place of long habitation and to the point of probably expansion. In my view, the Shawan Plateau was such a centre; it was here that the greater part of the development of the major *gosa* groups that constitute the Oromo nation today seem to have occurred, a long period of time before the Amhara conquest of the region in the fourteenth century.[78]

The above explanation neither establishes that the Shawan plateau was an Oromo cradleland nor does it prove that it was the centre of pastoral Oromo dispersal during the sixteenth century. What Bulcha's argument establishes is the long presence of several Oromo descent groups there. Yet, using Oromo *gosa* or descent groups (ethnonyms) and place names or toponyms , Bulcha concludes that

> the Shawan Plateau was the home of many well-known Oromo descent groups during the last one thousand years ... [S]ome of the largest Oromo descent groups such as Galaan [Galan], Yaayyaa, [Yaya], Waaj and Jidda live here ... This does not mean they did not exist elsewhere. What is remarkable is that they are clustered here more than in any other region. Although they are represented today in most of the other Oromo regions, they proliferate most on the Shawan Plateau, branching off into numerous sub-groups which in turn branch into sub-groups. That indicates the time depth of their presence in the region. Consequently, it seems that the plateau was, if not the centre, certainly one of the centres for the development of Oromo history and culture over a long period.[79]

[77] Ibid.
[78] Bulcha, *Contours of the Emergent and Ancient Oromo nation*, 209–10.
[79] Ibid., 219–20.

While the Shawan plateau may have been the centre of *some* Oromo groups' dispersal during the first half of the *fourteenth* century, it was not the centre of the sixteenth-century pastoral Oromo dispersal.

Cradleland conclusions

Thus, there are five suggestions for the location of the Oromo cradleland, including that of Bulcha. I.M. Lewis locates Oromo cradleland in northern Somalia. However, his conclusion is not supported by valid historical evidence. H.S. Lewis situates the original home of the Oromo people in the region around Lakes Shamo and Stephanie, the area of Galana Sagan and Galana Dulei (see Map 8, page 123, for the location of the two rivers), while Haberland posits that their ancestral home was in the cool highlands of Bali. Braukämper has argued that 'the homeland of the Oromo could … be identified as the highland area between the Darassa country and the upper Dawa in the west and the Gannale Valley in the east'.[80] While separately problematic in determining the exact location of the Oromo cradleland, taken together the conclusions of each of the four scholars contribute to a fuller view of the origins of the pastoral Oromo. Each refers to a different homeland for different pastoral Oromo groups, all of which were located in the present regions of Bale, Sidamo and Gamu Gofa.

THE OROMO CRADLELAND: A NEW ARGUMENT

The following section attempts to present a new argument for the location of Oromo cradleland based on oral traditions. Interestingly the oral traditions of all Oromo consistently assert that their ancestors came from southern Ethiopia. It was also in the same region that their ancient self-designation 'Oromo' appears to have originated.

The name Oromo

While Professor Bairu Tafla notes the obscurity of the origins of the name Oromo,[81] the Oromo themselves believe that their national name has always existed as the mark of their distinct identity and self-designation. According to Gemetchu Megerssa, Oromo is one of the 'conceptual categories by which the Oromo classify their people, their land and all other social and natural elements in their environment'.[82] It is the name that articulates the Oromo world-view, underpins their traditional religious, political and social institutions and conveys a sense of belonging, of complete unity. Above all, Oromo is the name inseparably linked to the Oromo myth of origin. In the words of Gemetchu Megerssa:

[80] Braukämper, 'Oromo Country of Origin', 35.
[81] Tafla, *Asma Giyorgis and His Work*, 52–53.
[82] Gemetch Megerssa, 'Knowledge, Identity and the Colonizing Structure: The Case of the Oromo in East and Northeast Africa' (PhD diss., University of London, 1994), 14.

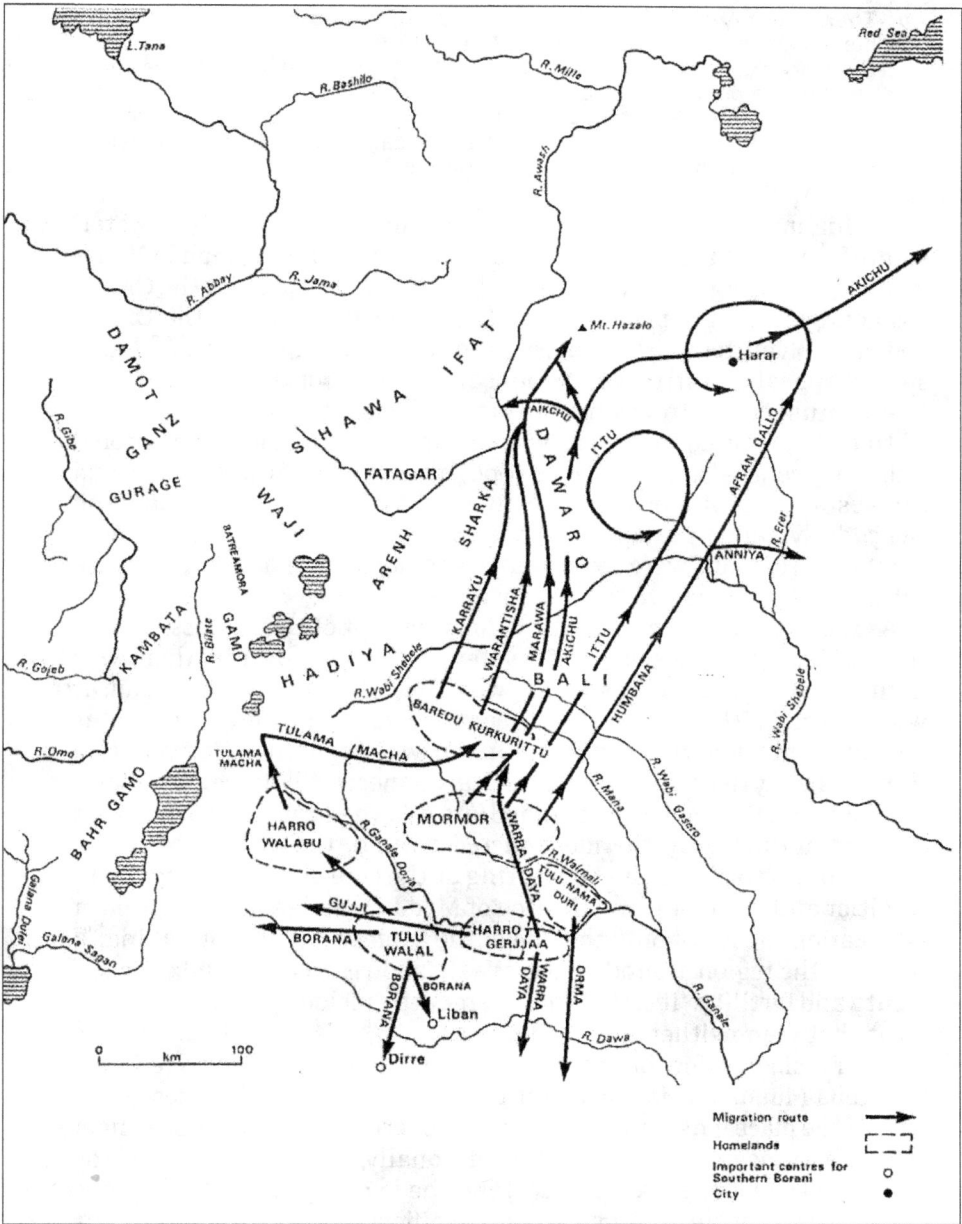

Map 8 The beginning of the sixteenth-century pastoral Oromo population movement (adapted from Hassen, 'The Oromo of Ethiopia, 1500–1850', PhD diss., University of London, 1983).

> The Oromo myth of origin takes different forms to accommodate the diverse human and natural phenomena. In terms of the origin of the Oromo people, the cosmic category of water is anthropomorphized and becomes the apical ancestor Horo. In another context, the first Oromo rises out of the water or is associated with the water body he crosses. It is therefore in this sense that Waallaabu the original water out of which Waaqa [God] created the universe becomes the origin of life and therefore of the Oromo.[83]

In this myth, the reference to Waallaabuu as the 'original water' signifies the spring located in the present region of Bale. Madda Waallaabuu (the spring of Waallaabuu) is the most sacred place in the Oromo cosmology. It is 'the place where God revealed Himself to the Oromo people'.[84] Even today the holy ground of Madda Waallaabuu[85] has a special appeal and strong emotional attachment for the Oromo. It was the spiritual centre from where the moral force, the collective strength of traditional Oromo religion, was generated. The traditional Oromo religion is centred around Waaqa (God), the Creator of the universe and the sustainer of life on earth. Although the Qaalluu institution and the *gada* system probably developed earlier, it appears that the fundamental institutions were consolidated at Madda Waallaabuu during the second half of the fourteenth century.

As indicated in Chapter 1, 'the Oromo concept of the process of creation begins with the element of water ... In the beginning, there was nothing but water.'[86] This water was that of Madda Waallaabuu. It was at Madda Waallaabuu that Waaqa created the eponym Horo. It is fascinating to note that the term 'Oromo' was apparently derived from 'Horo'. The myth establishes a mystical connection between the water of Madda Waallaabuu, the eponym Horo and the term Oromo; it makes Waallaabuu not only the most sacred ground, the birthplace of the nation, but also places the holy spring at the core of Oromo religion. In traditional Oromo religion, 'the God of Madda Waallaabuu is the God of all creation. He is not only the God of the Oromos but of all mankind.'[87] As such, the region around Madda Waallaabuu is an ideal land of peace, plenty and fertility. 'It is the land where cattle yielded so much milk and meat that men neither ploughed nor sowed.'[88] Waallaabuu is also the place of residence for the spiritual leader of traditional Oromo religion, the Abba Muudaa. It is important to note that the myth makes Waallaabuu the place where the *gada* form of government had its office under the majestic *oda* (sycamore) tree. Traditionally, the Oromo believed the *oda* to be the most sacred of trees, the shade of which was the source of peace, the centre of religion, and the official meeting ground for the democratically elected *gada* leaders.[89] There are still eleven massive

[83] Ibid., 145–6.
[84] Rev. Ronald Ward, 'Pilgrimage in Oromia – Madda Walaabuu', *Qunamtii Oromia*, Vol. III, No. 1 (September 1992), 14.
[85] Ibid.
[86] Megerssa, ibid., 91.
[87] Ward, ibid., 15.
[88] Yelma Deressa, *Ya Ityop iya Tarik Ba'asra Sedestannaw Kefla Zaman*, 212.
[89] Hassen, 'The Oromo of Ethiopia', 14.

oda trees around Madda Waallaabuu, 'where Gada, order, symmetry, and beauty happens'.[90]

> Traditionally, the land of the *Abba Muudaa*, which pilgrims have visited for centuries, has been located in the regions of Bali and Sidamo in southern Oromia. It is said to be a place of righteousness, wisdom, harmony, peace and *Gada* democracy. The land of the *Abba Muudaa* was the place where all the important Oromo religious and political institutions developed. It was the rich source of their historic beginnings and of their view of the universe. In short, the land of the Abba Muudaa provides the cultural templates for Oromo religious beliefs, their political philosophy, based on *Gada*, and their knowledge of themselves and their history.[91]

Finally, the Oromo myth of origin makes Madda Waallaabuu 'Heaven on Earth' where the Oromo lived in happiness for 'the God of the Oromo is a God of life and joy'.[92] It was there, most likely, that the name Oromo was popularized. Gemetchu Megerssa claims that the name 'Oromo' was derived from the eponym 'Horo'.

> In Oromo ... the phoneme (h) is not articulated before the vowels (a, i, o and u). This is not a phonologically relevant trait. Thus the name (H) Oromo could be pronounced both with and without the initial (H). The link between these two names is made clear in the ritual of adoption, when the verbal form of the word is used to describe the process of becoming a full member of the Oromo community. The ritual is known as horomassa meaning literally 'to let someone become part of (H) Oromo'. Horo, the root word from which (H) Oromo is derived can in turn be traced to the verb horru meaning 'to reproduce'. In the Oromo sense of this word, reproduction is not only a biological phenomenon; it is also a social one. By their incorporation into Oromo through the ritual of adoption, non-Oromo, even those captured in battle, can be socially transformed and acquire an ... equality of rights and privileges with those who are Oromo by 'biological descent': This includes the right to claim direct connection with the apical ancestor, Horo.[93]

Thus, the origin of Oromo is most probably connected with the eponym Horo, encapsulating the concepts of biological and social reproduction, and capturing in essence the Oromo vision of their identity.[94] While much remains to be understood about the great symbolic power of the Oromo name, it clearly has complex historical, social, cultural, political and religious significance for the people who bear it, with an evident link with the Oromo myth of origin and Madda Waallaabuu – the cradleland.

But where is Madda Waallaabuu? The famous Madda Waallaabuu is found in the Bale region, in the *awraja* (sub-province) of Dallo near the Gannale River.[95] The Guji, another Oromo group, claim that their original home was in Gerjjaa, in the valley of the Gannale River, in the

[90] Ward, 'Pilgrimage in Oromia – Madda Walaabuu', 15.
[91] Mohammed Hassen, 'Pilgrimage to the Abba Muudaa', *Journal of Oromo Studies* 12, 1–2 (July 2005), 144.
[92] Ward, ibid. 15.
[93] Megerssa, 'Knowledge, Identity and the Colonizing Structure', 24.
[94] Ibid., 25.
[95] Merga, 'Senna Ummata Oromo', 8.

awrajas of Dallo in Bale and Jamjam in the Sidamo region, indicating the importance of these regions in most Oromo oral traditions.[96] In short, the oral tradition of all Oromo, whether of Kenya or Ethiopia, are unanimous in their claim that their pastoral ancestors came from what are today the regions of Bale and Sidamo (see Map 4, page 87). These traditions reflect the Oromo view about their cradleland, and are confirmed by modern scholarship based on field data gathered from Bale and Sidamo regions.[97]

In the nineteenth century, European travellers and missionaries reported that the Oromo of Hararghe remembered, as they do even today, that their pastoral ancestors had come from Mormor in Bale. For the Hararghe Oromo, Mormor, in addition to being the original home and the point of their population movement in the sixteenth century, was a holy place of pilgrimage to the Abba Muudaa.[98] Today, Mormor is found in the Bale region in the *awrajas* of Fasil and Dallo, near the River Gannale. The Arsi Oromo claim that their original home was Baredu Kurkurittu in the highlands of Bale, on the side of Mormor, between the Walmali and Mana Rivers, two tributaries of the River Gannale.[99] The Borana in Kenya claim Tullu Nama Duri (the hill of the ancient people) as the place of their origin.[100] The Orma in Kenya similarly claim *Tullu* (hill) as their place of origin,[101] presumably the same Tullu Nama Duri that is located in Bale in the *awraja* of Dallo, between the Walmali and Gannale Rivers. Legend has it that the Borana came from *Tullu Nama Duri* in Bale region and settled in Liban, where today their important shrines are located.[102] It was from Tullu Nama Duri area that the Borana slowly moved to northern Liban where they must have lived for a long time, and from where, according to Haberland, they were driven by the Guji Oromo into the Dirre region.[103]

The Macha and Tulama, (the two major Borana groups that spread over central and south-western parts of Ethiopia) claim Tullu Walal as the place of their origin.[104] Tullu Walal, which is located in the area of the present Guji and northern Boranaland, was known to be the general area where the Borana lived during the fourteenth and fifteenth centuries and from where they launched their massive population movement in the sixteenth century.[105] Tullu Walal, though not a part of Tullu Nama

[96] Tasammaa and Waaqwayo, *Sena Saba Oromoofi Sirna Gadaa*, 26.

[97] Merga, ibid.

[98] de Salviac, *An Ancient People: Great African Nation – The Oromo*, 50.

[99] Merga, ibid., 8.

[100] Paul S.G. Goto, 'The Boran of Northern Kenya: Origin, Migrations and Settlements in the 19th Century' (BA thesis, University of Nairobi, 1972), 26–28.

[101] A. Werner, 'Some Galla Notes', *Man: A Record of Anthropological Science* 15 (1915), 10–11.

[102] Sahlu Kidane, *Borana Folk Tales: A Contextual Study* (London: Haan, 2002), 4.

[103] Haberland, *Galla Süd-Aethiopiens*, 779.

[104] Ibid., 24.

[105] Legesse, *Gada: Three Approaches to the Study of African Society*, 8.

Duri, is located just a short distance south of it. Some Macha and Tulama groups say '*Ani walaletin dhaladhe, dhalonniko Walla inqabu*'.[106] ('I was born at Walal'). 'My birth[place] does not suffer from lack of knowledge', others say, and '*Ummaan Waallaabuu baatee*' ('Creation came out of Waallaabuu').[107] This appears to suggest that it was at Madda Waallaabuu that the Oromo first became conscious of their distinct identity, separate from their neighbours. According to the Oromo myth of origin, it was at Madda Waallaabuu that Waaqa created the Oromo and their first Qaalluu or the Abba Muudaa. It was probably here that the national name of Oromo came into use as a way of distinguishing themselves from their neighbours. It appears that the Oromo creation myth was inextricably connected with the name 'Oromo' and the land of Mada Waallaabuu.

Of the four scholars detailed above, Professor Haberland's interpretation seems to me to be referring to the homeland of the farming Oromo community in the province of historical Bali. I say this for several valid reasons. First, we have already seen that the area that H.S. Lewis designates as the Oromo cradleland was the Borana homeland, while the region Braukämper makes the cradleland was actually occupied by the Darassa people before the latter were expelled by the Guji Oromo.[108] Future research may prove or disprove Bulcha's claim that the Shawan plateau was one of early Oromo homelands.

The land of Fugug
As can be seen from the traditions cited, all pastoral Oromo mention multiple places as their cradleland, though all locations are near each other. In one Oromo tradition there is a reference to a distant land, claimed to be the original home of the Oromo people, the birthplace of the nation. This land is known as 'Fugug'.[109] The noun *fugug* appears to have been a derivative of the verb *fago* (faraway). In the tradition it is said that the land of Fugug was 'endowed with grazing' and was famous 'for its suitability for human settlement and cattle rearing'.[110] What is clear from the tradition of Fugug is that it was a highland area. With the tradition of Fugug, it may be that we have an idea of considerable significance for identifying the location of the farming Oromo community. The tradition places Fugug in the regions of Shawa and the historical province of Bali. However, neither the eastern nor the western Oromo remember today the exact location of the land of Fugug. For the Oromo in the south-west, especially those in the Gibe region, 'Fugug was in the east near Tajurra, on the sea-coast'.[111] For those of Anniya in Hararghe, the land of Fugug lay to the west in the direction

---

[106] de Salviac, *An Ancient People: Great African Nation – The Oromo*, 181.
[107] Merga, 'Senna Umatta Oromo', 8.
[108] Ibid., 9.
[109] Abba Jobir Abba Dula, 'Unpublished Manuscript of Abba Jobir Abba Dula, the Last King of Jimma', 8.
[110] Alemayehu Haile, *History of the Oromo to the Sixteenth Century*, 2nd edn (Finfinne: Oromia Culture and Tourism Bureau, 2006), 58.
[111] Ibid., 58.

of Bale region. For the Afran Qallo Oromo in the central highlands of Hararghe the land of Fugug is in the direction of Bale and Arsi regions. For them, Fugug was a sacred land, the birthplace of the nation. Accordingly, Oromo pilgrims from Hararghe mention Fugug in their prayer chants on their way to and from the land of Abba Muudaa in Mormor in Bale. As late as 1875, the president of Afran Qallo government was known as Abba Fugug ('the father of Fugug'),[112] meaning the defender of the sacred land and the protector of the traditional religion. Among other Oromo, only fragmentary traces remain in their traditions. The Oromo had common ancestors who had lived in Fugug for a long time before they moved to Waallaabuu.[113] Today people ask someone who has stayed away from his or her village for a long time and returned, 'have you been to Fugug?' The question points to a tradition that makes Fugug a distant land, and perhaps reflects the time-span during which the ancestors of Oromo engaged in mixed economy had lived there.

Today we find the land of Fugug[114] (see Map 6, page 98) and Mount Fugug in Arsi and the northern part of the region of Bale, the heartland of historical Bali. Recent research in the region of Shawa has brought to light other highland areas that have Fugug as their suffixes. 'These are Badda Fugug – the settlement area of Salale Oromo in northern Shawa; Bacho Fugug – the settlement area of Bacho Oromo in Western Shawa; [and] Ribu Fugug – another name of a place in Shawa.'[115] These three places appear to have been the areas where some Oromo groups lived during the thirteenth century, possible earlier. Of the four areas that have some connection with the name of Fugug, it is difficult to establish with certainty which one was the original land of Fugug. However, the locations in Shawa suggest that it was the area in the heartland of historical Bali. This implies that the name of Fugug was brought to the region of Shawa earlier than the thirteenth century by Oromo immigrants from Fugug in historical Bali. Three important conclusions flow from this. First, the land of Fugug located in Bali was probably an important Oromo politico-religious centre long before the fourteenth century. Second, those Oromo who lived in Fugug were engaged in mixed economy farming and cattle keeping, while those who depended entirely on pastoralism moved to the lowlands around the River Gannale, where they had grass and water in abundance for their cattle. Third, and even more important, the pressure from the southward-expanding Christian kingdom and the intense conflict between the Christians and Muslims during and after

[112] Among the Afran Qallo Oromo in Hararghe, as late as 1875, the Abba Gada (the leader of the *chaffe* assembly) was also known as Abba Fugug. Interestingly, the name Fugug and the concept it represents, 'a far-away land', is still strong among the Afran Qallo Oromo.
[113] Abba Dula, 'Unpublished Manuscript of Abba Jobir Abba Dula', 8.
[114] de Salviac, *An Ancient People: Great African Nation – The Oromo*, 171. According to the same source, 157, the *jila*, the Oromo pilgrims to the land of their spiritual leader, Abba Muudaa, chanted the name Fugug on their way to and from the land of Abba Muudaa.
[115] Haile, *History of the Oromo to the Sixteenth Century*, 58.

the reign of Amda-Siyon (1314–44) seem to have further encouraged pastoral Oromo movement from the regions of Shawa and highlands of historical Bali, which was controlled by the Christian administration, to the region beyond their control and at the same time free from the devastating Muslim-Christian conflict of the time.[116]

Oromo oral traditions recorded by Cerulli reveal that the highlands of southern Ethiopia in general and those of Bale in particular have special appeal to the Oromo. They are regarded as land of peace, plenty and fertility.[117] These regions were also the spiritual centre from which the moral force – the collective strength of traditional Oromo religion – was generated. The extant literature reveals Oromo emotional attachment to the hills and mountains and to the rivers and the valleys of the land of Abba Muudaa – a feeling well preserved in Oromo oral tradition and religious songs.[118]

We have already seen that the lowlands of the present region of Bale were exceptionally important to the oral traditions of most Oromo. An important conclusion could be drawn from this. The main Oromo group, who practised a mixed economy, lived in the highlands of historical Bali, while the lowlands in the valley of the River Gannale became the grazing ground for the cattle of the pastoralists, who drifted away from the main group owing to the nature of their transhumant economy combined with the pressure from the southward-expanding Christian kingdom and the Muslim-Christian conflict in the region of historical Bali.

At this juncture, one point must be made absolutely clear. It seems that the homeland of the agricultural Oromo was small in size. It was the pastoral element of the Oromo society that, even at that early stage, moved far and wide, enlarging the frontier of their pastureland, probably covering a lot of space in keeping with their need for ample grazing land. In the process of this expansion of the grazing land, Oromo pastoralists encountered many other peoples whom they assimilated and Oromo-ized and by whom they were, in turn, influenced.

Agro-pastoralism

Eike Haberland's research establishes that the Oromo were originally agro-pastoralists who depended on a 'cattle-rearing and grain-growing economy'.[119] It appears that most, if not all, Oromo became pure pasto-

---

[116] See, for instance, Hassen, 'The Oromo of Ethiopia, 1500–1860', 16–18.

[117] E. Cerulli, *Etiopia Occidentale* (Rome, 1933), 169–72.

[118] de Salviac, ibid., 178–87.

[119] Haberland, *Galla Süd-Aethiopiens*, 772. When I mentioned this aspect in the preface to my first book, *The Oromo of Ethiopia*, Harold Marcus criticized me for not explaining 'such a surprising development, rare in world history'. See Marcus' review of *The Oromo of Ethiopia: A History, 1570–1860* in *The American Historical Review*, 97 Supplement (February 1992), 259. According to Jan Hultin, 'Marcus's statement is nonsense. Furthermore, his dismissal of Haberland's hypothesis misrepresents what the latter actually has written ... Adopting pastoralism is neither surprising nor a rare development in world history.' See Hultin, 'Perceiving Oromo Galla in the Great narrative of Ethiopia', in Baxter et al., *Being and Becoming Oromo*, 87, see note 6.

ralists only after they had embarked on the massive sixteenth-century population movement, as pastoralism fitted with their movements. This is similar to the Maasai who, long considered archetypical pastoralists, actually adopted a purely pastoral way of life only relatively recently.

> Originally agro-pastoralists, raising sorghum and millet along with their cattle and small stock, they came to specialize more and more in a pastoral way of life appropriate for the plains, leaving grain production to communities of farmers inhabiting the fertile highlands either side of the valley and hunting and gathering to specialized groups who lived in the forests bordering the highlands and plains.[120]

The Oromo, who were assumed to have been pure pastoralists before their sixteenth-century population movement, were agro-pastoralists. Most Oromo adopted a purely pastoral way of life partly to take advantage of the environment in which they found themselves and partly because it fitted with their movements during the sixteenth century. Haberland's research supports this conclusion.[121] In this regard Oromo oral traditions have proved their irreplaceable value. The data at our disposal are not sufficient to account for all the movements of the pastoral Oromo. Nevertheless, a tentative generalization can be made. It was probably the practice of *fora* that led to this development. As mentioned in Chapter 1, *fora* consisted of the division of the cattle into 'dry' and 'lactating' cows, taking the former to the lowlands where there was enough pasture in the wet season while keeping most of the latter near the village. In other words, *fora* was probably the time when young men took cattle to the untamed river valleys south of historical Bali as well as those in the regions of Sidamo and Gamo Gofa. While on expedition the young men had to learn the art of fighting and hunting as they had to protect themselves and their cattle from enemy raiders and wild animals. Those who participated in *fora* expeditions lived mainly on the game and on milk, dressing in the skins of the wild beasts they killed. The hardship and endurance in long-distance walking for which the Oromo warriors were famous [122] seems to have been acquired during the *fora* expeditions. In short, through killing an enemy or dangerous animals, young men distinguished themselves as brave warriors. Bravery was revered with near religious awe among pastoral Oromo. It was probably for this reason that Martial de Salviac commented: 'Every Oromo is a soldier. The warrior temperament is born with him.'[123] The warrior temperament, rather, was acquired through training from childhood and especially during *fora* expeditions.

---

[120] Thomas Spear and Richard Waller, *Being Maasai: Ethnicity and Identity in East Africa* (Athens, OH: Ohio University Press, 1993), 1.

[121] Haberland, *Galla Süd-Aethiopiens*, 772.

[122] Bruce, *Travels to Discover the Source of the Nile*, Volume 3, 240. See also E.A. Wallis Budge, *A History of Ethiopia, Nubia and Abyssinia*, Vol. 2 (London: Methuen, 1928), 614.

[123] de Salviac, *An Ancient People: Great African Nation – The Oromo*, 308.

As one aspect of the transhumant economy, *fora* may have led to the separation of the group into highland and lowland communities. It is impossible to know when this process began, but possibly well before the fourteenth century. The fourteenth-century expansion of the Christian state and the conflict between the Christians and the Muslims may have intensified the movement from the highland to the lowlands areas. Of course, we have no direct evidence that this happened. However, what Haberland wrote in the early 1960s about the contemporary transhumant economy may apply to the economy of early Oromo society.

> The main section of the tribe lives in the highlands and practices agriculture while the young manhood looks after the herds in the lowlands. Each group follows its distinct way of life and thus the cultural elements associated with cattle-rearing come more strongly to the fore in the lowlands. There are plenty of cases where whole groups settled down for long periods in the lowlands and later became separate tribes. Favorable grazing conditions had led them to settle in the lowlands in order to live exclusively by cattle-rearing ... The vegetable food-stuffs needed for nourishment are procured by barter with the highland tribe.[124]

Faced with a precarious economy and pressure from the Christian kingdom that had been expanding southward since the fourteenth century, some Oromo might have migrated from the highlands of historical Bali to the vast lowlands south of the same province. In other words, they moved from a region of conflict and control to a region of relative peace and freedom. In this regard, Bulcha's observation appears to be highly relevant.

> [Beginning] with the conquests of Amda-Siyon, the history of the Abyssinian expansion was also a history of Oromo displacement to the south and east, and perhaps, also to the west of the Shawan Plateau. The Oromo had moved away to avoid the predatory expeditions of the Abyssinian kings as well as the *chawa* [professional soldiers] garrisons they stationed in the conquered territories.[125]

FURTHER DEVELOPMENTS

In the vast lowlands south of Bali three developments appear to have taken place: population growth, the development of a possible mechanism for population control, and the militarization of the *gada* system.

Population growth
The factors that account for the perceptible increase in pastoral Oromo population have only recently been addressed. In a 2011 article, the historian Daniel Ayana explains 'why demographic factors favored the Oromo [to be a formidable force at the beginning of the sixteenth century] among the many contemporary pastoralist groups'. It reveals

---

[124] Haberland, *Galla Süd-Aethiopiens*, 772.
[125] Bulcha, *Contours of the Emergent and Ancient Oromo Nation*, 209.

'the factors that initiated and sustained the great human drama of the Oromo population movement'.[126] As indicated above, pastoral Oromo lived in the vast grazing land south of historical Bali. Ayana identifies five major factors that account for the increase in the pastoral Oromo population. The availability of abundant rainfall in the homelands of the pastoral Oromo was a key factor:

> The overlapping rainfall regime of the macro-region is an important factor in the emergence of the pastoral Oromo from among their numerous medieval neighbors as critical players in the human drama. The historic pastoral Oromo land lies at the intersection of the summer rains of the north and northeast, the spring rains of the south and southwest, and the autumn rains of the southeast.[127]

Ayana demonstrates that this rainfall regime maintained regularity from the twelfth to the sixteenth centuries. The availability of more than adequate rainfall and abundant pasturage created an ideal environment for a large increase in animal population, which in turn most likely 'created an optimum condition that spurred population growth'. [128]Asmara Legesse's detailed research demonstrates that the population increase caused the transformation of the *gada* system into a powerful 'mechanism for population control' through delaying the age of marriage to the mature age of forty and restricting child bearing.[129] In his own words:

> It seems evident that Gada system operated as a non-generational system of age-set for a major part of its history (i.e. during the fifteenth century and earlier). The rules restricting the position of the generations of marriage and child bearing were introduced sometime during the [second half of the fifteenth] century to set limits on the rapid expansion of the population occurred in that century.[130]

The *gada* system appears to have 'regulated the rate of pastoral Oromo population and saved them from engagement in most of the contemporary attrition conflicts.'[131] While contemporary nomadic groups, such as the Afar, the Gabal, the Somali and others were involved in internecine conflicts among the Christian and Muslim communities in the Ethiopian region during the thirteenth and fourteenth centuries, pastoral Oromo appear to have kept themselves from the conflict zones. Another important factor in the increase in the Oromo population was that their homelands were located in safe areas away from 'attack by the Christian and Muslim contestants'.[132] What is more, the vast

---

[126] Daniel Ayana, 'From Geographic Skirt to Geographic Drift: The Oromo Population Movement of the Sixteenth Century', *Journal of Oromo Studies*, 17, 2 (January 2011), 2–3.
[127] Ibid., 7.
[128] Ibid., 12.
[129] Legesse, *Gada: Three Approaches to the Study of African Society*, 8.
[130] Ibid., 154.
[131] Ayana, 'From Geographic Skirt to Geographic Drift', 15.
[132] Ibid., 19.

area south of historical Bali was easy to defend by pastoral Oromo and difficult for attack by the Christian forces. For example, there are accounts of a 1470s military expedition to Gam by a governor of Bali that led to defeat and death for him and all his forces.[133] 'Gam' was either a corruption of an Oromo place name of Qaqama located on the banks of Ganale River, or it was a corruption of an Oromo term of *gama*, which means beyond, that is, 'beyond' the southern boundary of historical Bali.

According to Daniel Ayana:

> The pastoral Oromo clans enjoyed not only relative safety from macro-parasitism, but also a gradient of autonomy from micro-parasitism ... By far the largest health benefit for pastoralists is their mobility which provides them safety from 'the burden of crowd diseases' that plagues farmers' settlements.[134]

Ayana goes on to discuss other factors that provided Oromo pastoralists with relative safety from malaria, which infested the valleys of major rivers in lowland areas of Bale and Sidamo regions. Oromo pastoralists also appear to have enjoyed relative safety 'from typhoid and relapsing fever':

> Two factors could have provided relative lee-way for pastoral Oromo against malaria. First, their regular mobility for transhumance might have included avoiding low-lying areas infested with *trypanosomiasis* pathogen inimical to their cattle. Second and probably more effective was *zoo prophylaxis*, the death of malaria parasite in animal blood stream. One can presume that the large cattle herds combined with regular mobility for pasture offered an epidemiological shield against malaria ... Dispersed settlement of clans and sub-clans and the general warm weather provided a gradient autonomy from typhoid and relapsing fever. The known pre-sixteenth century pastoral Oromo areas were generally warm at lower altitudes. Studies show that typhus outbreaks are concentrated in cold and wet months. [135]

With their protein-rich nutrition based on milk, meat and butter, supplemented by 'carbohydrate-rich cereals'[136] obtained from the neighbouring highland farming communities in exchange for their animal produce, pastoral Oromo probably were in better health than their settled neighbours, a fact reflected in population growth.

Pastoral Oromo population movement

By the 1430s and 1440s the growth of pastoral Oromo 'had reached a critical mass'[137] that could not be contained by the *gada* system's mechanism of population control. As a result, pastoral Oromo began raiding Bali. News of their attack on the provinces under Christian administration had reached Europe by 1441 or even earlier and, by the second half of

---

[133] Basset, *Journal Asiatique*, 96, 139.
[134] Ayana, ibid., 20–21.
[135] Ayana, 'From Geographic Skirt to Geographic Drift', 23.
[136] Ibid., 24.
[137] Ibid., 15.

the fifteenth century, Oromo pastoralists were already seen as the fierce enemies of the Christian kingdom.[138] What is not in doubt is that during the fifteenth century the pastoral Oromo population had increased very significantly. According to Asmarom Legesse, this increase in population may have triggered the massive pastoral Oromo movement at the beginning of the sixteenth century.[139] Evidence from Bahrey, writing in 1593 (only seventy-one years after 1522, when the major Borana attack on Bali was reported) supports this conclusion. He gives no less than thirty names of 'father' figures, or founders of confederacies that gave birth to 'numerous children' in the shape of numerous *gosas* and sub-*gosas* numbering today over two thousand.[140] Bahrey leaves no doubt that all left their home region within the short period of seventy-one years,[141] notwithstanding the fact that he was not well acquainted with the Barentu moiety. By contrast, he did not record the names of many fully-fledged confederacies and numerous *gosas* and sub-*gosas* that spread towards the sea on the northern Somali coast in the east and in the south, and towards the Malindi coast on the Indian Ocean in East Africa. A Portuguese source reports the presence of some Oromo groups there by the early seventeenth century. A Jesuit missionary traveller of the seventeenth century claims that the Oromo were the most numerous in the country.[142] If this claim is accurate, it must have been the result of the wide spread Oromo practice of adopting non-Oromo into their society through the institution of *moggaasa* (to be discussed in Chapter 4). This massive population movement can only be explained in terms of a large demographic change among pastoral Oromo during the fifteenth and early sixteenth centuries. As we have seen above, pastoral Oromo who lived beyond the reach of the long arm of the powerful Christian state enjoyed abundant rainfall and pasturage, which probably led to substantial increases in the number of livestock. The accompanying growth in the human population could have triggered the impulse for population movement.[143]

Militarization of the *gada* system

The militarization of the *gada* system was most likely a response to the pressure from the expanding Christian state. It appears to have been a process that developed over several decades. By militarization it is meant preparing young and adult Oromo men for warfare through arduous training which started, as indicated above, most likely when young men were on *fora* expeditions. Warfare had an important cultural

---

[138] D.P. Zurla, *Il Mappamondo di Fra Mauro Camaldolese*, (Venice, 1806), 136.

[139] Legesse, *Gada: Three Approaches to the Study of African Society*, 8.

[140] Alemayehu Haile, et al., *History of the Oromo*, Chapter 3. See also Levine, *Greater Ethiopia*, 79–80.

[141] Bahrey, 'History of the Galla', see the chart on pages 110–11.

[142] Jerónimo Lobo, D.M. Lockhart, trans., M.G. da Costa, ed., *The Itinerário of Jerónimo Lobo*, (London: Hakluyt Society, 1984), 159, quoted in Teodros Kiros, *Zara Yacob, A Seventeenth Century Rationalist: Philosopher of the Rationality of the Human Heart* (Lawrenceville, NJ: Red Sea Press, 2005), 34.

[143] See for instance, Haberland, *Galla Süd-Aethiopiens*, 772.

aspect as bravery became the highest virtue among pastoral Oromo. War produced heroes in whose honour boasting songs were sang. There were two kinds of these, *Farsa* and *gerarsa*. *Farsa* were 'poetical expressions of the bonds which united the members of the tribe. They were the boasting songs of the tribe as a whole.'[144] *Gerarsa* were 'boasting songs about a single warrior's "bravery"'.[145]

> Through *farsa* songs, eloquent heroes found their poetical expression, which set members of their tribes aflame with pride. Through these powerful songs the dead heroes of the nation were reincarnated and the living heroes were elevated to a higher plane; bravery was almost worshipped as a religion. Through *gerarsa*, individual warriors won the hearts of their mistresses and the respect and admiration of the [young and old].[146]

Pastoral Oromo exhibited a very effective guerrilla war tactic for dealing with the military forces of both the Christian and Muslim communities. They organized age-set as a fighting unit. Each age-set had its own leader, elected on the basis of distinction and courage in war. According to de Salviac:

> The Oromo is animated with warrior spirit in the highest quality. The vitality and the durability of this people, who have traversed centuries, maintaining [their]autonomy and the integrity of [their] customs, are due to the courage, to the bravery, to the energy which [they] deployed.[147]

The military dimension of the *gada* system was succinctly described by Abba Bahrey in a single sentence: 'All men, from small to great are instructed in the art of Warfare'[148] among the Oromo. Bahrey's observation touches on the essence of the system which was the militarization of the society. Pastoral Oromo divided fighting men into three categories: first the *qondalla* grade, the young warriors, who were hardened by the *fora* expedition, then the Raba grade, who were the junior warriors and the third, the Dori grade, the senior warriors. By this arrangement the system furnished leadership in offensive and retaliatory wars.[149] In any offensive the three grades coordinated their attack and retreat. In the process pastoral Oromo developed remarkably effective guerrilla warfare.

The movement of pastoral Oromo, as the respected scholar, the late Hussein Ahmed noted, was not motivated by the desire to 'extend political domination, to collect tributes or to impose a national religious culture',[150] but rather, was a movement in search of grazing land 'to

---

[144] E. Cerulli, *The Folk Literature of the Galla of Southern Abyssinia*, Harvard African Studies, 3 (Cambridge, MA: Harvard University Press), 58.

[145] Hassen, *The Oromo of Ethiopia A History 1570–1860* (Cambridge: Cambridge University Press, 1990), 12.

[146] Ibid., 13.

[147] de Salviac, *An Ancient People: Great African Nation – The Oromo*, 308.

[148] Bahrey, *Some Records of Ethiopia*, 126.

[149] Legesse, *Gada: Three Approaches to the Study of African Society*, 76.

[150] Hussein Ahmed, 'Clerics, Traders and Chiefs: A Historical Study of Islam in Wallo Ethiopia with Special Emphasis on the Nineteenth Century', PhD diss., University of Birmingham, 1985, 109.

accommodate a rapidly growing population' as observed by Donald Levine.[151] In their movements the two major Oromo moieties – the Borana and Barentu – seem to have emerged not by maintaining 'the pure blood' of the ancestors, but by successfully assimilating diverse groups. The oral traditions of the 2,800 Oromo *gosa*s or sub-*gosa*s[152] seem to be not just memorized legends of divisions or sub-divisions, but narratives of fusion and interaction by which the major divisions constantly increased in size. This was facilitated by the *gada* system, which mobilized the pastoral Oromo militarily and politically, and provided them with the mechanism for dynamic movement. The fusion and interaction among the Borana and the Barentu *gosa*s and sub-*gosa*s and their neighbours, coupled with the dynamic *gada* system, sustained the Oromo nation.

> A nation's history cannot be fixed at a certain starting point, nor can it be dated from a specific event. It rather comprises a continuum of events emanating from beginnings that may belong to remote past ... although the course of its history has not adhered to a single pattern. A nation may emerge from several separate groupings or from the coalescence of one large entity. It may produce a single political entity or find itself divided among several. A nation may find its unifying bond and a sense of fraternity in the origins of its people. And it may develop a single common language from which it proceeds to the formation of its own culture, the character and essence of which thus derive from that language.[153]

CONCLUSION

I conclude this chapter by stressing that the cradleland of the Oromo people, that is, where they appear to have become conscious of their separate identity, was located in southern Ethiopia. There is no doubt whatsoever that the Oromo did not originate from beyond the boundaries of modern Ethiopia. Their political, cultural, and religious institutions appear to have developed in the highlands of southern Ethiopia in general and the regions of Bale and Sidamo in particular. On the eve of the sixteenth-century population movement, pastoral Oromo lived in six homelands in the regions of Bale and Sidamo (see Map 4, page 87). Settled agricultural Oromo communities lived in the historical provinces of Bali, Dawaro, Fatagar, Ifat, Hadiya and Waj (located in what are today Shawa, Arsi, northern Bale and western Hararghe). These settled agricultural Oromo communities lived under the Christian administration, while the pastoral Oromo lived beyond its control. It was the

[151] Levine, *Greater Ethiopia*, 79–80.
[152] The names of the two thousand and eight hundred Oromo *gosa*s and sub-*gosa*s are identified in Haile, *History of the Oromo to the Sixteenth Century*, 85, 94, 114, 117–36, 146–59, 177–9,184–90, 198–230, 238, 240–52, 257–63, 269–77.
[153] I have drawn on Abd Al-Ziz Duri, Lawrence I. Conrad, trans., *The Historical Formation of the Arab Nation: A Study in Identity and Consciousness* (London: Croon Helm, 1987), 4.

pastoral Oromo who embarked on the sixteenth-century massive population movement.

Oromo population movement within and beyond Ethiopia followed patterns of population movements which were well established in the Horn of Africa. The Afar and the Somali, for example, migrated from southern Ethiopia to their present locations. A number of Semitic-speaking groups such as the Adare (Harari), the Gurage and the Amhara migrated from the north to the south, while the Oromo migrated from within the south. As stressed in the Introduction, population movement has always been the stuff of history[154] whether it was in Ethiopia, or Africa or the rest of the world. This is because 'Human history has always been shaped by the growth of and migration of population.'[155] Though unrecorded by historians there were population movements in the Ethiopian region for centuries. In fact, the fourteenth and sixteenth centuries Christian-Muslim conflicts in Ethiopia were partly a response to population movements.[156] Although overlooked in Ethiopian historiography between 1888 and 1892 no less than 200,000–300,000 people moved from northern Ethiopia to the region of Hararghe alone after King Menelik conquered and incorporated the region into the Ethiopian empire in 1887.[157] It is believed that since the early 1990s over 3 million people have moved and settled in the regional state of Oromia alone, which demonstrates that population movement still continues in Ethiopia.

During the course of their movement, the Oromo adopted various non-Oromo groups, and this was accompanied by Oromo-ization. The extensive movement of pastoral Oromo from Bale, Sidamo, and Gamu Gofa contributed to the Oromo-ization that embraced many other groups. Oromo pastoralists absorbed Cushitic- and Semitic-speaking groups into their social structure. Through the *gada* system, adoption brought new members from the periphery into the centre of communal life.[158] The Oromo pastoralists penetrated easily and assimilated quickly where there were already Oromo-speaking communities. This was particularly true of old Bali, Dawaro (Charchar in western Hararghe), Fatagar, Waj and other areas in and south of what is today the Shawa region.

---

[154] Olaniyan, ed., *African History and Culture*, 2.

[155] Paul Kennedy, *Preparing for the Twenty-First Century*, (New York: Random House, 1993), cover page.

[156] See for instance, Merid Wolde Aregay, 'Population Movement as a Possible Factor in the Christian-Muslim Conflict of Medieval Ethiopia', *Symposium Leo Frobenius* (Munich: Derlag Dokumentation, 1974), 261–81.

[157] Richard Caulk, *Between the Jaws of Hyenas: A Diplomatic History of Ethiopia (1876–1896)*, ed. and intro. Bahru Zewde, (Wiesbaden: Harrassowitz Verlag, 2002), 291.

[158] Hassen, *The Oromo of Ethiopia: A History, 1570–1860*, 21–22.

4

The Pastoral Oromo
Confront the Christian Expansion, 1440s–1559

The jihad of Imam Ahmad (1529–43) and the pastoral Oromo population movement made the sixteenth century one of turmoil and violent
changes in the Horn of Africa. Both events were the results of processes
that had been gathering momentum for over two centuries and they
came to a head almost simultaneously. The jihad dramatically influenced the outcome of pastoral Oromo population movement because
it was accompanied by warfare on a scale not previously witnessed in
the area and sent different groups fleeing from the 'storm centre', abandoning their ancestral homes. This caused a chain reaction over a wide
area. The dispersal of the refugees was accompanied by carnage and
destruction on an appalling scale. 'The immense toll that [it] had taken
in human lives and material wealth was'[1] beyond calculation. Untold
numbers must have died from famine during the jihad and the anarchy
that followed its failure. This was particularly true of the Harar and
Charchar regions, which were devastated. When Emperor Galawdewos
conducted extensive military campaigns in the region and destroyed
the Muslim city of Harar in 1550, thousands of people may have been
killed.[2] His actions precipitated a civil war among the Muslims out of
which Amir Nur (1552–67), the nephew of Imam Ahmad, emerged as
the third jihadic leader the city of Harar produced during the sixteenth
century. Amir Nur's 1559 jihadic war was to have catastrophic consequences for both the Christian kingdom and the Muslim state of Harar
(see Chapter 5).

As a result of the Christian and Muslim conflicts, a great number of
people abandoned their ancestral lands to seek refuge in difficult mountainous regions or other areas that held out hope of asylum.

> While some inhabitants fled to escape the sword, others fled famine and
> misery which had ruined much of the country ... In addition, aside from the
> war itself, mass movements and famine, epidemics played havoc in sections
> of the country as well. Whole villages were abandoned, the land left unculti-
> vated and the survivors migrated to other areas in the hope of finding some
> means of subsistence.[3]

[1] J.S. Trimingham, *Islam in Ethiopia*, 89.

[2] See for example, Boavida et al., *Pedro Páez's History of Ethiopia*, 303.

138 [3] J.A. Davis, 'The Sixteenth Century Jihad in Ethiopia and the Impact on its

This phenomenon changed the pattern of population distribution, particularly in historical Bali, Dawaro, Hadiya and the Harar-Charchar regions. Instead of a fairly even scattering of groups, with population densities varying according to the advantages of water and soil, great agglomerations of peoples emerged, often centred on a relatively difficult terrain, and separated from one another by considerable tracts of virtually empty land.[4]

The history of the Hadiya people offers a good example. These people, who now dwell in the region between Gurage and the upper Bilate River, are undoubtedly the scattered remnants of a formerly much larger ethnic complex, which probably constituted the majority of the once mighty Muslim principality called Hadiya. The histories of this principality and the people who shared its name were inextricably linked; the changes in the fortunes of the former brought about irreversible changes in the fortunes of the latter. This Muslim principality that had won fame in the Muslim world for its rich agricultural produce, its trade and its large cavalry and infantry forces (and notoriety for its production of eunuchs[5]) was located, according to Braukämper, 'between southern Haraghe, southern Arsi, and northern Bale and stretched for an unknown distance southward into Sidamo province'.[6] Hadiya formed the backbone of Muslim opposition against Christian domination for almost two centuries. When the victorious Imam Ahmad reached Hadiya in 1531, the Muslim ruler of the province submitted to his co-religionist without any resistance. The Imam rewarded the Hadiya leader by confirming him in his position, while the Hadiya chief cemented his tie with the Imam by giving his daughter Muris as a wife.[7] Abdul-Nasir, the Imam's famous general, also married the sister of a Hadiya leader, completing the marriage alliance between the ruling houses of Hadiya and the jihadic leaders from Harar.[8]

(contd) Culture', *Journal of the Historical Society of Nigeria* 3 (1964), 113. See also Trimingham, *Islam in Ethiopia*, 90.

[4] For similar phenomena, see J. Omer Cooper, *The Zulu Aftermath: A Nineteenth Century Revolution in Bantu Africa* (London, 1966), 1–7, and *passim*.

[5] Al-Umari, ibn Fadl Allah, trans. M. Gaudefroy-Demonbynes, *Masalik al-Absar fi Mamalik al-Amsar: L'Afrique moins L'Egypte* (Paris, 1927), 1–3. See also al Maqrizi, trans. and ed. F.T. Rinck, *Historia Regum Islamiticorum in Abyssinia* (Leiden, 1790); from this Latin version, G.W.B. Huntingford made an English translation in London, in 1955, 'The Book of the True Knowledge of the History of the Kings in Abyssinia'; I have consulted the typescript found at the School of Oriental and African Studies Library, 9–10: 'the king of Amhara forbids that slaves be castrated with a serious penalty have been established, but they were led secretly to the city of Vafhlu (Wafla?) [Kingdom of Hadiah], whose inhabitants are stupid and without any religion and they become eunuchs there. This is the only city in the whole region of Abyssinia which allows this to happen. Then, the castrati are brought to the city of Hadiah and are again subjected to the razor, until a passage for urine, which the pus-filled matter had obstructed is opened', (14–15).

[6] Ulrich Braukämper, 'Islamic Principalities in Southeast Ethiopia between the Thirteenth and Sixteenth Centuries', *Ethiopianist Notes* 1, 2 (1977), 15.

[7] She died a few months later.

[8] Arab Faqih, *Futuh al-Habasha*, 377.

After the formation of this alliance the Hadiya people, especially the Gudela who lived in the northern section of Dallo, left their country as auxiliaries to General Abdul-Nasir, who became the governor of Ganz. The Gudela occupied new grazing areas in Ganz, Kambata, and Waj. It is important to note that the Gudela who left Dallo were small groups of nomads who were under pressure from numerous other nomads from other groups, such as the Alba and Kabana, two sections of the Hadiya people who occupied the area between the Charchar range and eastern Arsi, and joined the Imam after his conquest of Dawaro. According to Braukämper, the turbulence of the jihad provoked such far-reaching population movements among the peoples of the area that the ethnic situation was radically altered. 'A part of the Alaba and Kabana at first moved to the southwest, where they left some of their clans in Gadab and the present Sidama country.'[9] Some of the Hadiya people still recall this time in their traditions as Daudi Galla (the time of dispersal, in their language). Thus, during the eventful jihadic years, different groups from Hadiya shifted to the north-west and south-west, where sometime later they were either absorbed by the Oromo or pushed westward by them.

The pastoral Oromo population movement, which began much earlier, took considerable advantage of the situation created by the jihad. The Christian military colonies in the southern provinces, which time and again in the fifteenth century had stopped the pastoral Oromo movement to the north, were dislodged. Their destruction at such a critical time was disastrous for both Muslims and Christians. The Christian kingdom took time to recover and was thwarted in its attempts at resettlement in the southern provinces by the pastoral Oromo. Regions that had been sparsely populated before the jihad had been left empty by the shifting of the population during the wars and the Oromo could thus easily settle large areas in a short time.

As has been indicated in Chapter 1, the Oromo consisted of two major moieties, the Borana and Barentu. There was no such thing as a 'pure' Borana or Barentu descended from a single founding father. It would seem that the history of the Oromo people is not a collection of histories of hundreds of *gosas* or descent groups, but a story of fusion and interaction by which all the major sub-moieties or confederacies and various descent groups were constantly altered and transformed.[10]

This chapter first attempts to explain why the Borana Oromo were unable to move through the Rift Valley before the 1530s. It then charts the beginning of the Barentu Oromo movement from three separate central *chaffee* assemblies (parliaments) in the province of Bali and discusses briefly the importance of the institution of *mogassa*, which enabled the Oromo to turn an enemy into an ally. Finally, we track movement of pastoral Oromo and Emperor Galawdeows' (1540–59) failed attempt at stopping it.

[9] Braukämper, 'Islamic Principalities in Southeast Ethiopia', 1, 2 (1977),12.
[10] Here we shall first deal with the Borana, who are not prominent in this chapter, and then with the Barentu, who are the central theme.

WHY WAS THE BORANA OROMO POPULATION MOVEMENT SLOW TO START?

Before attempting to answer this question, it is important to provide some information about the Borana moiety itself. It was divided into three sub-moieties or confederacies, namely, Macha and Tulama, the southern Borana,[11] and Gujji (see Map 4, page 87). The Macha and Tulama lived together under one *chaffee* assembly – the traditional Oromo government based on the *gada* system, under which leaders were elected for eight-year periods. It made laws, decided on issues of war and peace, and settled inter-clan disputes. The Macha and Tulama lived at Harroo Wallaabuu located some 30 to 40 miles (48 to 64 km) east of Lake Margherita.[12] The southern Borana lived in Tulul Wallal and the Gujji lived around Harro Gerjjaa on both sides of the Ganale River. Here, I only discuss the movement of the Macha and Tulama, who moved to the north in two stages, not that of the southern Borana and Gujji. During the first stage, the Macha and Tulama moved in small groups, while during the second stage they moved in large groups with many members. During both stages their custom was to set out to war together, although after a period they eventually separated[13] in the last quarter of the sixteenth century. The sources are unanimous in claiming that after their movement from Harroo Wallaabuu, the Macha and Tulama had a common *chaffee* assembly in Fatagar at a place called Oda Nabe, in Dukam, about thirty kilometres south-east of the village of Finfinnee, now the famous Ethiopian capital of Addis Ababa. Oda Nabe is constructed from *oda*, the holy sycamore tree, and *nabe*, derived from the Arabic *nabi*, a word for the prophet, which implies a strong Islamic influence. In fact, three recent studies establish that Oda Nabe was a very important political and religious centre for the settled Oromo communities who lived in Fatagar under Christian adminis-tration during the fourteenth century.[14] At Oda Nabe, the Macha and Tulama appear to have encountered many people who were Muslims. For instance, the clan of Ali of the Jidda group must have been Muslims, as it was only Muslim Oromo who used names such as Ali. Members of the Innaangoo clan also appear to have been Muslims.[15] From this it appears that pastoral Oromo in the course of their movements in the

[11] As can be seen, Borana was both the name of the major moiety, whose sub-moieties spread to the north (Macha and Tulama), as well as the name of the group that spread over southern Ethiopia and northern Kenya. The one difference is that the Macha and Tulama sub-moieties used the term Borana as the name of their common 'father' in relation to the Barentu Oromo, while the southern sub-moiety still use the term Borana as their own national name.
[12] C.F. Beckingham and G.W.B. Huntingford, 'Preface', in *Some Records of Ethiopia*, lxxvi.
[13] Bahrey, in *Some Records of Ethiopia*, 112.
[14] Gidada, *History of the Sayyoo*, 28. See also Alemayehu Haile et al., *History of the Oromo to the Sixteenth Century*, 90–91. See also Bulcha, *Contours of the Emergent and Ancient Oromo Nation*, 161–2.
[15] Gidada, ibid., 21.

regions of Bali and Hadiya adopted members of the Muslim population, whether through voluntary submission or defeat.

Bahrey makes a clear distinction between the first and the second stages of the Macha and Tulama movement to the north. Regarding the first, he states that 'the [Oromo] came from the west and crossed the river of their country, which is called Galana, to the frontier of Bali in the time of Hatse Wanag Sagad'.[16] That event most probably took place around 1522. For the second stage, he states that 'those of the Borana who stayed came out of their country by way of Kuera, that was the time when Fasil attacked them and was killed by them'.[17] Those who remained behind later came out of their country not by making a long detour towards Bali and returning once again to the west, as the earliest groups did, but by pouring out of Harroo Wallaabuu and Wallal via the short and direct route through the Rift Valley to Waj and Batera Amora. This took place between 1578 and 1586, when the powerful Birmaje Gada was in power. What is more, it was a section of this last Borana wave, known as Jaawwii,[18] that attacked Gamo, the homeland of Bahrey, thus forcing him to flee to the northern part of the Christian kingdom.[19] It must be clarified that Bahrey's homeland of Gamo was located not in the Gamu highlands in southern Ethiopia as many still believe but in the region of what is today Shawa, not far from 'the town of Shashmane'.[20]

Before discussing the movement of the Borana into Bali around 1522, it is necessary to examine briefly some errors that arose out of the extrapolation of the nineteenth-century situation backwards into the sixteenth century, as well as to consider the various factors influencing the Borana Oromo population movement. As mentioned above, the Borana crossed the river of their country, Galana, to the frontier of Bali in 1522. Different identifications have been given to this river. Huntingford, followed by H.S. Lewis, has identified it with one of three rivers called Galana. 'The first is the Galana Dulei, which flows into Lake Stefanie, the second is the Galan Sagan [for the location of the two rivers see Map 8, page 123], which enters the Galan Dulei from the east, and the third is the Galana which enters Lake Margherita.'[21] However, all three rivers are far away from the frontiers of Bali. Hence, the attempt to identify one or all of them as the Galana of Bahrey is untenable. We have seen in Chapter 2

[16] Bahrey, in *Some Records of Ethiopia*, 111.

[17] Ibid., 114.

[18] Bahrey, followed by numerous Christian chroniclers, called the Jawe 'Dawe'. The Oromo term Jaawwii is a name of a *gosa* (a descent group) while the Amhara term *dawe* is a name of a very serious and incurable skin disease. According to Tasawo Merga, 'The Oromo war on the Amhara had become an incurable skin disease with which they had to live'. Merga, 'Senna Umatta Oromo', 114–15.

[19] Since our concern here is with the first wave of Borana movement, we leave the second stage for the next chapter.

[20] Aregay, 'Southern Ethiopia and the Christian Kingdom', 309.

[21] Huntingford, 'Preface', in *Some Records of Ethiopia*, lxxii–lxxiii. See also H.S. Lewis, 'The Origins of Galla and Somali,' *Journal of African History* 7 (1966), 32.

that Schleicher identified Bahrey's Galana with Wabi Shebelle,[22] which is the most likely. Merid has identified it with the Ganale Doria, or the Galana Dida, its main tributary.[23] This identification with the Ganale is plausible, provided the reference is only to the upper Ganale. The lower Ganale is at a distance from historical Bali and any identification with it is untenable. By contrast, equating it with the upper Ganale would suggest that in the early 1520s the Borana crossed the upper part of this river and poured into the lowlands of Dallo, the region dominated mainly by the Barentu.

The Borana movement into Bali

Why did the Borana groups cross into Bali, a well-defended province,[24] instead of descending into the wide plains of the Rift Valley, a region well endowed with pasture and water – the two essential items needed by the pastoral Oromo for their cattle? What is more, the Rift Valley was more convenient both for attack and retreat. The second wave of Borana (1578–86) directly followed this path. In the light of these advantages, it is not easy to explain why the Borana crossed into Bali in the 1520s. Moreover, what sparked off the Borana Oromo population movement at this time?

Many scholars assume that both the Borana and Barentu moved from west of Ganale to Bali in these years. However, we have already shown in the previous chapter that the majority of the Barentu lived east of the Ganale River. Bahrey also specifically refers to the Borana coming to the frontier of Bali in 1522 for a joint war with the Barentu moiety against the Christian kingdom. So far two explanations have been given to the two questions raised above.

> It is probable that the migration of various peoples from Ifat, Adal, the Charchar-Harar highlands and the Danakil lowlands into the central plateau had forced a southward dislocation of the peoples of Hadiya, Kambata, Gamo and Kuera. This may also account for the fact that the [Oromo] took the more difficult route through Bali, since at least until the wars of Ahmad Gran it was a well-defended province.[25]

In the above explanation, the dislocation of the various Cushitic and Semitic-speaking groups due to the jihadic war is claimed to have sparked off the Borana Oromo population movement. However, this seems to be an anachronistic application of the situation in the 1530 and 1540s to that of the early 1520s. The explanation also fails to show how the dislocated and dispersed groups were able to put serious pressure on the Oromo who would eventually engulf the powerful Christian kingdom and the Muslim state of Harar. In addition, there are also sources that claim that the Borana were forced to change their course

---

[22] Schleicher, *Geschichte der Galla*, quoted in Tafla, *Asma Giyorgis and his Work*, 137, note 166.
[23] Aregay, 'Southern Ethiopia and the Christian Kingdom', 150.
[24] Ibid., 156.
[25] Ibid.

of movement due to the resistance of the Sidama people in general and that of the Walayita state in particular.

The Sidama people now dwell between Lake Abbaya, Lake Awasa, and the upper Ganale, although they were supposed to have had Bali as their original ancestral home. Cerulli, followed by many others, argued that the ancestors of the Sidama people were driven out from the north of the present province of Bale by the Oromo, thus migrating westward to their present dwelling areas.[26] However, this is incorrect. In fact, Stanley claims just the opposite – that it was the Sidama people who pushed the Oromo from the highlands on the upper Ganale.[27] In short, where Cerulli makes the Oromo population movement the cause for the exodus of the ancestors of Sidama from Bali, Stanley believes that the fleeing Sidama themselves sparked off the Oromo population movement. Some aspects of Stanley's argument seem partly correct. A portion of his argument is indeed supported by evidence that the ancestors of the Sidama, fleeing from the storm centre following the failure of the jihad,[28] assimilated Oromo groups such as the Hofa on the upper Ganale.[29] The assimilated Oromo groups seem to have been either isolated groups or the remnants of those Oromo who had earlier crossed into Bali and beyond Wabi Shebelle River between 1522 and 1546. The historical evidence, however, contradicts a key point in Stanley's argument. Although the consequences of the jihadic war during the first half of the sixteenth century were dramatic, the Oromo population movement had begun in an earlier period. What is more, Stanley fails to explain how the divided and disunited small groups were able to put pressure on the Oromo, who unquestionably were larger and possessed the very effective *gada* system that mobilized all able-bodied men for warfare.

It was the possession of the *gada* system that enabled the Oromo not only to prevail but also, through the practice of adoption, easily turn an enemy into an ally and war partner. What is more, it was from the Oromo, according to Braukämper, that the Sidama adopted the *gada* system. Above all, the Sidama people, who are an amalgam of thirteen small groups, did not form one ethnic body before 1650. Braukämper claims that there were no Sidama people to speak of in the 1520s.[30]

In 1980 Braukämper presented a hypothesis for why the Borana did not directly move to the north through the Rift Valley: 'The homeland of the Oromo ... [was] bordered by presumably rather densely populated domiciles of peoples of Hadiya-Sidama stock who prevented them from

---

[26] Cerulli, *Studi Etiopici I: la Lingua e la Storia di Harar*, 2.
[27] S. Stanley, 'History of the Sidama', MS 19, cited in Braukämper, 'Islamic principalities', 25–26.
[28] This may have taken place after 1543 in general and 1545 in particular, since the death of Abbas marked the end of a larger Islamic state in the southern region.
[29] Merga, 'Senna Umatta Oromo', 6–8.
[30] Ulrich Braukämper, 'The Ethnogenesis of the Sidama', *Abbay Cahier* 9 (1978), 128.

taking a direct northward route of expansion and induced them to turn to northeast via Dallo.'[31] Braukämper's views on this question are quite plausible. Hadiya groups lived west of the Urgoma mountain range, in Gadab and in Dallo, the western parts of the present region of Bale. It is certainly possible that, together with the support of the Christian military colonies, the Hadiya people helped force the Borana to change the direction of their movement. However, other elements of Braukämper's argument suffer from shortcomings. For example, he claims that the Hadiya people reached their climax by the middle of the sixteenth century by spreading to Bali, Dawaro and Fatagar: this, presumably, was before the Oromo overtook these provinces. As has already been indicated, by the middle of the sixteenth century the Hadiya state had shrunk drastically in size, the Oromo had effectively ended Christian administration in Bali, and lowland Dawaro and Fatagar was under their attack. What is more, Braukämper connects Hadiya and the Harla,[32] making them one people, but does not substantiate this with any concrete evidence.[33] He also claims that Hawasso was the Oromo name for the Harla people. In reality, Hawasso was the name of an Oromo clan that lived around the middle section of the Awash River, which the Oromo call Hawash, and thus they received the nickname Hawasso; they belonged to the Karrayyu[34] confederacy (on which see below).

As for the strength of the Walayita state, which prevented the Borana from moving directly to the north through the Rift Valley, it is stated that 'fortifications were made on the frontier as a defence against the [Oromo]. Ruins of some of them remain north of Lake Margherita between the rivers Wayo and Bilate and elsewhere.'[35] This again is an extrapolation of the eighteenth- and nineteenth-century situation into the early sixteenth century; there was no Walayita state at that time. At the beginning of the sixteenth century, Walayita was part of the Christian kingdom. There is in fact an indication that one of the founders of the Walayita dynasty, which claims a Tigray origin, 'may have been a renegade leader of an isolated group of Christian settlers cut off by the collapse of

---

[31] Braukämper, 'Oromo Country of Origin: A Reconsideration of Hypotheses', 29. See also *idem, Geschichte der Hadiya Sud-Aethiopiens*, 136–39; *idem*, 'Islamic Principalities', 27–28.

[32] The Harla were Semitic-speaking people, who lived in the region of Hararghe as early as the tenth century. They were sedentary farmers, town dwellers, merchants, and great warriors, who provided the leadership for the jihadic war of the sixteenth century, including Imam Ahmad and several other prominent generals.

[33] The evidence Braukämper presented in support of his assertion is the claim that the Karrayu Oromo call the Harla Hawasso (e.g. people who live around the Awash River). What is more, Hawasso was the general name by which Oromo pilgrims from Shawa and beyond were known in southern Ethiopia, when they visited the land of Abba Muudaa.

[34] Alemayehu Haile et al., *History of the Oromo to the Sixteenth Century*, 76.

[35] Beckingham and Huntingford, 'Preface', in *Some Records of Ethiopia*, lxvi.

the empire in the south'.[36] The Walayita state, founded sometime between 1650 and 1700, was centred around Kendo from where it began expanding in the eighteenth and nineteenth centuries. This state, like the Oromo Gibe states of the nineteenth century, was separated from its neighbours by strips of natural forest known as *mogga* (borderland in Oromo language) where only outlaws and wild beasts lived. Like the contemporary kings of the Gibe states, the Walayita kings built trenches and walls to defend their borders. Of all the kings of Walayita, the famous nineteenth-century king Damote is reported to have built deeper and wider ditches and trenches to defend the land he won from Kambata and the Arsi Oromo.[37] It is some of these nineteenth-century fortifications, one of which was observed by Azaïs and Chambard in the 1920s north of Lake Abaya,[38] which are supposed to have prevented the Borana from moving in that direction early in the sixteenth century.

The above explanation attempts to answer the question why the Borana crossed into Bali in 1520s. As to what sparked off the Borana population movement, very little has been said. We now turn to Borana tradition itself in the hope that it may help to answer both questions.

The legend of Liqimssa

Among the Borana, both in Ethiopia and northern Kenya, there is a strange legend that is difficult to explain. However, it holds the key to understanding a number of complicated questions. Stranger still, this legend, which appears to be distributed widely among the Borana, is unknown among the Barentu Oromo. This is the legend of Liqimssa (the swallower), which is set in Wallaabuu.[39] There are two contradictory episodes in it. On the one hand it is said that Wallaabuu, the original home of the Borana people, was the land of plenty (milk, meat and butter), peace and fertility. 'It is the land of Abba Muudaa, where white cattle yielded so much milk and meat that men neither ploughed nor sowed.' In this ideal land, which is characterized as 'heaven on earth', the Borana lived in happiness under one Abba Bokku (the leader of the *chaffee* assembly). On the other hand, this legend claims that the people

---

[36] Tsehai Berhane-Selassie, 'The Question of Damot and Walamo', *Journal of Ethiopian Studies* 13 (1975), 41–42.

[37] The numerous wars that the kings of Walayita conducted against the Arsi Oromo during the eighteenth and nineteenth centuries are depicted by Tasawo Merga. *Idem*, 'Senna Umatta Oromo', 113–74.

[38] R.P. Azaïs and R. Chambard, *Cinq années de recherches archéologiques en Ethiopie, Province du Harar et Ethiopie Meridionale*, vol. 1 (Paris, 1931), 272.

[39] Cerulli, *Etiopia Occidentale*, vols 1–2, 169–72 ; see also E. Cerulli, *Somalia: Scritti Vari editi ed inediti*, vol. 2 (Rome: 1964), 127; Yelma Deressa, *Ya Ityopya Tarik*, 212; B.W. Andrzejewski, 'Ideas about Warfare in Borana Galla: Stories and Fables', *African Language Studies* 3 (1962), 127; Beckingham and Huntingford, 'Preface', in *Some Records of Ethiopia*, lxxvi; V. Grottanelli, 'The Peopling of the Horn of Africa', in *East Africa and the Orient: Cultural Synthesis in Pre-Colonial Times*, ed. H. Neville Chittick and Robert L. Rotberg (New York: Africana Publishing, 1975), 55.

left their 'blessed' Wallaabuu because of a 'cursed' beast that ate people one by one[40] and could change its shape. It was called Liqimssa. The noun *liqimssa* is derived from the verb *liqimssu* meaning to swallow, to finish, or to destroy, in the sense of wiping out everything. It also has the implication of 'hunger' in the sense that everything is 'swallowed' by some powerful entity and therefore there is nothing left to eat. The concept embodied in the term is that hunger is an evil against which one cannot fight. 'The beast eats [people] one by one and men cannot fight against it. So they run away from the beast.'[41] Cerulli interpreted this legend as the 'Somali pressure' on the Oromo, which forced the latter to abandon 'their original home' in the central part of southern Somalia and to move to Ethiopia.[42] However, it has already been made clear that the theory of 'Somali pressure' does not have any historical support.[43] Huntingford, without contradicting Cerulli's interpretation, substitutes his 'Somali pressure' with 'Sidama pressure'.[44] The question of 'Sidama pressure' is equally untenable as shown above.

The absence of the 'Somali and Sidama pressures' tempts one to interpret the legend as either 'the pressure from the powerful Christian kingdom', most probably during the reign of Emperor Amda-Siyon (1314–44) and his successors, when the warrior Christian kings were expanding the frontiers of their state in all directions, notably to the south, where their country bordered with Oromo territory. Some sections of the Borana may have been the victims of the Christian state's southward expansion. This interpretation becomes plausible if we look at it in the light of an element in the legend, which seems to suggest long-standing pressure from the powerful 'beast' that forced people to flee their country. Or the legend could equally be interpreted as natural or ecological disaster. The natural disaster may have been war, with its far-reaching consequences, rinderpest that spread havoc in the animal and human population, or even an epidemic or some combination of the above factors. Whatever it was, the term *liqimssa* refers to an 'invincible' force beyond one's control, be it warfare or famine, both of which have catastrophic consequences. As E.A. Wrigley observes:

> The pressures of hard times and the opportunities of happier periods are reflected in historical demography like images in a camera obscura. The picture always, needs interpretation and may lack the polychrome fullness of historical reality, but it forms a clear and dependable outline to which colour may be added as the population characteristics are related to their social and economic setting.[45]

[40] Andrzejewski, 'Ideas about Warfare', 127; Grottanelli, 'The Peopling of the Horn of Africa', 55.
[41] Andrzejewski, 'Ideas about Warfare', 127. See also Cerulli, *Etiopia occidentale*, vols 1, 2, 169–72.
[42] Cerulli, ibid.
[43] Hersi, 'The Arab Factor in Somali History', 20–24.
[44] Beckingham and Huntingford, 'Preface' in *Some Records of Ethiopia*, lxxvi.
[45] E.A. Wrigley, *Population and History* (New York and Toronto: McGraw-Hill, 1969), 28.

Interestingly, the legend of Liqimssa is widespread among the Borana moiety both in Ethiopia and Kenya. It seems that this was a concentrated and dramatic retelling of a long history of 'crises' that crystallized in a single event, the catastrophe caused by the 'cursed beast.'

Finally, my interpretation of this strange Borana legend as the 'pressure of the powerful Christian state' is supported by the historical record. I have demonstrated in Chapter 2 the presence of some Oromo groups within the medieval Christian kingdom during the fourteenth century and possibly earlier. Amda-Siyon's Chronicle mentions Galla as people and Hagara Galla as the country of the Galla.[46] Amhara traditions mention a Galla River and a Galla Forest. Fra Mauro's map of 1460 refers to the Galla River, which has been identified with the headwaters of the Wabi Shabelle. P. Zurla, in his study of Fra Mauro's, concludes that 'the people described as fierce enemies of the Christians and located south of the Galla River were the Galla themselves'.[47] This important conclusion, which demonstrates the presence of some Oromo groups on the border with the Christian kingdom just south of the province of Waj and the Awash River, has the following significance. By the first half of the fifteenth century the Borana, from their base in Harroo Wallaabuu, had already embarked on their movement to the north via the short route. However, the Christian defence system in the Rift Valley seems to have frustrated their movement at this stage. This conclusion is also supported by information from another source.[48] The presence of the Borana on the border with the Christian kingdom not only shows the persistent struggle between the Christian military colonists and the Oromo, but also hints at the possibility that, as the Christian state checked the northward movement of pastoral Oromo, the latter may have slowed down the process of the Christian state's expansion to the south. The garrisoning of the frontier provinces did not totally stop the northward movement, since some elements of the Barentu section continued streaming to the north from the direction of Bali. In other words, the Borana were unable to move via the short route to the north as the Barentu did. As a result, the Borana turned towards Bali.

The main reasons why the Barentu Oromo were able to proceed with ease, in contrast to the difficulties faced by the Borana, seem to have been two-fold. First, it seems that most of the Barentu moiety were spread out over a large area in and south of the province of Bali, and it was almost impossible to control their movement over such a wide territory. The narrow Rift Valley, however, enabled Christian defence encampments to easily and effectively control the Borana movement. Second, members of the Barentu moiety were more numerous than the Borana and consequently stronger. This becomes clear from the fact that by the time of the sixteenth-century pastoral Oromo population movement, the Borana had three sub-moieties, although not yet

[46] Getatchew Haile, *The Works of Abba Bahriy*, 26.
[47] D.P. Zurla, *Il Mappamondo di Fra Mauro Camaldolese*, 136, quoted in Merid Wolde Aregay, 'Southern Ethiopia and the Christian Kingdom', 149–50.
[48] Yelma Deressa, *Ya Ityopya Tarik*, 225.

fully-fledged, while the Barentu had seven fully-fledged sub-moieties. It is clear from our sources that the smaller and relatively weaker Borana were not able to move directly to the north past the impregnable wall of the many Christian garrisons in the Rift Valley. Once that wall was demolished by the jihadic wars, the Borana fought their way north, devastating the small Christian colonies in Waj and other provinces (see Chapter 5).

THE BEGINNING OF THE BARENTU OROMO POPULATION MOVEMENT

The major sixteenth-century pastoral Oromo population movement was begun by the Barentu moiety with the support of the Borana. These Borana, who joined the Barentu in the early phase of pastoral Oromo movement to the north, fought as volunteers and adventurers who rallied to the call of their brothers. It seems that when the news of the Barentu success in moving to the north reached the Harroo Wallaabuu area, it stirred the Borana warriors to go and join them in the adventure.[49] From this it follows that, during the first phase of their movement, the officers of both the Borana and Barentu moieties met, discussed the route to follow, and fought jointly under a single command. According to Asmarom Legesse 'it is clear that *gada* regiments made up of fighters from both moieties, did their fighting not as two tribes with two parallel armies, but as a single nation governed by the same political and military institutions'.[50] This practice seems to have lasted until the 1580s, before they began occasionally fighting each other over scarce resources.

As indicated earlier, the members of the Barentu moiety lived mainly east of the Ganale River in what is today the Bale region. They lived in two areas. A section composed of three full-fledged sub-moieties lived in the highlands of Bale, with their common *chaffee* assembly at Bareda Kurkurittu, around the upper Ganale, the region that Haberland gives as the original home of the Arsi Oromo.[51] As indicated above, the *chaffee* assembly was the traditional Oromo government under which leaders were elected for eight-year periods. The elected leaders included the Abba Gada or Abba Bokku (the father of the *gada* in power), Abba Dula (the father of war), and Abba Sera (the father of law). It was from Bareda Kurkurittu that one section, due to the transhumant nature of their economy, moved to the lowlands of Bale. At first, both those who lived in the highlands and those in the lowlands seem to have had a common *chaffee* assembly at Bareda Kurkurittu. With the march of time, however, the importance and influence of the local *chaffee* seems to have increased at the expense of the central *chaffee*, and the political and the ritual units were split up, each division becoming a confed-

---

[49] Yelma Deressa, *Ya Ityopya Tarik*, 228.
[50] Legesse, *Oromo Democracy*, 161.
[51] E. Haberland, *Galla Süd-Aethiopiens*, 6 (map).

eracy with its own central *chaffee*. Thus, for all practical purposes, by the beginning of the sixteenth century there was no common *chaffee* for all the Barentu. Instead there were three central *chaffees* – one in the highlands and two in the lowlands of what is today the Bale region (see Map 4, page 87). This may explain why the major Barentu groups moved to the north in two different directions and why, after their settlement in the northern region, one section of the Barentu sent their representatives to the spiritual leader at Dallo (in the lowlands of the present Bale region) while the other section sent representatives to the spiritual leader at Bareda Kurkurittu in the highlands of Bale.

Central *chaffee* assembly at Bareda Kurkurittu

By the end of the fifteenth century the three major sub-moieties of the Karrayu, Marawa and Warantisha (Arsi) had one central *chaffee* at Bareda Kurkurittu. The Karrayu, who spearheaded the sixteenth-century pastoral Oromo population movement, are traditionally regarded as the first 'son' of Barentu. Karrayu in turn had six 'sons'. These were Liban, the most powerful of all the Oromo according to Asma Giyorgis,[52] with its own numerous divisions and sub-divisions, Wallo, another equally powerful group, then Jelle (Jile), Obo, Suba and Bala. All of these six 'sons' of Karrayu were already independent confederacies by the time of Bahrey. Marawa, the second 'son' of Barentu, had three 'sons', the Ana (or Anna), Uru and Abati. The Warantisha, from *warrana* (spear i.e. the warrior), were known for their fighting capacity, still proverbial among all Oromo, and were popularly called Arsi and formed the single largest and most powerful Oromo group. Braukämper claims that 'the formation of the Arsi as a separate ethnic entity'[53] did not develop until the seventeenth century. 'This simply is a historically untenable proposition.'[54] In fact, Professor Daniel Ayana maintains that the earliest reference to an Oromo *gosa* or clan in a Muslim source was that of the Arsi, which is mentioned 'in the hagiography of Sheik Ishaq Ahmed of Alawi', who is said to have travelled among the Arsi Oromo. This means the name Arsi was mentioned for the first time 'as early as the twelfth century'.[55]

As we have seen in Chapter 2, Liban, Galan, Yaya and Lalo were among the earliest Oromo clan names to be mentioned in Christian sources, while Arsi is the first to be mentioned in a Muslim source. In fact, Oromo oral tradition is unanimous in making Warantisha (i.e. the Arsi) the third son of Barentu. The Chronicle of Susenyos makes numerous references to the Arsi (see Chapter 7),[56] which leaves no doubt that they

---

[52] Tafla, *Asma Giyorgis and His Work*, 137.
[53] Braukämper, *Islamic History and Culture in Southern Ethiopia*, 153.
[54] Mohammed Hassen, 'The Oromo in Medieval Muslim States of Southern Ethiopia', *Journal of Oromo Studies* 15, 1 (March 2008), 213.
[55] Daniel Ayana, 'The "Galla" that Never Was: Its Origin and Reformulation in a Hinterland of Comparative Disadvantage', *Journal of Oromo Studies* 17, 1 (March 2010), 16.
[56] Pereira ed., *Chronica de Susenyos*, 105 and *passim*.

spearheaded the attack on the northern parts of the Christian kingdom during the second half of the sixteenth century.[57] Thus it appears that the Arsi Oromo's separate identity was formed, not in the seventeenth century, but during the twelfth and thirteenth centuries. Braukämper even accuses Asma Giyorgis of presenting anachronistic information by 'explicitly [linking] events of the 16th and early 17th centuries with the Arsi'.[58] It seems that

> Braukämper does not appear to have consulted the chronicle of King Susenyos (1607–32), which contains numerous references to the Arsi Oromo as part of the Barentu or eastern Oromo confederacy, but he is quick to fault Asma Giyorgis who apparently had read Susenyos' chronicle. If historical record is the test of historical accuracy, then Asma Giyorgis's conclusion about the Arsi Oromo is on a stronger foundation than Braukämper's assertion.[59]

In short, Braukämper does not seem to have realized that Warantisha was another name for the Arsi, who had spread out over a large territory. A section of Arsi were in the northern and western part of the Christian kingdom, while the rest were present in three regions in southern Ethiopia. In other words, it was the Karrayu, Marawa and the Arsi with their central *chaffee* assembly in the highlands of Bali that opened the theatre of sixteenth-century pastoral Oromo population movement.

Central *chaffee* assembly at Mormor

The second central *chaffee* for the other sections of the Barentu sub-moieties was located at Mormor in Dallo in the lowlands of the present Bale, on the boundary between Dallo and historical Bali. Three major sub-moieties that belonged to the *chaffee* at Mormor moved both to the north and to the east. These were the Akichu, the largest and the most powerful of this division, a section of which spearheaded the eastern Oromo population movement and eventually reached the sea coast in northern Somalia.[60] Another section of the Akichu moved to the north through Dawaro, Fatagar and Amhara. Together with the Karrayu, Marawa and Arsi, the Akichu were the scourge of the Christian kingdom as well as of the Muslim state of Harar. The second division at Mormor was Ittu, and the third Humbana. These three sub-moieties dominated the movement to the Charchar-Harar region. The Warra Daya (Warra Dhaayyee) was the seventh sub-moiety or confederacy of the Barentu moiety. By the time of Bahrey, it was a powerful and independent group that extended to the Christian kingdom in the north, to Harar region in the east, and to what is today northern Kenya in the south. The Warra Daya had its own central

[57] Aregay, 'Southern Ethiopia and the Christian Kingdom', 330.
[58] Braukämper, *Islamic History and Culture*, 154.
[59] Hassen, 'The Oromo in the Medieval Muslim States of Southern Ethiopia', 213.
[60] Tasawo Merga, 'Senna Umatta Oromo', 12. According to his source, the Gujji and the Warra Daya lived in the same region, though they did not have a common *chaffee* assembly. As we have already indicated, the Warra Daya belonged to the Barentu, while the Gujji belonged to the Borana moiety.

chaffee in the lowlands of Dallo by the side of river Ganale at a place called Harro Gerjjaa.[61]

Several important points can be concluded from what has been said about the beginning of pastoral Oromo population movement. First, during the second half of the fifteenth and definitely by the sixteenth century, large numbers of pastoral Oromo moved not only in the northern direction, as is usually supposed, but also southwards towards the region in what are today northern Kenya and southern Somalia. Such massive population movement in various directions may be taken as an unmistakable indication of the increase in population during the second half of the fifteenth and the beginning of the sixteenth century. Second, on the eve of the major population movement, not all the Oromo were under a common *chaffee* assembly. Instead there were different central *chaffees*, each with its own similar *gada* laws. The laws of the different sub-moieties came under the two categories of either Barentu or Borana law. For instance, if Arsi and Humabana quarrelled, their dispute was settled according to Barentu law, since both were the 'children' of Barentu. This was in regard to blood price, which varied according to the degree of relationship. Whether it was due to this law or otherwise, the 'children' of Barentu generally moved in one direction, and lived near to one another. Similar practices were also true of the Borana.[62] At the same time, *gosas* or clans of Borana and Barentu were distributed widely among all Oromo.

A cursory look at the genealogies of various Oromo confederacies demonstrates the extent of the diffusion of clans in all Oromo areas (see Map 5, page 96).[63] The moiety system among the Oromo was both *gosa*-based and non-*gosa*-based, because every Oromo area tends to be dominated by members of one moiety and non-*gosa*, and we find *gosas* or clans from both moieties and all the sub-moieties. Hence Asmarom Legesse's apt observation that Oromo 'moieties were not drifting apart, but rather they were reproducing themselves everywhere'.[64]

Finally, on the eve of the sixteenth-century major pastoral Oromo population movement, some sections of Barentu moiety lived within historical Bali, while others lived in its immediate environs. Historical Bali was located in the north-eastern part of the present regions of Arsi/Bale, between the Urgoma mountain range and the eastern Wabi bend. It was 'bordered in the north by Dawaro and Sharka, in the west by Hadiya, in the east by Adal and Dawaro, and in the south by regions which cannot be specified'.[65] According to Braukämper, the major part of Bali's territory was situated south of the Wabi Shabelle River, while Huntingford claims that the most of Bali was situated north of the

---

[61] Merga, 'Senna Umatta Oromo', 12.
[62] Merga, 'Senna Umatta Oromo', 12.
[63] Alemayehu Haile, *History of the Oromo to the Sixteenth Century*, 94,117–36, 146–7, 150–60, 177–9, 184–90, 198–230, 243–52, 260–3, 273–7.
[64] Legesse, *Oromo Democracy*, 163.
[65] Braukämper, 'Islamic principalities', 25.

river.[66] Both these scholars claim that the Oromo lived outside historical Bali. Cerulli, followed by Trimingham, has extended the southward
frontier of Bali up to the Ganale, which includes the lowlands of Dallo.[67]
If this is accepted, the entire Barentu Oromo seem to have been located
within the borders of historical Bali or in its immediate surroundings.
It is very doubtful, however, whether historical Bali exercised any
authority in the lowlands of Dallo. What is more, during the jihad of
Imam Ahmad, especially between 1529 and 1532, when Bali played a
role as a strategically important theatre of operations, there is no indication in *Futuh al-Habasha* that the Muslims had penetrated to the
lowlands. Nevertheless, the people of the lowlands of Bale may well
have been under the direct ideological influence of historical Bali.

THE BEGINNING OF THE PROCESS OF PASTORAL OROMO POPULATION MOVEMENT

The sources so far at our disposal have several major lacunae and contra-
dictions that make it difficult to describe the beginning of the process
of pastoral Oromo population movement. During the fifteenth century,
chroniclers depicted population movements that put pressure on the
Christian state as part of the 'Muslim rebellion'. This may have included
pastoral Oromo pressure. Furthermore, the Christian chronicles are
silent on the region south of historical Bali. There are hints, however, that
the pressure of the Oromo on Bali was increasing during the fifteenth
century. For example, according to a tradition collected by Haberland, the
Allabadu Oromo pastoralists from the northern Gujj had already reached
around Lake Langano by the middle of the fifteenth century. They
were driven back from the region, however, by the soldiers of Emperor
Zara Yaegob (1434–68).[68] As indicated in the previous chapter, during
the reign of King Baeda-Maryam (1468–78), the Christian governor of
Bali, Jan Zeg, is reported to have led a large military expedition into an
unknown country called Gam where he was killed with all his forces.[69]
The military expedition appears to have been sent to punish restive
pastoral groups. It was from south of Bali that the Oromo pastoralists
were pushing into that province. Thus it seems that this expedition was
for the purpose of stopping the Oromo. But the bold adventure backfired,
ending in a great disaster for the governor and his soldiers. This interpretation is supported by a theological dispute that reflected the Oromo
pressure on Bali during the reign of Baeda-Maryam (1468–78).

[66] G.W.B. Huntingford, *The Glorious Victories of Amda Seyon*, King of Ethiopia,
22.
[67] Cerulli, *Studi etiopici II: la lingua e la storia del Sidamo*, 3. See also Trimingham, *Islam in Ethiopia*, 67.
[68] Haberland, *Galla Süd-Aethiopiens*, 276.
Basset, R. 'Etudes sur l'histoire d'Ethiopie I, Chronique Ethiopienne', *Journal
Asiatique*, 7, 18 (1881), 96, 139.
[69] Ibid., 96, 139.

> A Venetian painter ... (whose) skill was greatly appreciated ... was commissioned by the king to decorate the walls of many churches with his paintings. One of his pictures, a Virgin and Child, caused a great commotion. According to Western convention he painted the infant Christ on the Virgin's left arm. Now the left arm is ... considered less honourable than the right, and the clergy raised a great outcry, declaring that Our Lord was dishonoured and demanding that the picture be destroyed.[70]

Indeed the picture, which deeply angered the Christian population,[71] appears to have been destroyed by the Oromo, who were also reported to have killed the priests and taken men and women captive. What is interesting about this tradition is that when in the third year of his reign Baeda-Maryam quarrelled with a certain Tewoflos (a religious man), the latter is reported to have called on the Oromo for help. Shortly after the death of Baeda-Maryam, it appears that there was a power struggle at the centre of the Christian kingdom in which one party also appears to have requested assistance from the Oromo.[72] From these references Basset concluded that the Oromo were in the Christian kingdom during the fifteenth century.[73] We have already seen in Chapter 2 that there were Oromo putative clans, such as Liban, Galan, Yaya, Lalo, Waji Oromo, Warra Qaalluu and others living within the medieval Christian kingdom. Meanwhile, during the second half of the fifteenth century, pastoral Oromo pressure on the southern Christian provinces, especially Bali, was increasing.

There is evidence that the Oromo attacked Bali in 1514, eight years before the date of Bahrey's history.[74] This is supported by information from other sources.[75] The Chronicle of Libna Dengel makes a clear reference to pastoral Oromo arrival early in his reign.[76] The manner in which this was reported leaves no doubt that the Oromo attacks in the southern provinces greatly concerned the Christian administration. 'By the early 1520s, Libna Dengel's camp was nearly always to be found in the southwestern Provinces [sic][77] of his kingdom ... It is possible that the king's presence in the area was necessitated by mounting [Oromo] pressure from the south'.[78] One author claims that Libna Dengel's victory over Amir Mahfuz in 1516 strengthened the Christian defences,

---

[70] A.H.M. Jones and Elizabeth Monroe, *A History of Ethiopia* (Oxford: Clarendon Press, 1955), 58.

[71] Basset, 'Etudes sur l'histoire d'Ethiopie', 96, 139.

[72] Basset, ibid. The Oromo were 'reported to have broken the gate of Atronsa Maryam [Dabra Libanos in the region of Salale] to have thrown away church paintings as well as the remains of Baa'eda [Baeda] Maryam', which may be historically untenable.

[73] Basset, ibid., 96, 139.

[74] Yelma Deressa, *Ya Ityopya Tarik*, 226.

[75] A. d'Abbadie, Nouv. Acq. Fran. No. 21300, folio 785.

[76] See Huntingford, *The Historical Geography of Ethiopia*, 111–12.

[77] Probably the author means south-eastern provinces.

[78] Abir, M., *Ethiopia and the Red Sea: The Rise and Decline of the Solomonic Dynasty and Muslim-European Rivalry in the Region*, (London: Frank Cass, 1980), 86.

thus deterring the Oromo.[79] Indeed, Amir Mahfuz, the leader of Harar (1490–1516), was the scourge of Dawaro, Bali, and Fatagar during his entire reign until his death in 1516 at the hand of Libna Dengel. The new self-confidence that the Christians gained by this victory[80] may have contributed to checking the Barentu Oromo population movement. This, and a number of other points to be discussed below, indicates that the Barentu were well informed about the situations both in the Christian kingdom and the Muslim state of Harar. What must be remembered is that the early Oromo military confrontations with both the Christians and Muslims in Bali essentially followed the traditional methods of border raids by neighbouring nomads, raids that were intended for booty and enlarging grazing grounds. This may have also discouraged King Libna Dengel[81] and the Muslim leaders who replaced him from taking the Oromo threat seriously.

This does not mean, however, that Muslim rulers had abandoned their concerns about the Oromo pressure on Bali. In fact, the *Futuh al-Habasha* presents evidence that the jihadic leaders, in response to the Oromo pressure on the Hadiya nomads, were forced to transfer the latter to Ganz, Kambata and Waj.[82] The transfer was inspired by both military and political considerations. The Muslim leaders from Harar, who seem to have had a long experience of the pressure that a powerful nomadic group could exert on their weaker neighbours, probably thought that the transfer of the weak groups was the remedy for easing the tension. However, the transfer backfired. Instead of easing the tension, it actually thinned the Hadiya population to such an extent that the Oromo easily absorbed those who remained.

It seems probable that the 1532 defeat of the Christian forces by Imam Ahmad in Bali irreparably harmed the defence of the province. This created a situation in which the various pastoral Oromo groups were easily able to enter Bali during the early phase of the jihad. Following this rapid advance, it seems that an extraordinary process of assimilation took place, by which the Oromo *gosas* or clans absorbed weak Hadiya nomadic groups. In certain areas strong Hadiya nomadic groups probably absorbed numerically weak Oromo clans, but were Oromo-ized in the process. The settled cultivators also underwent Oromo-ization, but they kept their distinctive Islamic way of life, which enabled them to superficially Islamize the Oromo.[83] The pastoral Oromo seem to have easily adapted to another environment and coalesced with the indigenous people while, at the same time, imparting their language and the complex *gada* system, which eventually replaced the Islam of

[79] Deressa, *Ya Ityopya Tarik*, 226.
[80] Hassen, Mohammed, 'The Oromo of Ethiopia, 1500–1850: With Special Emphasis on the Gibe Region', 153.
[81] Huntingford, *The Historical Geography of Ethiopia*, 111.
[82] Arab Faqih, *Futuh al-Habasha*, 377 and *passim*.
[83] Several genealogies of Wallo and Harar Oromo lineages begin with Muslim names, a fact that shows that the Oromo had absorbed Muslims in the course of their movement.

the Hadiya.[84] The desire to participate in the spoils of both the Christian and Muslim states may have attracted various non-Oromo groups to join the highly motivated Oromo warriors. An unusual aspect of Oromo-ization was that many of the absorbed groups were nomads. The *gada* system facilitated the process of assimilation through its effective mechanism of adoption. The Oromo genius for assimilation quickly claimed the non-Oromo, defeated or otherwise.

The institution of *moggaasaa*

Moggaasaa was an important institution within the *gada* system that facilitated the process of pastoral Oromo population movement. Broadly, *moggaasaa* means adoption, and there were two forms of this. The first form is a collective adoption. According to Mekuria Bulcha, the complex concept of *moggaasaa* indicates 'naming, "sharing" identity through adoption of a group of people into a clan and the nation, [the] Oromo tradition of the collective adoption of non-Oromos'.[85]

The second form of *moggaasaa* is known as *guddifacha* (to adopt a child as a foster parent). This still exists. Traditionally, the adopted son or daughter was looked upon as the parents' natural child. However, only the adopted son enjoyed all the rights of a son by birth. As a patrilineal society, the Oromo counted descent through the male line and inheritance passed from father to son. Even if foster parents produced a son of their own after they had adopted a son, the first remained *angafa* (the oldest son) with all the attached rights and privileges.[86] The collective form of adoption has special relevance to our subject. The individual(s) who were given name(s) were adopted into a clan or *gosa*. The adopted individual or group could be either Oromo or non-Oromo.

I have discussed the collective form of adoption into *gosas*/clans in detail elsewhere,[87] so here let me mention only a few salient points. First, the adoption was always undertaken by the leader of the *chaffee* assembly or the Abba Gada on behalf of his *gosa*.[88] Second, adoption was always held in public during the day under the shade of the *oda* tree. Third, before adoption, animal(s) were slaughtered and a knife was dipped in the blood of the victim and planted before the assembly of the *gosa* elders and representatives of other *gosas*. Then the leader of the *chaffee* assembly said a prayer, blessing the new members, and the adopted individual or groups touched the knife planted (in the place of assembly) repeating in chorus the following words as presented by Tasawo Merga: 'I hate what you hate, I like what you like, I fight whom you fight, I go where you go, I chase whom you chase',[89] etc. This oath, we are told, was binding and 'unbreakable' on both sides. The adopted groups now became collectively the 'sons' of the clan or confederacy

84 Braukämper, *Islamic History and Culture*, 85.
85 Bulcha, *Contours of the Emergent and Ancient Oromo Nation*, viii.
86 Merga, 'Senna Umatta Oromo', 78.
87 Hassen, 'The Oromo of Ethiopia', 21–22.
88 See for example, *The Journals of C.W. Isenberg and J.L. Krapf*, 256.
89 Merga, 'Senna Umatta Oromo', 70.

that adopted them. According to Tasawo Merga, blood symbolized the brotherly unity of the *gosa* and its new 'sons,' and the knife symbolized the readiness of the *gosa* to fight for the right of its new members, while the new members pledged themselves to fight for the rights and the cause of their new *gosa* members.[90] By this oath of mutual responsibility and obligation, clans quickly enlarged their members, while the weak Oromo or non-Oromo groups gained both protection and material benefit. The clan or the confederacy collected contributions of cattle and other property for the support of the new adoptive members.[91] Thus, it is clear that adoption was inspired by political, military and economic considerations on both sides. For the most part, the Oromo assimilated strangers with ease, but they too were assimilated into other groups (see Chapters 7 and 8). The reason for this is simple. The open, democratic, and egalitarian *gada* system encouraged and sanctioned adoption. After adoption, the concept of belonging was extended to include not only the clan that adopted, but also the confederacy to which that clan belonged. Through this new genealogy, the new members now became part of the Oromo people, counting their ancestors several generations back to the hypothetical founder of the confederacy. In short, it was the process of adoption that accounts for the rapid increase in the size of the Oromo population.

What this demonstrates is that both the Barentu and the Borana moieties were fluid groupings: some members left and others were incorporated through the continual process of population movement, conquest, assimilation and interaction with their neighbours. Thus there was no such thing as a 'pure' Barentu or Borana descended from a single founding father. It would seem to me that the history of the Oromo people is not a collection of 2,800 *gosas* but a story of fusion and interaction by which all members of the Barentu and Borana moieties were constantly altered and transformed.

Adoption was accompanied by Oromo-ization. The wide dispersal of the pastoral Oromo from the southern regions was mainly responsible for the Oromo-ization that embraced many non-Oromo groups. Oromo pastoralists absorbed both Cushitic- and Semitic-speaking groups as clients or serfs (*gabbaro*) into their clan structure. The importance of adoption is that it brought *gada* from the periphery into the centre of communal life for the new members. Although Oromo pastoralists of the sixteenth century were egalitarian, they excluded recently assimilated people from the office of Abba Gada, which was held only by the direct descendants of 'original' Borana or Barentu. Nor did assimilated members send their representatives (*jila*) as pilgrims to honour the Abba

[90] Ibid.
[91] Ibid. See also Angelo Mizzi, *Cenni Etnografici Galla ossia Organizzazione Civile, usi e costumi Oromonici*, 82; *idem, Semplici Constatazioni filologico-etnologiche Galla*, 62–63. Any cattle or property that was given to the adopted members were considered as *andhura*, meaning umbilical cord, thus expressing a special gift that a father gives his son at his birth. Any property that was given as *andhura* was untouchable by others.

Muudaa,[92] because they lacked roots that connected them with the lands of the Abba Muudaa. However, once the adopted people had been fully integrated into Oromo moiety system this changed, according to Asmarom Legesse.

> The most rudimentary stage in the development of moieties happens when Oromo rapidly adopt or incorporate aliens on a large scale. It takes assimilated aliens some time to gain full citizenship. During that transitory stage, they may be excluded from key Oromo rituals and/or institutions, they may create their own rituals, they may have their own qallus, and they may have only a partial role in Gada, or they may have their own Gada. In other words, their transitional situation may be revealed in partial or parallel participation in Oromo institutions.[93]

Oromo pastoralists penetrated easily and assimilated quickly where there were already pockets of Oromo-speaking communities. This was particularly true of historic Bali, Dawaro, Hadiya, Waj and other provinces. It was reported that in 1545 Emperor Galawdewos sent an army to fight against the allied forces of Hadiya and the Oromo. The emperor's soldiers, with their firepower, defeated and captured many Hadiya and Oromo prisoners.[94] Just as in Hadiya and other provinces, the migrating pastoral Oromo allied themselves with other groups for the purpose of attacking the Christian state. By the 1540s, Oromo pastoralists were mobilizing Cushitic- and Semitic-speaking groups for their war against both the Christian kingdom and Muslim state of Harar. This indicates that both Semitic and Cushitic groups, who had fought with each other in the name and interest of either Christianity or Islam since the fourteenth century, began to fight for the Oromo, who had no ideological axe to grind against either Christianity or Islam. The populations of Bali, Dawaro, Fatagar, Hadiya and Waj, who had earlier furnished 'volunteers, warriors of the faith' to defend the frontiers of either the Christian or Muslim states, now furnished warriors and not 'volunteers' to fight not for the defence of the frontiers of the states but for the destruction of those states.

THE CHRONOLOGY OF THE PASTORAL OROMO POPULATION MOVEMENT

The Melbah Gada (1522–1530)
According to the chronology of the Oromo population movement recorded by Bahrey, it was during the period of the Melbah Gada that the Borana attacked Bali. Bahrey did not realize that it was actually the Barentu groups who led the pastoral Oromo population movement, as indicated by their knowledge of the course of the jihadic war, which

---

[92] de Salviac, *An Ancient People: Great African Nation – The Oromo*, 178.

[93] Legesse, *Oromo Democracy*, 178.

[94] William Conzelman, *Chronique de Galâwdêwos, Roi d'Ethiopie* (Paris: Emile Bouillon, 1895), 141.

enabled the Oromo to avoid the zone of conflict. They do not appear to have attacked either Muslims or Christians, instead waiting in the wings for the two old enemies to destroy each other. What the Oromo probably did was to dislodge a few isolated communities. Since Bali was the theatre of jihadic operations between 1529 and 1532 the pressure from pastoral Oromo was probably limited.

The Mudana Gada (1530–1538)

During the time when the Mudana Gada was in power, it is recorded that the Oromo crossed the Wabi. The reference is certainly to the Shabelle, which means the northern 'frontier of Bali proper'.[95] This suggests that by this time the Christian administration in Bali had collapsed and the pastoral Oromo had already established themselves in that province. Two factors could have made this possible. First, after the fall of Dawaro to the Muslims in August 1532, the Christian force was wiped out by Wazir Adole, the Muslim general who became the first governor of Bali.[96] Second, once the people submitted to the victorious Muslims and accepted Islam, the leaders from Harar left behind only skeletal forces and moved on to the central and northern parts of the Christian kingdom. The Muslim leaders, who were accustomed to pastoral raids in their own country, did not develop any coherent policy towards the troublesome Oromo in Bali. As has already been indicated, the Oromo avoided confrontation with both the Muslim and Christian forces, and they were not willing to fight for the cause of Islam. As a result, Muslim leaders had difficulty recruiting any pastoral Oromo for their jihad. Since the theatre of the jihadic war shifted from Bali and Dawaro to the central and northern parts of the Christian kingdom, the Muslim leaders do not appear to have designed a policy to contain the Oromo in Bali. On the contrary, the Muslim leaders expelled some Hadiya groups from Bali, especially those such as the Gudela who had served the Muslims as auxiliary soldiers. In the process, they not only thinned the already sparse population of the region, but also contributed to the further weakening of the defence in Bali and Dawaro. Thus, it is safe to assume that between 1530 and 1538, when the Muslim leaders were at the height of their power, the path for pastoral Oromo population movement both to the north and north-east was wide open. Since the Muslims and the Christians focused on destroying each other, the pastoral Oromo movement continued unhindered.

The three stages of the pastoral Oromo population movement

Bahrey's account suggests that by the 1530s a three-stage process of pastoral Oromo population movement had taken shape: scouting, night-time surprise attack and settlement. I have discussed this process elsewhere.[97] Here let me mention a few important points. Pastoral Oromo

---

[95] Beckingham and Huntingford, 'Preface', in *Some Records of Ethiopia*, lxxiv–lxxv.
[96] Arab Faqih, *Futuh al-Habasha*, 380–81, 390, and *passim*.
[97] Hassen, 'The Oromo of Ethiopia', 23–24.

developed a very effective scouting mechanism that enabled them to surprise their enemies while avoiding surprise attacks on themselves. This development of a scouting strategy suggests that the Oromo were familiar with border warfare. Furthermore, the sophisticated guerrilla tactics used by the Oromo during the early phase of their movement were dependent on successful scouting activities. Scouts were sent long distances, sometimes taking many days, from the Oromo base area. Scouting was a preparatory stage during which information was gathered about the neighbouring territory, concerning the strong and weak points, the presence and absence of organized resistance forces, and the economic resources. It seems to have played an extremely important role in the early phase of the movement of pastoral Oromo, when they were bent on avoiding direct contact with both the Christian and Muslim forces who not only possessed abundant iron weapons, but also significant number of European firearms.[98]

The second stage was characterized by surprise attacks, carried out during the night so as to avoid detection and pursuit. The purpose of these attacks was to collect booty as quickly as possible, while at the same time unnerving the enemy. Since these attacks were carried out at a long distance and under cover of darkness, the Oromo's enemies were not able to pursue the attackers to their base areas and counterattack. Safe base areas, where women, children and animals were kept, formed a cornerstone of Oromo strategy. This effective policy indicates that the pastoral Oromo had a long experience of border warfare with the Christian kingdom. According to Bahrey, until 1554 the Oromo were returning to their safe base area near the Wabi Shabelle River after every campaign.[99] This demonstrates that once the Oromo crossed the Wabi between 1530 and 1538 the Muslim force in Bali was not able to repulse them, and that the Wabi Shabelle area, the boundary between Bali and Dawaro, became a safe base area for the Oromo during the time when Imam Ahmad was at the height of his power.[100]

This second stage in the process of pastoral Oromo population movement was doubly important. First and foremost, the evening surprise attacks were repeated on selected weak targets at intervals, until the resistance of the victims was broken. The victims either evacuated, fleeing to safer areas, or they submitted to the pastoral Oromo, accepting their supremacy, which was more apparent than real. Second, the defeated groups were turned into fighting units through adoption. Thus the conquered people joined the Oromo in the next attack on other groups. The conquered people increased the fighting capacity of the Oromo and widened their knowledge of the terrain. Adoption marked the loyalty of the vanquished and their eventual assimilation with the conquerors, while, for the conquered, it assured safety, protection and equal sharing of booty in the next raids.

[98] Ibid., 23.
[99] Bahrey, in *Some Records of Ethiopia*, 116–17.
[100] This section is summarized from Hassen, 'The Oromo of Ethiopia', 23.

The third stage in the process of pastoral Oromo population move-ment consolidated the earlier ones. The former frontier and enemy terri-tory won during the second stage was turned into the base from which the next war for new grazing areas and booty would be launched. The three-stage process would then be repeated, until the Oromo had vastly increased both the size of their territory and their people. It was these processes, coupled with the built-in dynamism of continual expansion within the *gada* system, that seem to have taken the pastoral Oromo through the length and breadth of a large amount of territory within half a century.[101]

As already indicated, the Mudana Gada (1530–38) took the campaign beyond the Wabi Shabelle River. Tasawo Merga suggests that this *gada* passed 'a fundamental law' stating that 'each new *gada* must pass beyond the territory already conquered and occupied by the previous *gada*.'[102] However, he does not provide any evidence in support of this claim. In fact, attacking a new territory constituted a ritual war and was an integral requirement of the *gada* system. Known as the *butta* war, conducted every eight years, it was preceded by a grand feast for which many animals were slaughtered.[103] The war was ritual in form and economic in content. Bahrey's statement suggests the immediate economic advantage for the Oromo: 'They attack the country which none of their predecessors have attacked.'[104] It thus appears that the direction of *butta* war was decided by the economic prospects of a new territory that had not previously been raided rather than practices or laws instituted by the Mudana Gada. What this *gada* did, in all proba-bility, was to establish the safe base area around Wabi Shabelle, in itself a considerable achievement. It opened the path for subsequent pastoral Oromo population movement in different directions.

The Kilole Gada (1538–1546)

The period of the Kilole Gada coincided with the drastic change in the fortunes of the jihad. Imam Ahmad, who had not suffered any defeats between 1529 and 1542, was utterly routed in March 1543. The 'fate of Abyssinia was decided by the death of the Imam Ahmad and the flight of his army.'[105] So finished, as abruptly as it had begun, the reign of the most powerful Ethiopian Muslim leader of the time, and his death ended his empire. Wazir Abbas, the nephew of the Imam, managed to regroup the surviving elements of the once mighty Muslim force and retreated to the southern regions, where he established Muslim authority. This restored some sort of authority in the provinces of Dawaro and Fatagar, but did not seem to have altered the progress of pastoral Oromo move-ment. There is every indication that Abbas did not wage war against the Oromo, who had by now fully occupied Bali. In the words of Bahrey,

101 Hassen, 'The Oromo of Ethiopia', 23.
102 Merga, 'Senna Umatta Oromo', 14–15.
103 Cerulli, *The Folk Literature of the Galla*, 68.
104 Bahrey, 'History of the Galla', 122.
105 Trimingham, *Islam in Ethiopia*, 89.

the Kilole Gada 'carried war towards the lowlands of Dawaro'.[106] This region was defined by Huntingford as included in the area between the Wabi Shabelle and the Harar plateau.[107]

What this implies is that Wazir Abbas, who was preoccupied by the menacing threat from the new Christian emperor, Galawdewos, did not attempt to push the Oromo out of the areas they occupied. While the Muslim force was pinned down in the north, Abbas left Bali to its fate and left the Oromo there undisturbed. It seems that they, in turn, did not harass his well-armed small force.[108] Wazir Abbas, with head-quarters in Dawaro, may have exercised some authority in Fatagar. However, evidence for his effective control of Bali is lacking.[109]

Emperor Galawdewos and the Oromo (1540–1559)

When Galawdewos[110] came to the south in 1545, having established his authority in the north and north-west, he probably had over 2,000 horsemen and 20,000 foot soldiers.[111] Although Galawdewos had superiority both in number and firepower, he was greeted with a threatening letter by Abbas warning him not to 'consider that the imam was dead, as he was his successor, and lest he should think these the words of a coward who threatens and does not act, he would come in search of him at once'.[112] True to his words, Abbas marched from Dawaro to Waj. He too believed that God was on his side, but he lacked firearms and a disciplined force. Portuguese musketeers (who came to Ethiopia in 1541 to fight against Imam Ahmad) triumphed easily with their iron determination and ruthlessness, eager to revenge the humiliation Christians had suffered during the jihad. Abbas was killed and the Muslim force routed.[113] With his death, what was left of the Muslim empire was divided into two parts: a small enclave in the region of Hadiya, and Harar. A stream of Muslim refugees overwhelmed the first while the second was beset by an internal power struggle. The Muslims in Bali, lowland Dawaro, and Hadiya, astounded by the Christian victory and harassed by the pastoral Oromo, fled to the mountainous region between the Bilate River and the Gurage highlands. Those who remained in Bali accepted the *fait accompli* and soon became part of the Oromo nation.

The victorious Galawdewos, alarmed at the rapid spread of the pastoral Oromo in lowland Dawaro, ordered his famous regiment Adal Mabraq to either drive the Oromo out of the province or stop them there.

---

[106] Bahrey, 'History of the Galla', 115.

[107] Beckingham and Huntingford, 'Preface', in *Some Records of Ethiopia*, lxxiv–lxxv.

[108] It was probably his obsession with Galawdewos that forced Abbas to relegate the defence of Bali against the Oromo pressure to such an unimportant position.

[109] The claim of the Christian chronicle that Abbas declared himself the king of the Muslims in Bali was probably theoretical rather than actual.

[110] Galawdewos seems to have been very hesitant to fight with Abbas.

[111] See, for example, Boavida et al., *Pedro Páez's History of Ethiopia*, vol. 1, 303.

[112] Whiteway, *The Portuguese Expedition to Abyssinia*, 199–200.

[113] Abbas was outgunned and outnumbered.

Unfortunately for Galawdewos, it was already too late. The Kilole Gada defeated and drove Adal Mabraq out of lowland Dawaro. This was the first major Oromo victory over a Christian force. Adal Mabraq was forced to cross the Awash River into Fatagar. It was at this stage that Galawdewos realized the seriousness of the situation and acted immediately. The Christian administration collapsed in Bali as well as in the lowlands of Dawaro. Galawdewos was determined to save highland Dawaro. Thus he built his palace in Dawaro and established his court at Agraro, a very fertile region, where he remained from 1545 to 1548.[114] Cerulli plausibly concludes that Galawdewos stayed in Dawaro for so long in order to defend it from the Oromo incursion from Bali.[115] There is no hint in his chronicle of the emperor setting foot in Bali during his three years in Dawaro, either to demand tribute or to punish its people for its non-payment. To all intents and purposes Galawdewos seems to have accepted the situation. As a realistic and practical man, he concentrated on saving Dawaro rather than trying to retrieve Bali.[116] In fact, according to Bermudez, after Galawdewos defeated and killed Abbas, he made Ayres Dias, the mulatto commander of the Portuguese force, the governor of Dawaro, Fatagar and Bali.[117] Although this appointment is not mentioned in the emperor's own chronicle, Dias' subsequent concentration on the building of settlements for the refugees from Bali and lowland Dawaro and his preoccupation with the pastoral Oromo movement indicate the validity of Bermudez's claim.

When the Kilole Gada defeated the Adal Mabraq regiment in 1545, Galawdewos himself led a victorious expedition against the Oromo.[118] It is significant that the chronicler notes that Galawdewos made the Oromo into obedient, tribute-paying subjects. This shows that the Oromo were not newcomers to the chronicler, but rather troublesome neighbours who had to be disciplined and transformed into subjects. It also reveals that the objective of Galawdewos was not to drive the Oromo out, but to stop them where they were. This means that the Oromo remained in the areas they had already occupied.

As far as the pastoral Oromo population movement is concerned, three directions are clearly discernible by 1545 (see Map 8, page 123). First, the spearhead of the northern movement, the Karrayu, closely followed by some sections of the Akichu, Arsi and Marawa, were on the border of highland Dawaro, preparing for the investiture of the new *gada*. Second, the major part of the Akichu, the spearhead for the eastern direction, closely followed by the Humbana and Ittu, were in the lowlands of Dawaro at striking distance from the highlands of Harar, also preparing for the new *gada*. This wing had not yet adopted

---

[114] Conzelman, *Chronique de Galâwdêwos*, 141–3.
[115] Cerulli, *Studi etiopici II: la lingua e la Storia dei Sidamo*, 30.
[116] According to James Bruce, Galawdewos was born in 1522, the year the Borana attacked Bali. Bruce, *Travels to Discover the Source of the Nile*, vol. 3, 197.
[117] Whiteway, *The Portuguese Expedition*, 202. Ayres Dias not only inherited Abbas' three provinces but also his wife, who was christened.
[118] Conzelman, *Chronique de Galâwdêwos*, 141–2.

an aggressive policy towards the Muslim state of Harar. The third direction was charted by the Borana from the Harroo Wallaabuu area. By this time, the Borana had slowly but surely begun moving to the region lying immediately to the north, from where their pressure was already felt in Waj. The rapid success of the Barentu must have encouraged the Borana to adopt an aggressive attitude. This, coupled with the rebellion in Hadiya, occupied the emperor's time and consumed his meagre resources.[119] Galawdewos' difficult situation must have created favourable conditions for the spread of the Borana. It was at this juncture, when serious threats faced three provinces of the Christian kingdom – highland Dawaro, Fatagar and Hadiya – as well as the Muslim state of Harar, that the period of the Kilole Gada expired and a new *gada* came to power.

The Bifole Gada (1546–1554)

In the words of Bahrey, it was the Bifole Gada 'which devastated the whole of Dewwaro [Dawaro and] began attacking Fetegar [Fatagar]. He began to take people captives, and made of them servants, and called them *geber* [serfs].'[120] At the start of the Oromo raids around 1522, capturing adult men was not only dangerous but also of little benefit. Dangerous because the Oromo could keep the captives only in the safe base areas, which meant that the men could function as a Trojan horse to bring in their own troops. If the Christian captives managed to escape, they could not only supply useful information about the nature and geography of the base area and the size of human and animal population to the Christian military leaders, but also direct the Christian force unnoticed to the area, thus providing the indispensable element of surprise attack.[121] Of little benefit, because there is abundant evidence of sufficient manpower in the Oromo base areas. Thus, in the first decades of raids, the adult men were probably killed, as they posed a danger to the Oromo warriors, while women, children and animals were captured.[122] The killing of adult men was undoubtedly intended to spread terror among the resisting population while the taking of cattle booty served to enrich the victors. The capture of women and children was possibly for the purpose of adoption into Oromo society. Once the newly conquered areas were turned into safe bases and the animal population began to increase, extra hands were needed for herding the cattle, producing grain and contributing fighting men. At that point, capturing vanquished people became an economic as well as military necessity. Only men who resisted were killed, and the rest were made *gabar* (serfs or clients) and eventually adopted as members of Oromo society. The Oromo term for *gabar* was *gabbaro*.

[119] Conzelman, *Chronique de Galâwdêwos*, 141–2.
[120] Haile, *The Works of Abba Bahriy*, 201.
[121] Coupled with this potential danger, there was probably mutual absence of communication owing to the language and religious differences, which may have widened the gulf of mutual suspicion and fear.
[122] Bahrey, in *Some Records of Ethiopia*, 116.

Bahrey's information highlights a number of important points. This *gada* not only overtook the whole of Dawaro, but also pushed the war across the Awash River into Fatagar. The latter would soon become the theatre of Borana operations, while Dawaro became the headquarters whence the Barentu movement radiated to the north, east and west. What is more, making the inhabitants *gabar* was an important indication of developments already taking place. This seemingly new institution appears to have been either a modification of the Christian *gabar* class system (which defined the relationships between lords, including professional soldiers, and peasants) or it was of Oromo origin. In Ethiopian Christian society, the labour of the peasants sustained the unproductive nobility and the professional soldiers. The system kept 'the professional soldiers [and nobility] free from agricultural and other domestic occupations'.[123] The victorious Oromo warriors abolished the Christian class system by merging the nobility, professional soldiers and the peasants and organizing them into age-sets. Each age-set was attached to the Oromo clan that had captured its members; they were then allowed to 'regulate their own affairs'.[124] It is also possible that the new institution was derived from the Oromo word *gabara*. This is the term used to describe the compulsory service and gifts owed by a man to the family of his would-be-wife. It also describes the relationship between a landlord and a tenant, and between a figure of authority and a common man. In this sense, Bahrey's *gabar* describes the obligatory relationship between the conquerors and the conquered. The vanquished, still owners of their plots of land, became the serfs or clients of the pastoral Oromo, who demanded service and tribute. The Oromo term for the conquered people was *gabbro*. The Oromo adopted the *gabbro* into the *gada* system, giving them a clan genealogy, and recruited the able-bodied men for military service. Thus the Oromo nation was being consolidated out of the debris of the shrinking territories of the Christian kingdom and the Muslim state of Harar.

During the Bifole Gada (1546–54) the Christian administration lost its control over Dawaro. This conclusion is supported by the report of Bermudez, the Portuguese missionary who lived in the region at this period of considerable historical change[125]. It has already been stated that since 1545 Galawdewos had been preoccupied with the pastoral Oromo population movement. His appointment of Ayres Dias, the prominent mulatto who commanded the Portuguese force at the battle of Wayna Dega in March 1543[126] as the governor of Bali, Dawaro and Fatagar, must be seen in this light. Ayres Dias must have had a special attachment to the emperor: he not only abjured Catholicism to embrace the Orthodox faith, but also changed his difficult name of Ayres Dias to a popular Ethiopian Christian name, Marcos.[127]

---

[123] Aregay, 'Southern Ethiopia and the Christian Kingdom', 419.
[124] Ibid.
[125] Whiteway, *The Portuguese Expedition*, 218.
[126] Imam Ahmad was killed in this battle.
[127] Takla Sadiq Makuria, *Ya gragn Ahmed warara*, 748.

Marcos, as commander in chief of the Portuguese forces, along with the emperor, fought against the Oromo in late 1547 or early 1548. The emperor lost many men. Marcos himself was wounded in this battle and later died.[128] His death makes Marcos the first prominent foreign casualty of an Oromo war. It must have deprived the emperor of a talented and loyal servant, a champion of his cause. Marcos' great attachment to the emperor was reciprocated by the respect, admiration, and love of Ethiopian Christians.

> I was seven months in that land [Gafate], during which the King went to make war on the [Oromos], as he had told me; but he returned wearied and almost defeated, without having accomplished anything of value. A short time after Marcos died, and he had him buried with great pomp in a church where the kings of that country are buried; he, and all his, showed as much grief at his death as if it had been their own brother or father; and they said that with him died all their defence and the protection of their country.[129]

Bermudez may have exaggerated the dire situation in order to downplay the capabilities of Galawdewos. However, subsequent daunting problems amply demonstrate that Galawdewos was in a critical situation. Repeated Muslim incursions from Harar distracted the emperor from war on the Oromo. Nevertheless, the ease with which the Christian governor of highland Dawaro routed the Muslim invaders from Harar in 1548[130] must have given Galawdewos some time to concentrate on the methods to be followed and new strategies to be adopted against the mounting pressure of the pastoral Oromo population movement. The new policy did not appear to have aimed at driving the Oromo from Bali and lowland Dawaro, but rather to contain them or to minimize the effect of their incursions through strengthening the defence system. Galawdewos was determined to save highland Dawaro. Accordingly, in 1548 he settled the entire Portuguese force in Dawaro, where he hoped their cannon and muskets would prove an impregnable wall against the pastoral Oromo. However, the new arrangement did not last for more than four months.

Bermudez's description of the situation reveals how the pastoral Oromo managed to exhaust and then crumble the defences of the Christian provinces:[131]

> [The Oromos] are a fierce and cruel people, who make war on their neighbours, and on all, only to destroy and depopulate their countries. In the places they conquer they slay all men ... kill the old women, and keep the young for their own use and service.[132]

In the above, reference is made not only to the exodus of sedentary communities from the region conquered by pastoral Oromo, but also to

[128] Ibid., 760.
[129] Whiteway, *The Portuguese Expedition*, 218.
[130] Conzelman, *Chronique de Galâwdêwos*, 141–2.
[131] This and a number of other points to be discussed show that Bermudez' information is more trustworthy than hitherto acknowledged.
[132] Whiteway, *The Portuguese Expedition*, 228–9.

their practices of killing men and keeping young women for their use and services. While these practices were confirmed by other evidence, the killing of old women was quite unlikely. According to unanimous Oromo oral traditions, royal chronicles, and Amhara traditions, women and children were not killed. On the contrary, old women were regarded as envoys of peace, acting as intermediaries between two fighting forces and leading caravans in danger zones, even during the height of war. Even Christian kings occasionally resorted to the Oromo practice of sending old women to an enemy when one party wanted to stop fighting or to make peace. Emperor Susenyos is reported to have used this strategy.[133] Furthermore, the killing of women in general, and that of old women and children in particular, was regarded as the most shameful act a warrior could commit. Such a man remained an object of ridicule and a laughing stock for the rest of his life.[134]

Bermudez explains why the area attacked by the pastoral Oromo was quickly depopulated through the rapid exodus of the inhabitants to other safer areas:

> We also cleared the country of women, boys, and everyone who could not fight; with these went nearly all the inhabitants, great and small, from fear of the cruelty of the [Oromos]. A country like that is quickly depopulated for the inhabited places have no buildings that are defensible, nor which cost much to rebuild, as they are all of wattle and straw. They have no other walls or fortresses.[135]

The absence of walls and fortifications around settlements made the inhabitants an easy prey for surprise night attacks. The above quotation hints at the significant fact that the region was thinly populated. Eighty years after the time of Bermudez, the missionary Pedro Páez reported that some areas of the Christian kingdom were densely populated, while in most areas 'settlements are small'.[136] The widely dispersed inhabitants were unable to marshal their resources to build walls, ditches and fortifications so as to resist night attack. Their flight not only made the task of the pastoral Oromo much easier, but unwittingly contributed to this rapid expansion; the Oromo soon overtook the unfortunate refugees in the new 'haven'. A significant conclusion is that safety was possible only in densely populated regions, where the inhabitants were able to build walls and fortifications.

Information provided by Bermudez demonstrates that by 1548 the Oromo had already begun to abandon their policy of avoiding an enemy that possessed firearms. He describes how, without risking total war, the Oromo warriors besieged such an enemy by maintaining constant pressure, eventually forcing them to either flee or submit:

> We were ready sometime, awaiting the [Oromos], when one day they appeared. They were innumerable, and did not come on without order like

---

[133] Pereira, *Chronica de Susenyos*, 143.
[134] Tafla, *Asma Giyorgis and His Work*, 327.
[135] Whiteway, *The Portuguese Expedition*, 229.
[136] Boavida et al., *Pedro Páez's History of Ethiopia*, vol. 1, 200.

barbarians, but advanced collected in bodies, like squadrons. When they saw us they halted, some waiting for the rest, and then marched in one mass and camped near us, at a distance where our shots could do them no harm. As they were many and we were few, we did not go out to attack them, but waited in our camp. At the most there were one hundred and fifty of us, as the rest were already dead, nearly all in war, some few of sickness ... Our camp was pitched on rising ground, whence we commanded the rest of the country, and stood over those that fought against us. We defended ourselves here for ten or twelve days, awaiting the king. During this time we killed many of them by shot, and by our artifices of fire, because they approached so fearlessly that we could aim every cast and shot. Meanwhile our powder failed, and as the king did not come, we had to leave the position in search of him. The [Oromos] did not pursue us: perchance because they also did not desire our company.[137]

Bermudez adds that when Galawdewos heard that the Oromo had become masters of Dawaro, he lost command of himself and wept like a child. Certainly it seems that there is an element of exaggeration in what Bermudez tells us. However, the shock from the loss of Dawaro must have been great. It was not only Dawaro that was lost, but Hadiya too. As we have seen above, Bahrey leaves no doubt about the loss of Bali and Dawaro, but does not mention Hadiya. Nevertheless, we know from other sources that after 1545 the Muslim forces split into two parts, one returning to Harar and the other taking refuge in the small mountainous region between the Bilate River and the Gurage highlands. To all intents and purposes, the Muslim province of Hadiya, that was conquered by Emperor Amda-Siyon in 1332, was dramatically reduced in size and population to such an extent that it becomes anachronistic to talk of Hadiya as a major political entity after 1545 (as Braukämper does).[138] What existed after this time was a small state that bore the historical name of Hadiya. However, even this much-diminished Hadiya resisted Christian domination and so bore the brunt of the struggle against Galawdewos.

Bali and lowland Dawaro were now totally occupied by the pastoral Oromo. The Christian emperor neither collected tribute from the two provinces nor returned refugees. Meanwhile the once large, powerful and rich province of Hadiya was reduced in size to a fraction of what it had been. Thereafter effective political control, i.e. collection of tribute and punishment for failure to pay, was limited only to this small entity that, with the grandiose name of Hadiya, projected an image out of proportion to its real size and importance.

In highland Dawaro, the Christian defence system had crumbled, but was not yet ruined. Some Christian political control was still exercised in the province, as the last remnants of Christian military colonists were not yet dislodged. By 1548, however, the defence system was on the verge of collapse. This conclusion is supported by two important facts. First, after the Oromo drove the Portuguese forces out of Dawaro in 1548, Galawdewos settled the soldiers in Beta Amhara, the province considered as the heart of the empire.

---

[137] Whiteway, *The Portuguese Expedition*, 229–30.
[138] Braukämper, *Islamic History and Culture*, 61.

Here the king made good to us the income we had lost in Doaro [Dawaro] by the incursions of the [Oromos]. The province of Bethmariam (Beta Amhara) is large and well peopled; the receipts from it are considerable; all these the king gave the Portuguese; the land was divided among us according to the recipient's position.[139]

Second, according to the Chronicle of Galawdewos, the emperor appointed 'Fanuel to govern in his place, the eastern provinces, Dawaro and the dependents, with full power and himself went to attack the people who lived on the borders of Damot'.[140] This was a critical time when the emperor himself should have remained in the province to defend it. Considering the gravity of the situation, which nobody knew better than the emperor himself,[141] it seems Bermudez is not exaggerating when he states that after the fall of Bali, Hadiya and Dawaro 'as he considered the [Oromo] war unlucky, he determined to visit certain kingdoms of his empire which he had not yet seen'.[142] Galawdewos abandoned his beautiful palace in Dawaro and his court at Agraro, the country that, in the words of the chronicler, 'is famous in all Ethiopia for its richness and prosperity'.[143] Shortly afterward Galawdewos built a city in Waj, where he settled permanently, abandoning the practice of moving the capital. He constructed his palace of stone and built stone fortifications around the town.[144] These were the first practical measures that he took to protect Waj, making it a safe headquarters from which to direct the campaigns against the Oromo. Even though Galawdewos failed to implement this strategy, he did succeed in making Waj a safe capital until his death in 1559.

Compared with his campaigns against the pastoral Oromo, Galawdewos achieved spectacular results against the Muslims. By defeating and killing Abbas in 1545, he not only devastated most of the Muslim forces, but also contributed to the decline of those that remained. In 1548, Fanuel, the governor of Dawaro, easily routed the invading Muslim force, capturing two of their prominent leaders. The following year, Fanuel led an expedition into Harar, where he is reported to have scored a brilliant victory over the Muslims. Encouraged by this success, Galawdewos led another expedition in 1550; he remained in Harar for five months, causing considerable damage. 'He destroyed their strong castle, and burned their wooden houses, took their king's property.'[145]

---

[139] Whiteway, *The Portuguese Expedition*, 240.

[140] Conzelman, *Chronique de Galâwdêwos*, 144.

[141] Galawdewos is reported to have said to Bermudez, 'Father, no outrage will be done you; but as you … know it is necessary to attend to the war which the Gallas are making on me'. Whiteway, *The Portuguese Expedition*, 216.

[142] Ibid., 230–1; Conzelman, *Chronique de Galâwdêwos*, 149.

[143] Ibid., 141–2.

[144] Ibid., 145–7.

[145] Conzelman, *Chronique de Galâwdêwos*, 145–7. It has also been reported by another source 'that Galawdewos burnt the grand mosque except one minaret, which was seen by Caghne Taurin in the early 1880s': see Papiers d'Abbadie, V., *Lettres par la mission Catholique au pays des Gallas 1845–1895*, II Nouv. Acq. Fran. No. 23852 fol. 329.

After him no other Christian king ever set foot in Harar in order to either demand tribute or punish the Muslims for their incursion. Thus Galawdewos' expedition of 1550 to Harar marks the last invasion of any Christian emperor until 1887, when King Menelik of Shawa brought to an end the independence of the Muslim city-state by incorporating the region of Hararghe into his expanding kingdom, a topic that is beyond the scope of this book.

According to his chronicler, upon his return from this successful expedition, Galawdewos was troubled by new incursions of the Oromo on the Waj frontier. 'Then the king treated with kindness those people affected by the [Oromo] incursion. He provided the refugees with whatever was possible. And he gave them a place to settle.'[146] It was at this time that he built the fortified capital in Waj. In 1554, when the period of the Bifole Gada was coming to an end, 'Galawdewos fought against the [Oromos], killing many and taking captives both animals and men. They fled to their country in the forest.'[147] Galawdewos did not follow up his victory with a strategy of either driving the Oromo out or returning the refugees back to their country in the lost provinces. The reason for his success against the Muslims and not against the Oromo was due to the nature of the war that he conducted against each.[148] The Muslims fought in a conventional style, against which Galawdewos had a considerable advantage in both men and firepower. Furthermore, the Muslims were settled in communities, and could therefore be pursued and punished in their own homes for their attacks on Christian territory. With the Oromo the situation was entirely different. The emperor had trained manpower, considerable firepower and large iron weapons, while the Oromo did not possess any firearms. However, the elusive character of Oromo warriors undermined this considerable advantage. Whenever possible they avoided engagement with his highly destructive striking force. Repeated Oromo attacks on settled Christian military colonists proved impossible to stop. Their night attacks caused considerable damage to men and property, and also eroded the morale of the Christian forces. By the time the local Christian troops recovered from the shock and were prepared to counterattack, the Oromo warriors would have disappeared from the area, taking away their spoils, usually many head of cattle. It was this elusive character of the Oromo warriors that gave urgency to the resettlement of the Christian victims in Waj, where the emperor had his fortified permanent capital.

The Michelle Gada (1554–1562)

The period of the Michelle Gada was a landmark in the history of the pastoral Oromo population movement. Both Christian and Muslim power substantially decreased during this period, while the power of the pastoral Oromo dramatically increased. The sudden and radical transformation in the balance of power quickly brought to an end two

---

[146] Conzelman, *Chronique de Galâwdêwos*, 149.

[147] Ibid., 157.

[148] This section is summarized from Hassen, 'The Oromo of Ethiopia', 24.

centuries of struggle between the Muslims and Christians, replacing it by the struggle of both against the Oromo for the next three centuries. For reasons to be discussed shortly, the Oromo became highly motivated during the period of the Michelle Gada. They continued their practice of terrifying the peasants, while at the same time totally abandoning their policy of avoiding imperial soldiers. On the contrary, the Christian regiments started avoiding the Oromo warriors. If a single event could demonstrate a tilt in the balance of power in favour of the Oromo, this is it. Among the first casualties of the aggressive pastoral Oromo was the already mentioned Jan Amora corps stationed in Fatagar.[149] In short, the period of this *gada* opened the chapter of the rapid expansion of the pastoral Oromo, changing the course of history in the region. In the words of Bahrey:

> It was he who killed the Jan Amora corps and fought against Hamalmal at Dago; he devastated all the towns and ruled them, remaining there with his troops, whereas previously the [Oromo] invading from the Wabi had returned there at the end of each campaign.[150]

A number of these developments require further discussion. The Michelle Gada that destroyed Jan Amora's corps in Fatagar also fought with Hamalmal at Dago. This not only signalled the disintegration of Christian administration in Fatagar, but also opened the path to Shawa, Ifat, Geshe, and Ganh.[151] In addition, Dawaro and Fatagar now became the operational headquarters of the pastoral Oromo, the former for the Barentu and the latter for the Borana. Dawaro, located in the Rift Valley, occupied an important strategic position, and it served as a safe base area from where the different regions were attacked. This province, which Merid Wolde Aregay describes as having been at one time 'virtually a military camp teaming with regiments',[152] became the Barentu country that divided the two traditional enemies of the Oromo, the Muslims of Harar and the Christian kingdom. Fatagar, the headquarters of the Christian court for almost a century, now became the headquarters of the Borana, with their famous *chaffee* at Oda Nabe.

Bahrey's statement that the Michelle Gada 'devastated all the towns and ruled them, remaining there with his troops', implies that the Oromo replaced the Christian administration with one of their own. Such a process would have required a high degree of organization and effective communication. Notwithstanding Bahrey's remarkable information, Braukämper claimed that 'the Oromo tribes have apparently never possessed a centralized political authority'.[153] Braukämper

---

[149] The Oromo victory over the Jan Amora corps has been described by one writer as the psychological material from which the fireworks for the great later victories were derived. See for example Tasawo Merga, 'Senna Umata Oromo', 17.

[150] Bahrey, in *Some Records of Ethiopia*, 116–17.

[151] Tasawo Merga, 'Senna Umatta Oromo', 17.

[152] Aregay, 'Southern Ethiopia and the Christian Kingdom', 88, 199.

[153] Braukämper, *Islamic History and Culture*, 143.

did not explain how they became such a formidable force in the Horn of Africa without centralized political authority. The Oromo created no kingdoms during the sixteenth century, but did have a centralized political authority, in the person of an elected Abba Gada (the leader of the *chaffee* assembly); his residence was the seat of government and the capital of a confederacy during an eight-year period. Other leaders of the *gada* government included Abba Dula ('the father of war'), Abba Sera ('the father of law'), and *saylon* or *sagalan* Borana or Barentu, the nine judges who were elected from retiring officers.[154]

> One thing that all authorities on the Oromo, apparently with the exception of Braukämper, agree is that the *gada* system was a political structure that made the Oromo militarily a powerful nation in the whole region of today's Horn of Africa from the sixteenth to the eighteenth centuries.[155]

Scholars of the Ethiopian history of this period normally observe little but destruction in the pastoral Oromo population movement. The only notable exception is Merid Wolde Aregay, who states that the Christian soldiery in some cases brought more ruin to the peasantry than did the pastoral Oromo who were moving in search of grazing lands.[156] In making their assessment, scholars such as Ullendorf[157] did not consider the continuous enslaving and pillaging to which the Christians and Muslims subjected each other.[158] They also spared only those who accepted their respective faiths. The pagans were fair game and easy victims for plunder and enslaving by both sides. From antiquity, the people of the four provinces of Bali, Dawaro, Hadiya and Fatagar, where both the Christian and Muslim administrations gave way to Oromo administrations, had witnessed intense rivalry between the Muslim and Christian rulers. Caught between these two forces, the people experienced collection of tribute, slave raids, and sometimes wanton pillaging by both. But after their recovery from the initial shock and attack of the pastoral Oromo, the people seem to have come to terms with their new masters. Adoption may have facilitated the process of integration. What cannot be doubted is that the inhabitants were left to manage their own affairs. They must have also been recruited in large numbers to staff the new administration. Without such recruitment it is difficult to see how the region could have been governed, since the pastoral people could not remain in these towns. Of the five *gada* that ruled between 1522 and 1562, Michelle was the most successful in defeating, and in some cases routing, both Christian and Muslim forces. Bahrey hints at the reason why this *gada* had

---

[154] Hassen, 'The Oromo of Ethiopia', 14–15.
[155] Hassen, 'The Oromo in Medieval Muslim States of Southern Ethiopia', 212–13.
[156] Aregay, 'Southern Ethiopia and the Christian Kingdom', 282, 311 and *passim.*
[157] Edward Ullendorff, *The Ethiopians: An Introduction to Country and People* (London: Oxford University Press, 1960), 73.
[158] Aregay, 'Southern Ethiopia and the Christian Kingdom', 279.

such success: 'this *luba mesele* (Michelle Gada) began the custom of riding horses and mules, which the [Oromo] had not done previously'.[159] Donald Levine even speculated that the Oromo acquired 'horses, presumably from the Somali'.[160] However, Levine does not explain how the Oromo acquired horses from the Somali, who did not live in a neighbouring region. In fact, even Bahrey's claim that the Oromo did not ride horses and mules before this *gada* is open to question. Ali Mazrui asserts that it was the Oromo use of horses in battle that 'eventually convinced Ethiopians of the military value of horses'.[161] This is historically inaccurate as horses had been used in warfare for centuries among the Amharas, the Tigrayans, the Muslim populations and the Oromo in Ethiopia. What is more, it was from the Oromo that the Christians in Ethiopia adopted the custom of using the names of their warhorses. Before the period of Michelle Gada the Oromo use of large cavalry formations was not evident to their enemies. This was because so far most of the Oromo campaigns had been conducted on the basis of nighttime guerrilla attacks, which made horses less important. Be that as it may, once horses were employed in battles, the Oromo seem to have made effective use of them. The horses enabled them to move fast and far. Between 1522 and 1554 the pastoral Oromo only overtook Bali, Dawaro, and Hadiya. But between 1554 and 1562 they repeatedly attacked Waj, dominated Fatagar and the whole of Harar, Ifat, Angot and Gedem, and the path to Shawa and Damot was laid open. This spectacular expansion within a mere eight years must have been greatly facilitated by the use of cavalry. Most probably the Oromo introduced two new innovations with their use of horses in warfare. Daniel Ayana argues that Oromo warriors began using the 'toe-stirrup, [which provided] the ability to stand on one's toe while throwing spears, then sliding left or right easily to avoid oncoming spears by clinging on [with the] big toe'.[162] What is more, the Oromo appear to have organized cavalry formations and cultivated vital skills through frequent drilling. Thus Oromo young men grew up practising throwing spears as well as riding horses. In the process, they became formidable horsemen (see Chapters 5, 7 and 8). Once the pastoral Oromo had expanded into areas where horses were bred, such as Dawaro, Fatagar, Angot, Ifat, Gedem, Amhara and Harar, they must have employed the animals

---

[159] Bahrey, 'History of the Galla', 117.

[160] Levine, *Greater Ethiopia*, 88.

[161] Ali A. Mazrui, *The Africans: A Triple Heritage* (London: BBC Publications, 1986), 117.

[162] Personal communication with Professor Daniel Ayana, dated March 21, 2014. I am deeply indebted to my friend Daniel Ayana for providing me with this information. Manoel de Almeida, a Spanish missionary historian, who was in the Christian kingdom during the 1620s says about Oromo cavalry: '[Their horses are] capable of enduring great fatigue to which the [Oromo] accustom them, making them trot at half speed for whole days at a time. The saddles they use are very light and very simply made; the stirrups of iron, very thin and narrow, for they do not put the foot into them, but only the big toe', Almeida, in *Some Records of Ethiopia*, 137–8.

on a large scale. Horses were valuable for their speed in scouting, for charging in battles, and for retreating quickly when overwhelmed by a superior enemy. Until 1538 the Oromo fought on the border so that, if defeated, they could disappear into the nearby forests. Neither Christians nor Muslims, whether or not mounted on horses, were thus able to follow the withdrawing Oromo, even if they had won the battle.

Mobilization of cavalry enabled the active military initiatives that characterized the Michelle Gada. In 1555 they fought against Galawdewos in Waj. He seems to have forced the Borana to retreat, but did not reap any lasting benefit from this victory, since their threat prevented him from attending to problems in the other provinces. In 1556 he fought another campaign from a base at Asa Zanab. In the words of Asma Giyorgis, 'he did not harm them, instead he quickly returned from the campaign'.[163] According to the monk Pawlos, in the seventeenth year of his reign (i.e. 1557), Galawdewos 'devastated the [Oromo] settlement area'.[164] This settlement must have been on the frontier with Waj. It is significant that Pawlos' account contains no hint whatsoever that the Oromo were regarded as an alien and unknown people. On the contrary, his material gives the general impression that the Oromo were well-known rebellious pastoral groups. In 1557 and 1558 the Borana descended into the Rift Valley plains, raiding several areas. According to the Chronicle of Galawdewos, in 1559, shortly before his death, the emperor was building a town for the refugees who fled from the new Oromo incursion.[165] He made no attempt whatsoever to return the refugees to their home region. What is more, the pressure from both the Borana and Barentu was mounting simultaneously. The pessimism expressed in the court at this time, depicted in the chronicle,[166] seems to reflect the grave situation created by the burden of refugees in the capital, the news of the approaching Muslim force, and the ever-mounting pressure of the Borana and Barentu, all of which will be discussed in the next chapter.

[163] Tafla, Asma Giyorgis and His Work, 143.
[164] Conti-Rossini, 'L'autobiografia di Pawlos monaco Abissino del secolo xvi', *Rendiconti della Reale Accademia dei Lincei* 27 (1918), 285–6.
[165] Conzelman, *Chronique de Galâwdêwos*, 173. It appears that by 1559 Galawdewos was in a real dilemma that he met by concentrating on helping the disaffected people.
[166] Aregay, 'Southern Ethiopia and the Christian Kingdom', 172.

5

Movements of Pastoral Oromo into the Christian Kingdom, 1559–1600

In the previous chapter the course of the pastoral Oromo population movement into Bali, Dawaro, Hadiya, and to some extent Fatagar was described. Here their movement will be charted into the rest of the Christian kingdom. Before doing this, however, it may be useful to take a brief look at the situation in the region in 1559, a watershed in the history of the Horn. In that year the Muslim victory had a significant impact on the Christian kingdom.

THE IMPACT OF THE 1559 MUSLIM VICTORY ON THE CHRISTIAN KINGDOM

In 1559 Amir Nur (1552–67) the Muslim leader from Harar, won a decisive victory over Galawdewos, the emperor who restored the Christian kingdom after it was nearly destroyed by Imam Ahmad between 1529 and 1543. There is a similarity between the Christian defeat of 1529 and that of 1559. In the first, the small but highly organized, well-trained and disciplined Muslim force under Imam Ahmad completely routed the ten-times-greater Christian force, which was loosely organized and badly led by Libna Dengel. A large number of Christian soldiers were slain, and many more were taken prisoner. The rest ran off in disarray and confusion. This utter defeat was a complete surprise for the Christians. It may be that the Christian leadership did not expect a great victory, but no-one seems to have been prepared for a defeat of such shattering proportions. The surviving Christian leadership, including the emperor, was shocked. With the Christian society in a state of total confusion, it was left to Libna Dengel to try and salvage something out of what remained.

In 1559, exactly thirty years after the victory of 1529, the Muslims under the leadership of Amir Nur (the nephew of Imam Ahmad) routed a hastily collected Christian force under Galawdewos. The emperor, most of his officers, and a great many of his men were slain. The rest were either captured or dispersed in panic and disarray. Galawdewos' camp was plundered, his capital looted, and its inhabitants put to the sword. In 1529, as in 1559, the morale of the Christian force was shattered.

According to Merid Wolde Aregay, the death of Galawdewos 'was the greatest opportunity which the [Oromo] were to have throughout the history of their [movement] into the north'.[1] In other words, the death of Galawdewos and the destruction of his army left the kingdom too feeble to stop the Oromo advance. Furthermore, the military disaster of 1559 and the pressure of pastoral Oromo movement generated intense civil wars within the Christian society itself, which 'after 1559 led to the destruction of the centralized system of government and the complete barbarization of the many bodies of professional soldiers'.[2] Thus the 1559 Muslim victory not only prepared the background for rapid Oromo victories, but was also a major turning point in the history of their movement into the heartland of historical Abyssinia.

There is general agreement among historians that in 1529 the Christian leadership was both weak and ineffective.[3] In 1559, however, the Christian leadership was in the hands of an able emperor. From 1543 to 1548, Galawdewos had gone from victory to victory. As we have seen in the previous chapter, in 1550 Galawdewos himself led a large force to Harar where he stayed for five months causing destruction to lives and property while shattering the morale of the Muslim population in the region.[4] Although Galawdewos was at the height of his power by 1550, his force underwent a number of marked changes. For example, the battles against the pastoral Oromo had also sapped the strength of the Christians, especially after 1548 when Galawdewos lost many provinces to the Oromo, and obsession with this made the Christians blind to the danger from the Muslims. They wrongly assumed that they could not be challenged and that they had the power to cope with any Muslim attack. Moreover after Galawdewos' victory of 1550, the way in which the Christian leaders routed the Muslims, the way in which they blindly gloried in their success of having penetrated Harar and burned the Muslim capital and massacring the inhabitants of the city[5] was calculated to impose the maximum humiliation on their defeated enemy. These successes lulled the Christian leadership into an exaggerated sense of strength.

Thus when Amir Nur attacked on 22 March 1559, the Christian force was caught off guard. This victory provided the Muslims with the opportunity to wipe out the stigma of defeat and humiliation under which their army had suffered over the prior sixteen years. The death of Galawdewos, a man 'victorious in every action he fought, except in that one only in which he died'[6] marked a turning-point in every sense

---

[1] Merid Wolde Aregay, 'Southern Ethiopia and the Christian Kingdom, 1508–1708, with Special Emphasis to the Galla Migrations and their Consequences' (PhD diss., University of London, 1971), 173.
[2] Ibid., 3.
[3] Taddesse Tamrat, *Church and State in Ethiopia, 1270–1527*, 295–96. See also Aregay, 'Southern Ethiopia and the Christian Kingdom', 113–17, 133–6.
[4] Boavida et al., *Pedro Páez's History of Ethiopia*, vol. 1, 303.
[5] Ibid.
[6] Bruce, *Travels to Discover the Source of the Nile*, vol. 3, 224.

of the term. Not only did his death produce terrible grief throughout the Christian land, it left the political scene uncertain and fluid. Furthermore, and more relevant from the point of our discussion, it left the Christian defence system in utter ruin, and marked the end of the era of Christian dominance. After this battle the Christian force was never able to regain its full strength and failed to win back an inch of land lost before 1559 to the pastoral Oromo. On the contrary, as the following discussion will show, the kingdom rapidly lost the best of its provinces, one after the other. The failure of the Christian state to protect its own frontiers had a devastating effect on the internal power structure of the kingdom, and opened a new chapter in the history of the Christian kingdom in which the landed nobility challenged the power and authority of the monarchy, leading as it did into bitter civil wars.

Two parallel crises faced the kingdom after March 1559. There was the immediate question of defending the frontiers of the kingdom from the active military initiatives carried out by pastoral Oromo who were rapidly expanding grazing lands for their cattle, while parallel with this there was a new crisis developing from within the kingdom, as a reaction to the inability of the leadership to defend the frontiers. The internal crisis was essentially military, political, economic and social, and it was looking for some new catalyst. The external and the internal crises found what they lacked in each other. The Oromo pressure found its strength in the internal troubles, while the internal crisis found its detonator in the success of the Oromo population movement; but the internal difficulties of the Christian kingdom owed more to the assault of the pastoral Oromo than the Oromo population movement did to the internal crisis of that kingdom. Be that as it may, the difference between the disaster of 1529 and 1559 was no less striking. In the former, the Christian force was routed, but its leadership was still intact. In the latter, the Christian force was both defeated and its leadership destroyed. The task that faced the kingdom was not just one of recruiting more men and rebuilding the army, the whole officer corps had to be recruited from the top to the bottom. Understandably, the most immediate issue was that of replacing the dead emperor.

KING MINAS, 1559–1563, AND THE OROMO

Galawdewos, having no son, was succeeded by his younger brother, Minas, a man with a rich repertoire of experience but unprepared for the task of sitting on the throne. It is significant that on the day of his coronation Minas remarked that he was 'not worthy of sitting on that great and 'honoured' throne'.[7] He intended these words to show his humility to the nobility who had made him king. His short reign proved his remarks to be true. Minas began his reign at Mengesta Semayat in eastern Gojjam, and it seemed on the surface that the country had

[7] F.M.E. Pereira, *Historia de Minas, Rei de Ethiopia*, (Lisbon, 1888), 27.

genuinely acquired a mature monarch who would rally the people around himself. However, Minas quickly proved himself to be the victim of the situation. The old spirit of Christian unity, of readiness to rally to defend the Cross against the Crescent, could still be evoked for a time, as it had been done during the times of Emperors Galawdewos and Sarsa Dengel (1563–97). However, the pastoral Oromo, whom the Christians faced was neither against the Cross nor desirous of imposing the Crescent. The fight against the mobile pastoral non-Muslim Oromo did not generate the same ideological passion as a fight against the traditional Muslim foe. Minas failed to infuse the Christian society with new dynamism. He had not moved far enough or fast enough towards meeting the challenge of the day. In fact, two diametrically opposed features of Minas' background combined to make him the man he was.

Minas had been captured in 1538 by the Muslim army, and had stayed for three years with Imam Ahmad and his wife Del Wanbara, both of whom appear to have liked him. Minas is reported to have married their daughter.[8] Portuguese missionaries, who had their own axe to grind against Minas, claimed that he was converted to Islam.[9] It is reasonable to assume that Minas may have been converted to Islam under pressure. It is doubtful that Imam Ahmed would have allowed Minas to marry his own daughter without his conversion to Islam. One thing is for certain, it seems that the Imam, who considered the presence of Minas in his camp a political asset, had treated him kindly.[10] In 1541 Imam Ahmad sent Minas to the Pasha of Yemen in exchange for military assistance. Then, in 1544 he was ransomed by Galawdewos in exchange[11] for Muhammad, the son of Imam Ahmad and Del Wanbara. Minas' short captivity among the Muslims seems to have left an indelible mark on him and created a complex personality. He responded eagerly to the call to be made king, but the spectre of previous experience dulled his initiative and inhibited him from taking any action that could possibly be construed as risky.[12]

When the Muslim force withdrew from Waj, in March or April 1559, he missed an opportunity to go back to the capital of Galawdewos. His return to Waj would have boosted the morale of his forces and gained him a strategic advantage against the Oromo, from which internal peace might have followed. Instead, he drew the wrong conclusion from the Muslim victory. Whereas he had expected them to follow up their success by moving deep into the heart of the kingdom, they withdrew from Waj and quickly returned to Harar.[13] Thus, as the victo-

[8] Aregay, 'Southern Ethiopia and the Christian Kingdom', 184. However, according to Takla Sadiq Makurya, the woman Minas married was the sister of Del Wambara. Makurya, *Ya Gragn Ahmed, Warara*, 650–60.

[9] Boavida et al., *Pedro Páez's History of Ethiopia*, vol. 2, 41.

[10] Pereira, *Historia de Minas*, 18.

[11] Galawdewos paid 4,000 ounces of gold in addition to releasing Muhammad, the son of Imam Ahmad.

[12] It seems that the security of his government may have weighed more heavily with Minas than trying to save the provinces under attack.

[13] In 1559, the victorious Amir Nur returned to Harar, because the city was attacked by the Oromo.

rious Muslims abandoned Waj, so did Minas, who moved the seat of his government from here to Mangesta Samayat in eastern Gojjam. His decision to transfer the capital across the Abbay (the Blue Nile) enabled him to get away almost unchallenged by his followers. He seems to have justified the move as a temporary measure that would on the one hand protect the safety of his government and, on the other hand, allow his remaining force to recuperate and replace their losses before meeting a new challenge. But, in the rushed transfer of the capital, he tacitly abandoned the provinces east of the Abbay. As we shall see below, this decision irreparably altered the political landscape of the kingdom. It is probably for this reason that Merid Wolde Aregay blames Minas for undermining the morale of his Christian subjects.

> Minas began his reign by a cowardly act which was to undermine the morale both of his armies and of the nobility. Instead of rallying around him whatever soldiers he could find and attempting to stop Nur, he and his mother hurriedly left Waj for the distant secure mountains of Mangasta Samayat in Gojjam. We do not know whether it was Minas himself or his mother who was responsible for this. He might have feared falling once more into the hands of the Muslims.[14]

After a short while the top Christian leaders, who escaped from the massacre of 22 March 1559, held a great council at the residence of Minas in eastern Gojjam. The participants included Kiflo, Takla Haymanot, Daglahan, Rom Sagad and Hamalmal.[15] The presence of the last-mentioned general in this council had far-reaching consequences for the future. Hamalmal, as the governor of Fatagar, had already witnessed the fall of Bali, Dawaro and other provinces to the pastoral Oromo. In fact he had already fought repeatedly against the highly mobile Oromo warriors. Hamalmal was reported to have been a man whose 'mind was dominated by the desire for horses'.[16] His obsession with horses may reflect his understanding of the nature of Oromo warfare, in which, after 1554, horses played a decisive role. On his way to and from Harar in 1559[17] he seems to have consciously avoided the Oromo. It also appears that he left Harar at about the time that the Oromo were on the verge of attacking that city.

By the time Hamalmal had returned to Fatagar he must have heard about the Muslim's disaster at Hazalo, where their victorious force under Amir Nur was completely routed by Oromo warriors. Of the formidable military force with which Amir Nur destroyed the Christian army and its leadership, only few men escaped from the battlefield of Hazalo and returned to Harar. If one event could be said to change the course of history by unceremoniously bringing to an end the era of long conflicts between the Christians and the Muslims in Ethiopia, the

[14] Aregay, 'Southern Ethiopia and the Christian Kingdom', 176.
[15] Pereira, *Historia de Minas*, 17.
[16] G.W.B. Huntingford, trans. and ed., 'The History of King Sarsa Dengel (Malak Sagad) 1563–1597', unpublished manuscript (School of Oriental and African Studies, University of London, 1976), 29.
[17] In 1559 Hamalmal attacked the city of Harar, and killed Barakat, the Sultan.

Battle of Hazalo was it.[18] After this, the Muslims from Harar were not able to create a strong striking force with which to invade the Christian kingdom. As will be shown below, their feeble attempt to invade the province of Bali in 1576 would end in tragedy. The Christians, too, were exhausted; their territory shrank and they were unable to field any army to invade Harar for over three hundred years, up to 1887.

It appears that Hamalmal may have known before he went to the council at the residence of Minas in 1559 that the danger from the Muslims was over. This assumption is strengthened by the fact that the outcome of the council seems to have been strongly influenced by the arguments of Hamalmal, who was best acquainted with the general situation in the provinces east of the Abbay River. This highest state council, in which all the top surviving Christian leaders – excepting *Bahar Nagash* Yeshaq the governor of the province of the Sea – took part, discussed the problems facing the kingdom and decided upon making the Dambiya region the rainy-season residence of Minas. The choice of Dambiya may have been influenced by the wealth and safety it provided. This decision also proved another major landmark in the history of the kingdom. Since 1270, and especially after Amda-Siyon (1314–44) established a strong Christian empire, the provinces east of the Abbay were the centre from which the expansion of the Amhara Empire was directed to the south. By the transfer of the residence of the king, the Christian nobility was unconsciously transferring the centre of political and military gravity of the kingdom across the great river. The queen mother and other high dignitaries followed Minas to Dambiya,[19] where he soon founded his capital at Gubay in Emfraz, 'a mountainous area overlooking the north-eastern shore of Lake Tana'.[20]

Hamalmal was created *dajazmach*, (commander of the vanguard) with authority over all the territory east of the Abbay 'up to the limit of his power'.[21] The last phrase expresses a series of accommodations that were being made to the situation on the ground. It implies that there was a reduction in the size of the kingdom. This becomes clearer from the fact that only a few decades before probably hundreds of *dajazmach*s used to be appointed over the provinces east of the Abbay. For example, Dawaro alone was controlled by about fifty *dajazmach*s in the early sixteenth century.[22] The appointment of Hamalmal over all the provinces east of the Abbay, but only with the title of *dajazmach*, may be a confirmation of what was taking place on the ground. Nevertheless, the decision to move the seat of the government deep into a more northern and safer area set a pattern for the chequered future of the kingdom

[18] Mohammed Hassen, 'The Oromo of Ethiopia, 1500–1850: With Special Emphasis on the Gibe Region', 186.
[19] Pereira, *Historia de Minas*, 27.
[20] Richard Pankhurst, *History of Ethiopian Towns from the Middle Ages to the Early Nineteenth Century* (Wiesbaden: Franz Steiner, 1985), 94.
[21] Pereira, *Historia de Minas*, 27.
[22] Ludolphus, *A New History of Ethiopia*, 16. See also Antoine d'Abbadie, *Géographie de l'Ethiopie*, (Paris: Martinet, 1890), 68.

and laid the foundation for the future expansion of the kingdom in the northern direction. Thereafter the kingdom did not expand an inch in the region east of the Abbay, but rather lost much territory held earlier. Thus, between 1559, when Minas first moved to Emfraz, and 1636, when Fasiladas founded Gondar as a permanent capital, five kings (Minas, Sarsa Dengel, Ya'eqob, Za-Dengel and Susenyos) had their courts either in one or two of these places, namely Gubay, Ayba, Wandege, Qoga, Gorgora and Danqaz.[23] The concentration of these royal towns in this region demonstrates beyond any shadow of doubt that after 1559 the centre of political power of the kingdom moved from the eastern provinces to the region of Lake Tana.

Within a few months, the transfer of the seat of power began to produce its effects. As time went by Minas' sense of frustration increased because he was unable to provide his soldiers with adequate provisions. His short-sighted solution for alleviating the situation was to embark on slaving raids on the non-Christian minorities in the region.[24] The first victims of Minas' slaving expeditions were the Falasha (who call themselves Beta Israel 'the house of Israel'). As we shall soon see, instead of rallying to the eastern provinces that were now attacked by the Barentu and Borana Oromo simultaneously, Minas gathered Christian forces from provinces not yet attacked such as Tigray and Amhara, to attack the Falasha in their impregnable Semien Mountains. The campaign lasted only for a short while, because 'the learned and respected men advised him to give up fighting Falasha since the right time had not arrived'.[25] This may have been an euphemism for the failure of the campaign and a justification for its failure. Minas also conducted slaving raids against the Nilotic inhabitants of the Balaya region in western Gojjam, where he captured cattle and enslaved their owners.[26]

Besides his unwarranted attack on Falasha and his slaving raids, Minas, who appears to have had a deeply seated fear of powerful governors, embarked upon 'the dangerous policy of at once removing from office all the important provincial governors'.[27] Some of the men who were removed from office were capable individuals who had long experience in the art of governing. By this rash policy, Minas alienated his governors, his peaceful subjects and, at the same time, failed to provide his soldiers with necessary provisions. In his frustration he even turned against the Portuguese, who then turned against him. Minas had the Portuguese Bishop Oviedo soundly beaten, imprisoned

[23] Pankhurst, *History of Ethiopian Towns*, 94–116.
[24] Minas' slaving raids seem to have deprived the state of the services of able manpower and reduced the revenues, all of which added to the weakness of the state.
[25] Pereira, *Historia de Minas*, 28 (translation by Aregay, 'Southern Ethiopian and the Christian Kingdom', 179).
[26] Tsega Endalew Etefa, *Inter-Ethnic Relations on a Frontier: Mätakkäl (Ethiopia) 1898–1991*, (Wiesbaden: Harrassowitz, 2006), 36.
[27] Aregay, 'Southern Ethiopia and the Christian Kingdom', 179.

him for six months and then exiled the bishop and his followers, all of whom joined the camp of Minas' enemies.[28] His volatile character and unwise relation with the nobility and the Portuguese made him very unpopular. Minas' own chronicler euphemistically admits that he made laws that angered and turned the great men of the kingdom against him.

> Soon after he sat on that most Christian throne he began to re-establish the law and constitution of the kingdom; but the great men of the realm like Keflo and his colleagues, began to criticize and grumble, and to promote sedition secretly until by act they made it manifest.[29]

When an attempt to assassinate Minas failed during the second year of his reign, the opposition that had been seething for some time exploded. The opposition was engineered by the same nobility who had put him on the throne,[30] though Hamalmal and few other top officials supported him. Of the king's powerful enemies, Yeshaq, the governor of the two parts of Tigray, was the most intractable one. A formidable warrior who, while his own father submitted to Imam Ahmad, who 'had held him in such esteem that he had made him his son [Muhammad]'s steward and captain of many men',[31] Yeshaq never submitted, even to Imam Ahmad. He it was who, in the early 1540s, brought Portuguese soldiers who helped Galawdewos in defeating and killing Imam Ahmad in 1543. Early in his reign Minas humiliated Yeshaq and commanded him to 'come anyway without making excuses about being sick'.[32] Minas led a military expedition against Yeshaq; while he was on his way to Tigray, Keflo and other powerful men put on the throne one Tascaro. Undeterred by this turn of events, Minas arrived in Tigray and soundly defeated Yeshaq, killing one of his sons while capturing another.[33] At his court, Minas' supporters easily defeated and executed the unfortunate Tascaro. Some of the Portuguese who were found with Tascaro were also hacked to death with axes.[34] Although Minas succeeded in defeating Yeshaq, the latter never gave him respite and his short reign was consumed by his efforts at destroying Yeshaq and for maintaining his throne. During this time the Oromo expanded through several provinces, but Minas never fought with them. In fact, during his second expedition to Tigray in 1562 Minas took the garrisons of the eastern provinces at the very time when the pressure from the pastoral Oromo population movement was gathering momentum in all the eastern provinces. There could not have been a worse time in which to have withdrawn the garrisons from the storm centre. In Tigray, Minas was defeated by Turkish soldiers, with superior firepower, who fought on the

[28] Bruce, *Travels to Discover the Source of the Nile*, vol. 3, 231, 234.
[29] Pereira, *Historia de Minas*, 28.
[30] Ibid.
[31] Boavida et al., *Pedro Páez's History of Ethiopia*, vol. 1, 302.
[32] Ibid., vol. 2, 39.
[33] Ibid., 40.
[34] Ibid., 41.

side of *Bahar Nagash* Yeshaq.[35] Thus, by his transfer of the capital from Waj to eastern Gojjam, and then to Emfraz, Minas neither contributed to the defence of the kingdom nor strengthened the institution of the monarchy. On the contrary, he undermined both. By alienating provincial governors, he planted the seed for civil war, and by alienating his peaceful subjects, he prepared the background for rapid pastoral Oromo movements. By his inability to provide military leadership to stem the tide of Oromo movement, he stripped the person of the king of his aura of respect.

THE PROGRESS OF THE BARENTU OROMO MOVEMENT (SEE MAP 9 BELOW)

Before closing our discussion of the developments during the short reign of Minas, it is necessary to mention some of the measures taken by Hamalmal, in order to protect the provinces over which he was appointed supreme. We have already shown in the previous chapter that, by 1546, the Karrayu, followed by some sections of Akichu, Warantisha and Marawa Oromo, were on the border of highland Dawaro, preparing for the investiture of the new *gada*. During the Bifole Gada (1546–54) the Oromo overtook the whole of Dawaro and during the Michelle Gada (1554–62) the balance of force was changed dramatically in favour of the pastoral Oromo. They not only devastated the Muslim force at Hazalo, but also destroyed the famous Christian force known as Jan Amora in the important province of Fatagar.

Bahrey makes it clear that the destruction of Jan Amora was followed by the Oromo attack on the small district of Dago.[36] The Oromo attacks on the garrison at Dago seem to indicate that the Christian defence establishment in Fatagar was irreparably destroyed. Most probably Fatagar was attacked from two directions at this time. First, the spearhead of the Borana movement, Macha and Tulama, which unsuccessfully attacked Waj but was repeatedly repelled by Galawdewos, had been forced to retire to the forest between the Awash River and Lake Zeway. They had been checked from crossing the river by the presence of Christian regiments in Fatagar. Once Amir Nur had destroyed the Christian force in Fatagar in March 1559, the Macha and Tulama overwhelmed the province from the south. At the same time, the numerous and more aggressive Barentu warriors, namely Akichu and Warantisha or Arsi, attacked Fatagar from Dawaro, east of the Awash River. Simultaneously overwhelmed, Hamalmal had no alternative but to transfer his headquarters to Shawa, abandoning Fatagar to its fate. Hamalmal's removal of the garrisons from Fatagar to Shawa suggests that the Christian soldiers were unwilling to fight with the Oromo on the plains. Apparently with the intention of raising the morale of his force

[35] Aregay, 'Southern Ethiopia and the Christian Kingdom', 193.
[36] Bahrey, 'History of the Galla' in *Some Records of Ethiopia*, 116–17.

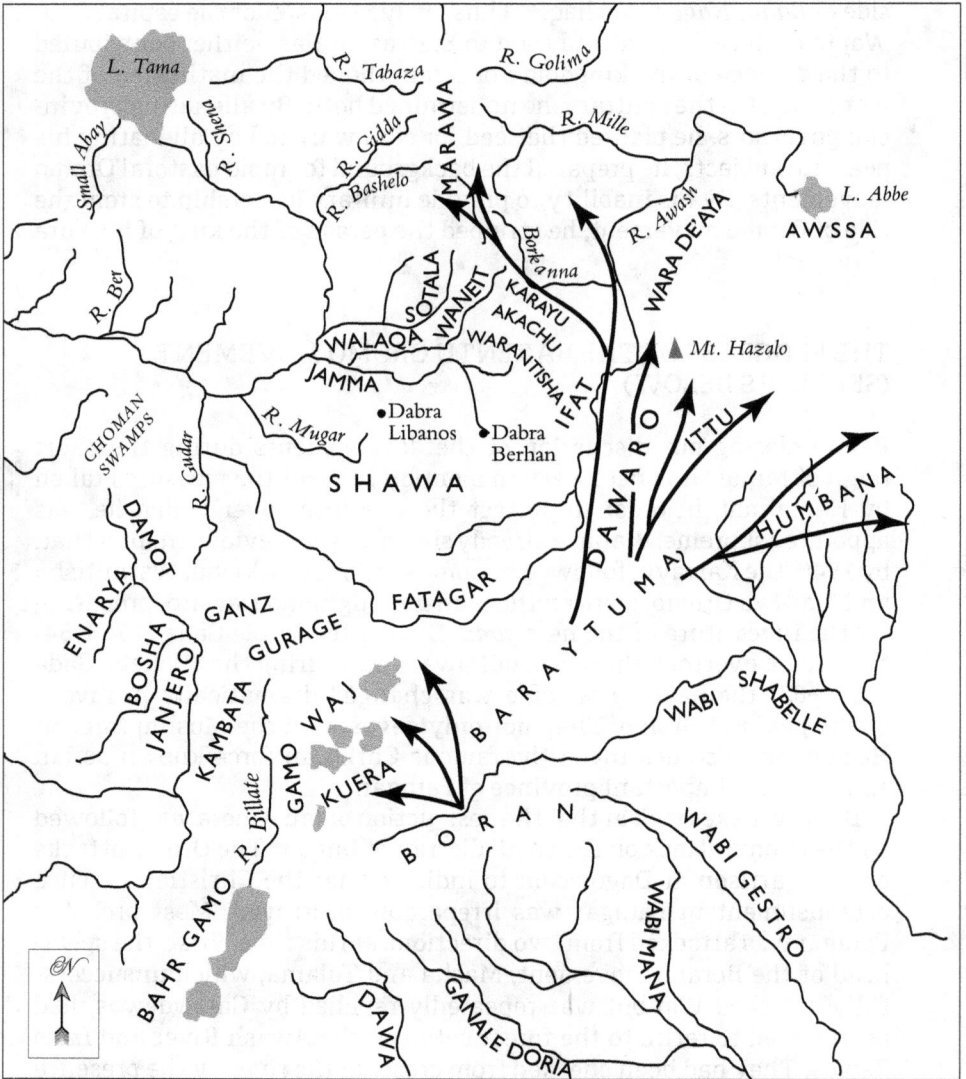

Map 9   The progress of the Barentu Oromo population movement, 1559–1563 (adapted from Aregay, 'Southern Ethiopia and the Christian Kingdom, 1508–1708', PhD diss., University of London, 1971).

and reducing the effect of the Oromo cavalry, Hamalmal abandoned the plains of Fatagar, where the Oromo cavalry would have had a significant advantage, and withdrew to the inaccessible mountains in Manz. This was a convenient place of refuge for several reasons. As well as being unsuitable for the pastoralists and their large herds of cattle, the various mountain chains in the region neutralized the effectiveness of the Oromo cavalry, and the bitter cold of the region would have forced them to look for better land. Besides, the new region was the frontier province between Fatagar, which had been abandoned, and other provinces such as Gedem, Geshe, Angot and Amhara, which had not yet been attacked. Hamalmal's withdrawal from Fatagar was not a cowardly act, but a pragmatic step designed to save his soldiers from the Oromo cavalry. Incidentally, this is another unmistakable confirmation for the correctness of Bahrey's assertion about the large-scale Oromo use of cavalry at this time.[37] It also demonstrates the effectiveness of the revolutionary innovations (mentioned in the previous chapter) that Oromo warriors appear to have introduced to their cavalry warfare, including their use of the toe-stirrup enabling them to stand on their big toes while throwing spears, and their cultivation of vital cavalry skills through frequent drilling of men and horses so that they achieved great prowess and were able to endure great fatigue.

Hamalmal's withdrawal from Fatagar was followed by an exodus of Christian refugees to safer regions inaccessible to the Oromo, and set a pattern for the future course of the history of the region. Only those communities that took shelter in the deep and inaccessible valleys or mountain tops escaped the intensity of the Oromo incursion. Soon Hamalmal's position became critical even in his inaccessible retreat. The battle of Dago that took place either towards the end of 1560 or 1561 is a good example. 'Dago was a small district to the east of Tagulat between Shawa, Gedem and Ifat'.[38] It was located in an unapproachable place, but this did not prevent the Oromo from attacking the region. The configuration of the land did, however, prevent them from effectively utilizing their cavalry. Here Hamalmal's strategy bore fruit, although the battle was indecisive. Bahrey makes it clear that it was the Michelle Gada and not Hamalmal that started hostilities. What is interesting to note here about Bahrey's information is not what he tells us about the battle, but about the presence of the Oromo in this region itself. This is one of the routes along which the Oromo movement spread into Geshe, Ganh and beyond. The aggressive Karrayu, followed by the Akichu and Marawa, attacked this region so repeatedly that Hamalmal was once again forced to abandon his base, this time withdrawing to Angot. Hamalmal, who only two years earlier was given authority over all the provinces east of the Abbay, had now withdrawn to the province of Angot. Here he again hoped to check the Oromo attack from Amhara, Tigray and Begameder. Angot was a large and mountainous province,[39]

---

[37] Ibid.

[38] Aregay, 'Southern Ethiopia and the Christian Kingdom', 204–5.

[39] Ibid., 32.

and its choice shows Hamalmal's determination to protect the provinces that had not yet faced an Oromo assault.

While Hamalmal was strengthening the defence of the strategically located province of Angot, Ifat was overtaken by large sections of Karrayu, Akichu and Marawa. Other warriors from Ittu and Warra Daya, also seem to have participated in the offensive against Ifat. Within a short time it was 'reduced to the escarpment, with its limits in the north and south at approximately the Robi and Qabanna Rivers'.[40] The Oromo advance on Ifat led to an exodus of Muslim refugees from the province. This exodus of both Christians and Muslims from Dawaro, Fatagar and Ifat seems to have revolutionized the relationship between the two communities. These traditional enemies who had been engaged in conflict for over two centuries now closed, albeit temporarily, the chapter of their former enmity, and for the first time formed a united front against a common enemy, the Oromo. Only two years earlier this could not have been dreamed of. Nothing could more dramatically illustrate how the times had changed than this Muslim-Christian alliance.[41] Both peoples resolved to stop the Oromo advance for their mutual safety, peace and survival. This alliance, however, was only formed at the last moment in a desperate attempt on the part of the refugee communities to salvage something from the wreckage of their provinces. But it was already too late. The wealth, especially the animal population, had already attracted the Oromo and whetted their passionate desire for cattle, horses, goats and sheep, and excellent pasturage. What becomes clear at this stage of the Oromo population movement is that the conquerors were guided more by the desire for resources, and the personal glory from the killing of enemies and grazing lands for their cattle, than by a desire to oppress the conquered people. Their resounding victories, which increased the prospect for rapid enrichment, attracted the highly organized and mobile pastoral warriors. The hunt for proceeds exceeded all expectations, and opened the era of rapid movement. The Oromo victories were partly secured by the previous mutual Christian and Muslim destruction of each other's power.[42] The Muslim-Christian wars and subsequent Oromo population movement had been followed by the decay of agriculture, commerce and consequently famine. These repeated miseries, which affected the thinly-spread inhabitants of the region, forced them to flee to

[40] Svein Ege, 'Chiefs and Peasants: The Socio-Political Structure of the Kingdom of Shawa about 1840' (MPhil thesis, Hovedoppgave i historie ved Universitetet i Bergen, 1978), 23.

[41] The history of north-east Africa seems to have a particular tendency to repeat itself though in a different form. More recently, in the late nineteenth century, the relationship between the Christian empire of Ethiopia and the Mahdist state of the Sudan was revolutionized as the result of European pressure on both. See for instance, G.N. Sanderson. 'Contributions from African Sources to the History of European Competition in the Upper Valley of the Nile', *Journal of African History* 3, 1 (1962), 69–85.

[42] Among other things, the slowness of the Oromo population movement before the Michelle Gada. (1554–62) could be explained partly by the fact that both Christian and Muslim forces were strong enough to stop Oromo advance.

safer areas. Thus the refugees were the victims of both wars and famine. Under such conditions the unarmed Christian peasants (see below) and the Muslim communities were no match for the ever-growing strength of the pastoral Oromo warriors. Only the king had the military might to check the Oromo advance. However, Minas was preoccupied with his internal enemies and as a result did not take any action against the Oromo. By 1562, only Shawa and a few other provinces alone remained in the hands of the Christian administration. The Christian leaders were unable to stop the pastoral Oromo advance on the provinces of Gedem, Geshe and Amhara.

The inability of the Christian administration to do anything coincided with Minas' reign. The leaders proved unequal to the task entrusted to them. For example, when Hamalmal was unable to reverse the tide of the Oromo incursion, he was forced to turn his attention towards the rebelliousness of his own soldiers, and he lavishly attempted to provide them with whatever was available. In doing so, he endeavoured to extract as much as possible from the peasants under his administration, who suffered from both the undisciplined nature of the soldiers and the lack of responsibility of their governors. Sometimes the interests of the soldiers and the defence of the provinces came into conflict. When this happened it was the interests of the latter which were ignored, despite the fact that ostensibly the soldiers were acting in its interests. The peasants, of course, did not remain indifferent to their suffering, and this became the cause of perpetual tension within the Christian society. The root cause of this tension was the weakness of the supply system which exposed the peasants to plunder. Because the peasants tended to resist when their cattle and crops were plundered, they were 'prevented by law from possessing and carrying any kind of arms'.[43] The unarmed peasantry was not a match for highly motivated and mobile Oromo warriors. The weakness of the Christian state's supply system was not a problem created by Minas. It had existed long before his reign. For instance, Francisco Alvarez, who lived in the Christian kingdom from 1520 to 1526 observed that foraging was practised by the soldiers. 'Because here there is no pay to be given, and every man brings with him what he is to eat, which consists of flour of parched barley and that is a good food, and parched peas or millet. This is their food at the wars, and the cows, where they find them.'[44] The provisions carried by the soldiers lasted only a few days. After their provisions were exhausted the soldiers 'on the march helped themselves to whatever cattle and crops they found on their way'.[45] Because the armies of Christian emperors were usually large, sometimes numbering 100,000 men[46], the territory through which they marched must have been extensively plundered.

It is Minas himself who must take some blame, in particular for the following. First, of his several political blunders, the one that

---

[43] Aregay, 'Southern Ethiopia and the Christian Kingdom', 81.

[44] Alvares, *The Prester John of the Indies*, 407.

[45] Aregay, 'Southern Ethiopia and the Christian Kingdom', 92.

[46] Alvares, *The Prester John of the Indies*, 407.

troubled him most was the conflict he created with *Bahar Nagash* Yeshaq, the powerful governor of the two parts of the northern region of Tigray. As already indicated, Yeshaq was among the very few top Christian leaders, who did not submit to Imam Ahmad during his jihadic war (1529–43). 'After the death of the Imam, Yeshaq had become one of the most important men in the country.'[47] Minas removed Yeshaq from his position and appointed him as the governor of the city of Axum. Humiliated and enraged, Yeshaq put a puppet king on the throne. Though his rebellion was crushed in 1561, Yeshaq escaped and put another puppet king on the throne. Second, Minas was unable to demand that his soldiers to carry their own provision even for a few days. Instead they depended on what they plundered from peaceful subjects, as when Minas decided to fight Yeshaq and the Turkish pasha in 1562.

> All the dignitaries of Shawa, Hamalmal, Taklo, Rom Sagad and others gathered and discussed with the king the provisions for the army. Minas sent Hamalmal and Zara Yohannes with many soldiers to go to Doba and capture animals so that these could serve as provisions for the descent to Tigray.[48]

As already indicated, Minas was defeated by the Turkish soldiers, who supported the rebellious Yeshaq. The Doba were peaceful nomads and fine fighters and by plundering them the Christian administration was weakening them. It was at this juncture, when Christian leadership had resorted to the unwarranted policy of looting its own peaceful subjects, that the period of the Michelle Gada came to an end.

THE HARMUFA GADA, 1562–1570

The Michelle Gada was succeeded by an equally victorious and highly mobile Harmufa Gada, which took the war into several provinces. In the words of Bahrey, 'Harmufa killed the soldiers of the regiment called Giyorgis Hayle at Qacheno',[49] located in the river valley of Wayat.[50] The soldiers of Giyorgis Hayle stationed at Qacheno were probably the best crack force in the kingdom. However, it seems they were not prepared for the assault of the new *gada*. The commander of this regiment was a certain Awssa, a friend of Hamalmal who, like the latter, believed in avoiding the Oromo warriors whenever possible. However, the Harmufa Gada suddenly surprised and destroyed a large section of Giyorgis Hayle. The sudden attack provided the survivors with an unlooked for spectacle and panic struck their hearts. With no time to organize resistance, Awssa turned his horse and fled and the rest followed. The leader and a number of his men escaped because of the swiftness of their horses. The credit for this Harmufa success must without doubt go to

---

47 Aregay, 'Southern Ethiopia and the Christian Kingdom', 180.
48 Pereira, *Historia de Minas*, 34.
49 Bahrey, 'History of the Galla' in *Some Records of Ethiopia*, 118.
50 Tafla, *Asma Giyorgis and His Work*, 149.

their scouts and war leaders. It was probably because of this success, and others to follow, that the Harmufa Gada was so boastful.[51] The manner in which Bahrey compares the defeat of Awssa with that of Amir Nur at Hazalo suggests that it was a major rout. What is more, from the manner in which the surviving soldiers of Giyorgis Hayle avoided meeting the Oromo thereafter, and from the way they marched through Ifat, Fatagar and Shawa to Waj, looting and plundering reportedly without mercy, they were very unsettled. With the defeat and dispersal of Giyorgis Hayle, the Oromo advance on Angot, Amhara, southern Tigray and Begameder was a foregone conclusion. Giyorgis Hayle was a protective shield stationed at the crossroads from where the passes to the northern provinces were controlled. Very soon the Harmufa 'devastated the countries of Gan (Ganh), Anguat (Angot) and Amhara'.[52] The attack on Angot and Amhara clearly implies that the Christian military establishments in the provinces of Gedem, Ganh and Geshe were already neutralized. These three small provinces 'were strategically important for the defence of the highlands against encroachments from the nomads and pastoralists of the eastern lowlands'.[53] As Awssa, the commander of Giyorgis Hayle, abandoned the strategic post at Qacheno so Hamalmal, his boss and friend, abandoned Angot to its fate. As already indicated, in a few years Hamalmal had abandoned Fatagar, the Manz area, and now Angot.

At this stage of Oromo population movement, which was still spearheaded by five Barentu sub-moieties, three directions of movement were observable (see Map 9 above). The first was the spearhead of the powerful Karrayu and Marawa groups, which entered Fatagar and fought Hamalmal at Dago. From here they managed to turn north between the inaccessible massif of Gedem on the east and the equally inaccessible and formidable massif of Manz on the west, passing through Geshe on the way to Angot. In all likelihood it was this group which attacked Giyorgis Hayle at Qacheno and later forced Hamalmal to abandon Angot. Second, another section of Karrayu and Marawa, together with Warantisha and Akichu groups, followed the route of the first group up to a point between the Chacha and Mofar Rivers, at which point they found it impossible to continue. From this it would seem that the second group was larger and accompanied by children, women and numerous cattle, while the first group was probably composed only of warriors. The second group turned to the east along the western Ifat, crossing the Robi River and leaving to the west the Gedem massif and then crossing the Borkanna River towards southern Amhara and beyond (see Map 9). Third, the Warra Daya (Warra Dayye) group that had been trailing behind the four sub-moieties followed the course of the Awash River along its course in the lowlands of Dawaro. To a large extent the movement route of Warra Daya was defined by the course of the Awash River.

[51] Bahrey, ibid., 118–19.
[52] Ibid.
[53] Aregay, 'Southern Ethiopia and the Christian Kingdom', 39.

Minas died in September 1563 while preparing to lead his third campaign against Yeshaq and his second puppet king. During his short reign Oromo pastoralists established themselves in the provinces of Fatagar, Ifat, Ganh, Gedem, Geshe and Angot, together with some parts of Shawa.[54] Minas 'never fought against the Oromo during his short reign'.[55] He died a frustrated man, unable either to defend his provinces or to raise tribute with which to maintain his soldiers.

Minas was succeeded by his son Sarsa Dengel, who came to the throne at the young age of 14 years and was a man of restless and bloodthirsty reputation. According to the monk Pawlos, the Oromo first entered the province of Angot in the year in which Minas died.[56] As we have already indicated, Hamalmal withdrew from the province before the Oromo occupied it. According to Merid, 'Hamalmal even encouraged some of the garrisons that had remained in the frontier districts to abandon their mountain strongholds ... He lacked the ability and boldness of his predecessor Fanuel.'[57] This may or may not have been the case. What is not in dispute is that Fanuel and Hamalmal faced the same problem but under entirely different circumstances. During the reign of Galawdewos, when Fanuel was the governor of Dawaro, the Christian kingdom was relatively strong. However, after 1559 when Hamalmal was appointed governor of the eastern provinces, the fortunes of the kingdom dramatically changed, and its military establishment was collapsing in the eastern provinces. Consequently, the defeated and demoralized garrisons in the eastern provinces did not need any encouragement from Hamalmal to abandon their post. On the contrary a number of garrisons had already voted with their feet, abandoning their mountain strongholds at the storm centre, in favour of an area not yet under Oromo assault, even before Hamalmal had abandoned Angot in 1563. The already-mentioned Giyorgis Hayle is the best example.

'Hamalmal had been one of the generals of Minas.'[58] From our sources it appears that Hamalmal was an intelligent man and a brave and good military leader who knew the reality, the limits and extent of his power. Undoubtedly he was haunted by the spectre of repeated Christian defeat, which may have inhibited him from taking anything that could possibly be construed as a risk. The security and the survival of the army may have weighed more with him than the bold adventure of meeting the fast-moving, highly motivated enemy, whose war strategy was still a mystery to the Christians (see Chapter 7 below). Some of the provinces might have been saved if the Christian politicians and military leaders had been united on a radical and new pragmatic policy, such as building strong fortifications at strategic points and maintaining them with thousands of soldiers. The annual upkeep of these fortifications would have required a great deal of resources

---

[54] On Shawa, see below,
[55] Tafla, *Asma Giyorgis and His Work*, 153.
[56] Conti-Rossini, 'L'autobiografia di Pawlos Monaco Abissino', 28.
[57] Aregay, 'Southern Ethiopia and the Christian Kingdom', 197, 212–23.
[58] Huntingford, preface, 'The History of King Sarsa Dengel', ii.

that would have laid a heavy burden on the people. Thus it appears the Christian kingdom lacked the means as well as the will for this. In any event, unity of purpose was lacking, and the politicians and military strategists were unable to generate a new defence policy. It took the Christian leadership several decades even to adopt to the highly effective Oromo *chibbra* (Amharic *chiffra*) fighting method.[59] Instead of coming up with new ideas, new strategies, the old and crude policy of slaving, which had been widely used during the heyday of colonization, was resuscitated with a new vigour born of desperation. This policy devastated the non-Christian minorities and depopulated vast areas that, in turn, contributed to the rapid spread of the pastoral Oromo.[60] Hamalmal alone cannot be blamed for this state of affairs. It was the economic disaster that drove the Christian leadership into this course of action. What Hamalmal could be blamed for is his revolt against the young king in 1563.

SARSA DENGEL AND THE OROMO: THE FIRST PHASE, 1563–1578

When Minas died suddenly there was serious disagreement among the nobility whether to put Sarsa Dengel on the throne immediately or to delay it until the arrival of Hamalmal. The Chronicle of Sarsa Dengel presents this disagreement among the nobility in the following terms.

> There were some who said, 'let us put on the throne at once the son of this king, the eldest among his brothers'. [There were others who said] 'it is not fitting that we alone should proclaim him king, since the great ones of the nation, Hamalmal and Zara Yohannes, Takla Haymanot and Mondolews are not here'. But the counsel of those who said, 'let us make him king at once' prevailed.[61]

Hamalmal's party within the court wanted his presence at the succession. Hamalmal had claim to the throne through his mother, Romana Worq, who according to Páez was a sister of Emperor Libna Dengel.[62] However, his ambition was not to be the king but probably aspired to be a sole regent, or co-regent with Sbla Wangle (the queen mother). Hamalmal was deeply offended by the decision, which did not take

[59] *Chibbra* was a traditional Oromo method of conducting warfare which was based on three elements: the first was gathering of information about enemy territory through a network of scouts; the second was organizing warriors in a line of six to a dozen deep, so that the first who fell were immediately replaced by other warriors who continued to advance unnerving the enemy. The third was a combination of choice of place and time, and speed in attack and retreat. *Chiffra* was the Amharic version. It was the adventurous prince Susenyos who lived among the Oromo and adopted their method of fighting. By adopting the *chiffra* system, Susenyos improved the speed, coordination and the capacity of his army to attack rapidly, or retreat expediently.
[60] Hassen, *The Oromo of Ethiopia*, 30.
[61] Huntingford, 'The History of King Sarsa Dengel', 2.
[62] Boavida et al., *Pedro Páez's History of Ethiopia*, vol. 2, 90.

his interest into consideration.[63] He felt insulted and humiliated when the final decision was reached without his presence. His scheme for stopping the spread of the Oromo movement failed and the problem of maintaining his numerous camp followers added to his difficulties. The restlessness of his soldiers increased his sense of frustration and in every sense his position became untenable. He believed he had to be in the decision-making council to steer the whole course of events in the proper direction. The news of his revolt and march towards the court sent a wave of terror through Mangesta Samyat in eastern Gojjam. Hamalmal's revolt was a nightmare that the Christians dreaded. He was a mature man and a calculating politician who was regarded as a father-figure. His revolt was the first conspicuous crack in the government of Sarsa Dengel. From the sources, it seems that Sarsa Dengel and his supporters were alarmed by Hamalmal's revolt, but not surprised. They were deeply frightened, but had prepared themselves in advance for something of the sort. Their reaction was very restrained. In the eyes of the Christian peasants this was a humiliating moment in their history, when their leaders failed to unite in the face of serious challenge from the pastoral Oromo population movement.

Hamalmal's arrival in eastern Gojjam, 'made the earth tremble' and the news of his arrival troubled the young king, who escaped and 'remained on the mountain with few officials and eight horsemen [who said] "we will die for you, we will not betray you, our master"',[64] The Christian peasantry, who feared Hamalmal's huge force even more than the young king on the run, told Sarsa Dengel 'do not come to us, but go where Hamalmal cannot find you. They spoke thus because they were frightened by the boldness of Hamalmal who had no shame in destroying the Christian kingdom.'[65]

Fortunately however, after Sarsa Dengel escaped Hamalmal showed wisdom by avoiding running after the fleeing king. In consequence, the original idea of an all-out war with Sarsa Dengel was watered down to a few skirmishes here and there. By this change of tactic Hamalmal once again demonstrated that he was a calculating man who did have the overall wisdom of avoiding total war at a risky moment. Hence, he compensated his lack of judgement in rebelling against Sarsa Dengel by his willingness to come to terms with reality. Very soon Hamalmal left eastern Gojjam, crossed the Abbay and settled down at Endagabatan where he built good fortifications.[66] Even though Aregay believes that Hamalmal's return to western Shawa was not motivated by a sense of duty,[67] his fortifications at Endagabatan were a timely measure that postponed Oromo occupation in the region for almost two decades. Hamalmal seems to have believed, as did Galawdewos, that there was

[63] Conti-Rossini, C. trans. and ed., *Historia Régis Sàrsà Dengel (Malak Sagad)* (Paris, 1907), 5.
[64] Huntingford, 'The History of King Sarsa Dengel', 5.
[65] Ibid., 13.
[66] Ibid.
[67] Aregay, 'Southern Ethiopia and the Christian Kingdom', 212.

neither a way of driving out the pastoralists from the areas they had occupied, nor a means of returning refugees to their provinces. The best course of action was therefore to settle the refugees in the provinces not yet attacked and strengthen the defences there. At Endagabatan, Hamalmal seems to have done just that. He pooled the isolated and scattered garrisons from the provinces where Christian administration had collapsed and stationed them behind fortifications at strategic points in defensible provinces.

While Hamalmal was strengthening the fortifications at Endagabatan – and at the same time preparing for some sort of final show-down with Sarsa Dengel – *Azmach* Taklo, the governor of Damot, abandoned the former's cause for that of Sarsa Dengel, and outmanoeuvred Hamalmal. Although Taklo was not one of the superior officers, he applied his strategy carefully to achieve his military ends. Beneath his adventurous exterior Taklo was a man of good experience who had grasped the essential implications of the Muslim and Christian alliance against the Oromo. He exploited the spirit of the alliance and, by so doing, contrived to get the Muslim leader of Waj, a certain Asma-ad-Din, to side with Sarsa Dengel against Hamalmal. Accordingly, Asma-ad-Din's force of 800 cavalry sided with Sarsa Dengel, thus out-numbering Hamalmal's 500 cavalry.[68] The chronicler of Sarsa Dengel praises the alliance engineered by the skillful *Azmach* Taklo. 'It was indeed wonderful that [Muslims] should help [Sarsa Dengel], while his own relatives, high officers of the state were fighting him.' Outmanoeuvred, Hamalmal was besieged in his own fortification. Harassed by misfortunes, shortage of food for his forces and the prospects of mass desertion of his soldiers, Hamalmal 'took the advice of the wise men'[69] and asked the queen mother, whom he had abducted from a convent earlier, to intercede on his behalf. Repentant for his rebellion Hamalmal submitted to Sarsa Dengel on 12 February 1564.[70] While submitting, Hamalmal 'handed over the old man whom he had made emperor and another boy [that Yeshaq] had sent him, whom they had also raised as emperor ... both as captives,[71] and seated Sarsa Dengel on his throne.

However, on 14 February 1564, Fasilo, one of the commanders of Hamalmal, attempted to kill *Azmach* Taklo, who had engineered Hamalmal's surrender. Though the attempt failed, Hamalmal's soldiers plundered the belongings of the queen mother and other royal children, as well as that of Taklo and his wife.[72] The treacherous plunder was undertaken with neither the knowledge nor approval of Hamalmal, who

---

[68] Conti-Rossini, *Historia Régis Sàrsà Dengel*, 19–20. From the size of Muslim cavalry, it would seem that the Muslim refugee population in Waj was probably large.

[69] Huntingford, 'The History of King Sarsa Dengel', 28, 30.

[70] Ibid., 35. However, according to Páez, Hamalmal's submission took place on 23 February. See for instance, Boavida et al., *Pedro Páez's History of Ethiopia*, vol. 2, 90–91.

[71] Huntingford, 'The History of King Sarsa Dengel', 36.

[72] Ibid, 36.

ordered his soldiers to return everything they looted from the court, which they did the next day.[73] From this sad incident Sarsa Dengel drew an important lesson. The very soldiers who looted the court without the knowledge of Hamalmal returned everything with his order. The lesson was that the soldiers respected Hamalmal more than they feared the young king. Sarsa Dengel needed soldiers who would respect and fear his orders. Above all, he needed disciplined loyal soldiers who carried out his will. As already indicated, it was the hunger of his soldiers that forced Hamalmal to sue for peace. He asked for pardon, and the queen mother and her son were magnanimous towards him. Hamalmal was pardoned and was appointed as governor of Gojjam. Hamalmal died there shortly after in November 1564.

However, the correctness of Hamalmal's new defence policy was evident immediately after he made peace with the young king. The garrisons of the threatened eastern provinces abandoned their posts and wanted to go across the Abbay for safety. The regiment known as Giyorgis Hayle, which had earlier demonstrated its lawlessness whilst fleeing through Shawa and Fatagar to Waj, once again abandoned their new haven for yet another one across the Abbay. Other regiments such as Batra Amora in Waj followed suit. There was a general flight from all the eastern provinces. Sarsa Dengel, who was now on good terms with Hamalmal, seems to have listened carefully to the advice of the old man. Sarsa Dengel soon intercepted the fleeing soldiers before they crossed the Abbay and followed the course, already mapped by Hamalmal, and settled them at Mugar in western Shawa. By his encounter with the demoralized and fleeing soldiers, Sarsa Dengel seems to have drawn two conclusions. First, it appears that he realized that there was no way of turning the tide against the Oromo. It was probably due to this realization, reached early in his reign, that Sarsa Dengel never seriously undertook either to return the refugees to their provinces, or to drive out the Oromo from the provinces they had occupied. Merid Wolde Aregay claims that 'strong feminine influence in his life left marked effects on his character'.[74] This may or may not have been the case, but what is not in dispute is that Sarsa Dengel was weak and indecisive. 'The only way he knew of winning or retaining the loyalty of the nobility and the soldiers was by heaping favours on them. He compromised and surrendered on important issues in order to please them.'[75]

Secondly, and more importantly, Sarsa Dengel seems to have realized from the mutinies of the disaffected soldiers and the rebellion of Hamalmal, that the loss of the eastern province would have serious internal repercussions for his administration. He soon saw that his rights to the throne were based neither on legal sophistry nor ideological rhetoric, but on the sword alone. He was obliged, therefore, to aim at the creation of an army devoted to him alone, and at the acquisition of the financial means indispensable for maintaining himself on the

[73] Ibid, 36.
[74] Aregay, 'Southern Ethiopia and the Christian Kingdom', 220.
[75] Ibid., 232.

throne. This he started at Mugar, where he had settled the deserting soldiers. He even raised a tantalizing hope among the demoralized soldiers by recruiting into his own army the young and virile elements from among them.[76] Sarsa Dengel's need for creating a personal crack force with which to discipline the disaffected soldiers became even greater when he temporarily put in chains Awssa, the commander of Giyorgis Hayle. The restless soldiers boldly

> attacked the king's camp, looting everything in the camp, and left nothing of the possessions of the king and the princesses, as well as taking people's goods from their houses and even from the church. ... After committing this offence they set off for Walaqa.[77]

Sarsa Dengel followed them into Walaqa, where he made peace with them. He did this by releasing Awssa from detention and pardoning those who looted his camps. After they were pardoned, Awssa ordered his soldiers to return the goods they looted from the queen mother and the princesses. No sooner had Sarsa Dengel made peace with Awssa and the Giyordis Haile regiment, than Fasilo, one of the commanders of Hamalmal, rebelled against him. Fasilo's rebellion ended when the king pardoned him. Fasilo, who mercilessly plundered the property of Christian peasants, shared his loot with the king and other court officials. Thus, when he arrived at the court, he 'filled the king's heart with joy because he gave them things which pleased them'. *Azmach* Taklo, the engineer of Hamalmal's surrender, was removed from his position of power and replaced by Fasilo, who commanded more soldiers. Not long after, Fasilo rebelled again and his soldiers 'surrounded the king's camp and looted everything ... One of the foot soldiers wounded the king's horse.'[78] That day Sarsa Dengel probably would have lost his life, if he had not mounted another horse quickly and fled through the rebel lines.[79] Sarsa Dengel was able to overcome these rebellions, because he created a crack force with which he disciplined the disaffected soldiers. The causes of repeated rebellions were many, but two were crucial. The first was the threat of hunger, which always provided a pretext for plundering the peasantry, which in turn, created perpetual tension within the Christian society. The second was the fear of Oromo cavalry. It is not an exaggeration to state that by the 1560s the restlessness of the regiments in the eastern provinces was the direct response to the Oromo military challenge to the Christian military establishment.

The Oromo warriors' movement was unpredictable. They depended on the guerrilla type of warfare. They were highly mobile, well trained, mounted and greatly motivated. Above all, they did not have any permanent settlement and it was very difficult for the garrisons to retaliate by going to Oromo territory. The effective spy-ring that the Oromo scouts

---

[76] Ibid. See also Conti-Rossini, *Historia Régis Sàrsà Dengel (Malak Sagad)*, Paris, 1907, 29–30.
[77] Huntingford, 'The History of King Sarsa Dengel', 45.
[78] Ibid., 46, 57, 54.
[79] Boavida et al., *Pedro Páez's History of Ethiopia*, vol. 2, 92.

employed at this stage helped them to disappear with their cattle deep into the bush before the Christians could retaliate. In their pursuit the Christian soldiers would be harassed suddenly and unexpectedly in a forested land they did not know, and by an enemy they could not see. Thus many a time the Christian forces had to abandon their pursuit in despair and hurry back to their post to escape starvation, since they could not find provisions in the land which had been devastated by an unsettled situation.

> As soon as the [Oromo] perceive an enemy comes on with a powerful army they retire to the farther parts of the country, with all their cattle, the Abyssinians must of necessity either turn back or perish. This is an odd way of making war wherein by flying they overcome the conquerors; and without drawing sword oblige them to encounter with hunger, which is an invincible enemy.[80]

Demoralized by hunger and frustrated by their inability to inflict any damage on the Oromo, the Christian soldiers were filled with a desperation that manifested itself in the form of rebellion against the state as well in looting or massacring the defenceless subjects of the Christian state itself.

THE PROGRESS OF BARENTU MOIETY'S NORTHWARD MOVEMENT

Before we close our discussion on the period of the Harmufa Gada (1562–70), we must again take up the progress of the Barentu moiety's movement to the north, where we left them in 1563, while they were spreading themselves rapidly. The Karrayu and Marawa together reached the valley of the Wanchite River, at which point the Karrayu turned west, while the Marawa continued through Makana Sellase, crossing the Borkanna River into a region bounded by rivers on three fronts and Angot in the north (see Map 9 above). Undoubtedly this group passed through densely populated areas in a very short time. This could have happened either because the Oromo avoided attacking strong points, as they did in many places, or because the group was large and powerful, as Asma Giyorgis claims.[81] We have already shown that the Marawa were divided into three sub-moieties, namely, Ana, Uru and Abati, while the Karrayu were in turn divided into six sub-moieties, namely, Liban, Wallo, Jille, Obo, Suba and Bala. Each of these sub-moieties was sub-divided into many smaller groups, The Wallo for example were divided into seven groups. Bahrey gives the following seven as the 'sons' of Wallo: Wara Buko, Wara Guera, Wara Nole and Wara Illu, these four calling themselves Wallo, while Wara Karrayu, Wara Illu and Nole Wara Ali are known as *Sadacha* ('the three').[82] In popular tradition the

---

[80] Tellez, *The Travels of the Jesuits in Ethiopia*, 66.
[81] Tafla, *Asma Giyorgis and His Work*, 139.
[82] Bahrey, 'History of the Galla' in *Some Records of Ethiopia*, 114.

Wallo are reported to have had seven 'sons,' as confirmed by Bahrey. What is interesting to note here is that, of all pastoral Oromo groups who settled in the north, the Wallo group had a very strong Muslim tradition. This may be partly because they were the first Oromo group to accept Islam. There is also another reason why this may be so. According to one tradition, Wallo was the head of an Oromo clan, which went to Harar, embraced Islam, and came to the Christian kingdom as one of the fighters of Imam Ahmad.[83] Legends such as this one reflect more about the changed value system than anything else. Some Wallo clans may have already embraced Islam even before their arrival in the northern region. For example, Nole Wara Ali seems to have been Muslim, Ali is an unmistakable Muslim name and usually only Muslim Oromo adopted Muslim names.

From the sources it is clear that a section of Karrayu and Marawa occupied southern Amhara while the rest moved on to Angot. From the manner in which Pawlos describes the first Oromo attack on Angot, it appears that the province was attacked suddenly, and the peasants did not put up a strong resistance.[84] Sarsa Dengel's court, which was embroiled both in the mutiny of the soldiers and Hamalmal's rebellion, had neither the will nor the means to alleviate the plight of the peasants of Angot. Left to themselves, the peasants were unable to drive out the strong warriors from the province. In one sense, the Oromo attack on southern Amhara and Angot was radically different from that of the southern provinces. In the latter, they repeatedly attacked and withdrew to their safe base areas, while in the former they attacked only during the Harmufa period, and then proceeded to settle. In other words, in southern Amhara and Angot the Oromo settled before commencing to break the backbone of peasant resistance by means of a long period of continuous attack and retreat. Considering the extremely difficult nature of the terrain for attack and retreat, and taking into account the large size of the peasantry in the region, the Oromo warriors' attack must have been a bold gamble generated by the degree of self-confidence gained from having won several victories. In the eyes of the unarmed peasants the Oromo were an 'invisible' enemy. The exaggerated reputation for the Oromo ability to do the 'utmost mischief possible in the shortest time',[85] their reputed cruelty during the initial stage of their attack, the lightning speed with which they could attack and retreat, all these seem to have contributed to create an impression of being invisible in the eyes of the untried peasantry.

> The report of their cruelty made such an impression upon the Abyssinians, that on their first engagements, they rarely stood firmly [against] the [Oromo's] first onset. Besides this, the shrill and very barbarous noise they are always used to make at the moment they charge, used to terrify the horses.[86]

[83] Domenico Brielli, 'Ricordi Storici de Wallo', in Conti-Rossini, *Studi Etiopici*, 87.
[84] Conti-Rossini, 'L'autobigrafia de Pawlos Monaco Abissino', 287.
[85] Bruce, *Travels to Discover the Source of the Nile*, vol. 3, 240.
[86] Ibid., 240-4.

The Oromo spy network seems to have been a very active and effective one. Without essential information concerning the provinces of Begameder and southern Tigray, we cannot see how the vanguard Oromo force was able to attack the two provinces within the Harmufa Gada period. At this stage in their movement our information on their assault in southern Tigray is too scanty to enable us to make any definite statement. However, we do have sufficient information of their attack on Begameder. Bahrey makes it quite clear that 'Harmufa of the Bartuma made war on Begameder, and killed Waka the brother of Harbo'.[87] Pawlos has also confirmed that the Oromo had defeated Harbo the governor of Begameder.[88] The first Oromo attack on Begameder must have been a very serious one. According to Merid, this attack 'was made shortly before the rainy season of 1569'.[89] The attack was made by the Karrayu and Marawa groups, which seem to have left southern Amhara and crossed the Borkanna River towards its source, then passing through the heart of Amhara and descending the valley of Bashilo, from where they crossed the river of the same name. From the manner in which they defeated and dispersed the Christian force and struck panic among the peasantry of Dambiya, and from the sheer devastation they caused, it would seem that the attack was undertaken suddenly and unexpectedly. We suspect that the long-distance attack in Dambiya was motivated purely by the hope of animal acquisition, because the region was famous for its animal population, and also the court of the late king Minas was located here. From this it would seem that they had the necessary information both on where to attack and or when to attack. The big group that attacked Dambiya withdrew quickly after taking significant booty and administering a quick, sharp shock to the peasants in the area.

THE ROBALE GADA, 1570–1578

Harmufa was succeeded by the Robale Gada. This came to office at the time when Sarsa Dengel had established his authority and, more importantly, had won a resounding victory over the governor of Hadiya. According to Bahrey, it was Robale 'who devastated Shoa and began to make war on Gojjam'.[90] This means Sarsa Dengel did not turn the tide against the Oromo, even after he had fully established his authority. By 1573, instead of rallying his force for the support of the eastern provinces, Sarsa Dengel 'began, or rather resumed, the predatory activities which were to become the main occupation of his life'.[91]

---

[87] Bahrey, 'History of the Galla' in *Some Records of Ethiopia*, 118.
[88] Conti-Rossini, 'L'autobiografia de Pawlos Monaco Abissino', 288.
[89] Aregay, 'Southern Ethiopia and the Christian Kingdom', 324.
[90] Bahrey, 'History of the Galla' in *Some Records of Ethiopia*, 119.
[91] Aregay, ibid., 277.

THE BORANA MOVEMENT TO THE NORTHERN PROVINCES
(SEE MAP 10 BELOW)

So far in our discussion of pastoral Oromo population movement, we have concentrated primarily on the Barentu moiety, for the simple reason that the Barentu formed the vanguard of the whole movement for almost four decades, both in the eastern and the northern directions. This does not mean that the Borana did not make a name for themselves. They were part of a population movement that engulfed the Horn in the second half of the sixteenth century. The major difference between the two moieties was that at the start of the movement the Barentu moiety had already more than thirty fully-fledged sub-moieties which were fighting in their names, and were looking for new grazing grounds for their cattle. Even though the Borana moiety had three sub-moieties on the eve of their movement only the Macha and Tulama charted their movement to the north, while the Gujji and the southern Borana remained in the southern region, from where sub-moieties directed the course of movements towards what is today northern Kenya and south-western Somalia.[92]

Our interest here, however, is with the Macha and Tulama movement to the north. The Macha and Tulama were collectively known as Borana. In this section we use Macha and Tulama and Borana interchangeably. We have already mentioned two points about the Borana moiety's movement to the north that are worth remembering at this point. First, from the clan genealogies of the various Barentu groups found in Arsi, Bale, Hararghe and the Wallo regions, we find numerous Borana clan names. For instance, in Hararghe we find clan names such as Macha, Tulama, Borana, Wayu, Galan, Arrojjii and so many others (see Map 5, page 96). In Wallo region there is even an *awraja* (sub-province) named after the Borana who settled there. Among the Arsi Oromo sub-moiety genealogies, we find Borana, Jaawwii, Wayu and Liban, to mention just a few examples. These are all important clan names of the Borana (Macha and Tulama) who settled either in what are today the regions of Shawa, Wallaga, Kaffa, Illu Abba Bora and Gojjam. What these clan names in Arsi, Bale, Hararghe and Wallo regions (where the Barentu sub-moieties mainly settled) indicate is that numerous groups of the Borana joined the Barentu on their march early in the movement.[93]

Second, we have also indicated that while warriors of the Borana moiety were joining the Barentu march, the Macha and Tulama were simultaneously moving to the north, fighting in their own name and winning new grazing lands for their cattle. Initially, the Borana were less successful in expanding their territory. The two most likely reasons for

[92] On the Oromo migration towards Kenya, see E.R. Turton, 'Bantu, Galla and Somali Migrations in the Horn of Africa: A Reassessment of the Juba/Tana Area', *Journal of African History* 16, 4 (1975), 519–37.

[93] The *gosas* of the Borana moiety kept their clan names even after they had joined with and settled among the Barentu. This was also true of the Barentu *gosas* who settled among the Borana moiety or sub-moieties.

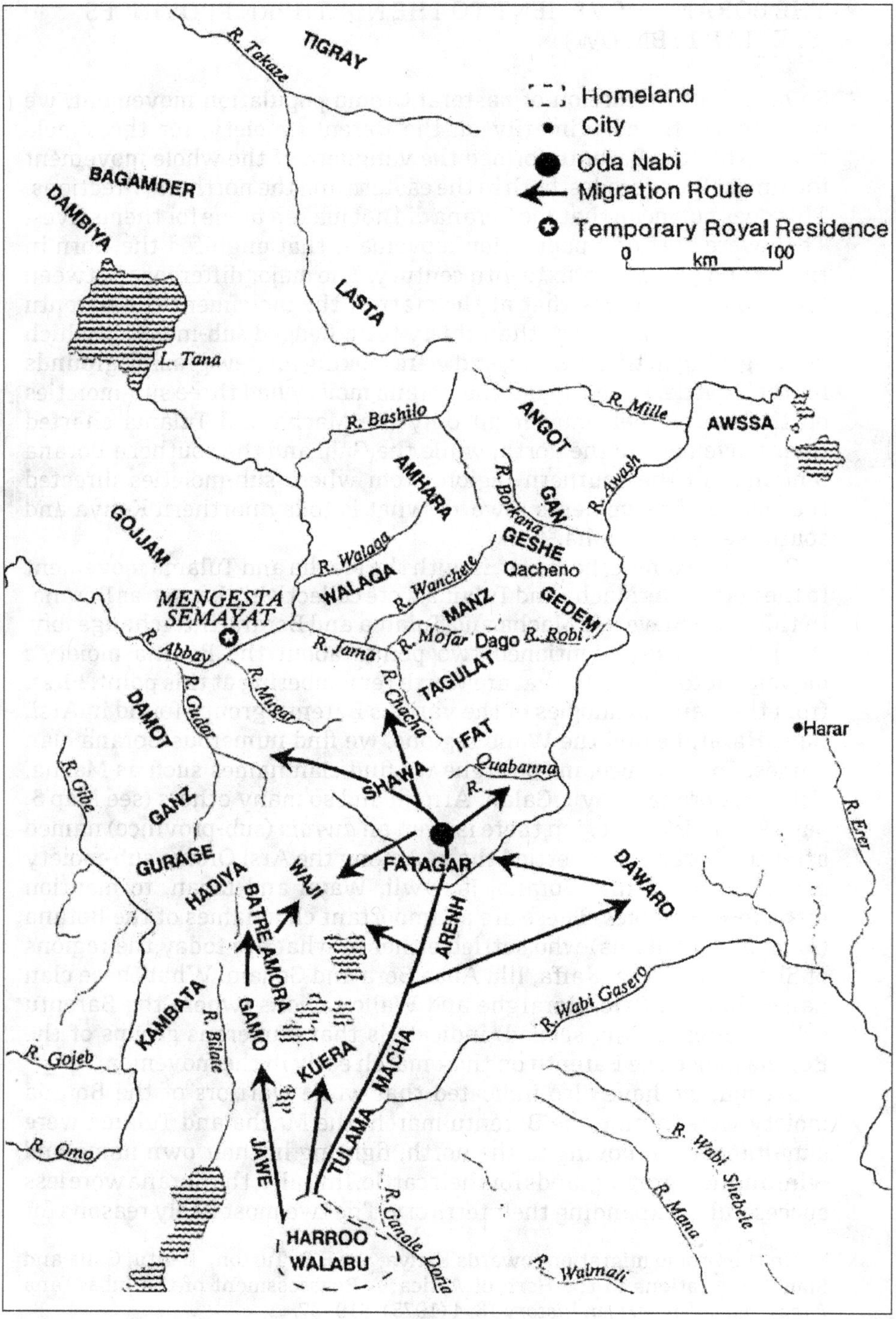

Map 10   The Macha and Tulama movement to Fatagar and other provinces (adapted from Hassen, 'The Oromo of Ethiopia, 1500–1850', PhD diss., University of London, 1983).

this were probably their relatively smaller size when compared to that of the Barentu. From their base at Harroo Wallabuu they progressed, therefore, rather slowly through the Rift Valley. The other reason for their slow progress was the presence of strong Christian regiments at various strategic positions. Following the jihadic wars, and repeated Barentu attacks, the Christian defence system in the eastern provinces collapsed. This facilitated the rapid spread of Borana during the period of the gada under discussion. However, before embarking on a discussion of the large Borana movement to the north during the Robale Gada (1570–78), we should clarify certain points that are relevant to our discussion.

In the 1920s, while visiting Ambo, E. Cerulli gathered the tradition about a beast called Liqimssa,[94] the central theme of which revolves around Harroo Wallabuu, the Borana point of dispersal. Cerulli correlates this tradition of the Borana, dispersal from Wallabuu with Bahrey's *Zenahu le Galla* and then charts the route that the Oromo followed in their northward movement. Cerulli bases the thrust of his argument on the following conclusion of Bahrey. 'Those of the Borana who stayed came out of their country by way of Kuera; that was at the time when Fasilo attacked them and was killed by them.'[95] By 'their country', Bahrey means the Harroo Wallabuu region and his statement does not have any other meaning. From internal evidence the death of Fasilo took place in late 1587. As indicated by Aregay, Cerulli has inaccurately identified the above-mentioned Kuera with the present

> Koira, a small district east of Lake Abaya, inhabited by a Sidama tribe called Koira or Baditu. He also thinks that Gamo refers to the Gamu highlands west of the same lake. On the basis of these identifications, Cerulli draws conclusions that contradict Bahrey's own history of the [Oromo].[96]

According to Aregay, Bahrey's home of Gamo was located 'somewhere to the south of Waj. It may have been on the plains between Lake Shala and the Bilate River.'[97] The district of Kuera where Fasilo was killed in 1587 was not far from Bahrey's home of Gamo. In fact, Kuera has been identified with 'the small village of Kuyera, situated between the Lakes of Shala and Awasa, near the town of Shashmane'.[98] On the basis of his inaccurate identification of Bahrey's home of Gamo with Gamu highlands, Cerulli makes the Jaawwii, a section of the Borana (who attacked Bahrey's home of Gamo in the late 1570s), the spearhead of pastoral Oromo population movement to the north, which is historically inaccurate. However, there is an element of truth in Cerulli's assertion that makes the route from Harroo Wallabuu through Kuera and Gamo the major path of the Borana sub-moieties movement to the north during

[94] Cerulli, *Etiopia Occidentale*, vol. 2, 169–73. For the interpretation of the legend of Liqimssa, see Chapter 4.
[95] Bahrey, 'History of the Galla' in *Some Records of Ethiopia*, 114.
[96] Aregay, 'Southern Ethiopia and the Christian Kingdom', 306–7.
[97] Ibid., 309.
[98] Ibid.

the 1570s, which Cerulli projected to the situation of the early 1520s. I do not think Cerulli was aware of the weakness of Bahrey's *Zenahu le Galla* regarding the Barentu moiety's movement to the north. This is probably why Cerulli makes Borana rather than Barentu the spearhead of Oromo movement.

What both Cerulli and Merid forgot to consider concerns the relevance of the above-mentioned tradition of the Borana movement into Shawa itself. In this tradition, it is stated that Shawa had a powerful king named Sarako, who prevented the people from bearing arms. A certain giant arose against Sarako and his children, and destroyed them. When the two groups of the Borana, Gombichu and Ada, entered Shawa, they found no-one to stop them since the children of Sarako had been killed. So the Borana entered Shawa without much difficulty.[99] What is important about this tradition is the part that refers to the fact that the people of Shawa were disarmed and that the Borana entered Shawa without experiencing much resistance.

There is a ring of authenticity to this tradition underneath its legendary shell. This was because Christian peasants were not allowed to bear arms.[100] The above-mentioned tradition may reflect this reality. The unarmed and un-drilled Christian peasants were not able to resist the rapidly moving Oromo cavalry. Besides, after the fall of Fatagar the defences of Shawa were under attack. Hamalmal's retreat from Shawa to Angot in 1560–61 implies that Shawa itself was no longer safe. What is more, since the time of Michelle Gada (1554–62), four Barentu sub-moieties, namely Karrayu, Wallo, Marawa and Warantisha were channelling their movement to the north. We have seen that some of these groups actually passed through Manz on their way to Geshe, Ganh, southern Amhara, Angot and beyond. Manz was an important part of historical Shawa. What all this amounts to is that, even before the Robale Gada, the defence of Shawa on the eastern front was in a shambles. This may be the reason why Hamalmal settled in western Shawa in 1563 rather than in any other place. It may also be why the notorious regiment of Giyorgis Hayle was settled in western Shawa after much persuasion by Sarsa Dengel in 1564–65. When the Borana Robale Gada overtook Shawa in the 1570s it seems that they did not find much resistance. The above tradition suggests this and Bahrey's history also implies the same thing.[101]

In his chapter on the Robale Gada Abba Bahrey makes two points very clearly. First, he mentions the Robale of Barentu that attacked Amhara, Angot and Begameder. Second, he also mentions that the Robale of Borana carried the war from Shawa to Gojjam.[102] I believe it was the weakness of the defence system or lack of strong resistance in Shawa which may have encouraged the Borana to cross the Abbay

[99] Cerulli, *Etiopia Occidentale*, vol. 2, 169–73. Amhara oral tradition blames an arrogant king for disastrous defeat by the Muslims. Cerulli believes that this tradition of the arrogant king relates to Emperor Libna Dengel (1508–40).
[100] Aregay, 'Southern Ethiopia and the Christian Kingdom', 81.
[101] Bahrey, 'History of the Galla' in *Some Records of Ethiopia*, 119.
[102] Ibid.

and attack Gojjam. According to Abir: 'Their ability to attack simultaneously in different areas made resistance to their raids almost impossible.'[103] To check the progress of such an enemy would have required a large cavalry and many foot soldiers in every province. King Sarsa Dengel lacked both the material resources and the necessary organization to undertake such a massive operation. Due to negligible tribute, Sarsa Dengel lacked both material resources and strong organization to conduct a sustained war against Oromo warriors.

> Nor does the revenue and tribute that I shall describe directly promise anything better. The kingdom of all others in this empire from which most gold comes is Narea [Ennarya]. From there none of the former emperors, so the present one states, ever received as much as Malaac Cequed [Malak Sagad], who reigned during the years 1563 to 1596. What Malaac Cegued received each year only once amounted to five thousand oquaeas, according to some people, for many do not think this is certain. For the rest of the time, he did not receive in any one year more than one thousand five hundred, which is fifteen thousand patacas.[104]

According to Pedro Páez, after the Oromo attacked Gojjam, Sarsa Dengel thought it best to excuse the tribute of three thousand horses so that the inhabitants of Gojjam could use the horses to defend themselves against the Oromo.[105] It appears that Sarsa Dengel possessed very little both in gold and horses – the two vital resources in strengthening the defence of the kingdom. The Oromo cavalry must have outnumbered the imperial force. If the Oromo started using horses only during the period of Michelle Gada (1554–62), as Bahrey claimed,[106] it would have not been possible for the Oromo cavalry to outnumber the imperial cavalry within such a short time during the period of Robale Gada (1562–70). Thus, Oromo warriors must have been using horses much earlier than hitherto believed. Be that as it may, let me briefly mention the sources of income of the government of Emperor Sarsa Dengel.

Generally speaking, Sarsa Dengel had three primary sources of income. The first included the revenue from the land and other taxes that were utilized for the upkeep of the army.[107] According to Almeida, the emperor received a great tribute in cows.[108] However, many of these were either consumed by tax collectors or ruined in the process by which they were gathered. In short, the income from the revenue had never been enough and it had to be supplemented from the third source of income. The second revenues came from the crown lands

[103] M. Abir, 'Ethiopia and the Horn of Africa', in *The Cambridge History of Africa*, vol. 4 (1600–1790), ed. Richard Gray (Cambridge: Cambridge University Press, 1975), 543.
[104] Almeida, 'The History of High Ethiopia or Abassia' in *Some Records of Ethiopia*, 87–88.
[105] Boavida et al., *Pedro Páez's History of Ethiopia*, vol. 1, 265. See also Almeida, ibid., 86.
[106] Bahrey, 'History of the Galla' in *Some Records of Ethiopia*, 117.
[107] Almeida, 'The History of High Ethiopia or Abassia' in *Some Records of Ethiopia*, 86–88.
[108] Ibid.

which went towards the upkeep of the court. The third, and the major sources of revenue, came from frequent plundering raids and slaving expeditions, and the confiscation of the property of the enemies of the throne. The revenue from commerce was insignificant due to the insecurity of travelling, which had dramatically reduced trade. From these three sources, rewards were made to the faithful servants, nobles and soldiers. The court was neither the centre of plenty as it had been in the early sixteenth century, nor threatened by starvation. It still attracted a large number of people. The soldiers in the frontier provinces became very restless due to the pressure of the pastoral Oromo movement. The restless soldiers had to be bribed with all sorts of favours. Thus the army was the object of Sarsa Dengel's special care. It received its pay whenever resources were available, and when resources were lacking the soldiers received his license to plunder peaceful subjects while, at the same time, his limited resources handicapped him from mounting any sustained offensive against the Oromo. Almost all his wars against the Oromo were either defensive or a nervous reaction to their bold incursions into the regions that were vital for his throne. For instance, when the Borana Robale entered Shawa, Sarsa Dengel did not come to the rescue of this province. However, when the same Robale took the war to Gojjam and Waj, Sarsa Dengel responded with a firm decision to punish the Borana. He mobilized fully and thoroughly prepared to humiliate them.

> He sent messages to all provinces of his kingdom telling [the governors] to assemble here, and also to the Chawa [professional soldiers]. He sent messages likewise to Zara Yohannes in Gojjam, to Takla Giyorgis, the Tsahefe Lam[109] of Damot, and to Dahragot the [governor] of Waj, ordering all of them to come with their troops … When he arrived in Waj he was told that the [Oromo] had occupied all the Maya country and Waj with their herds, their children and their women.[110]

The governor of Shawa was conspicuously omitted from this mobilization order. From all the eastern provinces it was only the governors of Waj and Damot who were included. This implies that either it was only these two provinces that were under his effective control or that he wanted just to defend them. His mobilization was particularly successful. Oromo warriors, who usually kept their children, women and cattle in safe base area, were caught off guard. They were devastated, their large herds of cattle captured and their women and children enslaved. Interestingly Sarsa Dengel captured several Oromo warriors and recruited them into his army. What is more, Sarsa Dengel adopted a new policy of settling pastoral Oromo groups both in Gojjam and Begameder, where he 'distributed the uncultivated and fallow lands' among the Oromo and 'mingled them with the Christians'.[111] Those who were recruited into his army and those who were settled

---

[109] This was the title used by the governor of Damot.
[110] Huntingford, 'The History of King Sarsa Dengel', 73–74.
[111] Tafla, *Asma Giyorgis and His Work*, 163.

among the Christians probably were required to accept Christianity, which marked the beginning of their integration into Christian Amhara society – a policy that was to be perfected during the reign of Emperor Susenyos (1607–32), which will be discussed in Chapter 7. In terms of Sarsa Dengel's victory, his chronicler claims that no Muslim or Christian leader did as much as Sarsa Dengel towards 'the eradication of the [Oromo]'.[112] However, Bahrey – a contemporary historian – describes Sarsa Dengel's victory in a more realistic manner. 'The king of Ethiopia gave battle to him [the Oromo] at Zeway, killed many of his men and captured many of his cattle; thanks to this booty many people became rich.'[113]

Sarsa Dengel was unable to derive much political and military advantage out of this resounding victory for three reasons. First, to the Oromo, this loss was only a temporary setback that affected only one of the several groups. The loss of men, women and cattle by one group could be replaced by the gain of another group. What is interesting to note here is that during the whole course of the pastoral Oromo population movement, women, children and cattle continued to pass over to new masters. Since women were in short supply among the moving pastoral Oromo, they were one of the prizes for which they were fighting. Accordingly women changed hands frequently. In the process languages got intermingled, different groups hopelessly mixed up, and customs interchanged. The captive youths became warriors under their new masters, the old were turned out to tend the flocks and herds, and the flocks and herds simply changed masters for a few years until they were taken by yet another master. It must be noted that during their movement to the north pastoral Oromo moved from place to place with their flocks of herds, always in search of rich pastureland for their cattle and avoiding their loss. Cows, horses, mules, sheep, goats and donkeys were their important possessions. Since they were on the move, they had no particular areas to defend and no towns to protect. In every sense, the pastoral Oromo had advantages over their settled enemies, who had to defend their villages or towns and protect their property. The second reason that Sarsa Dengel gained little political and military advantage was that, after his successful expedition to Waj in 1572, he and 'his soldiers withdrew to Damot and Bizamo and then to Gojam and Dambiya, not to return until 1577. By so doing Sarsa Dengel exposed 'all the provinces along the Awash [River] to renewed attack'.[114]

Third, while Sarsa Dengel was attacking them in Waj, the Barentu Robale crossed over from their base in Amhara into Gojjam and terrified the peasants. Zara Yohannes, who was probably on his way to help Sarsa Dengel, changed his course and followed the Barentu Robale across the Abbay into Amhara, where he was surprised and killed by the Oromo. Being the governor of Gojjam, he was the 'chief of the

[112] Huntingford, 'The History of King Sarsa Dengel', 73–74.
[113] Bahrey, 'History of the Galla' in *Some Records of Ethiopia*, 119.
[114] Aregay, 'Southern Ethiopia and the Christian Kingdom', 255, 265, 285, 306 footnote 1, 314.

dignitaries',[115] and his death must have been a considerable loss to Sarsa Dengel, who immediately went back to Gojjam to reorganize Zara Yohannes' dispersed force.

It was in 1577 that Sarsa Dengel decided to fight against the *Bahr Nagash* Yeshaq, who not only challenged the king's authority but also put on the throne two puppet kings one after the other. The king's court officials discussed this matter 'and said "how can the king set out and abandon the country to the [Oromo]?" But he refused to listen to them, since he had decided to fight Yeshaq.'[116] When the king's mother heard about his intention, she

> immediately left Gend Barat, where she was living at that time, and hastened to meet him at Sabrad. That day she said to him, 'my son, why have you decided to do this thing against me and your brothers? Do you wish to deliver us to the [Oromo]? Does not our possible doom distress you? By these and similar words she persuaded him to change his mind, for he was obedient to his mother ... Having given up his design to go to Tigre, he decided to go to Waj to fight the [Oromo] who were there.[117]

Sarsa Dengel's change of heart was only temporary and intended to mitigate mounting criticism against him and to allay the fear of the Christians in western Shawa.[118] His campaign against the Borana in Waj was partly successful in that, because he was able to kill many of them,[119] some fled from the province with their children, women and cattle. This implies that this time the Borana were not caught off guard. Immediately after Sarsa Dengel left the area, the Borana returned to Waj in large numbers demonstrating their determination to stay in that province. With his short-lived partial victory Sarsa Dengel assembled all the professional soldiers from all the provinces east of the Abbay River and marched to Gojjam for his planned war against Bahr Nagash Yeshaq.

While Sarsa Dengel was in Gojjam he received news that the Barentu Robale were attacking Dambiya, the seat of his court. He marched with full speed and fell on the Abati of Marawa division that invaded the province from across the Bashilo River. 'While the battle was at its hottest, for these rebellious slaves were redoubtable fighters, the powerful and victorious king penetrated into their midst and killed ... many.'[120] This is the first grudging acknowledgement by the chronicler that the Oromo were formidable warriors. It was in recognition of this quality that Sarsa Dengel started recruiting a large number of Oromo warriors into his army in 1572. However, during this battle with the Abati Sarsa Dengel did not think of taking Oromo prisoners of war. His goal was to exterminate them and leave 'their bodies

---

[115] Bahrey, 'History of the Galla' in *Some Records of Ethiopia*, 119.
[116] Huntingford, 'The History of King Sarsa Dengel', 90.
[117] Ibid., 91.
[118] Hassen, *The Oromo of Ethiopia*, 34.
[119] Huntingford, 'The History of King Sarsa Dengel', 91.
[120] Ibid., 92.

as the food of the birds of the sky and the beasts of the field'.[121] This victory is also confirmed by Abba Bahrey, a contemporary historian with these words: 'Sarsa Dengel attacked the Robale of the Abati at Wayna Daga and killed them, not sparing one; it is of them that they say not more than ten remained; they alone returned home to carry news of the defeat.'[122] This was the first major victory over the Abati. Several more were to follow before the aggressive Abati became a spent force, totally swamped by the Christian society among whom they had settled.

In the bitter conflict that developed between Sarsa Dengel and Bahr Nagash Yeshaq, the Oromo were deeply involved on both sides of the conflict. As already indicated, Sarsa Dengel started recruiting a significant number of Oromo warriors into his army since 1572. Yeshaq also discovered the advantage of involving the Oromo in his conflict with Sarsa Dengel. Between 1576 and 1578, with the promise of rich booty, Yeshaq lured Marawa and Karrayu Oromo warriors from their base in Amhara region. The Oromo involvement on both sides of the conflict is a good example of their participation in the politics of the Christian society. Thus, in 1579, Sarsa Dengel marched against Yeshaq and his Turkish allies, with all the regiments from the provinces east of the Abbay, 'together with many [Oromo]',[123] who were described as fierce warriors. 'Then all the relations of Yeshaq, all the leaders of his partisans came and submitted to the king, all the musketeers and all the [Oromo] came also, without exception.'[124] Sarsa Dengel defeated and killed Yeshaq, whose head was cut off[125] and put on display for others to see. In the clash that took place on 27 November 1579, one of the commanders of Sarsa Dengel named 'Gilo died after penetrating into the midst of the Turks, killing them on all sides. This man was well known to the Moslems for his strength.'[126]

Apparently Gilo was one of the military commanders of Sultan Muhammad of Harar, when the Muslim leader invaded Bali in 1576, plunging his feeble sword into the disintegrating body of the Christian kingdom. The invading Muslim force was liquidated. However, Gilo submitted to Sarsa Dengel and became one of his military commanders. From his unmistakable name, Gilo appears to have been an Oromo. What the war against Yeshaq clearly demonstrates is the deep Oromo involvement in Christian politics. During the same period, the Oromo were also deeply involved in the affairs of the city-state of Harar, which is beyond the scope of this book.

[121] Ibid., 96–7.
[122] Bahrey, 'History of the Galla' in *Some Records of Ethiopia*, 119.
[123] Huntingford, 'The History of King Sarsa Dengel', 113.
[124] Ibid., 116.
[125] Boavida et al., *Pedro Páez's History of Ethiopia*, vol. 2, 97.
[126] Huntingford, 'The History of King Sarsa Dengel', 116.

THE REIGN OF SARSA DENGEL AND THE OROMO:
THE SECOND PHASE, 1579–1597

Though victorious in his war against Yeshaq, Sarsa Dengel irreparably damaged the defence of all the provinces east of the Abbay River. This was because he mobilized and took all the regiments from them. According to Merid Wolde Aregay, the fate of the provinces of 'Arenh, Sharka, Waj and Shawa was decided when the emperor took the regiments stationed in them to Tigre.'[127] Some of these regiments were very small and one wonders why (if not to prevent their liquidation in his absence) that Sarsa Dengel took them all the way to Tigray. It seems he must have already formed the opinion that the fall of the eastern provinces was inevitable.

The Birmaje Gada, 1578–1586

The Birmaje Gada came to office at the time when Sarsa Dengel was marching to the north with the regiments of all the eastern provinces, including his Oromo soldiers and accompanied by Maya auxiliaries who used poisonous arrows. This *gada* adopted a revolutionary fighting method. I discussed this aspect elsewhere,[128] and it is sufficient here to note Bahrey's observation. 'This Birmaje of the Borana made ox-hide shields of body length and attacked the Maya, who were skilled archers, but were beaten because there was no place for their arrows to strike since the shields were made of stiff ox-hide.'[129] The Maya warriors served as auxiliaries of the Christian military. They were respected and dreaded by all for their poisoned arrows. The Borana adopted the full-length, stiff ox-hide shields probably after they had suffered repeatedly at the hands of the Maya warriors. It was probably the poisoned arrows of the Maya, together with the Christian soldiers, who prevented the Borana from moving through Waj during the 1520s. Once adopted, the new shield revolutionized the whole course of the Borana warfare. In every sense, this was a real turning point in the course of Borana sub-moieties' movement to the north. This revolutionary adoption of long shields enabled the Birmaje warriors to shorten Sarsa Dengel's control of the provinces east of the Abbay River. Bahrey states:

> Birmaje [gada] pressed hard on *Azmach* Daharagot, commander in chief of the king's army; and killed Zena and his guards. At first Daharagot defeated the [Oromo] many times; but by the will of God, because the sins of the Christians were not expiated, the [Oromo] devastated Aren, the country of which Dararagot was governor and killed Gato, Batro, Badlo, Amdo and other personages.[130]

[127] Aregay, 'Southern Ethiopia and the Christian Kingdom', 255.
[128] Hassen, *The Oromo of Ethiopia*, 35.
[129] Bahrey, 'History of the Galla' in *Some Records of Ethiopia*, 120.
[130] Ibid. For different spellings of the names of individuals mentioned in the quotation, see Haile, *The Works of Abba Bahriy*, 204.

Following the defeat, it appeared that Daharagot withdrew abandoning all the provinces over which he was appointed governor and, according to Merid Wolde Aregay, 'it is not known when and how he withdrew from Waj. Nothing is heard of him until 1590 when he reappears as *dajazmach* of Tigre.'[131] The Borana Birmaje, encouraged by victory over Daharagot, motivated by the huge resources they acquired in Waj, and trusting in their shield for more victories, prevailed in Damot. The Christians in Damot fled to Gojjam. 'Among the countless people who fled to Gojjam were ... (the mother of the king) and other members of the royal family.'[132] Encouraged by this turn of events, the Borana Birmaje simultaneously attacked Shawa, Waj and Damot. Shortly after, the Borana Birmaje 'occupied all of Shawa and Damot, up to the gorge of the Blue Nile'[133] (see Map 11 below). Sarsa Dengel did not react decisively to the bold Borana Birmaje's attack on the provinces east of the Abbay River. Militarily Sarsa Dengel was at the pinnacle of his power. During his war against Yeshaq in 1579, Sarsa Dengel captured 300 Turkish soldiers, and a large quantity of guns and artillery pieces. His army had never been so formidable or so well-equipped as it was at this time, but by his subsequent action he showed that he was more insecure than at any time since his accession to the throne. As a result he was more concerned about providing resources for his large army than defending the provinces east of the Abbay River. The news of the Borana victories caused considerable anger among his officials. To them it seemed as if the nightmare of the previous decades, that is to say the total loss of all the eastern provinces, was coming to pass. In 1580 Sarsa Dengel called a state council at Gubay to decide what to do.

> The idea of the emperor was to leave after the rainy season to go to fight the [Oromo] from Angot to Gedem, Ifat, Fatagar and Dawaro. He made and ratified this decision with all the chiefs from everywhere when he had sent each of them to their respective provinces.[134]

This was the first grand plan to attack the Oromo in the eastern provinces with the exception of Bali and a few other provinces. The future of these provinces and the hopes of their governors, as well as that of the displaced refugees, depended on the implementation of that plan. However, before the rainy season was over the king was already having second thoughts about the implications of the plan to attack the Oromo over such vast areas; in consequence the original decision relating to a massive expedition was watered down and replaced by a feeble attack on the Falasha, who time and again proved a timely scapegoat for the Christian rulers.[135]

[131] Aregay, 'Southern Ethiopia and the Christian Kingdom', 334.
[132] Ibid., 335.
[133] Bahrey, 'History of the Galla' in *Some Records of Ethiopia*, 119.
[134] Huntingford, 'The History of King Sarsa Dengel', 148.
[135] For an excellent history of the Falasha, see James Quirin, *The Evolution of the Ethiopian Jews: A History of the Beta Israel (Falasha) to 1920* (Philadelphia: University of Pennsylvania Press, 1990).

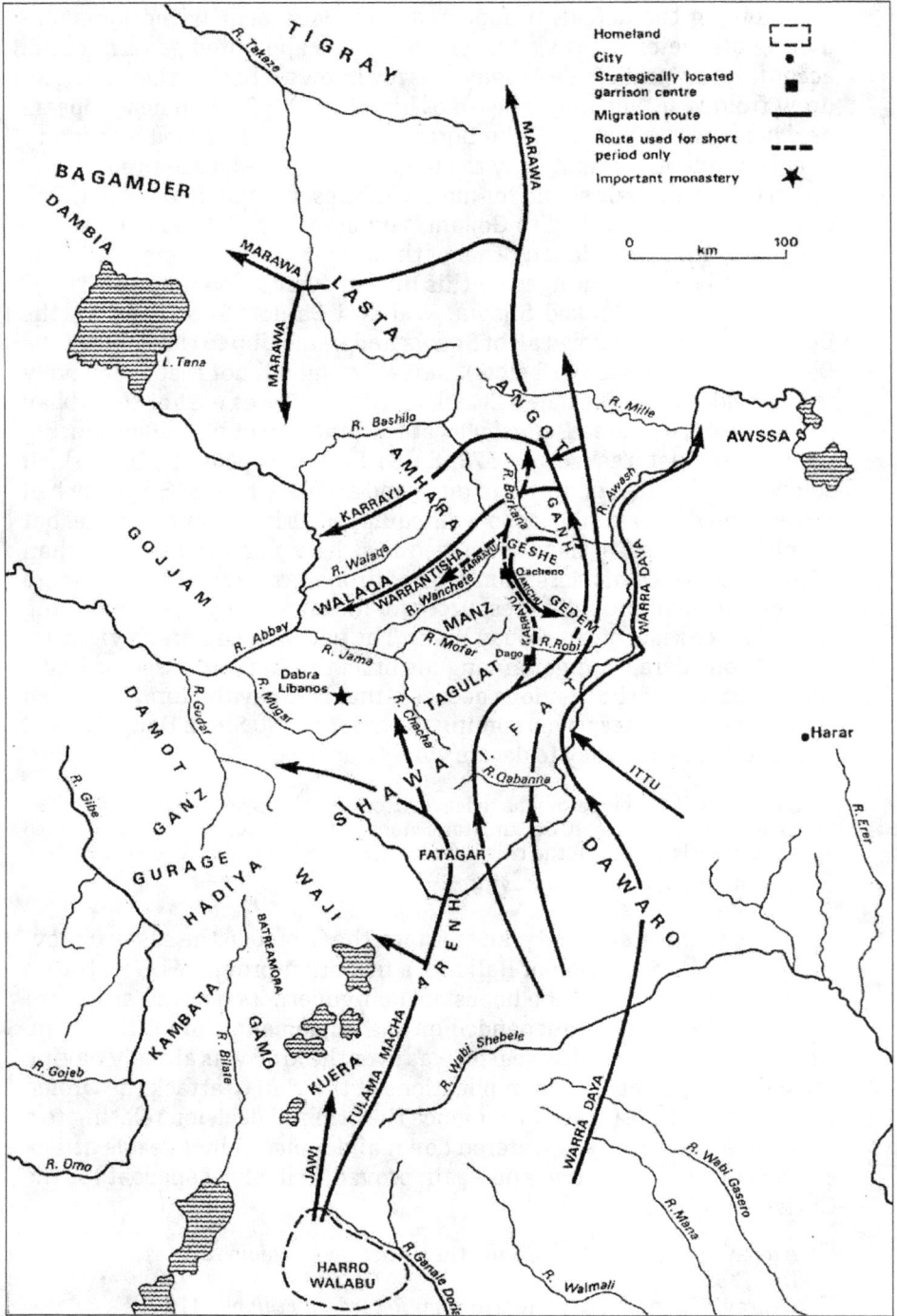

Map 11   The pastoral Oromo population movement to the central and the northern parts of the Christian Kingdom (adapted from Hassen, 'The Oromo of Ethiopia, 1500–1850', PhD diss., University of London, 1983).

The historian Merid Wolde Aregay criticizes Sarsa Dengel on five valid grounds. First, his removal of the regiments for the Tigray campaign was tantamount to 'abandoning all eastern provinces'. Second, the history of Sarsa Dengel's reign 'after 1579 is a history of lost opportunities in every sense of the phrase'. Third, the 'failure of Sarsa Dengel and his troops to show some of sort of reaction to the loss of all the provinces east of the Blue Nile defies not only justification but even understanding'.[136] Fourth, Aregay states that 'instead of defending the country, the emperor and his captains were destroying it' through their plundering and slaving raids on peaceful subjects. Finally, he argues that the 1579 campaign against the Falasha was 'a timely excuse to avoid returning to the frontier provinces'.[137] The reason for abandoning the campaign against the Oromo is given by the chronicler as the refusal of Radi, the leader of the Falasha, to pay tribute in cereals, honey, cattle and sheep. This infuriated the king so much that he immediately sent messages to all the regiments and governors of Tigray to come to his assistance. The ideological justification for his attack on the Falasha is given by Sarsa Dengel himself: 'It is better to me that I fight with the enemies of the blood of Jesus Christ rather than go to fight against the [Oromo].'[138] This implies either that his soldiers refused to go on the campaign against the Oromo, or he did not have provisions for them, or both.

Sarsa Dengel's slave raiding and its impact on pastoral Oromo population movement

It appears that Sarsa Dengel's reign after 1579 was dominated by the need for providing resources for his large army than defending the provinces east of the Abbay River. Resources were obtained mainly through slave raiding and campaigns against his non-Christian subjects, both of which appeared to have cleared the way for pastoral Oromo movement. This started immediately after his 1579 Tigray campaign, when the king promised his large army of soldiers that he would 'take them to the country of the pagans, so that they may eat their corn and loot their possessions'. He kept his promise and took them to Gojjam, where his large professional soldiers plundered the cattle of non-Christian subjects, looted their corn and enslaved their women.[139] This means the king was conducting raids against non-Christians subjects at the very moment when the victorious Borana were on the verge of overtaking Gojjam itself.

Sarsa Dengel's 1579 campaign against the Falasha, which was particularly devastating, set the pattern for the thoroughness of his campaign, killing all the captured livestock of the Falasha as well as the soldiers: '[n]one of those who would walk on their feet … [were] left alive'. Yonel, one of the commanders of the king, cut off the heads of brave Falasha

---

136   Aregay, 'Southern Ethiopia and the Christian Kingdom', 335.
137   Ibid., 215, 255, 285, 306 footnote 1, 464.
138   Huntingford, 'The History of King Sarsa Dengel', 148.
139   Ibid., 146, 147.

men and 'sent as a gift to the king nearly two hundred of the women whose husbands had been killed'. An enslaved Falasha woman threw herself over a precipice, 'dragging with her ... the man to whose hand hers was tied ... She was not alone in doing this astonishing thing'. After the war against the Falasha the king promised his soldiers: 'I will take you to where you will find riches, for so far you have not found riches, but only victory over the enemies of our Lord in the campaign in Semen'. The chronicler, who compares the wisdom of Sarsa Dengel with that of King Solomon, states that learning that his soldiers were 'unwilling to embark on a new campaign, he gave them the hope of finding cattle, slaves and much wealth'. He kept his promise and took them to the Balaya and Wambarya regions in Gojjam. In the former region a quarter of the houses of the people were destroyed by fire, while in the latter region the cattle of the Gafat people were plundered and their men, women and children enslaved. The loot was so huge that 'there was rejoicing in [the camp of the king] for seven days'. In 1581 Sarsa Dengel attacked the Basso people on the pretext that they resisted Galadewos during the 1550s! According to the chronicler, the devastation that was inflicted on the Basso in 1581 was 'a seven fold vengeance upon those who opposed [Galadewos]. Truly, truly our lord Malak Sagad [the king's throne name] is an avenging [king].'[140] After 1580 Sarsa Dengel conducted many campaigns in the land of non-Christian Agaw people in Gojjam, where his soldiers committed all kinds of outrages. His devastating

> raids into various districts of Gojjam and into provinces on the other side of the Blue Nile; against the Gafat in Shat in 1581, against the Agaw of Bed and Sarka in the following two years and against districts neighbouring on Enarya in 1584. More people in other regions were probably affected in these as well as in the years between 1585 and 1587.[141]

Sarsa Dengel's slave raids not only cleared the way for Oromo movement, but also intensified the export of slave trade from the Christian kingdom. According to Merid Wolde Aregay, slaves were exported through the kingdom of Funj in the Sudan and through the Turks who controlled Arkiko and Massawa on the Red Sea coast.[142] Through cruel and brutal slave-raiding campaigns, Sarsa Dengel inadvertently facilitated the rapid spread of the Oromo through his kingdom. The emperor, who perfected the policy of slaughtering, enslaving and plundering the Agaw people of Gojjam turned his attention against the Oromo only after his soldiers were enriched with their loot from his peaceful subjects.

In 1586, when the Marawa Oromo from their base in Amhara region attacked Begameder, Sarsa Dengel mobilized his forces 'and sent them with some [Oromo], who were experienced fighters, thirsting to shed human blood, and armed with shield, spear, and club'.[143] The chroni-

---

[140] Ibid., 153–4, 171, 175, 188.
[141] Aregay, 'Southern Ethiopia and the Christian Kingdom', 287.
[142] Ibid., 303–4.
[143] Huntingford, 'The History of King Sarsa Dengel', 186.

cler, who admires Oromo fighting quality, exaggerates their eagerness to shed human blood. His exaggeration has double ideological purposes. The first was to indirectly express his disapproval of Sarsa Dengel's use of Oromo warriors. The second was to present the Oromo as the enemies of the Christian society. Enemy or not, Sarsa Dengel discovered a new policy of using Oromo warriors against his other Oromo enemies. The king's campaign against the Marawa was not successful as they fled from Begameder with their loot before the thunderbolt intended for them was launched.

Unhappy with the failure of the campaign against the Marawa, Sarsa Dengel decided to boost the morale of his soldiers. He took them to the districts of Acahafar and Wambarya in Gojjam, where they enriched themselves plundering the Agaw people. The king took his share of slaves and cattle from his soldiers. The king also took his soldiers to the district of Wambarya in April 1586, where they again plundered and enslaved the Agaw people.[144]

Either in November or December 1586, Sarsa Dengel received news that 'the [Oromo] have come, arriving suddenly in Gojjam without anyone knowing; they have stolen a great many cattle from all the districts of Gojjam; they have taken people into slavery and killed others'. Among those who narrowly escaped capture by the Oromo was the mother of Sarsa Dengel herself, who became a refugee on a mountain top in the district of Wasan Amba in Gojjam. Sarsa Dengel quickly mobilized and arrived in Gojjam, where he brought a sigh of relief to his mother. Oromo warriors fought Sarsa Dengel's soldiers 'so hard that they put them to flight, and forced them back to where the king was. Then Sarsa Dengel adopted a new strategy, which would later be perfected by Susenyos. This strategy was based on picking the ground that was too narrow for Oromo cavalry, but good for Sarsa Dengel's foot soldiers and drilled musketeers, who routed Oromo warriors. Sarsa Dengel thanked God, who had given him 'the victory over the rebellious peoples'.[145] The phrase 'rebellious peoples', which is repeated a number of times in the king's chronicle, was an interesting development. By 1570s, it appears that Sarsa Dengel had slowly but surely come to believe that the Oromo were rebellious people, who had to be forced into submission, rather than enemies to be expelled. This may account why he did not conduct any sustained campaign against them. It may also reflect why the king's chronicler started admiring grudgingly the fighting qualities of Oromo warriors.

Before the end of 1586, the Borana Birmaje gada had crossed the Abbay River and attacked Gojjam. This Borana attack on Gojjam was devastating enough, but the rout and subsequent dispersal of the victims became still more so on account of two circumstances which attended it. The first of these was the death of Fasiladas, the cousin of Sarsa Dengel, who fell either in defence of his rich estate among the fleeing peasants, without having performed in his own name anything

---

[144] Ibid., 215, 216.
[145] Ibid., 218–19.

worthy of his long experience and the universal respect in which he was held, or died even possibly 'while rallying the people of Shawa to their own defence.'[146] The second factor was the capture of his son Susenyos, (whose history will be discussed in Chapter 7).

While Susenyos was still in captivity the Borana group among whom he lived went to attack the province of Damot. Dajazmach Asbo, the governor of the province, waited patiently until the Borana looted his province and had encumbered themselves with heavy booty. He then attacked them at the moment they were not suspecting at the place where they were busy sharing their acquisitions.[147] He easily dispersed the startled Borana, capturing many from among them.

> Dajazmach Asbo detained them under severe conditions, saying 'If you bring back the son of Fasilidas, I will release you from imprisonment and send you to your people, otherwise I will kill you. They [the Borana men] for their part replied to him saying, 'We will bring him for you, and if we do not bring him, kill us.' When Susenyos was set free and returned from captivity Dajazmach Asbo … released those [Oromo] and sent them to their own people in accordance with his words.[148]

After obtaining his goal of setting Susenyos free from captivity, Asbo, did not follow up his success with more boldness and imagination. His strategy against the Borana Birmaje brings to light the new defence measure that the Christian leaders were adopting slowly but surely. Since neither the peasants nor the soldiers could possibly withstand the first Oromo onslaught, with all its attendant consequences, the raiders were tacitly permitted to loot. Whilst they were doing this, the Christian soldiers went and hid along the route by which the heavily-loaded Oromo would make their return, waiting for an opportunity to take revenge on the plunderers. They usually waited at a difficult crossing, which was advantageous for their foot soldiers but perilous for the Oromo cavalry, where either fight or flight would be equally dangerous. This new strategy was perfected by Susenyos, who also introduced the Oromo *chibbra* (Amharic *chiffra*) fighting system, which improved the efficiency of the Christian force (see Chapter 7 below).

While the Borana Birmaje was attacking Shawa, Damot, Waj and Gojjam, the Barentu Birmaje was busy attacking Amhara, Begameder and Tigray. The Marawa group that had spread over lower Angot branched off mainly to the west where the vanguard group descended down to the valley of the Takaza, and kept up the pressure on Begameder and Dambiya. The latter was a fertile and rich province that had attracted the eyes of several kings. After his return from the Tigray expedition in 1579, Sarsa Dengel made Gubay the seat of his court. 'Gubay was located on top of a series of hills which faced towards Lake

---

[146] Aregay, 'Southern Ethiopia and the Christian Kingdom', 335.

[147] Bahrey, 'History of the Galla' in *Some Records of Ethiopia*, 120.

[148] Pereira, *Histoire de Minas*, 4–5. I am deeply indebted to Haile Larebo, who translated for me the relevant part of Susenyos' Chronicle from Geez into English.

Tana. The position and the impregnable castle which the emperor built there with the help of the Turks protected it from the assaults of the Marawa [warriors].'[149] However, Sarsa Dengel's s presence in Dambiya did not lessen the Marawa's burning desire to access the province, rich in cattle,[150] a prize considered worth fighting for by the pastoral Oromo. Accordingly, between 1585 and 1586 the Marawa took the war into Dambiya and 'killed Aboli of the royal family, Samra Ab the Bahr Nagash, and other personages'.[151] Of the other Barentu groups, the Warantisha had already started spreading, 'out along the valley of the Wancit, lower Jama and Walaqa Rivers; the Akachu [Akichu] to their west, in southern Amhara and in Gedem and the Karrayu throughout Amhara, Angot and Ganh'.[152] Together the Barentu sub-moieties spread over extensive mountainous areas in what are today, Wallo, Begameder and Tigray regions. Of the numerous Karrayu groups, the 'seven houses' of Wallo had started to establish themselves in the southern section of Amhara, the region known until then as Lakomalza. The Wallo settled here and gave their name to the region and the province.

> The area thus occupied by the Wallo consisted of the major localities known today as Jama, Laga-Mida, Laga Gora, Laga Ambo, Ali bet, Abay bet and Gimba. These seem to have been the original localities which constituted the so-called sabat bet Wallo (the seven houses of Wallo).[153]

The Mulata Gada, 1586–1594

The Mulata Gada came to office at the time when economic difficulties had forced Sarsa Dengel to become almost like a professional slave-hunter among non-Christian minorities west of the Abbay. 'While in 1585 his mother was homeless and a refugee at the Gojam village of Dajan, and while the Borana were completing their conquest of Damot, he was raiding for slaves across the river in Balya and Wambarma.'[154] The Mulata continued to wage war in all directions and during this *gada* period the Oromo in general, and the Borana in particular, won spectacular victories. The Borana Mulata Gada's spectacular victories in Waj, Shawa and Damot marked the beginning of the end of Christian administration in these provinces, which forced the emperor to conduct a spirited campaign against the Borana in late 1587 or early 1588. He attacked them with his crack force of musketeers and cavalry armed with iron helmets. The Borana shields and spears proved useless and irrelevant in front of fire power and the swords handled by drilled soldiers.[155] The Borana warriors who attacked Gojjam were devastated.

[149] Aregay, 'Southern Ethiopia and the Christian Kingdom', 328.
[150] Almeida, 'The History of High Ethiopia or Abassia' in *Some Records of Ethiopia*, 87–88.
[151] Bahrey, 'History of the Galla' in *Some Records of Ethiopia*, 120.
[152] Aregay, 'Southern Ethiopia and the Christian Kingdom', 330.
[153] Zergawa Asfera, 'Some Aspects of Historical Development in "Amhara Wallo" (c. 1700–1815)' (BA thesis, Addis Ababa University, 1973), 4.
[154] Aregay, 'Southern Ethiopia and the Christian Kingdom', 335.
[155] Hassen, *The Oromo of Ethiopia*, 36.

That day Sarsa Dengel distinguished himself by fighting like a common soldier. In the words of a contemporary historian:

> He did not act according to the history of the kings of his ancestors who, when making war, were in the habit of sending their troops ahead, remaining themselves in the rear with the pick of their cavalry and infantry, praising those who went forward bravely and punishing those who lagged behind. This time, on the contrary, our king put himself at the head of his brave troops and fought stoutly; seeing which the army threw itself like a pack of wild beasts on the [Oromo], who were killed without survivors. Most of them fell over a precipice, so that the inhabitants of the country and the labourers killed them wherever they found them. The king ordered the heads of the [Oromo] to be cut off [filling] Adora, a wide place.[156]

By his resounding victory, Sarsa Dengel restored his lost prestige, raised the morale of his Christian subjects and humiliated the Borana. He was determined to follow up his victory in Gojjam by waging war against the Borana across the Abbay River in Waj. After a long march, he arrived in Waj, but found no Borana to face him. 'But as soon as the [Oromo] learned of his arrival ... they were seized with fear and trembling, and they fled with their wives, their children, and their flocks ....'[157]

The slow-moving army of Sarsa Dengel often resorted to looting to replenish its supply, and this acted as an alarm bell to the Borana warriors who were seldom caught off guard.[158] Sarsa Dengel's army moved slowly because it included a large number of camp followers and a baggage train which hampered its movement.

> The number of men at arms ... even if it should be less, makes an excessively big camp because the camp followers and the baggage train amount to many more than the soldiers. The reason is that usually there are more women than men in the camp. Besides the king being accompanied by the queen and all or nearly all the ladies who are usually at court, widows, married ladies and even many unmarried ones, and the wives of the chief lords and captains, so that they go to war with their households and families, besides this, every soldier has one or many [women with him].[159]

The Borana did not have the problem of camp followers and a big baggage train, as they always left their women, children and flocks at a safe base area far from the zone of conflict. Any Borana warrior group usually numbered from six 'to eight thousand, but these are mostly picked young men'.[160] Oromo warriors carried dried meat prepared with butter that was nourishing and easy to carry. As a result, the Borana retreated when they got wind of Sarsa Dengel's arrival. Rapid movement was the source of their strength. The policy

---

[156] Bahrey, 'History of the Galla' in *Some Records of Ethiopia*, 123.
[157] Huntingford, 'The History of King Sarsa Dengel', 230.
[158] Hassen, *The Oromo of Ethiopia*, 40.
[159] Almeida, 'The History of High Ethiopia or Abassia' in *Some Records of Ethiopia*, 78. See also Alvares, *The Prester John of the Indies*, vol. 1, 320.
[160] Almeida, 'The History of High Ethiopia or Abassia' in *Some Records of Ethiopia*, 137–38.

of choosing a soft target and a right time was one of their greatest tactics.[161]

Having failed to punish the Borana in Waj, Sarsa Dengel decided to try his luck against the Jaawwii (a branch of the Borana) who were in the small district of Batera Amora. It was the Jaawwii (also spelled as Jawe) group that destroyed commander Fasilo and his army in late 1587. According to Bahrey, it was the Jawwii who 'devastated the two districts of the country of Gamo'.[162] However, when the Jawwii

> heard the news of the arrival of this terrible king, who is more terrifying than all the kings of the earth, [they] fled afar so that there was no traces of their existence. The great ones of the kingdom then deliberated and said, 'Where are we going to seek now'? All traces of [Oromo] have disappeared; no one knows where they have gone; there is no corn to pillage or to buy, and there is great hunger in our camp. Let us return to our camp [i.e. return to Gubay, the main residence of the king in Begameder].[163]

The Jaawwii disappeared before the arrival of Sarsa Dengel. With their dispersal there was neither grain nor cattle to buy or loot, thus exposing his soldiers to fear of hunger. We catch a uniform note of panic. 'Has it not been said that it is better to die by the spear than from hunger?'[164] From this it follows that the morale of Christian soldiers was undermined by the weakness of their supply system. The Christian leadership was unable to cope with the root of the problem – feeding its soldiers during their war against the Oromo. The hunger issue dominated all others. The soldiers' decision to return across the Abbay River was irrevocable. 'The king granted their request saying, "yes, let it be as you say." Having [said] thus, he turned around and went back to Gurage, travelling with speed.'[165] Sarsa Dengel crossed the Abbay without inflicting any injury on the Borana. Whatever hope he might have had of creating a semblance of authority east of the Abbay River could not be sustained once he had crossed the river because the dispersed Borana regrouped and decided to show him that to come back was well-nigh impossible.[166] According to Bahrey, the Borana devastated both Shawa and Damot,[167] and kept up the pressure on the Gibe region and Gojjam. As we have seen briefly above, since 1579 Sarsa Dengel spent most of the time west of the Abbay River, mainly conducting slave raids.[168]

While the Borana Multa Gada (1586–94) continued with its attack on Shawa, Damot, Gojjam and the Gibe region, the Barentu Multa Gada continued with its attack on the regions of Wallo, Begameder, Tigray

[161] Hassen, *The Oromo of Ethiopia*, 40.
[162] Bahrey, 'History of the Galla' in *Some Records of Ethiopia*, 114.
[163] Huntingford, *The History of King Sarsa Dengel*, 230. See also Conti-Rossini, *Historia Régis Sàrsà Dengel*, 144–5.
[164] Huntingford, The History of King Sarsa Dengel, 230.
[165] Ibid.
[166] Hassen, *The Oromo of Ethiopia*, 41.
[167] Bahrey, 'History of the Galla' in *Some Records of Ethiopia*, 127; See also Hassen, 'The Oromo of Ethiopia, 1500–1850', 252–3.
[168] Aregay, 'Southern Ethiopia and the Christian Kingdom', 287–97.

and the Awsa state in the Afar desert. Around 1590, while one section of the Wara Daya and Wallo warriors caused great trepidation among the Muslims in the Sultante of Awsa in the Afar desert,[169] the other section of Wara Daya attacked the district of which Walda Christos was the governor. The latter withstood the heavy storm of their first attack and forced them to retreat in disarray abandoning their booty.

> Walda Krestos ... conquered Mulata, recovered the booty which he had taken and killed a great number of the [Oromo]. He pursued a party of them and drove them over a precipice ... On his return [Sarsa Dengel] found that the country had been preserved by the readiness of Walda Krestos and the battles which he had fought; and for that reason he made him Ras, or head of his house, and set him at the head of the whole kingdom.[170]

Although Walda Christos was lucky in conflict against the Warra Daya Mulata, both he and Sarsa Dengel were unlucky in the case of the elusive Mulata of Marawa in Dambiya. The Marawa warriors, who acquired an intimate knowledge of the topography of the land through which they staged their attacks and retreats, kept up pressure on this province, while the emperor strengthened its defence. The Christian force soundly beat the Marawa time and again, but the defeat of one group never deterred the attack of the next. Perhaps the wealth of this province, especially its cattle, captured the attention of the Marawa. The elusive character of the Marawa presented the soldiers as well as the peasants with serious technical problems. The Marawa launched a series of raids which had little or no purpose in terms of actually making the province their own territory, such as characterized other Oromo attacks in other provinces, but they continued raiding by means of surprise attacks and sudden withdrawals, always taking back much booty and doing considerable damage to the peasants. By the time the soldiers had arrived on the scene of the raided area the victorious Marawa were already negotiating the Takaza River, for generally they crossed back into their own country with the spoils. It was essentially this elusive character of the Marawa attacks on Dambiya that forced Sarsa Dengel to change the seat of his court from Gubay to Ayba in 1590.

> The court was moved further north to Ayba in order to escape their raids which commenced once the rivers became fordable. The slaving activities in which the emperor became engaged, after moving to Ayba, show that he had not gone to Wagara to be nearer Wanya Daga and other nearby areas of Bagameder threatened by Marawa bands coming from the Takaza river ... Ayba was sufficiently distant from the Shena valley and protected by the mountains flanking it on the north and east from any bands which might come across Wayne Daga. At the same time it was not far removed from Alafa, Achafar Gojam and the provinces beyond, among the pagan peoples on which the emperor and his soldiers preyed.[171]

---

[169] Hassen, 'The Oromo of Ethiopia, 1500–1850', 212.
[170] Bahrey, 'History of the Galla' in *Some Records of Ethiopia*, 124.
[171] Aregay, 'Southern Ethiopia and the Christian Kingdom', 329–30.

In the Oromo tradition of the time, the killing of an enemy or a big and dangerous animal was considered to be an act of great courage, which qualified the killer to shave his head like a hero. However, the killing of women or children or animals – not considered as strong and dangerous – was a cowardly act that disqualified the killer from cutting his hair like a hero. Motivated by their repeated victories during and before the Mulata Gada, a group of Barentu even went to the extent of considering the inhabitants of Shawa and Amhara as ignominious animals not worthy of killing. 'One party said an outrageous thing when they declared, "let us not shave our heads when we kill the inhabitants of Shoa and Amhara, for they are but oxen which speak and cannot fight".'[172] During the period of the Mulata Gada, the Christian kingdom suffered repeated defeats and lost all of its provinces east of the Abbay. In the words of a contemporary historian:

> Mulata of the Borana afflicted the Christians of Damot, scattered them, and devastated their country; from his time Shoa and Damot were deserted ... The country submits to him, Mulata, and none remains without submission to him. When this book was written it was the seventh year [i.e. 1593] of the government of Mulata.[173]

The Dulo Gada, 1594–1602

The Mulata Gada was succeeded by the Dulo Gada. The Barentu Dulo Gada continued with its attack on Begameder, Tigray and Amhara region, while the Borana Dulo Gada directed the thrust of its attack into the area between Gojjam and Ennarya. By so doing the Borana threatened the disruption of communications, trade, revenue and travel between Ennarya (the centre of the economic life of Sarsa Dangel's government) and Gojjam. Sarsa Dengel, who, according to Merid Wolde Aregay, 'never once set foot in Amhara or Angolt'[174] (to rally assistance for Christians in the two provinces), hastened to re-open the communications between Ennarya and Gojjam. With the apparent intention of administering a quick, sharp shock to the Borana, the emperor led a large force into Damot in 1595. The Borana fled and prevented Sarsa Dengel from securing any decisive victory. However, after Sarsa Dengel withdrew from Damot, the Borana regrouped in 1596 and disrupted the flow of revenue and trade between Ennarya and Gojjam. This directly affected Sarsa Dengel, who in 1597 led a major expedition into Damot, the land occupied by the Borana. The Borana fled before the military action intended for them was launched. By their flight the Borana caused serious erosion in the morale of Christian soldiers, who were exposed to hunger and refused to fight in the land of the Borana.

Sarsa Dengel, after thirty-four year reign, during which he won several victories over the Oromo but ironically lost almost all the prov-

---

[172] Bahrey, ibid., 127.

[173] Bahrey, 'History of the Galla' in *Some Records of Ethiopia*, 127.

[174] Aregay, 'Southern Ethiopia and the Christian Kingdom', 322.

inces east of the Abbay River,[175] was exhausted by the slave-raiding campaigns and the war against the Oromo, frustrated by his failure, by the attitude of his soldiers, who were brave when plundering their peaceful subjects and cowardly when fighting in Borana land, died on 4 October 1597. It was the same Sarsa Dengel, who lost all the provinces east of the Abbay River to the Oromo, that Trimingham praised as 'one of the greatest warrior kings who ever occupied the throne'.[176] The above careful examination of his long reign does not support such generous conclusion.

The Oromo were able to conquer vast lands during the long reign of Sarsa Dengel for several reasons, chief among which the following three were very crucial. First, the Oromo warfare was based on the policy of gathering vital information through a spy network, accompanied by rapid movement in attack and retreat, and 'their strategy of choosing the least defended places and exhausting by repeated raids whatever strength the local inhabitants had'.[177] Second, the Christian peasantry did not appear to have put up stiff resistance because, they were unarmed, subjected to economic exploitation, terrorized by exaggerated cruelty of the Oromo warriors, all of which 'perhaps dulled their instinct for self-defence'.[178] Third and above all, it was Sarsa Dengel's endless slave-raiding campaigns that cleared the way for rapid Oromo movement through vast territory. What is not in doubt is that, through cruel and brutal slave-raiding campaigns, Sarsa Dengel inadvertently facilitated the rapid spread of the Oromo through his kingdom. When he died as a frustrated man in 1597, Shawa, which in more than one sense was the centre of the Christian kingdom since the time of Amda-Siyon[179] was no longer under Christian control. The Amhara population of Shawa, weakened by the continuous Borana assaults, and Sarsa Dengel's failure to help, was in no state to resist any longer. The Amhara, who did not flee across the Abbay

> took refuge in the deep and inaccessible valleys of the Jamma Addabay system, on inaccessible mountain plateaus in Manz and Geshe, and on the narrow plateaus of the eastern escarpment in Ansokiya, Ifreta and Gedem. Small groups also lived in the upper parts of the Qabanna and the Kassam valleys in the south. The terrain made it impossible for the Oromo to use their cavalry effectively, while their nomadic way of life led them to prefer the high plains. By about 1600 the Oromo controlled all the plains south of the Mofar, the central highlands up to Gedem, where the main route of their invasions seems to have turned down the escarpment to the eastern side of the Borkanna river, and the wide tract north-west of Shawa, in the west even settling south of the Wanchet river in Marhabete. They also occasionally crossed through Manz, although they do not seem to have settled there.[180]

[175] Hassen, *The Oromo of Ethiopia*, 34–36.
[176] Trimingham, *Islam in Ethiopia*, 95.
[177] Aregay, 'Southern Ethiopia and the Christian Kingdom', 170–1.
[178] Ibid., 199.
[179] Ibid., 312.
[180] Svein Ege, 'Chiefs and Peasants', 21.

When southern Amhara was lost to the Amhara authority during the Robale Gada (1570–78), it was a tremendous moral shock to the Christians, as well as a blow to the prestige of the Amhara dynasty. This was because this province, besides being the home of the Amhara people, was the area to which Amhara kings retreated in time of trouble. The graves of several prominent Amhara kings, the famous royal prison of Amba Geshen, the royal treasure of several centuries, rich and famous churches, were all located in the same area.[181] But the loss of Shawa further shocked the Christian morale in addition to shattering the prestige of the Amhara dynasty. The loss of Shawa meant not only the loss of the centre of the Amhara empire, and the springboard for the southward expansion, but also the end of Amhara authority east of the Abbay. The Amhara kingdom retreated beyond the Abbay, and afterwards crossing the Abbay to fight against the Oromo became an impossible task for many of the Amhara kings. Indeed, only few able and gifted Amhara kings managed to mount short campaigns in Shawa during our period. However, where the Gondar kings failed even to face the Oromo in Shawa, pockets of Amhara communities who survived in the inaccessible parts of Shawa succeeded. These Amhara communities, cut off from the rest of the kingdom, survived in their mountain stronghold until the beginning of the nineteenth century, when they started reversing the tide of events against the Oromo.[182]

---

[181] Makurya, *Ya Gragn Ahmed Warara*, 6–9.
[182] R.H.K. Darkwah, *Shewa, Menilek and the Ethiopian Empire, 1813–1889* (London: Heinemann, 1978), 1–54.

6

Abba Bahrey's *Zenahu le Galla* and its Impact on Emperor Za-Dengel's War against the Oromo, 1603–1604

Zenahu le Galla, Abba Bahrey's singularly most popular manuscript, which has been quoted several times in this study, deserves serious consideration. As will be shown further in the chapter, although Bahrey authored other works, it was *Zenahu le Galla* that made him very famous and a significant intellectual in the country during the second half of the sixteenth century. His manuscript was and remains one of the most original documents in Ethiopian historiography. However, three points should be made before advancing further. First, although the main focus of this chapter is examining the importance of *Zenahu le Galla*, it also attempts to explore briefly other works of Abba Bahrey, especially some of the prayers he marshalled against the Oromo. Second, in this chapter I have drawn on my previous short articles on Abba Bahrey.[1] Third, the title of Abba Bahrey's manuscript in its original Geez language is *Zenahu le Galla*, which is translated as 'History of the Galla'. 'Ethnography of the Galla' or 'News about the Galla'. However, according to Getatchew Haile, the Geez term Zena 'has multiple meanings such as news, epistle, prophesy, deed, narrative, and so forth'.[2] In this chapter, *Zenahu le Galla*, 'History of the Galla' and 'News about the Galla' are used interchangeably.

 Zenahu le Galla, written in 1593 contains the first detailed description of pastoral Oromo population movement of the sixteenth century and its impact on the Christian Kingdom of Ethiopia together with their history and their social organization. As the first detailed study

[1] This chapter draws heavily on my previous short articles on the works of Abba Bahrey, namely, Mohammed Hassen, 'The Historian Abba Bahrey and the Importance of His "History of the Galla"', *Horn of Africa* 14, 1 & 2 (1990/91), 90–106; Mohammed Hassen, 'The Significance of Abba Bahrey in Oromo Studies: A Commentary on *The Works of Abba Bahriy and Other Documents Concerning the Oromo*, by Getatchew Haile', *Journal of Oromo Studies* 14, 2 (July 2007), 131–55; Mohammed Hassen, 'Review Essay: Revisiting Abba Bahrey's "The News of the Galla"', *International Journal of African Historical Studies* 45, 2 (2012), 273–94.

[2] Getatchew Haile, *The Works of Abba Bahriy and Other Documents Concerning the Oromo* (Avon, MN: self-published, 2002), 56. Translation by Maimire Mennasemay, 'A Critical Reappraisal of Abba Bahrey's *Zenahu Le Galla*', *Horn of Africa* 29 (2011), 44.

of Oromo social organization of the time, *Zenahu le Galla* makes unprecedented claim to authority on pastoral Oromo population movements during the second half of the sixteenth century. It also contains the first rational thorough analysis of the class structure of the Christian society of his time, which demonstrates Bahrey's deep knowledge about his society and how he used that knowledge effectively for educating the elite at the court of Emperor Sarsa Dengel. As the first detailed historical document that dramatically presents the impact of Oromo warfare on the Christian kingdom, Bahrey's manuscript has been the most widely read and referenced source on Ethiopian history in general and early Oromo history in particular. The manuscript has been translated into three major European languages, German, French and English. It was first translated from Geez into Amharic in the 1940s. The 1954 English translation was reprinted in 1992, with a new introduction by Donald Levine. It was again translated into Amharic in the late 1990s by Aleme Eshete. In 2002, the manuscript was once again translated into Amharic and English by Getatchew Haile. Its several translations clearly indicate the uniqueness and the historical value of *Zenahu le Galla*. Written more than four hundred years ago, Bahrey's manuscript was and remains the most influential and enduring historical document that shaped the presentation of the Oromo in Ethiopian historiography. The first part of this chapter briefly looks at the intellectual stature of its famous author and examines the impact of the manuscript.

Abba Bahrey was an extraordinary monk, a historian, a court official who adored Sarsa Dengel, an intellectual driven with a passion against the Oromo. His *Zenahu le Galla* is simultaneously historical and ideological. Historical because his manuscript was written by a man who was himself the victim of the pastoral Oromo population movement, a man who was driven from his land, a man who lost everything he owned to the Oromo, and yet depicted the social structure of the Oromo society of his time as the foundation of their military victories. An ideological treatise because, his manuscript was written with a clear-cut and precise political objective – to arm the elite at the court of Sarsa Dengel with powerful ideas, for understanding the weakness of the class structure of their society and how to overcome its debilitating consequences. His political message was simple and its purpose clear: the class structure of the Christian society was the root cause of its military weakness. His desire was to educate the elite at the court of Sarsa Dengel on how to overcome the weakness of their society by providing them with his prescription and presenting them with a feasible course of action.

Abba Bahrey was probably the lone star on the intellectual map of the Christian kingdom during the second half of the sixteenth century. A scholar bent on marshalling *Zenahu le Galla* for characterizing the Oromo as a destructive primitive people[3] finds 'much to harvest' in Abba Bahrey's manuscript. There is no doubt that Bahrey's manu-

---

[3] See for instance, Haile, *The Works of Abba Bahriy*, 119.

script inspired and still inspires strong anti-Oromo feeling. It is not without reason that his *Zenahu le Galla* has been the lightning rod for the ideologically motivated attack on the Oromo at the beginning of the twenty-first century. I do not know of any historical document that has been translated so many times. Since 2001 Abba Bahrey's manuscript has been the most passionately discussed historic document among the Ethiopian diaspora internet audience. The passion Bahrey's manuscript still generates is testament to the sensitivity of the Oromo issue in Ethiopia. The manuscript's description of the events under discussion also has greater implications for the history of the seventeenth century than hitherto acknowledged.[4]

The importance of Bahrey's work is two-fold. First, it contains a detailed account of Oromo history, their social organization and the impressive progress of their population movements; second, his writing appears to have inspired several Amhara emperors to conduct spirited campaigns against the Oromo. The efforts of one of those emperors will be examined in this chapter, while that of another emperor will be examined in Chapter 8. Bahrey was a man of abundant religious faith and literary gifts, who became famous for discussing the military weakness of his society and the strength of its Oromo enemies. The central thesis of his work concerns not the Oromo strength per se, but rather what brought about their victories against the Christians, even though the latter were more numerous and better supplied with weapons than the former.[5] The value of his work stands out because of his ability to rise above the ignorance of his society about the Oromo and exhibit an understanding of the Oromo social organization, which was the source of their strength. He was extremely confident in his people's ability to mobilize their human, material and spiritual resources to turn the tide against the Oromo if they knew the source of their weakness. A deeply religious man, a gifted intellectual, a mature and wise man beyond his time, he articulated 'clear-cut political ideas' in *Zenahu le Galla* that Chernetsov, characterizes as 'a report to the monarch written by a proficient and knowledgeable secretary, well-versed in court politics'.[6] Beyond being well-versed in court politics, he was probably the first social historian who analysed the contemporary Christian society within a socio-political framework. Although the historical value of *Zenahu le Galla* has always been recognized, very little was known about its author until some years ago.

[4] The exceptions are S.B. Chernetsov, 'The "History of the Gallas" and Death of Za-Dengel, King of Ethiopia (1603–1604)' in *IV Congress Internazionale di Studi Etiopici* (Roma, 1974), 803–808; S.B. Chernetsov, 'Who Wrote "The History of King Sarsa Dengel"? Was it the Monk Bahrey?' *Proceedings of the Eighth International Conference of Ethiopian Studies, University of Addis Ababa, 1984*, ed. Taddese Beyene, vol. 1 (1988), 132–5; Joseph Tubiana, 'Un Ethnographe Ethiopien au XVI Siècle' in *De La Voute celeste au terroir, du jardin au foyer* (Paris: Editions de l'Ecole des Hautes en Sciences Sociales, 1987), 655–9: I am indebted to Professor Tubiana for sending me this paper.
[5] Boavida et al., *Pedro Páez's History of Ethiopia*, vol. 1, 173.
[6] Chernetsov, 'Who Wrote "The History of King Sarsa Dengel"?', 131.

Now thanks to the works of Takla Sadiq Makurya, S.B. Chernetsov and, especially that of Getatchew Haile, Abba Bahrey is emerging as a significant intellectual of his age who sought to inform and educate the elite at the court of Emperor Sarsa Dengel. Abba Bahrey channelled his intellectual creativity into writing about the greatness of Emperor Sarsa Dengel, while pioneering the spirit of resistance against the Oromo. As Chernetsov has noted, Bahrey's work: 'stands apart ... [among] the work of Ethiopian historiography ... [and] all of medieval Ethiopian literature, something that Bahrey must have been aware of'.[7] His slim manuscript

> contains a concise and thorough review of the structure and interrelationship of [Oromo] tribes, as well as an account of their conquests and wars with the Ethiopians. Bahrey's analysis of [Oromo] victories and Ethiopian defeats leads him to compare the two societies. As a result, he produces an interesting and in its own way a very precise picture of Ethiopian feudal society and its class structure. The whole is set forth with considerable skill and is marked by an objectivity quite rare for a work of medieval literature.[8]

We can observe four sections in Bahrey's *Zenahu le Galla*: a brief description of Oromo ethnography, the weakness and strength of his manuscript, a recording of the progress of pastoral Oromo population movement, and a call for the mobilization of Christian forces for the purpose of stopping the Oromo advance – the principal message of his work. In what follows, the salient points of each of the four parts is presented. However, this is preceded by information about Abba Bahrey, a learned monk and a poet, whose manuscript inspired and still promotes anti-Oromo prejudice.

ABBA BAHREY: A FASCINATING SCHOLAR OF HIS TIME

According to Getatchew Haile, Abba Bahrey was born in 1535[9] in the historic province of Gamo, when Imam Ahmad was at the height of his power, and the Christian kingdom probably at the darkest moment of its very existence. Bahrey tells us nothing about his parents nor about his siblings. His parents evidently provided him with the best available education in the land of his birth. All indications are that he was a gifted student who impressed his teachers with his thirst for knowledge. Impressed by other monks, he embraced monastic life at an early age.[10] After completing his education, Bahrey lived most of his life in the same land where he served as the head of Debra Mariam Monastery in Gamo. Most writers assumed and still assume that Bahrey's homeland of Gamo was located in Gamu highlands in the region of Gamu Gofa in southern Ethiopia. Those who are not familiar with historical geog-

[7] Ibid.
[8] Ibid.
[9] Haile, *The Works of Abba Bahriy*, 46.
[10] Ibid., 209.

raphy of the Christian kingdom during the sixteenth century may be surprised to realize that Bahrey's homeland was not located in Gamu highlands. In fact, the meticulous scholarship of the late Professor Merid Wolde Aregay establishes conclusively that Bahrey's homeland of Gamo was located near the modern town of Shashemene[11] in the region of Shawa. The implication behind this fact will become clearer further in this chapter. Here it should suffice to say that Bahrey introduces himself to us with these words:

> I am the youngest of the priests. I am a disciple of the monks. I am the one who composed the music for the songs of Debra Mariam Monastery, which corresponds to the Psalms of David. Dear reader of my book, do not be quick to condemn me about my wickedness. Rather, hasten to forgive me.[12]

As a thinker, a poet and a writer, Bahrey was indeed a rare bright star on the intellectual map of the Christian kingdom during the tumultuous second half of the sixteenth century. The remarkable thing about him was that he distinguished himself as a writer at the young age of 25, in 1561 when he composed his first song that ends with these words:

> This concludes the section five.
> Which serves as illustration.
> I named it the Song of Christ
> Because I was exhausted translating
> the holy song in your name.
> Provide me with rewards of flesh and spirit.[13]

He adds 'O Christ … In the time of joy give me twice the age of fifty'[14] i.e. allow me to live a hundred years! His life was not the time of joy. However, he lived for seventy years, which means by the standard of the time, Bahrey had a long and productive life.

Though a monk, Bahrey was not a poor man. He appears to have accumulated wealth for his old age. Unfortunately, when the Jaawwii Oromo attacked Gamo, in the late 1570s, they looted everything Bahrey owned and forced him to flee from Gamo to the court of Sarsa Dengel in Begameder. At this point it is important to stress that when Bahrey mentions the Jaawwii Oromo attack on his homeland of Gamo in the late 1570s, he is referring to their attack around what is today the town of Shashemene in Shawa rather than their attack in the region of Gamu highlands in southern Ethiopia. Bahrey never forgot nor forgave the Oromo group that looted his property.

> Thank you, O lord, Thank you
> I thank you by calling your name
> I speak about your graciousness
> Because you protected me
> For you did not let me down

---

[11]   Aregay, 'Southern Ethiopia and the Christian Kingdom', 309.
[12]   Haile, *The Works of Abba Bahriy*, 44.
[13]   Ibid., 47.
[14]   Ibid., 48.

> I beg you that you will not let me down in the future
> I beg you so that you save me
> From the thieves, who wounded me
> They took everything I accumulated for my future
> Please return to me everything
> The enemy took from me.[15]

Bahrey appears to have had a mastery of Geez literature. He displayed his knowledge of Geez literature while composing his famous songs of David. He acknowledged that this song was not the original product of his mind. He compiled it from the works of others.

> He mentions 91 books as his reference in the Introduction. He also indicates the number of times he quoted each book. What is most surprising is not only his knowledge of Geez literature, but also how he was able to remember each source of respective quotes.[16]

On the basis of clear and irrefutable internal evidence Professor Getatchew Haile establishes Abba Bahrey as the undisputed author of the works mentioned below whose authorship until recently remained unknown. They are:

1. Song of Christ, or Psalms of Christ
2. The Short Song of Christ
3. The Appearance [face] of Gabriel
4. The Peace of the Saint.[17]

Before Bahrey's time Christian chroniclers usually did not take credit for their works. In a radical departure from established literary tradition, Abba Bahrey mentions his name in at least four of his works, thus establishing his individual identity as an author. In the process, Bahrey pioneered a new period of literary tradition that marked the beginning of 'the high-point' in the art of historiography[18] during the second half of the sixteenth century. The following is an example of what Bahrey in his authorship of *the Songs of Christ* left for posterity.

> Those who remember me for good deeds, let them rejoice and be merry, likewise, those who wish me peace that is free of wickedness. Oh father, do not disregard the pleas of Bahrey, your servant. Do not delay your time of your favor upon me.[19]

By claiming authorship of his works, Bahrey appears to be a politically conscious man who was aware of his own place and contribution to the making of history. It appears that Abba Bahrey authored his first work, *The Short Song of Christ* at the age of 25 in 1561. Most probably he authored the *Long Song of Christ* in 1576 when he was more than forty

---

[15] Ibid., 39.
[16] Ibid., 46.
[17] i.e. *Mezmure Kiristos, Achiru Mezmore Kiristos, Melekhe Gabriel and Selame Qodusan* respectively.
[18] Chernetsov, 'Who Wrote "The History of King Sarsa Dengel"?', 131.
[19] Haile, *The Works of Abba Bahriy*, 38.

years old. It was in his *Long Song of Christ* that Bahrey articulated his Christian nationalism, his love for his country. Between the ages of 41 to 58 he was most productive as an author and as confessor of the emperor, which combined to insure his prominence in the inner circle of Sarsa Dengel's court.

It now appears that none other than Abba Bahrey was the author of the *History of King Sarsa Dengel*, 'which was written piecemeal – chapter by chapter – between 1579 and 1592.' Chernetsov presents a number of valid arguments all of which indicate Abba Bahrey was the author of the major parts, if not all, of the *History of King Sarsa Dengel*. These include: similar or identical literary devices to those used in *Zenahu le Galla*, similar or identical paired epithets were used in both works, and the emperor is always depicted as victorious. In both works, there is a 'similar attitude towards the prophetic gift of priests', 'similarity of language' is manifest, and similarity between the two works 'is no accident'.[20] According to Chernetsov,

> the *History of Sarsa Dengel* and 'Zenahu Le Galla'... are works not only literary in form, but historical in content. It is instructive to compare the two with regard to the latter aspect. One should bear in mind, however, the peculiarities of each. Though the History of the Galla is fifteen times less voluminous than the History of King Sarsa Dengel, it deals with a much lengthier chronological period – from 1523 to 1593. The latter work, on the other hand, is not only limited to the reign of Sarsa Dengel (1563–81, 1585–92), but focuses attention on the person of the monarch, mentioning other figures only insofar as they were involved with him. Thus, King Sarsa Dengel is mentioned in the History of the Galla six times in connection with historical events, five of which are described (usually at much greater length) in the History of King Sarsa Dengel ... Thus, we can say that the data of the history of the Galla are quite in conformity with the data of the history of Sarsa Dengel.[21]

It was not by accident that work began on the writing of the *History of King Sarsa Dengel* in1579. Most likely, it was that year that Abba Bahrey arrived in the court of Sarsa Dengel. As a learned man and a fascinating thinker of his age, Abba Bahrey must have charmed Sarsa Dengel with his manners, discipline, commitment to religious duties, and devotion to his king. Besides the king, Bahrey must have captivated the elite at the court with his education, wisdom, and wide experience. Bahrey loved King Sarsa Dengel, who, in turn, appears to have treated him with kindness – the man who became his confessor as well as the one entrusted with the task of writing the history of the king. Abba Bahrey not only adored Sarsa Dengel but also showered prayers on him. The prayers for the king were inspired not only by a sense of duty and devotion but also with incredible passion.

> Oh Lord, give your wisdom
> To King Sarsa Dengel
> To govern the people well
> To enslave the unbelievers

[20] Chernetsov, 'Who Wrote "The History of King Sarsa Dengel"?' 131, 133.
[21] Ibid., 133–4.

During his reign
Let honey drizzle from the mountains
Let milk gush out from the hills
Let there be peace in the country
Let there be reconciliation in all the districts
Let it be the end of suffering and abhorrence
Let everyone submit to him [...]
Let everyone gather to learn from his wisdom
Keep him from evil, all day and night
From illness and pain too.[22]

From internal evidence it appears that the above prayer was composed in 1576 together with the *Long Song of Christ*. Abba Bahrey mentions Sarsa Dengel's victory over Sultan Muhammad Nasir (1573–76) of Harar, who led a futile expedition into Bali, where the Muslim force was liquidated.[23] Harar's pretentions as a military power were thus ended.[24] If the above prayer was composed in the year in which Sarsa Dengel destroyed Sultan Muhammad Nasir's force, the author then must have been 41 years old instead of 46[25] as he tells us. What is interesting to note here is that in 1576 Bahrey was living in Gamo. According to Getatchew Haile, it was in 1576, while still living in Gamo that Bahrey wrote the following song,[26] a powerful plea for mercy from God.

Oh Lord, why have you forsaken us forever?
You gather the dispersed, bring back the lost
Remember your people
They have heeded your admonishment
Taken to heart your punishment
At no time have they gotten respite from
Turbulent times
And became the target of the infidel's radicals.
You need not be notified, for you know all
You know the injustice the enemy has perpetuated
Against your saints
And the blasphemy against the divine
Above all [the enemy] targeted your temple
Burned down its gates like a log in the wilderness
Destroyed its walls like a grain silo
Slighted its glory, defiled its holiness
Turned the sanctuary into a barn.[27]

When the above song was written in 1576, it appears that the Borana Oromo had already attacked the province of Gamo, causing scattering of

---

[22] Haile, *The Works of Abba Bahriy*, 40–41.

[23] Trimingham, *Islam in Ethiopia*, 96. See also James Bruce, *Travels to Discover the Source of the Nile in the Years 1768–1773*, vol. 3, 249.

[24] As a result of the 1576 jihadic gamble, Harar was exposed to devastating Oromo attack. Militarily defeated, economically damaged, politically undermined, the Muslim leaders abandoned the city of Harar and moved their capital to Awssa in the Afar desert in 1577. See Hassen, 'The Oromo of Ethiopia, 1500–1850', 206–9.

[25] Haile, *The Works of Abba Bahriy*, 46.

[26] It was probably in the late 1578 or early 1579 that Bahrey fled from his province of Gamo, which was a turning point in his life.

[27] Haile, *The Works of Abba Bahriy*, 120–1.

the Christian population. A few years later the Christian administration in Gamo collapsed. At the time when Bahrey wrote the song, he appears to have believed, like his contemporaries, that the Oromo dominance was God's punishment for Christian sins. In 1593, without rejecting this view, Bahrey came up with an ingenious explanation for the Christian defeat.[28] His claim that the enemy targeted the temple for destruction was probably motivated by his desire for Christian unity against a common enemy.[29] From what has been said thus far, it appears that Bahrey's thinking was dominated by his enduring affection for Sarsa Dengel and his prayer against the Oromo. There is no doubt that Bahrey's *Song of Christ* and prayer for the king and against the Oromo were probably known at the court of Sarsa Dengel. From this, it can be deduced that Bahrey's fame as a gifted writer must have preceded his arrival at the court of Sarsa Dengel by at least some years. This may explain why Sarsa Dengel took him into his service immediately after his arrival at the court. Another interesting point to note concerns Bahrey's prayer for his king 'to enslave the unbelievers'. From this it appears that the slaving expedition Sarsa Dengel was conducting against non-Christian communities of his kingdom was well known to Abba Bahrey, who supported it with his prayer.

For Abba Bahrey the well-being of the king was the well-being of the people, his happiness, their happiness, his safety the core of their existence:

> Keep him in peace all the time
> Is he is not shouldering power [authority]
> All our lives depend on him as a tree
> Branches dangle on the trunk
> Because to us he is like our head
> And we are to him, like the rest of the body
> Therefore let us always pray about this matter
> So that his kingdom will have peace
> When there is peace and stability
> In the kingdom it is not for him alone
> [Let us be with him in good and bad times]
> Because when there is change in the weather and
> Absolute change in the kinship[30]
> Everything of the past will change[31]
> During our prayer let us say
> Let your salvation and deliverance reach him soon [...]

---

[28] Ibid., 209–10.

[29] During the sixteenth century the Oromo believed in their traditional religion that was different from both Christianity and Islam. They did not have religious motives for destroying places of worship. For instance, the Oromo did not destroy Muslim shrines and mosques in the region of Hararghe. Churches may have been destroyed. However, it is very doubtful that the Oromo purposely destroyed churches. Yet, Bahrey makes them destroyer of churches, most probably because he wanted to mobilize the Christians against these destroyers of their churches.

[30] i.e. when leaders are removed from power either through coup or death.

[31] i.e. the change in leadership leads to political upheaval, which is characteristic of the history of Abyssinia.

Let there be unity between books[32]
And the sword[33] forever.[34]

The above prayer most likely expresses the upheavals of the early reign of Sarsa Dengel, when his authority was challenged by rebellious noblemen and his life threatened by the restless Giyorgis Hayle soldiers. Abba Bahrey, who lived through the chaotic reign of Minas and the upheaval of the early reign of Sarsa Dengel, appears to have longed for peace and stability in the kingdom.

He attributed Sarsa Dengel's victories to God's support for his cause:

O Lord let him be totally happy with your power
Anoint Sarsa Dengel, the son of the anointed
Let him accomplish everything with justice
And be happy with your enormous generosity
You blessed him with your support
You placed sparkling [shining] crown of victory on his head
More valuable than gold crown
You made him feared by the people of the south and east
And those in the west
He is hero in war
He has never been defeated, winning is his custom
He does not brag [not intoxicated] with his victories
He does not express contempt in his speech [...]
O Christ protect his reign, 'let it be a time when forgiveness reigns'
Distance danger from him
Embrace his soldiers as 'your people'
Fulfill all his wishes
For he has approached you with whole heartedness
He prayed to you in the name of your mother
Let his enemies and adversaries suffer in your hands
Let the fire of your anger eat them
All those who oppose him also.[35]

In the annals of the Christian kingdom, no comparable prayer for another king was ever offered like Abba Bahrey's prayer for Sarsa Dengel. It is an elegant prayer, in which Abba Bahrey expresses his profound love for the king. This prayer was written in 1576 as part of the *Songs of Christ*.

There is a strong hint in *Zenahu le Galla* that its author was an important official at the court of Sarsa Dengel. Bahrey closes his manuscript by writing his own name, and 'below the last line of the manuscript, on the right-hand side, is written faintly, in longer characters, the word *Yamen* 'right hand.'[36] This invaluable piece of information has hitherto been ignored. 'Right hand' in this sense means an important official who was close to the emperor and indeed Bahrey was such an official. This is indirectly supported by the Chronicle of Susenyos. In chapter twenty-two of that work it is stated that 'Azaj Bahrey ['commander' or Steward Bahrey] was present among the

---

[32] i.e. learned men of the books (the clergy).
[33] i.e. the warriors or soldiers.
[34] Haile, *The Works of Abba Bahriy*, 41.
[35] Ibid., 42–43.
[36] Bahrey, 'History of the Galla' in *Some Records of Ethiopia*, 129.

nobles, administrators, and advisors of the king at the ascension to the throne of Susenyos in 1604.[37] In addition Bahrey was the confessor of King Sarsa Dengel as referred to unmistakably in the king's abridged chronicle published by Conti-Rossini and Perruchon.[38] Further, Takla Sadiq Makurya confirms that Bahrey was both the confessor of Sarsa Dengel and an important official in his court.[39] As we have seen above Chernetsov clearly establishes that Bahrey was the chronicler of the *History of King Sarsa Dengel*.[40] In his *Zenahu le Galla* Bahrey makes it quite clear that he was very close to the court and knew about the burning issues of the day. In sum, it is safe to claim that Abba Bahrey, the author of the four major works mentioned earlier, an important official at the court, confessor Bahrey, the author of *History of King Sarsa Dengel*, and Bahrey the author of *Zenahu le Galla* were one and the same person – all of which would make him a productive scholar of his age, a fascinating thinker of the time and probably the most admired religious man at the court of Sarsa Dengel. In terms of addressing the Oromo issue, Abba Bahrey was the greatest influence on King Za-Dengel (1603–04).

Abba Bahrey represented the quintessential opposition to the Oromo. He was engaged in a battle of ideas on how best to mobilize Christian forces against the Oromo. Bahrey's manuscript provides a political vocabulary. Its message is uniform and cohesive. The manuscript framed the Amhara and Tigrayan view of the Oromo as dangerous enemies and destroyers. Other works may have shaped the images of the Oromo as dangerous enemies in the Christian minds, but Bahrey's *Zenahu le Galla* held and probably still holds special place because it enjoys the benefit of an eye-witness account and is considered as an objective work of an unbiased author. Toyin Falola observed 'The burden of history is remembrance, not by means of divination, but of evidence. The lessons of history are liberating in so far as we learn what not to believe about the past'.[41] The immediate lesson of history is to understand why the manuscript under discussion was written when it was written.

WHY WAS *ZENAHU LE GALLA* WRITTEN?

Before answering this question it is important to examine Bahrey's concerns and love for his country, his fear of that kingdom falling under

---

[37] Pereira, *Chronica de Susenyos, Rei de Ethiopia*, 57–9.

[38] Conti-Rossini, 'Due Squarci Inediti di Cronica Etiopica', *Rendiconti della Reale Academia dei Lincei* (1893), 18, Jules Perruchon, 'Notes pour l'histoire d'Ethiopie: Règne de Sarsa-Dengel ou Malak Sagad I (1563–1597)', *Revue Semitique* 4 (1896), 277.

[39] Takla Saqiq Makurya, *Ya Gragn Ahmed Warara*, 801–2.

[40] Chernetsov, 'Who Wrote "The History of King Sarsa Dengel"?', 131–5.

[41] Toyin Falola, *Tradition and Change in Africa: The Essays of J.F. Ade Ajaye* (Trenton, NJ: Africa World Press, 2000), vli.

Oromo control, all of which were articulated in his *Long Song of Christ* that was written in 1576.

> You elevated [this temple, the country] when she was still young
> Now you let her to be humiliated and her glory to dissipate
> Even though she [this country] provoked your wrath
> Is she better off the hands of the nomad
> I ask you to look upon her with favor, you who gave rest to Finhas.
> How long would it be before you revoke your wrath
> If you do not end your impatience with her
> What incentive do we have to keep your law
> To sanctify your name
> The books have been burned, and incinerated
> Forgive us, please; a mother cannot afford
> To ignore the plight of the products of her womb
> Of course, no master fails to discipline [his slave]
> No teacher refrains from correcting his disciple
> The rod and the stick were made in ancient times
> To punish the obstinate and the recalcitrant
> Your mercy is always abundant.[42]

The above quotation clearly demonstrates that Bahrey deep religious convictions. He was a man who believed that his people had been punished enough for their sins. Since the Oromo war was not an ideologically motivated religious conflict like a jihadic war, the Oromo had no interest in burning the books. If this occurred, most probably it was by accident rather than by design. Bahrey's claim that the books had been burned and incinerated was most likely a rhetorical device for appealing to Christian nationalism. In 1576, when Bahrey composed the above song, he may have believed that his country could be saved through his prayer. By 1593, he realized that prayer alone was not enough to stop the Oromo advance. Prayers had to be backed by practical measures to turn the tide against the Oromo. This in itself was an important discovery by a learned man with 'a sharp and observant intellect at work'.[43]

It is interesting to note in passing that Bahrey wrote *Zenahu le Galla* in 1593 'only one year after the completion of the *History of King Sarsa Dengel*'.[44] From internal evidence it appears that Bahrey wrote his manuscript for educational purposes. Who did he want to educate? Obviously it was the elite at the court of Sarsa Dengel. Chernetsov believes that it was precisely for that reason that Bahrey provides interesting information about himself.[45] His experience, the trial and tribulation of his life, the devastation of his land of Gamo, the exodus of Christian refugees from most of the provinces east of the Abbay River, were powerful material with which to move the court elite into action. Bahrey starts his manuscript with a short introduction in

---

[42] Haile, *The Works of Abba Bahriy*, 121–2.
[43] Mennasemay, 'A Critical Reappraisal of Abba Bahrey's *Zenahu Le Galla*', 46.
[44] Chernetsov, 'Who Wrote "The History of King Sarsa Dengel"?', 133.
[45] Ibid.

which he forcefully and logically justifies his reason for writing about the Oromo.

> I [hereby] begin to undertake the studies [I write] of the Galla [Oromo] in order that I may know the number of their tribes, their zeal to kill people, and the brutality of their demeanor. If there is anyone who would say to me, 'Why has he written about the wicked ones like the history of the good?', I will give him an answer, saying to him: 'Search in the books, and you will see that the history of Muhammed and the history of the kings of the Muslims have been written, although they are our enemies in religion.'[46]

Bahrey's unstated message is 'know your enemy', understand the source of your enemy's strength and discover the secret of your society's weakness; these are ideas manifestly stressed in his work. This, more than anything else, indicates what motivated him to write *Zenahu le Galla*. His manuscript is divided into twenty sections. Some of the sections are long while others are short, sometimes no more than two or three sentences. Bahrey's slim manuscript was written in a 'matter-of-fact style',[47] because his goal was to inform and educate the elite.

Bahrey opens his section 1, with this statement: 'The [Oromo] appeared from the west and crossed the river of their country that they call Gelena [Galana] to the frontier of [Bali].'[48] It was this simple statement that established as an ultimate truth the Oromo arrival on the border of the Christian kingdom in or around 1522. Bahrey did not mention the source of his information. Most likely it was what he gathered from others. The import of Bahrey's statement, 'they appeared from the west' has not been understood within its historical context. Most likely, Bahrey's statement deals more with the Borana attack on Bali than the Oromo presence within the medieval Christian kingdom. However, because of the weight given to Bahrey's authority, his speculative statement made it appear that the Oromo appeared on the scene for the first time only at the time sanctioned by his manuscript. Thus the statement about the Oromo appearance on the frontier of Bali took on the life of its own and became the single most-important factor in depicting the Oromo as 'newcomers to Ethiopia'. Of course, the Oromo presence within Ethiopia did not begin in 1522, nor with the Borana attack on Bali, nor with pastoral Oromo population movement of the sixteenth century. As an integral part of Cushitic-language speakers the Oromo have always lived within Ethiopia. As shown directly or indirectly in the first three chapters of this study, Oromo groups lived within the medieval Christian kingdom, especially in and south of the region of Shawa, at least since the thirteenth century, if not earlier.

> Indeed, the linguistic and historical evidence that Getatchew [Haile] presents suggests the presence of the Oromo in northern and central Ethiopia as early as perhaps the Zagwe dynasty [c.1000–1270] and certainly during the reign

---

[46] Haile, *The Works of Abba Bahriy*, 195.
[47] Chernetsov, 'Who Wrote "The History of King Sarsa Dengel"?', 133.
[48] Haile, ibid., 196.

of Yekuno Amlak (1285–85), implying that the Oromo are one of indigenous people of Ethiopia.[49]

In short, available evidence shows some Oromo groups' presence within the medieval Christian kingdom of Ethiopia for at least two to three hundred years before the time sanctioned by Bahrey's manuscript. Who is to say that the Oromo did not live in the region before their presence was recorded in Christian sources?

In sections 1 to 4, Bahrey discusses the division of the Oromo society into two moieties called Borana and Barentu (whom he calls Baraytuma) and the numerous sub-moieties into which both were divided. As we have seen in Chapter 4, the Barentu section lived in and south of the region of historical Bali, while the Borana lived in the region of Sidamo and Gomu Gofa. It was with the Borana group that Bahrey had first-hand experience.[50] It was one of the Borana clans, the Jaawwii, who looted his property, overtook his land and forced him to flee to the court of Sarsa Dengel. Bahrey did not have first-hand experience with the Barentu Oromo about which he gathered information from others. He was most probably at his best when he presented information based on his experience and first-hand observation.

In section 4, Bahrey also describes the *gada* system of government that was radically different from the monarchical institution of his society. Bahrey tells us that the Oromo changed their government every eight years,[51] which was an accurate observation. Of course, his concept of government was limited to that of monarchy, and the Oromo practice of changing governments every eight years was foreign to his society's political culture. Yet he tried to understand Oromo social organization. He was also the first man to understand the connection between Oromo social organization and their military strength, which in itself was an important discovery. Of course, Bahrey's interest was not the Oromo social organization per se, but its connection with their military strength. Maimire Mennasemay claims that Bahrey was 'tacitly impressed by the Oromo culture of freedom that seems to eschew the kind of voluntary servitude he observes in some of the classes of Christian Ethiopia he identifies in section nineteen'.[52] Such a claim may not be accurate. What is not in doubt is that Bahrey abhorred some aspects of Oromo culture, while at the same time he was also impressed with their social organization, which in his mind was the source of their military success. In short, Bahrey was the first man to write about the *gada* system. His 'attempts to explain the success of the [Oromo] by comparing their social organization with that of Abyssinia show a genuine sociological curiosity'.[53]

[49] Mennasemay, 'A Critical Reappraisal of Abba Bahrey's *Zenahu Le Galla*', 46, quoting Haile, *The Works of Abba Bahriy*, 97–98, 101.
[50] Aregay, 'Southern Ethiopia and the Christian Kingdom', 401.
[51] Haile, *The Works of Abba Bahriy*, 200.
[52] Mennasemay, 'A Critical Reappraisal of Abba Bahrey's *Zenahu Le Galla*', 51.
[53] Karl E. Knutsson, *Authority and Change: A Study of the Kallu Institution among the Macha Galla of Ethiopia*, 157.

In sections 5 to 18 Bahrey details the progress of the pastoral Oromo population movement. In fact, his greatest contribution to the history of the period was his impressive presentation of Oromo population movement. He did this in a very original way that demonstrated his literary talent. In a radical departure from the tradition of royal chronicles, Bahrey adopted an ingenious literary device that was based on the Oromo *gada* cycle of eight-year periods. In royal chronicles, 'theoretically a chapter corresponds to each year of the [monarch's] reign'.[54] Instead of writing about the population movement year by year, Bahrey devoted each section to an eight-year *gada* period for recording pastoral Oromo population movement and for registering the achievements of each *gada* in power. Only a gifted observer with a sharp mind could construct such an original device, an effective and appropriate format for telling the drama of the story of Oromo population movements in the second half of the sixteenth century.[55]

According to Bahrey's chronology of pastoral Oromo movement, which I have followed in the previous two chapters, it was during the period of the Melbah Gada (1522–30) that the Borana crossed the river of their country called Galana, and came to the frontier of Bali.[56] During the time when the Mudana Gada (1530–35) was in power, the Oromo crossed the Wabi Shabelle River, and opened the path for the subsequent pastoral Oromo population movement.

During the period of the Kilole Gada (1538–46) the Oromo carried the offensive towards the lowlands of Dawaro, where they defeated the famous Christian regiments of Adal Mabraq and drove them out of the area.[57] During the period of the Bifole Gada (1546–54) the Oromo dominated the whole of Dawaro and began to make war on Fatagar. The period of the Michelle Gada (1554–62) opened up the rapid spread of the pastoral Oromo that changed the course of history in the region. According to Bahrey, it was the Michelle Gada who destroyed 'the Jan Amora Corps and fought against Hamalmal at Dago; he devastated all the towns and ruled them, remaining there with his troops, whereas previously the [Oromo] invading from the Wabi had returned there at the end of each campaign'.[58]

Of the five *gada* that ruled between 1522 and 1562, Michelle was the most successful and Bahrey attributes its success to the Oromo use of cavalry'.[59] Between 1522 and 1544 the pastoral Oromo only entered Bali, Dawaro and Hadiya. The second factor, which Bahrey failed to account for, was the success of the Michelle Gada. In March 1559, Amir Nur (1552–67) the Muslim leader from Harar, destroyed the Christian military including its leadership. A few weeks later the Muslim force itself was liquidated at the Battle of Hazalo. This means the two traditional

[54] Tubiana, 'Un Ethnographe Ethiopen au XVI Siècle', 656.
[55] Ibid.
[56] Haile, *The Works of Abba Bahriy*, 196.
[57] Bahrey, 'History of the Galla' in *Some Records of Ethiopia*, 115.
[58] Ibid., 116.
[59] Ibid., 117.

enemies were exhausted and were unable to stop the Oromo advance. As a result, between 1554 and 1562 the Oromo repeatedly attacked Waj, moved into Fatagar and the whole of Hararghe, Ifat, Angot and Gedem. They not only inflicted serious defeats on both the Christians and Muslims but also laid open the path to Shawa, Damot and beyond.

The equally victorious and highly mobile Harmufa Gada (1562–70), who took the war into several new provinces, succeeded the Michelle Gada. According to Bahrey this *gada* destroyed the soldiers of the regiment called Giyorgis Hayle at Qacheno. The regiment, which acted as a protective shield, controlled the crossroads and the passes to the northern provinces. The Oromo dominated the provinces of Ganh, Angot and Amhara and entered Begameder, where they defeated the governor called Harbo, 'and killed his brother Waka'. The Harmufa Gada was succeeded by the Robale Gada (1570–78) who killed Zara Yohannes, the governor of Gojjam and the 'Chief of the Dignitaries'. The Robale Gada was succeeded by the Birmaje Gada (1578–86) who attacked Shawa, Waj, Damot and Gojjam. In the latter province they killed Fasiladas, the cousin of King Sarsa Dengel, and captured his son Susenyos (the future emperor) around1586. The same *gada* took the war to Dambiya and 'killed Aboli of the royal family, Sumra Ab, the Bahr Nagash, and other personages'.[60] The Birmaje Gada was succeeded by the Mulata Gada (1586–94) during which period the Christian kingdom suffered repeated defeats and lost all of its provinces east of the River Abbay. In the words of Abba Bahrey:

> The country submits to him, Mulata, and none remains without submission to him. When this book was written it was the seventh year [i.e. 1593] of the government of Mulata. They got ready to open the circumcision and investiture of the sons of Mesle [Michelle], and as to the battles and blood-shedding which will take place in their time, I shall write of them later, if I am still alive; and if I die, others will write their history for me, and that of future Lubas. But happy is he who dies, for he shall enter into rest.[61]

Bahrey ends his seminal presentation of pastoral Oromo population movement in sections 5 to 18 over a period of seventy years with this graphic picture. A number of interesting points emerge from the above quotation. First, by 1593, when Bahrey wrote his manuscript, he was 58-years old. By the standard of the time he lived into a ripe old age. Second, by 1593, the Christian administration had disintegrated in all the provinces east of the Abbay River. Third, and most important, Bahrey promised to write about the battles of the next *gada* period (1594–1602) if he was still alive. As we will see below, Bahrey was still alive in 1604, eleven years after he completed his manuscript. Why did he not write about the war of the next *gada*, the spirited war conducted by Dulo Gada (1594–1602)? It is impossible to know. However it is certain that either what he wrote was lost or he did not write of it at all. From internal evidence, it appears that he did not write anything about

[60] Ibid., 118, 119, 120.
[61] Ibid., 124–5.

the Oromo wars after 1593 because after the death of Sarsa Dengel in 1597 the triumvirate that held power abandoned all the wars against the Oromo. Bahrey appears to have been careful not to offend the most powerful court officials by writing about the need for conducting war against the Oromo. Be that as it may, in 1593, when he wrote his manuscript, Bahrey was very enthusiastic about waging war against the Oromo. In fact, he wrote his manuscript to inspire resistance against the Oromo as we will see in section 19. However, before presenting the arguments made there, we will examine the content of section 20, which is in line with Bahrey's descriptions in his previous eighteen sections.

BAHREY'S USE OF OROMO TERMS IN HIS SECTION 20

In section 20, Bahrey uses Oromo terms to describe Oromo activities in a village. This description implies that Bahrey either knew a few Oromo words, which he must have acquired from Oromo soldiers in the army of Sarsa Dengel, or Amharic-speaking Oromos provided him with Oromo terms. Either way his use of the following Oromo concepts demonstrate his remarkable sociological curiosity.

Bahrey starts his description of Oromo society with the terms the Oromo use for children. 'They call the small children *mucha*; and those who are older they call *elman*. And those who are older than these, who begin to do fighting, they call *gurba*.'[62] The Oromo term for children is *elman*, while *mucha* means a small boy who was from one to eight years old. This was the first stage in life through which a small boy had to pass. The Oromo term for this stage was *daballe*, which is derived from the verb *daballu* (jump about, dance around). The term *daballe* conveys a rosy picture of happy times, which elders envy. It was at this stage in life that boys were taught the family trees within an Oromo clan. It is said that a boy of five years knows the names of his forefathers to the depth of twelve or fifteen generations.[63] According to oral tradition through knowledge of the family tree within the clan, the boy establishes his place in the society.

Bahrey's claim that 'those who began to do fighting, they call *gurba*' is not quite accurate. *Gurba* means a male youth between the ages of eight and 16 years. It was at this stage that they participated in singing and dancing activities with their age mates, and learned how to throw spears and defend themselves. However, they did not participate in actual fighting as Bahrey suggests. What they did was to herd cattle, while acquiring the skills of fighting.

> The young men who are not yet circumcised are called *quandala* [*qondalla*] they dress their hair like soldiers ... if they kill a man, an elephant, a lion, a

[62] Haile, *The Works of Abba Bahriy*, 211.
[63] Haberland, *Galla Sud-Athiopiens*, 115. See also Bairu Tafla, *Asma Giyorgis and His Work*, 121.

rhinoceros, or buffalo, they shave the heads leaving a patch of hair on the top. But those who have killed neither man nor animal do not shave their heads; in the same way, married men do not shave themselves if they have killed neither man nor animal.[64]

The above is an accurate and excellent observation. Only someone who knew at least limited Oromo terms and observed Oromo tradition at close range could make such a description. It demonstrates beyond any doubt Bahrey's keen sense of observation and his contact or connection with some Oromo groups. However, what is puzzling is that he never acknowledges any connection or contact with any Oromo even with those who were converted to Christianity and served in the army of Sarsa Dengel. Of course, Bahrey was a man of his time, a product of his society, and a person who was victimized by the Borana Oromo. He claims that they wounded him.[65] It is not clear whether it was a physical wound or a psychological wound. The latter is the most likely case, as he was driven from his land, losing everything he had saved for his old age. Thus, for Bahrey, Oromos were enemies who kill people even when they suffer from lice. In his own words 'Those who have not killed man or large animals do not shave themselves and in consequences they are tormented with lice. That is why they are so eager to kill us.'[66]

Bahrey debased the moral character of the Oromo by describing them as merciless enemies of the Christians. His manuscript was instrumental in etching in the mind-set of his society a depiction of the Oromo as an 'enemy who is so zealous to do evil' (see below). Be that as it may, we continue with his description of Oromo social organization: 'All the unmarried [Oromo], whether Luba or *quendela*, are called *qero* [*qeerroo*] and live (together) in one dwelling, the *qero* of the Luba with the Luba, that of *quendela* with *quendela*, and the *geber* with the *geber*.'[67]

This description is interesting as it deals with Oromo warriors, though it is presented as if that was the Oromo mode of living. It is inaccurate because Bahrey was provided with incomplete information. For Bahrey, Luba means those who were circumcised. However, Luba has a 'much wider range of meanings' of which one is another name for *gada* classes, 'that succeeded each other every eight years in assuming political, military, judicial, legislative and ritual responsibilities'.[68]

We can define the gada class or Luba as a regiment of a generation that assumes power for a period of eight years, whereas gada is the years when the members of the class stay in power as the rulers. Stated differently, Luba is a group of people and gada is the term of office of the leader of that group, and by extension it is the name of the era during which that leader and his Luba were in power.[69]

---

[64] Bahrey 'History of the Galla' in *Some Records of Ethiopia*, 127.
[65] Haile, *The Works of Abba Bahriy*, 39.
[66] Bahrey 'History of the Galla' in *Some Records of Ethiopia*, 122.
[67] Haile, *The Works of Abba Bahriy*, 211–12.
[68] Legesse, *Oromo Democracy*, 31.
[69] Ibid, 116.

Bahrey is accurate when stating that all the unmarried [Oromo], whether Luba or *qondalla* 'are called *qero* [*qeerroo*]'. The term *qeerroo* means bachelor or unmarried man of fighting age. As warriors, the *qeerroo* may have lived together, as unmarried soldiers live together in barracks. The following description appears to reflect daily the activities of Oromo warriors.

> They appoint about twenty people to build the *sequela* [a rectangular house], and they call them *ajertu*[70] [builders]. Furthermore, they appoint (people) for killing cows; and they are called *qelta* [*qeltu* i.e. butchers]. Also, two people are appointed who roast the meat and cut it up, and distribute it in pieces equally to all; they call them *wajoz* [roasters].[71] Furthermore, they appoint five men to milk the cows of all; their name is *halebdo*.[72] Furthermore, they appoint (people) for scooping the milk and giving it to each in measurement ... Furthermore, they appoint seven people for bringing home the herds. They also search for the strayed. Their name is *berbado*.[73] They also choose from among themselves two and authorize them to admonish and punish the one who goes to a woman; these are called *gorsa*.[74] This abstinence is not righteousness, but so that they may be alert and diligent for fight. For he who is married thinks of that by which he would please his wife. Furthermore, they appoint about ten people to drive the cattle; their name is *tewwutu*.[75]

In the above long quotation Abba Bahrey presents an Oromo village as an armed camp of warriors, who are ready for waging war. Bahrey claims that even old men, 'do not rest from fighting, unless they are too feeble'.[76] This graphic description of an Oromo village had an intended purpose. It was to impress upon the elite at the court of Sarsa Dengel that the entire Oromo population – from young to old were mobilized as a single body to wage war against the Christians. Bahrey ends his section 20, which has 'great anthropological value'[77] with a single dramatic sentence that sums up the main argument of his manuscript. 'There is no one else who has found an enemy who is (so) zealous to do evil.'[78] As Merid Wolde Aregay accurately observed, Bahrey exaggerated Oromo eagerness to shed blood, because he 'had suffered from the [Oromo] raids and conquests'.[79] However, his exaggeration had an ideological motive, which gives staying power to his manuscript. That is why those who characterize the sixteenth-century pastoral Oromo population movement as a destructive force in Ethiopian history always marshal Abba Bahrey's manuscript in their arguments.[80]

[70] *Ajertu* were people who built roofs.
[71] The Oromo term is *Waadu*.
[72] The Oromo term is *elmitu*. *Halebdo* is a Geez word.
[73] It is *berbadu*, rather than *berhado*.
[74] It is *gorrssitu* rather than *gorsa*, which means advice, rather than adviser.
[75] Haile, *The Works of Abba Bahriy*, 212–13.
[76] Ibid., 213.
[77] Knutsson, *Authority and Change*, 157.
[78] Haile, *The Works of Abba Bahriy*, 213.
[79] Aregay, 'Southern Ethiopia and the Christian Kingdom', 315.
[80] For instance see, S. Gobat, *Journal of Three Years' Residence in Abyssinia* (New York: Negro Universities Press, 1969), 52.

What is interesting to note here is that, even though Bahrey describes Oromo social organization so meticulously, he does not appear to appreciate some natural qualities of at least those Oromo who were converted to Christianity and served in the army of Sarsa Dengel. In fact, it is not an exaggeration to state that Bahrey's description of the Oromo society of his time was devoid of any natural human qualities. Three decades after Bahrey's writing, Manoel de Almeida enumerates these qualities in these terms:

> [T]he [Oromo] have some natural good qualities, for they are men of their word and are not ill natured. This is seen in many of them who have been taken from their own people and brought up in the household of the Emperor or of other great nobles, and have always shown themselves so tractable that they are in no way inferior to the Abyssinians ... Generally speaking they are of good physique and courageous.[81]

THE MAIN MESSAGE OF BAHREY'S *ZENAHU LE GALLA* IN HIS SECTION 19

By 1593, when Bahrey wrote his manuscript, he was an old man whose years had coincided with the second part of the tumultuous sixteenth century. Except for the information on the Barentu Oromo, which he gathered from others, most of his account on the Borana appears to have been based on his own experience. He was a keen observer, with a deep sense of history, and highly articulate in expressing his ideas. Historical literature of a kind, of course, had developed within the Christian kingdom long before the time of Bahrey. What makes his work quite distinct and unique from other historical literature of the time is his serious concern with the Oromo as the major actors of the day. He was the prime mover at the court of Sarsa Dengel of the whole debate about the Oromo. As an official having inside access to what was happening in the court, he might have dwelled on all trivialities that took place there, as his contemporaries did. Instead, Bahrey concentrated on the Oromo question, which for him was the source of all the problems of the kingdom. On the one hand, he was deeply saddened by the inability of the Christians to stop the Oromo advance. On the other, he was disappointed and shocked by the division within the Christian society. In his eyes, the power struggle between the forces of centralization and those of decentralization made the Christians incapable of defending themselves.

> Bahrey's attempt ... at explaining the military prowess of the Oromo and the weakness of the state in a socio-political analytic framework ... is an expression of concern. Indeed, for Bahrey, it is an expression of protest against the existing form of the socio-political structure of the state, which in his eyes had become disastrously dysfunctional.[82]

---

[81] Almeida, 'The History of High Ethiopia or Abassia' in *Some Records of Ethiopia*, 137.
[82] See Hailu Fulas' review of R.K. Molvaer, *Tradition and Change in Ethiopia:*

At the imperial court, Bahrey observed that there were many persons who had their own axes to grind and complaints to make, none of which were contributing to the crucial issue of Christian defence. He saw that Christian salvation was possible only if their energy was harnessed for the common purpose of opposing the common enemy. It appears that he believed that a call for unity against the common enemy would have stimulated Christian nationalism. The creation of a state of psychological mobilization would have facilitated the closing of ranks and enabled the Christians to accept the sacrifices required. Behind Bahrey's presentation of this issue in section 19, one can see the serious thinking of an intelligent politician who had a precise grasp of the difficulties faced by the Christian kingdom, and who was suggesting an imaginative course of action. Notwithstanding all his love and reverence for Sarsa Dengel, Bahrey does not attempt to conceal the defeat of the Christians. He endeavours to represent events without bias, so that his fellow Christians could understand what was at stake and adopt measures commensurate with the danger they faced. He justifies his radical departure from the norm of the day on Biblical grounds:

> The reason why I have written at one time of the victory of the [Oromo], and at another time the victory of the Christians, is because it is the custom of the books which say, 'Today to you and tomorrow to the other.' Victory belongs at one time to this one, and another time to that one. He who conquers always is the one God who is above all.[83]

The Oromo population movement was of course also described by Muslim and Christian historians, including the Portuguese. However, where their strong prejudice or lack of insight prevented them from observing those organizational factors that enabled Oromo pastoralists to become formidable warriors, we find keen concern in Bahrey to understand the source of Oromo strength. This he rightly attributes to their social organization. Unlike *Zenahu le Galla*, *The History of King Sarsa Dengel* seldom mentions Oromo victory, and in it there is a continuous thread of triumph that, if it had really continued throughout his thirty-four year reign, ought to have checked the Oromo progress. With Bahrey the distinction between illusion and reality is clearly drawn. He knew why he was writing and for whom.

In the *History of King Sarsa Dengel* (1563–92), Bahrey follows the traditional genre of Christian chroniclers that depicts the greatness and glorious achievement of the emperor. He departed from that tradition in his ideologically inspired *Zenahu le Galla*, which urged the Christian intelligentsia at the court of Emperor Sarsa Dengel to understand the secret of Oromo strength and the weakness of their own society.

This intelligentsia split into two groups to account for the Christian defeat. One group ascribed it to the will of God as a punishment for the sins of the Christians, while the other attributed it to the large number

(contd) *Social and Cultural Life as Reflected in Amharic Fictional Literature ca. 1930–1974*, *Northeast African Studies* 4, (1982), 41.
[83] Haile, *The Works of Abba Bahriy*, 208.

of Oromo warriors. While the arguments of both camps can be detected in the Christian literature of the time, both standpoints found their fullest expression in Bahrey, who developed the arguments logically.

> The knowledgeable ones make an extensive inquiry, asking, 'How is it that the [Oromo] defeat us, although we are many, and many are our arms?' There are those who say, 'God has allowed them because of our sins.' And there are those who say, 'it is because of our nation's division into ten classes. Nine of these do not come close to any battle, and they are not ashamed of their fear. But the tenth class battles and fights to the best of its ability. Although our number is big, those who can fight are few, and those who do not come near the battle are many.[84]

In the above quotation, Bahrey clearly expresses the arguments of both groups. His observation captures the spirit of the moment and makes an interesting contribution to our knowledge of the class structure of the Christian society of the time.

With his intimate knowledge and beautiful writing, Bahrey expresses the core of the weakness of Christian defence. He took it upon himself as a special mission to enlighten and educate the elite on disparity in terms of fighting men between the Christians and the Oromo. Bahrey presented the nine non-fighting classes of his society in the following dramatic manner.

> One of these is the party of the monks, who are countless. There are those who become monks in their youth, when monks lure them while they are studying, like [the case of] the writer of this essay and those like him. There are also those who become monks because of fear of battle. The second group is called *debtera*. They study scriptures and all the profession of the clergy; they clap their hands and stamp with their feet;[85] they are not ashamed of their fear. They take as their model the Levites and priests, namely, the sons of Aaron. The third group called *jan hatsena* and *jan measere;*[86] These guard justice and guard themselves from battle. The fourth is the group of *deggafoch* of the women of the dignitaries and the royal ladies, powerful men and strong young men. They do not come near the battle; they say 'We are attendant to the women'. The fifth group is called *shimagille* [elders], *geze,*[87] and *beale rist* [landowners]. They give a portion of their land to the peasant and demand his services; they are not ashamed of their fear. The sixth group is the peasants. They spend their day in the fields and are oblivious about fighting. The seventh group is those who benefit themselves from commerce. They make profit for themselves. The eighth group[88] is the artisans, such as the smiths, scribes, tailors, carpenters and their like. They do not know fighting. The ninth group is the minstrels, those who play the *gende kebero* [drum] and the begena [harp], who making begging a profession. They bless the one who rewards them; they give him vainglory and idle praise. And when they curse the one who does not reward them, they are not charged, for they say, 'This is our tradition'. They keep themselves very far from battle. The tenth group is those who carry the shield and spear. These can do fighting, and 'follow the steps of the king to run.' Because of the fewness, of these our country is destroyed.[89]

---

84   Ibid., 209.
85   'i.e. when they chant and dance during religious feasts', ibid., 209.
86   'These are people of the law, judges', ibid., 209.
87   'A class of landlords', ibid., 210.
88   'included people who worked on leather', ibid., 210.
89   Ibid., 209–10.

In the above long quotation, Bahrey presents in graphical detail the disparity in terms of fighting men between the Christians, and the Oromo. The disparity may have been an exaggeration. For Merid Wolde Aregay, the disparity is a myth created by Bahrey.[90] Indeed it was a myth created for a purpose, i.e. promulgation of the main message: 'it is because of the fewness of our fighting men that our country is destroyed'. It is Bahrey's message of destruction of a country, which played an overarching role in shaping his society's attitude towards the Oromo. Never has a single work been so influential as Bahrey's short manuscript in determining Oromo representation in literature in subsequent centuries – as a destructive, barbarian force, lacking in the essential qualities of humanity.[91] Bahrey may not have intended it but his manuscript has become a frame of historical reference for limiting early Oromo history to the first half of the sixteenth century. Be that as it may, Bahrey's presentation of unparalleled disparity between the Christian and Oromo fighting men was meant to provide weight to his message impressing upon the elite the moral imperative for increasing the size of Christian fighting men. From this thesis flows another that he expressed eloquently in a single sentence. 'Among the Oromo all men – from young to old are trained in warfare, to kill and destroy Christians.'[92]

In the above quotation Bahrey not only demonstrates his knowledge of the class structure of his society, but goes to the heart of what he considers to be the weakness of its defence system. For him, the solution to this serious problem was to increase the number of fighting men. He made it clear that this policy could be instituted if the majority of the people were called upon to fight. Further, he implies that if the private soldiers of the landlords and governors were made to provide their services to the state directly, the king would be able to meet all the Oromo challenges whenever and wherever they occurred. In order to demonstrate the numerical disparity between the Christian fighting men and those of the Oromo, he gives the following graphic description:

> Among the [Oromo] on the contrary, these nine classes that we have mentioned do not exist; all men, from small to great, are instructed in warfare, and for this reason they ruin and kill us. Those who say that it is by God's command that they kill us, find their reasons in the fact that the Israelites were conquered and their ruin accomplished at the hands of the kings of Persia and Babylon. If brave warriors gain the victory, they say, 'who would ask help from God the exalted and most high?' And if those who are numerous always conquer those who are few, the words of Holy Scripture, which say, 'One man shall put a thousand to flight and two shall pursue ten thousand,' would be found to be in vain. However, you wise men, you can judge if the claim of the first of these arguers is right, or that of the second.[93]

[90] Aregay, 'Southern Ethiopia and the Christian Kingdom', 315.
[91] C.R. Markham, *A History of the Abyssinian Expedition* (London: Macmillan, 1869), 39–40.
[92] Haile, *The Works of Abba Bahriy*, 210.
[93] Bahrey, 'History of the Galla' in *Some Records of Ethiopia*, 126–7.

As noted, opinions in the court of Sarsa Dengel were divided along the lines of the above arguments. Bahrey did not go so far as to deny the validity of the first argument, but he clearly argued for the need to increase the Christian fighting force. Among the younger elements at the court, Bahrey's thesis became the impetus for a new course of action and there is every reason to believe that Bahrey wrote with this element in mind. As will become clear, this element argued that on the home front the first thing to do was to bolster up the monarchy, and restore the eroded Christian morale. Bahrey's ideas found favour at court with the ardent, revolutionary leader Za-Dengel, who gave his time and energy to implementing them. It appears that Bahrey's central thesis, that stressed the need for increasing the size of Christian fighting men appealed to Za-Dengel and his supporters. This element may have believed that the moment the size of fighting men increased morale would rise, confidence be regained and trust in and credibility of the leadership restored. With that, the initiative in the offensive would pass into Christian hands. For the moment that reality lay in the future. In the interim, Bahrey inspired Za-Dengel's spirited campaign against the Oromo, which will be discussed below.

SARSA DENGEL'S LAST CAMPAIGN AGAINST THE BORANA OROMO

The Dulo Gada (1594–1602) continued the advance in different directions. Its thrust into the area between Gojjam and Ennarya, the gold mine of Sarsa Dengel, threatened the disruption of communications, trade, revenue and travel between the two. From his chronicle, it does not appear that during his long reign Sarsa Dengel had set foot either in Amhara or in Angot in order to help the Christians against the Oromo. However, in 1597 while in poor health, he hastened to re-open the communications between Ennarya and Gojjam. This demonstrates how much he depended on the gold tribute from Ennarya. This last attempt was a grand project, by which he wanted to push the Borana Oromo from Damot, and the whole land between Abbay and Ennarya. With the apparent intention of pushing the Borana in order to guarantee the safety of the route to Ennarya, he left his court, in spite of a warning message from a priest, who told him that it would be bad for him to fight the Borana at that time. The warning seems to have been the veiled ideological expression of those elements that attributed every Christian defeat to their sins. The supporters of this fatalistic view argued against pushing the war into Oromo territory. In fact,

> a priest famous for holiness, and a talent for divination, ... warned [Sarsa Dengel] not to undertake that war. But the king, expressing his contempt of both the message and messenger declared his fixed resolution to invade Damot without delay.[94]

---

[94] Bruce, *Travels to Discover the Source of the Nile*, vol. 3, 254–5. See also Jules Perruchon, 'Notes pour l'histoire d'Ethiopie Règne de Sarsa-Dengel, 277–8.

Accordingly, the emperor persistently led a large force into Damot, but the flight of the various Borana groups prevented him from securing any decisive victory. The much hoped for gallant attempt to punish the Borana and guarantee the safety of the route to Ennarya did not materialize. Instead it boomeranged and caused serious erosion in the morale of the Christian army, which was exposed to hunger and refused to fight in the land of Borana. During thirty-four years of long campaigns against the Oromo, Sarsa Dengel won several victories as we saw in the previous chapter. However, ironically, he lost almost all the eastern provinces. Exhausted by arduous campaigns, frustrated by his failure to stop the Oromo, demoralized by the cowardly attitude of his force towards fighting in the Oromo territory, he died on 4 October 1597.

USURPATION OF ZA-DENGEL'S SUCCESSION IN 1597

When Sarsa Dengel died, a nineteen-year-old nephew of the king named Za-Dengel lived at court. Za-Dengel was born either in late 1577 or 1578.[95] His father, Lessana Chrestos, was the brother of Sarsa Dengel and an ordained priest 'well known for his literary achievements'. Za-Dengel received many years of 'extensive education from the monastery at Daga Island'.[96] Pedro Páez, who was impressed with Za-Dengel's interest in education and quick-wittedness states that he 'was very curious in matters of learning for he had always occupied himself with them as a boy, even while in prison.'[97] By all accounts, Za-Dengel was the best-educated man destined to sit on the Christian throne for a very long time. Besides his extensive education, Za-Dengel had the added advantage of growing up at the court of Sarsa Dengel, the political nerve centre of the kingdom. What is more, Sarsa Dengel, who did not have his own legitimate son, loved Za-Dengel 'like an only son'.[98] At the court of Sarsa Dengel, Za-Dengel distinguished himself in the debate over the question of why the Oromo were defeating the Christians. In addition, he 'had revealed that he possessed an upright character and deep love for justice'.[99] It was at the court of Sarsa Dengel that Za-Dengel came to know and admire Abba Bahrey, the confessor of the king. There is no doubt that Za-Dengel, as a learned man, was familiar with the works of Abba Bahrey, including *Zenahu le Galla*. Through his powerful works, Bahrey had exerted a strong influence on Za-Dengel, who had lived his whole life in those tumultuous decades and had shared with Bahrey all the currents of experience of the time and common trials of living in a rapidly changing kingdom. Observing in Za-Dengel the qualities of an able general and upright administrator, Sarsa Dengel seems to have maintained hope that his nephew

---

[95] Aregay, 'Southern Ethiopia and the Christian Kingdom', 357.
[96] Ibid., 371.
[97] Boavida et al., *Pedro Páez's History of Ethiopia*, vol. 2, 158, 166.
[98] Aregay, 'Southern Ethiopia and the Christian Kingdom', 355.
[99] Ibid., 371.

would take the charge to save the kingdom. Consequently Sarsa Dengel 'designated Za-Dengel, the son of his brother Lessana Chrestos as his heir and had him recognized as such by the nobility and by the Qurban soldiers'.[100]

Regardless, the queen mother, Empress Maryam Sena, and her two sons-in-law, Ras Atnatewos, (the governor of Amhara) and Keflawahd (the governor Tigray) usurped the order of succession as will be shown below. This indicates that the three powerful court officials saw a threat to their position in Za-Dengel's personality and tendencies.[101] As a learned man who revealed in the king's audience hall his 'astuteness in political and legal matters and sensibility against injustice and oppression',[102] Za-Dengel was unacceptable to the soldiers and the nobility, including women of the royal family. 'To the rapacious Qurban soldiers, the scheming ladies of the court, and the proud nobility of the provinces, Za-Dengel's concern for order and justice was a source of uneasiness.'[103] They persuaded the king to change his mind in favour of his seven-year-old son Ya'eqob. Yet, in his last moments, the king once again changed his mind in favour of Za-Dengel, saying,

> As I am sensible I am at the point of death, next to the cause of my soul, I am anxious for the welfare of my kingdom. My first intention was to appoint [Ya'eqob], my son, to be successor; and I had done so unless for his youth, and it is probable neither you nor I could have cause to repent it. Considering however, the state of my kingdom, I prefer its interest to the private affection I bear my son; and do, therefore, hereby appoint Za-Dengel, my nephew to succeed me, and be your king, and recommend him to you as fit for war, ripe in years, exemplary in the practice of every virtue, and as deserving of the crown by his good qualities, as he is by his near relation to the royal family.[104]

Merid Wolde Aregay claims that this speech was invented by James Bruce.[105] In reality, James Bruce could not have invented it in 1804. The same speech appears in Job Ludolphus' book, published in 1682.[106] Apparently, James Bruce merely rendered it in the English of the nineteenth century.

It is more than likely that Job Ludolphus got the speech from Abba Gregory, a learned Amhara priest whom Edward Ullendorff described as 'an informant of truth and reliability'.[107] He lived in Italy and worked with Ludolphus in 1652. For Abba Gregory, to remember this speech *verbatim*, it must have existed as a document most probably penned by Bahrey himself. It was Bahrey who put in the mouth of the dying king his deep admiration for Za-Dengel 'as fit for war, ripe in years, exemplary in the practice of virtue'. There is a contemporary eye-witness

---

[100] Ibid., 356. Qurban soldiers were the king's elite force.
[101] Boavida et al., *Pedro Páez's History of Ethiopia*, vol. 2, 146.
[102] Aregay, 'Southern Ethiopia and the Christian Kingdom', 358.
[103] Ibid.
[104] Bruce, *Travels to Discover the Source of the Nile*, vol. 3, 255–6.
[105] Aregay, 'Southern Ethiopia and the Christian Kingdom', 358, see note 1.
[106] Job Ludolphus, *A New History of Ethiopia*, 177.
[107] Ullendorff, *The Ethiopians*, 10.

account that confirms that on his death bed Sarsa Dengel told Ras Atnatewos and other nobility to put Za-Dengel on the throne.[108] Abba Bahrey not only supported this, but also inspired Za-Dengel to attempt the implementation of *Zenahu le Galla*'s principle of resistance against the Oromo,[109] an idea they shared in common. In more ways than one, their fate was also tied together.

KING YA'EQOB, 1597–1603

The queen mother and her two sons-in-law, Keflawahd and Atnatewos, in whose presence the king died, usurped the order of succession and enthroned the young Ya'eqob and exiled Za-Dengel in chains to an island in Lake Tana. The triumvirate denied Za-Dengel the throne, possibly wanting to exercise absolute power during the regency of 'a boy emperor'[110]. Nevertheless, there might have been a hidden motive behind their move. They had seen in Za-Dengel the burning desire to intensify the war against the Oromo. They had lived with the war and seen its consequences for their country, and were tired of it and wanted peace. In fact, it seems they represented the dogmatist element at the court, which attributed the Christian defeat to God's punishment. Bahrey was very careful in his presentation of the arguments. He did not dare to offend this entrenched power block (see Chapter 7 below).

With the death of Sarsa Dengel and the exile of Za-Dengel, Bahrey's influence at the court disappeared. It is not known whether he removed himself from court politics and maintained a very low social profile. Interestingly, he reappears on the political scene in 1603–04, when Za-Dengel was struggling to maintain himself on the throne.[111] During the seven years of Ya'eqob's regency (1597–1603) when Maryam Sena (the queen) and her two sons-in law were in control of the throne, campaigns against the Oromo were almost suspended. By placing the young Ya'eqob on the throne, the nobility thus achieved two inter-related purposes. They suspended the war against the Oromo and they kept Za-Dengel out of power, preventing him from implementing the principles of Bahrey's manuscript. As a result, during the seven years Gojjam, Amhara, Begameder and Walaqa were repeatedly inundated by both the Barentu and Borana groups, and the fate of each province was left to the inhabitants and their governors. In 1603, when Ya'eqob prematurely decided to end the regency, Ras Atnatewos, the governor of Gojjam, openly rebelled against the young emperor. The adventurous Za-Sellassie, the commander of Qurban soldiers 'and several corps of [Oromo] auxiliaries' abandoned the cause of Ya'eqob and 'made common cause with Atnatewos'.[112] Ironically, Ya'eqob

---

[108] Boavida et al., *Pedro Páez's History of Ethiopia*, vol. 2, 145.
[109] Chernetsov, 'The "History of the Gallas" and Death of Za-Dengel', 806.
[110] Boavida et al., ibid., 146.
[111] Aregay, 'Southern Ethiopia and the Christian Kingdom', 371.
[112] Ibid., 367.

defeated and captured his two powerful enemies. However, the inexperienced emperor made a poor judgement when 'he pardoned Atnatewos and reinstated him in his previous posts'[113] while he exiled Za-Sellassie to the distant kingdom of Ennarya. Shortly after, the empress and Ras Atnatewos removed Ya'eqob from power in disgrace.

Meanwhile, Za-Dengel used the seven years of his imprisonment for 'improvement of his knowledge on religious and secular matters'.[114] These were years of trial and preparation for Za-Dengel. He must have heard about the effects of the Oromo war on the peasants in Gojjam and Begameder. However, there was no action from the court. During these years, Gojjam became the scene of bitter fighting, with heavy casualties on both sides. To the Christians, the province was prized as the rich region that had become the home of Christian refugees from across the Abbay River. The Oromo valued the province as strategically pivotal for further entry into the Christian kingdom. As will be shown shortly, Za-Dengel wanted to save Gojjam and push the war back across the Abbay.

KING ZA-DENGEL, 1603–1604, AND THE OROMO

Amazingly the very nobility who exiled Za-Dengel in chains in 1597 'secretly brought him to the imperial city and proclaimed him emperor, and then they went to seize [Ya'eqob] who was still in his palace, quite unaware'.[115] Za-Dengel saved Ya'eqob from mutilation and exiled him, thus starting his short reign with a humane measure. While sending Ya'eqob into exile in the kingdom of Ennarya , Za-Dengel freed and brought back from exile in the same place the adventurous Za-Sellasie. Za-Dengel, who wanted to use the military talent and his leadership of the Qurban soldiers for his cause, not only brought back Za-Sellassie, but also 'appointed him over Dambiya and Wagara, where most of the [Qurban] units lived. [Za-Dengel] even gave him his sister in marriage, hoping thereby to attach him closer to himself.'[116] Ironically, as we shall see shortly and in the next chapter, Za-Sellassie was the man who destroyed Za-Dengel. But that, for the moment, lay in the future. For now it should suffice to say that Za-Dengel was the most educated and the best qualified man for the job. In him, writes Merid Wolde Aregay, 'we find a rare, humane and sensitive personality. He was undoubtedly one of the most interesting ... [and] also one of the most enigmatic men who ruled over the country'.[117] Enigmatic because very little was written about his short reign, and little was understood about his goal of implementing Bahrey's ideas. According to Aregay: 'When he was placed on the throne in September 1603, at the age of twenty-six,

---

[113] Ibid., 368.
[114] Boavida et al., *Pedro Páez's History of Ethiopia*, vol. 2, 157.
[115] Ibid.
[116] Aregay, 'Southern Ethiopia and the Christian Kingdom', 372.
[117] Ibid., 370–1.

[Za-Dengel] had a good understanding of the political situation. He may have admired the integrity and dedication of Galawdewos, whose throne name he adopted.'[118]

There is reason to believe that Bahrey was given the title of *azaj* ('commander' or 'steward') when he served at Za-Dengel's court.[119] Azaj Bahrey, most probably was the principal secretary and a confidante of Za-Dengel, who may have enjoyed great authority as an intellectual who inspired steadfast resistance against the Oromo. One thing is for certain: the title reflects the king's trust and confidence in Bahrey. Merid Wolde Aregay made an interesting observation when stating that Za-Dengel admired Emperor Galawdewos (1540–59). Like Galawdewos, he appealed to the sense of Christian unity against the common enemy. His knowledge of history made him realize that Galawdewos' victory over Imam Ahmad in 1543 could be repeated only with Portuguese and Spanish assistance, specifically their cannons and soldiers. To repulse the Oromo and push them back east of the Abbay, Za-Dengel knew that his soldiers needed guns and cannons and training in the use of the equipment. Above all, he knew that his forces lacked the will to fight. To infuse morale into his forces, he needed an ally. He quickly came to the conclusion that he could get all he needed by cultivating friendly relations with Spain, the major European power of the day. As the Portuguese had saved his country six decades earlier, Za-Dengel might have believed that Spain would save it again.

Accordingly, he invited Pedro Páez, the highly educated and industrious missionary, to his court shortly after he came to the throne with the following urgent message. 'We greatly desire that you come here at once and bring the books of justice of the kings of Portugal, if you have them, because we should like to see them.'[120] Páez was to be the link between his government and that of the Emperor of Spain and Portugal. Both men needed each other, the one for political goals, and the other for religious purposes. Páez was surprised by Za-Dengel eagerness to accept Catholic faith immediately. By embracing Catholicism, Za-Dengel might have believed that he would obtain quick and certain assistance against his internal and external enemies. In fact Pedro Páez was so worried that he had to caution Za-Dengel with these words. 'Lord, it does not seem to be time yet for your majesty to stake everything. I think it would be better to go more slowly, so that it may penetrate gently.'[121] Za-Dengel wrote to Pope Clement VIII and Philip III, Emperor of Spain and Portugal respectively, requesting aid. In his letter to the Emperor of Spain and Portugal, Za-Dengel stated that as the Portuguese saved our country from Muslim destruction,

> now too we have some enemies who are called [Gallas] and are destroying our land. When we go against them, we do not find them, because they flee, and

[118] Ibid., 371.
[119] Pereira, *Chronica de Susenyos*, 57–59
[120] Boavida et al., *Pedro Páez's History of Ethiopia*, vol. 2, 158.
[121] Ibid., 171.

when we return home, they fall like robbers upon those who are near them, and then withdraw. We therefore beg your majesty to send us ... many fighting men and craftsmen of all crafts; and may it be at once without delay.[122]

As the most educated leader with intimate knowledge of Orthodox Church doctrine, it is very difficult, if not impossible, to explain Za-Dengel's eagerness to embrace Catholicism, unless he was following the example of Galawdewos. At the height of the jihad of Imam Ahmad, when the very survival of the Christian kingdom was at stake, Galawdewos might have hinted at the possibility of embracing the Catholic faith.[123] However, once the threat from the Muslim force evaporated, Galawdewos denied making any promise about accepting the Catholic faith. As someone who admired Galawdewos and knew his history, Za-Dengel might have aspired to emulate his predecessor.

Some observers were not keen to see it that way. James Bruce, for instance, interpreted Za-Dengel's eagerness to embrace Catholicism as the unique accomplishment of Pedro Páez.[124] Merid Wolde Aregay suggested that Za-Dengel's flirtation with Catholicism was a tactical move to gain support against his internal enemies.[125] This is correct in part, but it is not the full explanation. The principal motivation must be seen in Za-Dengel's obsession with the Oromo and his desire for the defence of the kingdom. By eagerly embracing Catholicism, he believed he would ensure quick and certain assistance against his internal and external enemies. Beneath his acceptance of Catholicism and the edicts he issued, Za-Dengel was a visionary politician who saw the absolute necessity of getting foreign aid to stop the Oromo pressure and the means to attain that aid.[126]This is because, by the beginning of the seventeenth century, the Christian elite was already convinced that the Oromo would be defeated only with the use of imported firearms. For instance, on the basis of Tellez report, Ludolphus wrote in 1682, that the Abyssinians could defeat the Oromo if they 'have guns and know how to use them'.[127] Therefore, it is not far-fetched to suggest that Za-Dengel wanted firearms for his campaign against the Oromo. Páez' attitude towards him assured the forthcoming aid, while his acceptance of the Catholic religion provided the ideological justification to appeal on his behalf. Did Za-Dengel embrace Catholicism out of a genuine religious conversion or did he accept it because it was

[122] Ibid.,173. See also Girma Beshah and Merid Wolde Aregay, *The Question of the Union of the Churches in Luso-Ethiopian Relations 1500–1632* (Lisbon: Junta de Investigações do Ultramar & Centro de Estudos Históricos Ultramarinos, 1964), 75–6.

[123] Whiteway, *The Portuguese Expedition to Abyssinia*, 180–1, 183–4, 207. See also Tafla, *Asma Giyorgis and His Work*, 695.

[124] Bruce, *Travels to Discover the Source of the Nile*, vol. 3, 263–5.

[125] Aregay, 'Southern Ethiopia and the Christian Kingdom', 382–5.

[126] Boavida et al., *Pedro Páez's History of Ethiopia*, vol. 2, 171–2.

[127] Ludolphus, *A New History of Ethiopia*, 218. It was in the 1880s that King Menelik of Shawa vanquished the Oromo with superior firepower fulfilling what was anticipated two centuries earlier.

the means to Spanish support? What is clear is that Za-Dengel was concerned with the defence of his throne and his country. The tragedy lies in hasty acceptance of Catholicism and his launching the crusade against the Oromo too quickly and wanting to accomplish everything too soon as envisioned by his mentor, Abba Bahrey. As Chernetsov puts it, 'The reign of Za-Dengel is very interesting because he was the very first king' who made an attempt to realize the ideas of *Zenahu le Galla* and 'its principles of resistance'[128] against the Oromo.

Once Ya'eqob was replaced by Za-Dengel, the Oromo in Amhara, Walaqa and Bizamo, who were following closely developments within the Christian kingdom decided to take advantage of the change of government. They organized a three-pronged coordinated attack on Gojjam. Their goal appears to have been to 'control' the lands of Gojjam. Za-Dengel quickly mobilized a large force and left for Gojjam in a hurry. Meanwhile, he ordered Ras Atnatewos, the governor of Gojjam, 'not to give battle until he arrived ... [but] he gave battle and was defeated with loss of many men.'.[129] Oromo warriors were elated with their victory over the governor of Gojjam. They were so confident that Za-Dengel was weak that they decided to attack his force at once.

> Splitting into three squadrons, they advanced to where the emperor was, and when he saw this he commanded his men to form three squadrons as well and, taking his place in the middle one, he went forth to encounter them. On coming close, one squadron of [Oromo] charged so furiously that it soon put the [emperor's] left-hand squadron to flight; they then did the same to the right-hand squadron, so that the emperor remained alone with his squadron facing the [Oromo] battle corps. When the captains saw that they decided to turn ... , but when he heard this he dismounted from his horse, ... saying 'I shall die here fighting. The rest of you can run away to the mountain..., but ... people will say that the emperor whom you made yesterday was abandoned by you today at the start of battle'. At this, they all resolved to die without turning tail, and they attacked and fought so valiantly that they put the [Oromo] to flight.[130]

By his quick action, undisputed bravery and an inspiring speech, Za-Dengel restored the courage of his men, who then resolved to die with their emperor, thus turning an obvious disaster into a remarkable victory. For their over-confidence, Oromo warriors paid with the lives of 1,700 men that day. Za-Dengel followed up his victory by defeating two other Oromo warrior groups who were simultaneously attacking Gojjam. His attack on one Oromo group was so furious that he was reported to have slaughtered all of them.[131] The first partial mobilization against the Oromo proved spectacularly successful and was interpreted by Za-Dengel as a test of the workability of Bahrey's ideas (more on this below). Meanwhile, while conducting war against the Oromo, Za-Dengel adopted measures with which he intended to maintain law and order and protect commerce. It was reported that

[128] Chernetsov, 'The "History of the Gallas" and Death of Za-Dengel', 806.
[129] Boavida et al., *Pedro Páez's History of Ethiopia*, vol. 2, 159.
[130] Ibid., 159–60.
[131] Ibid., 160.

his majesty was seen and heard in his kingdom, and he accomplished deeds pleasing to God. He abhorred evil and loved righteousness; he considered thieves as devils and robbers as demons. His reign became a period of blessing to the poor and of malediction to the wicked. The farmers and traders loved him and praised him.[132]

ZA-DENGEL'S FULL MOBILIZATION AGAINST THE OROMO

While Za-Dengel was conducting the political and military war against the Oromo, Susenyos, his rival was helping Oromo warriors defeating Christians. Early successes inspired Za-Dengel to try his fortune against the Oromo in Walaqa and the rebellious Susenyos.[133] At this time, (1603–04) Susenyos was in the service of various Oromo groups helping them to reduce mountain strongholds in the regions of Amhara, Shawa and Walaqa, where Christian communities had taken refuge. After his three victories in Gojjam, Za-Dengel proclaimed the most revolutionary decree of the seventeenth century, a call to full mobilization. It was directly based on the content and spirit of Bahrey's *Zenahu le Galla*.

> If every man who is of age who lives in any land of my kingdom does not come, not only the chawa [professional soldiers], whose task has always been warfare, but also the farmers as well as the retainers of the ladies, and the servants of the monks, if any one stays behind and does not heed this call-up, his house shall be pillaged and his property confiscated. All men who were of age for fighting and who carried instruments of war came and joined him. None stayed behind in the villages except the lame, the paralyzed, the blind and the sick. The retainers of the lords, he took all of them, and he made them chawa and called them Malak Hara.[134]

What was radically different about this mobilization from all others of the time was that the call was made to every able-bodied citizen. All other call-ups before and after this were directed mainly to the ranks of professional soldiers, but Za-Dengel had seen in his own lifetime their ineffectiveness. He might have read and pondered over Bahrey's history, in which was stressed the need for a new course of action. It was Bahrey's observation that the existence of the nine non-fighting

---

[132] Tafla, *Asma Giyorgis and His Work*, 273. See also Aregay, 'Southern Ethiopia and the Christian Kingdom', 372–3. Za-Dengel is also reported to have made a 'New Version' of the Agaya book – a small manuscript originally written during the second half of the fifteenth or early sixteenth century, or possibly even later. Its core message is the prophecy made to King Libna Dengel (1508–40) that the Oromo would rule Ethiopia for 250 years. The prophecy may reflect the Oromo pressure on the Christian society. According to Asma Giyorgis, those who made a new version of Agaya book claimed that they were forced by Za-Dengel 'to write it'. It is not far-fetched to suggest that Za-Dengel probably wanted to use this work as part of his powerful campaign against the Oromo.

[133] See the beginning of the next chapter for a description of Susenyos' captivity and return.

[134] Pereira, *Chronica de Susenyos*, 50, trans. Aregay, 'Southern Ethiopia and the Christian Kingdom', 398.

classes had hampered every Christian effort against the Oromo.

Among the nine classes, Bahrey stressed the absolute necessity of making good use first of the escorts of the wives of dignitaries and princesses since 'they are vigorous, brave and strong men who nevertheless do not go to war'. Bahrey also stressed the importance of mobilizing the peasants, 'who have no thought of taking part in the war'.[135] In Za-Dengel's proclamation, all nine classes were included and even servants of the clergy were not excluded. Herein lies the tremendous impact of Bahrey's *Zenahu le Galla* on Za-Dengel, whose revolutionary measures 'testify that he not only knew, but shared the ideas of Bahrey'.[136]

What is striking about Za-Dengel's mobilization proclamation is not only its heavy reliance on Bahrey's *Zenahu le Galla*, but also its implication for allowing the peasants to bear arms. As indicated in the previous chapter, the Christian peasants were not allowed to bear arms, and were therefore easy prey for the Oromo warriors. Probably influenced by Bahrey's ideas, Za-Dengel appears to have wanted the peasants to defend themselves, a very practical idea. 'According to the abridged history, the law intended to enable the peasants to bear arms was proclaimed in words that suggest complete and permanent emancipation.'[137] The proclamation appears to have not only the goal of giving peasants the right to bear weapons, but also to emancipate them from their traditional obligation of providing goods and services for the soldiers. Though never fully implemented, this proclamation was truly radical and was far ahead of its time. The peasants responded eagerly to Za-Dengel's 'call to arms'.[138]

The implementation of Bahrey's ideas enabled Za-Dengel to raise an enormous number of fighters who, in the words of Susenyos' chronicler, were 'as numerous as a swarm of locusts'.[139] Unfortunately for Za-Dengel, he now had more fighting men than he needed, and lacked the organization and necessary logistical support with which to maintain the flow of supplies to this large army. It is one thing to raise an army, but quite another to supply it and maintain its discipline. Za-Dengel's purpose was to use this mass of untrained men against Susenyos and his Oromo supporters, and accordingly he led his followers against them. He crossed the Abbay River and reached the land of Darra in Walaqa. After a short engagement, Susenyos fled with his Oromo supporters. Deeply saddened with the escape of his enemies, Za-Dengel had to content himself with the large herds of cattle he plundered from the Oromo.[140]

While Susenyos was rallying the various Oromo groups against Za-Dengel, the latter made the struggle against the Oromo his battle cry. In this, he became over-ambitious and committed five errors. First,

[135] Bahrey, 'History of the Galla' in *Some Records of Ethiopia*, 125–6.
[136] Chernetsov, 'The "History of the Gallas" and Death of Za-Dengel', 806.
[137] Aregay, 'Southern Ethiopia and the Christian Kingdom', 378.
[138] Ibid., 381.
[139] Pereira, *Chronica de Susenyos*, 52.
[140] Tafla, *Asma Giyorgis and His Work*, 277.

his emancipation of the peasants may have had an immediate impact on the soldiers, who depended on what the peasants produced and on their services. Merid Wolde Aregay believes that 'the peasants not only refused to render the customary domestic services but also made it clear to the soldiers that as tax payers they were no longer obliged to maintain them'.[141]

Second, while Za-Dengel was unaware, on 9 August 1604, the leaders of his large force sent a secret message to Susenyos urging him not to go deep into Oromo territory as they were planning to rebel against Za-Dengel. They justified their planned rebellion on the ground that Za-Dengel deprived them of their servants and caused the peasants to become soldiers.[142]

Third, the news of his letter to the king of Spain and the Pope became known. It became a very powerful weapon in the hands of his enemies and provided the ideological justification for his excommunication. Interestingly, it was Za-Sellassie, the commander of the Qurban soldiers, and the brother-in-law of Za-Dengel, who persuaded

> the Bishop Abuna Petros to release all men, great and small, from their oaths of loyalty to the emperor. The clergy in general was affected by the emancipation of the peasants and the bishop in particular may have been offended when the emperor published his religious proclamations without consulting him.[143]

Once the Orthodox Church establishment turned against Za-Dengel, even Abba Bahrey may have questioned the king's wisdom for abandoning the Ethiopian Orthodox faith. Though Bahrey inspired Za-Dengel's spirited campaign against the Oromo, by his reckless action, the king may have turned against himself even his staunchest supporters such as Abba Bahrey. What is not in doubt is that, by his rash inclination to embrace Catholicism, he either neutralized or diffused his potential supporters who then became indifferent to his cause. Za-Dengel wanted to use Christian nationalism for his grand campaign against the Oromo but he undermined his purpose by accepting Catholicism.

Fourth, by taking the retainers of the lords and constituting them under the command of a new *chawa* (professional soldiers') grouping named Malak Hara, he offended both the lords and the retainers. The lords were offended because by taking away their men he was limiting their power, and the retainers because he gathered them under his own command, but then was unable to provide them with sufficient provisions. His treasury was empty and was not even replenished with tribute from those provinces he controlled. As a result, he was able to rally the retainers to his call by capturing their imagination with his nationalistic propaganda. However, hunger cut deeply into their morale and sapped their support for him. The very men who only a short time

[141] Aregay, 'Southern Ethiopia and the Christian Kingdom', 385–6.
[142] Boavida et al., *Pedro Páez's History of Ethiopia*, vol. 2, 216.
[143] Aregay, 'Southern Ethiopia and the Christian Kingdom', 387.

before had given their full support to Za-Dengel's revolutionary ideas, now began to suspect them.

Fifth, and most importantly, by his overzealous action against the Oromo, Za-Dengel incurred the deep mistrust of his most elite force, the Qurban soldiers. The reason for this disaffection had a lot to do with the campaigns in which they had fought for their king so valiantly. Za-Dengel had led them into Gojjam on a number of expeditions against the Borana and Barentu groups.[144] He had led them across the Abbay River into Walaqa. Although the latter province was under the nominal Christian administration until the beginning of the seventeenth century, by the closing decade of the sixteenth century, 'the effective frontiers of the empire were limited to the Abbay River, with the [Oromo] groups established on the western spurs of the plateau'.[145]

Even during the reign of Sarsa Dengel, especially in the 1590s, the professional soldiers had already become very nervous about crossing the Abbay River to fight against the Oromo. Whenever possible, soldiers resisted crossing the river. Amazingly by the beginning of the seventeenth century, professional soldiers had already started avoiding Oromo warriors even west of the Abbay in Gojjam. Za-Dengel's expedition into Walaqa must have been seen as a reckless act by the Qurban soldiers. What is more, Za-Dengel did not allow his soldiers to loot and plunder his Christian subjects. The soldiers were already used to looting even their fellow Christians, and by refusing them permission, it seemed to the Qurban soldiers that he was encroaching on their rights. The disaffected soldiers found their champion in Za-Sellassie, the famous adventurer. Za-Dengel marched against Za-Sellassie but on his way he was deserted by other noble men of the kingdom and many of their soldiers.

> On the 13th October 1604, the king, after drawing up his army in battle order, placing 200 Portuguese with a number of Abyssinian troops on the right, took to himself the charge of the left. The engagement began with the appearance of great success. On the right, the Portuguese led by old and veteran officers destroyed and overturned everything before them with their firearms, but on the left ... things went ... otherwise. He and his attendants being surrounded by the whole army of Selassie ... were unable to support any longer such disadvantage.[146]

Although Za-Dengel was killed in a gruesome manner on 13 October, he was buried only on 15 October. His death shocked his own Christian population as well as Pedro Páez, who had cautioned him to move slowly about embracing Catholic faith. Grief stricken, Páez wrote the following words about the tragic end of Za-Dengel: 'It was spectacle to be pondered deeply, that he who shortly before had been the emperor of

---

[144] Ludolphus, *A New History of Ethiopia*, 179–80.
[145] Darkwah, *Shewa, Menilek and the Ethiopian Empire*, 4. See also Trimingham, *Islam in Ethiopia*, 94.
[146] Bruce, *Travels to Discover the Source of the Nile*, vol. 3, 267–8.

Ethiopia should be left at the level of the most miserable and hopeless slave who died in the battle'.[147]

The death of Za-Dengel closed a year of ambitious campaigning against the Oromo. It also ended the first attempt at experimenting with Catholic faith by the king. Above all, Za-Dengel's death ended the first dramatic attempt to implement the far-reaching implication of Bahrey's theory of raising a large army. 'Both have outrun their historical time by far, and this was their tragedy. We know nothing of Bahrey's fate, but King Za-Dengel fell on the battlefield for the unity of his motherland like a patriot and a soldier'.[148]

To conclude, in this chapter an attempt has been made to show that Abba Bahrey was a learned monk, a social historian, a court official who adored Sarsa Dengel, and an intellectual driven with a passion against the Oromo. As indicated at the beginning of this chapter, Bahrey's manuscript is simultaneously an historical and an ideological document. Historical because his manuscript was written by a man who was an eye witness to the drama of pastoral Oromo population movement, and victimized by them, a man who was driven from his land losing everything he owned to the Oromo, and yet depicted the social structure of the Oromo society of his time as the foundation of their military victories. It was an ideological treatise because, his manuscript was written with a clear-cut and precise political objective – to educate the elite at the court of Sarsa Dengel on how to overcome the weakness of their society by providing them with his prescription and presenting them with a feasible course of action for harnessing the human and material resources of their society for the purpose of turning the tide against the Oromo. In short, Bahrey's *Zenahu le Galla* appears to have three goals. The first was to educate the elite at the court on the source of Oromo military strength. Second, Bahrey appears to have wanted the elite to turn their society's source of weakness into its strength. Third, he characterized the Oromo as a dangerous enemy to be defeated, and wrote the following prayer for their defeat in 1576.

> Oh Christ, the fountain head of life
> Have mercy on your people, dislodge their enemy
> Gather them from scattering
> The wayward deserves mercy, the beggar a helping hand
> Please do not do to us what the prophets have spoken
> 'Even when they stand in supplication before me
> As the righteous ones of the Old Testament – Noah, Job and Daniel
> I will not forgive this people'
> Even though our sin is heavy
> Heavier than the righteousness of these great ones
> Remember your mother's purity
> For that exceeds everything
> Remember the scars of your hand
> To have mercy on us and to deliver us
> The only Child of God the Father.[149]

[147] Boavida et al., *Pedro Páez's History of Ethiopia*, vol. 2, 181.
[148] Chernetsov, 'The "History of the Gallas" and Death of Za-Dengel', 808.
[149] Haile, *The Works of Abba Bahriy*, 121–2.

Finally, we have seen above the fate of King Za-Dengel, who attempted to implement the far-reaching ideas of Bahrey's manuscript. In the next chapter, we will briefly look at the fate of Abba Bahrey, whose slim manuscript, to a large measure, has shaped for centuries how the Oromo were presented in Ethiopian historiography.

7

The Oromo
and the Christian Kingdom, 1600–1618

In Chapters 4 and 5, we followed the progress of the pastoral Oromo population movement from 1522 to 1597. In this chapter, we continue with their settlement in Gojjam, Begameder and other northern provinces and its impact on the political landscape of the Christian kingdom up to the beginning of the eighteenth century. In this, as in the previous chapters on pastoral Oromo population movement, we follow the *gada* periodization cycle.

The Melbah Gada (1602–10) came to power at the time when power struggle was further weakening the Christian kingdom. After eighty years, during which ten successive *gada*s had carried out, with varying degrees of success, a population movement into the east, north and western parts of what is today Ethiopia, a new cycle of *gada* names now began repeating the same series in the same order. So, as we opened our discussion on pastoral Oromo movement with the Melbah Gada (1522–30), now again, in 1602, we start with another Melbah Gada. However, the distance from Bali where we first started observing the activities of the Melbah Gada in 1522, and the place where the cycle begins again is vast. The Melbah of the Borana and Barentu continued with expansion in several directions. The major advance of this *gada*, and of several subsequent ones, was concentrated on the areas west of the Abbay (the Blue Nile). In the region east of the Abbay River, the Oromo cavalry remained invincible[1] up to the first half of the nineteenth century. In the region west of the Abbay, the Christian kingdom was at its weakest at the beginning of the seventeenth century and the Oromo benefited from their enemy's weakness. As a result a number of pastoral Oromo groups managed to settle both in Gojjam and Begameder.

Tsega Etefa rightly argues that between 1597 and 1607 the 'Oromo attacks on Amhara, Bagameder, [Begameder], Enarya [Ennarya], Gojjam and Walaqa ... were essentially associated with Susenyos'.[2] The

---

[1] Getahun Dilebo, 'Emperor Menelik's Ethiopia, 1865–1916: National Unification or Amhara Communal Domination' (PhD diss., Howard University, Washington DC, 1974), 20–21.

[2] Tsega Etefa, 'Pan-Oromo Confederations in the Sixteenth and Seventeenth Centuries', *Journal of Oromo Studies* 15, 1 (March 2008), 26.

Oromo used Susenyos' firepower to capture *amba*s (fortified mountain tops) in Shawa and Amhara, while Susenyos used Oromo cavalry and foot soldiers for making himself the emperor of the Christian kingdom. It was the same Susenyos who perfected Emperor Sarsa Dengel's policy of settling friendly Oromo groups, both in Gojjam and Begameder and did so much to make them part of the Christian political establishment. The larger part of this chapter is devoted to Susenyos' fighting for the Oromo, his numerous campaigns against the Oromo, his failure at turning the tide against them and his success in turning some Oromo groups into ardent defenders of the Christian kingdom west of the Abbay River. The first section of the chapter deals with Susenyos' struggle for power using Oromo warriors. Without the Oromo warriors and his use of Oromo war strategy, most likely Susenyos would not have come to power. It is to demonstrate precisely this aspect that in this section we discuss his power struggle.

THE BEGINNING OF SUSENYOS' STRUGGLE FOR POWER, 1597–1604, AND THE OROMO

Susenyos was born in 1569 on the vast and rich estate of his father in Gojjam. His father, Fasiladas, was the cousin of Emperor Sarsa Dengel (1563–97). He was a learned man, who was highly respected for his knowledge, wisdom and wealth. Fasiladas' mother, according to the Chronicle of Susenyos, was called Hamalmala Warq. She was the daughter of Azaj Kolo, who was admired for his wealth. Susenyos was the youngest of Fasiladas' five sons. His brothers – Afa Chrestos, Sela, Yamana and Malka – were destined to serve as prominent officials in the government of Susenyos, even though the last two rebelled against their brother during the 1620s because of his religious policy. The universally admired Fasiladas was killed in 1586 on the border of Shawa, while fighting against the Oromo, who also captured his 16-year-old son, Susenyos. In many ways, it was his capture by the Oromo, which catapulted Susenyos onto the political stage.

Susenyos lived in captivity for two years, during which time he was adopted and became the 'son' of a Borana[3] Oromo clan, thus becoming the first Amhara prince to have been adopted by the Oromo. For the Oromo, once adopted, Susenyos was one of them. According to his chronicle, 'the [Oromo] who captured him liked and treated him as his child'.[4] His adoption by and the two-year stay among the Oromo at this formative age clearly and demonstrably had a lasting impact upon him. He was the first Amhara prince who had command of the Oromo language, learned their manners and acquired their fighting

---

[3] The Borana adoption ceremony was undertaken by the Abba Gada on behalf of his *gosa* (clan/confederacy). Once adopted, Susenyos became the 'son' of the group that adopted him. By their adoption criteria, Susenyos was the first Oromo 'son' to be the emperor of the Christian kingdom.

[4] Pereira, *Chronica de Susenyos*, 4.

skill. He was also the first Amhara prince to marry an Oromo woman, a daughter of an influential *gada* official.[5] In the process, Susenyos initiated a tradition of an Amhara prince marrying a woman from an influential Oromo clan, the process by which enterprising Oromo leaders came to dominate the Christian kingdom itself by the middle of the eighteenth century. Above all, Susenyos was the first Amhara prince who discovered first hand the secret of Oromo strength, their effective fighting method, which he adopted and made an integral part of his war strategy, and was followed by his successors. According to the knowledgeable traditional historian Asma Giyorgis, Susenyos 'had learned' Oromo

> language and the history of their great men and knew all the great heroes in whose honour songs were sung. He understood their traditions and their administration of justice ... He had become a good horseman, all well versed in the arts of war. He had killed a lion and wore a Qunco [shaved his head leaving a patch of hair on the top, as per the Oromo custom of a brave warrior].[6]

Susenyos returned from captivity when he was about 18 years of age in 1588, and some of his father's *gult* (estate) in Gojjam was given back to him.[7] He lived on his estate but did not appear to have improved his rudimentary education. 'He could read, and, perhaps, write.'[8] During the next ten years, Susenyos may have visited the court of Sarsa Dengel a number of times. At the court, Susenyos was well known for his courage, physical fitness, fighting skill and knowledge of the Oromo language, customs and the secret of their strength. Although a formidable horseman, a famous swimmer and a great warrior, Susenyos was not admired in the court of Sarsa Dengel. In fact, Susenyos was not considered at first for the throne when Sarsa Dengel died in 1597. Instead, it was the learned and universally admired Za-Dengel, who succeeded to throne. As we saw in Chapter 6, Za-Dengel's succession to the throne was immediately usurped by the Empress Maryam Sena, and her two sons-in-law, Ras Atnatewos, the governor of Amhara and Keflawahd, the governor of Tigray. They replaced Za-Dengel with Ya'eqob, Sarsa Dengel's seven-year-old illegitimate son, because they wanted power for themselves during his regency. Later on, to further consolidate power, the empress added the adventurous Za-Sellassie to the triumvirate. However, even before the young Ya'eqob was put on the throne, the empress and her sons-in-law, sent 'a large army, including 25 riflemen'[9] to seize Susenyos. But the adventurous prince escaped from a death trap and fled to and stayed among the Oromo in Walaqa for months.

[5] Harold Marcus, *A History of Ethiopia* (Berkeley, CA: University of California Press, 1994), 39.
[6] Tafla, *Asma Giorgis and His Work*, 187.
[7] Ibid.
[8] Aregay, 'Southern Ethiopia and the Christian Kingdom', 395.
[9] Tafla, *Asma Giorgis and His Work*, 189.

THE CHRONICLE OF SUSENYOS

At this point in our discussion, it is relevant to mention the activities of Susenyos, the man who had lived among the Oromo for a number of years, fought for them several times, and fought against them more than any Christian king fought prior to the beginning of the nineteenth century. No other Amhara prince or warlord served the Oromo cause as much as Susenyos did. With his firepower, he helped various Oromo groups in penetrating the Christian strongholds in the provinces of Walaqa, Gojjam, Shawa and Amhara. Our main source for Susenyos' history is his own chronicle of more than ninety chapters.[10] The largest of its kind, it contains very important geographical literature. It also contains information on the names of the rivers Susenyos crossed, the hills he ascended and the slopes he descended, all of which were undertaken either in flight from his enemies or in pursuit of them, or in his effort to raise taxes (for that was how he rewarded his loyal servants and punished disloyal elements). It also relates how he administered the country through his close relatives, how he abandoned the idea of fighting the Oromo east of the Abbay River, and how he even settled a large number of Oromo clans on the western side of the Abbay River in Gojjam,[11] as the safest bulwark against the attack of their own brethren. All of this is an important data for the study of government in the seventeenth-century Christian kingdom. For our purpose, its chief importance lies in the fact that it contains the most detailed account of campaigns against the Oromo.

The writers of Susenyos' voluminous chronicle were two: Abba Mehereka Dengel, the confessor of Empress Maryam Sena, wrote the first part of the chronicle.[12] The second and larger part was written by Azaj Tino ('chief steward' Takla Sellassie). Interestingly, Tino was the confident and the 'principal secretary'[13] of Emperor Susenyos. He was among the top dignitaries at court of Susenyos who embraced Catholicism and became one of its ardent defenders.[14] Azaj Tino appears to have known the Oromo society, its language and culture. As indicated in Chapter 1, Azaj Tino probably belonged to the second generation of converted Oromo. Most likely his father may have been among the first generation of Oromo, who were settled by Sarsa Dengel, either in Gojjam or Begameder. What is for certain is that Azaj Tino was brought up in a Christian household and was provided with the best Christian education. His mastery of and eloquence in the Geez language, suggests that he was highly educated man (this is confirmed by Pedro

---

[10]   I am indebted to Haile Larebo for his translation of the relevant sections of Susenyos' Chronicle from Geez into English.

[11]   Tafla, *Asma Giyorgis and His Work*, 281.

[12]   Aregay, 'Southern Ethiopia and the Christian Kingdom', 357.

[13]   Boavida et al., *Pedro Páez's History of Ethiopia*, vol. 1, 34.

[14]   Ibid, vol. 2, 259. See also Bartnicki and Mantel-Niećko, 'The Role and Significance of the Religious Conflicts and People's Movements in the Political Life of Ethiopia', 29.

Páez).[15] He was also the most knowledgeable person about the Oromo society of his time. We have already said that Azaj Tino's representation of Oromo history is radically different from that of Bahrey (see pages 75–6). The latter dated the ingress of the Oromo into the Christian kingdom as 1522. Tino does not set Oromo origin outside of the Christian kingdom. He makes Lalo their father and Dawaro 'his original home'. However, one thing remains certain. Tino's central thesis that establishes the presence of some Oromo groups within the Christian kingdom, even as early as the thirteenth century, is not disputed, and in fact there is ample evidence to support it as we have seen above in Chapters 2 and 3. In this way, Azaj Tino's contribution towards refuting the fallacious claim about the sudden arrival of the Oromo in the sixteenth century is quite invaluable.

Azaj Tino, who seems to have been impressed by the Oromo belief in one Waaqa (the Oromo God), describes the Oromo Abba Muudaa (ritual leader) in glowing terms. According to Tino, all Oromo go to Abba Muudaa, from far and near, to receive his blessings for victory. This blessing is contained in the form of myrrh, on which he spat his saliva, and distributed it to the delegates. The delegates brought back this treasure to their respective clans, who used the blessings of the spiritual father in their war against their adversaries. His blessings were associated with success in warfare,[16] and therein lies the ideological role of the Abba Muudaa in the great war of pastoral Oromo population movement. In this sense the Abba Muudaa represented the ideological fountainhead that generated the spur for conquest, and he interpreted success or failure in terms of their willingness to stick to his advice in their daily life. The kernel of his advice consisted in the dictum, 'do not fight among yourselves'.[17] By the first half of the seventeenth century, this advice was more honoured in its breach than in its observance.

A constant theme throughout the chronicle is the fact that warfare was at the centre of Susenyos' life. His was an exuberant nature, endlessly appreciative of, and delighting in, every war situation. Pedro Páez accurately states that Susenyos was 'experienced in matters of war, because he has spent most of his life in it'.[18] According to his chronicler, he was a warrior in the highest degree, brigand by necessity, and self-made emperor. Even after making himself the emperor, 'Susenyos's long reign was a period of incessant warfare'.[19] The chronicle does not omit even some of the emperor's profoundly shocking barbarity, graphically expressing that he executed his wars with a thoroughness and cold-bloodedness of a monster. Such a depiction probably was not an exaggeration. As will be shown further in

[15] Boavida et al., *Pedro Páez's History of Ethiopia*, vol. 2, 259.
[16] Pereira, *Chronica de Susenyos*, 214.
[17] Ibid.
[18] Boavida et al., *Pedro Páez's History of Ethiopia*, vol. 2, 204.
[19] Caraman, Philip, *The Lost Empire: The Story of the Jesuits in Ethiopia, 1555–1634* (Notre Dame IN: University of Notre Dame Press, 1985), 58.

this chapter and the next, Susenyos even attempted to build a hill with Oromo skulls. As horrifying as such a tale is, the shocking part is the accounts of the endless pillaging, looting and massacring of the weak 'pagan' minorities. Of all the successes and victories attributed to Susenyos, and celebrated in this chronicle, his repeated victories over various Agaw groups and the Oromo constitute a consistent thread, the ideal most manifestly embraced. In the end, according to what is mentioned in his chronicle, defeat by the Oromo, or victory by Susenyos, turned out to be equally ruinous to the peasantry.[20]

SUSENYOS' POLITICAL HISTORY

Susenyos' political history begins with the death of Sarsa Dengel in 1597 and his escape to Walaqa. While he was there, the Kano group of the Borana sub-moiety attacked the province, under their Abba Gada (leader) named Buko,[21] who was to become the highest-ranking official of Oromo origin in Susenyos' future government. It was among this same group that the latter lived during the years of his captivity. As an adopted 'son', he was treated with kindness. For his alertness, vibrant personality, energy and enthusiasm in warfare, boldness and courage in the face of danger and quality of leadership, he was much admired by Oromo warriors. The various Oromo warriors who wanted to capture the Christian mountain-top strongholds found in him an able and ruthless leader who knew well how to lead attacks against such. It was for this reason that Merid Wolde Aregay describes him as a condottiere 'who proved useful to the various [Oromo] tribes whom he served. He helped the Afre tribes against the strongholds in Walaqa and Gojam and against the Gafat and the Shenacha.'[22]

As the first Amhara prince to be adopted by the Oromo, Susenyos enjoyed all the available privileges and protection among the Oromo in Walaqa. With Oromo support, Susenyos declared open rebellion, plundered the tribute that was going to the royal treasury and started exacting his own tribute from the Christian peasants in Walaqa. It appears that the Oromo wanted to use the adventurous Amhara prince for the purpose of moving into both Gojjam and Dambiya,[23] while Susenyos wanted to use Oromo warriors for his rise to power. Empress Maryam Sena and her two sons-in-laws sent Be'ela Chrestos, the governor of Gojjam, with a large army to capture or kill Susenyos in Walaqa. At the head of all the Oromo warriors Susenyos fought fiercely against Be'ela Chrestos, 'but neither was victorious. The latter crossed into Goggam [Gojjam] while Susenyos went over to Dabra Libanos where the monks received him with honour.'[24] From there Susenyos went

[20] Pereira, *Chronica de Susenyos*, 106, 235–6.
[21] Ibid., 44–49.
[22] Aregay, 'Southern Ethiopia and the Christian Kingdom', 439.
[23] Tafla, *Asma Giyorgis and His Work*, 191.
[24] Ibid.

'to his Oromo allies in western Shawa'.[25] Susenyos' alertness, quick action, self-reliance, intrepid spirit and instinct for self-preservation, all of which he acquired during his captivity among the Oromo, saved him from capture or death as they would save him time and again from imminent danger in the future. During the years (1588–97) when Susenyos lived on his father's estate, he had already distinguished himself as a fighter in his war against the Oromo in Gojjam. He assisted Be'ela Chrestos, the governor of Gojjam, 'in defeating the [Oromo] who had overrun that province, and by his courage and conduct that day had left strong impression on the minds of the troops'.[26]

It was the same governor of Gojjam that Susenyos fought against with his Oromo warriors in Walaqa. Considering his apparently capricious behaviour and sudden change of sides, it is quite evident that Susenyos was a very different man from Za-Dengel. The latter was committed to waging war against the Oromo, while the former was helping the Oromo. His opinion on everything varied and changed rapidly with the state of his mind. He had espoused the idea of helping the governors of Gojjam and Walaqa. But Susenyos soon changed not only his ideas, but also his loyalties, and joined the Oromo in attacking the provinces for which he had just been fighting. After 1597, the constant factor in Susenyos was lust for power. Unlike Za-Dengel, who was an intellectual with a good knowledge of history of his society, Susenyos lacked much on the intellectual side before he ascended the throne in 1607. He was ruthless towards both his Christian subjects and Oromo enemies. Among those who were devastated during the years of Susenyos' banditry were the non-Christian Gafat people in western Shawa and Walaqa. Susenyos and his soldiers killed people, burned their houses, captured cattle, and

> broke into a stronghold called Yazambal that belonged to the Gafat and where a great store of wealth was found. Then he camped at Mugar and fought the Gafat called Asama [four Gafat tribes joined their forces] ... and showered their poisonous arrows on him like hail. After bitter fighting he crossed over and camped in Walaqa. He attacked the Abadray and the Gambo, and plundered them and seized all they possessed ... He annihilated those called Den and all the Gafat. The few that survived crossed into [Gojjam].[27]

Through his plunder and merciless attack Susenyos forced the various Gafat groups to abandon their land and flee across the Abbay into Gojjam, clearing the land in western Shawa and Walaqa for the Oromo (see Map 11, page 210). In short, Susenyos subjected both allies and enemies to his own ends. His two backgrounds, his father's estate in Gojjam, and his long banditry, combined to make him the man he was. The Gojjam estate was under heavy Oromo attack even before the death of his father in 1586, and it was there that he received the

[25] Etefa, 'Pan-Oromo Confederations in the Sixteenth and Seventeenth Centuries', 25.

[26] Bruce, *Travels to Discover the Source of the Nile*, vol. 3, 259.

[27] Tafla, *Asma Giyorgis and His Work*, 199.

first training in the art of the sword, which was perfected during his two years (1586–8) stay with the Oromo. From 1597 to 1603 Susenyos raided and plundered several provinces. He used his Oromo warriors for forcing the Christian peasants to submit to him.[28] The following is a typical example of how he used Oromo warriors to force the Christians in Manz to submit and pay tribute to him. Susenyos led a very large number of Tulama Oromo warriors to Manz in northern Shawa.

> But when the people of Manz saw the size of his army-indeed the Teloma [Tulama] were as numerous as the sands of the sea-they trembled before him and submitted to him thinking, 'He will bring in the [Tulama] and make them settle at our river, take away our country and force us to cross into [Gojjam], for he previously made our brothers, the Gafat, cross over into [Gojjam]. They paid tribute to him and used all the arts of persuasion and he sent the [Tulama] back to Belat and so they returned complaining of not being allowed to plunder, kill, devastate, and take over the country.[29]

While Susenyos camped with his Oromo warriors in Walaqa, he was approached by Malaka Chrestos, to reconcile himself with King Ya'eqob and the powerful men who controlled the young king's government. Malaka Chrestos, 'maternal half-brother' of Susenyos, was sent by Empress Maryam Sena, Atnatewos and Keflawahd, the three most dominant king makers of the time and Za-Sellassie, the commander of the notorious Qurban regiment. By opening negotiations with Susenyos, the most powerful officials probably wanted Susenyos to abandon using Oromo warriors for destroying what was left of the Christian kingdom. Susenyos responded favourably to the call for abandoning the Oromo warriors. 'I agree, I have no objection. If [Ya'eqob] gives me the whole of [Shawa] and the rest of my father's [estate in Gojjam], I shall be reconciled with him and abandon the [Oromo] army.' However, the powerful officials, who initiated negotiation with Susenyos rejected his demand, most probably because they did not want to give him all his father's estate in Gojjam. They were willing to give him Shawa, which after all, was not under effective Christian administration. Susenyos was not willing to abandon his father's estates in Gojjam, in return for the unrealizable dream of taming the Oromo and establishing his full control in Shawa. Deeply disappointed with the rejection of his demand, Susenyos mobilized huge numbers of Barentu Oromo warriors and marched 'to the land of Amhara, which he devastated and laid waste'.[30]

The removal of Ya'eqob from power and his replacement by Za-Dengel in 1603 created a conducive environment for Susenyos struggle for power. This was because some officials of Ya'eqob who feared Za-Dengel's reprisal fled and joined Susenyos' campus east of the Abbay River. Even Be'ela Chrestos, the brother of Za-Dengel, who earlier fought against Susenyos, fled to the camp of the adventurous prince. Emboldened with this turn of events and relying on his Oromo warriors, Susenyos 'crossed

[28] Ibid., 193, 197.
[29] Tafla, *Asma Giyorgis and His Work*, 245.
[30] Ibid., 245, 247.

into [Gojjam] and devastated it. He crossed a second time and laid waste half of [it] from the Suha River to the Cu River. He returned and made his camp at Darra' east of the Abbay River. When Za-Dengel 'heard how Susenyos had twice crossed into [Gojjam] and devastated it and how powerful he had become, he shook his head and was filled with wrath'.[31] In fact, it was Susenyos' devastation of Gojjam and his growing power that forced Za-Dengel to follow Susenyos across the Abbay to Darra in 1603. With his large force, Za-Dengel nearly defeated Susenyos and his intrepid Oromo warriors. However, using the cover of 'heavy rainfall and hail',[32] the adventurous prince and his Oromo warriors, escaped and saved themselves from destruction. Za-Dengel was deeply saddened because he was unable to kill Susenyos and destroy his Oromo allies. Although Za-Dengel was unable to eliminate the threat from Susenyos, what he did achieve was plundering Oromo cattle[33] and exhausting and alienating his huge force. Shortly after Za-Dengel was brutally killed by his own elite soldiers. Those who engineered the death of Za-Dengel, even planned the unthinkable radical idea of abolishing the institution of monarchy.

> Henceforth let us no longer be ruled in the name of a king; let no bastards rule over us; let us continue in our respective positions and provinces; let us have liberty; to consult among ourselves and give judgment as the [Oromo] do, with [their Abba Gada and *chaffee* assembly].They concluded this agreement.[34]

The above statement is quoted by Asma Giyorgis from the pen of Azaj Tino, who wrote the greater part of the Chronicle of Susenyos. It was a remarkable admission on his part to openly state that the non-Christian Oromo, enjoyed more political liberty than his own Christian society of the time. This was because among the Christians all important issues were decided upon by the king, who was also the source of the law and above the law. In contrast to the Christian society, the Oromo were able to discuss every important issues through their *chaffee* assembly, including, but not limited to, declaration of war and conclusion of peace, making of laws and adoption of non-Oromos, all based on the consensus of those who participated in the assembly deliberation. In the above statement Azaj Tino reflects his profound understanding of Oromo political culture of his time.

EMPEROR SUSENYOS, 1604: THE FIRST PHASE AND THE OROMO

As we noted in the previous chapter, the tragic death of Za-Dengel was brought about by the rebellion of his own soldiers known as Qurban.

[31] Ibid., 273–5.
[32] Etefa, 'Pan-Oromo Confederations in the Sixteenth and Seventeenth Centuries', 27.
[33] Tafla, *Asma Giyorgis and His Work*, 277.
[34] Ibid., 279.

One cause of that rebellion was Za-Dengel's spirited war against the Oromo. The commander of the Qurban soldiers was Za-Sellassie, an enterprising warlord, who was notorious for changing his loyalty for or against the person on the throne. Za-Dengel, who wanted to use the military talent and his leadership of the Qurban soldiers for his cause, not only freed and brought back Za-Sellassie from exile in Ennarya, but also 'appointed him over Dambiya and Wagara, [and] even gave him his sister in marriage, hoping thereby to attach him closer to himself'. [35] Ironically, it was Za-Sellassie himself, who administered the final deathblow to Za-Dengel, not only betraying his brother-in-law but also causing his death, thereby demonstrating his ultimate perfidy. Za-Dengel's premature death was followed by an interregnum, that lasted from 13 October to 13 December 1604, the longest period when the Christian kingdom existed without its monarchic institution. Once Susenyos heard about the death of Za-Dengel, he wrote the following bold letter to Ras Atnatewos, the governor of Gojjam.

> I am coming. Receive me so that you may crown me, for the throne of my fathers has become vacant and remained empty without a king ... It is proper now that you crown me. I did not previously desire the vacant throne of my ancestors, but wished for the [estate] of my father with [Shawa] so that I might live by working and farming. But now I am coming; receive me, and do not try to fabricate any excuses. [36]

Susenyos quickly mobilized his Oromo and Amhara warriors and crossed the Abbay River and arrived in Gojjam. He wanted to back up his claim to the throne with a show of force on the ground. While crossing the Abbay River, Susenyos met the Liban Oromo from among whom about 400 *qeerroo* (the best cavalry) joined him on his march on Gojjam. Ras Atnatewos 'met [Susenyos] as required and joined his army ... and saluted him king' in the midst of repeated cheerful congratulations of both armies, now united. [37] After seven years on the run, Susenyos sat on the Christian throne, with the backing of the Oromo, whom he made *chawa* (professional soldiers) in Gojjam. [38] He was crowned on 14 December 1604 in the presence of several dignitaries, including the famous writer, Abba Bahrey. What Abba Bahrey wanted to achieve by supporting Susenyos, instead of Ya'eqob, the son of Sarsa Dengel, whom Bahrey adored, is not clear from the sources. What is clear is that Bahrey had to run from the sword of the unscrupulous prince (see below). Shortly after the coronation, Za-Sellasie and the Qurban soldiers asked Susenyos to lay down the crown in favour of Ya'eqob. [39] Za-Sellassie promised Susenyos that if Ya'eqob does not show up by June 1605 they will swear an oath of loyalty to

---

[35] Aregay, 'Southern Ethiopia and the Christian Kingdom', 372.
[36] Ibid., 279–81.
[37] Bruce, *Travels to Discover the Source of the Nile*, vol. 3, 271.
[38] Tafla, *Asma Giyorgis and His Work*, 201.
[39] Aregay, 'Southern Ethiopia and the Christian Kingdom', 390.

him. In response Susenyos sent the following message to Za-Sellassie with firm determination.

> You tell me to wait until June and give up the crown of empire if my cousin [Ya'eqob] comes back. Not if he comes back, I say, but even if Emperor [Sarsa Dengel] who was the greatest of all, were raised from the dead, I would not give up the command that God has given me or take off the crown that He has placed on my head.[40]

Susenyos marched from Amhara with his huge Oromo and Amhara warriors to Begameder and devastated the land.[41] And yet he was defeated by Za-Sellassie's party. Amazingly when Ya'eqob failed to show up, Za-Sellassie sided with Atnatewos and all the dignitaries swore on behalf of everyone under excommunication to die with Susenyos and never to accept any other lord.[42]

Rarely did fortune change so dramatically for Susenyos from jubilation to disgust when 'those who ate oaths like bread and drank excommunication like wine'[43] deserted him. They included Atnatewos,[44] who first crowned him on 14 December 1604. With the support of Za-Sellassie and his Qurban soldiers, Ya'eqob was enthroned for the second time. Ya'eqob repaid his indebtedness to Za-Sellassie by making him governor of Gojjam as well as first minister.

KING YA'EQOB, 1604–1607

With Ya'eqob's second return to power Susenyos was abandoned by all his erstwhile Amhara allies, including his own brothers,[45] and resumed his 'old occupation. He began to help the various [Oromo groups] in reducing strongholds throughout Shawa, Walaqa and Amhara.'[46] Susenyos had to flee to Amhara where a large force of Karrayu Oromo from the clans of Bila and Jelle (Jille) joined him. Though his people rejected him, Susenyos became a hero among the Oromo, who clearly used his leadership for the purpose of defeating and occupying the provinces of Gojjam and Begameder. When Susenyos fled into the Oromo territory across the Abbay, he did not renounce his claim to the throne. This means that, in effect, there were two kings, one on the throne and the other in exile among his Oromo and Amhara supporters.

---

[40] Boavida et al., *Pedro Páez's History of Ethiopia*, vol. 2, 218.
[41] Tafla, *Asma Giyorgis and His Work*, 287.
[42] Broavida et al., *Pedro Páez's History of Ethipia*, vol. 2, 189.
[43] Ibid., 220.
[44] Tafla, *Asma Giyorgis and His Work*, 281.
[45] Pereira, *Chronica de Susenyos*, 75–7. For instance, Susenyos requested his brother Yamana Chrestos not to leave him when Ya'eqob threatened to march on Susenyos. The latter is reported in the chronicle to have said: '"Please, do not abandon me, my brother and the son of my mother." But Yamana Krestos said to him "It is impossible for me to be with you." After this exchange of talk, they separated, and each went his own way.'
[46] Aregay, 'Southern Ethiopia and the Christian Kingdom', 392.

Abba Bahrey also fled across the Abbay with his followers and camped on the *amba* (fortified mountain top) of Badabaj in or near the region of Manz.[47] Ironically, it was the same Susenyos who besieged Bahrey on his fortified *amba*. Sensing the sword of Susenyos falling on his neck, Bahrey abandoned his fortified mountain top, probably in 1605. That was the last time Bahrey was mentioned in the literature of the time.

As an exiled emperor and an adopted 'son' Susenyos was popular among the Oromo. Adventurous Oromo warriors flooded to Susenyos' domain and within a short time outnumbered his Amhara followers. His standard became their standard, the noise of his drum their incitement for action. His oratory in their language made him their natural leader.[48] Once the Oromo accepted him, Susenyos started taxing the indigenous peasants in Walaqa. From the latter province he went to Debra Selalo, where famine forced his followers to abandon him. What attracted different Oromo and Amhara groups around him was the prospect of rich booty. When that hope dwindled, time and again, all but a few intimate friends deserted him. From Debra Selalo, he went to Mugar, where he impressed some Oromo fighters that soon flocked to his standard. With his new followers, he pillaged Christian peasants on fortified *ambsa* (flat mountaintops) in Shawa and returned to Walaqa, where he mercilessly looted a large commercial caravan. As indicated earlier, Susenyos forced the Gafat people to abandon their country of Amonat to seek refugee across the Abbay in Gojjam. Once the Gafat were driven out of their land, 'the country became a wasteland'.[49] Shortly after, Oromo pastoralists settled in the land of Amonat. When the Amhara peasants on fortified mountain tops in Shawa revolted against him, he surprised them with his large force of Oromo warriors. At the very sight of his Oromo followers, the peasants fell into submission.[50] This brings to the fore a key element in his policy. Whenever and wherever the Christian peasants revolted against him he attacked them with his Oromo fighters and settled those fighters in the territory of the peasants. The strong suspicion, enmity and deep prejudices that divided the Oromo and the Christians created situations so tense and explosive that on the slightest pretext the Oromo warriors would loot and massacre the peasants. This gradually evolved into a government policy for settling Oromo warriors on the land of his Christian enemies.

In the words of the chronicle, the Christians would submit to him 'after they had seen the massacre of their children, the death of their friends, the enslavement of their women, destruction of their property and rustling of their animals'.[51] It seems that Susenyos forced the Christian peasants into submission by repeatedly holding up before their eyes the spectre of settling among them Oromo warriors. This was his notorious policy to 'divide and destroy' all opposition. It had

[47] Crawford, *Ethiopian Itineraries circa 1400–1524*, 54.

[48] Tafla, *Asma Giyorgis and His Work*, 197.

[49] Ibid., 325.

[50] Ibid., 325. See also Pereira, *Chronica de Susenyos*, 44–49.

[51] Pereira, *Chronica de Susenyos*, 60.

another side to it. Once Susenyos established himself on the throne, a large part of his followers became Amhara soldiers. He played on their fear and enmity of the Oromo, and with them he successfully managed to contain the Oromo takeover of Gojjam and Begameder.[52]

In 1605 Susenyos went to Amhara province with a large army of Barentu Oromo warriors. The Christian governor of the province fled to Walaqa, where Susenyos followed him, destroying many of the fortified mountain-top strongholds with his Barentu followers. From there, he went to Ennarya,[53] where he was defeated, and then went to Gurage, from where he went on to Enamore, where all except two of his followers deserted him. It was during these years that the adventurer prince learned to live without bitterness with the changing fortunes of war. 'Susenyos ... never felt ashamed of his defeat nor proud of his victory he understood that he has his day, as others, in turn, have their days'.[54]

Susenyos was soon joined by the Wallo Oromo, who desired to occupy Begameder. While these happy events gradually accumulated for Susenyos, Ya'eqob tried to make peace with him. He employed Susenyos' mother in 'an application to her with an offer of peace and friendship; promising besides that he would give him ... Amhara, Walaqa and Shoa, and all lands that his father had ever possessed in any other part of Abyssinia'.[55] In this peace offering (with the exception of Susenyos' father's estate in eastern Gojjam), Ya'eqob was not actually giving anything to Susenyos. Nobody knew better than Susenyos, who had travelled and lived in the three provinces, that none of them were under the effective control of Christian administration anyway. In essence Ya'eqob was making Susenyos king over the lost provinces. Susenyos knew this very well. He wanted to be the king of the Christian kingdom in its proper place across the Abbay. Accordingly, Susenyos answered Ya'eqob 'that what God had given him no man could take away from him; that the whole kingdom belong to him, nor would he ever relinquish any part of it but with his life'.[56]

In early 1606 when various Oromo warriors joined him, according to Pedro Páez, Susenyos was overjoyed, but without trusting them too much.[57] It was at that point that Emperor Ya'eqob decided to deal with Susenyos and his Oromo allies once and for all. When Ya'eqob arrived with huge force to attack him, Susenyos saved himself and his men by fleeing. Susenyos requested his Brother Yamana Chrestos to accompany him. He 'insisted so much that he even kissed his hand and took hold of his foot, saying, "Do not leave me, my brother. If you go, who will accompany me?"'[58] Yamana Chrestos refused to accompany

[52] Tafla, *Asma Giyorgis and His Work*, 311.
[53] Hassen, *The Oromo of Ethiopia*, 52–3.
[54] Pereira, *Chronica de Susenyos*, 27–30.
[55] Bruce, *Travels to Discover the Source of the Nile*, vol. 3, 274.
[56] Ibid. See also Tafla, *Asma Giyorgis and His Work*, 287–9.
[57] Boavida et al., *Pedro Páez's History of Ethiopia*, vol. 2, 221.
[58] Ibid.

his brother. Unfortunately, three days later Yaman Chrestos himself was disastrously defeated by Za-Sellassie and 'escaped with just a few servants, losing all the horses and mules that he had.'[59] In February 1606, Ya'eqob's general Za-Sellassie, with his Amhara followers, met Susenyos, with his mainly Oromo followers, at the field of the latter's choice. In the words of the chronicler, 'Susenyos organized his army like that of the [Oromo *chibbra*, Amharic] *chifra* fighting system. But neither the army of Za-Sellassie, nor any of the Amhara at that time knew anything about the *chifra* fighting method. They used to mix up like people in a market place',[60] which meant that they were not organized like the Oromo warfare. The *chiffra* fighting method was organized in such a way that all warriors advanced in a great line of six to a dozen ranks deep, so that, without confusion or panic, the first who fell were immediately replaced by other fighters who continue to advance with great courage and launch audacious attacks that unnerves the enemy. Choice of place and time, speed in attack and retreat, blood curdling battle cries when charging, and coordination in attack were all integral parts of the *chiffra* system. By adopting it, Susenyos improved coordination and the capacity of his army to attack rapidly, or retreat in time. These changes enhanced his capacity to surprise his enemies. The effect was rapid and quite dramatic. Susenyos, who 'had spent most of his formative years in banditry, an occupation in which an agile mind and strong arms are indispensable',[61] attacked Za-Sellassie

> while in the pass so rudely that his axes entangled in broken ground ... [he] was surrounded and almost cut to pieces. Za-Sellassie, with a few followers, saved themselves by the goodness of their horses and joined the king, being the first messengers of their own defeat.[62]

Instead of helping the defeated Za-Sellasie, Ya'eqob humiliated him thus creating division within his own camp. Besides the huge booty he captured from Za-Sellassie, Susenyos' opportunity for defeating Ya'eqob improved greatly when a large number of Oromo warriors, who 'thought victory was certain' came to help him. Susenyos 'also saw victory was certain with their help, but he said in his heart, "After I have defeated Emperor [Ya'eqob] these men will fall on me and kill me, and they will be left as the lords of the lands."'[63] Simmering suspicious between Susenyos and Oromo warriors would later develop into intermittent warfare between them. Three short weeks after Susenyos defeated Za-Sellassie, he forced Ya'eqob to repeat the blunder of Za-Sellassie by falling into a trap fighting on the battle field chosen by the adventurous prince. Susenyos' mainly Oromo warriors, his choice of the battlefield and his *chiffra* fighting method combined to defeat Ya'eqob. The unfortunate and inexperienced young king 'blamed his captain for [his own

---

[59] Ibid.
[60] Pereira, *Chronica de Susenyos*, 79.
[61] Aregay, 'Southern Ethiopia and the Christian Kingdom', 545.
[62] Bruce, *Travels to Discover the Source of the Nile,* vol. 3, 275.
[63] Boavida et al., *Pedro Páez's History of Ethiopia*, vol. 2, 221.

defeat] and went so far as to order the execution of a few'.[64] Ya'eqob's irra-tional behaviour provided timely justification for Za-Sellassie once again to change sides. From Gojjam, where he was viceroy, Za-Sellassie sent a secret message of friendship to Susenyos, pledging his loyalty to him as emperor, which greatly pleased him.[65] Then Susenyos joined Za-Sellassie in Gojjam. After avoiding the final blow with Ya'eqob for months, on 10 March 1607, Susenyos, at a mature age of thirty-five, met Ya'eqob's depleted and demoralized forces, at an ideal battlefield of his own choice. What followed was written by Azaj Tino, as reported by Pedro Páez.

> As they began to fight, the Turks who were with Emperor [Ya'eqob] fired ... [but] only killed one man. [Susenyos] then attacked with his men ... with such great fury that he soon turned Emperor [Ya'eqob's] men, and they fell before his face ...like locusts falling into the sea.[66]

On that fateful day several principal political and religious leaders, including Ya'eqob and Abuna Petros, the Patriarch of the Ethiopian Orthodox Church, were killed. Ras Atnatewos, who fought on the side of Emperor Ya'eqob, 'escaped and went to enter the monastery of Dima, and took monks as mediators. Afterwards, [Ras Sela Chrestos] took him to his brother [Susenyos], and made him pardon him and he also pardoned all those who had escaped from the battle.' Fortunately for Susenyos, Empress Maryam Sena died while Susenyos was celebrating his victory over Ya'eqob. Even though Susenyos temporarily left Za-Sellassie in his position of power as the governor of Gojjam, he soon discovered that the ungrateful warlord 'intended to rise up against him, as he had against two previous emperors, and he commanded his men to seize him and hold him under guard'.[67] After a year in detention, the adventurous warlord escaped from his confinement only to be killed either by the Oromo who were attacking Gojjam at that time or 'the peasants and soldiers of a Gojam village that he and his followers tried to plunder'.[68] The death of Za-Sellassie must have brought a sigh of relief to the emperor. 'His head was sent to Susenyos, who fastened it on a lance for all to see.'[69] This means that, by the time Susenyos came to power for the second time in 1607, all the most powerful officials who could have become his implac-able enemies were dead, neutralized or removed from the political stage.

EMPEROR SUSENYOS, 1607–1632: THE SECOND PHASE AND THE OROMO

With the death of Ya'eqob, and his principal political and religious officers, the short period of dual kingship came to an end. The problem

[64] Aregay, 'Southern Ethiopia and the Christian Kingdom', 394.
[65] Boavida et al., *Pedro Páez's History of Ethiopia*, vol. 2, 223.
[66] Ibid., 224.
[67] Ibid., 225–6.
[68] Aregay, 'Southern Ethiopia and the Christian Kingdom', 398–9.
[69] Caraman, *The Lost Empire*, 57.

of succession resolved, Susenyos adopted several policies with which he intended to consolidate his hold on power. First, in acknowledgement of Oromo support, Susenyos settled several Oromo groups, both from the Barentu and Borana moieties, in Gojjam and Begameder. 'They were so numerous that Susenyos had to confiscate church land to satisfy his Oromo allies, which highly angered the clergy.'[70] While settling his Oromo allies in the heart of the Christian kingdom, Susenyos turned against other Oromo who wanted to conquer and occupy both Gojjam and Begameder. The Oromo quickly realized that Susenyos had betrayed them and they decided to remove him from power. According to Asma Giyorgis, 'those of the [Oromo] who favored Susenyos remained with him but the rest decided to oppose him. [Those who opposed him] decided to overthrow him once and for all.'[71] For that purpose the Oromo appear to have adopted two policies against Susenyos. The Oromo provided support to pretenders to the throne and those Christian elements who opposed Susenyos for various reasons. It is believed that within the 'first two years of Susenyos's reign sixteen or eighteen pretenders were proclaimed emperor in the various parts of the country'.[72] Many of those pretenders sought and received support from various Oromo groups. The Oromo goal in supporting the pretenders appears to have been to weaken and destabilize Susenyos' government. For instance, in 1608, the Oromo groups who conquered and settled in Angot and Amhara provided support for 'a pretender of Amba Geshan',[73] foreshadowing the massive Oromo involvement in Christian affairs during the 1620s and after. More importantly, the Oromo formed a number of confederacies that conducted spirited warfare against Susneyos for several years. Their immediate goal was to overthrow him, while their ultimate objective was to occupy both Gojjam and Begameder. In response to the Oromo challenge, Susenyos adopted a very aggressive policy towards his Oromo enemies.

His aggressive policy was a political expediency, dictated by the circumstances. It was common knowledge to all the Christians in the kingdom that Susenyos came to the throne with massive Oromo support. 'The indiscriminate pillaging committed by Susenyos'[74] during the years of his banditry was still fresh in the minds of Christian peasantry. Additionally, there was a sense of deep fear among the Christians as to why Susenyos settled such large numbers of friendly Oromo both in Gojjam and Begameder. The presence of large Oromo groups in his army, after his grasping for power, intensified the Christian suspicion and fear. In order to allay their fears and dilute opposition, Susenyos had to demonstrate his concern for defending the country by initiating a relentless attack on the Oromo. Few Amhara kings of the

---

[70] Etefa, 'Pan-Oromo Confederations in the Sixteenth and Seventeenth Centuries', 28.
[71] Tafla, *Asma Giyorgis and His Work*, 311.
[72] Aregay, 'Southern Ethiopia and the Christian Kingdom', 396.
[73] Ibid., 513.
[74] Ibid.

century had been more driven by the desire to 'recover territory lost [to] the [Oromo]' at best,[75] or to make them loyal subjects at worst, than Susenyos. He was an irritable, impatient and at times a sadistic man, whose mind was obsessed with the need to provide sufficient provisions for his troops. For him warfare and the welfare of his troops were organically linked. As we shall see further in this and the next chapter, it was through warfare that Susenyos plundered resources with which he bought the loyalty of his soldiers. That was why he took full responsibility for warfare and for the welfare of his troops.[76] He knew he was a self-made man, who during the years of his banditry had been wretchedly poor at times,[77] yet managed to keep followers around himself precisely because he was always able to provide for them in some way. After he came to the throne, he was obsessed with the same thing. Now there was a surge of interest and hope that the shattered empire might reconstruct itself, that order and stability might be restored and that revenue would flow again. As the following discussion will show, his wars with the Oromo and embroilment with all sorts of internal opposition[78] shattered all that hope.

Even though, a day after the death of Ya'eqob, Susenyos had him buried with honour,[79] rumour quickly spread that Ya'eqob 'fell unknown among a herd of common soldiers ... the consequence of which was, that he was believed to be alive many years afterwards'.[80] Within a year a pretender calling himself Ya'eqob arose in Tigray and caused a considerable problem. It is said that by the middle of 1608 both parts of Tigray were more or less under his control.[81] How did the pretender win so much support and sympathy within such a short time? The answer is quite simple. He played on the fundamental fear of the Christian peasants with regard to Susenyos. The pretender's platform could be summed up in the following words that are attributed to him:

> 'I am Yaeqob, the son of Malak Saggad. The son of [an Oromo] called [Susenyos], defeated me with [an Oromo army] at the Ber river, and I escaped in flight, but now, you people of Tegre [Tigray] who love the descendants of ... Zara Ya'eqob and ...Wang Saggad, how can [an Oromo] sit on the throne of Yikunno Amlak? No alien has so far ever reigned in Ethiopia'. And they followed him, for the people of Tegre were true sons of [Ethiopia] who loved their country and their rulers.[82]

There is clear evidence that shows that the content of this propaganda had powerful impact on the Christian peasants in Tigray. The pretender's propaganda appealed to their anti-Oromo prejudice and played on Christian peasants underlying fear of the attack of Oromo warriors.

---

[75] Caraman, *The Lost Empire*, 59.
[76] Boavida et al., *Pedro Páez's History of Ethiopia*, vol. 2, 204.
[77] Pereira, *Chronica de Susenyos*, 21–2.
[78] Caraman, *The Lost Empire*, 58–9.
[79] Boavida et al., *Pedro Páez's History of Ethiopia*, vol. 2, 204.
[80] Bruce, *Travels to Discover the Source of the Nile*, vol. 3, 277.
[81] Aregay, 'Southern Ethiopia and the Christian Kingdom', 397.
[82] Tafla, *Asma Giyorgis and His Work*, 311.

Ras Sela Chrestos, the governor of Tigray, appealed to Susenyos for his immediate arrival in Tigray.

> Behold, all of Tegre [Tigray] has gone mad, and followed the impostor. Tens of thousands have been killed as if they were martyrs who have heavenly hope. Hence, look to your kingdom and come quickly to pacify their agitation, and to calm the mad ones by the sight of your face and by the news of your coming. But if my lord do not come, there is no wisdom or power that can stop this thing'... [The people of Tigray] have gone mad; they have lost their sense and gone mad; and if they die they regard it as martyrdom.[83]

Once Susenyos arrived in the region and, through diplomacy and show of force, calmed the people of Tigray, he had to intensify his spirited campaign against the Oromo. To dispel the doubt about his being 'pagan Oromo', Susenyos had to show that he was not. He had to reveal his passions and make his most intimate desire the will to fight against the non-Christian Oromo. He had to show that he was a man of high morals with a burning desire to put his country back where it once had been. He had to play on a blend of nostalgia and fear: on the one hand the possibility of restoring the old frontiers, and on the other hand the Christian fear of, and anger against, the Oromo. This he clearly expressed in his letters of 14 October and 10 December 1607, to the Pope and to the king of Spain and Portugal respectively.

> These letters say not a word of his intended conversion nor of submission to the See of Rome; but complain only of the disorderly state of his kingdom, and the constant inroads of the [Oromo]' earnestly requesting a number of Portuguese soldiers to free them from their yoke, as formerly, under the conduct of Christopher de Gama they had delivered Abyssinia from that of the [Muslims].[84]

Susenyos was drawn to the Catholic faith not only under the influence of the learned and wise Jesuit missionary, Páez, who was in Ethiopia (1603–22) and had good command of both Amharic and Geez languages, 'but also by the hope of military assistance against the [Oromo]'.[85]

The precarious alliance between the various Oromo groups and Susenyos came to an end as soon as he came to the throne. Those who allied with him and settled both in Gojjam and Begameder supported his cause. Those who decided to overthrow him forced him to seek the military support of the Emperor of Spain and Portugal in the very year in which he came to power. While conducting spirited war against his Oromo enemies, Susenyos treated the Oromo among his soldiers just as he treated his Amhara or Tigray soldiers. In fact, Susenyos 'filled practically all the court offices with boys from among the [Oromo], Agaw, Gafat and Gonge captives of his slaving expeditions'.[86] What is more, Susenyos promoted his Oromo benefactor, Buko to the rank of *dajaz-mach* and appointed him as the governor of Damot, then located south

---

[83] Ibid., 313.
[84] Bruce, *Travels to Discover the Source of the Nile*, vol. 3, 285.
[85] Caraman, *The Lost Empire*, 80.
[86] Aregay, 'Southern Ethiopia and the Christian Kingdom', 456.

of the Abbay River. Although tens of thousands of Oromo served in armies of Christian emperors since the time of Sarsa Dengel, Buko was most probably the first highest-ranking individual of Oromo origin to serve as a governor of an important province.

While treating his Oromo soldiers with respect, Susenyos tried to stop his Oromo enemies across the Abbay from attacking Gojjam. The first major challenge came when the Warantisha Oromo warriors from Walaqa attacked Gojjam. The governor of the province appealed urgently for help. Susenyos rushed to the area, and gave battle to the Warantisha on 10 February 1608. Even though Oromo warriors fought bravely, Susenyos was victorious.[87] From the chronicle, it appears that the place Susenyos had chosen for the battle was the bank of a river that was rugged and precipitous, and the Oromo cavalry suffered more by falling than by the muskets and spears of Susenyos' men. While escaping, many Warantisha fell over a very high precipice, dashing themselves to pieces on the plain below or in the river, until the river became full of blood.[88] This was his first major victory against the Oromo. He wanted to exploit the benefit of this victory by pushing the war across the Abbay into Walaqa. The history of the previous kings repeated itself. His soldiers refused to go with him. So Susenyos had to content himself with shelving the plan for future action. When he had been a bandit, and with small band of followers, he crossed the Abbay whenever he wanted. Now as an emperor with a large army, it was not easy to cross the Abbay, as it was difficult to find food there. The Amhara soldiers were very nervous about going to war east of the Abbay River because of the superiority of Oromo cavalry and the threat of hunger in an enemy territory. By the time Susenyos embarked on his offensive against the Oromo, their cavalry 'outnumbered and outclassed the cavalry troops of the emperor and his governors'.[89]

To prevent the Oromo from conquering Gojjam, Susenyos adopted four defensive measures early in his reign. First, he sought foreign military assistance against the Oromo. In his letter of December 1607, he appealed to the king of Spain and Portugal, requesting about a thousand soldiers 'to help him save the Christian empire'.[90]

Second, Susenyos ordered his provincial governors to adopt the defensive measure of intercepting Oromo warriors at strategic locations. This measure depended on the knowledge of the dynamics within Oromo society, their settlement patterns, the timing and the direction of their attack. For that purpose, Susenyos expanded and intensified the settlement of friendly Oromo groups in both Gojjam and Begameder, who made the policy of interception to be met with repeated success.

Third, Susenyos 'realized the advantages of building stone walls early in his reign' and sought the advice of Jesuits missionaries 'on methods of improving and strengthening the traditional mud and

---

[87] Boavida et al., *Pedro Páez's History of Ethiopia*, vol. 2, 227.
[88] Pereira, *Chronica de Susenyos*, 105.
[89] Aregay, 'Southern Ethiopia and the Christian Kingdom', 502.
[90] Pereira, *Chronica de Susenyos*, 105.

stone walls'.[91] He ordered his provincial governors to build stone walls at 'strategic passes and locations'. For instance, the fortifications built by Sela Chrestos, the governor of Gojjam, did not stop Oromo warriors from across the Abbay from attacking central and southern Gojjam. However, because of the preponderance of mounted Oromo warriors, the fortifications may have limited the effectiveness of surprise Oromo attacks. What is more, 'the warning given by the small detachment of soldiers posted [at the fortifications] helped many people in the interior to move to secure places, and enabled the governor or his lieutenants to make timely interceptions'.[92]

Finally, Susenyos intensified his offensive war against his Oromo enemies. It was by the combination of these defensive measures that Susenyos hoped to prevent the Oromo from occupying the northern central provinces. These measures may not have 'provided protection to the beleaguered' Christian population, but they 'may have contributed towards checking further territorial encroachments'[93] by the Oromo. We will check the effectiveness of these measures towards the end of his reign.

While Susenyos was camping at Suha, he heard that the Liban Oromo warriors had spread across Wasan Amba along the banks of the Abbay River. The Liban, according to the chronicler, were 'as numerous as locusts, masters of warfare and military strategists, the strongest of all the strong [Oromo]'.[94] The Liban warriors that poured over eastern Gojjam were so numerous that Susenyos was forced to let them loot and ruin Gafates, Chome, Agaw, Damot up to Sakala' and Gabarma. He met them only after they had destroyed these lands and captured their cattle, women and children.[95] The reason for his action is not hard to find. In fact it was part of his new strategic policy, by which he wanted to save Begameder and Gojjam. This was part of the policy of fighting with the Oromo after they had looted, for then they would be exhausted and burdened with their loot. Susenyos himself told Almeida why he adopted this policy.

> What makes the [Oromo] much feared is that they go to war and into battle determined and firmly resolved to conquer or die. The Emperor [Susenyos] recognized this quality in them and in most of the Abyssinians the exact opposite. To this he used to ascribe the victories of the [Oromo] and defeats and routs of the Abyssinians, though the latter are usually much more numerous, and have better horses, muskets, helmets, and coats of mail in plenty. The [Oromo] do not usually come in bands of more than six or seven or eight thousand, but these are mostly picked young men. The same emperor used therefore to say that the Abyssinians could not possibly withstand their first onslaught. So he used to let them invade the country and steal the cattle and whatever else they found. He used then to wait for them on their return.

---

[91] Aregay, 'Southern Ethiopia and the Christian Kingdom', 504–5.
[92] Ibid., 505.
[93] Ibid., 508–9.
[94] Pereira, *Chronica de Susenyos*, 105. See also Bruce, *Travels to Discover the Source of the Nile*, vol. 3, 284–85, and Abir, *Ethiopia and the Red Sea*, 200.
[95] Pereira, *Chronica de Susenyos*, 105.

> Their first fury was broken and they were thinking of reaching their country and securing and preserving the booty with which they were loaded. In this way he often defeated them.[96]

The above long quotation needs some elaboration. In most of his engagements with the Oromo, Susenyos was victorious. He employed their own *chiffra* fighting system against them. By choice of place, time and good use of the firearms, which the Oromo lacked, he neutralized the effectiveness of their cavalry. Hence, it was only on some occasions, as we shall see below, that the Oromo warriors were able to defeat him. However, the Oromo warriors had repeatedly defeated several Christian regiments and routed provincial governors. The difference between the imperial army and those of the provincial governors was that the former was larger in number, better equipped with firearms, better trained and mounted. The provincial regiments or the retainers of the landlords were usually small, they had limited muskets and their cavalry were inferior to those of various Oromo fighters. These regiments and retainers were usually defeated and scattered by highly mobile Oromo warriors.[97] The Oromo had additional advantage over the Christian soldiers and peasants. Because of their diet based on milk, meat, butter and grain, and their training in the art of warfare, 'their physique was good and they were courageous in battle'.

> In spite of their strength in numbers, the Ethiopians had a great fear of the [Oromo] and fought well against them only when they were inspired by the emperor ... Primarily peasants, they were man for man no match for the fierce and more professional [Oromo] ... When they marched it was always at night yet they were able to cover twice the distance that Ethiopians did in a day. In this way they could surprise them in a sudden raid.[98]

Because of the speed of Oromo warriors and their unnerving assault, the regiments and retainers of lords were never a match for the formidable Oromo cavalry. However, the same Oromo warriors defeated the army commanded by Susenyos only on some occasions. The reason for this is obvious. Generally, Oromo warriors numbered from 6,000 to 8,000 men, while Susenyos had three to four times that number. For instance, by the middle of 1608, he had an army of 25,000 fighting men, while by 1622 this had grown to around 40,000 strong.[99] Of this force, four to five thousand were cavalry, and the rest foot soldiers. Of the cavalry, as many as 700 or 800 wore coats of mail and helmets. They had no less than 1500 muskets, of which probably only 400 to 500 were in good working order.[100] In every respect Susenyos was superior to

[96] Almeida, 'The History of High Ethiopia or Abassia', in *Some Records of Ethiopia*, 137–8.
[97] Aregay, 'Southern Ethiopia and the Christian Kingdom', 503.
[98] Caraman, *The Lost Empire*, 76.
[99] Aregay, 'Southern Ethiopia and the Christian Kingdom', 475–6. See also Caraman, *The Lost Empire*, 75.
[100] Almeida, 'The History of High Ethiopia or Abassia', in *Some Records of Ethiopia*, 77–8.

his Oromo enemies, except in terms of the cavalry, in which the various Oromo warriors outnumbered those of Susenyos, since most of the Oromo warriors were mounted. As indicated in Chapter 5, it was most likely because of their use of the toe-stirrup that Oromo warriors were famous for taking naps while riding their horses. Emboldened by their over-confidence in their horses, Oromo warriors inadvertently provided Susenyos with added advantage. They did this by offering 'pitched battles in open places, often dividing themselves into two massive and unwieldy wings of footmen and horsemen'.[101] The size of Susenyos' army, its weapons, training and his military leadership, all contributed towards the succession of victories he won against the Oromo. But ironically his Oromo campaigns were equally ruinous to his subjects. Herein lies the major weakness of his administration.

> The people take no provisions and as far as those who do take some, when they are finished, they all live on what they are given, and they usually leave places through which they are marching almost as much ruined and plundered as the [Oromo] might have done if they had invaded them. This is specially so if the army remains in a district for some days, for there is no solution but for the emperor or captain major to assign certain places to it, which they rob of all the kinds of provisions found there ... This is also the reason why the [Oromo] easily invade the territories of the empire, and why, on the other hand, the imperial armies cannot invade those of the [Oromo] far; they do not cultivate at all, and have no stock of provisions on which to feed, but live entirely on the milk of their cows. When necessary they easily take them wherever they like, retreat with them and leave the deserted meadows to the imperials, so that in time they are forced to retreat and, if they do not, die of sheer hunger.[102]

Whenever Oromo warriors were surprised, they were slaughtered by Susenyos, as will be shown below. When not caught suddenly, Oromo warriors generally avoided Susenyos' army in the field. In this they were helped by his large, slow-moving army, which included, the queen, priests, the wives of important officials, married and unmarried ladies of the court.[103] It is said that the court of Susenyos functioned as a market place, which included numerous 'traders, retailers, scroungers and prostitutes'.[104] Thus when Susenyos marched with his entire camp followers, 'the whole multitude is over a hundred thousand or a hundred twenty thousand'.[105] Oromo warriors did not have this type of problem. Their women, children and cattle were kept in their safe base areas. Rapid movement was the source of their strength. The policy of choosing a soft target and a right time was one of their greatest tactics.[106]

Susenyos, whom we left on the bank of a river waiting for the retreating Liban on very rugged and precipitous ground, met the

---

[101] Aregay, 'Southern Ethiopia and the Christian Kingdom', 503.
[102] Almeida, 'The History of High Ethiopia or Abassia', in *Some Records of Ethiopia*, 79–80.
[103] Ibid., 78.
[104] Aregay, 'Southern Ethiopia and the Christian Kingdom', 470.
[105] Caraman, *The Lost Empire*, 78.
[106] Hassen, *The Oromo of Ethiopia*, 40.

heavily loaded warriors and dealt with them very severely. What is very interesting to note here is that Susenyos left all his cavalry on safe ground in hiding. The Liban warriors committed the classic blunder of engaging with Susenyos in conventional battle at which he had advantage both in number and firepower. Susenyos' numerous foot soldiers suddenly poured themselves on the Liban from all sides, in a situation where fighting or flight posed equal danger. On this day, his muskets, arrows, spears and stone missiles and wooden clubs all contributed in their own way to the slaughter of the day. According to his chronicle, there was no soldier who did not cut off one or more enemy heads and present them to Susenyos, who heaped them up and made a hill out of them.[107] The once powerful Liban were greatly reduced[108] and eventually absorbed into Amhara Christian society. A few days later he also met the Digalu Oromo warriors in the lowlands of Kundel, at a place called Zaragam. This group, which may have already heard of the fate of the Liban, fled at the first sight of Susenyos, abandoning all its booty. With these victories to his credit and the retrieved booty for his soldiers, Susenyos once again decided to push the war across the Abbay River into Walaqa. When his soldiers knew about his intention they rejected it openly. In the words of the chroniclers, they said 'this one year only we have defeated the [Oromo] four times. Why then now is he taking us for another military expedition against the [Oromo]?' When he realized that they were not interested in the project he dropped it.[109]

Between 1608 and 1611, Susenyos tried and failed at least on three occasions to persuade his soldiers to follow him across the Abbay. To counter the resistance of professional soldiers against Oromo campaign, Susenyos developed and perfected the policy of using Oromo warriors in his numerous wars against other Oromo groups. Oromo settlers in both Gojjam and Begameder and soldiers who served in his army were converted at first to Orthodox Christianity and later to Catholic faith, and in the process they were permanently alienated from their brethren, who now became their enemies. Those Christianized Oromo were slowly integrated into Amhara and Tigray society. According to Merid Wolde Aregay, 'the large number of units of [Oromo] warriors which the emperor and his governors kept with them'[110] may indicate the extent of Christian leaders' dependency on their Oromo warriors for the protection of the Christian kingdom itself.

During the third year of Susenyos' reign, after the rainy season, Susenyos went to Ayba, where he received a letter containing an urgent appeal from his brother, the governor of Begameder. According to this letter, large numbers of Marawa warriors from Ana, Uru and Abati, were wasting Begameder. Susenyos hastened with full speed to help his brother. Upon arrival near where Oromo warriors camped, Susenyos demonstrated his understanding about the famed Oromo 'intelligence

[107] Pereira, *Chronica de Susenyos*, 106.
[108] Tafla, *Asma Giyorgis and His Work*, 309.
[109] Pereira, *Chronica de Susenyos*, 108.
[110] Aregay, 'Southern Ethiopia and the Christian Kingdom', 475.

gathering strategy ... that fed commanders not only with information relevant to military operations but also concerning locations of fertile lands for occupation and settlement'.[111] The strategy also helped Oromo warriors to avoid conventional war with Susenyos. The emperor ordered his soldiers 'not to kindle fire' and prohibited them from talking among themselves[112] so as to deprive Oromo intelligence officers the opportunity to provide timely warning for their commanders. Taking advantage of the element of surprise, Susenyos wanted to catch the Marawa unprepared. Unluckily for him, this was not a field of his own, but of his Oromo enemy's choosing. Usually every Oromo warrior group in enemy territory would choose a plain convenient for cavalry. Susenyos, who wanted to prevent the Marawa from escaping, hastily ordered a cavalry attack. What followed was succinctly expressed by James Bruce, who carefully consulted Susenyos' chronicle.

> They received the kings cavalry so rudely ... they were beat back, and obliged to fly with considerable loss, being entangled in the bushes. No sooner did the king observe that his horse were engaged than he ordered his troops to pass the ravine to support them ... but a panic had seized his troops. They would not stir, but seemed benumbed and overcome by the cold of the morning, spectators of the ruin of the cavalry ... And those of the cavalry that had escaped the massacre repassed the ravine, and dispersed themselves in the front of the foot; while the victorious Marawa ... pushed their victory to the very front of the king's line.[113]

Even though Susenyos ordered all the drums to be beaten and the trumpets to sound to excite his soldiers into action, nothing stopped the desertion of his soldiers. It was a total rout, the first major Oromo victory over Susenyos. The casualty list included several of the nobility, numerous elite of his cavalry and 'countless foot soldiers'. As a result of the disaster, 'there was no house [family] in the camp of the king that did not mourn the death of someone'.[114] The victorious Marawa not only decimated his army, but also captured huge booty including weapons and Susenyos' war drums and the royal tents. Susenyos fled and saved himself from the fury of excited Marawa warriors, who devastated extensive territory and burned down the royal town at Qoga.[115] Pedro Páez, who accompanied Susenyos on several military expeditions, attributed Susenyos' defeat to the fact that Christian soldiers did not fight 'in a united way'; nor did they keep military order so much that a retreat by those in the front ranks would be followed by the others.[116] Asma Giyorgis interpreted Susenyos' utter defeat as God's punishment for pride that 'had entered his heart. It seems that he thought his

---

[111] Etefa, 'Pan-Oromo Confederations in the Sixteenth and Seventeenth Centuries', 33.
[112] Tafla, *Asma Giyorgis and His Work*, 315.
[113] Bruce, *Travels to Discover the Source of the Nile*, vol. 3. 291. See also Pereira, *Chronica de Susenyos*,117–18.
[114] Pereira, *Chronica de Susenyos*, 118.
[115] Tafla, *Asma Giyorgis and His Work*, 319, 317.
[116] Boavida et al., *Pedro Páez's History of Ethiopia*, vol. 1, 173.

bravery and wisdom were part of his nature and that he did not humble himself before God'.[117] Pedro Páez was puzzled why Susenyos' formidable force that enjoyed superiority both in number and weapons were not always victorious against the Oromo, and sought explanation from the emperor himself, who blamed the soldiers for being disorderly. [118]

THE MUDANA GADA, 1610–1618

The Mudana Gada came to power after Susenyos had inflicted four defeats on the Melbah Gada (1602–10), while the latter administered one telling blow on the former. The new *gada*, who wanted to take advantage of the recent humiliation of Susenyos, were eager to wage war in all directions, thus sending a wave of terror throughout the land. Susenyos accepted this challenge seriously, and appealed to all his governors to rush to his assistance. His soldiers who had been nursing their wounds since the last disaster went to Dangaz, where they were joined by a new force that came to their assistance. In response to Susenyos' request, Keflo, an important official brought a large number of professional soldiers from Gojjam. Yolyos, Susenyos' son-in-law, 'came to his assistance with a countless multitude, the earth swarming with them'.[119] To counter the growing power of Susenyos, the victorious Marawa and 'other Oromo groups formed a confederation to [occupy]... all lands between the Takaze River and Lake Tana. They pursued Susenyos as he retreated, obliterated Enfraz, [Emfraz] and [even] burnt down the royal settlement at Qoga',[120] further humiliating Susenyos. The Oromo victory and their unchecked burning and looting is interpreted by the chronicler as 'God's warning for Susenyos to repent'.[121] But Susenyos had his own plan. He wanted to meet them on the field of his choice. When his soldiers realized that he was determined to take revenge for his humiliation, they were very nervous and did not hide their fear. 'We cannot fight against the [Oromo] after the last disaster. We are shocked and shattered by the number of men who died last time. Would you like the destruction of your remaining soldiers?'[122] Susenyos was not discouraged by the cowardice of his soldiers. At a distance, he pursued the Oromo warriors. When he arrived in Ebenaat, his numbers were increased by the arrival of fresh soldiers from two provincial governors, boosting the morale of his troops. He met the Oromo warriors near Tiqin, where he chose the best ground and made good use of his superiority in weapons.

> The [Oromo] presented themselves to Socinos [Susenyos] in battle, in a plain below Ebenaat, surrounded with small hills covered with wood. The [Oromo]

[117] Tafla, *Asma Giyorgis and His Work*, 321.
[118] Boavida et al., *Pedro Páez's History of Ethiopia*, vol. 1, 173.
[119] Tafla, *Asma Giyorgis and His Work*, 319.
[120] Etefa, 'Pan-Oromo Confederations in the Sixteenth and Seventeenth Centuries', 30. See also Tafla, *Asma Giyorgis and His Work*, 319.
[121] Pereira, *Chronica de Susenyos*, 119–20.
[122] Ibid., 121.

filled the plain, as if voluntarily devoting themselves to destruction, and from the hills and bushes were destroyed by fire-arms from enemies they did not see, who with strong body took possession of the place through which they entered, and by which they were to return no more ... no general, or other officer, thought himself entitled to spare his person more than the king: all fought like common soldiers; and being the men best armed and mounted, and most experienced in the field, they contributed in proportion to the slaughter of the day. About 12,000 men on the part of the [Oromo] were killed upon the spot ... whilst 400 men only fell on the part of the king; so it was a massacre rather than a battle.[123]

In this resounding victory, Susenyos not only massacred the earlier victorious Oromo warriors themselves, but also retrieved much of their booty and set free their captives. Susenyos was able to retrieve weapons and his war drums from his defeated enemies. Only royal tents were not retrieved.[124] The chronicler says that 'the king returned the booty' to their owners and divided the [Oromo] cattle among his soldiers'.[125] The presence of Oromo cattle, separate from their booty in the province, seems to suggest that the warriors who were exterminated probably did not come to attack and then return. They probably wanted to stay in the province, which was why they brought their huge herds of cattle with them. Asma Giyorgis claimed that by his resounding victory, Susenyos changed the Marawa's 'happiness and pride ... to shame and tribulation; and the sorrow, shame and tribulation of [Susenyos] ... to happiness and glory'.[126] Shortly after his victory, Susenyos arrived in Tigray, where he was crowned in the city of Aksum.

By insisting upon punishing the overbearing Oromo who formed a confederacy against him, Susenyos had shown a determination in coping with the situation. By their cowardice his soldiers had shown that they had none. They did not lift their fighting spirit either during the heat of the fighting or the beating of the drums and sounding of the trumpets. Among his soldiers there was an absence of any true desire to continue the war with the Oromo. The following incident may show the pervasiveness of this feeling. After the Easter of 1611, Susenyos wanted to push the war across the Abbay River into Walaqa and Shawa. This was the first time that he had shown any desire to go as far as Shawa, and his advisors, whose opinion was based on the feelings of their soldiers, suggested to Susenyos that it would be better to go to Bizamo than to Walaqa and Shawa. Accordingly Susenyos was forced to change his course, and the journey towards Bizamo was commenced, seemingly with high spirits. However, within a few days, by the time he arrived at the river Abbay, the fire had already gone out of his soldiers. They were looking for any pretext to disrupt the journey and avoid crossing the Abbay, and they found it in the shortage of provisions. The soldiers mutinied and looted Susenyos' stores, thus exposing the nobility, including the king himself, to the bitter taste of hunger.

---

[123] Bruce, *Travels to Discover the Source of the Nile*, vol. 3, 294–5. See also Pereira, *Chronica de Susenyos*, 121–2.

[124] Tafla, *Asma Giyorgis and His Work*, 319.

[125] Pereira, *Chronica de Susenyos*, 122.

[126] Tafla, *Asma Giyorgis and His Work*, 321.

Susenyos had no alternative but to abandon the campaign to cross the river, and return to Dambiya, where he soon sanctioned the pillaging, looting and destruction of the unfortunate Shankillas, on the pretext of their having attacked a caravan, though in reality it was a desire to please his soldiers.[127]

SUSENYOS' SLAVE RAIDS AND THEIR IMPACT ON OROMO SETTLEMENTS IN GOJJAM

During the sixteenth and seventeenth centuries, several Amhara emperors were involved in both slave raids and slave trade. As we saw in Chapter 2, the first Amhara emperor who embarked on slave raiding was Amda-Siyon (1314–44). However, according to Merid Wolde Aregay, the first Christian emperor to embark on the practice of slave trade was Liban Dengel (1508–40).[128] Slave raids and slave trade continued during the reigns of Minas (1559–63), Sarsa Dengel (1563–97) and Ya'eqob (1597–1607). However, it was during the reign of Susenyos that the slave raids and slave trade developed into a major source of revenue for the state. The emperor was engaged in these practices for several reasons. As 'a man fully shaped and fashioned by his long career as a brigand and condottiere, [Susenyos] was guided by no principle or objective but his own interests. The country was to him a rich spoil to be shared with his companions.'[129] In the very year in which he came to power, Susenyos left his court at Qoga 'with his army in order to pursue the inhabitants of the lands of Alafa, who did not want to pay the customary tribute'.[130] In reality the Agaw inhabitants of Alafa did not refuse to pay. They were too poor to pay the exorbitant tribute demanded from them, thus providing a pretext for Susenyos to destroy their lands. After several months of plundering and enslaving the non-Christian Agaw people and fighting against a number of Oromo groups, Susenyos jubilantly returned to his court at Qoga, 'where he shared out among his men all the gold, slaves, cattle and other things that he had captured in war'.[131]

Even Christian refugee inhabitants of Gojjam did not escape from Susenyos' brutal raids and enslavement. For instance, at the end of 1610 when the Gonga refugees along the Abbay River failed to pay their tribute in full, Susenyos was so angry that his soldiers 'slaughtered a large number ... and brought their heads to the emperor ... After marching all night into Guman, they suddenly fell on the land when dawn broke and killed and captured many people.'[132] Pedro Páez was an eye witness to the tragedy that befell the Gonga people. He was so

---

[127] Pereira, *Chronica de Susenyos*, 139–41.
[128] Aregay, 'Southern Ethiopia and the Christian Kingdom', 106.
[129] Ibid., 395.
[130] Boavida et al., *Pedro Páez's History of Ethiopia*, vol. 2, 226.
[131] Ibid., 228.
[132] Ibid., 236.

moved by their sufferings that he begged Susenyos to have mercy upon and free thousands of 'beautiful children' and women'.[133]

Pedro Páez's intercession gained freedom for about 12,000 captives in 1610. However, Susenyos continued with his policy of plundering and depopulating many areas of Gojjam. For him, banditry, plunder of property and slave raids were all part of his strategy for attracting followers to his standard. It was with looted cattle and captive-victims of slaving raids that Susenyos won the loyalty of his soldiers and attempted to finance his wars against the Oromo. The reason for his policy was obvious.

> Because of the chaotic conditions which preceded and followed his accession, he found himself without the means to maintain those whom he had succeeded in gathering around him. Inevitably, therefore, he resorted to the well-tried expedient of living at the cost of the various pagan peoples who had neither the organization nor the strength to resist any concerted attack made against them. Susenyos's reign was inaugurated by a general license of pillage and plunder, followed immediately in December of the same year, by systematic raids on the pagan Agaw living between Alafa and Bure. The emperor and his soldiers did not leave Gojjam until they had taken many captives from the Shinasha and other Gonga peoples who had taken refuge in the southern parts of the province.[134]

In June 1612 Susenyos once again took his soldiers to land of Achafar, where so many Agaw inhabitants were killed or enslaved that the land was said to have been deserted.[135] Merid Wolde Aregay, an authority on the history of the period, argues convincingly that 'Susenyos's slaving campaigns ... resulted in unparalleled destruction to life and property'.[136] By depopulating many areas, Susenyos created a vacuum into which pastoral Oromo groups moved easily in southern Gojjam. Thus slave raids not only facilitated pastoral Oromo movements but also contributed to their speedy settlement in vast areas of Gojjam.

> Unable to think of any alternative means for supporting his army, the emperor increased the frequency and range of his pillaging and slaving expeditions. The raids of the 1610, like those of 1607 and 1608, extended from Alafa, to the west of Dambiya, all the way south to the camps of the Gonga refugees along the Blue Nile ... but [Páez'] warning that these raids were opening the way to the [Oromo], who were massed on the other side of the Blue Nile, went unheeded. The 1614 expedition against all the Agaw of Gojam, allegedly brought about by their lawlessness and insubordination, was particularly destructive. The Agaw of Achafar, considerably debilitated and reduced by earlier raids, abandoned their homes and sought refuge among the Agaw of Chara and the Shanqela of Matakal. Not contented with the cattle and slaves he and his soldiers acquired in all these places, he then devastated the extreme southwestern parts of the province.[137]

---

[133] Ibid., 237. See also Aregay, 'Southern Ethiopia and the Christian Kingdom', 470.
[134] Aregay, 'Southern Ethiopia and the Christian Kingdom', 470.
[135] Boavida et al., *Pedro Páez's History of Ethiopia*, vol. 2, 240.
[136] Aregay, 'Southern Ethiopia and the Christian Kingdom', 472.
[137] Ibid., 479.

As part of his slaving raids, Susenyos developed cruelty to the 'art' of government. With his insatiable thirst for slaves and strong desire for buying the loyalty of his soldiers, he made the weak and defence-less Agaw peasants the victims of his devastating raids. His own chronicle describes in a horrifying manner, the thoroughness with which his slaving raids were planned and carried out methodically as follows.

> And after this he arose and descended into the land of Lala and Abola, in which were three pagan tribes which were the Agaw, the Gonga and the Jagat. The king then divided his army into two sections. He made *belatenoch geta* Yonael commander of the soldiers in one section. The king himself took the other section of the army and he went down leaving the impedimenta with the spoils he took from such places as Matakal to follow behind. Upon his arrival the king sent out *warari* [a raiding party] to the right and to the left. So many cattle were taken in this very *warari* that they offended the eye. Many men and women slaves, who looked like the grape and fruit of the *doqma* tree [*Syzygium guineense*[138]] which were not fully ripe, were also captured. There was much rejoicing in the camp because of the large quantity of takings. There was not a man in the army of the king who did not, from the spoils then taken, come into possession of cattle and slaves. On the second day after the day of the *warari*, the *belatenoch geta* Yonael returned to the king his lord, with large booty of cattle and people. And the king made gifts of all the cattle which were taken to those who had caught them. As for the slaves he reserved them for himself and did [with them] as he wanted.[139]

Some of the unfortunate Agaw inhabitants of Chara, who escaped from slaughter and enslavement sought their safety in a cave. When they were found, Susenyos ordered his soldiers to burn them[140] and they were consumed by fire. Azaj Tino, the writer of the greater part of Susenyos' chronicle, told Pedro Páez that he had seen with his own eyes many of the events depicted in the Emperor's Chronicle,[141] prob-ably including the above-mentioned incident of destroying helpless people with fire. Be that as it may, according to Merid Wolde Aregay, Susenyos used the slaves from this expedition for buying horses from the merchants that came from the kingdom of Funj, in what is today the Sudan, to bolster his cavalry strength. His soldiers dreaded Oromo cavalry and by strengthening his cavalry, Susenyos was attempting to boost the morale of his soldiers. However, the horses purchased with Agaw victims of his raids did not turn the tide against the Oromo. On the contrary, his endless predatory activities depopulated many areas

---

[138] I am deeply indebted to Dr Gobana Huluka for providing me with botan-ical name of Amharic *daqoma* tree, *Badessa* tree in Afaan Oromo, as well as for the following information: the '*doqma* tree has fruits that almost look like and taste like a black cherry or small version of a black plum but with rich juice. It has bigger size and bigger seeds than black cherry. A not fully ripe *doqma* fruit could be a reddish-dark color or one that is not too dark/black.'

[139] Pereira, *Chronica de Susenyos*, 145–46 (translation by Aregay, 'Southern Ethiopia and the Christian Kingdom', 480).

[140] Boavida et al., *Pedro Páez's History of Ethiopia*, vol. 2, 240.

[141] Ibid., 259.

in Gojjam. As noted above, Susenyos settled several Oromo groups in the very areas his slaving raids depopulated. There are many examples of such an arrangement in the Chronicle of Susenyos, of which, as we will see below, the case of Warantisha Oromo is a classic one. In his effort to capture cattle and slaves, which were employed in buying the loyalty of his large army, Susenyos depopulated the vast districts of Wambarya and Wambarma, thus facilitating the settlement of the Oromo in these districts.

> In the process, he left behind him in the districts of Wambarya and Wambarma carnage unprecedented in the history of the Agaw people ... In other words, the conquest of pastoral Oromo was the object of his hopes and preparation; but he ruined the Agaw without achieving anything. It is no exaggeration to state that the wars which the [Oromo] conducted from Bizamo into Wambarya and Wambarma and other districts along the Abbay for almost three decades before Susenyos came to power were much less destructive than the slaving raids which were conducted between 1607 and 1616 by the Christian emperor.[142]

During the long reign of Susenyos, the slave trade played a significant role in shaping the economy of the Christian kingdom,[143] – in fact constituting the most-important export from the kingdom. It was for the purpose of exporting slaves to and through the neighbouring countries that Susenyos appears to have cultivated friendly relationship with the Muslim rulers of the Kingdom of Funj, the leaders of the port city of Zayla on northern Somalia coast, and the small port of Arkiko on the Red Sea coast of what is today Eritrea: Aregay concludes that Susenyos' 'assiduous cultivation of the friendship of his neighbours ... have been connected with the export of slaves'.[144] According to Aregay, the two main causes for the outbreak of hostilities in 1618 between Susenyos and the king of Funj 'were connected with poaching on Ethiopian territories'. Taking advantage of the outbreak of hostilities, Susenyos and his governors led devastating expeditions, 'which yielded immense number of slaves, became necessary as a result of the cessation, albeit temporary, of slaving raids on the pagan Agaw'.[145] Through the intercession of Pedro Páez, those Agaw groups who embraced the Catholic faith were spared from Susenyos' slaving raids. According to Aregay, these slaving activities 'came to an abrupt end sometime in 1619',[146] but, of course, his slave raids against the Agaw and other non-Christian minority population did not end altogether then. With only a few years of interruption, it continued to the end of his reign, thus financing his continued campaign against the Oromo, as well as his rebellious Christian subjects. Some aspects of Susenyos' slave raids will be mentioned in the next chapter.

---

[142] Hassen, *The Oromo of Ethiopia*, 70–71.
[143] Boavida et al., *Pedro Páez's History of Ethiopia*, vol. 1, 265.
[144] Aregay, 'Southern Ethiopia and the Christian Kingdom', 482.
[145] Ibid., 483–4.
[146] Ibid., 484–5.

SUSENYOS' CAMPAIGN AGAINST THE OROMO 1612-1618

Around 1612, the pressure of the Borana on Gojjam became intense. At the same time, the Warantisha Oromo, from their bases in Jamma and Amonat land in Walaqa, captured almost all Christian strong-holds in the province. As indicated above, it was Susenyos himself who drove the Gafat people 'out of Amonat to [Gojjam]' clearing the land for the Warantisha Oromo settlement.[147] Susenyos wanted to contain the Warantisha in the land of Amonat, which he thought had enough pasture for their large cattle. The Warantisha pastoralists, however, desired to extend their domain to Gojjam. Susenyos received alarming news that the Warantisha had invited the Ittu from Adal[148] (from Char-char in western Haraghe) to join them in their attack on Gojjam. The prospect of the Borana, Warantisha and Ittu attacking Gojjam simul-taneously made the defence of the province a nightmare for Susenyos and his brother Sela Chrestos, the governor who had accepted Catholi-cism during the time of crisis. Susenyos was determined to attack the Warantisha before the arrival of their allies, the Ittu from Charchar. He ordered full mobilization in order to attack them separately. Thus after Christmas of 1612, he crossed the Bashilo River from Begameder into Amhara, from where he crossed over into Walaqa. The detour was intended to deceive the Warantisha and take them by surprise. However, his soldiers 'had a false alarm of [an Oromo] attack and they all fled, leaving the emperor alone, but later, when they saw that nobody was pursuing them, they came back'[149] to where Susenyos was. The next day Susenyos caught the Warantisha by surprise. 'Although the battle was very hard fought, in the end the emperor won ... killing so many that [the] water was left with red blood.'[150] Thus the unsus-pecting Warantisha men were massacred, their women and children and cattle were taken captive by the victorious army and the survivors fled in total disarray.

What is interesting to note here is that Susenyos opened negotiations for peace with the vanquished Warantisha. His knowledge of Oromo customs and way of life becomes clear from the way he sent an old captive woman to ask the Warantisha to make peace. In Oromo society of the time, women and children were not killed in a war situation. On the contrary, they were considered as the torch of peace.

> Among the [Warantisha] captives was a widow named Fato. She had a son named Karrayu. [Susenyos] sent her to the [Warantisha] saying, 'you deserted me, invaded my country, Walaqa, and destroyed all the amba, and I came to fight you. Now, I pardon you; come and be my subjects'. The [Warant-isha] received the message through the widow and sent about 30 people who made peace with [Susenyos].[151]

---

[147] Tafla, *Asma Giyorgis and His Work*, 325.
[148] Pereira, *Chronica de Susenyos*, 139–41.
[149] Boavida et al., *Pedro Páez's History of Ethiopia*, vol. 2, 239.
[150] Ibid., 227.
[151] Tafla, *Asma Giyorgis and His Work*, 327.

From the manner in which the chronicler mentions the name of Karrayu, Fato's son, it seems he was probably a leader of the Warantisha. It was most likely for that reason that Susenyos ended his message with a plea. 'Please, come and make peace with me.'[152] The terms of the agreement are not spelled out clearly in the chronicle, but it seems that three important conditions were probably included. First, Susenyos seems to have returned their children and women to the Warantisha. Second, the Warantisha agreed to live in peace, and third and most important, Susenyos seems to have promised them his support in any future conflict with their enemies. With this commendable victory against the Warantisha, and a huge booty of cattle that enriched his soldiers, Susenyos returned to his court.

The dispossessed and weakened Warantisha had to replace their lost stock for their survival. They were too weak to attack their brethren, the numerous Borana, and too feeble to cross the Abbay to attack Gojjam. They had no alternative but to turn against the Ittu, who came all the way from Charchar to help them. The Ittu were caught off guard and looted. It was probably because of their restlessness that Asma Giyorgis blamed the Warantisha as 'the most cunning, the most given to conspiracy and tale-bearing, and the most treacherous'.[153] The Warantisha were restless because of their small size and their huge cattle population, which whetted the appetite of their powerful neighbours. It took some time before the Ittu had gathered enough strength to repay the Warantisha in kind. The Warantisha appealed for help. Accordingly, Sela Chrestos, the governor of Gojjam went to Walaqa with a large force. The Ittu refused to meet him in the field. The Warantisha were too frightened to remain in the province without his presence. Hence, Sela Chrestos took thousands of them with their cattle across the Abbay and settled them in eastern Gojjam sometime in 1614.[154] In a way, this was part of Susenyos' grand plan to create a secure bulwark against other Oromo warriors. According to Asmarom Legesse, it was also part of Susenyos' strategy for reversing the momentum of Oromo expansionism. 'He had first-hand knowledge of their culture and had in some measure become Oromized. He was using Oromo techniques of mass adoption and military strategy to reverse Oromo expansion and to try to bring them under his dominion.'[155]

As part of the Oromo nation, the Warantisha, were very familiar with Oromo warfare. They knew when and the most likely place where Oromo warriors choose to attack. They knew the Oromo scout system and the signals they used for communicating with each other. The Warantisha not only provided the Christian administration with useful information as to how to ring the alarm bell and intercept Oromo warriors but they also furnished the administration with needed fighting men. From this perspective, Susenyos was the first Amhara

[152] Pereira, *Chronica de Susenyos*, 146–7.
[153] Tafla, *Asma Giyorgis and His Work*, 325.
[154] Pereira, *Chronica de Susenyos*, 146–7.
[155] Legesse, *Oromo Democracy*, 179.

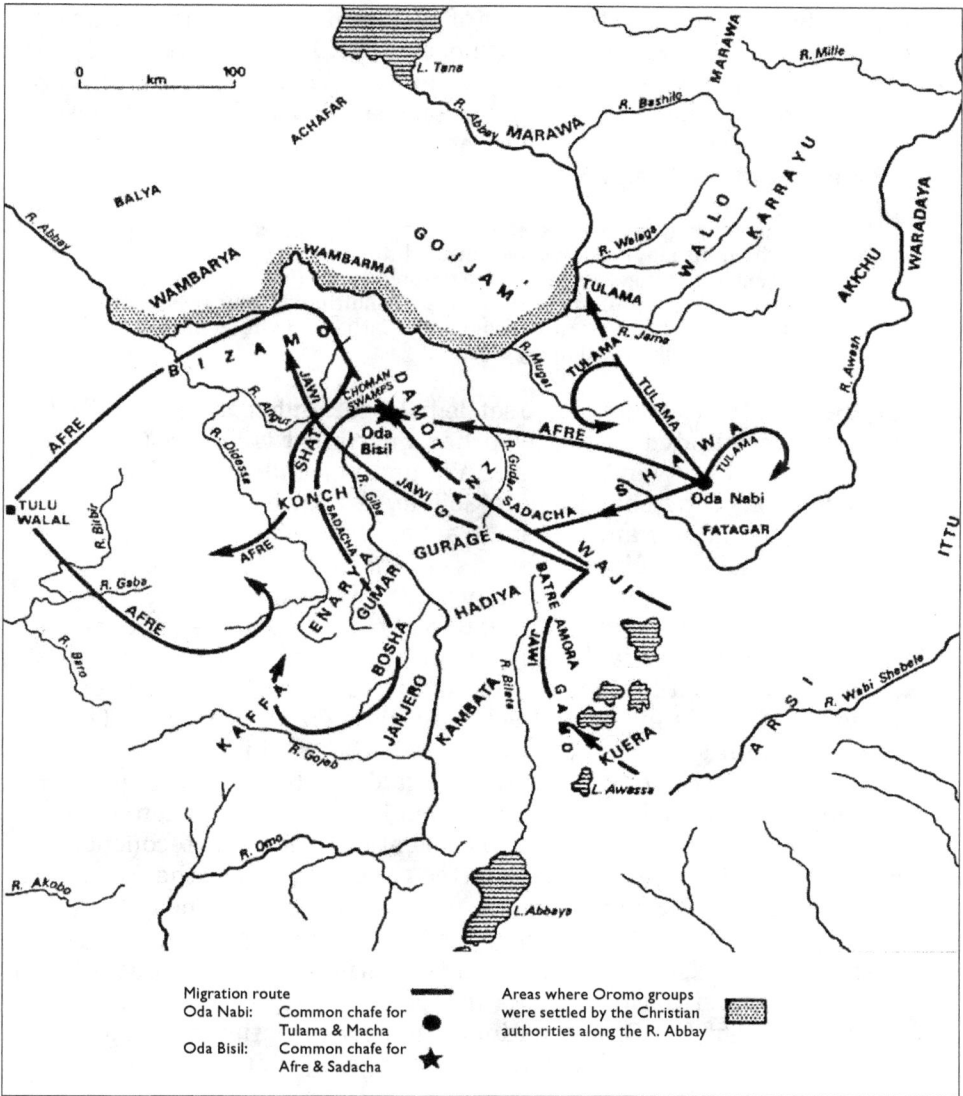

Map 12 The Macha and Tulama population movement to the south-western provinces (adapted from Hassen, 'The Oromo of Ethiopia, 1500–1850', PhD diss., University of London, 1983).

emperor who discovered the policy of turning his own victims into defenders of his kingdom, as mentioned above. He was particularly successful in this field. He even took the trouble to gather together the scattered Maya, the experts in poisoned arrows, and settled them together with the Warantisha and other Oromo groups in Achafar and Kurbaha (see Map 12 below).

> The arrangement was advantageous to him, as it enabled him to populate an area which his slaving raids had turned into an empty waste land. Their participation in slaving raids and in the suppression of rebellions suggest [sic] that the rendering of military service was a condition of their resettlement. Their conversion to Christianity [obviously Catholic] in 1619 marked their initiation into highland sedentary culture.[156]

In 1617 and 1618 Susenyos also settled a large number of *Yahabata*[157] and other assimilated groups who had quarrelled with the Oromo in the districts of Wambarya and Wambarma and other districts bordering along the Abbay River in Gojjam.[158] The obvious reason for doing so was that he wanted them to act as shield against the Oromo incursion from across Bizamo. Because of the Yahabata's long association with the Oromo they knew their war tactics as well as the likely time they would make raids. Thus, it was not difficult for the Yahabata to intercept the Oromo raiding party before it caused any damage.[159] However, the deeper reason for settling the Yahabata in the districts mentioned above is given indirectly by his own chronicler.[160] The Agaw inhabitants of these districts were either sold into slavery or exterminated in the continuous slaving raids that Susenyos and his governor of Gojjam had conducted between 1607 and 1616. When some of those who were settled in the above-mentioned districts reconciled themselves with the Oromo and started returning across the Abbay to the province of Bizamo, Susenyos was so alarmed, that he quickly moved many of them and settled them in Begameder and central Gojjam in the midst of a predominantly Christian Amhara population. Their conversion to Christianity permanently alienated them from the body of the Oromo nation. The new Christianized Oromo furnished the Christian kingdom with an ongoing or steady supply of soldiers against other Oromo.

In 1614 Susenyos ordered *Rases* Yaman Chrestos, the governor of Begameder, Sela Chrestos, the governor of Gojjam, Afa Chrestos, the governor of Amhara province, and Dajazmach Walda Hawariat, the

---

[156] Aregay, 'Southern Ethiopia and the Christian Kingdom', 512.

[157] The *Yahabata* were assimilated non-Oromo groups. They were given this name, meaning 'those who are mounted' by the Macha Oromo, because they were excellent cavalry men.

[158] Pereira, *Chronica de Susenyos*, 195–7.

[159] Hassen, *The Oromo of Ethiopia*, 69.

[160] See Pereira, *Chronica de Susenyos*, chapter 45, which states that Susenyos stayed for a month in 1614 in Agaw land, during which time the Agaw were exterminated and their land became a desert. Those who survived the slaughter were sold into slavery.

emperor's son-in-law, to go to Grarya in western Shawa and fight against the Tulama. The four senior officers of the kingdom (the first three were his brothers) led a large coordinated force into western Shawa. They surprised and defeated a section of the Tulama; the rest saved themselves by fleeing the battlefield. This was the first major expedition into western Shawa, after Susenyos had acceded to the throne in 1607. The four most powerful men not only devastated Tulama land but also 'captured women, children and cattle'.[161] However, the defeated and dispersed Tulama warriors, taking advantage of their knowledge of the topography of their land, regrouped within few weeks and started harassing, cutting off stragglers and ambushing military units that were detached from the main body of the army thus increasing the causality list of the victorious army. Thus, the victory in western Shawa was a short-lived success as the expeditionary forces were compelled to withdraw quickly.[162]

After Easter of the same year, Susenyos ordered Ras Sela Chrestos and Keflo (an official) to attack the Borana in Bizamo, for killing the emperor's messengers and disrupting the flow of tribute from the rich province of Ennarya. More than revenge for the death of his messengers, Susenyos wanted to open the route to Ennarya, the main province from which he received tribute of gold. The two powerful officials crossed the Abbay with a large army attacked 'the land as far as Baro. They captured cattle, women and children and returned singing triumphantly.'[163] However, the two officers inflicted very little damage on the Borana warriors, since they avoided conventional war and fled into dense forests, where the Christian soldiers could not follow them. Nevertheless, the expeditions to western Shawa and Bizamo clearly indicate that Susenyos' long-expected offensive against the Oromo, both to the east and south of the Abbay had commenced.

By early 1616, the Borana and the Barentu formed a league to attack Tigray, Begameder and Gojjam simultaneously. The news of the league sent a wave of terror throughout the three provinces. What inspired the formation of the league at this time most probably was part of the Oromo attempt to overthrow Susenyos. It may have also been the Oromo response to Susenyos' offensive across the Abbay. However, two things can be said with certainty. First, the league included Karrayu, who poured into Tigray, the Marawa, who had gathered on the frontier of Begameder, the Ittu, and the Borana themselves who attacked Gojjam. Second, it appears that the leadership of all the groups had met and discussed the details of the operation, including even the timing of the attack. Susenyos received the news of the formation of the league very seriously. He was determined to either dismantle it or minimize its effectiveness. According to his chronicler, after receiving the news, Susenyos went to Begameder, which was strategically located between Tigray and Gojjam. The

---

[161] Tafla, *Asma Giyorgis and His Work*, 331.
[162] Pereira, *Chronica de Susenyos*, 149.
[163] Tafla, *Asma Giyorgis and His Work*, 333.

presence of Susenyos in Begameder deterred the Marawa once again from exposing themselves to destruction. Susenyos wanted to march to Tigray. However, his officers told him it would be impossible to march to Tigray at that time.

> We cannot save [Tigray]. If we go down by Wag Meder and Abargalle we shall not find enough water and grass for our camp. It will not even suffice for the merchants, let alone for us. If we descend via Lemalmo it will be too far, and the [Oromo] will have returned, having done what they set out to do. Let us save [Gojjam] which is nearer to us, lest both countries be lost.[164]

With the safety of Begameder assured, Susenyos left Tigray to its fate and rushed to Gojjam. In Tigray the series of fortifications that were built at strategic positions by the energetic and able Takla Giyorgis, the governor of Endarta, and the son-in-law of the emperor[165] acted as an effective means of checking the flow of the Karrayu into the land. Takla Giyorgis carefully planned and built fortifications at strategic locations where mountains and valleys provided security. He even moved the provincial court near the frontier so as to galvanize his people and lead resistance against the Oromo. To limit the damage from the attack of Oromo warriors, Takla Giyorgis 'moved people from open and exposed plains into more defensible locations'.[166] The walls built around the fortifications made the Oromo spears, arrows and stone missiles useless. The few muskets that were used in the fortifications kept the Oromo cavalry at bay and the surrounding trenches punished their horses. The sheer determination of the Tigray peasants to keep the Oromo out of their land forced the latter to look for softer targets. These they found in the sparsely populated lowlands of Tigray, where the Oromo easily dislodged the Doba nomads.

When the Ittu warriors from Walaqa launched their long-expected attack on Gojjam, Hadaro, Ras Sela Chrestos' general, suddenly attacked them while they were crossing the Abbay and put them to flight. The Ittu warriors saved themselves from destruction by quickly returning to Walaqa. Upon Susenyos' arrival in Gojjam, he received the good news about the defeat and disorderly flight of the Ittu warriors. In 1616, Susenyos ordered all his senior officials to push the war across the Abbay to Walaqa and Shawa against the Ittu. Susenyos wanted either to 'destroy the Ittu or convert them to Christianity, and then settle them in Danbiya [Dambiya] and Begameder, for he knew that the Ittu and [Warantisha] ... could not live in harmony with the rest of the [Oromo] ... He thought that if he could control the Ittu, the rest were not powerful enough to be a threat to him.'[167]

Ras Yaman Chrestos, Susenyos' elder brother, and the governor of Begameder, the first minister and the most powerful man after the

[164] Ibid., 333–5.
[165] Aregay, 'Southern Ethiopia and the Christian Kingdom', 506–7. See also Pereira, *Chronica de Susenyos*, 149.
[166] Aregay, 'Southern Ethiopia and the Christian Kingdom', 507.
[167] Tafla, *Asma Giyorgis and His Work*, 335.

emperor, refused to go to Shawa on the ground that his soldiers were unwilling to follow him.[168] The Ras may have had his own axe to grind, since he did not like Susenyos' attitude towards the Orthodox Church. However, his refusal must have been prompted by practical difficulties that he had faced in western Shawa in 1614. For his insubordination, Ras Yaman Chrestos was removed from the office of first minister, which was filled by his younger brother Ras Sela Chrestos. The latter led a huge imperial army to Walaqa, from where he went on to Mugar in western Shawa. Everywhere the Ittu Oromo fled before him. Whatever cattle, women and children he gathered during his long expedition, Sela Chrestos returned to Gojjam without achieving the smashing victory he had wanted. Yet, his spirited campaign both in Walaqa and Shawa indirectly encouraged a significant number of the Ittu to return to Charchar in western Haraghe, while the rest were settled by Susenyos in Dambiya,[169] where they were converted to Christianity and became an integral part of the Christian Amhara society.

THE FAILED CONSPIRACY TO OVERTHROW SUSENYOS, 1617

In 1617 there was a conspiracy to overthrow Susenyos, organized by some of his close relatives, his officials and nobility who opposed his religious policy, and by those who were disaffected by his wars against the Oromo. Those who conspired to overthrow Susenyos included, but were not limited to, his own brother, Ras Yamana Chrestos, Yolyos, his son-in-law, Abuna Semon, the Patriarch of the Orthodox Church, Atnatewos and Keflawahad;[170] the last two dominated the regency of Ya'eqob, 1597–1603. As we saw above, it was Ras Atnatewos, who first crowned Susenyos in 1604. Interestingly even 'Walatta Giyorgis', the sister of King Ya'eqob, whom Susenyos defeated and killed in 1607, and the wife of the adventurous Za-Sellassie was involved in the conspiracy. Ras Yamana Chrestos was chosen to lead. According to Asma Giyorgis:

> The conspirators made the following pact: 'After killing the *Negus* [king], we shall also slay these others and after this we will never again crown a *negus*; we will live in our respective governorates; we shall also come to terms with [Oromo] on our respective frontiers. How can we bear three or four military expeditions a year?' They swore an oath to one another on the golden cross of Abuna Semon [the Patriarch].[171]

According to Pedro Páez, a confidante of Susenyos, the principal leader of the conspiracy was Yolyos, a powerful official who was prone to rebellion. For instance, in 1612, Yolyos and Keflo rebelled against Susenyos. They were tried and found guilty and sentenced to death. However, Susenyos spared their lives, exiling Keflo for a short time. Yolyos was

---

[168] Aregay, 'Southern Ethiopia and the Christian Kingdom', 501.
[169] Tafla, *Asma Giyorgis and His Work*, 337.
[170] Aregay, 'Southern Ethiopia and the Christian Kingdom', 464.
[171] Tafla, *Asma Giyorgis and His Work*, 339, 341.

pardoned and released from detention after eight days, Susenyos' daughter (Yolyos' wife) having pleaded with her father for his life.[172] When a genuine religious issue was added to his earlier humiliation and thwarted ambition, Yolyos was determined to kill his father-in-law.[173]

However, before they were ready to strike, the conspirators encouraged Patriarch Abuna Semon to hastily excommunicate Susenyos. Surprised by the seriousness of the challenge to his authority, Susenyos gave the Patriarch the option of immediately removing the excommunication, threatening his life if he did not comply.[174] Frightened, the Patriarch removed his excommunication and Yolyos then declared open rebellion. It was probably Yolyos' uncontrolled desire for killing Susenyos which at the last minute persuaded Ras Yamana Chrestos to abandon the cause of the conspirators for that of his brother, thus dooming the conspiracy.[175] In the battle that followed on 11 May 1617, Yolyos and the Patriarch were killed. The soldiers cut off the heads of both men and gave them to Susenyos, who displayed them on a mat[176] next to each other. The above-mentioned sister of Ya'eqob and Ras Atnatewos were tried and executed.[177] Along with other powerful officials, Keflo was beheaded in the palace compound and his body thrown into the forest to be food for wild animals. Susenyos spared the life of Ras Yamana Chrestos and sent him into exile.[178] His victory over the conspirators convinced Susenyos to move decisively against the Orthodox Church establishment (see Chapter 8). The next chapter will examine Oromo Christianization, the beginning of the breakdown of their social organization, their deeper involvement in the religious conflict of the time and the conflation of Oromo interests with those of the people they wanted to conquer.

---

[172] Boavida et al., *Pedro Páez's History of Ethiopia*, vol. 2, 234–5.
[173] Boavida et al., Pedro Páez's History of Ethiopia, vol. 1, 340
[174] Ibid., 341.
[175] Aregay, 'Southern Ethiopia and the Christian Kingdom', 465.
[176] Boavida et al., *Pedro Páez's History of Ethiopia*, vol. 1, 344. Páez, who had his own axe to grind against the head of the Ethiopian Orthodox Church, states that the Patriarch had 'a wretched end'.
[177] Tafla, *Asma Giyorgis and His Work*, 345.
[178] Boavida et al., *Pedro Páez's History of Ethiopia*, vol. 1, 345–6.

8

Oromo Christianization, Conflict and Identity, 1618–1700

As we have seen in the previous three chapters, Oromo pastoralists maintained a remarkable unity that enabled them to conquer all the provinces east of the Abbay River, while managing to settle in Amhara, Angot, Walaqa, Begameder and Tigray provinces. Job Ludolphus has summarized the factors within the Oromo society that enabled them to be formidable warriors.

> An encouragement of boldness and hardiness to adventure that by such a conspicuous mark, the sluggish and cow-hearted should be distinguished from the bold and daring. In their banquets and feasts the best bit is always set in the middle and he that takes it must be the first in any previous undertaking, nor is there any long consideration; every one person prepares to win honour to himself, ambition stimulating their fortitude ... But their most prevailing encouragement in battle is that because no man should be thought to fight for base hire, or out of servile obedience for another man's honour, but only for his own reputation, plunder is equal divided among all. They go to war, as if they had devoted themselves for victory, with a certain resolution, either to overcome or to die. From whence proceeds great obstinacy in combat.[1]

Ludolphus must have gathered the above information from his Amhara informant, Abba Gregory. This indicates that the learned Abba Gregory was knowledgeable about the Oromo society. It was probably such knowledge that convinced Abba Gregory and Ludolphus that the Oromo could be conquered only by use of European firearms and knowledge of its use.[2] What they did not realize at the time was that the factors that made for the strength of the Oromo society earlier were becoming a source of weakness for a society that had spread over such a vast territory. As I discussed elsewhere,

> when the Oromo were on the move, fighting for individual honour unleashed a dynamic spirit to push forward; but once they began settling down, fighting for individual honour became the source conflict among themselves. When common interest united them, the Oromo posed formidable challenges to the Christian state. With their spread over wider territory, it became very difficult to reconcile the interests of various groups. Clan interest, replaced the wider interest of the confederacy. Disharmony undermined their unity and their

---

[1] Job Ludolphus, *A New History of Ethiopia*, 83–4.
[2] Ibid., 218.

fighting capacity. With the break-up of confederacies, different groups fought against each other as much as they fought their enemies.[3]

Pedro Páez interpreted the beginning of the breakdown of Oromo unity in terms of their lack of a unifying king. In his own words, if the Oromo 'were all to unite and attack together, not even the emperor [would be able to face them], but since they do not have a king ... they never unite'.[4] A few years after the death of Pedro Páez in 1622, Alemeida, a Jesuit missionary historian who was in the Christian kingdom during the 1620s and early 1630s, explained the beginning of the breakdown of Oromo social organization in terms of the will of God: 'If God had not blinded them and willed that certain families and tribes among them should be at war with one another constantly, there would not have been an inch of land in the empire, of which they are not masters.'[5] By turning against each other, the Oromo gave breathing space to their enemies and encouraged the rebellion of their subjects, as will be shown further in this chapter.

While the Oromo strength was consumed in their own quarrels, their enemies rejoiced in the discovery of this weakness. It was Susenyos who, through his long contact with them, made the discovery and tried to turn it to his own advantage. His long experience with the Oromo enabled Susenyos not only to exploit the breakdown of their social organization, but he also adopted their effective *chiffra* fighting system, which improved his soldiers' speed, the coordination and the capacity to attack rapidly, or retreat in time.[6] We have seen in the previous chapter how Susenyos recruited Oromo soldiers and settled a large number of friendly groups in both Gojjam and Begameder. In the process, Susenyos succeeded not only in dividing the Oromo, but also in making a significant number of them defenders of the Christian state. Yet Aregay claims that 'Susenyos had no premeditated political or military plan for dealing with the [Oromo]. Throughout his long reign he did not contemplate any idea of recovering the provinces occupied by the [Oromo] by subduing and subjugating the conquerors.'[7]

On the contrary, Susenyos had a clear-cut military and political plan for dealing with the Oromo. He tried and failed to 'recover territory lost to the [Oromo]'.[8] Aregay himself acknowledges that 'Susenyos was the first emperor after Galawdewos who took seriously his responsibility for the [defence of] his provinces'.[9] By the time of Susenyos, Oromo warriors were a highly mobile force, whose striking power was still impressive. Their cavalry outnumbered even his. What is more, the Oromo mastered the technology of crossing the Abbay River. It was

[3] Hassen, *The Oromo of Ethiopia*, 58.
[4] Boavida et al., *Pedro Páez's History of Ethiopia*, vol. 1, 306.
[5] Almeida, 'The History of High Ethiopia or Abassia', in *Some Records of Ethiopia*, 149–51.
[6] Pereira, *Chronica de Susenyos*, 79.
[7] Aregay, 'Southern Ethiopia and the Christian Kingdom', 500.
[8] Caraman, *The Lost Empire*, 59.
[9] Aregay, 'Southern Ethiopia and the Christian Kingdom', 504.

said that they crossed the Abbay 'at all times without difficulties by swimming, or on rafts or inflated skins, or by clinging to their horses' tails.'[10] It is precisely for this reason that a significant number of Oromo groups settled in Gojjam, where they maintain their identity to this day. However, in the more northern rugged regions such as Begameder, Amhara, Angot, Gojjam, Tigray and few other areas Oromo cavalry was less effective. What is more, in the above-mentioned areas, the Oromo infantry had to abandon the secret of their strength. 'Many of the elements of surprise, such as mobility, flexibility and night attacks, which had hitherto made the [Oromo] foot bands invincible, had to be abandoned'.[11] For Almeida, a contemporary Portuguese missionary historian, it was God who ordained that the above-mentioned regions are 'very mountainous and consist of very steep ranges where the [Oromo] cavalry cannot readily make raids, which is the kind of fighting they practise'.[12]

Militarily, Susenyos realized that without formidable firepower, it was impossible to turn the tide against the Oromo. It was precisely for that reason that he sought foreign weapons and soldiers early in his reign. That support never materialized. Once Susenyos realized recovering the lost provinces was well-nigh impossible, he focused on the second-best option, which was settling various Oromo groups both in Gojjam and Begameder, where they defended the Christian kingdom from attack by other Oromo groups. In other words, there was no other Amhara emperor before his time (and those who followed him adopted his policy) who had a better strategy for settling the Oromo and integrating them into the Christian society.

Aregay himself admits that the 'settlement of the [Oromo] in specific areas, and their knowledge of the raiding habits of the bands, enabled the defenders to anticipate the time of incursions and the directions the bands would follow'.[13] Furthermore, there was no other Amhara emperor before the time of King Menelik of Shawa (1865–89) and later emperor of Ethiopia (1889–1913) who deepened division within the Oromo society itself as Susenyos did. His policies caused irreparable damage to their unity, permanently alienating a significant section of the Oromo from their nation and distracting their interest by involving them in the factional and brutal Christian religious conflict from 1626 to 1632 (see below). In short, Susenyos not only dragged some Oromo groups into the bitter internal Christian conflict, but also conflated their interests 'with those of [the] people they wanted to conquer'.[14] Consequently, Oromo interests and their remarkable unity of the earlier period would never be the same again. In the following section we will

---

[10] James Bruce, *Travels to Discover the Source of the Nile*, vol. 3, 646–7. See also Wallis Budge, *A History of Ethiopia, Nubia and Abyssinia*, 614; Tsega Etefa, 'Pan-Oromo Confederations in the Sixteenth and Seventeenth Centuries', 33.
[11] Aregay, 'Southern Ethiopia and the Christian Kingdom', 502–3.
[12] Beckingham and Huntingford, *Some Records of Ethiopia 1593–1646*, 135.
[13] Aregay, 'Southern Ethiopia and the Christian Kingdom', 501.
[14] Ibid., 440.

see how Susenyos further involved the Oromo in the bitter Christian religious conflict.

THE KILOLE GADA, 1618–1626

The period of the Mudana Gada (1610–18) came to an end at the time when the Borana were embroiled with the rebellion of their own subjects, discussed elsewhere.[15] Here it should suffice to say that the famous assimilated group, known as the *Yahabata*, who were excellent horsemen, quarrelled with their Macha brethren and sought military support from Sela Chrestos. The governor of Gojjam sent Dajazmach Buko, the highest-ranking Christianized general of Oromo origin, and Asagdir, another general, to fight against the Macha groups in Bizamo (see Map 12, page 291). With the assistance of expert *Yahabata* guides,[16] the two generals defeated two Macha groups and captured their cattle and women. Not long after, Sela Chrestos himself led a large army and devastated a number of Macha groups in Bizamo. The *Yahabata*, who feared Macha revenge if they were to remain in Bizamo, asked Sela Chrestos to take them across the Abbay. They were conducted without delay and settled in Gojjam. Susenyos was overjoyed with Ras Sela Chrestos victories over the Macha and for settling the *Yahabata* in strategic districts. Susenyos and Sela Chrestos 'camped on the broad plain of Wanbarma',[17] where the *Yahabata* warriors had an impressive audience with the emperor.

> 'Thanks be to God for having spared you from death and liberated you from enslavement by your overlords. From now on, may you be completely delivered from bondage to the devil. Enter the land of baptism. Embrace Christianity so that we may be equal in the Kingdom of Christ.' When he thus addressed them, they answered, 'Let it be as you say.' When they had thus agreed ... lands were assigned to them, each according to his due: Wasan Amba [Machakel], Fatabaden ... and Yamakal. He assigned all these districts to them.[18]

Most of the *Yahabata* were baptized increasing the size of the Oromo-speaking Catholic population within the Christian kingdom. What was Susenyos' motive for settling the *Yahabata* in the districts mentioned above? The answer is very simple and his purpose very clear. Susenyos wanted the *Yahabata*

> to act as a shield against the Matcha incursion from across Bizamo. The *yahabata* were excellent horsemen and brave fighters and above all they had a unique advantage: because of their long association with the Matcha they knew their war tactics as well as the likely time they would make raids ... However, the deeper reason for settling the *yahabata* in the districts mentioned above is given indirectly by his own chronicler.[19] The Agaw

---

[15] Hassen, *The Oromo of Ethiopia*, 62.
[16] Ibid., 66. See also Pereira, *Chronica de Susenyos*, 191.
[17] Tafla, *Asma Giyorgis and his Work*, 351.
[18] Tafla, *Asma Giyorgis and his Work*, 353.
[19] See Pereira, *Chronica de Susenyos*, chapter 45.

inhabitants of these districts were either sold into slavery or exterminated in continuous slaving raids which Susenyos and his governor of Gojjam had conducted between 1607 and 1616.[20]

As indicated above, Mudana was succeeded by the Kilole Gada (1618–26). Due to the internal crises that afflicted the Oromo at this time (briefly mentioned above and to be further discussed below), the Borana were unable to mount any attack against Gojjam. However, the Borana in Bizamo disrupted the flow of gold tribute from Ennarya to the treasury of Susenyos in 1619. Angered by this, Susenyos ordered Sela Chrestos, the governor of Gojjam and other officers to punish the Borana and restore the flow of gold tribute. They led a strong military expedition to Bizamo and dispersed the Borana.[21] It was probably in response to the expedition to Bizamo that, in 1620, the Oromo planned to attack Gojjam itself. Sela Chrestos received wind of their plan through his elaborate security system. He soon appealed to Susenyos for assistance.

> Macha, after having won their battle against Hadiya, Gurage, Barentuma and Tulama, had turned towards Bizamo, where [they] stayed and wanted to fight Gojjam and Ennarya. Please, come and reach me soon with all your army. We have duty and obligation to fight together and save Gojjam and Ennarya.[22]

By means of a hasty mobilization, Susenyos raised a large force and marched to Gojjam. But the Macha did not show up. The level of the river and the prospect of the Borana flight forced them to abandon the plan of crossing over to Bizamo at that time of the year. Sela Chrestos returned to his headquarters at Debra Abraham, and Susenyos went in another direction. The failure of the Borana to attack Gojjam became deceptive, and Susenyos' quick return proved to be a mistake. Eight days after their separation, Sela Chrestos bombarded Susenyos with an urgent plea for help.

> Half of the Macha have crossed via Guman to attack Gonga and Jigat, Agaw as far as Zigan, Min, Matakal ... and Dagar. The other half had crossed via Machakal and had camped in the highland ... Now I have decided to fight either for life or death. This is the time and hour to come and reach us soon.[23]

With his determination to prevent the disaster and punish the Macha, Susenyos rapidly marched in full battle order towards Debra Abraham, and arrived at a critical point, when Sela Chrestos and his men were under the rain of numerous Macha arrows, spears and stone missiles. The arrival of a fresh, large and better-armed imperial force turned the tide against the Macha who were compelled to flee in disorder. In the ensuing confusion and darkness the soldiers of Sela Chrestos, startled by the speed and sound of the flying Macha, abandoned their leader in a wild escape from their fleeing enemy and ended up chopping off each

---

[20] Hassen, *The Oromo of Ethiopia*, 69.
[21] Tafla, *Asma Giyorgis and his Work*, 333.
[22] Pereira, *Chronica de Susenyos*, 217.
[23] Ibid., 220–1.

other's heads. It was only the presence of Susenyos on the other side of the town that stopped the panic-stricken residents of Debra Abraham from joining the flying soldiers. This victory represented a well-known, yet sad story of the whole campaign. Well-known, because Susenyos' victories over the Oromo were very frequent and there was nothing new about this one. A sad story, because his subsequent action distressed the people of Gojjam who thanked Susenyos for saving them from the Macha attack. In less than a week, his soldiers finished their provisions, and Susenyos called together the people of the area and asked them 'to give him a country by lot where his army could go and plunder. It is only if my soldiers eat that I can protect you. The people of Gojjam felt sad and did not give him any country to plunder. Susenyos ordered his soldiers to plunder.'[24]

This must have outraged the Christian population of the area, as it did the chronicler, who did not hide his disapproval of the plunder of fellow Christians. From what followed this sad spectacle, it appears as if the Oromo were monitoring the movement of Susenyos at a distance. A day after Susenyos left Debra Abraham, the Tulama poured into Gojjam and destroyed half of the province, from Baranta as far as Debra Warq.

> They also destroyed and devastated the country of Nagashat and Manqorqorya, Enqora, Enset, Yashur, Zangema and Yakubbat. All the countries inhabited by Shinne, Chome, Gafat and Dabana Ansa were devastated. Since the [Oromo] first attacked Gojjam, they had never killed so many men and captured so many women, children and cattle. There were people from Gojjam who knew of the coming of the [Oromo], but they hid it from the emperor, since they feared his plunder.[25]

The above quotation reflects a number of interconnected sad stories. It appears that the peasants in Gojjam (and probably in other provinces as well) feared Susenyos' plunder as much as they feared Oromo looting. For instance, in 1620 there was a strong fear of a combined Sadacha and Afre Oromo attack on southern Gojjam. Sela Chrestos, the governor appealed to his brother, the emperor for an urgent help.

> Susenyos left at the head of all his soldiers. Despite the urgency of the appeal, he marched very slowly, evidently giving his men time to loot everything on the way. When he finally reached those parts of the province inhabited by refugees from Shawa and Damot the people, unable to sustain the violence of the soldiers, forced the emperor to take away his men and to leave them to their fate. At about the same time the Tulama were making devastating raids on the eastern districts of the province. The inhabitants, all of them Christians, abstained from asking for any help. The emperor and his brother were not far away, but the [Oromo] were feared less than ... [Susenyos' soldiers].[26]

The people who were devastated by the Tulama were almost all refugees who fled to Gojjam, either from Damot, Bizamo, Shawa or from other provinces (see Map 12, page 291). They had fled to Gojjam, because Sela

---

[24] Ibid., 222–3.
[25] Ibid., 223–4.
[26] Aregay, 'Southern Ethiopia and the Christian Kingdom', 493–4.

Chrestos and Susenyos had encouraged them to do so and had instigated their rebellion against the Borana.[27] However, both Susenyos and Sela Chrestos failed these refugees, unable to give sustained assistance to the victims in their respective provinces, and exposed them to Borana revenge. Instead of supporting them with whatever resources they had, they encouraged them to flee either to Gojjam or to Ennarya. By so doing, they exposed Gojjam to attack and endangered the defence of Ennarya, which was by now greatly reduced in size.[28] Gojjam, the haven for all refugees, seems to have lulled these victims into an unguarded state, giving them a false sense of security. The Tulama attacked only a day after Susenyos had left. He did not come back to assist the unfortunate victims. Although the reason for this callous behaviour is not given in the chronicle, it may have been caused by inter-related factors. First, the people of Gojjam displeased Susenyos by their refusal to give him a country to plunder voluntarily. Second, the Tulama who poured into Gojjam at this time were very numerous and this may have frightened Susenyos' soldiers. Third, the Tulama probably attacked with lightning speed and withdrew with the same speed, in order to reach their home with their booty. Finally, the death of Susenyos' brother at this time may also have affected his attitude.

In the same year (1620), while Susenyos was in Bure, he heard about the coordinated Oromo plan to attack the provinces of Tigray, Begameder and Gojjam simultaneously. While the Karrayu Oromo were descending upon Tigray, the Marawa warriors were on their way to attack Begameder. At the same time, 'the Ittu and the [Borana]'[29] warriors were marching to invade Gojjam. The defence strategy of Takla Giyorgis, the able governor of Enderta, once again checked the Marawa warriors from engulfing this province. According to the chronicler, Takla Giyorgis made errors that contributed to his defeat. Instead of remaining in his strategic fortifications, he met them in the plain, where the numerous Oromo cavalry caused havoc. What is more, Takla Giyorgis met the Marawa before they encumbered themselves with booty, and consequently their first assault was tougher and more difficult to withstand. However, with a heavy defeat Takla Giyorgis was able to retreat to his strategic strongholds, where his men fought bravely and prevented the Marawa from taking the booty they so much desired.

Alarmed by the bad news from Tigray, Susenyos dispatched two urgent letters, one to Sela Chrestos in Gojjam, and the other to *Dajazmach* Walda Hawariat, his favourite son-in-law and trusted lieutenant. He had been appointed to defend and protect Dambiya from his headquarters at Danqaz. In his first letter, Susenyos told Sela Chrestos that the Wallo and Jille had invaded from Amhara up to the frontier of Lake Tana and that he needed his urgent assistance. In the second and more interesting letter, he included the following warning: 'Do not fight with the [Oromo] face to face. If possible attack them when they descend a

---

[27] Hassen, *The Oromo of Ethiopia*, 68.
[28] Ibid., 78.
[29] Tafla, *Asma Giyorgis and his Work*, 333.

slope: otherwise attack them in a narrow pass, which is suitable to you and inconvenient to them.'[30] These few lines sum up the foundation of Susenyos' strategy against the Oromo. It demonstrates his profound knowledge of Oromo warfare and his strategy based on neutralizing Oromo cavalry. In most of his wars, Susenyos either attacked Oromo warriors at a point when they were crossing a big river, or after they were loaded with booty, or when it was scarcely dawn of day, when they were unsuspecting of any attack, or when they were in a narrow pass or on rugged and precipitous ground, etc. What the choice of these types of situations have in common is that they are inconvenient for cavalry warfare. Susenyos always tried to immobilize the Oromo cavalry, which the Christian troops dreaded.

Walda Hawariat did not heed Susenyos' wise instructions. When the former knew about the arrival of the Wallo and the Jille to attack Begameder, he hurriedly mobilized and rushed to stop them. The very sight of the large Oromo force put his men to flight. Oromo warriors fell upon Walda Hawariat and his remaining soldiers 'like a tidal wave'.[31] The casualty list included Walda Hawariat, many of his brothers, and other members of the royal family. Susenyos was deeply angered by the disastrous defeat of his son-in-law.[32] Resolved on revenge, he marched against the Wallo and Jille. The latter were caught suddenly, before they had time to finish the celebration of their victory and the sharing of the booty. Susenyos closed all the passes with his strong cavalry and organized his force into three flanks, the right and left flanks commanded by his brothers, and the centre by himself. This was rudely received by the Oromo cavalry, which put up short but most-obstinate resistance during which the Turkish and Portuguese musketeers caused havoc and put them to flight. This flight of the cavalry had the effect it regularly had on Oromo foot soldiers: nobody considered which way to go but only that he had to get away. In the general panic and flight that followed, a number of Oromo were crushed to death by the stampede of their own cavalry. Those who escaped from the massacre by the speed of their horses under the cover of darkness found themselves in a deadly trap since all the passes were guarded by strong cavalry units. They were easily cut to pieces. That day Susenyos, his two brothers and his 17-year-old son Fasiladas had distinguished themselves by contributing to the slaughter of the day. Fasiladas is reported to have killed three brave Oromo warriors, thus inspiring Susenyos' soldiers to spontaneously sing a praise song in honour of the young prince.[33] On the day of his victory, Susenyos is reported to have made a mountain out of the skulls of Wallo and Jille,[34] which was evidence sufficient of the greatness of the slaughter.

There is an interesting episode that shows how Susenyos treated his captives in a partial way. The groups that attacked Begameder at

---

[30] Pereira, *Chronica de Susenyos*, 225–34.
[31] Tafla, *Asma Giyorgis and his Work*, 375.
[32] Pereira, *Chronica de Susenyos*, 233–4.
[33] Tafla, *Asma Giyorgis and his Work*, 371.
[34] Pereira, *Chronica de Susenyos*, 235–6.

this time included Oromo and Amharic language speakers. The latter were the subjects of the former. Susenyos captured both groups, but he ordered the emasculation and mutilation of the Oromo and the adornment of the Amhara with beautiful ornaments.

> After this ... victory ... the king ... ordered that they cut off the genitals and chopped the noses and ears of the [Oromo] who were taken prisoners. Those who were *talata* [*dhalatta*] and *gabar*, he had them adorned with beautiful ornaments. And he sent the [Oromo] who were emasculated and the [*dhalatta*] who were adorned on their way to their homes. Because of this all the tribes of the [Oromo] became very sad and all the children of Amhara, those who were born here or those who were captured overjoyed, because of his love for and kindness to them. At that time all the people of the realm praised [and] loved him for saving the country and rescuing it from the [Oromo].[35]

A few points from the above quotation need elaboration. First, *talata* is an Amharic version of the Oromo term *dhalatta* ('he who is born'), and describes the status of the conquered, who were adopted as the 'sons' of a particular clan by the Oromo. 'The phrase "he who is born" does not have anything to do with real birth. It only describes the ideal type of relationship that should exist between the conquered and the conquerors after the latter adopted the former.'[36] Once adopted by the Oromo criteria of defining who is an Oromo, the *dhalatta* were part of the Oromo people. Oromo pastoralists also adopted *gabars* (tenants or serfs) but they abolished Christian society's class division under which the tenants provided labour and produced for the professional soldiers and nobility. The victorious Oromo pastoralists made the tenants, professional soldiers and the nobility equal and demanded services from all of them, including planting and harvesting and herding cattle for the Oromo. From the sources, it is not clear why the Oromo organized *dhalatta* and *gabars* into separate age regiments. By emasculating and chopping of noses and ears of Oromo captives while adorning the *dhalatta* and the *gabars*, Susenyos was aiming to achieve three interconnected purposes. The first was to raise the morale of Christians in Oromo-held territories. The second was to discourage the Oromo from attacking Begameder. Third, it would seem that thirteen years after he came to the throne Susenyos was still haunted by the campaign of his enemies who accused him of being 'a pagan Oromo'. His horrible treatment of Oromo war captives appears that it was intended to both frighten the Oromo and silence his internal enemies. For his mutilation of the Oromo, Susenyos is reported to have been praised by his people as 'a patriot warrior and hero ... who ruled with such brilliance and wisdom'.[37]

With his resounding victory over the Wallo and other groups, Susenyos resolved to try his fortune against the Oromo in Amhara, Angot, Damot and Walaqa. These campaigns, which took place from 1620 to 1622, had two interconnected purposes. First, he was seeking

[35] Ibid.
[36] Hassen, *The Oromo of Ethiopia*, 64.
[37] Tafla, *Asma Giyorgis and his Work*, 379.

out Yona'el, a rebellious relative, who sought refuge among the Karrayu Oromo in Amhara. On his way to the province of Amhara Susenyos ordered the collection of the remains of dead Oromo, who were 'piled up so that they might be a memorial for posterity'.[38] Upon his arrival in the province of Angot, Susenyos got an opportunity to widen the division between the Oromo and the assimilated *dhalatta* and *Yahabata* groups. Susenyos appointed an Amhara governor over the *dhalatta* and *Yahabata* with responsibility for guarding the monastery of Hayq[39] from Oromo attack. Using the pretext of that rebellion, Susenyos allowed his soldiers to plunder indiscriminately both Christian peasants and the Oromo in Amhara, Angot and Lasta districts.[40] Second, Susenyos wanted to punish those Oromo who had given refuge to Yona'el and other rebellious Christian elements, while at the same time striking at the Wallo, Karrayu, and the Marawa in their base areas, so as to decrease the pressure they were exerting both on Tigray and Begameder. He succeeded in doing both. He also succeeded in discouraging the Oromo from giving refuge to his enemies. 'The king laid waste the country of the [Oromo], who had protected [Yona'el]. This occasioned a division among the [Oromo] themselves.'[41] Susenyos went into Angot from where he passed into Amhara where he devastated 'the three houses' of Wallo, namely Warra Kiyo, Warra Nole and Warra Illu. The devastated Wallo groups tried their luck on him by resorting to night attack. They were beaten back. This continuous train of successes against the Oromo produced its desired goal. Susenyos soon received the head of Yona'el, his arch-enemy, in search of whom he was devastating province after province. Yona'el was killed by a member of the Wayu (Waayyyuu) *gosa*, who wanted to make peace with Susenyos and obtain the release of their twelve leaders whom he had taken hostage.[42] Susenyos returned to Begameder with numerous victories to his name and Yona'el's head in his hands. However, his victories were achieved at a price. His soldiers' indiscriminate plunder of both the Christians and the Oromo united both groups in their opposition to his regime.

SUSENYOS' ATTACK ON THE ETHIOPIAN ORTHODOX CHURCH AND ITS IMPACT ON OROMO INVOLVEMENT IN RELIGIOUS CONFLICT

Susenyos, who was barely literate, does not appear to have received good religious education as a young man. As we have seen above, Susenyos spent his formative years in banditry. During those years,

---

[38] Ibid., 383.
[39] Ibid.
[40] Aregay, 'Southern Ethiopia and the Christian Kingdom', 494.
[41] Bruce, *Travels to Discover the Source of the Nile*, vol. 3, 350–51.
[42] Pereira, *Chronica de Susenyos*, 255–8. See also J. Perruchon, 'Notes pour l'histoire d'Ethiopie: Règne de Susenyos ou Seltan-Sagad (1607–1632)', *Revue Sémitique* 5 (1897), 185.

Susenyos did not hesitate in plundering monasteries. When Susenyos was struggling for power, the Orthodox Church clergy remained loyal to Emperor Ya'eqob. This was demonstrated by the fact that, when Susenyos defeated and killed Ya'eqob on 10 March 1607, the Patriarch of the Ethiopian Orthodox Church Abuna Petros was killed on the battlefield as well.[43] Consequently, Susenyos does not appear to have 'fully forgiven the indigenous clergy for the loyalty they had shown to Ya'eqob'.[44] Susenyos also knew that the clergy fomented the Qurban soldiers' rebellion against Za-Dengel (see Chapter 6). Besides lacking strong attachment[45] to the Orthodox Church, Susenyos had a practical need for turning against church property. As a self-made emperor, his priority was to ensure the security of his throne, which depended on the loyalty of his Oromo allies and his soldiers. It was for that purpose that he settled his Oromo allies on the land he confiscated from the church in 1607, 'which highly angered the clergy'.[46] The key to winning the loyalty of his soldiers was through distribution of resources. However, he faced formidable obstacles in that regard.

> Lacking the former revenue from the provinces, the maintenance of the army became, after the security of his throne, the second major cause of concern for the emperor. The situation was desperate from the start, for early in 1608 he tried to despoil the church. He made a proclamation ordering the expulsion of unchaste monks from the monasteries and the transfer of their share of the church's income to his treasury.[47]

Because Susenyos suspected indigenous clergy of fomenting rebellions against him, he depended on the famous Spanish missionary, Father Páez, for advice and guidance. His interest in Catholicism started in 1609. He was drawn to the Catholic faith not only under the influence of the learned and wise Jesuit missionary, Páez, who was in Ethiopia (1603–22) and had good command of both Amharic and Geez languages, 'but also by the hope of military assistance against the [Oromo]'.[48] In his 1609 letters to Pope Paul V as well as Philip III, the Emperor of Spain and Portugal, Susenyos 'had asked for one thousand Portuguese troops'.[49] In his response the Pope gave Susenyos 'some hope of military aid. "As you asked us to do," he wrote, "we have commended the present needs of your kingdom to our very dear son in Christ, Philip the Catholic and [mightily] king of Spain, who, we trust ... will give you effective help."'[50] However, learning from the tragedy of Za-Dengel, Susenyos 'did not intend to embrace [the Catholic faith] until he had the

[43] Caraman, *The Lost Empire*, 57.
[44] Aregay, 'Southern Ethiopia and the Christian Kingdom', 460.
[45] Caraman, *The Lost Empire*, 58.
[46] Tsega Etefa, 'The Oromo of Wanbara: A Historical Survey to 1941' (MA thesis, Addis Ababa University, 1997), 17.
[47] Aregay, 'Southern Ethiopia and the Christian Kingdom', 478.
[48] Caraman, *The Lost Empire*, 80.
[49] Ibid.
[50] Ibid., 80–81.

backing of a strong contingent of Portuguese musketeers'.[51] In short, like Za-Dengel before him, Susenyos appealed to the Pope as well as the Emperor of Spain and Portugal for 'at least a thousand Portuguese soldiers'[52] and weapons with which he intended to secure his throne, turn the tide against the Oromo and impose Catholicism on the indigenous Christians.

Neither weapons nor soldiers came from Spain and Portugal, yet Susenyos' interest in Catholicism continued, primarily because of the influence of Pedro Páez, the learned Jesuit missionary and Susenyos' younger brother, Sela Chrestos. The latter was the governor of Gojjam and the most powerful man after the emperor, as he was made the first minister in 1616. He was converted to Catholicism in 1612. His conversion was sincere and it was inspired by spiritual yearning. According to Páez, Sela Chrestos was a well-educated, highly courageous man[53] who was devoted to the cause of Catholic faith. Bella Chrestos, the half-brother of Susenyos, who 'was highly regarded for his sharp intellect, theological learning and skill as a military tactician',[54] was also converted to Catholicism in 1612. In 1613 Susenyos confided in absolute secrecy to Sela Chrestos and the Jesuit missionary Páez, that

> he had taken an oath to become a Catholic ... Unable to commit this to writing for fear that secrecy would be breached, as had happened when Za Dengel wrote to Rome in June 1604, he decided to send an oral message through an ambassador. The envoy chosen was Fecur Eczie [Fequre-Egzi], a man of courage and intelligence, the convert to Catholicism.[55]

In a letter he wrote to Spanish emperor on 13 January 1613, Susenyos stressed that he cannot publically embrace Catholic faith without Portuguese military support. By then some prominent personalities who served in Susenyos' administration believed that, without the assistance of Portuguese soldiers, 'they would have no law and no empire'. In his letter to the king of Portugal, Susenyos complained about the power of the Oromo and requested him to save his kingdom[56] as the previous Portuguese kings saved his country in the 1540s. Amazingly, Susenyos even blamed the Oromo for hindering his enterprise of replacing the Ethiopian Orthodox Church by the Catholic Church. He urged the Spanish emperor: 'as swiftly as your Majesty can, you may send us valiant soldiers who are zealous of our holy apostolic faith'.[57] Susenyos never received the military support he sought from the Spanish emperor of the time yet, under the influence of Sela Chrestos and Pedro Páez, he started believing that he was powerful enough to impose Catholicism on the Ethiopian Orthodox Christians. For that

---

51   Aregay, 'Southern Ethiopia and the Christian Kingdom', 460.
52   Caraman, *The Lost Empire*, 94.
53   Boavida et al., *Pedro Páez's History of Ethiopia*, vol. 2, 289.
54   Caraman, *The Lost Empire*, 85.
55   Ibid., 93.
56   Boavida et al., *Pedro Páez's History of Ethiopia*, vol. 2, 282
57   Boavida et al., *Pedro Páez's History of Ethiopia*, vol. 2, 284.

purpose, in 1614 Susenyos started harassing the clergy on the pretext that they were 'indulging in sins',[58] and this was accompanied by brutal measures, all of which were meant to slowly but surely replace the Ethiopian Orthodox Church with Roman Catholicism.[59] Susenyos' unmitigated attack on Ethiopian Orthodox Church turned a number of prominent governors, including Yamana Chrestos, his brother, and Yolyos, his son-in-law and the former governor of Tigray and Begameder, against his religious policy. Both men rebelled in 1617, and they hoped to use Oromo cavalry against Susenyos. Yamana Chrestos boasted that the Karrayu and Marawa Oromo supported his cause.[60] The Karrayu and the Marawa at that time were not yet converted to Christianity. By supporting Yamana Chrestos, they had nothing to gain except deeply involving themselves in the religious conflict of the time. As we saw in the previous chapter, at the most decisive moment Yamana Chrestos betrayed the cause of the conspirators, and the rebellion ended with the death of Yolyos and the Patriarch of the Ethiopian Orthodox Church.

> Believing that he was now invincible, the emperor proceeded to issue inter-dicts against the clergy and the laymen who upheld the old church. By 1620 churches and monasteries throughout Damhiya, Emfraz, and most parts of Wagara and Gojam were closed. The recusant clergy and their lay supporters, who had become liable to imprisonment, flogging, mutilation and even hang-ing.[61]

Many of the people who were affected by Susenyos' religious policy sought refuge among the Oromo, thus involving them in the bitter religious conflict of the time. The Christian refugees sought to gain Oromo support for their cause, while, the Oromo probably planned to channel the anger of refugees against their own state. 'The result, however, was that the [Oromo], whose unity was already breaking down from their own dispersal, were dragged into the interminable conflicts in which their interests [were distracted by the religious conflicts] of the people they wanted to conquer.'[62] In short, the Oromo allowed themselves to be distracted by Susenyos' religious policy from those goals that served their interests.

On the one hand, the Oromo who served in his army and those who were resettled in Gojjam and Begameder, were converted to Catholicism. They became staunch defenders of the new faith. On the other hand, as will be shown below, tens of thousands of the Oromo fought on the side of those who supported the Orthodox Church. Thus, the Oromo were deeply involved on both sides of the religious conflict, further confusing their interest. While various Oromo groups were deeply

---

[58] Ibid., 242.
[59] Aregay, 'Southern Ethiopia and the Christian Kingdom', 461. See also Pereira, *Chronica de Susenyos*, 170–71; Boavida et al., *Pedro Páez's History of Ethiopia*, vol. 2, 242.
[60] Aregay, 'Southern Ethiopia and the Christian Kingdom', 464.
[61] Ibid., 465.
[62] Ibid., 440.

involved in the bitter religious conflict, Susenyos' campaign against the Oromo intensified. In June 1620 he issued a proclamation commanding his governors that if they failed to force the peasants to work on Saturdays, they would forfeit their lands and the peasants would also be penalized.[63] This measure further outraged the clergy, especially the monks, many of whom fled as refugees into Oromo areas. The flight and pleas 'of proscribed clergy' for deliverance from persecution created tension even among Susenyos' soldiers at the court. Fearing 'mutiny by his soldiers, [he] agreed to issue an injunction against further preaching and proselytism by the missionaries. He had thought of this step only as a measure to ease tension.'[64] This is confirmed by Azaj Tino, the principal secretary and the confident of Susenyos, who was with the emperor at that time and said: 'The emperor could issue a thousand proclamations that the fathers should not teach, but I would not stop asking them to teach me their doctrine.'[65] What is more, Susenyos' injunction was limited mainly to his court and lasted only for a short time. Unhappy with this systematic attack on the Orthodox Church, Yonael, the governor of Begameder rebelled on 1 October 1620, and fled to the Oromo in Angot. Susenyos followed him to Angot and devastated the Oromo who provided protection for Yonael.

Between 1620 and 1622, Sela Chrestos, the governor of Gojjam, had also conducted a number of campaigns against the Borana in Damot and the Ittu in Walaqa. When the Ittu Oromo saw Sela Chrestos' 'army from a distance, they fled, leaving their baggage behind. Ras Se'ela [Chrestos] and the army captured all their cattle, and the women and children also, in such numbers that it was difficult to drive them along. Having fought the Ittu, they crossed to [Gojjam] via Darra.'[66] Not long after, Sela Chrestos led a very successful expedition against the Oromo and even pushed the war into Shawa.[67]

In 1622, it appeared that Susenyos was at the height of his power. However, this power was more apparent than real. According to Caraman there were 40,000 soldiers under his command at the time,[68] but notwithstanding his military advantage, he was at his weakest politically, because his open hostility against the Orthodox Church turned the Christian society against himself, while economically he faced the formidable task of maintaining his large force. Between 1607 and 1622, in spite of his repeated victories, Susenyos was neither able to win back any of the lost provinces east of the Abbay, nor be guaranteed the safety of the route to Ennarya, his economic base. There was no progress in commerce or improvement in his revenue either. Due to the chaotic conditions that preceded and followed his accession, the treasury was almost empty. What is more, he was not able to wisely

63 Boavida et al., *Pedro Páez's History of Ethiopia*, vol. 2, 261.
64 Aregay, 'Southern Ethiopia and the Christian Kingdom', 466.
65 Boavida et al., *Pedro Páez's History of Ethiopia*, vol. 2, 303.
66 Tafla, *Asma Giyorgis and his Work*, 337.
67 Pereira, *Chronica de Susenyos*, 255–68.
68 Caraman, *The Lost Empire*, 75.

use the small amount of gold tribute he received from Ennarya. Accordingly, his war machinery became a deadly parasite on his own subjects. There was one treasure not greatly affected by Susenyos in his attempt to maintain his army. This was the wealth of the Orthodox Church. As early as 1607, he had already turned his eyes towards the wealth of the Church. By 1622 there was no alternative left, but to appropriate the property of the church. His embracing of Catholicism in the same year provided him with the ideological justification to dispossess the Orthodox Church. In March, Susenyos publically converted to Catholicism in the presence of palace officials and the governors and ended his first speech as Catholic emperor with this warning: anyone 'who does not hold this faith of mine shall not enter my palace because I shall cut off his head with this sword, "for he has his in his hand," because he is my enemy'.[69] By openly embarking on the destruction of the Orthodox Church, Susenyos turned the Christian society against himself. In so doing, he sold the ground that he had bought so dearly. The strength of the Christian society was rooted in its unity nurtured by the Orthodox Church. The monks and priests provided the ideological rationale for revolution. They ignited the revolutionary fire among the peasants[70] and fled to the Oromo areas. Susenyos followed them with devastating raids against the Oromo. This in turn alarmed the Oromo, and the need for self-preservation forged alliances between rebellious Christian elements and the Oromo, and it was these alliances that ended his regime ten years later.

By 1622 Susenyos must have foreseen something of his impending failure. Maddened by his inability either to restore the lost provinces, or to stabilize the remaining ones, Susenyos turned on the weak and defenceless minorities, the easy scapegoats who became the victims of his terrible wrath.[71] He dealt with his formidable problems of revenue by endless looting, pillaging and killing. To him these were necessary and essential. Susenyos was unable to think of massacre as a terrible thing to which other Christian rulers had resorted only on some occasions. He saw it as a weapon of government to be used against both internal and external enemies. It is not an exaggeration to state that Susenyos was an embodiment of the law of the jungle. He was a bandit first and emperor second. He presented a perfect blend of banditry with the excesses of an autocratic kingship. Insecurity and uneasiness became so strong in him that he had no choice but to rely upon his soldiers, treating them as his only shield in an otherwise hostile country. Their maintenance was his highest priority next only to his throne.[72] Pedro Páez, a confidante of Susenyos, expressed it best by writing that the emperor spent most of his life in warfare 'and he has made it his office to govern an army'.[73]

---

[69] Boavida et al., *Pedro Páez's History of Ethiopia*, vol. 2, 272.

[70] See for instance, Levine, *Wax and Gold*, 18.

[71] See Pereira, *Chronica de Susenyos*, chapter 41, where the destruction of the Agaw people is depicted.

[72] Aregay, 'Southern Ethiopia and the Christian Kingdom', 478.

[73] Boavida et al., *Pedro Páez's History of Ethiopia*, vol. 2, 204.

Between 1623 and 1625 his soldiers indiscriminately plundered 'all the districts between Walaqa and Ifat'. They even ravaged 'some stronghold of Amhara and Angot'.[74] The Oromo were greatly affected by the soldiers' ravages, yet they were unable to respond by mounting any armed raids into Gojjam and Begameder during this time. They were unable even to storm and take fortified mountain strongholds, known as *ambas*, within their own territories. The *ambas* are mountain tops that are 'lofty and steep on all sides [and] have on top a level space of sufficient size for people to live there'.[75] All passes to the *ambas* were guarded with men armed with inexhaustible and irresistible stone munitions. Hence, they were natural fortresses and quite impregnable to an enemy not armed with muskets. In Shawa, Amhara and Angot provinces, the topography of the land, including the *ambas*, allowed the Christian population 'to fortify themselves and to avoid complete subjugation by the [Oromo]'.[76] The presence of Christian elements on these *ambas* represented only a shadow of Christian administration because their presence neither affected the surrounding Oromo nor benefited the kingdom in the form of raising taxes and maintaining law and order. Some elements from among the rebellious Christians who took refuge among the Oromo had muskets, with which they rendered a great service to the Oromo by enabling them to weaken the Christian fortresses within Oromo territory. However, the Oromo were unable to push this advantage west of the Abbay. This was due to a misfortune of another kind, a consequence of the 1624 famine, which was caused by a long drought that devastated the animal population. The famine and the destruction of the animal population were catastrophic to the Oromo, since they depended heavily on their animals. According to his chronicle, instead of taking the trouble to kill them, 'burying the dead [Oromo] became the major task of Susenyos'.[77] However, he was not able to derive much military or political advantage out of the calamity that struck the Oromo. His hands were tied by the effects of the famine, as well as by the mounting internal opposition. On 11 February 1626 Susenyos officially submitted to the See of Rome, thereby disestablishing the Orthodox Church. With that move he consolidated the camp of his enemies.

THE BIFOLE GADA, 1626–1634

The period of the Kilole Gada (1618–26) ended before the Oromo recovered from the effect of the famine. It was succeeded by the Bifole Gada. Due to the effect of the famine, the new *gada* was unable to mount strong raids on the provinces west of the Abbay. The attempt made by

---

74 Aregay, 'Southern Ethiopia and the Christian Kingdom', 494.
75 Almeida, 'The History of High Ethiopia' in *Some Records of Ethiopia*, 97.
76 Aregay, 'Southern Ethiopia and the Christian Kingdom', 512.
77 Tafla, *Asma Giyorgis and his Work*, 381. See also Perruchon, 'Notes pour l'histoire d'Ethiopie: Règne de Susenyos', 185.

the Borana in 1626 was repelled by Susenyos without much difficulty. It was only in 1627, after they had recovered fully from the famine, that they were able to make a devastating raid on Gojjam. To deal with this situation, Susenyos appointed the Christianized Oromo, *Dajaz-mach Buko*, 'as the governor of New Damot [north of the Abbay River] replacing [Sela Chrestos] who was nevertheless ordered to assist Buko when called upon'.[78] When multitudes of Borana crossed the Abbay, Buko called upon Sela Chrestos, but the latter was not willing to stand in the way of such an onslaught. Thus he took shelter in the land of Gambatta in order to avoid the fury of their first assault. *Dajazmach* Buko, one of the most trusted and able generals of Susenyos, found his small force of 1000 foot soldiers and 200 cavalry surrounded by a large Oromo force. Any thought of flight was too late, nor was there any way to escape. The greatest part of the Christian force was cut to pieces, including their leader.

Buko, who was probably an Abba Gada leader, treated Susenyos with kindness during his years of banditry. After Susenyos came to power, he rewarded his benefactor by appointing him as one of his most trusted officials. Buko was converted first to Orthodox Christianity, given the second-highest most-important title of *dajazmach*, and was appointed as *Sahaflam*, or governor, of old Damot south of the Abbay River. When his province was permanently lost, Buko was moved to Gojjam, where he served as the most able general of Sela Chrestos. Most likely it was after the loss of old Damot that Susenyos divided the administrative areas of Gojjam into three regions, namely, Gojjam, 'Damot and the Agaw districts'.[79]

While Sela Chrestos was the governor of the region of Gojjam, Buko was that of Damot. Under the influence of Sela Chrestos, Buko converted to Catholicism and became one of its ardent defenders. Buko 'acknowl-edged Sela Chrestos as his lord' and became his most able general. In 1621, Buko dedicated 'thirty recusant laymen [who he] killed with his own hands', to Sela Chrestos, Susenyos and the Catholic Church.[80] Next to Sela Chrestos, Buko was thought to be the torch for the spread of Catholicism in the country. His death must have been a terrible blow to the fate of Catholicism. A previous *gada* leader, the defender of the Christian kingdom against the Oromo now became the defender of Catholic faith demonstrating the profound cultural and ideological change Christianized Oromo underwent within two to three decades, and this reflects on the breakdown of Oromo social organization.. The victorious Borana, loaded with whatever booty they found, retired to their country in Bizamo across the Abbay. Susenyos, who was deeply grieved by the death of Buko, left his town Danqaz in the hands of his son Fasiladas, and marched towards Zantra.[81] He expected that the Borana would spread

[78] Etefa, 'Pan-Oromo Confederations in the Sixteenth and Seventeenth Centuries', 34.
[79] Aregay, 'Southern Ethiopia and the Christian Kingdom', 538.
[80] Ibid, 444.
[81] Pereira, *Chronica de Susenyos*, 289–91.

themselves to loot Gojjam, but the Borana feared his retaliation and contented themselves with what they had got and retired. Susenyos was not willing to cross the Abbay after 1626. Even when he

> defended Bagameder from incursions by [warriors] of the Marawa and the Karayu, he was thinking mainly of keeping them out of Dambiya and Emfraz. His brothers, Yamana Chrestos [before his rebellion] and Afa Chrestos, seem to have carefully avoided provoking the [Oromo] within their respective provinces into open wars with them. They probably defended the districts unoccupied by the [Oromo] by building fortifications and by intercepting raiders. They increased the size of their armies by incorporating several units of [Oromo] warriors.[82]

In 1627, taking advantage of the conflict between the Tulama and Macha confederacy, several Oromo clans from both Macha and Tulama sections 'went over to Susenyos', who gladly settled them in Begameder, 'so as to prevent them from returning to their kinsmen. It was probably the warriors of these clans who made up the squadrons known as Boran in the chronicle.'[83] Those who were settled in both Gojjam and Begameder were converted to Christianity. They provided invaluable services to the state. Many were recruited as soldiers into the imperial army while others became retainers of provincial governors. The policy of settling the various Oromo groups in both Begameder and Gojjam continued under Susenyos' successors. The loss of all the eastern provinces was tacitly accepted. The offensive measures across the Abbay had become part of history, at least until the time of Iyasu I (see below).

In 1629, Takla Giyorgis, the son-in-law of the emperor, and the able governor of Enderta, revolted because of Susenyos' religious policy. His rebellion was unexpected as it was unnerving, because of the special relationship the governor had with the emperor. For instance, when Susenyos' daughter, whom Takla Giyorgis had married, died, 'the emperor obtained a special dispensation from Rome, and married him to another of his daughter[s]'. The rebellion of the governor of Enderta, 'of whose loyalty Susenyos was never in doubt, finally convinced the latter that the coercive methods he had employed for the propagation of Catholicism had only increased the opposition to the religion and to himself'.[84]

Takla Giyorgis, who by his selfless efforts in building walls and fortifications at key passes saved highland Tigray from constant Oromo raids, now appealed to the Oromo for help. His promise of rich booty attracted many to his standard and, as a result, 'the greater part of his supporters consisted of [Oromo] warriors from the clans that had settled in the Azabo and Doba plains'. The irony of ironies was that Takla Giyorgis, helped the Oromo to reduce some of the walls and fortifications that he had built and defended so bravely. This only

---

[82] Aregay, 'Southern Ethiopia and the Christian Kingdom', 513.
[83] Ibid., 523.
[84] Aregay, 'Southern Ethiopia and the Christian Kingdom', 506, 527–8.

shows the bitterness of the religious conflict of the time. It also demonstrates the degree of Oromo involvement in the Abyssinian fratricide with no benefit to their common interest. Accordingly, when Takla Giyorgis' rebellion was crushed in the same year, the Oromo warriors constituted the largest section of his fighters.[85] He was captured and hanged.[86]

Takla Giyorgis' rebellion was followed by that of the peasants of Lasta and Amhara provinces, in which tens of thousands of Oromo warriors were deeply involved. The peasant rebellion and 'the ravages of Susenyos's soldiers' are believed to have led to the death of 'more than 100,000 non-Catholic Christians of these provinces'.[87] Although this rebellion was temporarily quelled with heavy loss of life, the involvement of the Oromo on both sides of the religious conflict increased. In the meantime, when the Macha Oromo spies reported the absence of strong military force in Gojjam, because its governor left for Lasta, the Macha Oromo crossed over from their base in Bizamo to Gojjam, and 'they badly ravaged the Province'.[88]

> The misfortune was followed by another in Gojam, great to the nation in general, and greater still to the Catholic cause in particular ... the [Oromo] from Bizamo ... passed the Nile, laying the whole province waste before them. [Fequre-Egzi], lieutenant-general under Sela Christos ... [was] slain ... He was reputed a man of the best understanding, and the most liberal sentiments of any in Ethiopia; a great orator, excelling ... in the gracefulness of manner ... He was among the first that embraced the Catholic religion ... and was the principal promoter of the translations of the Portuguese books into Ethiopic assisted by the Jesuit Antonio de Angelis.[89]

As we saw above, in 1613 Fequre-Egzi was appointed as an ambassador and entrusted with the most secret task of reporting to the Pope in person Susenyos' profound determination to embrace Catholicism, and his unshakeable commitment for imposing it on his people. Though Fequre-Egzi's delegation was unable to leave Ethiopia[90] for Rome, his appointment as an ambassador reflects his closeness to the emperor and the latter's confidence and trust in Fequre-Egzi's commitment to Catholicism. His death was a terrible blow to the cause of Catholicism in Ethiopia. However, neither Sela Chrestos nor Susenyos even tried to follow the Borana into Bizamo to punish them for the death of the general, or to retrieve the booty they had taken. The repeated Oromo inroads into Gojjam continued. Apparently during this period that the Macha Oromo

---

[85] Ibid., 516–17. See also Bruce, *Travels to Discover the Source of the Nile*, vol. 3, 374.

[86] Caraman, *The Lost Empire*, 150–1.

[87] Aregay, 'Southern Ethiopia and the Christian Kingdom', 495.

[88] Etefa, 'The Oromo of Wanbara', 26.

[89] Bruce, *Travels to Discover the Source of the Nile*, vol. 3, 385.

[90] His mission was condemned to failure from the beginning because of Susenyos' insistence that the delegation to Rome must travel by land route to Malindi on the coast of the Indian Ocean. For detailed information, see Caraman, *The Lost Empire*, 94–103.

'ravaged Min, Gonga, Matakkal, Cara, Dangla, Kwakera, Ankasa, Dagar, Lala and Abola as far as the Gumuz country in the far west and south-west of the region of Gojjam'.[91] Susenyos, under fire from the rebellion of his own Christian subjects, left the defence of Gojjam to his brother and concentrated on crushing the Lasta peasant rebellion. The latter was spearheaded by a pretender named Malka Chrestos, who had the full support of both the Christians and Oromo of Amhara and Angot. Fasiladas, the crown prince, 'was given the overall command of the campaign against the pretender. The army of the latter was composed of [Oromo] warriors and poorly equipped, inexperienced Christian peasants.'[92] Yet Fasiladas was unable to defeat the pretender, who took over the important province of Begameder and established his court on the strategic 'hills of Wayna Daga overlooking the plains of Emfraz and Dambiya'.[93] This forced Susenyos personally to command the war against the intractable pretender. In June 1632, Susenyos won a decisive battle in which he slew between 6,000 and 8,000 followers of the pretender.

> [The n]ext morning the king went out, with his son, to see the field of battle; where the Prince Facilidas [Fasiladas] is said to have spoken to this effect, in the name of the army: 'These men whom you see slaughtered on the ground, were neither pagans nor Mohametans [Muslims], at whose death we should rejoice – they were Christians, lately your subjects and your country men, some of them your relations. This is not victory which is gained over ourselves. In killing these, you drive the sword into your own entrails.'[94]

Susenyos understood the true meaning of Fasiladas' words. There and then, he decided not to drive the sword into the entrails of what was left of the Christian kingdom. Susenyos not only lost 'faith in his cause' but he was unnerved by the combined Christian and Oromo opposition to his religious policy. 'Blaming himself for the rebellions and wars that had occurred ... he empowered his son to take whatever steps would end the fratricide.'[95] Without officially abdicating, Susenyos left the whole matter to his son, who soon summoned

> a council of state to consider the restoration of the old faith. The assembly voted overwhelmingly in favour of this proposal. Susenyos accordingly issued a final decree, on 25 June 1632, re-establishing the Orthodox faith. Referring to Roman Catholicism he declared: 'We first gave you this faith believing it to be good. But innumerable people have been slain ... for which reason we restore to you the faith of your forefathers. Let the former clergy return to their churches, let them put in their altars [i.e. tabots, or holy of holies], let them say their own liturgy. And do you rejoice.'[96]

In short, the restoration of the Orthodox Church was received with universal joy among Ethiopian Christians, the measure saving what

---

[91] Etefa, 'The Oromo of Wanbara', 24.
[92] Aregay, 'Southern Ethiopia and the Christian Kingdom', 528–9.
[93] Ibid., 530.
[94] Bruce, *Travels to Discover the Source of the Nile*, vol. 3, 385.
[95] Aregay, 'Southern Ethiopia and the Christian Kingdom', 530–1.
[96] Pankhurst, *The Ethiopians*, 107.

was left of the kingdom from consuming itself with wasteful religious war. Depressed by the collapse of his religious policy and his failure to turn the tide against the Oromo, Susenyos died heartbroken in September 1632 at the age of sixty-three.[97] He had been a captive for two years, a bandit for almost ten years among the Oromo, and a king for twenty-five years, during which time he led numerous campaigns against the Oromo. He repeatedly inflicted crushing defeats on them, but ironically he was never able to win back any of the lost provinces. He did his best to stop the Oromo advance with whatever resources he had, and even sought foreign aid that never materialized. Even his official submission to the See of Rome failed to deliver the desired goods. In the end Susenyos left behind a kingdom that was weaker, and more troubled by problems of religious controversies,[98] than the one he had inherited.

Susenyos was successful in respect of his aims in two ways. On the one hand, he settled various Oromo groups in both Begameder and Gojjam, where they converted to Christianity and became part of the Amhara society, thus remaining permanently alienated from the Oromo nation. In other words, Oromo settlements in Gojjam, Begameder, Angot, Amhara and Tigray provinces and their massive involvement in Christian affairs is a clear indication of the breaking up of their unity. As we have seen in the previous three chapters, it was Oromo unity maintained by the *gada* system, their military strategy and their speed in attack and retreat, which enabled them to conquer vast areas. Those who settled in the above-mentioned provinces, not only abandoned the *gada* system, but were converted to Christianity, or Islam in the case of Wallo (see the Epilogue). On the other hand, Susenyos' religious policy deeply involved the Oromo in the affairs of the Christian society, thus distracting them from their national interest. Several Amhara emperors followed Susenyos' policy of attracting the Oromo and turning them into staunch defenders of Abyssinian society and its heritage. In the remaining part of this chapter I will not follow the *gada* periodization, which I have followed from 1522–1632.

EMPEROR FASILADAS, 1632–1667, AND THE OROMO

Fasiladas was the second son of Susenyos. He was born in 1603, while his father was engaged in banditry. Like other Christians kings and

---

[97] In one sense he died in June 1632. His pride had been hurt as never before. His dream of establishing the Catholic faith became the nightmare for his people. The events that led to the re-establishment of the old Ethiopian Church probably finished him off.

[98] Donald Crummey, *Priests and Politicians: Protestant and Catholic Missions in Orthodox Ethiopia, 1830–1868* (Oxford: Oxford University Press, 1972), 18–19. See also Levine, *Wax and Gold*, 20–21. The religious controversy that bedevilled the Christian society between 1632 and 1706 is discussed at some length in Aregay, 'Southern Ethiopia and the Christian Kingdom', 531–83.

princes, Susenyos had many wives and numerous concubines, 'who bore him ... twenty-five sons, who outlived him'[99] and numerous daughters, who were given as wives to able generals, administrators and trusted servants of the emperor. Susenyos' eldest son, Kanafre, was brought up on the spiritual diet of Catholicism. The Jesuit 'missionaries had lavished their attention and favour on Kanafre',[100] the heir apparent to the throne. According to Pedro Páez, an eye-witness historian, the 14-year-old prince was an ardent supporter of the Catholic cause whose sudden death on 24 December 1614, deeply saddened his father and the Jesuit missionaries.[101] His death made Fasiladas successor to the throne. Like his elder brother, Fasiladas was converted to Catholicism. He was educated by the Jesuit missionaries and brought up in their faith. In fact, in November 1621, it was Fasiladas and Susenyos, who jointly 'laid the foundation for a Catholic Church in [the region of] Azazo'.[102] However, when Fasiladas realized the intense hatred his father's religious policy generated in his people, he abandoned the cause of Catholicism in favour the Orthodox Church. In 1628 those who opposed Susenyos' religious policy

> offered to the prince the leadership in the struggle for the reestablishment of the old church. Fasiladas needed such an alliance in case the Catholic faction objected to his succession. But loyalty and devotion to his father, and above all, the fear of being disinherited if discovered, made him refuse the offer. In effect, his cautiousness saved him from being implicated in the palace conspiracy of 1628, in which a rejected wife and a daughter of the emperor were involved.[103]

After coming to power, Fasiladas rounded up rival claimants to the throne (all his brothers, except one) and confined them to 'a mountain stronghold'. Even then, Fasiladas faced three major challenges. The first was the pretender who caused so much trouble for his father and continued with his claim for the throne. Fasiladas wisely restored the Orthodox Church, and this significantly reduced the support the pretender had enjoyed. The other serious challenge was the handling of the Catholic party led by his nephew, Sela Chrestos, and the Jesuits, 'who were desperately trying to bring soldiers from Goa', the Portuguese headquarters on the western coast of India. Fasiladas' fear of the Portuguese soldiers invading the country never materialized, yet he 'safely' confined Sela Chrestos 'in a mountain stronghold'[104] in Gojjam for three years, 'until he discovered that [Sela Chrestos] corresponded secretly with the Jesuits at the Red Sea coast'[105] for which he was hanged. Fasiladas is reported to have put to death 'not only Catholics, but anyone not a Catholic who was related to a Catholic or

[99] Caraman, *The Lost Empire*, 59.
[100] Aregay, 'Southern Ethiopia and the Christian Kingdom', 527.
[101] Boavida et al., *Pedro Páez's History of Ethiopia*, vol. 2, 242.
[102] Ibid., 271.
[103] Aregay, 'Southern Ethiopia and the Christian Kingdom', 527.
[104] Ibid., 535–7.
[105] Tafla, *Asma Giyorgis and his Work*, 407, see note 586.

in the service of one'.[106] The Jesuit missionaries were exiled to Tigray, four were killed by the people and the rest eventually expelled from the country.

The third challenge Fasiladas faced was the Oromo attack both on Gojjam and Begameder. Either in 1632 or early 1633, in order to deter the Oromo attack on Gojjam, Fasiladas sent one of his officials across Abbay, which ended in disaster. 'The Minister Walda Giyorgis lost practically all the soldiers he had with him while campaigning against the Tulama in Walaqa.'[107] However, as a result of a serious famine that lasted from 1633 to 1638, the Oromo were unable to mount any coordinated attack on either province. During the five years of that famine, Fasiladas took a number of defensive measures, all of which contributed to lessening the effects of Oromo raids on the provinces west of the Abbay. The failure of Fasiladas' first attempt to take the war across the Abbay convinced him to adopt five inter-related policies towards the Oromo. As a pragmatic leader, Fasiladas came to terms with the reality of the situation. He accepted the loss of all the provinces east and southwest of the Abbay.[108] Instead of trying to save them, he concentrated on saving Gojjam and Begameder. In 1635, Fasiladas appointed a certain Asgader, most likely a Christianized and Amharized Oromo, as the governor of Gojjam. Asgader recruited his soldiers from among the Christianized Oromo, so much so that one of his squadrons was known by the famous Oromo name of Asgader Qeerroo. Thus Fasiladas continued with his father's policy of fighting the Oromo with his Oromo soldiers. What is more, Fasiladas took defensive measures consisting of building walls, fortifications, and trenches at strategic positions west of the Abbay. During his long reign, the province of Gojjam, attacked by the Karrayu from Amhara, the Tulama and Ittu from Walaqa, and Macha groups from Damot and Bizamo, captured his attention. It was here that he developed his highly complex defensive measures. 'A long line of fortified strongholds shielded Gojam, in the east against the Tulama, and Itu, and in the southwest against the bands of the two Macha confederations.'[109] These measures failed to stop the Oromo from raiding deep into Gojjam. However, according to an eye-witness report, the warning given by the armed men posted at fortified strongholds helped the inhabitants of the region to flee to places of safety in time.[110] Finally, along with his policy of building walls and strong fortifications in the provinces of Gojjam and Begameder, Fasiladas intensified his father's

---

[106] Ibid.
[107] Aregay, 'Southern Ethiopia and the Christian Kingdom', 544.
[108] Abir, *Ethiopia and the Red Sea*, 231–2.
[109] Aregay, 'Southern Ethiopia and the Christian Kingdom,' 542, 545.
[110] Richard Pankhurst, *An Introduction to the Economic History of Ethiopia from Early Times to 1800* (London: Lalibela House, 1961), 171. What is more, in 1648 the Yemeni ambassador, 'Hasan bin Ahmad el Haimi ... had seen one of the frontier posts ... guarded by ten armed men who were changed every month.' See J. van Donzel, *A Yemenite Embassy to Ethiopia 1647–1649* (Stuttgart: F. Steiner, 1986), 113.

policy of settling large Oromo groups in the provinces of Gojjam, Bega-meder, Angot and Amhara, where they were made to accept Orthodox Christianity, gradually integrating them into the mainstream of Christian Amhara society. Fasiladas is remembered for establishing Gondar as his capital in 1636.

The 35-year reign of Fasiladas was marked by continuous Oromo attacks on the frontiers of different provinces, though he 'did not fight much against the [Oromo]'.[111] To deter the Oromo attack on Gojjam, sometime before 1645 Fasiladas sent a military expedition against the Afre Confederacy, purportedly to punish them for giving support to Qerlos, the son of Sela Chrestos. It is interesting to note that Qerlos, whose father defended the Christian kingdom against the Oromo for more than twenty years, was leading spirited Oromo attacks on Gojjam. 'Greatly frustrated by the hit and ran strategy of the Oromo, [Fasiladas] decided to mount a frontal attack on the Oromo, south of the Abbay. In 1645, he led a strong expedition to [Bizamo] and defeated [Hakako clan] at a place called Sobe.'[112] His goal was to deter the Oromo 'from crossing into Wambarya and Wambarma.'[113] In response to Fasiladas' expedition across the Abbay, the Oromo mounted what appears to have been a coor-dinated military action by 'staging more attacks'[114] on Gojjam, Ennarya, Dambiya and Begameder (see Map 12, page 291). Their goal probably was to convince Fasiladas that crossing the Abbay to attack them was well-nigh impossible. Thus, after 1645, he did not attempt this again. When Yemeni ambassador, Hasan bin Ahmad el Haimi, visited Gondar in 1648, he reported that the Oromo were 'exerting strong pressure on the Christian [kingdom] from all sides and borders of their territory, none of these regions being devoid of them'.[115] The ambassador's report confirms that the Oromo were firmly established in all the northern rugged regions of the Christian kingdom. Instead of conducting military expeditions against the Oromo across the Abbay, Fasiladas focused on providing land for a number of Oromo migrant groups for the purpose of 'reinforcing the fortified strongholds that were created during the time of his father. At the same time he strengthened and extended the fortifications.'[116] Unable to stop the Oromo attacks on Gojjam and other provinces, as early as 1636, Fasiladas embarked on slaving raids on the Agaw.

> Raids on the Agaw and Shanqula tribes of Gojam were regularly undertaken until 1652, but on a much smaller scale than those made by Susenyos. Fasi-ladas and his captains seem to have limited themselves to attacking one or, at most, two tribes each year. This would mean that Fasiladas did not conduct the raids for the purpose of supplying and maintaining his soldiers. The proceeds from the sale of slaves may have been used for financing the constructions at Gondar and the restoration of churches in the various parts of the county.[117]

111 Tafla, *Asma Giyorgis and his Work*, 407.
112 Etefa, 'The Oromo of Wanbara', 26.
113 Aregay, 'Southern Ethiopia and the Christian Kingdom', 545.
114 Etefa, 'The Oromo of Wanbara', 26.
115 Donzel, *A Yemenite Embassy to Ethiopia 1647–1649*, 113.
116 Aregay, 'Southern Ethiopia and the Christian Kingdom', 545.
117 Ibid., 542–3.

So, like his father, Fasiladas was unable to turn the tide against the Oromo. For instance, in or around 1662, the Oromo attacked Gojjam from across the Abbay River. While, Fasiladas was fighting against the Borana in Gojjam, the Marawa and the Wallo attacked Begameder.[118] The Warra Himano Wallo warriors fought against Fasiladas' general in Begameder, which resulted in a 'great slaughter on both sides'.[119] In Gojjam, Fasiladas' 'system of fortification had failed to check [the Oromo]'.[120] It was precisely for this reason that the Oromo remained a significant part of the population of Gojjam, especially in the districts of Wanbara, where they maintained their language and even the *gada* system, up to now. During Fasiladas' long reign, the Oromo made significant territorial gains.

> The Wallo and the Wechale [Wuchale] spread over all of southern Amhara and the whole of Ganh. Some Marawa and Karayu clans pushed northwards from Azabo and established themselves in the lowlands of Serae and Manbert, districts of Tigre. Those clans which were already established in northern Amhara and in Angot extended their conquest into various parts of Lasta and Bagemeder.[121]

However, the Oromo who settled in central parts of Gojjam, Begameder and Lasta, were converted to Christianity and became part of the Amhara people. Interestingly, it was the Christianized and Amharized Oromo elements that established their own dynasty in Gojjam during the eighteenth century (see Epilogue).

EMPEROR YOHANNES I, 1667–1682, AND THE OROMO

Fasiladas died in October 1667 and was succeeded by his son Yohannes. The latter was a deeply religious man, who 'paid a lot of attention to church matters and to ways of regulating them'.[122] Yohannes does not seem to have chosen his Amhara provincial governors for their military abilities. Though not a military man, Yohannes conducted 'serious of expeditions against the Oromo, the Gumuz and the Agaw of Matakkal',[123] in western Gojjam. He abandoned military expeditions across the Abbay, and instead focused on rebuilding some fortifications in eastern Gojjam, and also massively recruited Christianized Oromo into his army. Yohannes' reign was characterized by the internecine religious conflict and the Oromo involvement in the fratricide. A brief discussion of the religious controversy is necessary as Christianized Oromo were involved on both sides of the conflict as will be shown further in this chapter.

[118] Etefa, 'Pan-Oromo Confederations in the Sixteenth and Seventeenth Centuries', 35.
[119] Tafla, *Asma Giyorgis and his Work*, 409.
[120] Aregay, 'Southern Ethiopia and the Christian Kingdom', 545.
[121] Ibid., 547.
[122] Etefa, 'The Oromo of Wanbara', 27.
[123] Aregay, 'Southern Ethiopia and the Christian Kingdom', 547.

The origin of religious conflict goes back to the time when Susenyos imposed Catholicism on the Orthodox Christians, who for centuries believed in the Monophysite faith based on the doctrine of the single nature of Christ. The Monophysite doctrine among Ethiopians was and still is known as *Tawahdo*. While, the Catholic missionaries preached about the human and the divine nature of Christ, the tenet of the Ethiopian Orthodox Church was 'that the human nature [of Christ] was made perfect by its union with divinity and that the two natures were united in such a manner that they could not be distinguished or separated from each other'. To explain the union of the humanity and divinity of Christ, some Orthodox clergy developed the doctrine of *Qeb'at* or unction. In 1620 the Jesuit missionaries condemned the *Qeb'at* doctrine together with that of the *Tawahdo*. It was during 'the years of persecution and exile [that] the geb'at [*sic*] doctrine was accepted by many of the exiled communities of'[124] the Ewostatewos monastery in Tigray, while the monks at the monastery of Takla Haymanot in western Shawa adhered to the *Tawahdo* doctrine. The conflict between the followers of the *Qeb'at* and *Tawahdo* doctrines came to head during the reign of Yohannes.

The proponents of the *Qeb'at* doctrine argued that 'it was not Christ's humanity but Christ himself who was glorified by unction and made the son of God'. Such interpretation was seen as the threat to 'the basic Christian doctrines of the Trinity and of the Redemption'. The controversy between the proponents of the *Tawahdo* and the *Qeb'at* pitted the order of the monasteries of Takla Haymanot in western Shawa against those of Ewostatewos in Tigray. 'Since monasteries of both orders were found in all the [Christian] provinces, every part of the country began to feel the divisive effects of the controversy.'[125] Thus, to the doctrinal dispute was added a regional aspect of the conflict fuelled by monks and monasteries, which combined to make the conflict a very bitter 'civil war'.[126]

> Probably for the first time in the history of the country wounded and captured Christians were mercilessly emasculated by their neighbours and fellow Christians ... The forces pitted against each other were more or less well balanced, and each side sought the assistance of neighbouring [Oromo] tribes and clans ... Their participation in the wars was not prompted by motives of territorial expansions. The veteran [Oromo] were attracted by the prospects of looting. For the young men, apprenticed in the lower age-sets, these wars provided opportunities for the first killings that would transform them into proud members of the warrior age-sets.[127]

Yohannes sided with the faction that espoused the *Qeb'at* doctrine. He appointed the ardent supporters of the *Qeb'at* faction to the highest positions in his government. In order to divert attention from the doctrinal religious conflict that divided the Christian society, he

[124] Ibid., 549–51.
[125] Ibid., 552, 554, 555.
[126] Tafla, *Asma Giyorgis and his Work*, 409.
[127] Aregay, 'Southern Ethiopia and the Christian Kingdom', 570.

adopted two measures, the first being the expulsion of the descendants of the Portuguese who had lived in Ethiopia since the time of Emperor Galawdewos (1540–59), together with the persecutions of the Muslim and Falasha minorities. According to the Chronicle of Yohannes I, as reported by Pankhurst, the Catholic descendants of the Portuguese settlers were given the option of leaving the country or conversion to Orthodox Christianity.

> As for Muslims, they are prohibited from living with the Christians; they must remain separate and live apart, forming a village of their own; no Christian may enter their service, neither a free man nor a slave may serve them, and neither husband nor wife may live with them. As for the Falashas, called Kayla, who are of the Jewish religion, they must not live with the Christians, but must separate themselves from them, and live apart, forming a [separate] village.[128]

In short, while the Muslim and Falasha minorities were 'forced to live in segregated quarters' of Gondar the 'various descendants of the Portuguese were rounded up from where ever they lived and escorted, at gunpoint, past the frontier with Funj',[129] a kingdom in the Sudan.

The second measure Yohannes adopted was to indulge his soldiers embarking on the tried and tested policy of enslaving and plundering the various Agaw groups. His slaving raids against the Agaw were conducted

> with the frequency and thoroughness of Sarsa Dengel and Susenyos. The raids of Yohannes were so devastating that, after the second expedition into Gojam, the pagan Agaw begged to be made Christians ... The raids brought gold and silver needed for donations and for the maintenance of the imperial household. But the extent to which he indulged in them suggests that the raids also served to distract the attention of the soldiers.[130]

Yohannes is reported to have 'abandoned the war'[131] against the Oromo. In fact, militarily Yohannes depended on his Christianized Oromo subjects. In Gojjam, Walle, the leader of the Macha groups, which Susenyos or Fasiladas had settled in Gojjam, was made *dajazmach* of the southern districts. As during the time of Susenyos, a Christianized Oromo, with the highest Abyssinian title, was made the governor of an important province. Yohannes also formed a number of squadrons from among the Marawa and Karrayu Oromo, who had settled in some parts of Begameder, Lasta and the adjacent districts. These were the backbone of his force in the northern provinces. However, the supporters of the *Tawahdo* doctrine, in Tigray and Lasta, rebelled against Yohannes and secured the support of the Marawa and Karrayu Oromo of Angot and Tigray[132]. During the three years of factional war, Yohannes received assistance against the *Tawahdo* faction from the Oromo in Amhara and Angot. In short, the Oromo were deeply involved in the bitter factional

---

[128] Pankhurst, *The Ethiopians*, 118.
[129] Aregay, 'Southern Ethiopia and the Christian Kingdom', 565.
[130] Ibid., 566.
[131] Tafla, *Asma Giyorgis and his Work*, 409.
[132] Aregay, 'Southern Ethiopia and the Christian Kingdom', 571.

conflict of the time. They would soon try to be king makers for their own faction.

IYASU I, 1682–1706

Yohannes died on 19 July 1682, and was succeeded by his 22-year-old son, Iyasu I, who was the eldest of three surviving sons of Yohannes. Though his father had supported the *Qeb'at* doctrine, Iyasu was an ardent supporter of the *Tawahdo* doctrine. In 1680 he had rebelled against his father and together with his followers, had fled to the Oromo 'in Walaqa and Amhara. With the help of the [Oromo], the rebels destroyed the fortifications in eastern Gojam that Yohannes had rebuilt.' Iyasu soon made peace with his father and returned to the imperial court. However, within a year he 'rebelled again and was caught while trying to reach the [Oromo] in Amhara'. Once again, the merciful father pardoned his restless son, who succeeded to the throne as the champion of the *Tawahdo* doctrine. The *Qeb'at* doctrine was condemned and those *Tawahdo* partisans who had lost their positions of power under Yohannes regained them. Iyasu needed strong military power for policing his fractured society. As part of his defence strategy, he had 'many squadrons of Christianized'[133] Oromo warriors, which suggests that he used them for imposing the *Tawahdo* doctrine on the supporters of the *Qeb'at* doctrine. What is more, to integrate Christianized Oromo into his administration, Iyasu elevated an enterprising warrior, *Dajazmach* Tige, 'to the prestigious rank of *Behtwaddad*, or 'Beloved' of the king, apparently the first Oromo to enjoy the highly esteemed status.'[134]

THE FIRST ATTEMPT OF THE CHRISTIANIZED OROMO ELITE TO BE KING MAKERS

The *Qeb'at* monasteries were numerous in Gojjam, where the Oromo 'become staunch partisans of the doctrine'.[135] The leader and the champion of the cause of *Qeb'at* faction was none other than the famous *Dajazmach* Walle, the Christianized Oromo governor of the southern districts in Gojjam. Walle wanted to be a king maker of the *Qeb'at* faction. For that purpose, he crossed the Abbay and appealed to his Macha brethren to support him in his scheme to put on the throne a man of his choice. In this he was not disappointed. 'The [Oromo], who sought but a [pretext] for invading Abyssinia readily embraced this opportunity, and rallied to him on all sides. His army, in a very short time, was exceedingly

---

[133] Ibid., 573, 574, 546.
[134] Pankhurst, *The Ethiopian Borderlands: Essays in Regional History from Ancient Times to the End of the 18th Century* (Lawrenceville NJ: The Red Sea Press, 1997), 317.
[135] Aregay, 'Southern Ethiopia and the Christian Kingdom', 578.

numerous.'[136] Amidst them Walle proclaimed one Yeshaq an emperor, and started cautiously marching towards Gojjam with the intention of marching on Gondar. The first wing of Walle's force arrived in Gojjam, while its leader remained behind in Macha land. Iyasu, an energetic and very brave young man, who had already distinguished himself as an able horseman and 'the best marksman with passion for war'[137] marched with full speed and 'met them just after they had crossed the river. He succeeded in dispersing them before they and their allies could organize themselves for an orderly march.'[138] The unfortunate Yeshaq was captured and executed, while Walle continued mobilizing support for his cause from among his Oromo allies. To reduce the pressure on Gojjam, Iyasu opened negotiation for reconciliation with Walle. We do not know the terms of reconciliation. What is certain is that Walle repented and made peace with Iyasu, who pardoned him. This demonstrates the assimilation of the Christianized Oromo into the Amhara political culture.

While Walle was trying to be a king maker on his own, the Christianized Oromo soldiers which Yohannes had settled in Lasta and the adjacent districts were also preparing to put on the throne a man of their choice. For this purpose they appealed to their brethren in Amhara and the surrounding areas. The Karrayu and the Marawa soon joined with them and with a king of their choice at their head, 'they began to move towards Bagameder, probably with the intention of reaching Gondar'.[139] Once again Iyasu intercepted and dispersed them. However, these two attempts by the Christianized Oromo to be the force behind the throne was the signal for what was to come. Within a few decades, the Oromo leaders of first Wallo and then Yajju, were to become the regents of the puppet Amhara kings of Gondar.[140] Nevertheless, in the short run, Iyasu's easy victories encouraged him to try his luck against other Oromo across the Abbay. There were also five other factors that seem to have influenced his decision.

Iyasu appears to have carefully read Bahrey's *Zenahu le Galla*. Like Za-Dengel, eighty years earlier, Iyasu was inspired by Abba Bahrey's manuscript. Like Abba Bahrey and Za-Dengel, he was a Christian nationalist who 'appears to have been moved by deep religious feeling'.[141] Although the Oromo treated Iyasu kindly in 1680 when he was a refugee[142] among them across the Abbay, he forgot their generous hospitality and just like Za-Dengel, eight decades before him, Iyasu conducted spirited wars against them. His objective was to reverse

---

[136] Bruce, *Travels to Discover the Source of the Nile*, vol. 3, 458–9.
[137] Ibid., 453.
[138] Aregay, 'Southern Ethiopia and the Christian Kingdom', 578–9.
[139] Ibid., 579. See also I. Guidi (trans.), *Annales Yohannis I, Iyasu I et Bakaffa* (Paris: 1905), 106. I am indebted to Abou Bamba for his translation of this text for me.
[140] Bruce, *Travels to Discover the Source of the Nile*, vol. 4, 146–88.
[141] Levine, *Wax and Gold*, 25.
[142] Pankhurst, *The Ethiopian Borderlands*, 309.

the tide to be against the Oromo, and to force them into submission. That task would be accomplished two hundred years later, with modern Europeans weapons of destruction. Nevertheless, Iyasu's spirited campaigns against the Oromo demonstrate the striking impact Bahrey's *Zenahu le Galla* likely had on him too. Iyasu was the most powerful Christian emperor since the time of Susenyos, and he was able to marshal a significant number of fire arms, probably including even a few artillery pieces, which were effectively used to his 'full advantage'.[143] Thus, Iyasu 'marshalled considerably greater strength, and many more firearms, than his predecessors. He was therefore militarily in much better position than the Oromos, many of whom he sought to assimilate or bring under his control.'[144]

What is more, Iyasu appears to have had real passion for war, especially against the Oromo. This becomes obvious from the French physician Charles Poncet's description.[145] He had evidently been overflowing with an inborn exuberant energy and an ardour and imagination for which slave-raiding expeditions west of the Abbay provided little outlet. What is more, he was easily bored with sedentary life at his palace in Gondar. 'In the rare times when he was not warring against the [Oromo] around Gojam or raiding the Shanqela and the Dubani of the western regions, he preferred to go on hunting expeditions rather than to stay in Gondar.'[146]. During his short stay with the Oromo across the Abbay in the land of the Tulama, when he rebelled against his father, Iyasu realized that his Christian subjects in the land of the Oromo were restive and expected assistance from the Christian leadership. At this time he soothed the Christians in Tulama land with his now famous promise to free them from the oppression of the Tulama.[147] Finally, Iyasu needed a cause to serve, a cause involving extensive military campaigns. This he found in the Christians' appeal for assistance against the Oromo, and his own secret ambition to force the Oromo into submission. Thus, more than half a century after it was abandoned, Iyasu resuscitated the campaign across the Abbay River. It was perhaps because of this that he was known as 'Iyasu the Great'.

Iyasu got the opportunity to launch his anti-Oromo campaign when the Liban from Bizamo crossed the Abbay and attacked Gojjam in 1683. He left Gondar and swiftly marched towards Gojjam and his sudden and unexpected arrival itself forced the Liban to abandon everything and flee across the Abbay to their country.[148] Determined to take advantage of this

---

[143] Ibid., 315.

[144] Pankhurst, *The Ethiopian Borderlands*, 309.

[145] See for instance, 'Charles Jacques Poncet's Journey from Cairo into Abyssinia and back in 1699–1700' in William Foster, ed. *The Red Sea and Adjacent Countries at the Close of the Seventeenth Century as Described by Joseph Pitts, William Daniel and Charles Jacques Poncet* (London: The Hakluyt Society, 1949), 130–1.

[146] Aregay, 'Southern Ethiopia and the Christian Kingdom', 582.

[147] Guidi, *Annales Yohannis I, Iyasu I*, 132.

[148] Ibid., 72

easy victory, Iyasu decided to push the war across the Abbay. There and then, the history of the previous kings repeated itself. His soldiers refused to cross the Abbay. It took him a year to convince them to change their minds. During that time he showed them unprecedented kindness, entertain them lavishly, 'passing the day and night in continual festival'.[149] In 1684, Iyasu marched towards Amhara at the head of an army animated by the generosity of the young king, and motivated for battle by the rhetoric of his Christian nationalism. Iyasu surrounded and surprised the Wallo, attacking them with a speed at a moment when they least expected or suspected it. The Wallo lost about 6,000 men on this day.[150] This resounding victory was Iyasu's first major success against the Oromo, but he failed to move fast and take advantage of it. It was only in 1688 that he was able to cross the Abbay with a firm determination not only to free the Christian subjects of the Oromo, but also to force the latter into submission. Upon his arrival in the Tulama land, Iyasu was jubilantly received by the people who are called *Kordida* in the chronicle. Apparently, they were descendants of former Christians who did not flee across the Abbay after the Tulama occupied their land. *Kordida* is an Oromo term consisting of *kor* 'to mount' and *dida* 'who refuse', so 'those who refuse to mount', meaning those who do not ride horses in battle. The Tulama, who did not regard these people as good fighters, called them by this name. According to the chronicle, they were as many as 100,000. They seem to have appealed to Iyasu to rescue them from the Tulama.[151] With the support and guidance of the *Kordida*, Iyasu inflicted a number of defeats on the Tulama.[152] The former, who feared Tulama revenge if they were to remain on their land, begged him with one voice to take them across the Abbay. Accordingly, 'thousands of families of the *Kordida* were brought back from the Tulama lands'.[153] Iyasu went to Tulama land with the intention of forcing the Oromo into submission, but returned from it by transporting away the very people who would have helped him with the task. In this sense, the expedition of 1688 was a failure.

While Iyasu was conducting war against the Tulama, their brethren the Macha, took advantage of his distraction and initiated 'significant … settlements in Gojjam, Agawmeder, Damot, and Wanbara'.[154] Most likely, it was during this time that 'a certain Ibido is reported to have crossed to Damot with all his family and livestock from Amuru. As we shall see later, it will be the descendants of Ibido who laid down the early foundations of the ruling dynasty of Gojjam.'[155] It was in response to their continuous settlements within the Christian kingdom, without his authorization, that Iyasu made spirited campaigns against the Macha south of the Abbay River.

[149] Bruce, *Travels to Discover the Source of the Nile*, vol. 3, 453.
[150] Ibid., 457. See also Guidi, *Annales Yohannis I, Iyasu I*, 75–7.
[151] Ibid., 132.
[152] Ibid., 132–8.
[153] Aregay, 'Southern Ethiopia and the Christian Kingdom', 584.
[154] Etefa, 'The Oromo of Wanbara', 27.
[155] Ibid.

In 1690, Iyasu and his ablest general, named Yohannes, surprised and routed a number of Oromo groups with real carnage.[156] Perhaps encouraged by repeated Oromo defeats, their subjects both in the Tulama and Macha lands rose up in arms against them. This rebellion, which reached its climax in 1692, was spearheaded by the people who are called *Qala Ganda* in the chronicle.[157] *Qala Ganda*,[158] was the term the Tulama used to describe those Christians who, when their lands fell to the Oromo, avoided capture by fortifying themselves within the mountain strongholds that dot the western parts of the Tulama lands. In all likelihood, the Tulama, who had superior cavalry in the plains, were unable to dislodge them from their strongholds and force them into submission as long as they stayed on the mountains. As a result of Iyasu's successful campaigns against the Oromo, the precarious balance between the two gave way to the *Qala Ganda*'s offensive against the Tulama. They sent the following message to him: "'Behold, we are your servants; we have exterminated the [Tulama] and the Liban tribe ... from Halqa as far as Genda Barat." The [king] rejoiced when he heard what they had to say.'[159] What is more, in a message to Iyasu in 1692, the *Qala Ganda* vaunted their role in the conquest of the Tulama and proposed to him to force them into submission.[160] They expected him to mount an immediate military expedition against the Tulama. Instead, Iyasu sent them large quantities of gifts and promised them future military assistance. In short, he failed to take advantage of the *Qala Ganda*'s readiness to fight for his cause. It was only in 1696 that Iyasu led an expedition into Tulama land. By then the momentum had already gone out of the *Qala Ganda*'s offensive.

Iyasu realized that the Wallo, Karrayu and Marawa Oromo groups who settled between Shawa and Tigray 'were already well integrated with the Amhara, Doba and Tigre peoples near them'. Instead of trying to subdue them through military force, Iyasu resorted to diplomatic methods of maintaining peace with them. For that purpose Iyasu gave the Oromo more lands 'in addition to those which they had received from Yohannes'.[161] His goal was to deter the Oromo from providing support for the rebellious Christian elements. However, when some Wallo and Karrayu groups gave support for a rebel known as Takla Haymanot, Iyasu embarked on a military expedition that appears to have taken him all the way to Shawa and Ifat.[162]

Iyasu's 1696 expedition into Tulama land was famous because this was the first time since the 1620s that a Christian king led such an

---

[156] Guidi, Trans. *Annales Yohannis I, Iyasu I*, 154–5.

[157] Ibid., 174.

[158] Ibid. *Qala* and *ganda* were terms of Oromo origin. *Qala* has two meanings. It means 'thin' and it also means 'a tableland on a mountain' (or plateau). *Ganda* also has a double meaning. It means a 'village' as well as 'villagers'. Taken together the two terms describe the people who lived on a mountain stronghold in Tulama land.

[159] Tafla, *Asma Giyorgis and his Work*, 411.

[160] Guidi, *Annales Yohannis I, Iyasu I*, 174.

[161] Aregay, 'Southern Ethiopia and the Christian Kingdom', 585.

[162] Guidi, *Annales Yohannis I, Iyasu I*, 189, 194.

expedition into Shawa and beyond. It was unproductive because, as we shall soon see, Iyasu did not achieve anything by it. 'While camped in Ifat, he is said to have proposed to his soldiers, and to the governors of Shawa and Amhara, who had joined him with their retainers, a plan for pushing the [Oromo] beyond the Awash [River].'[163] Such a grand scheme had not been attempted since the time of Galawdewos (1540–59). Iyasu did not fully appreciate the dramatic changes that had taken place since then. According to his chronicle, it was the governors and the people of Shawa and Amhara who advised him not to try it.[164] The king had no alternative but to accept the wise counsel of the governors and their people who well knew the cavalry power of the Oromo. During his long march to and from Shawa, Iyasu did not fight with any of the Oromo groups. In this sense, he did not achieve anything apart from exhausting his own soldiers. The failure of his expedition had an immediate impact on the relations between the Oromo and their subjects, and on the morale of his own soldiers. Some of the subjects of the Oromo, who earlier sought support from Iyasu, recognized the failure of his offensive against the Oromo, repented for their past mistakes and made peace with the Oromo.[165] The chronicler heaps insults and imprecations upon these people, who betrayed their erstwhile Christian ally and made peace with the Oromo. However the decision of these people to come to terms with reality is an unmistakable indication of the collapse of Iyasu's crusade against the Oromo across the Abbay. This, in turn, affected the morale of his soldiers. When Iyasu wanted to lead an expedition across the Abbay into Damot in 1697, his soldiers

> refused to accompany him beyond the Blue Nile. The soldiers complained that the expeditions into distant lands were taking them away from their farming occupations. They also told him that they would only fight in defence of their homes and lands, and that, although their profession was soldiery, they were not obliged to respond to every mobilization. They justified their refusal to help Iyasu in his [Oromo] campaigns by referring to the very decree that had brought the swift and terrible anger of the Qureban soldiers upon Za-Dengel.[166]

As noted earlier, Za-Dengel's ambitious Oromo campaigns led to his untimely tragic death at the hands of his own soldiers. The same fate awaited Iyasu who had neither learned the lesson from the history of Za-Dengel, nor taken heed of his soldiers' warning.[167] his second attempt to cross the Abbay in 1698 ended ignominiously.

> He gave orders to the commanders to count all the *chawas* [professional soldiers] from various squadrons who had responded to the call. In the past, he had often asked them to call up swiftly all the *chawas*. But only one-fifth

[163] Aregay, 'Southern Ethiopia and the Christian Kingdom', 586–7.
[164] Guidi, *Annales Yohannis I, Iyasu I*, 189–90.
[165] Ibid., 200–1.
[166] Aregay, 'Southern Ethiopia and the Christian Kingdom', 585. See also Guidi, *Annales Yohannis I, Iyasu I*, 201.
[167] As will be shown below, Iyasu was removed from power and assassinated cruelly in 1706.

or one-tenth in each squadron responded. Seeing this, all the commanders were disgusted because they knew that the king was planning for a great expedition. They also knew that the king had an appointment with an individual who was to lead him to the country on which he was planning to attack during Easter Week (the week of Passion). They told the king that in each squadron they were not able to mobilize even one-fifth or one-tenth of the soldiers as we stated earlier. On learning this, the king lost his temper and his face changed [because of his anger]. He admonished them because the *chawas* against their orders have not responded to the call. He cursed the world and cried heavily with tears coming from his eyes. His heart was inflamed and was burning like fire because he had to abandon his expedition and see his plan ruined.[168]

From the above long quotation, it is clear that Iyasu's professional soldiers, the very instrument with which he had hoped to force the Oromo into submission, opposed his spirited campaign. It is stated that Iyasu had an appointment with an individual, who was to lead him to a country he planned to attack. The name of that individual is not mentioned in Iyasu's chronicle. However, it is very likely that he was either an Oromo or an assimilated individual of previously non-Oromo background, who had knowledge of the topography of the land to be attacked, its resources to be plundered and its strengths and weaknesses.

Iyasu's campaign against the Oromo alienated both his soldiers, and the Christian peasants, who were to be protected. His soldiers were alienated because his campaigns were frequent and at least on two occasions they took from four to six months. That is precisely, why in 1698, 'the soldiers in Begameder, Wagara, Dambiya and Gojjam practically ignored his orders of mobilization'.[169] What is more, the soldiers had other difficulties.

> The forced marches were exhausting. And as they could not carry sufficient supplies to last them for such long periods, they often found the emperor's efforts to maintain discipline quite exacerbating. Besides, unlike the emperor and his men, the [Oromo] were fighting in familiar terrain. They were successful in cutting of stragglers and in ambushing squadrons which they found detached from the main body of the army.[170]

In reality, the soldiers carried supplies that lasted them at best for three days, which brings us to the alienation of Christian peasantry. While on campaign, the soldiers depended mostly on what they plundered from the peasants, supplemented with what they looted from the Oromo and other non -Christian people such as the Agaw. It was the soldiers' indiscriminate plundering that turned the Christian peasants against Iyasu's Oromo campaign. This was demonstrated in the following incident.

In 1700, when some Macha warriors from Bizamo attacked Gojjam, Iyasu left Gondar with speed and secrecy so as to surprise and destroy the Macha warriors. Ironically, the people of Gojjam themselves told

---

[168] Guidi, *Annales Yohannis I, Iyasu I*, 203–4.
[169] Aregay, 'Southern Ethiopia and the Christian Kingdom', 589.
[170] Ibid., 586.

the Macha groups that Iyasu was coming to attack them.[171] The groups fled and saved themselves. The action of the people of Gojjam naturally incensed and deeply hurt Iyasu. This episode (and it is not an isolated one) seems to suggest that his Oromo campaign was unpopular even among the people it was supposed to protect.

Iyasu led two more expeditions against the Oromo, in 1702 and 1704. The first campaign was directed against the Gudru Oromo confederation in Bizamo. At that time the Gudru were involved in conflict with their brethren the Basso Oromo. Taking advantage of the conflict between the two groups, Iyasu sided with the weaker Basso group. In terms of dividing the Oromo, his first expedition was successful. The Gudru were attacked both by Iyasu's soldiers and Basso warriors. Although Iyasu was victorious at first, he was quickly defeated by the Gudru warriors in an ambush. According to Asma Giyorgis, 'the Gudru lay in ambush in a narrow defile, and the [Oromo] fell on the [king's] army and completely annihilated the regiments called the Bursa and Cafanta ... None were spared from the [king's] army. It was a tragic and shameful defeat, and he returned to Yebaba having brought about the annihilation of his army.' [172] Iyasu barely escaped with his life from the Gudru warriors who surrounded him, while many of his prominent officers 'perished in the fray'.[173] Stunned by his disastrous defeat, the Basso, who feared the Gudru revenge, begged Iyasu with one voice to rescue them. They were moved 'as a body and resettled in Gojam'.[174] Like several other Oromo groups who were resettled in Gojjam, the Basso were converted to Christianity and integrated into the Christian Amhara society.

Iyasu's Gudru campaign appears to have been followed by a terrible famine that devastated Gondar when Iyasu and his officials were obliged to feed, from their own supplies, 'an innumerable multitude of destitute for two months'.[175] That famine was given the name of Gudru, reminiscent of Iyasu's humiliation at the hands of Gudru warriors.[176] Iyasu was burning with desire for revenge. For that purpose he visited 'monasteries to make a vow and pray, and to remind the monks not to forget him, for he feared the issue of the war he was going to make against Gudru, Gibe and Ennarya'.[177]

Then Iyasu went to Yebaba in Gojjam, where he joined with his army and began serious deliberation with the most famous Christianized Oromo man known as Tullu, who was earlier given the title of *dajaz-mach* (commander of the vanguard) and appointed as the governor of the region of Damot in Gojjam. Emperor Iyasu gave in marriage his own

[171] Guidi, *Annales Yohannis I, Iyasu I*, 213.

[172] Tafla, *Asma Giyorgis and his Work*, 413.

[173] Pankhurst, *The Ethiopian Borderlands*, 313.

[174] Aregay, 'Southern Ethiopia and the Christian Kingdom', 592.

[175] Richard Pankhurst, 'The Great Ethiopian Famine of 1889–1892: A New Assessment', *Journal of the History of Medicine and Allied Sciences* 21 (1966), 97. See also Guidi, *Annales Yohannis I, Iyasu I*, 231.

[176] Tafla, *Asma Giyorgis and his Work*, 415.

[177] Ibid.

favourite daughter, known as 'Walata Sellase' to Tullu, who was praised as 'an extremely wise and powerful'[178] [Oromo]. Tullu's marriage to Iyasu's daughter demonstrates the undeniable rise of the power of Christianized Oromo elite . While conducting a spirited campaign against non-Christian Oromo, Iyasu was the first Amhara emperor to give his own daughter in marriage to a Christianized Oromo, thus starting a practice of integrating powerful individuals of Oromo origin into the royal family. We have seen in the previous chapter that Susenyos was the first Amhara prince to marry an Oromo woman, while Iyasu was the first Amhara emperor to give his own daughter to a Christianized Oromo. In the process Iyasu seems to have acknowledged 'the ascendancy of' Oromo power and the relative decline of the power of the Christian emperor,[179] which will be discussed briefly in the Epilogue.

Besides consulting with *Dajamch* Tullu, his son-in-law, about his decisive war against the Macha Oromo, Iyasu carefully consulted with the governor of Gojjam and several Oromo groups who settled in Gojjam, including but not limited to, the Basso, Liban, the *Qala Ganda* and the *Yahabata* (who were earlier adopted into the Oromo nation). Then Iyasu issued a proclamation stating: 'Let it be known that I shall take revenge upon anyone who does not take provisions sufficient for four months, and who does not bring with him a sickle and an axe.' Iyasu crossed the Abbay River into Bizamo with determination to humiliate the Oromo (see Map 12, page 291). The Macha Oromo warriors rallied behind their famous Abba Gada, Dilamo, who was a tall, powerful, eloquent and brave warrior. In order to undermine the effectiveness of Iyasu's fire power, Dilamo resorted to attacking his force during the night, which for about ten nights 'caused trouble' for the well-armed large imperial force. However, when Iyasu arrived at a locality known as Tullu Amhara (the hill of Amhara), Dilamo exchanged his effective nightly attack for a head-on attack on Iyasu's force, which cost his life and exposed his brave warriors to destruction'. When battle was joined, 'there was heavy musket fire ... a heavy salvo of shots. All the warriors of [Macha] fell, hit by spears or by musket shots. First of all Dilamo fell; Zamubate, from the Basso clan, castrated him ... After defeating the [Macha warriors] ... Iyasu plundered all the peripheral regions of the Gibe.'[180]

The castration of Dilamo is the first example of the horrible practice committed against an Oromo Abba Gada mentioned in a Christian source. It reflects the gulf of the alienation that divided the Basso from their brethren the Macha Oromo. Be that as it may, Iyasu's last expedition across the Abbay appears to have been motivated by inter-related factors. The first was his burning desire to humiliate those who humiliated him in 1702. Another was connected with the terrible famine of 1702. Thus his Macha campaign that followed this famine seems to have been motivated more by the prospect of rich spoils to replace the

178 Ibid., 417.
179 Ibid.
180 Tafla, *Asma Giyorgis and his Work*, 417

depleted supplies of the king and his officials than by a desire for a military conquest. Furthermore, Iyasu was deeply angered with the Oromo victory over the kingdom of Ennarya, which was the main source of gold for the Christian kingdom. He was trying to salvage whatever was possible out of the wreckage of the kingdom of Ennarya. Finally, his 1704 expedition to the Gibe region was perhaps influenced by the effect of wild smallpox, which wrought havoc among some Oromo groups. According to one source: 'It raged among them with such violence, that whole provinces, conquered by them, became half desert; and in many places, they were forced to become tributary to those whom before they kept in continual fear.'[181] It is not far-fetched to assume that, in his grand design, Iyasu intended to conquer all the Macha in 1704. He may have thought that the smallpox might have weakened the Macha resistance. Whatever, the case may have been, his 1704 expedition was directed against the Macha Oromo in Damot. Iyasu's presence in Damot encouraged the assimilated *dhalatta* ('he who is born') groups to rebel against their masters – the Macha. With the assistance and guidance of the *dhalatta*, Iyasu inflicted 'severe decisive defeats upon the various [Oromo] armies which tried to stop his progress'.[182] The *dhalatta* expected Iyasu to stay in their land longer than his soldiers would endure. In fact, those of his soldiers who were opposed to the expedition to the Gibe region continuously urged him to return to Gondar.[183] To quicken Iyasu's departure from the Gibe region, his soldiers embarked upon the indiscriminate plundering of *dhalatta*'s property and enslaving of their women and children. Iyasu's attempt at protecting the *dhalatta* was totally ignored by his soldiers.[184] The *dhalatta* recognized their mistake of exchanging their Macha brethren for indiscriminate plunder of Iyasu's soldiers. They quickly abandoned his lost cause. They made peace with the Macha and remained an integral part of the Oromo nation. Thus 'Iyasu achieved hardly anything worthwhile'[185] with the expedition of 1704.

Iyasu's Oromo campaign failed to achieve its military objective. However, politically his campaign was successful in two respects. First, he was able to widen divisions within the Oromo society south of the Abbay River. Second, he brought and settled a number of Oromo groups in Gojjam, especially, the Jaawwii,[186] who were converted to Christianity. Iyasu carefully settled the various Oromo groups along the bank of the Abbay River, where they shielded both Gojjam and Damot from non-Christian Oromo attack.[187] His policy towards the

---

[181] Bruce, *Travels to Discover the Source of the Nile*, vol. 3, 246–7.

[182] Aregay, 'Southern Ethiopia and the Christian Kingdom', 592.

[183] Guidi, *Annales Yohannis I, Iyasu I*, 267–8.

[184] Ibid., 254. See also Aregay, 'Southern Ethiopia and the Christian Kingdom', 594.

[185] Aregay, Ibid., 594.

[186] Guidi, *Annales Yohannis I, Iyasu I*, 138–40. See also Etefa, 'The Oromo of Wanbara', 28.

[187] Aregay, 'Southern Ethiopia and the Christian Kingdom', 595.

Christianized Oromo was very interesting. For his spirited campaign against the Oromo both in the regions of Shawa and the Gibe region, Iyasu depended heavily on Christianized Oromo and other partisans of the *Qeb'at* doctrine in Gojjam. For that purpose, he relaxed 'all the restrictions which he had imposed on the *Qeb'at* clerics. The injunction against upholding the doctrine was ignored, and its advocates were allowed to defend and propagate it openly.'[188] After the death of Walle, the leader of the *Qeb'at* faction in Gojjam was the highly respected leader of Christianized Oromo known as Tullu, widely admired for his wisdom and military power.[189] As mentioned above, Iyasu appointed Tullu *dajazmach* and the governor of the district of Damot in Gojjam, and gave him in marriage his own favourite daughter. In the process Iyasu seems to have realized the importance of integrating powerful individuals of Oromo origin into the Amhara royal family and harnessing their talents for defending the Christian state against non-Christian Oromo attack. It was precisely for that purpose that 'Tullu shared the leadership of the *Qeb'at* faction with Eleni, Iyasu's favoured sister'.[190] This means that Tullu was integrated into the inner circle of the royal family, demonstrating that before the end of the seventeen century the Christianized Oromo were integrated into the Christian Amhara society and they became the ardent defenders of the Christian state.

By 1705, both the *Qeb'at* and *Tawahdo* partisans were very unhappy with Iyasu. The former for his not totally reversing his anti-*Qeb'at* policy and the latter for his favouring the governors of the *Qeb'at*-dominated Gojjam. As a result, Tullu, the first Christianized Oromo to marry into the royal family, rebelled against his father-in-law and crossed the Abbay to seek support among his Oromo brethren. Support for his cause was not lacking. When Iyasu realized the seriousness of the situation, he sent a *Qeb'at* monk and a spiritual father of Tullu with a peace offer to his rebellious son-in-law. To calm the charged atmosphere of factional conflicts, Iyasu 'began preparations for a council over the religious issue. It is very unlikely that he wanted to bring about the condemnation of the *Tawahdo* doctrine. He probably wanted to satisfy the demands of his *Qeb'at* [favourites]. The partisans of the *Tawahdo* doctrine rejected Iyasu's plan for a council. The leaders of the *Qeb'at* partisans wanted Iyasu 'to turn against the *Tawahdo* clerics'. In March 1706, the leaders of the *Tawahdo* faction, who feared that Iyasu may have 'committed himself to the *Qeb'at* cause', crowned his eldest son Takla Haymanot. 'Iyasu was prevented from marching against his son by the desertion of Tullu and the many squadrons of [Oromo] and *dhalata* Oromo warriors under him.' He was exiled to a monastery in one of the islands in Lake Tana. Most probably Tullu rebelled against his father-in-law for the second time because he may have wanted to put a supporter of *Qeb'at* faction on the throne. Tullu was outmanoeuvred by those who deposed Iyasu and imprisoned him. In fact, it was Tullu's

---

[188] Aregay, 'Southern Ethiopia and the Christian Kingdom', 595.
[189] Ibid.
[190] Ibid.

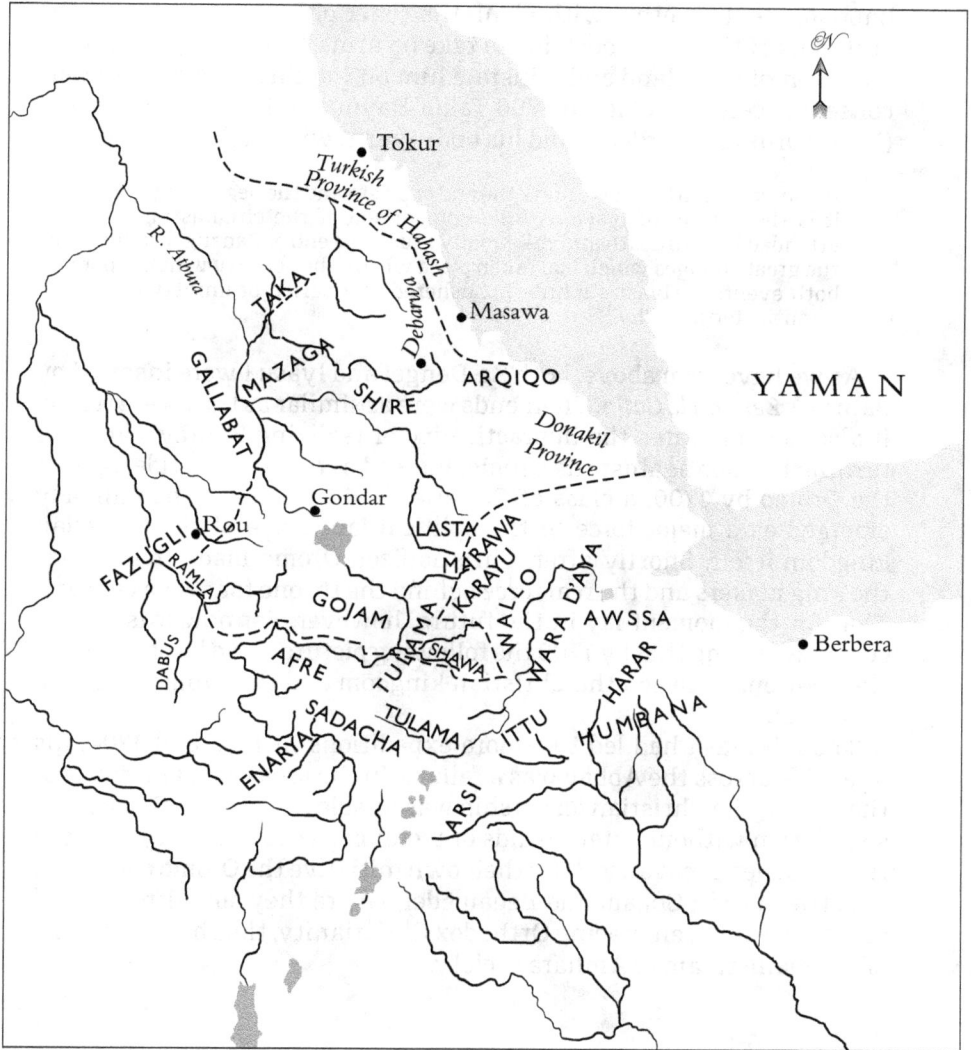

Map 13   The position of the Oromo in the northern parts of the Christian kingdom
c. 1700 (adapted from Aregay, 'Southern Ethiopia and the Christian Kingdom, 1508–1708',
PhD diss., University of London, 1971).

imprisonment together with Eleni, the sister of Iyasu, that forced the partisans of the *Qeb'at* doctrine to take up arms. 'Their attempt to take Iyasu out of the island and reinstate him on the throne had disastrous consequences.'[191] In March 1706 Takla Haymanot had his own father (Iyasu) brutally murdered and his body 'burnt with fire'.[192]

> If one event can be said to mark the end of an era and the beginning of another, it is the murder of Iyasu. A brief comparison of the circumstances which attended Iyasu's death and the equally gruesome end of Zadengel would show the great changes which had taken place within the century which separated both events ... [Iyasu's murder] ... ushered in a period of uninterrupted and unmitigated anarchy.[193]

As we have seen above, both Za-Dengel and Iyasu I were inspired by Bahrey's *Zenahu le Galla*. Their ends were as similar as they were tragic. It also demonstrates the impracticality of realizing Bahrey's ideas of turning the tide against the Oromo. Instead of turning the tide against the Oromo by 1700, a class of Christianized Oromo elite had already emerged as a major force in the political landscape of the Christian kingdom itself. Shortly after, Christianized Oromo made themselves the king makers and the real force behind the throne for over a century. That for the moment lay in the future, however. For now it is safe to conclude stating that by 1700 the following picture could be observed in the relations between the Christian kingdom and the Oromo (see Map 13 above).

Though Iyasu had led two more expeditions in 1702 and 1704, his offensive across the Abbay was a failure. In the areas east and south of the Abbay, the Christian leadership was unable to force the Oromo into submission without external aids or technological superiority over the latter's superior cavalry.[194] By their own initiative the Oromo continued to settle both in Gojjam and Begameder, where they submitted to and served the state, embracing Orthodox Christianity, thus becoming part of the mainstream of Amhara society.

---

[191] Ibid., 596–9.
[192] Tafla, *Asma Giyorgis and his Work*, 421.
[193] Aregay, 'Southern Ethiopia and the Christian Kingdom', 600.
[194] Getahun Delibo, 'Emperor Menelik's Ethiopia: 1865–1916: National Unification or Amhara Communal Domination', PhD Diss., Howard University, Washington DC, 1974, 37.

Epilogue

The history of the Oromo and the Christian kingdom (*c.* 1300–1700), which has been reconstructed in the foregoing chapters, is the story of long contacts and warfare between the Oromo and the Christian society. The warfare between the two communities entered the Christian society's cultural universe and coloured what the chroniclers wrote about the Oromo. Since the Oromo, as a preliterate society, did not write about their encounter with the Christian society, what was written about them reflects only one side of the encounter and thus planted the seeds of hatred, fear and prejudice that resulted in the deliberate distortion of Oromo history and their way of life in Ethiopian historiography. In the twenty-first century, when the political landscape of Ethiopia is changing, there is clear need for a paradigm shift in Ethiopian historiography, with the goal of moving away from a history that is based on incomplete records and prejudice. A history that is based on the achievements of only the Amhara and Tigrayan national groups does not serve a national purpose in the twenty-first century. What is needed for 'the essential task of building'[1] an enduring nation out of several nations and nationalities that is not threatened with the spectre of disintegration of every generation is the creation of an intellectual climate in which the achievement of all Ethiopian peoples can be recognized. This can be achieved by teaching an accurate history of the various Ethiopian peoples in such a way that it makes all of them conscious of their dignity, enjoying unity in diversity, promoting respect for each other's cultural heritage, and strengthening mutual understanding and trust among all.

THE PRESENCE OF OROMO COMMUNITIES WITHIN THE MEDIEVAL CHRISTIAN KINGDOM

Christian and Muslim influences are reflected in Oromo traditions and their key institutions going back to the thirteenth and fourteenth centuries, a time when the Oromo were said not to have been within

---

[1] I have drawn on Tamrat, *Church and State in Ethiopia*, 302.

the medieval Christian kingdom of Ethiopia. Amhara Christian traditions show the existence of contact between some Oromo groups and the Amhara communities during the thirteenth and fourteenth centuries. Muslim narratives from Harar mention an Oromo presence in the Ramis River Valley during the fourteenth century. Somali traditions also mention an Oromo presence within the Muslim states of southern Ethiopia during the fourteenth century. Oromo oral narratives, which provide the Oromo view of the universe presented in the form of legends and myths, show, on closer inspection, Christian and Muslim influence on Oromo traditions and on some of their basic institutions, including the Oromo creation myth, their sacred book, the two moiety systems, the Qaalluu institution. It is the story of pre-sixteenth-century Oromo groups' presence within the medieval Christian kingdom of Ethiopia. The 'Hagara Galla' of *Amda Siyon's Chronicle*, the 'Galla River' and the 'Galla Forest' of the local Christian literature, and the 'Galla River' of Fra Mauro's map all point to a long contact between the Amhara and some Oromo groups.

Arab Faqih, the historian of the sixteenth-century jihad, refers to a number of sedentary Oromo groups who lived under Christian administration. The sedentary agricultural Oromo communities, who were in and south of the present region of Shawa in the pre-sixteenth-century period, lived under the control of a Christian administration. However, the pastoral Oromo groups who lived in some parts of what are today the regions of Bale, Sidamo, and Gamu Gofa lived beyond the boundaries and outside the control of the Christian kingdom.

Most likely it was around Madda Wallaabuu where the Oromo first became conscious of their distinct identity, separate from their neighbours, with their own political, cultural and religious institutions, from where, owing to the pressure of the expanding Christian kingdom coupled with their transhumant economy, pastoral elements moved to six separate homelands, where favourable factors account for pastoral Oromo population increase, leading to massive population movements during the second half of the fifteenth century and most spectacularly during the first half of the sixteenth century, changing the history of the Oromo and radically altering the political landscape of the Christian kingdom itself.

The Impact of Jihadic war on Oromo population movement

The story of the large pastoral Oromo population movement, which started much earlier, took considerable advantage of the situation created by the jihad, and reached its climax during the tumultuous sixteenth century, following the carnages of the jihadic wars of Imam Ahmad (1529–43) and of his nephew Amir Nur (1559). The pastoral Oromo population movement, which started much earlier, took huge advantage of the situation created by the jihad. The Christian military colonies in the southern provinces were dislodged by the jihadic wars. Time and again these military colonies had stopped the pastoral Oromo movement to the north during the fourteenth and fifteenth centuries. The destruction of the Christian military colonies at a most critical time was equally disastrous to both the Muslims and Christians. Before the Christian kingdom could recuperate and re-establish its military colonies in the southern provinces, the pastoral Oromo who were moving to the north dislodged what remained after the jihadic wars and thwarted new attempts at resettlement. The regions that had been sparsely populated before the jihad were left empty by the shifting of population during the jihad. Between 1522 and 1554, the Oromo pastoralists easily penetrated and quickly assimilated into areas where there were already pockets of Oromo-speaking communities. This was particularly true of historical Bali, Dawaro, Hadiya, Waj and other provinces.

The decade of the 1550s was a real landmark in the whole history of the pastoral Oromo population movement. A landmark, because the power of both the Christians and the Muslims was dramatically decreased during this period, while the power of the pastoral Oromo similarly increased. The sudden and radical transformation in the balance of power quickly brought to an end two centuries of struggle between the Muslims and Christians, replacing it by the struggle of both against the Oromo for the next three centuries. This was brought about by the destruction of Christian military establishment by the Muslims and the destruction of Muslim force by the Oromo. In 1559, the Muslim forces under the leadership of Amir Nur (the nephew of Imam Ahmad) routed a small hastily collected Christian force under Galawdewos. The emperor, most of his officers, and a great many of his men were slain. A few weeks later, the victorious Muslim army was itself liquidated by Oromo warriors at the Battle of Hazallo. The death of Galawdewos and the destruction of his army left the Christian kingdom too feeble to stop the Oromo advance. Furthermore, the military rout of 1559 and the pressure of pastoral Oromo movement generated intense civil wars within the Christian society itself, which 'after 1559 led to the destruction of the centralized system of government and the complete barbarization of the many bodies of professional soldiers'.[2] Thus the 1559 Muslim victory not only prepared the background for rapid Oromo victories, but was also a major turning point in the history of their movement into the heartland of historical Abyssinia. During his long reign Emperor Sarsa Dengel (1563–97) tried and failed to stop the pastoral Oromo population movement into the heartland of Christian kingdom. However, he discovered the policy of recruiting some Oromo into his army, settling some Oromo groups among the Christian society and converting them to Christianity, which marked the beginning of their integration into Christian Amhara society.[3] It is the story of Abba Bahrey, the author of *Zenahu le Galla* and other works, which inspired two Amhara Emperors – Za-Dengel (1603–04) and Iyasu I (1682–1706) – to conduct spirited warfare against the Oromo. Their ends were as similar as they were tragic.

[2] Aregay, 'Southern Ethiopia and the Christian Kingdom', 3.
[3] Tafla, *Asma Giyorgis and his Work*, 163.

The undermining of Oromo unity by militarization and settlement among Christians

Sarsa Dengel's policy of settling the Oromo among the Christians was perfected by Emperor Susenyos (1607–32) who, as a young man, was adopted by and became part of the Oromo people. He was the first Amhara prince who had command of the Oromo language, learned their manners and acquired their war strategy and fighting skill. He was also the first Amhara prince to marry an Oromo woman, a daughter of an influential *gada* official.[4] No other Amhara prince or warlord served the Oromo cause as much as Susenyos. With his firepower, he helped various Oromo groups destroy the Christian strongholds in the provinces of Walaqa, Gojjam, Shawa and Amhara.[5] In return, Oromo warriors flooded into Susenyos' domain and within a short time outnumbered his Amhara followers. His standard became their standard, the noise of his drum their incitement for action. His oratory in their language made him their natural leader.[6] Susenyos fought for the Oromo several times, and it was mainly with Oromo support that he was able to come to power. In gratitude for Oromo support, Susenyos settled several Oromo groups both from the Barentu and Borana moieties in Gojjam and Begameder. 'They were so numerous that Susenyos had to confiscate church land to satisfy his Oromo allies, which greatly angered the clergy.'[7] While settling his Oromo allies in the heart of Abyssinia, Susenyos turned against other Oromos who wanted to conquer and occupy both Gojjam and Begameder. He fought against them more than any other Christian king prior to the beginning of the nineteenth century. Like Za-Dengel before him, Susenyos realized that without formidable firepower, it was impossible to turn the tide against the Oromo. It was that realization that appears to have inspired both emperors to abandon Ethiopian Orthodox Christianity and to convert to Catholicism, in the hope of securing Portuguese and Spanish weapons and soldiers for their campaign against the Oromo and other enemies.[8] That support never materialized; Za-Dengel was killed by his own soldiers.[9] Susenyos' religious policy was disastrous for his society. Once he realized that recovering the lost provinces was well-nigh impossible, he focused on the second-best option, which was settling various Oromo groups in Gojjam, Begameder, Amhara and Angot. The Oromo who settled in those provinces were converted to Christianity. Susenyos' religious policy deeply involved the Oromo in the affairs of the Christian society, thus conflating their national interest with those of the people they wanted to conquer.

[4]   Marcus, *A History of Ethiopia*, 39.
[5]   Aregay, 'Southern Ethiopia and the Christian Kingdom', 439.
[6]   Tafla, *Asma Giyorgis and his Work*, 187.
[7]   Etefa, 'The Oromo of Wanbara', 17, 28, 52.
[8]   Bruce, *Travels to Discover the Source of the Nile*, vol. 3, 285. See also Caraman, *The Lost Empire*, 80.
[9]   Bruce, *Travels to Discover the Source of the Nile*, vol. 3, 267–8. See also Boavida et al., *Pedro Páez's History of Ethiopia*, vol. 2, 181.

Other Amhara emperors during and after the period covered by this study followed Susenyos' policy of settling the Oromo, which resulted in their becoming defenders of the Christian society and its heritage. For instance, Emperor Fasiladas (1632–67) along with his policy of building walls and strong fortifications in the provinces of Gojjam and Begameder, intensified his father's policy of settling several Oromo groups in the provinces of Gojjam, Begameder, Angot and Amhara, where they accepted Orthodox Christianity, and gradually integrated them into the main stream of Christian Amhara society. Militarily Emperor Yohannes (1667–82) depended on the Christianized Oromo, who constituted the backbone of his force in the northern provinces. During his reign Christianized Oromo were involved on both sides of bitter religious conflicts such as that between supporters of the *Tawahdo* and the *Qeb'at* doctrines. Yohannes, as supporter of the *qeb'at* doctrine, appointed Walle to be *dajazmach* of the southern districts in Gojjam. He was the champion of the *Qeb'at* doctrine and the leader of the Macha Oromo groups, who had settled in Gojjam earlier. In northern provinces, the supporters of the *Tawahdo* doctrine also found ardent Oromo supporters, reflecting the degree to which Christianized Oromo were integrated into the body politic and religious fabric of the Christian society. Emperor Iyasu (1682–1706) as the champion of the *Tawhdo* doctrine, appears to have relied upon his Christianized Oromo, one of whom was promoted to the highest rank of '*Behtwaddad*, or the king's Beloved Courtier'.[10] In Gojjam, Christianized Oromo 'had become staunch supporters of the *Qeb'at* doctrine'.[11] *Dajazmach* Walle, the Christianized Oromo governor of the southern districts in Gojjam, rebelled against Iyasu's religious policy and attempted to be a king maker by proclaiming one Yeshaq an emperor.[12] Christianized Oromo in Lasta also attempted to be king makers. Although Iyasu easily defeated Christianized Oromo attempts at overthrowing him, these two attempts by the Christianized Oromo to be the force behind the throne was the signal for what was to come by the middle of the next century. While appointing Christianized Oromo individuals to the highest position of power in his government, Iyasu conducted a spirited campaign against non-Christian Oromo for the purpose of forcing them into submission. In this, he was encouraged by the increased importation of firearms to Gondar[13] and, like Za-Dengel in early seventeenth century, appears to have been inspired by Abba Bahrey's *Zenahu le Galla* for waging war against the Oromo. Like Za-Dengel a century earlier, Iyasu's attempt backfired and his end was as similar and tragic as that of Za-Dengel.[14]

After 1700 the Oromo continued to settle in Gojjam, Damot, Agawmeder and Begameder, where they were converted to Christianity, adopted the Amharic language and became part of the dominant

[10] Pankhurst, *The Ethiopians*, 125.
[11] Aregay, 'Southern Ethiopia and the Christian Kingdom', 578.
[12] Bruce, *Travels to Discover the Source of the Nile*, vol. 3, 458–9.
[13] Pankhurst, *The Ethiopians*, 125.
[14] Aregay, 'Southern Ethiopia and the Christian Kingdom', 600.

Amhara population of those regions. Those who settled in 'Balaya, Zigam and Ganga districts in Matakkal were assimilated into the Agawna-speaking society', while those who settled in Wanbara and Dabale districts 'have kept their identity and culture ... intact, still practising some aspects of the gada rituals, while believing in traditional Oromo religion based on Waaqa'.[15] Among those who settled in Damot was a very wealthy Oromo individual called Ibido, who married 'a local woman' by whom he had a son named Walda Abib, whose son Yosedeq, was a founder of 'the ruling house of Gojjam'. His successor, Haylu was later appointed Ras and ruled over 'Agawmeder, Damot, Gojjam and [Macha] up to Dangalbar'. Another descendent of Oromo settlers in Gojjam, Dajjazmach Zwide, had by 1800 emerged as a powerful lord whose descendants established a long-lasting ruling house of Gojjam. This means that most of the Oromo settlers in Gojjam were integrated into the dominant Christian Amhara society for which they 'provided active leadership skills to the extent'[16] of founding two local dynasties in Gojjam.

PASTORAL OROMO SETTLEMENT IN THE REGION OF WALLO

While most Oromo who settled in Gojjam and Begameder underwent profound cultural change along with frontier change, i.e. that they were absorbed into the dominant Amhara society, losing their language and other cultural heritage, the Oromo who settled in the region of Wallo maintained their identity and independence up to the first half of the nineteenth century and challenged the Christian establishment in two major ways: politically and religiously. To demonstrate these two aspects the rest of the Epilogue is devoted to pastoral Oromo settlement in the region, their state formations and the challenge they posed for the Christian kingdom itself.

In Chapter 2 above, we have seen evidence for some Oromo language-speaking communities' presence in southern Wallo before the sixteenth century. Most likely the Qaalluu Oromo, in whose name an *awaraja* (district) was named, arrived in Wallo during the early phase of the jihadic war (1529–43). We have also seen evidence for the Yajju Oromo settlement in Angot in 1532 (see page 91). The meticulous scholarship of the late Hussein Ahmed also supports the presumption of their 'earlier than is usually thought' settlement in the provinces of Amhara and Angot. This indicates that the Qaalluu and the Yajju Oromo were converted to Islam before their settlement in the region of Wallo. However, pastoral Oromo groups' arrival in the region took place mainly during the Birmaje Gada (1578–86) when the sub-moieties of the Barentu, such as Marawa, Karrayyu, Akichu, Warantisha and Warra Daya (Warra Dhaayyee) settled in a large number in the region

---

[15] Etefa, *Inter-Ethnic Relations on a Frontier*, 31.
[16] Etefa, 'The Oromo of Wanbara', 52, 91.

of Wallo. The region then was divided into a number of provinces, such as Amhara, Bugna, Wag, Lasta and Angot. Of the several Oromo groups who settled in Wallo, the Yajju – who wielded major military and political power within the Christian kingdom during the eighteenth century – settled in Angot, while the seven houses of Wallo settled in Amhara. In Wallo, the Oromo settled among a large sedentary Christian and Muslim population. They kept the original population on the land as 'tribute-paying subjects'.[17] As originally agro-pastoralist, the Oromo gradually embarked on sedentary agriculture. In Wallo, during the second half of the seventeenth century, the Oromo appear to have abandoned their *gada* system and its ideological foundation and traditional religion in favour of Islam or Christianity. Generally, the Oromo adhered to their own traditional religion as long as their *gada* system and religious institutions were intact and they were militarily powerful enough to maintain their independence from their Christian neighbours.

The rugged and mountainous topography of the Wallo region undermined the effectiveness of the *gada* system by the first half of the seventeenth century. By the second half, the Oromo mode of production in Wallo was based on well-developed agriculture, combined with 'horse breeding, cattle-rearing and warfare'. This transformation, coupled with the growth of trade, created the material basis for the formation of a class-based society. In other words, when social stratification, based on wealth and privilege and differences in status corresponding to the distribution of power and authority, broke up the *gada* system, Islam not only provided an ideology for the new nobility, it also served as a focus of clan loyalty. Christianity probably would have served the same purpose, had it not been the religion of their Amhara and Tigrayan neighbours, with whom they were involved in a bitter struggle for power and territorial expansion. It was in Wallo that the Oromo first embraced Islam in large numbers. The reasons for this are persuasive. They settled among a large Christian and Muslim population, whose religious practices exerted considerable influence on them. According to Hussein Ahmed, Islamization of the Oromo in Wallo 'took place at a much earlier date'. This is because some of the Oromo settlers in Wallo appear to have been Muslims even before their settlement in the region. For instance, Nole Warra Ali, one of the seven houses of Wallo were Muslims. The Qaalluu Oromo were converted to Islam most likely before their settlement in the region of Wallo. 'Moreover, the Yajju – or their ancestors – were already Muslim at the time of Oromo settlement.'[18] This means, the Islamization of the Oromo in Wallo was in full vigour during the second half of the seventeenth century. This explains why the Oromo states in Wallo were based on Islamic ideology (see Map 14 below). This brings us to the other reason why the Oromo in Wallo embraced Islam. This was because they seemed to have perceived Ethiopian Orthodox Christianity as an ideological arm of the

[17] Ahmed, *Islam in Nineteenth-Century Wallo*, 4, 15, 22.
[18] Ibid., 28, 121, 126, 133.

Amhara and Tigray society and a pillar of their unity and strength. The Oromo appear to have wanted to counter Christian unity and strength by making Islam a major unifying factor, part of their cultural life, and a mark of their independence. Trimingham's observation is accurate when he writes that the Oromo in Wallo 'reinforced their independence by the adoption of Islam'. He goes on to argue that the Oromo in Wallo accepted Islam 'as [a] bulwark against being swamped by Abyssinian nationalism'.[19] Indeed, Islam appears to have served as a powerful symbol of Oromo identity and a reliable fortress against the domination of their Christian neighbours. According to Hussein Ahmed:

> Their early Islamization, and their active role in the subsequent consolidation and expansion of Islam not only within their own cultural environment, but also in other areas under their domination such as Bagemder served to extend the reach of Islam. They helped to change the status of Islam from that of a religion of disparate communities to that of a dynastic ideology relevant to the entire region.[20]

The Yajju state

In Wallo there were two Oromo states that challenged the Christian state in two major ways. While the Yajju Oromo nobility dominated the political landscape of Christian kingdom for decades, the Warra Himano dynasty championed the cause of Islam in northern Ethiopia. By the 1720s, the Oromo who settled in northern regions among the Christian society were becoming a force to be reckoned with, which became very obvious during the reign of Bakaffa (1721–30). It has been said that:

> Young Bakaffa had taken refuge among the [Yajju Oromo] after his escape from the mountain prison, and when he became king the [Oromo] were welcomed at his court. He not only recruited a regiment of [Oromo] soldiers, but employed [an Oromo] as Master of the Palace and surrounded himself with [an Oromo] praetorian guard. Although he had Amharic Christian names as well, the name by which he was chiefly known, Bakaffa, was itself [an Oromo] name, meaning 'inexorable.'[21]

During the years when Bakaffa 'spent part of his youth among'[22] the Yajju, he was probably adopted and Oromized, which explains his Oromo name. All historical sources confirm that Bakaffa was heavily dependent on his Oromo soldiers, whom he armed 'with muskets [in order] to use them against the corrupt imperial guard and household units' and cow the nobility of Wag, Lasta, 'Tigray and Bahir Meder into submission'.[23] Thus during the reign of Bakaffa, the imperial crown rested upon Oromo support. Bakaffa married a brilliant Oromo woman, Empress Mentewab, who brought her brother and other relatives to high positions of power.[24] Their son, Iyasu II (1730–55) married Wabit,

[19] Trimingham, *Islam in Ethiopia*, 107, 109.
[20] Ahmed, *Islam in Nineteenth-Century Wallo*, 27.
[21] Levine, *Greater Ethiopia*, 83.
[22] Pankhurst, *The Ethiopians*, 125.
[23] Marcus, *A History of Ethiopia*, 46.
[24] Ibid.

the daughter of Amitto, the founder of the Qaalluu Oromo dynasty, who 'controlled a large part of southeastern Wallo'.[25] Iyasu II was succeeded by his Oromo-speaking son, Iyo'as (1755–69), whose reign 'saw the beginning of the rise of Wallo political dominance in the court of Gondar, when Iyo'as' maternal uncles, Lubo and Berelle, secured important positions of authority'.[26] Thus it was that, during the reign of Iyo'as, Gondar was full of Oromo soldiers and nobility whose language for the first time eclipsed Amharic at the palace. According to James Bruce (who was in Gondar in 1769), 'nothing was heard at the palace but [Oromo]', and that Iyo'as 'affected to speak nothing else'.[27] The rise of Oromo nobility's power in Gondar heightened the anxiety of the Amhara and Tigray nobility, who 'believed that the [Christian] state was sliding down a rapidly inclining slope toward Islam, a conclusion amplified when Iyoas removed a popular figure from the governorship of Christian Amhara, the only remaining bulwark against Muslim [Wallo] expansion westward'.[28]

It was such anxiety and strong anti-Oromo prejudice that brought Ras Mikael Sehul, the ruler of Tigray to Gondar. With the arrival of his 30,000-man army, the Tigrinya (Tigrigna) language replaced Oromo as the dominant language at the palace.[29] With superior firepower and his large army, Ras Mikael was determined to destroy the Oromo nobility's hegemony in Gondar. He got that opportunity when civil war broke between the Oromo nobility of Begameder who were thoroughly assimilated into Amhara culture and language and Wallo Oromo nobility who were not fully assimilated,[30] which provided Ras Mikael with a golden opportunity to destroy both groups. In the battle that followed, the 'bodies of those killed by the sword were hewn to pieces and scattered about the streets being denied burial'. The victorious Ras is reported to have pulled out the eyes of forty-four Oromo leaders who were captured on the battle field. According to James Bruce, 'The old tyrant' had 'the stuffed skin of the unfortunate' Oromo leader who was captured while fighting. The unfortunate man 'had been flayed alive and his skin had then been stuffed with straw'.[31] It was in 1769 that Ras Mikael deliberately murdered Iyo'as and poisoned his successor,[32] 'ushering in a century of feudal anarchy and mayhem, the Zaman Masafent, the "age of the princes," which lasted until 1855'.[33] Ras Mikael himself was defeated by a coalition of Oromo and Amhara nobilities.[34] However, the

[25] Ahmed, *Islam in Nineteenth-Century Wallo*, 126.

[26] Ibid.

[27] Bruce, *Travels to Discover the Source of the Nile*, vol. 3 658–9, 665, 667. See also Pankhurst, *The Ethiopians*, 126.

[28] Marcus, *A History of Ethiopia*, 47.

[29] C.F. Beckingham, ed., *Travels to Discover the Source of the Nile by James Bruce* (New York: Horizon, 1964), 49.

[30] Marcus, *A History of Ethiopia*, 47.

[31] Beckingham, *Travels to Discover the Source of the Nile*, 51, 111, 186, 187.

[32] Bruce, *Travels to Discover the Source of the Nile*, vol. 3, 200.

[33] Marcus, *A History of Ethiopia*, 47.

[34] Abir, *Ethiopia: The Era of the Princes*, 30.

destruction of the Wallo nobility's power in Gondar was followed by the rise of the power of Yajju Oromo nobility in the late 1770s.

The Yajju Oromo nobility rose to power when their leader Ali was converted to Christianity and appointed as Ras-Bitwoded (the highest Abyssinian title below that of a prince). Ras Ali (*c.*1779–88) took over the role of 'the guardianship of the king of kings' in Gondar. According to Abir, Ras Ali created the new Yajju dynasty at the very core of the Christian kingdom and 'ruled the province of Begamder and Amhara from his centre in Debra Tabor'.[35] The Yajju nobility's domination of Christian politics was bitterly resented by the Amhara and Tigrayan nobilities. That bitterness was succinctly expressed by a chronicler in the following words.

> How is it that the kingdom has become contemptible to striplings and slaves? How is it the kingdom is a laughing stock to the uncircumcised ... ? How is it that the kingdom is the image of a worthless flower that the children pluck in the autumn rains. I lament as I ponder over the kingdom, for I was present in its trial and tribulation. And I weep always without ceasing.[36]

From the above quotation it appears that even though Ras Ali and his successors had been Christians for decades, their Christianity was never accepted as genuine. The cultural gap and the rivalry between the Abyssinian nobilities and the Yajju nobility was so deep that it could not be bridged by the Yajju's Amharization and their conversion to Christianity. That was why the Yajju leaders derived their power from both Christian and Muslim Oromo in Begameder, Amhara, Wallo and Yajju.[37] The mainstay of the Yajju nobility's power, however, was their superior cavalry and that of northern Wallo. Up to the early 1850s, 'when firearms began to alter the balance of power',[38] the Yajju nobility remained a dominant force in the political landscape of the Christian kingdom. In fact, it was the Yajju nobility's domination in Gondar that partly inspired the rise of Christian nationalism by the middle of the nineteenth century. The other factor contributing to the rapid rise of Christian nationalism in the early 1850s was the phenomenal growth of Islam in Wallo.

THE WARRA HIMANO DYNASTY, *c.* 1700–1916

While the Yajju nobility dominated the politics of the Christian state at its centre, their kinsmen, and the Muslim rulers of the Warra Himmano dynasty, 'consistently employed Islam ... as an ideology of political legitimacy and territorial expansion', championing the cause of Islam

[35] Ibid.
[36] Pankhurst, *The Ethiopians*, 131–2, quoting H. Weld Blundell, *The Royal Chronicle of Abyssinia 1769–1840* (Cambridge: Cambridge University Press, 1922), 471–2.
[37] Abir, *Ethiopia: The Era of the Princes*, 30.
[38] Ahmed, *Islam in Nineteenth-Century Wallo*, 133.

in northern Ethiopia. Of the six Oromo states or principalities in Wallo (i.e. the Arreloch, the Warra Himano, the Yajju, the Qaalluu, the House of the Gattiroch, and the Borana), it was the Warra Himano dynasty that used Islam as a resistance ideology with vigour, creative dynamism and ingenuity for the purpose of resisting Christian territorial expansion and cultural encroachment. It was 'Godana Babbo, a Muslim Oromo cleric who' established the foundation of Warra Himano dynasty, whose successors used Islam 'as an ideology for building up a local power base and for pursuing a policy of territorial expansion'. Islam succeeded in solidly establishing itself among the Oromo in Wallo, who 'had become so powerful that they briefly dominated the imperial court at Gondar until they were superseded by their kinsmen, the Yajju'.[39]

The Warra Himano Dynasty was the second Muslim Oromo dynasty to be established in Wallo, the first to declare jihad in the name and interest of Islam, the first to adopt the prestigious title of Imam, and the longest-surviving Oromo dynasty.[40] The dynasty reached the zenith of its power during the reign of Muhammad Ali (1771–85) who was a far-sighted leader, a resourceful politician and a fervent Muslim. He was not only the first leader who attempted uniting the various Oromo principalities under his administration but also 'successfully mobilized the loyalty of his own followers and the support of the Muslim religious notables in order to achieve territorial and political aggrandizement'.[41] Muhammad Ali is

> remembered as a fervent Muslim ruler who appointed religious notables and attempted, through them, to eradicate certain vestiges of animist worship, practices and traditional customary laws, and to impose Islamic law ... [He] used Islam as a basis for consolidating his power by seeking and obtaining the support and sanction of Muslim scholars and jurists.[42]

Although Islam had a long existence in Wallo, it was after the conversion of Oromo that a favourable political situation led to the development of Islamic education in the region. As in other parts of Ethiopia and many other parts of Africa as whole, it was in Sufi centres where Islamic education flourished in Wallo. Muslim scholars established *zawiyya*,[43] where itinerant students studied at the feet of their teachers.

> The range of subjects offered, and the nature and aims of the educational system, are similar to those of other centres of learning in the Islamic world.

[39] Ibid., 17, 117–18, 125–6, 126.

[40] Mohammed Hassen 'Islam as a Resistance Ideology among the Oromo of Ethiopia: The Wallo Case, 1700–1900', in Said S. Samatar, ed., *the Shadow of Conquest: Islam in Colonial Northeast Africa*, (Trenton, NJ: Red Sea Press, 1992), 86–92. In the following section, I have heavily drawn upon this work.

[41] Ahmed, *Islam in Nineteenth-Century Wallo*, 119.

[42] Ibid., 121.

[43] *Zawiyya*, according to Hussein Ahmed is 'a multi-functional institution which served both as a prayer house, a study and meditation centre, and a venue for a general meeting for the faithful where occasional and regular religious festivals and ceremonies were held', ibid., 92.

> Besides the Qur'an and its exegesis (*tasfsir*), *Fiqh* (Islamic jurisprudence), *Nahw* (Arabic grammar and syntax), *Sarf* (morphology) and *Tawhid* (theology) are widely taught, usually each under a separate master.[44]

Of the many learning centres in the region, Dawway 'in southeastern Wallo' was the most famous among all Oromo in Ethiopia (see Map 14 opposite). During and after the 1870s the Oromo *ulama* (scholars) of Dawway were responsible for the spread of Islam among the Oromo in Western Hararghe,[45] Arsi-Bale as well as for the expansion of Muslim education in the Gibe region.[46] They were also 'responsible for the thorough Islamization of some of the neighbouring Afar nomadic groups of the Lowlands'.[47] Muslim scholars in Wallo used both Arabic and Ethiopic scripts to produce religious literature,[48] thus creating a literary tradition, which became the basis for Muslim education in Wallo. During the 1830s and 1840s the region was the centre of learning not only for the Oromo but also for Amharic- and Tigrinya-speaking Muslim populations in Ethiopia. In short, Wallo became the most famous centre of learning in northern Ethiopia. In this, it paralleled the role of the city of Harar, serving as the centre of Islamic diffusion to southern and south-western Ethiopia.

Muslim scholars not only indigenized Islam in Wallo, but also started an original form of Islamic poetry known as *Ajam*, which 'forms an important body of literature'.[49] It was through *Ajam* poetry, which was short enough for the people to learn by heart and chant it in *Manzuma*, 'a didactic poem recited at religious festivals',[50] that Muslim scholars introduced the Oromo into the world of Islam and made the early history of Islam intelligible to them.

Muhammad Ali not only made *sharia* (Islamic law) the basis of the prevailing legal system but also used Islam for uniting Oromo principalities for the purpose of resisting Emperor Takla Giyorgis, who 'aimed at the subjugation of the Wallo and the Wuchale'.[51] It was in the fierce battle of Legot in March 1783 that Muhammad Ali was defeated by Takla Giyorgis. However, it was a pyrrhic victory as the former went on not only resisting the latter but also consolidating his power over a wider territory.[52]

Muhammed Ali was succeeded by his son, Batto (1785–90), who was defeated by Emperor Takla Giyorgis and forced to embrace Christianity.

[44] Ahmed, *Islam in Nineteenth-Century Wallo*, 93.

[45] Trimingham, *Islam in Ethiopia*, 123.

[46] Mohammed Hassen, *The Oromo of Ethiopia: A History 1570–1860*, 158.

[47] Ahmed, *Islam in Nineteenth-Century Wallo*, 88, 144.

[48] Ibid., 94–5, 98.

[49] Alula Pankhurst, 'Indigenising Islam in Wallo: *Ajam* Amharic verse written in Arabic script', in *Proceedings of the Eleventh International Conference of Ethiopian Studies*, ed. B. Zewde, et al. (Addis Ababa: Addis Ababa University Press, 1994), 259.

[50] Ahmed, *Islam in Nineteenth-Century Wallo*, 205.

[51] Ibid., 120.

[52] Hassen, 'Islam as a Resistance Ideology', 87. See also Ahmed, *Islam in Nineteenth-Century Wallo*, 121.

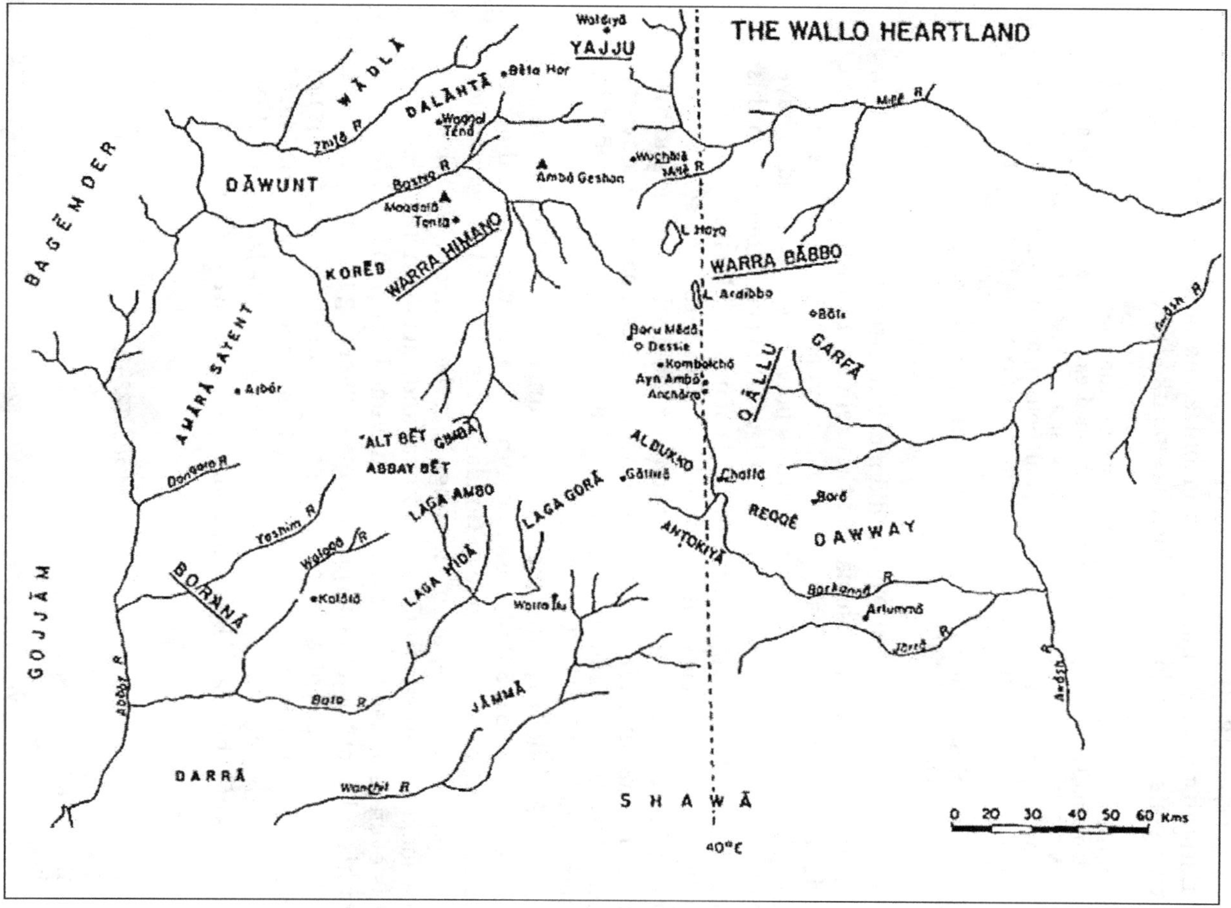

Map 14   Central and southern Wallo region (adapted from Ahmed, *Islam in nineteenth-century Wallo, Ethiopia*, Boston: Brill, 2001, reproduced by kind permission of Brill).

This was a major setback for Islam and the dynasty that championed it. However, the setback was short-lived as Batto's brother and successor Amade (1790–1803) avenged his predecessor's forced conversion to Christianity. Amade managed to mobilize the military forces of all Oromo states in Wallo, with which he embarked upon

> territorial aggrandizement by incorporating the districts of Amhara in his domain. The imamate which he established extended as far south as the Wanchit and Jama Rivers and as far west as the Abbay ... in 1798 he even managed to capture the imperial capital, Gondar, on two different occasions, and to put his own nominee on the throne ... According to a local tradition, Amade had the call to the Islamic ritual prayer as a symbolic gesture of his triumphal entry into the city [and perhaps] ... to avenge Batto's forced conversion to Christianity.[53]

There is no doubt that Amade did much to strengthen the position of Islam in northern Ethiopia and that religion in turn strengthened and sanctified the hereditary power of his dynasty in Wallo.[54] 'In order to legitimize and sanctify his hereditary power, he is believed to have obtained a written authorization from Mecca that permitted him and his descendants to assume the honorific title of imam.'[55] Imam Amade died in 1803 and was succeeded by Imam Liban (1803–15), whose 'religious enthusiasm ... led him to desecrate some of the local churches and turn them into mosques. In fact he died ... while on a campaign to convert a local Christian community to Islam.'[56] He, in turn, was succeeded by Imam Amade II (1815–38).

Imam Amade II 'headed the regency council on behalf of the young Ras Ali II'[57] (1831–53) of the Yajju dynasty, who was the real power behind the Christian throne in Gondar. Thus Amade II wielded enormous power and it was during his reign that the Oromo of Wallo became the 'most active centre of Muslim propaganda in East Africa'.[58] Amade II is even reported to have asked Muhammed Ali (1805–48) of Egypt for his collaboration in conquering and converting northern Ethiopia to Islam.[59] The Egyptian leader's response to this ambitious task is not known. What is known for certain was that Amade II 'was considered by many the most important Muslim ruler if not the leader of all the Muslims of Ethiopia'.[60] By then, Wallo 'had become a veritable Islamic

---

[53] Ahmed, *Islam in Nineteenth-Century Wallo*, 122–3.
[54] Hassen, 'Islam as a Resistance Ideology', 87–88.
[55] Ahmed, *Islam in Nineteenth-Century Wallo*, 123.
[56] Ibid., 124.
[57] Ahmed, *Islam in Nineteenth-Century Wallo*, 124.
[58] Arnauld d'Abbadie, Jeanne-Marie Allier, ed., *Douze ans de Séjour dans la haute-Ethiopie (Abyssinie)*, (Vatican City: Biblioteca Apostolica Vaticana, 1980), vol.2, 200–201. Hussein Ahmed, 'Clerics, Traders and Chiefs: A Historical Study of Islam in Wallo (Ethiopia) with Special Emphasis on the Nineteenth Century' (PhD diss., University of Birmingham, 1985), 273.
[59] Abir, *Ethiopia: The Era of the Princes*, 105, 114–15, 117.
[60] Ibid., 33.

state within the heartland of Ethiopia'.[61] It was most likely the Yajju nobility's domination of the Christian state politics and the rise of Muslim Oromo power in Wallo which was instrumental in the revival of Christian nationalism in historic Abyssinia. European missionaries who 'tended to relate the success of their own cause to political support for the ambitions of the indigenous Christian polities'[62] provided ideological justification for supporting the Christians in northern Ethiopia against Islam and Muslim power in Wallo. 'For the sake of Christianity and civilization, these Christians in Africa have to be helped. To help them is to destroy Islam and strengthen Christianity.'[63] So it was in the early 1850s when the clouds had already gathered thick and low over the once powerful Oromo cavalry in Wallo that resurgent Christian nationalism consolidated itself in northern Ethiopia.

EMPEROR TEWODROS, 1855–1868, AND THE REVIVAL OF CHRISTIAN NATIONALISM

It was Emperor Tewodros who expressed and represented the revival of Christian nationalism in historical Abyssinia. From the very beginning of his reign, 'Tewodros's treatment of the [Oromo] in general and the Wallo in particular, differed from his treatment of the Amhara'.[64] Tewodros had four inter-related goals in terms of the Yajju nobility and Muslim leaders of Wallo. The first was to break the power of the Yajju nobility over the Christian state; the second to destroy the power of the Muslim leaders of Wallo, which developed into 'a war of extermination'.[65] The third was to make a frontal assault on Islam with combined forces of the resurgent state and church and, finally, to convert or expel all other Muslims from his land.[66] Trimingham argues that, for Tewodros 'Christianity and Abyssinia were synonymous'.[67] As an emperor who called himself 'the slave of Christ',[68] it was Tewodros' political calling to end the domination of the Yajju nobility, his religious duty to destroy both Islam and Muslim power in Wallo. This explains his intense hatred of Islam and his decade-long devastation of Wallo (see below). In short, it appears that Tewodros saw Wallo and Islam as synonymous and made a frontal assault on Islam with the combined forces of the resurgent state and the church.

---

[61] Zewde Gabre-Sellassie, *Yohannes IV of Ethiopia: A Political Biography* (Oxford: Clarendon, 1975), 100.

[62] Richard Greenfield and Mohammed Hassen, 'Interpretation of Oromo Nationality', *Horn of Africa* 3, 3 (1980), 6.

[63] 'Afrique Memoirs et Documentes Abyssinia, 1838–1850', *Archives des Affaires Etrangers*, Paris, vol. 1, no. 13, folios 129 and 130.

[64] Donald Crummey, 'The Violence of Tewodros' in *War and Society in Africa*, ed. Bethwell A. Ogot (London: Frank Cass, 1972), 68.

[65] Ibid., 73.

[66] This section summarized from Hassen, 'Islam as a Resistance Ideology', 89.

[67] Trimingham, *Islam in Ethiopia*, 118.

[68] Ahmed, *Islam in Nineteenth-Century Wallo*, 164.

It has been said, and rightly, that Emperor Tewodros united historical Abyssinia on a 'clearly anti- Islamic, and even anti-Oromo, stance',[69] which was

> supported by the contemporary Protestant missionaries for three reasons: firstly because they hoped that the subjugation of Wallo could inaugurate a period of tranquility; secondly, because they saw the struggle in terms of a confrontation between Christianity and Islam; and thirdly, because they believed that Wallo was the spearhead of the Muslim drive to take over Ethiopia.[70]

According to his chronicler, Tewodros broke the power of Amharic-speaking Christianized Oromo nobility in Begameder, Gojjam, Lasta and Yajju.[71] Tewodros instituted a policy of converting the Muslims to Christianity and destroying the power of Muslim leaders and Islam in Wallo. He even extended his extermination of the Oromo in Shawa, when he decimated the Oromo living between Dabra Berhan and Angolala,[72] where 'the dead bodies appeared [on the ground] like a carpet'.[73] After smashing the power of the Yajju ruling dynasty, Tewodros' ultimate aim was to destroy Muslim Oromo power in Wallo. For that purpose, shortly after his coronation in 1855, Tewodros conducted a punishing military expedition in Wallo and fought against three rival Muslim leaders, killing one, capturing the second and defeating the third.[74] For the next ten years Tewodros conducted several devastating campaigns, which were accompanied by the burning of houses, looting of property and massacring of the people. In the end Tewodros 'degenerated into a cruel tyrant', who 'pitilessly exterminated'[75] even his own Christian subjects. According to Donald Crummey, 'Tewodros is one of the most violent of all monarchs – probably the most violent'.[76] Of all regions of northern Ethiopia, violent terrorism characterized his campaigns in Wallo.[77] His policy towards Muslims in Wallo affected the region in two major ways. First, 'the extent of physical and material destruction and pillaging of the Wallo countryside affected the demographic, economic and political vitality of the region for the remaining part of the century'.[78] Second, Tewodros instituted a policy of physically destroying Muslim leaders. His policy, in fact, became the working model for Emperors Yohannes and Menelik, based as it was upon the elimination or conversion of

---

[69] Ibid., 166.
[70] Ibid., 165. See also Donald Crummey, 'Tewodros as Reformer and Modernizer', *Journal of African History* 10, 3 (1969), 466–7.
[71] M.M. Moreno, 'La Cronaca Di Re Teodoro Attribuita Al Dabtara "Zanab"', *Rassegna Di Studi Etiopici* 2, 1 (1942), 158. Trans. B.J. Yates, as 'Invisible Actors: The Oromo and the Creation of Modern Ethiopia (1855–1913)', 46.
[72] Crummey, 'The Violence of Tewodros', 69.
[73] Yates, 'Invisible Actors', 47.
[74] Hassen, 'Islam as a Resistance Ideology', 89–90.
[75] Trimingham, *Islam in Ethiopia*, 119.
[76] Crummey, 'The Violence of Tewodros', 65.
[77] Ibid., 74.
[78] Ahmed, *Islam in Nineteenth-Century Wallo*, 167.

both the leaders and the Muslim population in the region of Wallo to Christianity, the destruction of mosques, and complete subjugation of the Muslims to the Christian Amhara political, economic, cultural and social domination.[79]

Finally, it may be appropriate to end this Epilogue with Professor Taddesse Tamrat's apt observation: 'Ethiopian history has a particular tendency to repeat itself.'[80] Although history repeats itself in different ways, it was the Amharic language-speaking Christianized Yajju nobility's predominance within the Christian political establishment, and the rise of Muslim power in Wallo that gave birth to strong Christian nationalism, which not only destroyed Muslim power in Wallo during the reign of Tewodros and Emperor Yohannes (1872–89) but it also led to the destruction of Muslim power in northern Ethiopia. It was the Amhara ruling elites' domination of the Ethiopian political landscape that precipitated the events of 1974 and more profoundly their loss of state power in 1991. The fate of the current Tigrayan ruling elite's domination of the Ethiopian state is not demonstrably different from that of the previous Amhara ruling elites. What will save Ethiopia from another cycle of destruction inspired by domination either by the Tigrayan, the Amhara or other elites will be genuine implementation of the federal system that exists only on paper in Ethiopia. The strength of federalism lies in the fact that it is the only practical way for the Amharas, the Oromos, the Tigrayans and the other peoples of Ethiopia to live together, instead of killing each other and destroying their future. It remains to be seen, however, whether the current Tigrayan leaders and those who aspire to replace them will be able to rise to the challenge of building a better future for all the peoples of Ethiopia through a functioning democratic federal system.

---

[79] This section summarized from Hassen, 'Islam as a Resistance Ideology', 91.
[80] Tamrat, *Church and State in Ethiopia*, 302.

Bibliography

Abba Dula, Abba Jobir, 'The Unpublished manuscript of Abba Jobir Abba Dula, the last king of Jimma Abba Jifar'.

Abbadie, Antoine d'. 'On the Oromo: Great African Nation Often Designated Under the Name "Galla"', trans. Ayalew Kanno. *Journal of Oromo Studies* 14, 1, March 2007: 117–46.

Abbadie, Antoine d'. 'The papers of Antoine and Arnauld d'Abbadie', Bibliothèque Nationale (Paris) Nouvelles Acquisitions Françaises, no. 21300.

Abbadie, Antoine d'. Nouv. acq. tran. No. 238452. 'Lettres sur La Mission Catholique du pays des Galls, 1845–1895', letter of Taurin Cahagne Harar, 3 December 1883.

Abbadie, Arnauld d'. *Douze ans de séjour dans la haute-Ethiopie (Abyssinie)*, ed. Jeanne-Marie Allier. Vol. 2. Vatican City: Biblioteca Apostolica Vaticana, 1980.

Abdul Rahman, Hadj Yousuf, ed., *Kitab Rabi al-Qulub fi Dhikr Manaqib Fada'il Sayyidina al-Shaikh Nur Husain*. Cairo, 1927.

Abdullahi Rirash, Sheikh Ahmad. *Kashf as Sudul Can Tarikhas-Sumal: Wahamalikahumas-Sabca.* (Uncovering Somali History and their Seven Kingdoms.) Mogadishu, 1974.

Abir, Mordechai. *Ethiopia: The Era of the Princes – The Challenge of Islam and the Re-Unification of the Christian Empire, 1769–1855*. New York: Frederick A. Praeger, 1968.

Abir, Mordechai. 'Ethiopia and the Horn of Africa'. In *The Cambridge History of Africa*. Vol. 4, *1600–1790*, ed. Richard Gray. Cambridge: Cambridge University Press, 1975 : 537–77.

Abir, Mordechai. *Ethiopia and the Red Sea: The Rise and Decline of the Solomonic Dynasty and Muslim-European Rivalry in the Region*. London: Frank Cass, 1980.

Achebe, Chinua. 'Chi in Igbo Cosmology'. In *From Morning Yet on Creation Day: Essays*: 93–103. London: Heinemann, 1975. Reprinted in A Norton Critical Edition: *Things Fall Apart: Authoritative Text Contexts and Criticism*, ed, Francis Abiola Irele. New York: W.W. Norton, 2009: 159–69.

Adveniat Regnum Tuum, 30, 1975: 49–51; 31, 1976: 38–42.

'Afrique Memoirs et Documentes Abyssinia, 1838-1850', *Archives des Affaires Etrangers*, Paris, vol. 1, no. 13, folios 129 and 130.

Ahmed, Hussein. 'Clerics, Traders and Chiefs: A Historical Study of Islam in Wallo Ethiopia with Special Emphasis on the Nineteenth Century'. PhD diss., University of Birmingham, 1985.

Ahmed, Hussein. *Islam in Nineteenth-Century Wallo, Ethiopia: Revival, Reform and Reaction*. Boston, MA: Brill, 2001.

Al-Umari, ibn Fadl, Allah, *Masalik al-Absar fi Mamlik el Amsar: L'Afrique moins L'Egypte*, trans. M. Gaudefroy-Demonbynes (Paris: 1927), 1-3.

Ali, Abdullah Yusuf. *The Meaning of the Holy Qur'an*, New Edition with Revised Translation, Commentary and newly compiled Comprehensive Index. Beltsville, MD: Amana, 1996.

Almeida, Manoel de. 'The History of High Ethiopia or Abassia Book IV'. In *Some Records of Ethiopia 1593–1646*, trans. and ed. C.F. Beckingham and G.W.B. Huntingford. London: The Hakluyt Society, 1954: 133–9.

Alvares, Francisco, trans. Lord Stanley. *The Prester John of the Indies: A True Relation of the Lands of the Prester John being the Narrative of the Portuguese Embassy to Ethiopia in 1520*, revised and edited with additional material by C.F. Beckingham and G.W.B. Huntingford. 3 vols. Cambridge: The Hakluyt Society / Cambridge University Press, 1961 [1881].

Andrzejewski, B.W. 'Ideas about Warfare in Borana Galla Stories and Fables'. *African Language Studies* 3, 1962: 116–36.

Andrzejewski, B.W. 'Sheikh Hussein of Bali in Galla Oral Tradition'. In *IV Congresso Internationale di Studi Etiopici*. Rome: Accademia Nazionale dei Lincei, 1974: 463–80.

Arab Faqih (Chihab Eddin B. Abdel Qadir). *Futuh Al-Habasha (Histoire de la conquête de l'Abyssinie XVI siècle)*, trans. and ed. M.R. Basset. Paris, 1897.

Arab Faqih. *Futuh Al-Habasha: The Conquest of Abyssinia by Sihab ad-Din Ahmad bin Abd al-Qader bin Salem bin Utman* (Arabic text), Cairo: 1974, *also known as Arab Faqih*, trans. Paul Lester Stenhouse with annotations by Richard Pankhurst. Hollywood, CA: Tsehai, 2003.

Aregay, Merid Wolde. 'Southern Ethiopia and the Christian Kingdom, 1508–1708, With Special Reference to the Galla Migrations and Their Consequences'. PhD diss., University of London, 1971.

Aregay, Merid Wolde. 'Political Geography of Ethiopia at the Beginning of the Sixteenth Century'. In *IV Congresso Internazionale di Studi Etiopici*. Rome: Accademia Nazionale dei Lincei, 1974: 613–31.

Aregay, Merid Wolde. 'Population Movement as a Possible Factor in the Christian-Muslim Conflict of Medieval Ethiopia'. In *Symposium Leo Frobenius*. Munich: Derlag Dokumentation, 1974: 261–81.

Aregay, Merid Wolde. 'Military Elites in Medieval Ethiopia'. In *Land, Literacy and the State in Sudanic Africa*, ed. Donald Crummey. Trenton, NJ: Red Sea Press, 2005: 159–86.

Arnesen, Odd Eirik. 'The Becoming of Place: A Tulama-Oromo Region in Northern Shoa'. In *Being and Becoming Oromo: Historical and Anthropological Enquiries*, ed. P.T.W. Baxter, Jan Hultin and Alessandro Triulzi. Uppsala: Nordiska Afrikainstitutet, 1996: 210–38.

Asfera, Zergawa. 'Some Aspects of Historical Development in "Amhara Wallo" *c.* 1700–1815'. BA thesis, Addis Ababa University, 1973.

Ayana, Daniel. 'The "Galla" that Never Was: Its Origin and Reformulation in a Hinterland of Comparative Disadvantage'. *Journal of Oromo Studies* 17, 1, March 2010: 1–40.

Ayana, Daniel. 'From Geographic Skirt to Geographic Drift: The Oromo Population Movement of the Sixteenth Century'. *Journal of Oromo Studies* 17, 2, January 2011: 1–38.

Azaïs, R.P. 'Study of the Religion of the Oromo People', trans. Ayalew

Kanno. *Journal of Oromo Studies* 19, 1–2, July 2012: 175–87.

Azaïs, R.P. 'Etude sur la religion du peuple Galla'. *Revue d'ethnographie et des traditions populaires* 7, 26, 1926: 113–20.

Azaïs, R.P. and R. Chambard. *Cinq années de recherches archéologiques en Ethiopie, provinces du Harar et Ethiopie Méridionale.* Vol. 1. Paris, 1931.

Bahrey, Abba. *Zenahu le Galla* 'History of the Galla'. In *Some Records of Ethiopia, 1593–1646*, trans. and ed. by C.F. Beckingham and G.W.B. Huntingford. London: The Hakluyt Society, 1954: 111–29.

Bartels, Lambert. *Oromo Religion: Myths and Rites of the Western Oromo of Ethiopia – An Attempt to Understand.* Berlin: Dietrich Reimer, 1983.

Bartnicki, A. and J. Mantel-Niećko. 'The Role and Significance of the Religious Conflicts and People's Movements in the Political Life of Ethiopia in the Seventeenth and Eighteenth Centuries'. *Rassegna di Studi Etiopici* 24, 1970: 5–39.

Basset, M.R. *Études sur l'histoire d'Éthiopie I, Chronique Éthiopienne* (d'après un manuscript de la Bibliothèque Nationale de Paris), extrait du *Journal Asiatique* 18, 1882.

Bassi, Marco. 'On the Boran Calendrical System: A Preliminary Field Report'. *Current Anthropology* 29, 4, August–October 1988: 619–24.

Bates, Darrell. *The Abyssinian Difficulty: The Emperor Theodorus and the Magdala Campaign.* Oxford: Oxford University Press, 1979.

Baxter, Paul. 'Social Organization of the Galla of Northern Kenya'. PhD diss., Oxford University, 1954.

Baxter, Paul. 'The Problem of the Oromo or the Problem for the Oromo'. In *Nationalism and Self-Determination in the Horn of Africa*, ed. I.M. Lewis. London: Ithaca Press, 1983: 129–50.

Baxter, Paul. 'Butter for Barley and Barley for Cash: Petty Transactions and Small Transformations in an Arssi Market'. In *Proceedings of the Seventh International Conference of Ethiopian Studies*, ed. Sven Rubenson. East Lansing, MI: Michigan State University, 1984: 459–72.

Beckingham, C.F., ed. *Travels to Discover the Source of the Nile by James Bruce.* New York: Horizon, 1964.

Beke, Charles. 'On the Origin of the Galla'. Report to the 1847 meeting of The British Association for the Advancement of Science. London, 1848: 3–33.

Bekerie, Ayele. 'Ethiopica: Some Historical Reflections on the Origin of the word Ethiopia'. *The International Journal of Ethiopian Studies* 1, 2, 2004: 110–21.

Berhane-Selassie, Tsehai. 'The Question of Damot and Walamo'. *Journal of Ethiopian Studies* 13, 1975: 37–45.

Beshah, Girma and Merid Wolde Aregay. *The Question of the Union of the Churches in Luso-Ethiopian Relations (1500–1632).* Lisbon: Junta de Investigações do Ultramar & Centro de Estudos Históricos Ultramarinos, 1964.

Beyene, Asfaw. 'Oromo Calendar: The Significance of Bita Qara'. *Journal of Oromo Studies* 2, 1–2, July 1995: 58–64.

Bitima, Tamene. *A Dictionary of Oromo Technical Terms.* Cologne: Rüdiger Köppe, 2000.

Black, Paul. 'Linguistic Evidence on the Origins of the Konsoid Peoples'. In *Proceedings of the First United States Conference on Ethiopian Studies 1973*, ed. Harold G. Marcus. East Lansing, MI: Michigan State University, 1975: 291–302.

Blanc, Henry, *A Narrative of Captivity in Abyssinia*. London: Smith, Elder and Co., 1868.

Blundell, H. W. *The Royal Chronicle of Abyssinia*, Cambridge, 1922.

Boavida, Isabel, Hervé Pennec and Manuel João Ramos, eds, trans. Christopher J. Tribe, *Pedro Páez's History of Ethiopia, 1662*, 2 vols. London: Ashgate / The Hakluyt Society, 2011.

Braukämper, Ulrich. 'Islamic Principalities in Southeast Ethiopia between the Thirteenth and Sixteenth Centuries'. *Ethiopianist Notes* 1, 1, 1977: 17–55; 2: 1–43.

Braukämper, Ulrich. 'The Ethnogenesis of the Sidama'. *Abbay Cahier*, 9, 1978: 123–30.

Braukämper, Ulrich. *Geschichte der Hadiya Süd-Aethiopiens: Von den Anfangen bis zur Revolution 1974*. Wiesbaden: Franz Steiner, 1980.

Braukämper, Ulrich. 'Oromo Country of Origin: A Reconsideration of Hypotheses'. In *Ethiopian Studies: Proceedings of the Sixth International Conference, 14–17 April 1980*, ed. Gideon Goldenberg. Boston: Balkema, 1986: 25–40.

Braukämper, Ulrich. *Islamic History and Culture in Southern Ethiopia: Collected Essays*. New Brunswick, NJ and London: Rutgers University Press and Transaction, 2002.

Brielli, Domenico, 'Ricordi Storici dei Uollo'. In *Studi Etiopici (Racco da C. Conti-Rossini*. Rome: Istituto per l'Oriente, 1945: 78–110.

Bruce, James. *Travels to Discover the Source of the Nile in the Years 1768, 1769, 1770, 1771, 1772, and 1773*, 3 vols. London: J. Ruthven for G.G.J. and J. Robinson, 1790.

Budge, E.A.W. *Life and Miracles of Takla Haymanot*. London: Methuen, 1906.

Budge, E.A.W. *A History of Ethiopia, Nubia and Abyssinia*, Vol. 2. London: Methuen, 1928.

Budge, E. A.W., trans. and ed. *The Book of the Mysteries of Heaven and Earth*. London: Oxford University Press, 1935.

Bulcha, Mekuria. *Contours of the Emergent and Ancient Oromo Nation: Dilemmas in the Ethiopian Politics of State and Nation-Building*. Cape Town: Centre for Advanced Studies of African Society, 2011.

Caraman, Philip. *The Lost Empire: The Story of the Jesuits in Ethiopia 1555–1634*. Notre Dame, IN: University of Notre Dame, 1985.

Caulk, Richard. 'Harar Town and its Neighbours in the Nineteenth Century'. *Journal of African History* 18, 1977: 369–86.

Caulk, Richard. *'Between the Jaws of Hyenas': A Diplomatic History of Ethiopia (1876–1896)*, ed. Bahru Zewde. Wiesbaden: Harrassowitz Verlag, 2002.

Cecchi, A. *Da Zeila alle Frontiere del Caffa: Viaggi di Antonio Cecchi*. 3 vols. Rome: Ermanno Loescher, 1886–87.

Cerulli, E. *The Folk Literature of the Galla of Southern Abyssinia*. Harvard African Studies, 3. Cambridge, MA: Harvard University Press, 1922.

Cerulli, E. 'Documenti Arabi per La Storia dell'Etiopia'. *Memorie della Reale Accademia dei Lincei* 4. Roma: G. Bardi, 1931: 37–101.

Cerrulli, E. *Etiopia Occidentale*. 2 vols. Rome, 1932–33.

Cerulli, E. *Studi Etiopici I: La Lingua e La Storia di Harar*. Vol. 1. 1936. Rome: Istituto per l'Oriente, 1938.

Cerulli, E. *Studi Etiopici II: La Lingua e La Storia del Sidamo*. Rome: Istituto per l'Oriente 1938.

Cerulli, E. *Somalia: Scritti Vari editi ed in diti*. Vol. 2. Rome: 1964 [1959].

Chernetsov, S.B. 'The "History of the Gallas" and Death of Za-Dengel, King of Ethiopia (1603–1604)'. In *IV Congress Internazionale di Studi Ethiopici*. Rome: Accademia Nazionale Dei Lincei, 1974: 803–8.

Chernetsov, S.B. 'Who Wrote "The History of King Sarsa Dengel"? Was it the Monk Bahrey?' In *Proceedings of the Eighth International Conference of Ethiopian Studies* (University of Addis Ababa, 1984), ed. Taddese Beyene, vol. 1. Addis Ababa: Institute of Ethiopian Studies, 1988: 131–5.

Chopra, Deepak. *Buddha: A Story of Enlightenment*. New York: HarperCollins, 2007.

Cohen, M. *Etudes d'Ethiopien méridional*. Paris: Paul Geuthner, 1931.

Cohen, D.W. 'Lwo speakers'. In *Zamani: A Survey of East African History*, ed. B.A. Ogot. Nairobi: Longman Kenya, 1974: 136–49.

Conti-Rossini, C., trans. and ed., *Historia Régis Sàrsà Dengel (Malak Sagad)*, 2 volumes, Paris, 1907.

Conti-Rossini, C. *L'autobiografia di Pawlos, Monaco Abissino del secolo XVI*. Rendiconti della Reule Accademia dei Lincei 27. Rome, 1918: 279–96.

Conti-Rossini, C. *Storia d'Etiopia*. Milan: Istituto Italiano d'Arti Grafiche, 1928.

Conzelman, William, trans. *Chronique de Galâwdêwos (Claudius), roi d'Ethiopie*. Paris: Emile Bouillon, 1895.

Crawford, O.G.S., ed. *Ethiopian Itineraries circa 1400–1524 including those collected by Alessandro Zorzi at Venice in the years 1519–1524*. Cambridge: Hakluyt Society / Cambridge University Press, 1858.

Crummey, Donald. 'Tewodros as Reformer and Modernizer'. *Journal of African History* 10, 3, 1969: 457–69.

Crummey, Donald. *Priests and Politicians: Protestant and Catholic Missions in Orthodox Ethiopia, 1830–1868*. Oxford: Oxford University Press, 1972.

Crummey, Donald. 'The Violence of Tewodros'. In *War and Society in Africa*, ed. Bethwell A. Ogot. London: Frank Cass, 1972: 65–84.

Darkwah, R.H.K. *Shewa, Menilek and the Ethiopian Empire, 1813–1889*. London: Heinemann, 1978 [1975].

Davis, A.J. 'The Sixteenth Century Jihad in Ethiopia and the Impact on its Culture'. *Journal of the Historical Society of Nigeria*, Part One 2, 4, 1963: 567–92; Part Two, 3, 1, 1964: 113–28.

Dilebo, Getahun. 'Emperor Menelik's Ethiopia, 1865–1916: National Unification or Amhara Communal Domination'. PhD diss., Howard University, Washington DC, 1974.

Deressa, Yilma. *Ya Ityopya Tarik Ba'asra Sedestannaw Kefla Zaman*. Addis Ababa: Berhanena Selam Printing Press, 1967.

Deressa, Belletech. *Oromtitti: The Forgotten Women in Ethiopian History*. Raleigh, NC: Ivy House, 2003.

de Salviac, Martial. *Un Peuple Antique au Pays de Ménélik: Les Galla Grande Nation Africaine*. Paris: H. Oudin, 1905.

de Salviac, Martial, trans. Ayalew Kanno. *An Ancient People: Great African Nation – The Oromo*. Self-published, 2005.

Dhugumaa, Anga'a. From the Revised Gadda to Macca-Tuulama Association. New York: self-published, 1998.

Donzel, E.J. Van. *A Yemenite Embassy to Ethiopia 1647–1649*. Stuttgart: F. Steiner, 1986.

Doyle, L.R. 'The Borana Calendar Reinterpreted'. *Current Anthropology* 27, 3, June 1986: 286–7.

Duri, Abd Al-Ziz, trans. Lawrence I. Conrad. *The Historical Formation of the Arab Nation: A Study in Identity and Consciousness*. London: Croom Helm, 1987.

Ege, Svein. 'Chiefs and Peasants: The Socio-Political Structure of the Kingdom of Shawa about 1840'. MPhil thesis. Hovedoppgave i historie ved Universitetet i Bergen, 1978.

Ehret, Christopher. 'Cushitic Prehistory'. In *The Non–Semitic Languages of Ethiopia*, ed. M. Lionel Bender. East Lansing: African Studies Center, Michigan State University, 1976: 85–96.

Ehret, Christopher. *The Civilizations of Africa: A History to 1800*. Charlottesville: University of Virginia, 2002.

Etefa, Tsega. 'The Oromo of Wanbara: A Historical Survey to 1941'. MA thesis, Addis Ababa University, 1997.

Etefa, Tsega Endalew. *Inter-Ethnic Relations on a Frontier: Mätakkäl (Ethiopia) 1898–1991*. Wiesbaden: Harrassowitz, 2006.

Etefa, Tsega. 'Pan-Oromo Confederations in the Sixteenth and Seventeenth Centuries'. *Journal of Oromo Studies* 15, 1, March 2008: 19–40.

Falola, Toyin. *Tradition and Change in Africa: The Essays of J.F. Ade Ajayi*. Trenton, NJ: Africa World Press. 2000.

Ficquet, Eloi. 'Fabrication of Oromo Origins', *The Journal of Oromo Studies* Volume 14, Number 2 (July 2007): 105–130. Translation from French by Ayalew Kanno 'La Fabrique des origines Oromo', *Annales d'Ethiopie*, Vol. 18 (2002): 55–71.

Foster, William, ed. *The Red Sea and Adjacent Countries at the Close of the Seventeenth Century*. London: The Hakluyt Society, 1949.

Fulas, Hailu. 'Review of R. K. Molvaer, *Tradition and Change in Ethiopia: Social and Cultural Life as Reflected in Amharic Fictional Literature ca. 1930–1974*'. In *Northeast African Studies* 4. 1982: 39–44.

Gabre-Sellassie, Zewde. *Yohannes IV of Ethiopia: A Political Biography*. Oxford: Clarendon, 1975.

Gidada, Negaso. *History of the Sayyoo Oromoo of Southwestern Wallaga, Ethiopia from about 1730 to 1886*. Addis Ababa: Mega Printing Enterprise, 2001.

Gnamo, Abbas, H. *Conquest and Resistance in the Ethiopian Empire, 1880–1974. The case of the Arsi Oromo*. Boston: Brill, 2014.

Gobat, S. *Journal of Three Years' Residence in Abyssinia*. 2nd edn. New York: Negro Universities Press, 1969.

Goto, Paul S. 'The Boran of Northern Kenya: Origin, Migrations and Settlements in the 19th Century'. BA thesis, University of Nairobi, 1972.

Gragg, Gene. 'Oromo of Wellegga'. In *The Non-Semitic Languages of Ethiopia*, ed. M. Lionel Bender, 166–95. East Lansing: African Studies Center, Michigan State University, 1976.

Gragg, Gene. *Oromo Dictionary*. East Lansing, MI: Michigan State University, 1982.

Greenfield, Richard and Mohammed Hassen. 'Interpretation of Oromo Nationality'. *Horn of Africa* 3, 3, 1980: 3–14.

Grottanelli, V.L. 'The Peopling of the Horn of Africa'. In *East Africa and the Orient: Cultural Synthesis in Pre-Colonial Times*, ed. H. Neville Chittick and Robert I. Rotberg. New York: Africana Publishing, 1975: 44–75.

Guidi, I., trans. *Annales Yohannis I, Iyasu I et Bakaffa*. Paris: 1905.

Haberland, E. *Galla Süd-Aethiopiens*. Stuttgart: W. Kohlhammer, 1963.

Haile, Getatchew. *The Works of Abba Bahriy and Other Documents Concerning the Oromo*. Amharic. Avon, MN: self-published, 2002.

Haile, Alemayehu, et al., eds. *History of the Oromo to the Sixteenth Century*. 2nd ed. Finfinne: Oromia Culture and Tourism Bureau, 2006.

Halévy, J. 'Notes pour l'histoire d'Ethiopie Le pays de Zague'. *Revue Sémitique* 5, 1897: 275–84.

Hammond, Dorothy and Alta Jablow. *The Africa that Never Was: Four Centuries of British Writing about Africa*. Prospect Heights IL: Waveland Press, 1992 [1970].

Harris, W.C. *The Highlands of Ethiopia*. Vol. 3. London: Longman, Brown, Green and Longman, 1844.

Hassen, Mohammed. 'The Oromo of Ethiopia, 1500–1850: With Special Emphasis on the Gibe Region'. PhD diss., University of London, 1983.

Hassen, Mohammed. *The Oromo of Ethiopia: A History 1570–1860*. Cambridge: Cambridge University Press, 1990.

Hassen, Mohammed. 'The Historian Abba Bahrey and the Importance of His "History of the Galla"'. *Horn of Africa* 13, 3–4; 14, 1–2, 1990–91: 90–106.

Hassen, Mohammed. 'Islam as a Resistance Ideology among the Oromo of Ethiopia: The Wallo Case, 1700–1900'. In *In the Shadow of Conquest: Islam in Colonial Northeast Africa*, ed. Said S. Samatar, 75–101. Trenton, NJ: Red Sea Press, 1992.

Hassen, Mohammed. 'Some Aspects of Oromo History that Have Been Misunderstood'. *The Oromo Commentary* 3, 2, 1993: 24–31.

Hassen, Mohammed. 'The Pre-Sixteenth Century Oromo Presence Within the Medieval Christian Kingdom of Ethiopia'. In *A River of Blessings: Essays in Honor of Paul Baxter*, ed. David Brokensha. Syracuse, NY: Maxwell School of Citizenship and Public Affairs, Syracuse University, 1994: 43–65.

Hassen, Mohammed. 'Pilgrimage to the Abba Muudaa'. *Journal of Oromo Studies* 12, 1–2, July 2005: 142–57.

Hassen, Mohammed. 'The Significance of Abba Bahrey in Oromo Studies: A Commentary on *The Works of Abba Bahriy and Other Documents Concerning the Oromo*'. *Journal of Oromo Studies* 14, 2, July 2007: 131–55.

Hassen, Mohammed. 'The Oromo in Medieval Muslim States of Southern Ethiopia'. *Journal of Oromo Studies* 15, 1, March 2008: 203–14.

Hersi, Ali Abdurahman. 'The Arab Factor in Somali History: The Origins and the Development of Arab Enterprise and Cultural Influence in the Somali Peninsula'. PhD diss., University of California, Los Angeles, 1977.

Hodge, Carleton T. 'Lisramic (Afroasiatic): An Overview'. In *The Non-Semitic Languages of Ethiopia*, ed. M. Lionel Bender. East Lansing: African Studies Center, Michigan State University, 1976: 43–66.

Hultin, Jan. 'Man and Land in Wallaga, Ethiopia'. Working papers of the Department of Social Anthropology, University of Gothenburg, 10, 1977.

Hultin, Jan. 'Perceiving Oromo: "Galla" in the Great Narrative of Ethiopia'. In *Being and Becoming Oromo: Historical and Anthropological Enquiries*, ed. P.T.W. Baxter, Jan Hultin and Alessandro Triulzi. Uppsala: Nordiska Afrikainstitutet, 1996: 81–91.

Huntingford, G.W.B., *The Galla of Ethiopia: The Kingdoms of Kafa and Janjero*. London: International African Institute, 1955.

Huntingford, G.W.B. *The Glorious Victories of Amda Seyon, King of Ethiopia*. Oxford: Clarendon, 1965.

Huntingford, G.W.B., trans. and ed. 'The History of King Sarsa Dengel

(Malak Sagad) 1563–1597'. Unpublished manuscript. School of Oriental and African Studies, University of London, 1976.

Huntingford, G.W.B. *The Historical Geography of Ethiopia from the 1st Century A.D. to 1704*, revised and ed. R. Pankhurst and D. Appleyard. London: Oxford University Press, 1989.

International Bible Society, *The Holy Bible: New International Version*. London: Hodder & Stoughton, 1986.

Isaacs, Harold. *Idols of the Tribe: Group Identity and Political Change*. New York: Harper & Row, 1975.

Isenberg, C. W. and J.L. Krapf. The Journal of C. W. Isenberg and J.L. Krapf Detailing Their Proceedings in the Kingdom of Shoa and Journeys in Other Parts of Abyssinia in the Years 1839-1842, London, 1968.

Jones, A.H.M. and Elizabeth Monroe. *A History of Ethiopia*. Oxford: Clarendon, 1955.

Kammerer, A. *La Mer Rouge, l'Abyssinie et l'Arabie depuis l'antiquité. Essai d'histoire et de géographie historique*. 3 vols, Cairo, 1929–52.

Kelly, Hilarie Ann. 'From Gada to Islam: The Moral Authority of Gender Relations among the Pastoral Oromo of Kenya'. PhD diss., University of California, Los Angeles, 1992.

Kennedy, Paul. *Preparing for the Twenty-First Century*. New York: Random House, 1993.

Kidane, Sahlu. *Borana Folktales: A Contextual Study*. London: Haan, 2002.

Kiros, Teodros. *Zara Yacob, A Seventeenth-Century Rationalist: Philosopher of the Rationality of the Human Heart*. Lawrenceville, NJ: The Red Sea Press, 2005.

Knutsson, Karl. 'Authority and Change: A Study of the Kallu Institution among the Macha Galla of Ethiopia'. Gothenburg: Etnografiska Museet, 1967.

Landor, A.H.S. *Across Widest Africa: An Account of the Country and the People of Eastern, Central and Western Africa, as seen during a twelve-months journey from Djibuti to Cape Verde*. London: Hurst and Blackett, 1907.

Legesse, Asmarom. *Gada: Three Approaches to the Study of African Society*. New York: The Free Press, 1973.

Legesse, Asmarom. *Oromo Democracy: An Indigenous African Political System*. Trenton, NJ: Red Sea Press, 2006 [2000].

Leus, Ton and Cynthia Salvador. *Aadaa Boraanaa: A Dictionary of Borana Culture*. Addis Ababa: Shama Books, 2006.

Levine, D.N. *Wax and Gold: Tradition and Innovation in Ethiopian Culture*. Chicago, IL: University of Chicago Press, 1972.

Levine, D.N. *Greater Ethiopia: The Evolution of a Multiethnic Society*. 2nd edn. Chicago, IL: University of Chicago Press, 2000.

Lewis, H.S. 'The Origins of the Galla and Somali'. *Journal of African History*, 7, 1, March 1966, 37–46.

Lewis, I.M. 'The Galla in Northern Somaliland'. *Rassegna di Studi Etiopici* 15, Rome: Istituto per l'Oriente, 1959, 21–38.

Lewis, I.M. *A Pastoral Democracy: A Study of Pastoralism and Politics among the Northern Somali of the Horn of Africa*. Oxford: Oxford University Press, 1960.

Lewis, I.M. 'The Somali Conquest of the Horn of Africa'. *Journal of African History*, 1, 2, July 1960, 213–30.

Lobo, Jerónimo, D.M. Lockhart, trans., M.G. da Costa, ed., *The Itinerário of Jerónimo Lobo*. London: The Hakluyt Society, 1984.

Ludolphus, Job, trans. J.P. Gent, *A New History of Ethiopia: Being a Full and Accurate Description of the Kingdom of Abessinia, vulgarly, though erroneously called The Empire of Prester John*. London: Samuel Smith, 1682.

Lynch, B.M. and L.H. Robbins. 'Namoratunga: The First Archeoastronomical Evidence in Sub-Saharan Africa'. *Science* 200, 4343, 19 May 1978: 766–8.

Makurya, Takla Sadiq. *Ya Ityopiyya Tao Rik Ka Aste Aste Lebna Dengel Eska Aste Tewodros*. Addis Ababa: Berhanena Selam Printing Press, 1945 (i.e. 1952/53).

Makurya, Takla Sadiq. *Ya Gragn Ahmed Warara*. Addis Ababa: Artistic Press, 1975/76.

Maqrizi, *Historia Regum Islamiticorum in Abyssinia*, ed. and trans. F.T. Rinck, Leiden: 1790.

Marcus, Harold. 'Review of The Oromo of Ethiopia: A History, 1570–1860'. *American Historical Review* 97, 1, supplement, February 1992: 259–60.

Marcus, Harold. 'Does the Past Have any Authority in Ethiopia?' *The Ethiopian Review*, April 1992: 18–21.

Marcus, Harold. *A History of Ethiopia*. Berkeley, CA: University of California Press, 1994.

Markham, C.R. *A History of the Abyssinian Expedition*. London: Macmillan, 1869.

Massaja, G. *Lettere e scritti minori, 1836–66*. Vol. 1, *A cura di Antonino Rosso*. Rome: Istituto Storico dei Cappuccini, 1978.

Mazrui, Ali A. *The Africans: A Triple Heritage*. London: BBC Publications, 1986.

Megerssa, Gemetchu. 'Knowledge, Identity and the Colonizing Structure: The Case of the Oromo in East and Northeast Africa'. PhD diss., University of London, 1994.

Megerssa, Gemetchu. 'The Oromo World View'. *Journal of Oromo Studies* 12, 1–2, July 2005: 68–79.

Melbaa, Gadaa. *Oromia: An Introduction to the History of the Oromo People*. Minneapolis, MN: Kirk House Publishers, 1999 [1988].

Mennasemay, Maimire. 'A Critical Reappraisal of Abba Bahrey's Zenahu Le Galla'. *Horn of Africa* 29, 2011: 38–63.

Merga, Tasawo. 'Senna Umatta Oromo: Jalqaba jarra kudha Jahafti hamma dhumiti jarra kudha Sagalafanti'. Unpublished manuscript, 1976.

Metaferia, Seifu. 'The Eastern Oromo (K'ottus) of Ethiopia and their Time Reckoning "System"'. *Africa Rivista trimestrale di Studi e documentazione dell'Istituto Italo-Africano* 33, 4, 1978: 475–507.

Mizzi, Angelo. *Cenni Etnografici Galla ossia Organizzazione Civile, usi e costumi Oromonici*. Malta: Empire Press, 1935.

Mizzi, Angelo. *I proverbi Galla*. Prima serie. Malta: The Empire Press, 1935.

Mizzi, Angelo. Semplici Constatazioni Filologico-etnologiche Galla. Malta: The Empire Press, 1935.

Mizzi, Angelo. *L'apostolato Maltese Nei secoli Passati, con speciale riguardo all'azione missionaria svolta nel bacino Mediterraneo*. Vol. 2, *Menologio Missionario*. Malta: The Empire Press, 1938.

Mokhtar, G., ed. *UNESCO General History of Africa*. Vol. 2, *Ancient Civilizations of Africa*. Berkeley: The University of California Press, 1981.

Mokhtar, M. 'Notes sur le pays de Harrar'. *Bulletin de la Société Khedevile de Géographie*. Cairo, 1877: 357–97.

Moore, Richard B. *The Name 'Negro': Its Origin and Evil Use*, edited with an introduction by W. Burghardt Turner and Joyce Moore Turner. Baltimore, MD: Black Classic Press, 1992 [1960].

New Jerusalem Bible. Darton: Longman & Todd, 1985.

Olaniyan, Richard, ed. *African History and Culture*. Lagos: Longman, 1990 [1982].

Oliver, Roland. *The African Experience*. New York: HarperCollins, 1991.

Omer-Cooper, J.D. *The Zulu Aftermath: A Nineteenth Century Revolution in Bantu Africa*. London: Longman,1966.

Pankhurst, Alula. 'Indigenising Islam in Wallo: *Ajam* Amharic verse written in Arabic script'. In *Proceedings of the Eleventh International Conference of Ethiopian Studies*, Vol. 2, ed. B. Zewde, R. Pankhurst and T. Beyene. Addis Ababa: Addis Ababa University Press, 1994: 257–73.

Pankhurst, Richard. *An Introduction to the Economic History of Ethiopia from Early Times to 1800*. London: Lalibela House, 1961.

Pankhurst, Richard. 'The Great Ethiopian Famine of 1889–1892: a new assessment'. *Journal of the History of Medicine and Allied Sciences* 21, 2, 1966: 95–124.

Pankhurst, Richard. *History of Ethiopian Towns from the Middle Ages to the Early Nineteenth Century*. Wiesbaden: Franz Steiner, 1982.

Pankhurst, Richard. *The Ethiopian Borderlands: Essays in Regional History from Ancient Times to the End of the 18th Century*. Lawrenceville, NJ: Red Sea Press, 1997.

Pankhurst, Richard. *The Ethiopians*. Malden, MA: Blackwell, 1998.

Paulitchke, P.V. *Die Wanderungen der Oromo oder Galla OstAfrikas*. Vienna: Perham, 1889.

Pereira, F.M. Esteves, ed. *Chronica de Susenyos, Rei de Ethiopia*. Lisbon: Impresa National, 1892–1900.

Pereira, F.M.E. *Historia de Minas, Rei de Ethiopia*. Lisbon: 1888.

Perruchon, J., trans. and ed. 'Histoire des guerres d'Amda Syon, roi d'Ethiopie'. *Journal asiatique* 8, 14, 1889: 271–363, 381–493.

Perruchon, J. *Les chroniques de Zar'a Yâ'eqôb et de Ba'eda Mâryâm, rois d'Ethiopie de 1434 à 1478*. Paris: Emile Bouillon, 1893.

Perruchon, J., trans. and ed. 'Histoire d'Eskender, d'Amda-Seyon II et de Nâ'od, rois d'Ethiopie'. *Journal Asiatique* 9, 1894: 316–66.

Perruchon, J. 'Notes pour l'histoire d'Ethiopie: Règne de Sarsa-Dengel ou Malak Sagad I (1563–1597)'. *Revue Sémitique* 4, 1896: 177–85, 273–8.

Perruchon, J. 'Notes pour l'histoire d'Ethiopie: Règne de Susenyos ou Seltan-Sagad (1607–1632)'. *Revue Sémitique* 5, 1897: 360–72.

Perruchon, J., trans. 'Bahaya Mika'el, Mashafa Mistirata–Samay Wamider'. *Patrologia Orientalis* 1, 1904: 1–97.

Phillipson, David, W. *Foundations of an African Civilisation: Aksum & The Northern Horn 1000BC–AD 1300*. Woodbridge: James Currey, 2012.

Quirin, James. *The Evolution of the Ethiopian Jews: A History of the Beta Israel (Falasha) to 1920*. Philadelphia: University of Pennsylvania Press, 1990.

Reid, Richard J. *Frontiers of Violence in Northeast Africa: Genealogies of Conflict since c. 1800*. New York: Oxford University Press, 2011.

Rikitu, Mengesha. *Oromia Recollected: Culture and History*. London: Magic Press, 1998.

Rochet d'Héricourt, C.E.X. *Voyage sur la Côte Orientale de la Mer Rouge dans le pays d'Adel et le Royaume de Choa*. Paris: Arthus-Bertrand, 1841.

Sanderson, G.N. 'Contributions from African Sources to the History of European Competition in the Upper Valley of the Nile'. *Journal of African History*, 3, 1, 1962: 69–85.

Scarin, E. *Hararino: Ricerce e Studi Geografici*. Florence: Centro di Studi Colonial, 1942.

Schleicher, A.W. *Geschichte der Galla. Bericht eines abyssinischen Monches uber die Invasion der Galla im sechzehnten Jahrhundert*, Berlin: 1893.

Sellassie, Gabra. *Tarika Zemen Ze Dagmawe Menelik Nigusa Nagast Ze Ityopya*. Addis Ababa: Berhanena Selam Printing Press, 1965.

Sellassie, Sergew Hable. *Ancient and Medieval Ethiopian History to 1270*. Addis Ababa: Addis Ababa Printing Press, 1972.

Smith, Anthony. *The Ethnic Origins of Nations*. New York: Basil Blackwell. 1987.

Soleillet, Paul. *Voyages en Éthiopie Janvier 1882 – Octobre 1884: Notes, Lettres et Documents Divers*. Rouen: Cagniard, 1886.

Spear, Thomas and Richard Waller. *Being Maasai: Ethnicity and Identity in East Africa*. Athens, OH: Ohio University Press, 1993.

Starkie, Enid. *Arthur Rimbaud in Abyssinia*. Oxford: Oxford University Press, 1937.

Sumner, Claude. *Oromo Wisdom Literature*, Vol. 1, *Proverbs: Collection and Analysis*. Addis Ababa: Gudina Tumsa Foundation, 1995.

Sumner, Claude. *Proverbs, Songs, Folktales: An Anthology of Oromo Literature*. Addis Ababa: Gudina Tumsa Foundation, 1996.

Tablino, Paul. 'The Reckoning of Time By the Borana Hayyantu'. Unpublished manuscript.

Tafla, Bairu, ed. *Asma Giyorgis and His Work: History of the Galla and the Kingdom of Šawā*. Stuttgart: Franz Steiner, 1987.

Tamrat, Taddesse, ed. *Alaqa Tayya's Ye Ityopya Hizeb Tarik*. Addis Ababa: Berhanena Selam Printing Press, 1971/72.

Tamrat, Taddesse. *Church and State in Ethiopia, 1270–1527*. Oxford: Clarendon, 1972.

Tasmaa, Toleera and Hundassa Waaqwayoo. *Sena Saba Oromoo fi Sirna Gadaa*. Addis Ababa: Artistic Press, 1995.

Tellez, F.B., trans. J. Stevens. *The Travels of the Jesuits in Ethiopia*. London: J. Knapton, Bell and Baker, 1710.

The Holy Bible: King James Version

The Holy Bible Revised Standard Version containing the Old and New testaments. Toronto: Thomas Nelson & sons, 1952.

The Jerusalem Bible. Darton: Longman & Todd, 1966.

Tibebu, Teshale. *The Making of Modern Ethiopia, 1896–1974*. Lawrenceville, NJ: Red Sea Press, 1995.

Trimingham, J.S. *Islam in Ethiopia*. London: Oxford University Press, 1952.

Triulzi, Alessando. 'Toward a Corpus of Historical Source Materials in Wallaga: a preliminary report'. *Proceedings of the Eighth International Conference of Ethiopian Studies*, vol. 2, ed. Taddesse Beyene. Addis Ababa: Addis Ababa University Press, 1984: 319–29.

Triulzi, Alessandro. 'Oromo Traditions of Origin'. In *Etudes Ethiopiennes*. Vol. 1, *Actes de la Xe Conference Internationale des études Ethiopiennes* (Paris, 24–28 August 1988), ed. Claude Lepage et al. Paris: Société Française pour les Etudes Ethiopiennes, 1994: 593–601.

Tubiana, Joseph. 'Un ethnographe Ethiopien au XVIe siècle'. In *De la voûte céleste au terroir, du jardin au foyer,* 655–59. Paris: L'Ecole des Hautes Etudes en Sciences Sociales, 1987.

Turton, E.R. 'Bantu, Galla and Somali Migrations in the Horn of Africa: A Reassessment of the Juba/Tana Area'. *Journal of African History* 16, 4, 1975: 519–37.

Tutschek, Carl, ed. Lorenz Tutschek. *A Grammar of the Galla Language,* Munich: published privately, 1845.

Ullendorff, Edward. *The Ethiopians: An Introduction to the Country and People.* London: Oxford University Press, 1960.

van de Loo, Joseph with Bilow Kola. *Guji Oromo Culture in Southern Ethiopia: Religious Capabilities in Rituals and Songs.* Berlin: Dietrich Reimer, 1991.

Vansina, Jan. *Oral Tradition as History.* Madison, WI: The University of Wisconsin Press, 1985.

Verharen, Charles. 'Comparing Oromo and Ancient Egyptian Philosophy'. *Journal of Oromo Studies* 15, 2, July 2008: 1–31.

Wagner, E., trans. and ed. *Legende und Geschichte der Fatah Madinat Harar von Yaha Nasrallah.* Wiesbaden: Steiner, 1978.

Ward, Ronald. 'Pilgrimage in Oromia – Madda Walaabuu'. *Qunamtii Oromia* 3, 1, September 1992: 14–15.

Wario, Hassan. 'Journey to the Shrine of Nura Symbols of Gada Ornaments, Space and the Puff Adder in Somatic and Ritual Transformation'. MA thesis, University of East Anglia, 1998.

Werner, A. 'The Galla of the East African Protectorate'. *Journal of African Society* 13, 50–51, 1914: 121–42; 262–87.

Werner, A. 'Some Galla Notes'. *Man: A Record of Anthropological Science* 15, 1915: 10–11.

Whiteway, R.S., trans. and ed. *The Portuguese Expedition to Abyssinia in 1541–1543 as Narrated by Castanhoso with some Contemporary Letters, the Short Account of Bermudez and Certain Extracts from Correa.* London: The Hakluyt Society, 1967 [1902].

Wrigley, E.A. *Population and History.* London: New York and Toronto: McGraw-Hill, 1969.

Yates, Brian. 'Invisible Actors: The Oromo and the Creation of Modern Ethiopia (1855–1913)'. PhD diss., University of Illinois at Urbana-Champaign, 2009.

Zitelmann. Thomas. 'Re-Examining the Galla/Oromo Relationship: The Stranger as a Structural Topic'. In *Being and Becoming Oromo: Historical and Anthropological Enquiries,* ed. P.T.W. Baxter, Jan Hultin and Alessandro Truilzi, 103–13. Uppsala: Nordiska Afrikainstitutet, 1996.

Zitelmann, Thomas. 'Oromo Religion, *Ayyaana* and the Possibility of A Sufi Legacy'. *Journal of Oromo Studies* 12, 1–2, July 2005: 80–99.

Zurla, D. P. *Il Mappamondo di Fra Mauro Camaldolese.* Venice, 1806.

Index

EASTERN AFRICAN STUDIES

These titles published in the United States and Canada by Ohio University Press